Praise for *Alice* by Stacy Cordery

"One of the most _____ of the past year, *Alice* is proof that scholarl_____ that popular biographies need not be frivol_____ ave relished, and one its readers will finish v_____ *'ichmond Times-Dispatch*

"The best aspect of _____ ....ait it presents of a long-vanished Washington where politicians from both parties would work out solutions at social events brilliantly orchestrated by the social lioness. Until her death at ninety-six in 1980, she reigned as 'the other Washington monument.' . . . For interested readers, it offers a wealth of insight into the politics and culture of twentieth-century America."   —*USA Today*

"To grasp the longevity of 'Princess Alice' upon the Washington scene, one must imagine either Jenna or Barbara [Bush] showing up for a party at 1600 Pennsylvania Avenue in the year 2071, the way Alice Roosevelt Longworth took her seat in the Rose Garden for Tricia Nixon's White House wedding sixty-five years after her own. . . . Stacy A. Cordery has had more access to Mrs. Longworth's private papers than previous writers, [and] notes . . . [that she was] 'the first female celebrity of the twentieth century.' "   —*The New York Times*

"It is to Cordery's credit that she puts her subject in the context of the times, so that one can understand the public's indulgence and sympathize with a woman who felt abandoned most of her life. . . . She writes with flair worthy of her subject. Alice was not simply a witness to great events. She was a player, igniting fires and stirring the political pot."   —*The Providence Journal*

"With graceful prose, commanding diction and psychological acuity, author Stacy Cordery . . . follows the fortunes of Alice Roosevelt Longworth in this absorbing and rigorously researched biography. . . . Cordery lends valuable but cautious psychological insights to all the climactic events in Alice's life— disappointments, weddings and the deaths of family members and friends. Most important, she takes a woman most remembered for her one-liners and, for the record, details her considerable contributions to U.S. politics and discourse."
                                                —*Star Tribune* (Minneapolis)

"Utilizing Alice's personal papers, Cordery [shows how] . . . Alice's independence of mind often led her against the grain: she worked to defeat Wilson's League of Nations and was a World War II isolationist and America First activist. Her witty syndicated newspaper columns criticized FDR and the New Deal, and she betrayed her cousin Eleanor by encouraging FDR's liaison with Lucy Mercer Rutherford. Cordery (*Theodore Roosevelt: In the Vanguard of the Modern*) pens an authoritative ~~San Diego Christian College~~ who broke the mold."
                                                —*Publishers Weekly*

ABOUT THE AUTHOR

Stacy A. Cordery is a professor of history at Monmouth College. She is the author of two books on Theodore Roosevelt and is the bibliographer for the National First Ladies' Library. She lives in Monmouth, Illinois, with her husband and son.

Alice

Alice Roosevelt Longworth,

from

White House Princess

to Washington Power Broker

Stacy A. Cordery

PENGUIN BOOKS

PENGUIN BOOKS

Published by the Penguin Group

Penguin Group (USA) Inc., 375 Hudson Street, New York, New York 10014, U.S.A.
Penguin Group (Canada), 90 Eglinton Avenue East, Suite 700, Toronto,
Ontario, Canada M4P 2Y3 (a division of Pearson Penguin Canada Inc.)
Penguin Books Ltd, 80 Strand, London WC2R 0RL, England
Penguin Ireland, 25 St Stephen's Green, Dublin 2, Ireland (a division of Penguin Books Ltd)
Penguin Group (Australia), 250 Camberwell Road, Camberwell,
Victoria 3124, Australia (a division of Pearson Australia Group Pty Ltd)
Penguin Books India Pvt Ltd, 11 Community Centre, Panchsheel Park, New Delhi – 110 017, India
Penguin Group (NZ), 67 Apollo Drive, Rosedale, North Shore 0632,
New Zealand (a division of Pearson New Zealand Ltd)
Penguin Books (South Africa) (Pty) Ltd, 24 Sturdee Avenue,
Rosebank, Johannesburg 2196, South Africa

Penguin Books Ltd, Registered Offices: 80 Strand, London WC2R 0RL, England

First published in the United States of America by Viking Penguin,
a member of Penguin Group (USA) Inc. 2007
Published in Penguin Books 2008

1   3   5   7   9   10   8   6   4   2

Grateful acknowledgment is made to the following for permission to use copyrighted works:
"The Return" from *Personae* by Ezra Pound. Copyright © 1926 by Ezra Pound. Reprinted by
permission of New Directions Publishing Corp.
Joanna Sturm for the use of selections from the Joanna Sturm Papers.

Photographic sources: Page numbers refer to the photo inserts between pages 110 and 111 and 430 and 431.
Joanna Sturm: 1 (top), 6 (top), 7, 8 (top), 11, 12, 13 (bottom), 15 (bottom), 17, 19, 20 (top),
21 (top), 24 (both), 25 (top), 26 (top), 27, 28 (both), 29 (both), 30 (both), 31 (both)
Library of Congress: 2 (both), 3 (both), 4, 5 (top), 9, 10 (bottom), 13 (top), 14 (both),
15 (top), 16, 18 (bottom), 22, 23 (bottom), 26 (bottom)
Theodore Roosevelt Collection, by permission of the Houghton Library,
Harvard University (bMS Am 1541.9 [142]): 1 (bottom)
Georgetown University Art Collection and Deborah Vollmer: 32
All other photographs are from the author's collection.

THE LIBRARY OF CONGRESS HAS CATALOGED THE HARDCOVER EDITION AS FOLLOWS:
Cordery, Stacy A.
Alice : Alice Roosevelt Longworth, from White House princess to Washington power broker / Stacy A. Cordery.
p.   cm.
Includes bibliographical references and index.
ISBN 978-0-670-01833-8 (hc.)
ISBN 978-0-14-311427-7 (pbk.)
1. Longworth, Alice Roosevelt, 1884–1980.   2. Children of presidents—United States—Biography.
3. Roosevelt, Theodore, 1858–1919—Family.   I. Title.
E757.3.C67 2007
973.91'1092—dc22
[B]   2006103087

Printed in the United States of America
Set in Fournier
Designed by Francesca Belanger
Family tree by Jeffrey L. Ward

To
Lewis L. Gould, mentor above all
and
Simon Cordery, partner in all

Preface

FOR NEARLY ALL of her ninety-six years Alice Roosevelt Longworth occupied a unique place in the nation's culture. Part Old Guard, part New Woman, Theodore Roosevelt's eldest daughter embraced her celebrity status and understood the constraints of fame but still did precisely what she wanted. At the turn of the twentieth century she became America's Princess Alice, the intrepid First Daughter who flouted social rules and thereby invited other women to challenge convention. She married Representative Nicholas Longworth in the White House as "the nation's bride," showered with fairy tale presents from governments and citizens around the globe. Torn between her Republican husband and her Progressive father in the 1912 election, she personified the agony of the divided GOP. Meetings in her drawing room helped to change the course of history, as she fought successfully to keep the United States from joining the League of Nations in the early 1920s. Her syndicated newspaper columns criticizing the New Deal programs of her cousins Franklin and Eleanor Roosevelt found a receptive audience and cemented her reputation as a wit. When war erupted again in Europe, Alice Longworth became a founding member of America First to keep the United States neutral in that overseas conflagration. In her sixties during the early cold war years, she campaigned for Robert Taft, boosted Richard Nixon, and became a passionate anti-Communist. Through the Kennedy and Johnson years, she was an institution in the nation's capital and her salon continued to bring together the powerful and the amusing. She embraced her most comfortable role: the other Washington monument.[1]

This book is the first full biography of Alice Roosevelt Longworth based on her personal papers. Access to these untapped sources, not previously available to other biographers and scholars, has opened the way to a more nuanced view than formerly possible of the career of this remarkable American woman. Her tart witticisms were important and influential, but Alice Longworth's sway over governmental policy makers and Washington society was due to her incisive intelligence, eclectic interests, and personal magnetism. Alice's emotional connections with family members and friends, among them leading politicians and journalists, are also revealed in her letters and diaries.

Alice Roosevelt Longworth was the social doyenne in a town where socializing was state business. She had a habit of "taking up" promising public servants. Her approval meant instant access to insiders' Washington. Every president and countless foreign dignitaries requested audiences with her. Politicians, writers, scientists, journalists, and social climbers coveted invitations to her teas. It was worse to be ignored by "Mrs. L" than to be skewered by her, and her rapier-sharp dismissals were reserved for the pompous and the obsequious. She could help dispatch an ineffectual politician to an early professional death—who remembers Thomas Dewey today as anything but "the groom on the wedding cake"? The hundreds of gatherings she hosted played their part in the smooth workings of the American government. Alice collected Republicans and Democrats, hawks and doves, people with and people lacking society's approbation. Talk flowed freely around her, connections were made, deals struck. For five decades, the Longworth home was ground zero for serious socializing among politicians and those who sought to influence them; her salon bridged the two worlds of Washington—society and politics. Alice Longworth ignored the Junior League and women's clubs. She had no need of them: leaders of the free world came to her dinner table.

They came because she was a politician; never elected, always involved. The *Oxford English Dictionary* defines *politician* as "one versed in the theory or science of government and the art of governing." Alice Longworth read political philosophy and avidly followed the course of legislation and foreign affairs. Her patriotism and her partisanship burned like twin flames at the center of her philosophy. She cared deeply about the preservation of the United States and never took its continuation for granted. She grew up knowing Civil War veterans, lived through two epic world wars, and faced the cold war with trepidation and resolve. Alice Longworth expected to be disappointed by elected officials, but she never lost her love for the political game.

She had a cheerful countenance, and that sometimes disguised her habit of looking on the world with what she called "detached malevolence."[2] She laughed easily and often, finding humanity wryly funny in its capricious and frequently self-destructive march. She was personally shy—just one reason she never sought elected office. Alice brooked weakness from no one, least of all herself. She was a mother, a grandmother, an important aunt for younger Roosevelts. And, in the same way that Eleanor Roosevelt had a platform because of her husband's position, Alice was the eldest daughter of a charismatic president, the wife of the Speaker of the House of Representatives, the sister of the assistant secretary of the navy, and the lover of the chair of the Senate Foreign Relations Committee during the heady interwar years when foreign policy was debated fiercely across the nation. But it wasn't simply her name or her connections that made Alice a celebrity and a power broker. Pulitzer Prize–winning author Paul Horgan believed "her spirited character, her civilized gaiety, and her all-out convictions" made "her a figure of political consequence—one of the first American women to achieve this position." It also took her intellect. She was widely considered the most brilliant of her siblings; even Eleanor—who had no reason to love her cousin—admitted that Alice had "an extraordinary mind."[3]

Like all Roosevelts, Alice had wide-ranging interests. An autodidact with a lifelong passion for knowledge, she taught herself Greek at age eighty. Filling her bookshelves were tomes historical, philosophical, literary, and scientific—theories of evolution were a particular interest. She retained a fascination for subjects that had grabbed her as a girl: Romany culture, fairies, poetry. In common with all her clan, Alice could and did quote quite liberally great passages from Alexander Pope, William Shakespeare, Rudyard Kipling, Charles Lamb, Niccolò Machiavelli, Sir Thomas

Browne, and others. And the amount and type of poetry she cherished and recited from memory was staggering—from Ogden Nash's limericks to G. K. Chesterton's "Lepanto." Alice Longworth's extensive library contained battered and marked copies of anthologies such as *The Oxford Book of English Verse*, Burton Stevenson's *Home Book of Verse*, the Modern Library edition of *Anthology of Famous European and American Poetry*, and volumes from poets like E. A. Robinson, Ezra Pound, and Alfred Austin, usually inscribed to her by the authors. Alice and her brother Ted coedited a volume of poetry. She loved words and word games; dog-eared and annotated in her angular handwriting were *Brewer's Dictionary of Phrase and Fable*, *The Oxford Book of Green Verse in Translation*, and *Aesop's Book of Fables*.

Essentially, though, she was always, always Theodore Roosevelt's daughter—the first-born and the longest-lived of his children. Theodore Roosevelt is the key to understanding Alice. Her formative years were shaped by abandonment. The three pivotal adults in her young life—her mother (involuntarily), her father, her aunt—abrogated their principal duties as parents: they failed to love her unconditionally and they all left her prematurely. Alice grew up with no reason to trust anyone. "To thine own self be true" became the motto of a girl who was motherless; rejected by her father; forsaken by her surrogate mother, Auntie Bye; and widowed young by her unfaithful husband. The acting out that Alice did as a teenager in the White House was only partly to gain the attention of the father she so desperately needed to notice her. It was also the logical modeling of a child after her elders, in this case Theodore Roosevelt and his elder sister, Bye. Denied the example of her mother, Alice Hathaway Lee Roosevelt, who died in childbirth, and disinclined to follow any lead provided by her withdrawn and puritanical stepmother, Edith Kermit Carow Roosevelt, Alice looked instead to her distant father and her beloved aunt. They bequeathed to Alice tremendous cerebral and political gifts in lieu of reliable emotional sustenance. TR and Bye were lighthearted intellectuals who thrived on new ideas, interesting people, and challenging situations. Both loved life. Both had what a relative called "tremendous vitality" that they could impart to others like "a shot in the arm."[4] Both appreciated their social positions but fought injustice when they saw it. Bye's happy home, where Alice lived from birth to age three, had a revolving door. Through it came and went good friends and fascinating achievers of all sorts. Conversation at the dinner table danced along a wide collection of topics, setting an example Alice would emulate. After marriage, Bye relocated to Washington, D.C., and became the center of a constellation of brilliant people, especially politicians. When Roosevelt was president, her home was the "other White House."

Theodore Roosevelt was much like his elder sister, Bye: iconoclastic, boisterous, energetic, and larger than life, yet thoughtful, well read, disciplined, and charming. He was the unmistakable sire of Princess Alice. The fact that she did not wholly share his sense of noblesse oblige was perhaps a sign of the lack of nurturing she received when young. The ideas of duty and service that Edith and Theodore imparted to their own children Alice understood. But rejecting them was part of her fractured birthright. When she wanted to, she could be as proper as her perfect half sister, Ethel. But she had to want to. Independence was the substitute for parental love that Alice generated out of self-defense. Thus independence could be a mask— but more often it was a prop.

Alice Roosevelt Longworth decried sentimentalism and neediness. Her father's famous strenuous life was transmuted in her to a hyper-self-reliance. The torrent of books and articles he published was echoed in her newspaper columns, but even more in her famous wordplay. Weathering one of her gibes was the best letter of recommendation to her salon. She was a survivor; she was tough; she was impenetrable. Morbid grief about a dead mother won no points in a nursery fast filling with half siblings. Her own father never mentioned her mother to her; it was a clear sign to Alice that the unhappy past was gone—literally dead and buried. Alice lived in the present. Her friend journalist Bill Walton said she seldom indulged in reminiscing.[5] She sought to please herself, having learned early that adults could not be trusted. IF YOU CAN'T SAY SOMETHING GOOD ABOUT SOMEONE, SIT RIGHT HERE BY ME read the legendary needlepoint pillow in her sanctuary. Though she did not originate the phrase, she adored the pillow. Stepmother Edith would not have approved. But then the sanction of others never meant much to Alice.

Mrs. L of the barbed tongue, the heterodoxy, the one who, as she said, left the good deeds to Eleanor, is only the tip of the complex woman who was Alice Lee Roosevelt Longworth. "Her interest in politics is nothing less than joyous," a reporter wrote in 1929.[6] Politics was about power, about an agenda for the nation, about morals, about civic duty, but it was also about politicians. The human condition intrigued her. As a friend put it, tapping her temple, "She liked to be amused, but she would muse—deeply—about everything."[7] Alice Longworth immersed herself in books and took seriously the obligation to be an informed citizen in the democracy she loved. She commands our attention not only because of her many achievements, her position and use of power at the epicenter of the nation's capital, her inherently interesting and often sorrow-filled life, but because she was an early-model bad girl who snarled instead of smiling, who spoke up rather than shut up, and who surrounded herself with men and women of ideas rather than a house full of children.

In 1966, at age eighty-two, Alice Longworth had tea with two old friends. As the water boiled, the subject turned to historical memory and the tendency to Bowdlerize to protect heroes. "Mrs. L remarked that 'I can assure you *nothing happened*' was the most insidious phrase possible. She poked her hands, clenched, into the wine-colored velvet cushions of her sofa, darted a glance from one to the other, and said, 'If anyone ever brings forth my name into such a conversation, I want them to say, "Believe me, *plenty happened*.'" "[8]

Contents

Alice

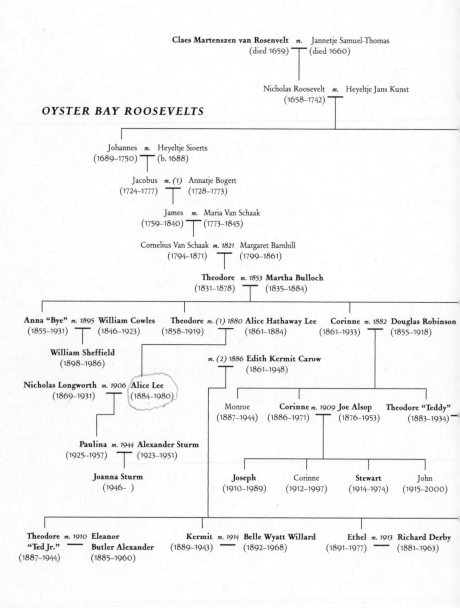

Claes Martenszen van Rosenvelt *m.* Jannetje Samuel-Thomas
(died 1659) (died 1660)

Nicholas Roosevelt *m.* Heyeltje Jans Kunst
(1658–1742)

OYSTER BAY ROOSEVELTS

Johannes *m.* Heyeltje Sioerts
(1689–1750) (b. 1688)

Jacobus *m. (1)* Annatje Bogert
(1724–1777) (1728–1773)

James *m.* Maria Van Schaak
(1759–1840) (1773–1845)

Cornelius Van Schaak *m. 1821* Margaret Barnhill
(1794–1871) (1799–1861)

Theodore *m. 1853* **Martha Bulloch**
(1831–1878) (1835–1884)

Anna "Bye" *m. 1895* **William Cowles**
(1855–1931) (1846–1923)

Theodore *m. (1) 1880* **Alice Hathaway Lee**
(1858–1919) (1861–1884)

Corinne *m. 1882* **Douglas Robinson**
(1861–1933) (1855–1918)

William Sheffield
(1898–1986)

m. (2) 1886 **Edith Kermit Carow**
(1861–1948)

Nicholas Longworth *m. 1906* Alice Lee
(1869–1931) (1884–1980)

Monroe
(1887–1944)

Corinne *m. 1909* Joe Alsop
(1886–1971) (1876–1953)

Theodore "Teddy"
(1883–1934)

Paulina *m. 1944* **Alexander Sturm**
(1925–1957) (1923–1951)

Joseph
(1910–1989)

Corinne
(1912–1997)

Stewart
(1914–1974)

John
(1915–2000)

Joanna Sturm
(1946–)

Theodore *m. 1910* Eleanor
"Ted Jr." Butler Alexander
(1887–1944) (1885–1960)

Kermit *m. 1914* **Belle Wyatt Willard**
(1889–1943) (1892–1968)

Ethel *m. 1913* **Richard Derby**
(1891–1977) (1881–1963)

HYDE PARK ROOSEVELTS

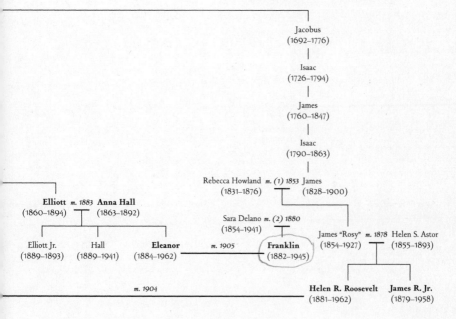

Jacobus
(1692–1776)

Isaac
(1726–1794)

James
(1760–1847)

Isaac
(1790–1863)

Rebecca Howland *m. (1) 1853* James
(1831–1876)   (1828–1900)

Elliott *m. 1883* **Anna Hall**
(1860–1894)   (1863–1892)

Sara Delano *m. (2) 1880*
(1854–1941)

James "Rosy" *m. 1878* Helen S. Astor
(1854–1927)   (1855–1893)

Elliott Jr.   Hall   **Eleanor**   *m. 1905*   **Franklin**
(1889–1893)   (1889–1941)   (1884–1962)   (1882–1945)

m. 1904

Helen R. Roosevelt   **James R. Jr.**
(1881–1962)   (1879–1958)

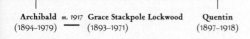

Archibald *m. 1917* **Grace Stackpole Lockwood**   **Quentin**
(1894–1979)   (1893–1971)   (1897–1918)

Names in boldface are mentioned in *Alice.*

Chapter 1

"It Was Awfully Bad Psychologically"

AN APPALLING double tragedy overshadowed the joy that should have welcomed Alice Lee Roosevelt's entrance to the world on February 12, 1884. The popular, young New York assemblyman Theodore Roosevelt lost both his beautiful wife, Alice Hathaway Lee, and his beloved mother, Martha Bulloch Roosevelt, on Valentine's Day 1884. He gave the infant her mother's name, a wet nurse, a temporary home, and then relegated her to an afterthought. The family turned in upon itself, lost in grief at the sudden and unexpected deaths, too heartbroken to celebrate Alice's birth. It was the last time anything would eclipse Alice Roosevelt.

The grieving family into which Alice was born boasted a long pedigree with fascinating forebears and a comfortable wealth. Dutchman Claes Martenszen van Rosenvelt arrived in colonial America in the 1640s, well over a century before the thirteen colonies declared independence from Great Britain. Claes and Jannetje Samuel-Thomas van Rosenvelt's son Johannes became the paterfamilias of the Theodore Roosevelt side of the family (the Oyster Bay, Long Island, Roosevelts). Another son, Jacobus, sired what would become the Franklin D. Roosevelt side (the Hyde Park Roosevelts). Five generations of Roosevelt merchants and businessmen, trading in hardware, glass, and other goods, culminated in Cornelius van Schaak Roosevelt. In 1840, he was one of the founders of Chemical National Bank and the father of Theodore Roosevelt Sr., the future president's father. The Roosevelt family grew in size and wealth. By the time Theodore Roosevelt Jr. was born, the family was one of New York's oldest and most socially prominent.

Alice Roosevelt was descended on her mother's side from a Boston Brahmin banking family, the Lees, and through them the Cabots and the Lowells, the families immortalized in John Bossidy's poem about Boston, "Where the Lowells talk only to the Cabots / And the Cabots talk only to God." On Alice's father's side, New England Dutch merchants and patrician Bourbons met. Her paternal grandmother was Martha Bulloch Roosevelt, descendent of an established Southern family whose ancestor James Bulloch had come to America in 1729. Thus Alice enjoyed impeccable membership in the American aristocracy.[1]

Consciousness of their tenure in North America—a fundamental part of what made patricians patricians—suffused the Roosevelt clan. Alice would later jest that the Roosevelts had managed to stay "one step ahead of the bailiff from an island in the Zuider Zee."[2] Still, the family was one of New York's oldest and most socially prominent and such a long line of antecedents gave the Roosevelts an unshakeable social stature and the certainty of belonging. Even encroachment by nouveau riche industrial capitalists could not threaten their standing. The Roosevelts might be outspent but not outclassed, and no amount of money earned by an upstart Scottish immigrant such as Andrew Carnegie would ever erase the fact that the Roosevelts beat him to America. The Vanderbilts could not buy, after the fact, a generalship in the American Revolution, or a seat at the Philadelphia convention. Alice's ancestors had both.

Around Alice's unchanging and insular world, the rest of the United States was rapidly transforming under the combined forces of industrialization and urbanization, fueled by immigrants from all over the world. Industrialization brought new inventions such as the telephone, indoor plumbing, electric lights, and central heating. Urbanization crowded people into cities, and tenements piled family on top of family. Horse cars, electric trolleys, and suburban trains ferried the middle classes to work. Seventeen million immigrants came to the United States between 1900 and 1917. They powered America's second industrial revolution, but their different languages, religions, and expectations gave rise to labor unrest and cultural upheaval. The Republican Party controlled the presidency in eight out of ten elections between the end of the Civil War and Theodore Roosevelt's ascension to that office in 1901. The Grand Old Party was the pro-business advocate of national expansion and high tariffs. The GOP considered itself the moral arbiter for the nation, having successfully guided the country through the 1898 Spanish-American War and begun America's rise to world prominence. Although they could not vote, women entered college and the workforce in small but increasing numbers. Family size decreased as mothers chose to bear fewer offspring. The average life expectancy at the turn of the century was forty years for men and forty-eight years for women. African Americans, struggling under legal segregation after 1896, confronted increasing hostilities. Resistance took organized form in the 1890s, as the Afro-American Council and later the National Association for the Advancement of Colored People fought the uphill battle against institutionalized racism.

Roosevelt wealth and status protected Alice from such changes. In 1896, 5.5 million of America's 12.5 million families were working class, earning less than $500 annually. The Roosevelts were among the 1.5 million families bringing in more than $5,000 per year and owning 86 percent of the nation's wealth.[3] They ran the banks and the railroads, the law firms and the politicians. They also governed the social code. Victorian morality was synonymous with honorable men, demure women, and docile children. Etiquette prescribed a precise system of behavior appropriate to baptisms, funerals, and every life situation in between. Good breeding entailed hewing closely to the moral code, instilling class values in children, and never causing a public scandal. Women's names were to appear in newspapers only at marriage and death.

The Roosevelt family belonged to a social circle of New Yorkers called Knickerbockers. Like their Massachusetts counterparts, the Boston Brahmins, they constituted a closed society. Knickerbockers and Brahmins conducted business among themselves and spent their leisure time together. Parents pressured children to marry within their stratum, a frequent occurrence as the Old Money elites did not consistently mingle with the nouveaux riches until the late 1880s. In that decade, the arrivistes, such as the

Vanderbilts, the Harrimans, and the Goulds, amassed so much money that it became possible for them to "buy" their way into society—or so fretted conservative Knickerbockers.

Theodore Roosevelt was born just as the upstart Robber Barons were starting their fortunes. The elder son of Theodore Roosevelt Sr. and Martha "Mittie" Bulloch Roosevelt, Teedie, as he was called as a young boy, grew up in a loving and sheltered environment, blemished only by his physical condition. Asthma and his undersized body contributed to making him an advocate of "the strenuous life." As a young man, he was closest to his father and to his elder sister, Anna, called Bamie or Bye. Their father gave his time and money to charities like Mrs. Slattery's Night School for Little Italians and cofounded cultural institutions such as the Metropolitan Museum of Art. Inheriting his father's altruistic nature and sense of duty, Theodore would see beyond his class.

Mittie was a transplanted Southerner. She filled her children's heads with the escapades of their swashbuckling Confederate uncles. Her appreciation for their heroics took root especially in her eldest son, who avidly read sagas and legends of many cultures. Mittie and her children shared a close bond. She was their first teacher and a model of the ideal wife who provided support for her husband's activities and managed the family's networks. While Mittie had her quirks—she was consumed with a passion for cleanliness and depended greatly on her eldest daughter for assistance with household tasks—her husband and children adored her and her impish sense of humor.

Teedie's relationship with his brother, Elliott (who would be Eleanor Roosevelt's father), was affectionate but competitive. Elliott seemed to have all the good looks, the charisma, the physical prowess, and the sense of fun. Young Theodore was bookish. He immersed himself in heroic literature and nature studies, and these came to supplement a later love of hunting, taxidermy, and histories of warfare. However, Elliott lacked Theodore's tenacity and his moral core. Elliott died at the age of thirty-four, an alcoholic, drug addict, and adulterer, possibly also suffering from undiagnosed epilepsy.[4]

When TR was twenty years old and halfway through his degree at

Harvard College, his father succumbed to stomach cancer. The inheritance TR gained could not make up for the loss of "the best man [he] ever knew," the father of whom he did not feel worthy. His grief was profound. Less than five months after his father died, he mused to his diary, "Had a very good sermon. I was much struck with one remark, that Christianity gave us, on this earth, rest in trouble, not from trouble."[5]

After his father's death, Roosevelt could live lavishly. His $8,000 annual trust income was $3,000 a year more than the salary of the president of Harvard. The Brahmins were happy to claim him as one of their own, giving him an immediate circle of like-minded gentlemen friends. All of the best Harvard clubs, including the Porcellian and the Hasty Pudding, inducted Theodore into their ranks. He joined the Rifle Club, the Art Club, the Glee Club; served as president of the Natural History Society; and helped found the Finance Club. His habits were not those of a raucous student. Roosevelt did not smoke, detested "low humor," and taught Sunday School classes. He studied biology but found his love of the outdoors thwarted by Harvard's theoretical scientists, who preferred the classroom. Roosevelt turned to history and government. His undergraduate thesis, "The Practicability of Equalizing Men and Women Before the Law," considered the topic of women's rights, including property ownership, and argued that women ought to keep their birth names upon marrying. Roosevelt was an excellent student in the era of the "gentleman's C," but something about him always stood out. He lacked the undergraduate savoir faire that marked his sophisticated classmates, and was known for single-minded intensity in almost every task he approached. This was not a compliment.

Theodore Roosevelt never concentrated quite so hard as during his courtship of the striking and athletic Alice Hathaway Lee. Theodore met Alice when he was nineteen and she was seventeen. His diary rarely ran on a one-woman track, and very few days passed without mention of other females who caught his fancy, but when Roosevelt began a serious pursuit of Alice, he could confide to his diary, "Thank Heaven I am absolutely pure."[6]

Alice Hathaway Lee was born in Chestnut Hill, Massachusetts, on July

29, 1861. She was the daughter of George Cabot Lee and Caroline Watts (Haskell) Lee. Alice Lee was called Sunshine by family and friends, who all agreed it perfectly described her cheerful disposition. She was young, charming, independent minded, and beautiful. Photographs prove her to have been slim and delicate of feature. As a young woman, Alice was tall for the era, almost Theodore's height of five feet, eight inches. Her daughter would inherit her nose, mouth, and slender build. George Lee was a wealthy Boston banker whose affluence allowed Alice and her sisters to live well but not ostentatiously. The Lees prepared their daughters for marriage—a woman's career then—by making them practice ramrod-straight posture and probably by learning other "finishing" skills, such as embroidery, music, and a little French. Alice excelled at archery and tennis, and during walks could cover ground as rapidly as her swain.

Alice attended many balls and parties that featured Harvard's best young men. Her next-door neighbor and cousin, Dick Saltonstall, introduced her, in October 1878, to third-year student Theodore Roosevelt. Roosevelt's father had died nine months earlier, and TR's grief was still raw. He confided to his diary in April, "I have lost the only human being to whom I told *everything*, never failing to get loving advice and sweet sympathy in return; no one, but my wife, if ever I marry, will ever be able to take his place. I so wonder who my wife will be! 'A rare and radiant maiden' I hope; one who will be as sweet, pure and innocent as she is wise."[7]

While "absolutely pure," Roosevelt was clearly not immune to the charms of women. On New Year's Day 1878, TR chronicled his "twenty calls," including one on Edith Carow.[8] He and Edith had grown up together. One of her earliest memories was a visit from the Roosevelts. Four-year-old Edith immediately bonded with Teedie, age seven. But the Knickerbocker Carows were starting to feel the effects of the patriarch's alcoholism. Charles Carow's drinking interfered with his transatlantic shipping business, and the family fortunes suffered. Between her father's mounting troubles and her deepening friendship with the Roosevelt children, Edith became a sort of charity case in the Roosevelt household. Tutored alongside the Roosevelt children, active in their childhood games and able to match them at intellectual pursuits, Edith grew closest to Theodore's sister Corinne, but never lost her initial response to Theodore.

Edith was sweet on him then and until they were teenagers. During two weeks together in the summer of 1878, TR and Edith rowed, swam, and took companionable walks in the way of longtime friends. He drove her out to pick water lilies and spent, as he recounted to his diary, "a lovely morning with her."[9] But Edith and TR quarreled frequently, and one of their rows, Edith always maintained, resulted in the breaking off of what she called their engagement. Edith remembered later that TR proposed several times in 1877 and 1878, but got nowhere because of objections, based either on her youth or on some unsuitable characteristics of the Roosevelts, made by Edith's maternal grandfather. Corinne later suggested that it was *her* father who forbade marriage because of Charles Carow's alcoholism.[10] TR never spoke to his daughter about her mother so Alice Roosevelt Longworth would only have heard her stepmother's side of the story—the side that hurt the most. In this version Alice's mother was TR's second choice: her father picked Alice Lee only after Edith, his first love, had spurned him.

No hint of an engagement appears in TR's diary—but he was never candid there on the most intimate matters until after the fact. There is the intriguing notation from Thursday, August 22, 1878, that "Edith and I went up to the summer house," presumably to have the talk that resulted in their estrangement. This was followed immediately by, "My ride today was so long and hard that I am afraid it may have injured my horse." The next entry is dated two days later: "The other day a dog annoyed me very much while on horseback, and I told the owner I should shoot it; which threat I fulfilled while out riding with [cousin] West today, rolling it over with my revolver very neatly as it ran alongside the horse."[11] A horse lamed and a dog dead because of Roosevelt's fury at Edith's rejection? He had known Edith longer than any other woman. To tender a marriage offer to one like kin not long after his family circle was broken is not farfetched, and of the women he knew, he would have expected Edith to be the most sympathetic. For her to reject his attempt at patching the circle back together must have seemed both incredible and cruel to the grieving young man.

After Edith and TR's argument, fifty-six days passed without female companionship.[12] Instead, Roosevelt took twenty-mile horseback rides and rowing excursions, a five-day "yachting cruise," and a three-week hunting trip through the Maine woods. It wasn't until his eventful junior year at Harvard that he met the scintillating Alice Lee. On the eighteenth of October, TR confided that Saltonstall drove him over to the family manse at Chestnut Hill in Boston, where "all his family are just too sweet to me for anything," and where he met Alice Lee. It was truly love at first sight for TR. "I fell in love with her then," he recounted to a cousin, ". . . and only the third time I had seen her, I registered a vow in my journal that win her I would. . . ."[13]

He became a regular presence at Chestnut Hill. "I really feel almost as if I were at home when I am over there," he wrote during one palliative stay. In the wake of his father's absence, he found patriarch Leverett Saltonstall "one of the best examples of a true, simple hearted 'gentleman of the old school' I have ever met." But Alice was the real enticement. The more he saw of "pretty Alice," the more he was certain in his objective toward her. And he saw quite a lot of her. By the end of April, TR and Alice sought time alone. At a theater party they "sat just behind the others," and during a walk, "Alice and I soon separated from the others and we did not return till nearly six."[14] They had their photographs taken together—that is, Alice and Theodore and the ubiquitous Rose, with some other friends. Dick's sister Rose Saltonstall was the socially dictated third person, since suitors of that class were not often allowed to be alone together.

Theodore's pursuit of Alice became ever more fervent, but she turned down his proposal. Roosevelt was distraught. He rode his horse back to Harvard in the "pitch dark" and "fell, while galloping down hill." It was, he chided himself, "a misadventure which I thoroughly deserve for being a fool."[15] It cost him another horse lamed.

Why Alice Lee declined Theodore's offer is not wholly apparent. George and Caroline Lee considered their daughter too young to know her mind. She hadn't even come out to society yet. It may be that the Lees wanted proof that Theodore would settle into a career that could provide for their daughter. What he would do to increase the Roosevelt fortune was not obvious when he asked for Alice's hand in marriage. Perhaps they objected to the peculiar mannerisms of the prospective son-in-law. His busy mind was occupied always with a plurality of thoughts, and they tumbled out of his mouth at such a rate that others sometimes had trouble understanding him. In TR's case, one avocation led to another. His childhood interest in the natural world grew into a serious study of the surrounding fauna. To learn better the science behind nature, Roosevelt studied Latin. To examine the animals he shot, he took up taxidermy, making his expensive clothes smell oddly of chemicals. His commitment to charitable work was also a bit strange to the other young men in Harvard Yard. The zealous way in which he lived his life applied to sports as well: he boxed, rowed, hunted, rode, walked (strenuously), and enjoyed every sport but baseball.

Yet Alice didn't reject him absolutely. In the miserable way of young love, TR was happy—and undeterred. Bubbling with optimism at the end of his junior year, he marveled, "I doubt if I ever shall enjoy myself so much again. I have done well in my studies and I have had a most royally good time with the Club, my horse, and above all, the sweet, pretty girls at Chestnut Hill, etc." After a summer spent at Oyster Bay—during which time he remembered to send Edith Carow a book for her eighteenth birthday—Roosevelt reappeared in Boston for his senior year. Of course it wasn't long before he and Dick Saltonstall presented themselves at Chestnut Hill, but Roosevelt's diary continues to provide evidence that while Alice Lee held his heart, his oldest friend still impressed him: "Had a most delightful call on Edith Carow; she is the most cultivated, best read girl I know."[16] Adjectives such as these he reserved for Edith alone.

He continued to see both women. In November 1878, he hosted a luncheon at the Porcellian in honor of his visiting sisters, who were charmed by Alice Lee. He whirled Alice across the floor at her coming-out party on December 2. At home over the Christmas holidays, TR saw Edith more than once. He lunched with her on Boxing Day, but spent the afternoon preparing for the arrival of Alice Lee, Rose and Dick Saltonstall, and three other friends. They "danced the old year out and drank the new year in," and a great party of them went out for a spree and supper.[17]

Finally—finally—on January 25, 1880, his exultant diary entry reads,

"I am so happy that I dare not trust in my own happiness. I drove over to the Lees determined to make an end of things at last; it was nearly eight months since I had first proposed to her, and I had been nearly crazy during the past year; and after much pleading my own sweet, pretty darling consented to be my wife. Oh, how bewitchingly pretty she looked! If loving her with my whole heart and soul can make her happy, she shall be happy." The success of his conquest freed Roosevelt's pen, and he confessed that "it was a real case of love at first sight—and my first love, too."[18] So much for Edith.

The weeks passed deliciously. Alice received a gratifying number of congratulations and basked in engagement parties in her honor. The women of the family tightened their circle around her. One week after the engagement, Bye sermonized, "Theodore is the one most truly like Father and the one from whom Father expected so much and on whom we all greatly lean; and now I feel sure you will help him lead a true and noble life worthy of his Father's name."[19] Alice understood. She never offered a challenge to the Roosevelt women, but seems to have blended into the family with ease; while her relatives provided Theodore with a true second home.

Theodore managed to tear himself away from the happy socializing to take one last hunting trip as a bachelor. "I do not know what I will do when you go out West for six weeks," Alice lamented. "What a good time we did have at Oyster Bay, I loved so much our pleasant little evenings in the summer house and all our lovely drives together. Teddy I love you with my whole heart and am never happier than I am when I am with you," she wrote. Their letters attest to their twin worries: his health and their fitness for marriage. On the eve of his departure, he confided, "I hope we have good sport, or, at any rate, that I get into good health. I am feeling pretty well now; and the Doctor said the very best thing for me was to go."[20]

In the fall of 1880, TR reluctantly left her side again and returned to New York to see about wedding plans. He also enrolled in law school at Columbia University—but without much enthusiasm and with no plans to practice law.[21] He called on his mother, for the two had much to discuss. Mittie and Caroline Lee assisted with the wedding preparations, and the latter had her hands full with a deluge of more than 250 wedding presents.

Early in the process, Alice crowed to TR, "Just think Teddy we have got 79 presents, I had them all out this afternoon for different people to see." In addition to her wedding gift, the groom gave the bride a "beautiful ring." "What an extravagant boy you are, Teddy," Alice purred.[22]

The wedding took place at noon on Wednesday, October 27, 1880, Theodore's twenty-second birthday. Elliott was his brother's best man, and Corinne was one of the four bridesmaids. The crowd overflowed Brookline's Unitarian church. Edith Carow was there and danced the soles off her shoes, subduing her lingering feelings for Theodore.[23] If the bridegroom noticed, he did not leave a record. The newlyweds spent a fortnight at the family home in Oyster Bay, New York, which Bye had prepared for them. "Teddy and I take lovely drives every morning and in the afternoon we either play tennis or walk," Alice wrote to thank her sister-in-law. "I never saw time go faster," she gushed to Bye. "I am so happy."[24] Alice and TR took a proper five-month European honeymoon in the spring of 1881, characterized apparently by the sweet harmony between them. The only trouble came from a physician who warned Theodore that his heart was so weak he should never undertake strenuous exercise. Characteristically, TR ignored him and climbed the 14,693-foot Matterhorn.

When they returned, glowing with good health and contentment, Theodore and Alice moved in with the Roosevelt family at 6 West Fifty-seventh Street. They had their own suite on the third floor. It was an idyllic time. The two began to entertain, going out most nights to join other society leaders. Alice attended meetings of her sewing circle.[25] Occasionally, she visited her family in Boston. She was busy there, with twenty callers in one day, she marveled once, and "everyone is so kind to me." But she worried about her husband stuck at home "making your little <u>boats</u>, up to all hours in the night; with no one to call you to bed." The nighttimes were hardest for them both. "I miss you so much more at night," the new bride confessed.[26] TR was researching and writing *The Naval War of 1812*—his "little boats." He found the project much more engrossing than law school, from which he eventually withdrew, degreeless.

In search of a useful career, Theodore Roosevelt won election to the New York State assembly from the Twenty-first District in 1881, one year after he had formally joined the Republican Party. He spent that fall at the state capital in Albany immersed in his political education. Bye conscientiously cut out newspaper clippings featuring TR and pasted them into her scrapbook. Roosevelt, at twenty-three, was the youngest assemblyman, and he had powerful backers among conservative Knickerbocker elites who tried to gauge his potential. His beautiful wife was by his side for that first winter of 1882. They lived in a boardinghouse that rang with tales of the days' business as Alice absorbed the Byzantine world of New York politics.

On weekends they returned to New York City and the family, where Bye hosted gatherings of politicians, writers, journalists, intellectuals, and reformers to help advance her brother's career. Bringing together influential people from many walks of life was a gift of Bye's, one she used quite freely on her brother's behalf throughout the rest of his life. Educated briefly at Les Ruches in Fontainebleau under the eagle eye of Marie Souvestre, Bye had been given an excellent grounding both in political philosophy and the social graces.

Older Roosevelts provided two different paths to politics. Theodore Sr. had been a Republican delegate to the GOP convention that kept two corrupt nominees—James G. Blaine and Roscoe Conkling—away from the presidency; later Roosevelt paid the price by being denied the position of collector of the Port of New York by Conkling. Still, he had no regrets. In the last letter he ever wrote to TR, Theodore Sr. told his impressionable son that he was proud of the fight he had made against "machine politicians" who "think of nothing higher than their own interests. I fear for your future," he worried. "We cannot stand so corrupt a government for any great length of time."[27]

A second path came from the example of TR's uncle Robert B. Roosevelt, who fought from the other side of the aisle. A lifelong Democrat, Uncle Robert was already well known for his commitment to the conservation of wildlife—he may have been TR's inspiration for his college plan of becoming a scientist—and his service in the U.S. Congress from 1871 to 1873. He was the author of such works as *Is Democracy Dishonesty?*, *The Washington City Ring*, and *Progressive Petticoats*. For the young assemblyman, Theodore Sr. and Robert set two examples of Roosevelts with a reform bent.

TR's background predisposed him to voting on behalf of his class. Nevertheless, he surprised many people, including his working-class constituents, when, during the Westbrook scandal, he made a name for himself as a reformer dedicated to clean government. After conducting his own research, Roosevelt concluded that Judge Theodore R. Westbrook was the pawn of Robber Baron Jay Gould and had profited illegally because of their business dealings. Roosevelt stood before the Albany assembly shaking with passionate indignation and called for the judge's impeachment. He lost, outmaneuvered by his senior colleagues, some of whom were themselves in Gould's pocket. But as a result, TR became a leader of the reform faction—cheered by some and hissed by others, whose class interests they accused Roosevelt of betraying.

Roosevelt turned a deaf ear to the "old family friend" who warned him to give up "the reform play" because he had "gone far enough, and that now was the time to leave politics and identify myself with the right kind of people, the people who would always in the long run control others...."[28] Roosevelt had intended to vote against a bill that would outlaw cigar making in homes, but he changed his mind after labor activist Samuel Gompers took him on a tour of the hovels where cigar makers, mostly Jewish immigrants, lived and worked. Aghast at the squalor, Roosevelt, taking a page from his father's book, decided the sweatshop system was immoral. People could not live healthily enough to participate in the democracy in such conditions. Between Westbrook and Gompers, Roosevelt found the gumption to step outside of himself and view life through the eyes of others. Thus began his career in public service, one in which he generally put the needs of the many above the greed of a few. The fork in TR's political road bent pragmatically leftward until very late in his life.

In October 1882, Assemblyman Roosevelt and his wife left Mittie and moved into their own home, a rented house at 55 West Forty-fifth Street. Alice's charm and beauty made them leaders of, in the jargon of the day, "the young married swells." Quiet evenings at home were the exception, but both husband and wife continued to delight in each other. In the summer of 1883, after undergoing an undefined gynecological surgery, Alice became pregnant. She couldn't find the words to tell Bye "how happy" the knowledge had made her.[29] Theodore's asthma resurfaced at the news. He threw himself into his second term in the legislature. When the session was over, Roosevelt returned to the Dakotas to hunt buffalo and regain his equilibrium. Having fallen in love with the wildness and the open skies around Medora, he invested ten thousand dollars in a ranch and began to animate it with cattle. He expected both a large return on his investment and to enjoy, once a year or so, the life of a cattle rancher.

The couple had also purchased more than fifty acres of land at rural Oyster Bay on which to build a home for their family. They joined other Roosevelts who had chosen the northern shore of Long Island for its proximity to Manhattan. The house was to be called Leeholm in Alice's honor, and would boast ten bedrooms and a large wraparound porch. They dreamed of a home filled with children—many of their own, and their nephews, nieces, and eventually grandchildren, too. Leeholm was a tangible commitment to their future, as tangible as the baby Alice carried. "My own tender true love," Roosevelt wrote Alice, "I never cease to think fondly of you; and oh how doubly tender I feel towards you now! You have been the truest and tenderest of wives, and you will be the sweetest and happiest of all little mothers."[30]

The Roosevelt family correspondence recorded nothing unusual during Alice Lee Roosevelt's pregnancy. Her mother-in-law remarked once about "how very large" Alice looked. She may have been commenting on the way Alice looked in a particular dress on a particular day, or she might have been viewing one of the symptoms of chronic nephritis. Theodore was not overly concerned about his wife. She had moved back into Mittie's house, and had Mittie's sister Anna Bulloch Gracie, Anna Hall Roosevelt (Elliott's wife), Mittie, Bye, and Corinne close by. Her own mother was a short train ride away in Boston. Theodore spent his weeks in Albany, rushing home for the weekend, except for the times an important bill kept him in the capital.

On February 6, 1884, Roosevelt wrote to his wife, "I look forward so much to seeing you tomorrow; I wish I could be with you to rub you when you get 'crampy.' " Theodore apparently understood the cramps as a normal part of pregnancy, not a warning sign of illness. He spent the weekend of February 9 to 11 with Alice in New York City. Corinne and her new husband, Douglas Robinson, had left their infant son in Bye's care while they were away in Baltimore. Mittie took to bed with what everyone thought was a severe cold. On Monday, the eleventh, Caroline Lee arrived to help her daughter through childbirth. Roosevelt attended hearings downtown that day and then left for the legislature, confident that the women were being well tended.

As he raced away toward Albany, Alice penciled what would be her last letter to her husband: "Darling Thee—I hated so to leave you this afternoon, I dont think you need feel worried about my being sick as the Dr told me this afternoon that I would not need my nurse before Thursday—I am feeling well tonight but am very much worried over the ~~baby~~ your little mother, her fever is still very high and the Dr is rather afraid of typhoid, it is not in the least catching. I will write again to-morrow and let you know just how she is—dont say anything about it till then. I do love my dear Thee so much, I wish I could have my little new baby soon.—ever Your loving wife, Alice."[31]

That evening at 8:30 p.m. Alice gave birth to a healthy, eight-and-three-quarter-pound girl. Anna Gracie bustled about taking care of the infant, while the doctor tended to Alice. Aunt Gracie wrote down an account of the birth. She described Alice crying "I <u>love</u> a little girl," and begging the doctor to tend to the infant as it was sneezing. As Aunt Gracie swaddled the newborn in flannel and set her down in an armchair the infant sneezed again. Alice begged, "Oh, don't let my baby take cold." Gracie remembered Alice remonstrating with the doctor to see to the infant. But he was concerned about the mother. While Aunt Gracie "made up the little Basinet with all the dainty, pretty little things her sweet little mother had laid aside," the family sent a telegram to Albany bearing the good news to the father, but advising him that Alice was "only fairly well." According to Aunt Gracie, "at eleven o'clock the baby's grandmother Lee told me 'Alice has had her child in her arms and kissed it.' "[32] The telegram reached Theodore on the thirteenth during the morning session of the legislature. This great news was stolen from him by the arrival of a second, dire telegram in midafternoon saying Alice had taken a turn for the worse.

Roosevelt left Albany in a fury to make the five-hour train trip home in ghastly weather. Dense fog and rain slowed all traffic in and out of New York. Roosevelt managed to arrive at 11:30 p.m. One hour earlier, Corinne and Douglas had returned home from Baltimore. Elliott threw open the doors of the house and warned them to go see their baby—who had been moved to another relative's home—before entering: "There is a curse on this house," Elliott cried to his sister. "Mother is dying, and Alice is dying too."[33] Inside, the women kept the vigil; Corinne at Alice's bedside and Bye at their mother's. Alice was a victim of an undiagnosed kidney ailment called Bright's disease. Mittie suffered from typhoid, an illness that annually killed several hundreds of city dwellers in the days before sanitation became a civic virtue.

Theodore gazed helplessly at his unconscious wife until called away for the last moments of his mother's life. All four of her children were present when Mittie died at 3:00 a.m. Theodore barely had time to register her death before he scaled the stairs to Alice's room. Eleven hours later, held tenderly by her devastated husband, Alice died. Their infant daughter remained—a living reminder that their joyous life together had not been a dream.

Two thousand people crowded the nave for the double funeral at the Fifth Avenue Presbyterian Church. Theodore suffered impassively through the eulogies and the burials. Four days later, he was back at the legislature. One grueling March day, TR reported twenty-one bills out of committee, and then stayed up all that night redrafting another bill. He couldn't think of his daughter—What did he know of infants? He couldn't face the horrible task of tending to the worldly affairs of his mother. The child and the legal responsibilities reminded him paralyzingly of his double loss. The routine of the statehouse, its masculine culture, and the endless work provided him with the stability to continue. "I think I should go mad if I were not employed," Theodore swore. "The more we work the better I like it," he wrote to Bye.[34]

As he poured himself into his career, he left much to his twenty-nine-year-old sister. Bye responded to the hundreds of condolence letters. It fell to her to organize and distribute their parents' possessions, including the house. Less than a fortnight after Mittie's death, it was done. Bye monitored the building of Leeholm. The agonizing chores were hers because Bye was the least encumbered—no family of her own, no remunerative employment—and because she was the responsible one, the eldest child, who had been more like an adult to her three siblings than one of them when they were younger. As she divided up the property of two lifetimes, Bye became the inheritor of the most painful and precious part of her brother's broken life: the infant Alice. "Her aunt can take care of her better than I can," Roosevelt morosely wrote a friend. "She would be just as well off without me."[35]

The baby had been christened the day after the funerals. Alice Lee Roosevelt was held by her dazed father and wore a smocked gown, "the one her sweet Mother liked more than anything else," Aunt Gracie recalled. The vicar poured water over her forehead from the family's heirloom silver bowl, the newly baptized infant also wore a locket with Sunshine's "golden hair in it."[36] The family usually called her Baby Lee when she was very young, Sister or Sissy when she was a child, and Auntie Sister when she was an adult. Although these are common enough names to give to the eldest daughter in a Southern household, the Roosevelts—with the exception of Mittie—were Northerners. It is more probable that Theodore found it painful to hear the name Alice. It is also curious that Alice was called Baby Lee, and not Baby Roosevelt, as though Theodore could not claim her.

Indeed, he did not act as a father to her for the first three years of her life. Bye moved with Alice into a new house on Madison Avenue, and although Theodore stayed there when he was in New York, he was not often in the metropolis. Theodore, in May, attended the Republican national convention in Chicago, but in the fall he went back to Medora, seeking the solace of the empty spaces and the hard, physical labor that running a cattle ranch entailed. His thoughts turned inward. He tried to put the brief time of happiness with Alice Lee into perspective. The last words he ever wrote about her came in the form of a memorial, penned in the Dakotas and privately published: "Her life had always been in the sunshine; and there had never come to her a single great sorrow; and none ever knew her who did not love and revere her for her bright, sunny temper and her saintly unselfishness. Fair, pure, and joyous as a maiden; loving, tender, and happy as a young wife; when she had just become a mother, when her life seemed to be but just begun, and when the years seemed so bright before her—then, by a strange and terrible fate, death came to her. And when my heart's dearest died, the light went out from my life forever."[37]

With these words, Theodore Roosevelt resolutely closed the book on Alice Hathaway Lee Roosevelt. Ten weeks after she died, he wrote bleakly in a "sketch" of his life: "I married Miss Alice Lee of Boston on leaving college in 1880. My father died in 1878; my wife and mother died in February 1884. I have a little daughter living."[38] Alice Lee Roosevelt does not appear in his published autobiography. Theodore did not speak of her again. His own daughter clearly did not substitute for his "heart's dearest." Even when Bye reminded her brother, "You have your child to live for," Theodore stayed out West.[39]

Anna Roosevelt was three years older than her brother and possessed of the same intelligence, intensity for life, and internal strength. She had overcome infantile paralysis that left her with a hunched back and a hearing problem. As an adult, Alice always held that "if Auntie Bye had been a man, she would have been president."[40] Bye kept the family together throughout its crises. She had been the apple of her father's eye, and the family treated Bye with awe and deference, which she earned through being wise, capable, organized, and less judgmental than Theodore. Bye handled Theodore's finances after Alice Lee's death (although not his investments). She and TR were very close. Bye believed firmly that TR should stay in politics, and she supported friendships and career moves that kept him there. Theodore consulted with Bye, not Elliott's wife, when the family finally had to make decisions about Elliott's wastrel lifestyle. Bye was the logical choice to raise Baby Lee.

Alice filled a deep void in Auntie Bye's life. Except for part of the summers, which Alice spent with her Lee relatives in Boston, the girl lived with her aunt steadily for three years and sojourned there regularly in her youth.

Alice thought Bye "the single most important influence on my childhood," and "the only one I really cared about when I was a child." Bye called Alice her "blue-eyed darling."[41] The bond between Alice and Auntie Bye was deep, strong, and lasting.

Bye's home presented a marked contrast to the one Alice would soon inhabit. Her aunt was outgoing and warm, witty and charming, passionately interested in civic affairs, able both to soothe and to scorn. From Bye Alice learned how to preside over tea and how to butter bread, *then* cut it into the thinnest slices. From Bye Alice studied the art of leading conversation. And from Bye Alice knew that there could be few taboo topics among those truly interested in the world and all its possibilities. With Bye there was, as Alice later put it, "a wonderful feeling of warmth and ease and hospitality."[42] Bye spoiled Alice, just as her Lee relatives did. Until she moved into the White House, Alice's later surroundings as a young girl were devoid of the sophisticated elegance that made a lasting impression on her at Bye's.

Her aunt held a special place in Alice's heart because she told her stories of her mother. Bye assured Alice that her Alice Lee was beautiful and charming, and Alice needed to hear that, for as an adult she recalled:

My father never told me anything about this. In fact, he never ever mentioned my mother to me, which was absolutely wrong. He never even said her name, or that I even had a different mother. He was so self-conscious about it. And my maternal grandparents, with whom I stayed every year in Boston, never mentioned her either. Nor my aunts. Finally, Auntie Bye did tell me something very revealing, such as that she had been very pretty and attractive. And she gave me some of her things . . . from my father I suppose. The whole thing was really handled very badly. It was awfully bad psychologically. There was I, laden with photographs of my late lamented mama, which I had to stick on my dressing table and on the wall above the bed. And I was always being exhorted, particularly by my Irish nurse, to 'say a prayer for your mother in heaven.' It was all quite awful.[43]

It helped, no doubt, that Bye and Alice Lee had been friends. Sensing Alice's pain and the confusion about her absent father and her deceased mother, Auntie Bye channeled all her resources to compensate for Alice's losses, to create a happy home filled with entertainments and interesting people, and to prove to Alice that she was deeply loved. Aunt Gracie remembered young Alice's joy in Anna's presence and how the two-year-old "was prone to laughing until 'her little sides shook.' "[44]

Under Bye's care, Alice experienced warmth, love, and undivided attention for the only time in her life. For the rest of her days, Alice sought, unsuccessfully, to duplicate that unconditional love.

Chapter 2

"Sissy Had a Sweat Nurse!"

WHEN THEODORE ROOSEVELT returned to reclaim his daughter, he did so at the insistence of his new wife, Edith Kermit Carow Roosevelt, already pregnant with their first child. Theodore felt guilty about his first wife's death, ambivalent about his remarriage, and irresolute about his daughter. Alice longed for Theodore's time—what three-year-old doesn't crave her father's undivided attention?—but she never got enough of it. Edith freely admitted that she was not the best kind of mother for a spirited child like Alice. Relinquished by her beloved aunt, Alice grew up a virtual orphan in a clannish family. She was plagued by self-doubt and a haunting sense that she never compared favorably to her siblings or her girlfriends. This would be the theme of her childhood—and the reason for her rebelliousness—which was part self-protective armor and part desperation caused by feeling she had little to lose. The strong-willed young woman who ultimately evolved delighted onlookers as much as she exasperated her parents.

Edith Kermit Carow always knew she would marry Teedie. When he went off to Harvard and fell in love with Alice Lee, no one was more surprised than she. In the small world of the American East Coast elite, Edith and Alice became social acquaintances. They all traveled in a group together to Canada. Edith even hosted a party for Theodore and Alice just after their wedding.

When Alice died, however, Theodore went out of his way to avoid Edith because of the Victorian moral code that dictated a long mourning period, and that he interpreted also to mean that he should be faithful to his wife until death. In 1885, after a nineteen-month separation, TR and Edith accidentally bumped into each other. They fell cautiously but thoroughly in love. TR had to tell his sisters, especially Bye. She and Corinne had long been skeptical of Edith's influence on their brother. They worried that she would try to isolate him from them. While Edith and Corinne had been best friends in their youth, Edith was always more standoffish and private than the Roosevelts. This was hardly surprising, given her father's alcoholism and death, and the family's reduced circumstances. Corinne told Alice years later that she and Anna "feared" that Edith would "come between" the sisters and their brother. "She did in a way," Alice conceded. To soften the blow for the one who would take it the hardest, Theodore wrote Bye a letter of appeasement: "As I have already told you, if you wish to you shall keep Baby Lee, I of course, paying the expense."[1]

Theodore assumed that Edith would not want the lively, toddling reminder of his first marriage around, or perhaps *he* did not want Alice with them. In any event, Roosevelt failed to ask his future wife's opinion before he wrote to Anna. "He obviously felt tremendously guilty about remarrying," Alice believed, "because of the concept that you loved only once and you never loved again." In his attempt to try to forget that he had ever been married, Theodore considered cutting himself off from its most obvious sign. Edith, it turned out, had decided feelings about her duty toward Baby Lee and wanted to bring her into the new family. It was all his fault, he wrote Bye sheepishly, and pleaded with her not to blame Edith.[2]

On December 2, 1886, in England, Theodore and Edith were wed. Bye accompanied TR across the Atlantic, leaving Alice in Aunt Gracie's care. Bye returned alone, as Edith and Theodore explored Europe until March 1887. Forever after, Edith mistily recalled her "honeymoon days, and remember them all one by one, and hour by hour." From abroad, Theodore had to write Bye an embarrassed letter: "I hardly know what to say about Baby Lee. Edith feels more strongly about her than I could have imagined possible. However, we can decide it all when we meet."[3] The newlyweds returned to New York City on March 27. Edith's wishes prevailed. Alice remembered being dressed in her best frock, handed a bouquet of pink roses, and being sent down the stairs of Auntie Bye's home—her home—to welcome Mother, as Edith insisted upon being called.

Bye had seen Alice's first steps, heard her first words, dressed her, fed her, tended her through her sicknesses—including an illness that deformed her legs—for three years. The whole family knew Alice as "Bye's Baby Lee."[4] Now, Theodore, the brother she admired, was coming home with a woman she mistrusted to take "her" child away from her. Almost thirty years later, Bye empathized with the parents of a bride-to-be, "for," she recalled achingly, "it is hard to face parting with one's daughter." In her memoir, Bye explained that "it almost broke my heart to give her up. Still I felt perfectly sure that it was for her good, and that unless she lived with her father she would never see much of him, and as my father and I had had such a close relationship, this would have been a terrible wrong to her...."[5]

Did Alice feel Bye's sadness or Edith's nervousness? Alice remembered Bye telling her, "Remember darling, if you are very unhappy you can always come back to me."[6] The child barely had time to adjust to her situation, for after a week, on April 4, TR and Edith left again to go on holiday, not to return until May, when they finally claimed her. This time, Bye was not present for Alice's final move away from Madison Avenue. She could not bear another wrenching parting as Alice, Theodore, and Edith left for Sagamore Hill (the new name for Leeholm) to live together as a family for the first time. Alice felt abandoned by the woman who had served as both mother and father for her profoundly important first three years.

After only a fortnight at Sagamore Hill, however, Edith shipped Alice off to her Lee grandparents for the annual summer visit. At least Chestnut Hill and Grandma and Grandpa Lee and her Lee aunts were familiar. Alice was their first grandchild and particularly special because she was what remained of their daughter. Alice remembered loving the "three enchanting weeks with everyone trying to make me deliriously happy. I was treated there as *belonging*. Everything belonged to me. I would come in and jump up and down on the sofa, hoping the springs would break, and they would merely smile indulgently."[7] Alice played with her mother's dollhouse and her mother's dolls, perhaps providing her with the sense of continuity that she lacked at Sagamore Hill. Alice romped with the children of the Brahmins, would make her debut alongside them, and continued the friendships into her old age. It is hard to know what some of them thought about her robust Roosevelt upbringing. Mary Lee recalled that Alice and another friend were great pranksters who delighted in upsetting the schoolroom routine from which they were exempt: "The 'fiend and the pirate' of my youth were Alice Roosevelt... and Molly Lowell. I remember one warm spring day when voices arrived in our schoolroom, coming apparently from nowhere, laughing voices shouting remarks not calculated to keep our minds upon our studies. The [schoolmistresses] deployed as usual around the school house.... At last the culprits were discovered, dirty but cheerful, crammed into the air box in the cellar."[8]

Throughout her childhood, Alice understood that in Boston she had her own separate relatives, her own grandparents, her own friends, and her own time with them. Although she later thought of the Lees as rather stuffy, "at least they were *mine* and I didn't have to share them with my siblings."[9] Alice felt an ambivalence: *different* meant "strange," but it also meant "special." The two feelings warred for the upper hand in her childish understanding.

Caroline Haskell Lee and George Cabot Lee provided for their granddaughter out of their substantial wealth. Alice received her mother's portion of her inheritance in a lump sum, from which she was given an allowance. The money was doled out by her grandfather Lee. When Alice was young, TR and Edith used to joke about the imperative of being nice to her. Edith was grateful for the infusion of Lee funds, since she had to stretch the tight Roosevelt family budget. A note Edith wrote to Bye gives some idea of the workings between the Lees and the Roosevelts: "Thank you for your letter which came today enclosing Mrs. Lee's. The green [coat] is exceedingly shabby and only fit for the country. The faithful Jacob brought me the little dresses [from the Lees] tonight. They are very pretty. Will you send a postal asking Tiffany's to forward Alice's gold beads to Boston...." At another time, Edith sought Bye's help because "I could not trust any one here with Alice's lace dress which is the reason I had to bother you. You will judge what it requires as you know money is no object."[10] Despite their ability to turn Alice's head with extravagant gifts, and whatever their feelings about Theodore's remarriage, the Lees never tried to win Alice away from Edith. Their letters consistently referred to Edith as "your Mother."

Yet the Lees wanted their granddaughter to appreciate her Lee ancestry. Accompanying a gift, Grandma provided a genealogy lesson: "I sent yesterday... a present from Mr. and Mrs. F. E. Haskell. In acknowledging it, they are your Mother's Uncle Fred and Aunt Margaret. I write this, as you seem to have no knowledge of your relatives on our side of the family."[11] Grandma Lee sent this letter in 1906, when Alice was no longer a child but still lacked the appropriate grasp of her mother's kin.

Rejoining the Roosevelt family entailed a mental readjustment. The first time she returned from the Lees' to Sagamore Hill, in late summer 1887, Alice had to reacquaint herself with her new situation—no comfortable, well-loved Auntie Bye (for anything more than a visit)—and a stepmother who was expecting a baby and preoccupied. Edith had suffered a miscarriage with her first pregnancy, and she and TR were understandably apprehensive about her health that summer. Of course, Theodore also had the specter of his first wife's mortal pregnancy before him. He responded with a severe asthma attack. Alice distracted her father by monitoring his morning shaving ritual, by waylaying him for rides on his shoulders, and, in her four-year-old way, forcing him to remember that life goes on.

On September 13, 1887, Edith safely delivered a boy, Theodore Jr. Aunt Gracie came over to care for the infant. Despite Theodore's urging, Edith did not want Bye's assistance. That meant Bye could not be there to help Alice with yet another profound transition. Edith slipped into postnatal depression, as she would do to varying degrees after each of her children's births. She accordingly devoted less of her time to Alice, at exactly the moment her stepdaughter most needed reassurance about the security of her place in the family. There is no evidence that Theodore compensated to help his daughter.

Alice pronounced her brother "a howling polly parrot" and was interested in watching him, "especially when he 'eats Mamma.'" After he was born, Alice sat by his bassinet, guarding, "lest someone should take baby brother away."[12] This fear was rooted in her own experiences. Life was precarious, unpredictable—a mother "taken away" by an incomprehensible thing like death, and herself "taken away" from her home with Auntie Bye just a few months earlier. Ted and Alice grew to be "boon companions," as Alice phrased it, and remained so until Ted's death. Other pregnancies followed: Edith had a miscarriage in 1888, gave birth to Kermit in 1889, Ethel in 1891, Archie in 1894, Quentin in 1897, and had miscarriages in 1902 and in 1903. Alice's own needs had to fit within the spiral of her stepmother's confinement, pregnancy, postnatal depression, and decreased attention. Nursemaids and eventually governesses tended the growing brood since Edith was frequently emotionally withdrawn and Theodore was physically absent. He continued his annual autumn hunting trips, regardless of domestic upheavals.

Even when Theodore was at home his burgeoning political career meant spending more and more time away from his children. In 1889, President Benjamin Harrison appointed him civil service commissioner. Alice was "distressed" that her father wasn't home for Ted's birthday—and Edith wasn't having an easy time without him either. She wrote to TR, away in the Rocky Mountains, "I am trying to make Alice more of a companion. I am afraid I do not do rightly in not adapting myself more to her....I wish I were gayer for the children's sake. Alice needs someone to laugh and romp with her instead of a sober and staid person like me." But, Edith suggested flatly, "I am not myself when you are away."[13]

Alice also needed attention and guidance to help her understand why she felt like the outsider in the nursery. What Alice craved was recognition of her differences, open discussion of the events of her birth, and reassurance of her place in the family. She was confused at one point about Edith's identity, thinking that she was "Papa's sister," just as Auntie Bye and Auntie Corinne were. "My brothers used to tease me about not having the same mother. They were very cruel about it and I was terribly sensitive," Alice recalled as an adult. Young Ted taunted her because the infant Alice had had a wet nurse. In her seventies, Alice remembered this childhood hurt: "So this horrid little cross-eyed boy of about five would go around to all and sundry exclaiming, 'Sissy had a sweat nurse! Sissy had a sweat nurse!' It was frightfully wounding to the character!"[14]

Theodore and Edith actively contributed to Alice's sense of unease. Theodore's silence about Alice Hathaway Lee complemented Edith's acerbic comments. Alice remembered Edith making it plain to the family that she and Theodore had been in love long before TR ever met Alice's mother. Once, in a fit of pique about Alice's behavior, Edith told Ted that if Alice Hathaway Lee had lived, she would have bored Theodore to stupefaction.[15] Ted lost no time in telling his half sister. The story is unfortunate enough, but it becomes sinister if Edith phrased it as a comparison: Alice took after her dull, empty-headed mother. Alice insisted that incidences such as these accounted for her attitude in later life: "It's not surprising that early on I became fairly hard-minded and learnt to shrug a shoulder with indifference. I certainly wasn't going to be a part of everyone saying, 'the poor little thing.' "[16]

As an adult, Alice thought that Edith resented being second choice, and had never forgiven TR his first marriage. Alice's later remembrances of Edith are unsympathetic: "In many ways she was a very hard woman... and she had almost a gift for making people uncomfortable." She had a "withdrawn, rather parched quality.... My stepmother made an enormous effort with me as a child but I think she was bored by doing so...[and] she could be mean."[17] Alice dutifully called Edith Mother when she was alive. After Edith's death, however, she referred to her as "my stepmother," as though the latter term more adequately reflected Alice's feelings. Letters during Alice's childhood show a warmer version of Edith. Once Edith was past childbearing, the two settled into a relationship that had fully as much mutual fondness and respect as it had tension. But the crucial years of Alice's childhood were fraught with her need for love and attention, neither of which she received in sufficient quantity. Edith wrote to Bye about the nine-year-old Alice's attempts to comprehend her situation: "I do feel quite as sorry for the poor child as for myself and the other inhabitants of the nursery, for she realizes that something is wrong with her, and goes through a real mental conflict trying to get straightened out."[18] If Edith looked at her nine-year-old stepdaughter as though something were "wrong" with her, it adds another layer of ambivalence where there would have ideally been unstinting love. It all made for parlous times as a teen.

Glimpses of the troubles between them can be seen in Edith's and Alice's contrasting attitudes toward convention. A Roosevelt cousin wrote that "Edith was relentless in her disapproval of transgressors of the established code of morals and conduct." He viewed it as a personality—perhaps a generational—clash: "To a brilliant stepdaughter who at the turn of the century was imbued with the same kind of revolt against parental authority that has been widespread among teen-agers of the last half-century, the cold and detached insistence on standards of conduct by the wife of her adored father must have been trying—all the more so in that Edith Carow had a gift of seeing through people, old or young."[19]

It was at that moment in Alice's life that Auntie Bye married. Bye's friendship with a naval attaché serving at the American embassy in London, Lieutenant Commander William Cowles, had blossomed into a love affair. Bye left for England at Christmastime in 1894. Alice could not stop crying long enough to see her off. In England Bye spent her time taking care of cousins Helen and James Roosevelt, whose mother had recently died. Helen was nearly a teenager when Bye arrived, and Alice could not have helped feeling jealous at the attention Helen received full time from Bye—even though Helen and Alice were warm friends at various points in their lives. But even Helen and James could not block the effect of the lieutenant commander on Bye. Though some in the family suggested the middle-aged Bye married Cowles so that she could stay in London rather than because she passionately loved him, their wedding, on November 25, 1895, began a solid and affectionate partnership. And while it was Ted who said it, all of the children habituated to Bye's attention must have felt it: "Aunty Bye won't love us as much now."[20]

Alice had to look elsewhere. By all but her own adult accounts, Alice worshipped Theodore. "I loved my father but I was never particularly close to him," she told reporter Sally Quinn late in life. When she was forty-three years old, journalist Charles Selden interviewed Alice and her best friend, Ruth Hanna McCormick, about their famous fathers. He concluded that Alice was a chip off the old block, who had "what the modern psy-

chologists call 'the father complex.' " Alice thought of her father as her
hero, according to Selden, which she denied.[21] When she was a child, Alice
seems to have loved her father in the extravagant way many girls do. She
could, then, only have sensed how TR's Victorian code became entangled
in his feelings for her. "My father," Alice contemplated, "obviously didn't
want the symbol of his infidelity around. His two infidelities, in fact: infidelity to my stepmother by marrying my mother first, and to my mother by
going back to my stepmother after she died."[22] Alice and Theodore's relationship was complicated by nineteenth-century morality, by the physical
distance between them for the first years of her life, by Edith, by the addition of five half siblings, and later by Theodore's ineptitude in the face of
Alice's teenage rebellion. Perhaps Alice's intelligence—evident as a child—
highlighted the similarities between them. TR was so like her, intellectually and temperamentally, that in Alice he saw his own faults mirrored.

One of Alice's earliest memories of her father occurred when she was
still living with Auntie Bye. For the first time in months, Alice was about to
see her father. The two-and-a-half-year-old waited at Auntie Bye's side by
the stables at the Meadowbrook Hunt Club to greet TR when he completed
the fox hunt. Theodore had ridden furiously that day, and returned with a
broken arm, torn clothing, and a bloody face. As he ran toward his daughter, Alice screamed. He caught her tightly. Helpless in the grip of the blood-
ied, sweaty man who did not look anything like her father, Alice screamed
again. Theodore shook Alice to quiet her. She screamed louder. He shook
harder. "It was a theme," Alice commented wryly, "which was to be repeated, with variation, in later years."[23]

Where TR had been an asthmatic child, Alice labeled herself a physical
coward as a girl. She wore a brace on her legs, the result of undiagnosed
polio as a child, which contributed to her unease around the strenuous life
at Sagamore. The contraption worked, and Alice eventually walked perfectly, but the memory of it stayed with her. At eighty-three, she recalled
feeling "like a tenement child...deformed with my legs...and I was always very conscious of that." When Alice was eight or nine, she had to
wear braces to keep her feet from turning out. Edith stretched Alice's
Achilles tendons each night, spending five minutes on one leg and seven

and a half on the other. Edith explained the device to Bye, who had suffered from a similar childhood disease: "They reach half way up her leg, and consist of two iron bars screened to the bottom of her shoe and connected by a leather strap around her leg. They have a hinge so she can move her foot freely up and down, but not sideways." Two weeks later Edith wrote again, with a dismal progress report: "Alice suffers far less with her foot but I fear it will be a long, long time before there is any permanent relief— one day she will walk quite easily and the next can hardly hobble. The Doctor thinks she does not have enough cartilage but I feel there may be rheumatic pains beyond the muscular trouble which he recognizes."[24]

Alice referred to the apparatus as a medieval torture instrument that made her self-conscious. She could not take walking for granted, for even on level ground the braces would lock up and throw her to the pavement. The braces did make good weapons, though, when employed to clunk her little brothers over the head. A more positive update on Alice came later: "She does not mind her braces the least bit in the world. Evidently they give her rather a distinction than otherwise among the children." This was another example of Alice learning to shrug her shoulders with indifference— and another case of *strange* simultaneously meaning *special*, just as it had done for TR when he suffered from childhood asthma.[25]

Shy because of her braces, Alice used to "spend hours of time pretending that I was a fiery horse, preferably cream colored, like Cinderella's horses, able at a bound to cover vast regions of the earth, and also at will to turn into something quite different, such as a princess with very long hair, or an extremely martial prince." All of these imaginary roles involved legs that worked: legs that bounded over the earth, danced like a princess, or fought in battle like a prince.[26] As an adult, Alice had little sympathy for people who wallowed in their illnesses. She had the example of Auntie Bye, who suffered pain every day of her life but never complained. Alice also had the opposite image of her stepmother. More than once, Alice's routine was disrupted and she was sent away because of Edith's various conditions. It was a point of pride with Roosevelts to bear physical ailments stoically.

Alice did not enjoy competing with her siblings and cousins at noisy, outdoor games, but she loved horses and was an excellent rider. She threw herself into nursery pillow fights, played with her dolls, and spent wonderful hours reading in the hayloft. In 1891, Edith described Alice and Ted with a new gift: "Alice liked the Buffalo Hunt better than anything she had....Ted's sharp eye noted what excellent horse blankets the cotton wadding in which it was packed made, and Alice...became absorbed for the rest of the afternoon in helping him construct them." A formative memory was of being carried up the hill at Sagamore on the shoulders of Auntie Bye's tall butler, seeing the sunset and thinking she'd never seen anything so exquisitely beautiful. She dreamed about sunsets after that.[27]

When Alice was six, on a trip with the family, her stepmother wrote to Auntie Bye: "The children were asleep but Alice waked from a doze in a state of joy, and was up at an unheard of hour next morning to get her new horse and cart in bed to play with. She looks splendidly, very clear, which means she feels well, and so bright and happy. She has improved much in her riding and seems to have more elasticity and spring of health than I have ever known." Nine-year-old Alice scrawled to her stepmother with creative spelling: "Yesterday morning all of us went up to see Ethel. I had a very nice time plying with her. In the afternoon we went to the centtrel park. I brought my houp with me. I know how to role it quit nicely now. We are going out driving this morning in Auntty Byes little yeller wagon." In 1891, Edith had reported: "The afternoon was stormy but Alice was happy as possible playing with Kermit. It is most lucky for her that she has such a flair for little children! She is so well and happy and really enjoys her lessons." As the eldest, she was occasionally pressed into service as a babysitter while Edith was away. Alice wrote sagely about a squabble she had overseen between Archie and Ethel: "She knocked him down but the thing he hurt was his feelings."[28]

The children played together frequently, but they did not study together often. Alice received sporadic tutoring when she was young and occasional lessons when she was older, but did not attend a formal school. Theodore and Edith provided Alice's first education. They taught her how to read and instilled intellectual discipline by having Alice recite her lessons to them. They read to her from *Grimm's Fairy Tales*, *Tales from the Arabian*

Nights, Milton, Scott, Dickens, Twain, Longfellow, Kipling, the *Nibelung-enlied*. She belonged to, she said, "the Andrew Lang period of the Blue Book. He translated these lovely folk tales . . . from every known language." Theodore acted out tales of George Washington, the Revolutionary War, the War of 1812, Davy Crockett and the Alamo, the Civil War, and Custer and the Indian wars. Edith instructed Alice in the Bible, which Alice read from cover to cover more than once, just to say she had. Alice inhaled books, as all Roosevelts did. She was given free rein in the library at Saga-more Hill, and was the only child allowed to interrupt her father when he was closeted there.[29]

A related love was wordplay. From riddles to anagrams, Alice enjoyed the intellectual delight of manipulating letters and phrases. Her papers are punctuated with examples of diversions such as illustrated limericks and acrostics. Alice was fluent in French, and had been introduced to German. Latin she swore she never liked "because I was made to do it." She recalled a "marvelous little book called *La Grecque Sans Larmes*, which of course meant we dripped with larmes getting through it. . . ." History delighted her, too, and she wrote to her father proudly of the time she soundly beat her cousins at a game they created of writing down "as many names as we could in history of mythology beginning at A, and going through the al-phabet, spending two minutes on each letter."[30] She also studied music, geography, and some of the sciences, particularly astronomy and geology. Alice later regretted the lack of formal schooling, but her intellectual curi-osity lasted her entire lifetime.

Just once, in 1898, Alice enrolled in school. A letter from a classmate remains from that time that gives an indication of how well the fourteen-year-old socialized with other children:

Most adorable Alice: This just shows how devotedly I love you—wasting my valuable time in school writing to you. Our hearts are all broken—mine especially—to small bluggy fragments over your leaving us. I forward some valentines that were in the box for you, I know who they both came from too, so I labelled them. I have the "itsy bitsy turtles" done up tight in a handkerchief to keep them from crawling out and getting squashed and broken like our hearts. Send me a bottlefull of your tears, if you please. . . . I feel quite sure I will break down and blubber at roll call to-morrow when your sweet name isn't called. In other words, "A place is vacant in our school, which never can be filled" (until you come back). Weepingly, sufferingly, hastily, Patty.[31]

Other letters written by childhood friends attest to her popularity. Alice did not detail her school experiences, but was adamant about the one school she did *not* want to attend: "The summer before Father was in Cuba I had been told that I was to be sent to boarding school in New York at Miss Spence's school. I had seen Miss Spence's scholars marching two by two in their daily walks, and the thought of becoming one of them shriveled me. I practically went on a strike. I said that I would not go—I said that if the family insisted, and sent me, I would do something disgraceful."[32]

The stubborn streak in Alice had been strengthening throughout her childhood. She might have quaked inside, but on the outside, Alice stood firm. Edith wished she would evince the proper, docile behavior of a Victorian girl. However, by the time Alice was fourteen, she was entering the turbulent waters of young womanhood where boys turned from adversaries to heartthrobs, and families became a place to run from rather than to. A portrait of "the model girl," common in etiquette books of the time, may have been Edith's ruler by which to measure her stepdaughter's shortcomings. Alice did not adhere very closely to the ideal—Ethel did. As a young teenager, Alice had learned to live for herself, and she preferred fun to duty. Bye, the independent salon mistress, was Alice's role model.

When Bye and Will Cowles returned from England in 1897, they moved into their Madison Avenue house. Will docked with his ship, the gunboat *Fern*, in Hampton Roads, Virginia, leaving TR and Bye time in New York to catch up. During the winter of 1897 to 1898, brother and sister were together a good deal, discussing the navy, its war readiness, and politics in general, often with congenial guests around Bye's dining table. Since 1895, TR had served as head of New York City's Board of Police Commissioners, and the family alternated between Sagamore Hill and the city. Roosevelt continued to make a name for himself among reform-minded Republicans.

While at Bye's, Theodore came to appreciate once more the salubrious effect that the calm and straightforward Anna Roosevelt Cowles had on all those around her. In April 1897, TR became assistant secretary of the navy and moved the family to Washington, D.C. The change, according to her parents, was not good for Alice. When she became too difficult to handle, TR thought immediately of his sister. Preoccupied with the tumultuous decisions leading up to American entry into the Spanish-American War, TR could not manage Alice. Edith could not control her either, for after Quentin's birth, she was sick in bed for weeks. Then around Christmastime, Ted grew ill. In the ensuing absence of parental guidance, Alice reacted to Edith's withdrawal from the family and the temporary loss of her "boon companion" with anger. She disobeyed curfew, rode up and down the hills of Washington on her bicycle with her feet on the handlebars, and fearlessly led a gang of boys—she was the only female member—into local mischief. When one of the boys dressed as a girl and knocked on the door asking for Alice, Theodore reached his limit. He and Edith despaired of Alice's attitude and her actions, called her a "guttersnipe," forbade her to communicate with her co-conspirators, and sent her to New York. Auntie Bye would have to work a miracle.[33]

A letter written in turns by Alice and Helen R. Roosevelt to their relative Franklin Delano Roosevelt in 1897 gives a sense of Alice's spirits. Helen began:

Alice spent last night here, and we sat out on the doorstep till nearly 10 o'clock, and whistled and made remarks to the passers by, some of which they heard!...Yesterday we went out alone in a cab and winked at all the men we passed....Alice is going to write now, as she has a few important questions to ask you. HRR

I want to know the name of the girl who James told me you were stuck on instead of me. Have you pro[posed] and has she acc[epted]? Please write and tell us her name as we are very anxious to know....I suppose

James told you all the pleasant little things I said about you, they are all true. A.L.R.

Isn't she bad? Have you <u>really</u> given her up or not? Please answer <u>all</u> these questions carefully, they are <u>so</u> important, and we are curious. HRR

I hope you have given me up, if not you had better. Have you seen the piece of poetry that James wrote.... It is dedicated to me and is perfectly horrid and silly, that is if he means it. A.L.R.

Of <u>course</u> he means it! He wouldn't have written it otherwise. For fear you have <u>not</u> heard it, I am sending it to you: "A noun has got a meaning too. / It's verb I'd like to do to you. / If I succeed, why there I'll see / That you shall never part from me." Isn't it beautiful? Alice sings it all the time to the tune of "Ta ra ra boom de ay." Affectionately, Helen R. Roosevelt.[34]

This letter of youthful flirtation and general silliness contrasts with a note to her father a month earlier, showing that Alice was perfectly capable of acting the ideal eldest daughter. She described the riding lessons she was giving Ethel and Kermit, her discovery of a nest of baby raccoons "in the tree where you shot Ted's 'coon,'" and the menacing weasel that escaped her pitchfork at Sagamore.[35]

The headstrong Alice was sent to live with Bye the day after her fourteenth birthday, two days before the battleship *Maine* exploded in Havana's harbor. She spent the rest of the winter and all of the spring with her favorite aunt. Uncle Will left shortly for Cuba, to investigate the ill-fated *Maine*. Alice had become accustomed to her freedom and enjoyed being a tomboy. Under Bye's ministrations an extraordinary transformation occurred. Alice became more tractable, polite, and agreeable. Theodore could not understand how Bye had wrought such a change, but Alice always behaved better with someone's undivided attention. And it helped that Bye was one of those remarkable adults who never forgot her own youth: "Have you shocked [cousin] Elfrida," Bye wrote to Alice conspiratorially after she left, "by telling her any of the bad things we did?" She could enter into their little love affairs, too. Bye was certain, for example, that James Roosevelt was "madly gone on" Alice, not another girl—and she was sure that Teddy Robinson, Auntie Corinne's son, was pairing up with Helen.[36]

Bye was great friends with all the young nieces and nephews, and because she understood them, she could also gently teach and enforce the rules. There was no "running riot" with Bye. Previsit instructions in 1897 consisted of these stiff lines and a nocuous comparison: "Now darling, I am too happy you are coming, but, there will be a few rules and regulations.... You know dearie Auntie does not believe in a great party just tearing around all day and so you and Helen will have a couple of hours music and reading." She expected them "to put everything nicely in order whenever you all have put it wrong, hats etc all must be put in their places and you girls have to try and help Auntie about everything. Helen understands and I would not for all the world feel that she was more help and more careful and dependable than you."[37]

Alice's dutiful updates amazed TR. "Her letters are really interesting and amusing," he wrote his sister gratefully. "Evidently you are doing her a world of good and giving her exactly what she needed. I quite agree with what you say about her; I am sure she really does love Edith and the children and me; it was only that running riot with the boys and girls here had for the moment driven everything else out of her head." Meanwhile, TR kept his daughter apprised of family matters—the boys' flying squirrels, Edith's health, Ted's recovery, his own romps at the Lodges' home, where the children stayed while Edith was recovering. When Edith was well enough, she wrote, too, although she couldn't resist a good swipe. Alice's last letter, Edith bantered, was so lovely she "thought it must have been done by Helen...."[38]

Perhaps war fever added to Edith's edginess. The constant talk in Washington, Edith wrote on April 14, was of war. It came one week later, to the whoops and hollers of the Roosevelt children. Thinking of the *Maine* blown up by Spanish imperialists, and patriotically taking on the cause of the Cuban freedom fighters, Theodore quit his desk job at the navy, declaring, "I have a horror of people who bark but don't bite."[39] He and his friend Colonel Leonard Wood formed the First U.S. Volunteer Cavalry, nicknamed the Rough Riders. Because Edith was recovering from surgery and could not take care of Ted, he joined Alice at Auntie Bye's—who by this time was coming to grips with the astounding fact that, at age forty-three, she was pregnant. Bye, Alice, and Ted made a happy household.

Letters flew thick and fast among the family members. Alice wrote TR about her lessons and regaled him with accounts of goldfish on the roof, a riotous game of follow the leader until Archie cut his lip and howled ("I told him that his teeth were crying red tears [the blood, you know], that made him laugh and then I gave him a ball"), and Archie's excessive repetition of songs on the hand organ until they all became "quite sick of those tunes. . . ." In response TR sent what the family called "posterity letters"— ostensibly intended for his children, but really addressed to future readers. For example, this from the battleground to his fifteen-year-old daughter: "I have had a hard and dangerous month. I have enjoyed it, too, in a way. . . . My own men are not well fed, and they are fierce and terrible in battle; but they gave half they had to the poor women and children. I suppose a good many of them thought, as I did, of their own wives or sisters and little ones. War is often, as this one is, necessary and righteous; but it is terrible."[40]

Meanwhile, the family (including Bye) had migrated back to Sagamore to await the return of the heroes. Alice passed the time teaching herself to ride astride on her father's saddle, until she could do it "almost as easily as I can girls' way." Girls generally rode sidesaddle, not astride, but that made the boys' way more interesting. After the battles, Colonel Roosevelt led his men, quarantined for yellow fever, to Long Island. The family visited him there. Alice particularly enjoyed that, for she was allowed to see her father's tanned and handsome troops on review. "If I was in love with one Rough Rider, I was in love with twenty, even though I did have a pigtail and short dresses," Alice later sighed.[41]

That fall, Alice turned philosophical and decided to "keep a diary or journal or whatever you wish to call it." She thought it would "amuse" her when she was older. The catalyst was her tremendous sorrow at leaving Sagamore Hill for Boston for the summer. She said good-bye to all the relatives and then to all the animals. She was diverted slightly from her sadness by the Dewey Naval Parade in New York City featuring veterans of the Spanish-American War. She got to ride in one of the boats, just behind her father on the *Monmouth*. The day was exciting, culminating in fireworks over the dark river that reminded her of Romantic poet Thomas Hood's "a lake and a fairy boat."[42] New Yorkers were glad to celebrate Admiral George Dewey, victor of Manila Bay—but just as pleased to get a look at the conqueror of Kettle Hill, whose next adventure was the race for governor of their state. Colonel Roosevelt's campaign kicked off in the fall of 1898 with a speech at Carnegie Hall. Edith, aware of the "many forces at work in New York politics," cared only that her husband was "safe at home."[43]

Winning the governorship of New York was relatively easy for the newly minted war hero. His Rough Riders helped him campaign, swearing earnestly that they would have "gone to hell with him." Everyone was caught up in TR's charisma and the excitement of the race, even Alice's teenaged friends who eagerly requested his "signature." Alice assisted Edith and TR's secretary, Amy Cheney, with the mounting correspondence. All efforts paid off. A Roosevelt cousin celebrated by naming her new guinea pig "Governor Roosevelt—Gov. for short."[44] Alice attended the swearing in, flanking Edith in Albany's assembly chamber.

"We have never been happier in our lives than we are now," Edith wrote six months into TR's tenure. Perhaps part of their contentment was a result of the good relations with their eldest daughter. Theodore boasted to a friend about his nearly sixteen-year-old child: "My big girl is a very big girl indeed now, almost grown up, and yours must be, too. I wish they could be together. Alice, I am sorry to say, does not show any abnormal activity, but is a good rider, walker and swimmer, and has an excellent mind and I think I could say that she is by no means bad looking." Edith concurred. She told her friends Alice was indeed "pretty and she is certainly intelligent."[45]

Their time in Albany was Alice's last fling at childhood, and she enjoyed being a governor's daughter. The executive mansion was commodious and full of interesting nooks and crannies calling out to be explored. Alice participated in some of the younger children's pranks, such as sneaking out of the bedrooms for a pajama-clad snowball fight. Under the watch of her omnipresent governess, Miss Young, her days were spent lunching, walking, shopping, writing letters, playing tennis and basketball (she was captain of her team), ice skating, and horseback riding. Alice was "fired by reading *Antigone* with a desire to study Greek," and pondered taking up Latin again, too. She loved the opera *Faust* and judged a play, *The Colonial Girl*, "quite amusing and good for an entirely second rate company."[46]

She was still the big sister, and she wrote often to homesick Ted, who was then attending Groton School in Massachusetts. He filled pages with his exploits, mostly football and visiting during half holidays, or "half hollerdays" as he more colorfully put it. When her parents were away Alice stood in for Edith. In letters to her absent parents she faithfully chronicled all the children's activities—from new pet lizards to art lessons. With some enjoyment, Alice shared that "Quentin now has a trick of whenever he sees me, of putting his thumb in his mouth and then taking it out and offering it to me to suck! I don't think it's at all nice, so I offer him mine to disgust him, whereupon he grows quite infuriated and beats his hands up and down at me and yells, 'Do you want my thumb? Do you want my thumb?' It's as good as a circus." As First Daughter of New York, she helped her mother in various capacities, for example, serving tea and cakes to the great lacebedecked phalanx from the "State Association of Mothers."[47]

In 1900, to Edith's dismay, as a result of the enthusiasm of midwestern and western Republicans and to the relief of party bosses in New York State, Theodore was tapped to run for vice president on William McKinley's ticket. Alice loved Washington, D.C., and was thrilled at the prospect of returning, but Edith did not wish to lose the good life they had in Albany. The long campaign trail took TR away from the family. This made all of them, including the candidate, "melancholy." He wrote to Alice from Fargo, North Dakota, that he enjoyed "meeting these crowds of funny old farmers and cowboys," because he felt "thoroughly at home with them." "West Virginian republican supporters" sent Alice a "small bear" that the family named Jonathan Edwards, "partly because we think he shows a distinctly Calvinistic turn of mind." It was all very exciting, but Alice, who had a deep sense of family honor, was offended at Theodore's second-place spot. Edith, too, did not relish the thought of her husband stuck "in such a useless and empty position."[48]

Nevertheless, after the electoral victory, the new vice president and his family arrived in the nation's capital on March 2, 1901, just before McKinley's inauguration. They stayed with Bye and Will at their rented home at 1733 N Street, for Edith wanted to spend the summer at Sagamore as usual and move into Washington properly in the fall. The family (minus young Quentin), surrounded by friends and relatives, attended the swearing-in at the Senate chamber. Quentin rejoined the others in the room above Thompson's Drug Store that Edith had rented for its view of the inaugural parade. The day concluded, for Alice and the adults, with a seat in the presidential box at the inaugural ball, held at the Pension Office Building. Alice envied the girls there who nonchalantly wore old dresses, and not the "excessively new white point d'esprit" gown Edith had made for her. Absorbed in watching the dancers, Alice perched on the arm of a chair until admonished not to, because First Lady Ida McKinley was sitting in it. That fact had escaped Alice. At sixteen years of age, Alice had only just begun to take an interest in politics beyond her father's fortunes. She considered the McKinleys "usurping cuckoos," but that night Alice had eyes only for the dance floor.[49]

The next morning, they returned to Oyster Bay, with its delights of berry picking, swimming, picnics, and general family togetherness. The summer was tainted by a painful abscess in her jaw that would trouble her intermittently for years. Alice, growing more impatient for Washington, enjoyed watching dancers perform the newest fad called the hootchy-kootchy. Always a quick study, she would tuck that away in her repertoire of actions to cause parental consternation.

A family vacation to the Tahawus Club in the Adirondack Mountains was rounding out the summer when news of an assassination attempt on President McKinley, in Buffalo, arrived. At the confirmation of his death, Alice and the rest of the children did a little selfish jig of happiness at their elevated status. She wrote when she was an adult that she was "not particularly elated" in the knowledge of her father's assumption of the presidency. "I was having a delightful time with a band of cheerful young people; greedy for sensation, centered upon myself, I was not merely an egotist, I was a solipsist."[50]

At the time, however, the local newspaper carried a story that probably gave a truer flavor of Alice's feelings than she admitted to as an adult. Alice and her friend Sarah Boneditch were driven forty miles in a buckboard by Michael F. Cronin, the proprietor of the Alden Lair Lodge, where TR had paused on his way from Tahawus to Buffalo. The girls wanted to follow Roosevelt's path toward the beautiful Wilcox mansion in Buffalo, where he was sworn in as president on September 14, 1901. "At the request of Miss Roosevelt," Cronin revealed to the reporter, he "retold the story of [TR's] midnight ride." Upon hearing the thrilling tale, "Miss Roosevelt asked the driver to give her one of the eight shoes worn by the horses that night." Cronin had already given the horseshoes away. Another guest overheard the request and recognized the appellant. He generously surrendered his trophy to Alice. Asking for the story and the historic horseshoe demonstrates an involvement in the events swirling around her that her later memories contradict. Perhaps the seismic battles that take place within a teenager's psyche in the war for personal independence explain the contradiction. When she was eighty-four, she told an interviewer that her response to the news of McKinley's shooting was "sheer rapture." She began, in what she later called an "amiably ghoulish" way, to let her finger fall on calendars at random, hoping to predict the day McKinley would die.[51]

The teenaged Alice might be forgiven for harboring a partly jaded view. After all, she had been the daughter of the governor of New York and the daughter of the vice president. So, although her sense of family honor was assuaged by Theodore's assumption of the presidency, Alice had no reason to think that her life would necessarily be any more fun. The McKinley White House had been a somber one. Because of the First Lady's illness, the McKinleys hosted few lavish gatherings. Further, Alice heard Edith fretting over the impending loss of privacy. Alice may have felt that her new position would circumscribe her ability to do as she pleased, but the possibility of a White House debut was promising. As an intelligent, well-read member of a political family, Alice had some idea of the opportunities that would occur as the Roosevelts became the First Family. Her childhood had ended with President McKinley's death. She lamented neither.

Chapter 3

"Something More Than a Plain American Girl"

It was the start of a new age; the first year of the twentieth century and less than two weeks after Theodore Roosevelt assumed the nation's highest office, his rambunctious family members hurled themselves into the White House. The Roosevelts' excitement was at odds with a nation grieving for its fallen president. Among the family, only Alice wore the subdued mien of a mourner, but McKinley wasn't the cause. Alice felt a characteristic isolation from this tremendous family event. She lingered with friends, she went to Auntie Bye's, and then to Chestnut Hill. By letter Edith tried to keep her stepdaughter informed of family news. "Father looks very serious—naturally—but is not at all nervous," as he took up his new duties. Thinking ahead, she suggested to Alice that "in one way you will find this a hard position, but in others it will be delightful, and I can do much for you that would have been financially impossible otherwise" because of TR's salary increase.[1] This was a considerate note from a busy woman. The spotlight was about to be fixed relentlessly on the First Family, and Alice would need guidance and support from Edith. When they clashed, Alice felt shy and alienated and turned to friends who did not always meet with her parents' approval. Yet none of them could have predicted Alice's rapid rise to international celebrity, nor what it would mean to the teenager struggling to mature.

Alice remembered the first time she realized her father was truly the president. She had been staying with Auntie Bye at her Connecticut home throughout September and October, and when TR was on his way to Yale University's bicentennial celebration, he stopped for a day with his sister and his daughter. "I had not expected him to be changed and, of course, he was not," Alice recalled. "There was no atmosphere of worry about his new responsibilities; not a trace of the solemnity that so often seems to afflict those in high position. He was, as always, full of the buoyancy and zest that swept everything along with it. However, much else was very different since I had last seen him at Sagamore in the backwater of the Vice-Presidency—the stir that accompanied his arrival, the crowds of politicians, newspapermen, and other visitors." She would soon enough know what it was like to attract the same stir, the same newspapermen, and similar crowds. Alice concluded in those early weeks that she, in fact, rather liked the "feel" of the ruckus caused by traveling with the president.[2]

By mid-October Alice had entered fully into the spirit of things. The new First Lady made the room assignments in the White House, and then decided to renovate the historic mansion, which she had found in "disarray." Alice occupied the large bedroom on the northwest side. Ethel's was next to hers, and they both overlooked Lafayette Square and the palatial homes of John Hay and Henry Adams across the street. Alice disparaged the furnishings of the White House when the Roosevelts arrived as "late General Grant and early Pullman," both "ugly and inconvenient." Her bedroom held "cumbersome black walnut pieces and two brass beds."[3] Compared to her cheery room at Sagamore, decorated as it was with floral wallpaper and chintz curtains, her bedroom in the White House was spartan.

But the White House was a paradise for children, and teenaged Alice could occasionally be convinced to join in games with the younger set. She careened down the main stairway on the large tin trays borrowed from the pantry, and raced along the upstairs hall on stilts and bicycles.[4] Boisterous games of hide-and-seek and tag spilled into every room. Leaping out of the circular upholstered seats in the East Room to scare visitors was a favorite pastime. Uproarious pillow fights made the White House attic ring with laughter. Many of the children's animals took up residency, too. The blue macaw, Eli Yale, ruled the conservatory.

The children loved living in the Executive Mansion, and their antics were soon widely reported. Americans found them a fascinating family, especially after the McKinleys, whose daughters had died in infancy. "Baby Ruth" Cleveland was a distant memory, and while the Lincoln boys were well known in their day, they had left the Executive Mansion four decades earlier. American voters liked to know that their president was one of them, and that their elected leader shared an empathetic understanding of the joys and sorrows of raising children. In January 1902, Edith's candid letter to a friend assessed her children's first half year in the White House: "Alice is exceedingly pretty, and has a remarkable steady head though in some ways very child like. Ted is a good boy and stands well at school. Kermit is odd and independent as always, and Ethel is just a handful. She is a replica of Mrs. Cowles. Archie we call 'the beautiful idiot' and Quentin is the cleverest of the six."[5]

The much-needed renovation was one of Edith's initial acts as First Lady, and although she carried off a widely acclaimed transformation, it meant moving her family into, out of, and then back into the White House. For Edith, it was worth it. The First Lady likened the old Executive Mansion to "living over the store," because when the Roosevelts arrived, the main floor of the White House consisted of public rooms and executive offices. The family would never have the privacy that Edith treasured unless some significant steps were taken, but the conversion from "gilded barn to comfortable residence" would not be completed until November 1902.[6]

Despite the upheaval, life took on a pattern for Alice. She began to perceive great possibilities in being First Daughter of the land. Added to her social calendar would be occasions of state, visits with dignitaries, and special perks yet to be discovered. She continued to see Auntie Bye at the Cowleses' comfortable N Street home, where President Roosevelt held his first cabinet meetings and where he met with members of Congress whose morals or reputations did not measure up to Edith's standards.

Alice similarly used the sympathetic Bye when she wanted to entertain friends. She had no sitting room of her own at the White House. Moving back to Washington meant reunions with particularly congenial friends, especially a group calling itself the Gooey Brotherhood of Slimy Slopers. Comprised of young women and men, the Slopers all went by nicknames.

Agile Ali was president, and her comrades included Dusky Dick, Betty Bright, Bill the Lizard, May Merrylegs, Presumptuous Pete, Jerky Jake, Sami the Sloper, and perhaps others. The only Slopers who signed their names to extant letters were Roger Alden Derby and Richard Derby. They had tongue-in-cheek meetings with matching minutes, and a newspaper spoof entitled *The Sloping Gazette*. The latter included such bits of nonsense as this:

> Three Slopers went off on a sloop
> But one slipped while ascending the poop
> Now in torment he lies
> Giving vent to sad cries
> Why?
> Because he can't be with his troop.

When they gathered at Auntie Bye's for "slopes," they shared tea, literary allusions, and dancing. They met up frequently at Washington entertainments. Their letters to each other were full of inside jokes and references to each other's suitability as Slopers—but, as Dusky Dick wrote, "'Tis better to have sloped and slipped than never to have sloped at all."[7] He may have been referring to a Sloper who married, for once that happened, the Sloper was cast out of the ranks. May Merrylegs gave a sense of the Sloper attitude when she wrote to Agile Ali: "Alice—I loff you! I feel like a champagne cork with the wire taken off—If I don't do something or write something I shall burst. You are a congenial soul.... I shall shortly repair to my room and dance. I am quite mad. And it is Sunday evening too. (How shocking)."[8] While she took pleasure in her friends, Alice could not enter fully into society until her debut.

First Lady Edith Roosevelt had officially ended the mourning period for William McKinley by throwing open the White House doors for the traditional New Year's Day Reception. From 11:00 a.m. until 2:00 p.m. on January 1, 1902, President Roosevelt and the First Lady received the brilliantly dressed line of foreign ambassadors, Supreme Court justices, senators, representatives, military officers, and other dignitaries. On the night of the second of January, Theodore and Edith presided over their first cabinet dinner. The following evening, the Roosevelts introduced their daughter into society. Alice's was the first debutante ball ever held at the White House, and Washington society considered it the most distinctive dance at the Executive Mansion since the days of legendary hostess Dolley Madison.[9]

Edith and Alice had been planning for months. Alice could hardly wait. She was "enchanted" by the thought of a Washington debut, and "to come out at the White House made it something to look forward to with even more excited anticipation," she explained in her autobiography. The coming-out ball was a defining moment in every debutante's life. For Alice, this was certainly true, as it began her rapid rise to national—ultimately, international—prominence. Her debut turned her into a celebrity, which then both complicated and enhanced her life. Celebrityhood threw into question family relationships. It circumscribed her actions while it presented opportunities. It made her courtship and marriage laborious. It made it harder to form new friendships and more difficult to trust the friends she had. By the time she left the White House, the *Richmond Times-Dispatch* insisted, "There have been few young women in America, or for that matter in any other country, who have received so much newspaper attention as has Miss Roosevelt."[10]

Debutante balls were a traditional rite of passage among the elite, symbolically demonstrating that the young woman was grown up and eligible for marriage to the right man. The social season provided numerous opportunities for striking, well-bred women to shine, but at the debutante's own ball the spotlight was hers alone. Alice's cousins Corinne Robinson (Auntie Corinne's daughter) and Eleanor Roosevelt (her uncle Elliott's daughter) made their debuts around the same time Alice did. For them, coming out was "a terrifying ordeal." As an adult, Corinne remembered that a debutante "was simultaneously made aware of the great and depressing obligations that family and social position imposed upon her. Society was a serious business and upon entering it a girl lifted her share of the city's poor, beleaguered, and untidy masses upon her fragile and well-bred shoulders."[11] Once a young woman debuted, she was automatically placed on the roll of the Junior League, a charitable organization begun by Alice's friend Mary Harriman in 1901 when she was nineteen.

Most parents of debutantes impressed upon their daughters the importance of aiding those less fortunate, but few eighteen-year-olds took to the selfless grind of charity work like Corinne and Eleanor. Alice dismissed such social obligations. The education in national and international politics she eventually received as First Daughter more than replaced visiting settlement houses and teaching dance to immigrants, as Eleanor did. As there existed no tradition of First Daughters taking up benevolent causes, Alice did not labor under a national expectation to devote herself to charity. And that simply wasn't her personality. She had no qualms about dedicating her young life to more pleasurable pursuits.

Normally, a Knickerbocker daughter would debut at Delmonico's in New York City at age eighteen. For Alice, there would be a second coming-out dance in December 1902 at the Assembly Ball as one of the "Magic Five" Roosevelt women. A debut en masse in a crowd of cousins did not suit her. Instead, she scheduled her White House ball for early January 1902 to take advantage of the Christmas holiday when enough young men could attend without shirking their schooling. The First Lady was willing to go along with Alice's wishes—although perhaps Edith was motivated by the chance to marry off her stepdaughter a year early. It was also a perfect vehicle for announcing the tone of entertainments hosted by the new First Lady. Staging such an important evening required great attention to details. Edith Roosevelt hired Isabelle "Belle" Hagner to help. The competent and charming Belle Hagner had worked for Auntie Bye and would become Edith Roosevelt's indispensable social secretary. Hagner was "the first salaried government official answering to the First Lady as her boss," and so presaged the extensive East Wing staff enjoyed by modern First Ladies.[12]

Even with the help of a secretary, the debut preparations were staggering. A guest list had to be drawn up, invitations issued, and décor and food planned. At least the U.S. Marine Band was an obvious choice, but a list of dances had to be chosen and ordered. Alice's expectations for every moment were understandably high. "A young girl should be treated like a bride when she makes her debut into society," social critic Ward McAllister decreed. "Her relatives should rally around her and give her entertainments to welcome her into the world which she is to adorn."[13]

As plans commenced, it became clear that Alice could not have everything she desired. The most alarming problem was the dance floor. Because of the White House renovation, the ballroom lacked a proper wooden dancing floor. The alternative to hardwood was a makeshift floor of coarsely woven linen "crash" laid over the old mustard-yellow carpet. Unlike other debutantes, who had to negotiate only with their parents for the fulfillment of their debutante dreams, Alice had to seek the approval of Congress. Thus, at one of the first White House dinner parties, Edith gave the First Daughter the task of charming the monies for the hardwood out of the redoubtable Congressman Joseph G. Cannon. Alice remembered that she "worked every ploy [she] knew on him, including Auntie Corinne's 'elbow-in-the-soup' treatment." Alice rather enjoyed this early taste of lobbying, but she was unsuccessful. The First Daughter made do with linen crash. Alice found it "personally humiliating."[14]

Not having a cotillion was worse. A cotillion was a formalized dance that entailed an elaborate concatenation of steps and a series of partners, with the debutante leading off. Cotillions usually included the presentation of flowers or favors for the dancers paid for by the hosts and could include expensive baubles, such as jewelry, watches, combs, purses, or stickpins made of gold and silver. Eleanor Roosevelt remembered that "your popularity was gauged by the number of favors you took home." Cotillions were de rigueur for debutante balls: the White House debutante could not fail to have one. But Edith, always anxious about money, said no.[15]

Adding insult to injury, for Alice, was the embarrassing substitution of punch for champagne. At the elegant New York debutante balls, champagne was served, Alice reminded her stepmother, and she thought it was terrible for the Roosevelts to be so rustic. The First Lady may have had an eye to cost or to pro-temperance Republican voters. Aping the sophisticated customs of New York might increase the status of the capital city, or it could be perceived as unseemly. For Alice, it was the ultimate disgrace. She offered to pay for the cotillion favors and the champagne out of her Lee allowance, but her stepmother forbade it. Edith maintained that the debutante ball was the duty of the parents. Thus Alice must make do with what the Roosevelt budget would allow.

What Alice's debut lacked in the accoutrements of maturity, it made up for in White House ball tradition. Approximately six hundred people attended the unofficial White House event.[16] The receiving line began at the customary time of 10:00 p.m. Edith and Alice stood in the Blue Room to greet the guests, a combination of her friends such as Helen Cutting, Robert Goelet, Arthur Iselin, Edith Root, Alice Warder, Robert Gerry, and Daisy Leiter; her relatives—Auntie Corinne and Uncle Douglas, Auntie Bye and Uncle Will, cousins Helen and James Roosevelt, Franklin Delano Roosevelt; and political and diplomatic officers who were also friends of the Roosevelts. "Miss Ruth Hanna," daughter of Republican Senator Marcus Hanna, attended wearing a gown of "liberty pink." The Blue Room boasted potted palms and the bright green leaves of smilax vines wrapped around the chandeliers and wound across the ceiling, decorating the pictures of George and Martha Washington, Abraham Lincoln, and Thomas Jefferson in the East Room. Holly graced every lintel. More than two thousand flowers—roses, carnations, hyacinths, and narcissus—completed the lavish decorations.

The First Daughter wore a traditional pure white taffeta gown with a white chiffon overskirt and a bodice appliquéd with white rosebuds. Around her neck hung a simple diamond pendant. One of Alice's guests, her soon-to-be friend Marguerite Cassini, thought Alice underwent an apotheosis: "Under the lights of the heavy chandeliers in the East Room, the tomboyish-looking girl I have seen around Washington is transformed into an assured, sparkling young woman in a stiff white satin gown and long white gloves ruffled on her arms. Her hair is of an indefinite blond and her skin lacks color but her eyes are a queer, attractive long shape, a phosphorescent grayish blue, changing color according to her mood, edged by long black lashes. Her smile curls up in mischief." The *New York Tribune* concluded: "A more charming debutante has rarely been introduced in Washington. She was as attractive in her dignified simplicity and natural grace as she was beautiful. Tall, with a striking figure, blue eyes, and a fine fair complexion, she is certainly one of the prettiest girls in Washington."[17]

The Marine Band struck up the first waltz, "The Debutante," at 11:00 p.m. Lieutenant Gilmore of the Artillery and Major Charles McCauley of the Marine Corps vied for the honor of dancing with the White House debutante for the first german. Lieutenant Gilmore won—a victory the artillery celebrated manfully. After dancing, the guests enjoyed a buffet supper that one of Alice's girlfriends called "sumptuous." Couples could then promenade in the White House conservatories or recommence dancing. Auntie Corinne thought that "Alice had the time of her life, men seven deep around her all the time." Franklin D. Roosevelt, an enthusiastic dance partner of Alice's, called it "glorious" from beginning to end.[18]

Alice, much later in life, admitted only to "enjoy[ing] it moderately."[19] Perhaps she remembered the crash, the punch, the absence of a cotillion, and the next day's newspaper coverage. In its front-page article, the *New York Times* called Alice's debut "one of the most charming social events Washington has ever seen," but declared that the decorations "seemed extremely simple." Adjectives suited to the innocence of a debutante ball, no doubt, but for Alice, hardly satisfying. The *New York Tribune* perhaps thought its article complimentary when it called the ball "a homelike affair, with an entirely unofficial air," but guessing Alice's response to this review is not difficult. Ironically, besides the debutante herself, the only thing the press was effusive about was the crash, "waxed so perfectly that dancing on it was a delight."[20] Small comfort, no doubt. The First Lady, too, must have resented being damned with faint praise. Six years later, when Theodore and Edith sponsored their second daughter's debutante ball at the White House, Alice couldn't help comparing. Ethel Roosevelt danced her cotillion on a hardwood floor while her guests refreshed themselves with "buckets of champagne."[21]

The front-page coverage introduced the First Daughter to America. She became known everywhere as Princess Alice. It was undemocratic, but spoke to her unique position. Alice received the first of hundreds of requests for her autograph and photograph. Americans had a taste for sensational journalism that did not go unnoticed by those assigned to report on the First Daughter's activities. Charging into the new century, Alice seized her chance. She was the first White House teenaged daughter since the demure Nellie Grant had graced Washington twenty-five years earlier, and that was enough to cause a stir. Soon, however, Alice's distinctive temperament manifested itself, and the press corps knew it was watching someone—something—brand new.

Alice was the first female celebrity of the twentieth century. Her name had "attention-getting, interest-riveting, profit-generating value."[22] In print, Alice Roosevelt was seldom identified as "daughter of the president." Her name—sometimes only her first name—was sufficient; an early Cher or Madonna. Americans recognized her face from the rotogravure section of the newspapers. Of all the Roosevelt family members outside the president, it was Alice who monopolized the dailies. By mid-1902, crowds gathered wherever she went. Alice's entrée to the larger world was through the doorway of celebrityhood, foisted upon her not-unwilling self, beginning with her White House debut.

Fans provided a market for Alice-inspired goods. She was the subject of popular songs that were turned into sheet music with her picture on the cover. "The Alice Roosevelt March" featured a lithe Gibson girl drawing of her. "The American Girl" was "respectfully dedicated to the First Young Lady of the U.S.A.," and on the cover her photograph was patriotically flanked by two buglers.[23] She became famously linked with the color "Alice blue," the blue-gray of her eyes, which became the most popular shade for dresses and gowns. Alice's face gazed steadily out from a French chocolate card—an early-model baseball card—tucked inside a Guerin-Boutron candy bar. Many different photos of the First Daughter were made into postcards sent by admirers and collected—then and now—by postcard aficionados and autograph seekers.

It was awkward for Alice to walk the fine line between her parents' desire for privacy and her own need for attention. She did not always enjoy being pursued by reporters and photographers. She worried that people liked her only because she was a daughter of the president. As she traversed the rocky years of young adulthood and the relationship with her parents temporarily worsened, choosing public approbation over parental approval became easier. As a young woman, Alice was confused by Edith and Theodore's attitude:

> The whole attitude toward publicity was so ridiculous. I was brought up on the principle that "nice" people didn't get their names in the papers except when they were born, when they married, or when they died. We were always being enjoined not to talk to reporters and to avoid photographers. At the same time there was all this interest in our every move. The family was always telling me, "Beware of publicity!" And there was publicity hitting me in the face every day.... And once stories got out, or were invented, I was accused of <u>courting</u> publicity. I destroyed a savage letter on the subject from my father, because I was so furious with him. There was he, one of the greatest experts in publicity there ever was, accusing me of trying to steal his limelight.[24]

Edith was not at all ambivalent about publicity. She cherished her privacy. Her feelings were well known to Alice and everyone else. Edith remodeled the White House in part to cut down on the number of citizens trooping through their new home. She responded to certain types of mail with form letters to discourage the formation of an entourage. She gave no interviews and was never tempted to write her autobiography. Edith took care to see that her family was similarly sheltered—as much as was possible for a woman who once complained, "Not one of my children ever wants to be told or directed about anything whatever!"[25]

Edith knew that she could not protect her children from publicity once they left the grounds of the White House, and she was unable to stop the press from writing about her family. Quentin penned a letter to Alice with a telling postscript: "05¢ five cents for the signature please."[26] For a twelve-year-old, he had a cynic's understanding of First Family fame. One way Edith could exercise control was to monitor the photographs of the children that the press printed. Edith hired Frances B. Johnston and other professional photographers to take still shots of them. She vetted Alice's choices. These became the official photographs released upon request. Alice's were always the most sought after, both by individuals and newspapers.

Theodore believed that there were appropriate and inappropriate times for publicity. He was masterful at manipulating the media, and his daughter learned everything she knew about the subject from him. As an adult, Alice quipped only half jokingly that her father had to be the bride at every wedding, the baby at every christening, and the corpse at every funeral. Alice, as strong-willed as her father, absorbed but did not always adhere to his definitions of acceptable and unacceptable. A battle of wills ensued. Alice did as she pleased, and took the consequences when the press reported it. "Do not like the advertisements of you appearing at portrait show," TR once wrote her sternly. "They distinctly convey the impression that any person who wishes to pay five dollars may be served tea by you and Ethel Barrymore. I cannot consent to such use of your name and must ask you not to serve tea."[27] But Alice wanted to participate in this charity event for the New York Orthopedic Hospital. She telegraphed sweetly to her father that his note had arrived too late.

Torn between her family's accusations of courting publicity and her own assimilation of her father's tactics, Alice's young adulthood was complicated in a way that her peers could not fathom. The subtle dynamics of Theodore's lingering guilt over his remarriage, Alice's fears of abandonment, and Edith's distant mothering made the relationship between Theodore and Alice precarious. Alice competed for TR's attention with her half brothers and sister, and with all his constituents. Unlike a father who leaves home to work, Roosevelt's office was partly their home: the governor's mansion, the White House. The boundary between home time and work time was fluid, with office seekers, politicians, private citizens, diplomats, and cabinet members in various combinations over for dinner nightly.

Despite her parents' objections, Alice made her own rules. "Being the offspring of a very conspicuous parent, I wasn't going to let him get the better of me," Alice remembered.[28] She did engage the press even if she couldn't help at least some of what was written. Reporters followed her. They invented stories about her. Their attention constrained her actions. As a young woman, Alice was both typical and exceptional. She was a normal teen, with periods of depression and rebellion alternating with phases of longing for parental guidance and family togetherness. Of course, most of her friends had not lost their mothers and none were daughters of presidents. In Alice, these tensions left her sometimes moody and morose, sometimes feeling lighthearted and giddy. It was the self-possessed, daring young woman with a zest for living who became the role model for young Americans.

Alice's first diary entry for 1902 explained the effects of the sudden and continuing press coverage. She lamented that the congressional daughters who lunched with her had the "pleasure of meeting (not me, but) the 'President's Daughter.'" With unconscious irony, Alice noted afterward she went to Auntie Bye's to talk over plans for her invitation to the coronation of Edward VII. As she had in Albany, Edith requested Alice's help for official events such as "a card reception where however, the people only passed through, Mother and I shaking hands with them...." About this same time, Alice's name first appeared as an enticement for charity purposes. "To the lucky drawer of this prize will also go Miss Roosevelt's card," the article in the *New York Tribune* promised.[29]

In early February, after Alice's debut, the focus of the family turned to Ted Jr., who became very ill with pneumonia at Groton School. Edith went to nurse him, and Theodore soon joined his wife and eldest son. Alice worried because TR would not take her to stay with her "own darling Teddy Brother." Edith sent her long letters from Ted's bedside, with details of the patient's pulse, respiration, medications (morphine and milk with whiskey), and temperature—and how "in his sleep he called loudly for 'Sissie.'" Only the little children and Auntie Bye and Uncle Will were around as Alice turned eighteen on February 12, 1902. On the fourteenth, TR returned from Groton and had lunch with Alice, Auntie Bye, Secretary of War Elihu Root, and Attorney General Philander Knox, Alice recorded, but she left immediately after dinner—finally—to see her brother. Upon her reaching Boston, the *New York Tribune* featured a story on the Roosevelts at Groton. The title concluded triumphantly: "Miss Roosevelt Arrives." For the next week, Alice devoted herself to the care of her stepmother and brother. "I do love that boy," Alice worried.[30]

Private concerns yielded to Alice's public service debut when she christened Germany's American-made imperial yacht the *Meteor*. The initial overture came from Kaiser Wilhelm II through American ambassador Andrew D. White.[31] Roosevelt immediately saw diplomatic advantages and gave his consent. If Roosevelt ever thought of his daughter's role only as an attractive accompaniment to the christening, it is certain that the French knew that the *Germans* did not. The French ambassador to Washington, Jules Cambon, wrote with a mixture of envy and apprehension to the minister of foreign affairs, Theophile Delcasse, on January 15: "It is the completion in a series of acts [by Germany] calculated to win over the public opinion of the country." The Russians worried that the event would crystallize German Americans into a force that would eventually support the fatherland.[32]

For all her bravado, Alice was shy and nervous at the actual event. Prince Henry, representing his brother the kaiser, arrived in Washington on February 23, 1902. Alice spent part of that day practicing by smashing bottles in Auntie Bye's backyard. Alice met the prince the next afternoon and thought him "a most cheerful soul."[33] That night, President Roosevelt gave a stag dinner for the prince and other foreign dignitaries who had gathered for the yacht's launch. The First Lady had the East Room decorated with thousands of tiny red, white, and blue electric lights in the shapes of anchors, ropes, and other nautical emblems. The menu consisted of duck, terrapin, and "filet de boeuf Hambourgeoise," enhanced by punch served in little boats that flew the *Meteor*'s flag. Dessert was a coup: colored ice cream molded into fruit shapes and served in spun sugar seashells with the German eagle on one side and American insignia on the other.[34]

The morning of the twenty-fifth, the participants and the observers made their way to the ceremony. Alice relished the day, evident in her effusive diary entry:

> Got to Jersey City at almost seven, had breakfast in the car. Then we all, the Prince, Father, Mother, myself and the parties got on the ferry boat to go to Shooters Island. Had bully fun going over. [C]hatted... with the Prince. Got to Shooter's Island about 10.30. I christened the

yacht. First I smashed the bottle of champagne on the bow saying "In the name of his Majesty the German Emperor I christen this yacht *Meteor*," then I cut the last rope which held it.... Everyone says I did well and successfully. The Prince then gave me a bunch of pink roses, and when he congratulated me both shook and kissed my hand.... [W]ent over to the *Hohenzollern* (the Emperor's yacht) and had lunch. The Prince gave me (from the Emperor) a bracelet with a miniature of the Emperor set in diamonds. Got more roses from the officers of the boat. Also a book of views of Berlin from the Emperor and a cable at lunch from him too. I sent him one directly after launching the boat. At lunch sat on the Prince's left, his Admiral von Eisendech on my right. He drew a picture for me on the back of his lunch card. The Prince made a speech to Father then Father one to him and then he made one about me. I should say toast, not speech.[35]

The newspapers chronicled the day in even more detail. The front pages of the *Washington Post*, *New York Tribune*, and the *New York Times* cleared column inches for sprawling diagrams of the *Meteor* and the *Hohenzollern*, descriptions of the women's dresses, Alice's comportment, and exactly how often the prince took Alice's arm. For her part, the *Times* commented, "Miss Roosevelt was the most self-possessed person on the stand."[36]

Alice enjoyed the prince, the publicity, and the diamonds. Henry Adams acerbically commented, "Of Prince Henry I know next to nothing except that he brought damnable weather and left diamond bracelets galore, with his dear brother's self-satisfied face on them. Alice Roosevelt wore hers to a... dinner, and excited the derisive howls of my niece Elise for its hideousness."[37] The *New York Tribune* editorial was kinder: "It is only a few weeks since Miss Roosevelt left the schoolroom and in a day she has become one of the most regarded women in the world, replacing the young Queen of Holland in popular favor. She is seeming unaffected by the sudden notoriety thrust upon her, but stands in the glare of the footlights without flinching." Because the ship was the private yacht of the kaiser and the sponsor was the daughter of the president, the "gala affair" was newsworthy. Half a world away, Frenchwomen could purchase a stylish cloak named the "'Miss Roosevelt' Wrap," by Beneson of Paris. "Alice," Marguerite Cassini conceded, "became a star overnight. The country fell in love with her."[38]

The only unhappy segment of the American population was the Women's Christian Temperance Union (WCTU). "It does not seem necessary to say what I am going to write to the daughter of the President, who is herself such a reformer," the national general secretary wrote to Alice. She claimed to represent the wishes "of the fifty thousand young women in the country who wear the white ribbon" of the temperance pledge. They begged Alice to use a nonalcoholic substitute for the christening champagne.[39] The good women of the WCTU were destined to be disappointed in Alice.

After the christening, Roosevelt's friend Whitelaw Reid, owner of the *New York Tribune,* watched Alice's deportment with approval and commended the president on the larger effects: "I fancy that the Prince's visit has been internationally useful, and I am sure it has given almost wholly unmixed pleasure in this country. Of course, you had no thought of political advantage in it anymore than the Prince had; yet I believe that it will also be found to have been of great political use."[40] It was the first example of the First Daughter's usefulness in foreign relations, the side of politics she found most absorbing as an adult, and the first time Alice's fame proved a boon to her father's presidency.

Immediately after the prince's departure, a tempest in an English teapot beset the president. Alice received an invitation from Whitelaw Reid, TR's special ambassador, to attend Edward VII's coronation. The idea thrilled her. She had never been overseas, and by the time her father was her age, he had been through Europe and East Asia. Alice and her aunts excitedly discussed appropriate attire. Then word came that England wanted to seat the famous daughter of their ally in Westminster Abbey with the rest of the world's royalty. The *Literary Digest* reported Europeans believed that Alice should be thought of as "a princess of the blood" who deserved "the honors due to the oldest daughter of an emperor."[41]

The Irish-American population wielded its considerable clout by inundating the White House with complaints about the anticipated trip. The

Sons of Erin believed that Alice should not go unless she took with her a petition signed by a million American mothers in protest of the English treatment of Ireland and South Africa. Irish-American societies across the United States condemned Alice's proposed attendance at the coronation as an unacceptable show of support for England. The chair of the Republican National Committee at the time, Marcus Hanna, dragged a bag of "several hundred letters [from] Irish organizations and individuals" to the White House. After hearing the first few, Roosevelt knew he could not send his daughter.[42]

TR cabled Britain and refused the invitation. "It is...likely," the *New York Times* suggested, "that the President on reflection became disinclined to have his daughter placed in a position where necessarily she would be regarded as something more than a plain American girl visiting London on a sightseeing trip." In fact, as TR explained to Ambassador Joseph H. Choate, he decided that "both the attentions which through courtesy would be shown her, and the fact that other attentions could not be shown her, would be misunderstood." Roosevelt allowed that his daughter's instant celebrity status took him by surprise. Reid frowned on the "misrepresentations and falsehoods" told by the press about Alice just "to make a political point."[43]

Alice was crushed. She confided to the back of her diary—the place she wrote her most secret vows so the maids wouldn't see—"I swear by all I believe in that if it is any way feasible I will go to the coronation of the next king, he who comes after the present Edward the seventh. [signed] Alice Lee Roosevelt." Half a year later, Alice had not forgotten her lost opportunity. When Edith would not permit Alice to accept an invitation to visit Jamaica, she complained, "Mother says I can't [go], as it is English territory and they would make a fuss about me. I don't give a hoot if they did. It's all because the newspapers kicked up such a row about my going over to the coronation in the spring."[44]

This seating question at Edward VII's coronation marked the first time that Alice became a pawn of pro- and anti-administration newspapers. Roosevelt's fans took great pleasure in the First Daughter's internationally recognized status, while his detractors accused TR of undemocratic aspirations and suggested that Princess Alice's father would soon proclaim himself king. London's *Daily News* gloomily recalled the cancellation of fetes planned in Alice's honor and England's disappointment at her absence. But the paper understood that the "fuss" over Miss Roosevelt "would seem to be not in accordance with the simplicity which marks American republicanism, and, if permitted, it might excite some unfriendly remarks in circles in America which the President would desire to conciliate."[45]

After that unsuccessful foray into the international spotlight, in early March, Alice embarked on a month-long consolation trip to Cuba. She packed six dozen photographs of herself. Former Rough Rider Leonard Wood communicated to Roosevelt that he and his wife would happily entertain Alice as their guest in the governor's palace over Easter. The Woods's gesture significantly cheered her. Wood had been the military governor in Havana since December 1899. American occupation of the island would end in May 1902, a month after Alice left. Once in Cuba, she was a faultless First Daughter. Although Cubans expressed ambivalence toward the American troops, Alice encountered only well-wishers. She viewed exercises at a school for orphans; presided over a charity reception; attended teas, parties, balls, and a cavalry review given in her honor. She also had her fortune told, an outgrowth of her enduring fascination with Romany culture. Another American visitor to the island at the same time vouched, "There was always plenty doing wherever Alice appeared—like her father, she was a center of activity." Alice's diary displayed her delight: "Several awfully nice Cuban men and girls out there. Had bully fun as I always enjoy meeting them."[46]

Alice and her chaperone shopped, ate spicy Cuban food, and followed jai alai games closely. Alice knew that "as the daughter of the President, I was supposed to have an intelligent interest in such things as training schools, and sugar plantations, the experiments with yellow fever mosquitoes." But the young men—and the betting—on the jai alai fields were never far from the teenager's mind.[47] As she left the island, Alice received a telegram from the governor of Matanzas asking for her help in revoking the death sentence of a local man convicted of murder, and a letter from a prisoner in Havana's "City jail" pleading for her intercession. The historical record is silent as to whether or not Alice assisted these men, but her celebrity status clearly preceded her. The condemned man and his allies surely hoped that their public appeal—it was the subject of a *New York Times* article—and Alice's proximity to the U.S. president would bring about their pardons.[48]

Alice began in earnest her life as the First Daughter upon her return. In that role, she had to balance the self-absorption of an eighteen-year-old with the demands of celebrity. She, and thousands of other Americans, read about herself in an illustrated, page-long *Ladies' Home Journal* article where she was described as "warm-hearted, impulsive and demonstrative," "gracefully slender," "an excellent horsewoman," fond of "outdoor exercise and all forms of wholesome athletic sport," in short, "the typical American girl of good health and sane ideas."[49]

On April 13, 1902, Alice made a confession to her diary: "I dressed up this evening in my Spanish white lace mantilla and wound my hair and dress with brilliant pink roses. No one saw me, I simply paraded up and down and looked at myself in the glass. This, I think, is a case of 'confession is good for the soul.' 'Vanity of vanities,' saith the preacher, 'all is vanity.' And I have absolutely no reason at all to be vain. These last remarks are decidedly in the school girl 'my diary thoughts,' my opinion on life and that sort of thing. I have decidedly fallen."[50] It was a Sloperesque dance, but framed in guilt. Only to her diary could Alice, raised by a famous father and a puritanical stepmother, confide her confused attempts to understand what the rest of the world suddenly saw in her.

Chapter 4

⛤

"I Tried to Be Conspicuous"

ALICE ROOSEVELT'S INABILITY to trust wholeheartedly created a potent and troubling mix when added to the celebrity status that caused her to question the intentions of friends and suitors. Her ferocious desire to be free of confining rules may have been a test: who would love her even when she pushed the furthest boundaries? Alice's teenage years predated the 1920s and the 1960s, two eras famous for youth rebellions. In the first decade of the twentieth century, a woman's goal was marriage, which required behavior beyond reproach. But Alice had a special worry: she could never trust that any man loved her for herself. The more she gave in to her fears and became a female caricature of her father's most criticized traits—impetuosity, stubbornness, insensitivity—the more she alienated some men, and perversely, the more she also became a hero to others. The end result would be a woman who fit no mold. The journey to that late-life, serene self-possession was painful; all the more so because so much of it occurred in public.

The First Daughter could turn to neither her father nor her stepmother for help in making sense of her situation. While he could find a moment for the occasional Highland fling with his daughter, TR was unavailable for the heart-to-hearts that she craved. And Edith, Alice recorded on April 30, 1902, was "in bed all day with a headache and dead tired." Tensions were high in the Roosevelt household. On May 8, Alice noted that she had a "foolish temper fit this morning with Mother. A newspaper paragraph saying [two different men] in love with me." Edith, unbeknownst to Alice, was pregnant—this explained her ongoing "headaches." But the next day, Edith miscarried, and remained in bed and downcast for a fortnight.[1]

Throughout her four years there, Alice served as White House hostess on various formal occasions, just as she had assisted at Auntie Bye's functions. The First Lady found Alice so useful that she vowed that she would "not have a big dinner till you are here to help me again." Edith was ill when an illustrious French commission visited the capital to unveil a statue of General Jean de Rochambeau, the French nobleman who fought beside George Washington. Lying on his back on the sofa in the Executive Office, energetically "kicking his heels in the air," TR accepted the invitation of the French ambassador Jules Cambon by shouting, "All right! Alice and I will go! Alice and I are toughs!" On the morning of May 22, 1902, Alice stood proudly beside Theodore to receive their visitors. In Edith's stead, the commission presented Alice with a pair of exquisite Sevres figurines. The next day, a host of Washington dignitaries, including the president and First Daughter, went to Annapolis to admire the French ship *Gaulois*. Before the commission departed, Alice attended a dinner at the French embassy and sat next to Charles de Chambrun, a man she found particularly handsome.[2]

In early June, she left for Boston and her summer visit to her Lee relatives. Alice had three good weeks in Chestnut Hill, watching country club boat races, dining with friends, flirting with Harvard men, and driving to the Pops concert in an automobile. What really helped her vacation was the announcement from Grandpa Lee that he would raise her allowance by five hundred dollars, to two thousand dollars a year. This increase represented a figure greater than the yearly salary of the average American worker in 1902. "I am happy!" Alice exclaimed to her diary, and used the funds to shop "madly."[3]

Despite her relatively substantial income, Alice worried about money. When her allowance arrived at the beginning of each month, she, like her friends, paid her bills and bought new clothes. Alice occasionally exceeded her budget, but living within her means was not arduous at first. In October 1902, for example, she noted that two days before the end of the month, she

was "so far only about fifty dollars over my allowance." That did not cur-
tail a spree on the thirty-first, when she "shopped all morning at three different stores." Nevertheless, she never felt she had enough money. Her
diary is full of promises to marry only very wealthy men, and plans as to
how she would spend a lot of money, if she only had it. "I pray for *money*!"
Alice confessed as she watched her bills mount.[4] It became less feasible to
meet her desires on two thousand dollars a year when she broadened her
circle of friends to include wealthy Washington socialites such as Eleanor
"Cissy" Patterson and Countess Marguerite Cassini. Theodore and Edith
criticized Alice for her choice of friends, while Grandma and Grandpa Lee
lectured their granddaughter on her financial profligacy.

National interest in the First Daughter amplified as her socializing increased. The "Alice Roosevelt Waltz" by composer Ferdinand Sabathil debuted on Independence Day 1902.[5] Newspapers were particularly interested
in who might be dancing with the First Daughter. On July 19, the *New York
Times* had to retract an earlier story claiming to announce Alice's engagement, only one of several incorrect guesses by newspapers. She told family
friend John Greenway in December 1902 that she had "been reported engaged five times in the last eight months!" But the fact that the rumors
were printed at all made her parents uncomfortable—and so did her summer of parties, boat races, dances, and other frivolities. "Got a talking to
this evening at having no interests in life from Mother and Father. Not at all
unexpected nor yet in the least undeserved; only I am afraid I just about
care. I wish I did. No hope for Alice."[6] Alice's tone wavered from sarcastic
to penitent, but the next day she left for Newport, the resort city of the very
wealthy—where few other Roosevelts, save Auntie Bye, ever went.

The Vanderbilts and similarly monied families escaped from the heat of
Boston and New York to play the whole summer long on the beaches of
Rhode Island. Alice enjoyed Newport—even though she knew that she
did not have the income to keep up with its inhabitants. Betting was a prime
sport at Newport. Women gambled at bridge, tried their luck in the casino,
and played the odds on yachting races. Vacationers spent their time
battling at croquet, driving cars, having their horoscopes read, dining, pic-

nicking, sleeping late, dancing, horseback riding, playing tennis, and sailing. In the summer of 1902, Alice created a mild scandal when she and her friend Ellen "Lila" Paul drove unchaperoned from Newport to Boston in Lila's automobile. The *New York Tribune* covered the news in a tone of astonishment on its front page: "In a big red automobile which snorted and bounced its way along the country roads leaving a cloud of dust in its wake, Miss Alice Roosevelt traveled yesterday afternoon from Newport to [Boston]. Miss Ellen Drexel Paul, of Philadelphia, was her companion and drove the machine. Tired, but thoroughly delighted with automobile riding, Miss Roosevelt arrived last evening at the home of her grandfather, George C. Lee."[7]

Alice's pleasure in the new sport led her to purchase her own touring car in 1904, an expensive, long, sleek, $2,500 "red devil" automobile. Alice loved driving cars—fast. Whenever she could she drove a car rather than a horse-drawn vehicle. More than once Alice paid fines for excessive speed while driving. "It must be great fun to run an auto," Auntie Corinne wrote dryly, "but do think of the life and limbs of your victims." Yet it was the unchaperoned drive from Newport to Boston that made the biggest impression on America. A writer for *Motor* magazine in 1907 asserted, "It needed only this edict from the White House to completely establish [women's driving] among those whose puritanical scruples had kept them reluctant lest in some occult manner this highly masculine pleasure should reflect against them."[8] The First Daughter thus added a legitimacy to the heretofore risqué combination of women and automobiles, and opened the avenues for women drivers.

Alice returned to Washington, where the remodeling of the White House continued. She did not shake her Newport schedule immediately. "Drank three cups of coffee for breakfast and then had a scrap with Auntie Bye," Alice noted in early September 1902. On the third, Theodore Roosevelt's carriage was hit by an electric trolley in Massachusetts. Roosevelt appeared unhurt, but the accident killed a Secret Service agent of whom the younger Roosevelt children were particularly fond. Alice's diary entry was strangely unemotional. However, the accident must have shaken her, for her diary is full of her father's activities for the next few weeks. Alice noted that "Father very busy writing the speeches for his western trip," on September 16, and the next day that "Father and the Senators yesterday were going over the revision of the tariff. He is having a pretty hard time." She even changed her habits to be able to see her father, having been reminded horribly of his mortality: "Have begun to get up for breakfast." Theodore did not approve of his daughter's increasingly busy social schedule. It prohibited her from breakfasting with the entire family, the one meal that the Roosevelts tried to eat alone together. It was not Alice's style to wax sentimental about her feelings for her father. However, she did try to prove to herself that she was capable of loving him. She feared that she was not capable of loving anyone.[9]

About this time Alice also broadened her talents in another area of which TR disapproved. "Read a lot about draw poker and poker dice throwing," the First Daughter wrote. The next day she "dealt [her]self poker hands all morning." Later in her life, Alice intimated that she learned to play poker only after she was married.[10] Although others may have helped to hone her skills, Alice taught herself while still a teenager. Poker was a way for Alice to enter the men's sphere, to prove that she was a good sport. Alice preferred to be on the inside of any group of men, and she knew that she would never be happy simpering on the outside, especially if their activity looked amusing. It didn't matter to her that the fun—playing poker and betting, in this case—was considered an unacceptable pastime for women in 1902. Ladies bet on bridge discreetly. Alice bet on poker and bragged about her winnings.

At the end of September, Theodore Roosevelt had to undergo a procedure because of an abscess caused by the trolley car accident. Alice supported her father by sitting with him through the trying ordeal of the doctor scraping the bone of his left leg. She wrote he was "getting on splendidly" after the operation.[11] Father and daughter must have talked together about the overarching domestic crisis of the moment as the physician operated, for Alice's diary entry contained what was for her then an unusual statement of position on a political issue. The anthracite coal strike, begun in Pennsylvania, threatened to cause a shortage of home heating fuel across the nation. Opinions warred as to whether the miners' rights, in such a case, could outweigh the specter of Americans freezing to death. Alice understood that her father "of course has no legal rights. But," she continued, "I think it is time that the government should have something to say about a thing which so much concerns all the 'people' as the great coal industry does." Alice wrote this down in her diary because she was trying to take an interest in something outside herself, as her parents suggested she should. Alice confided the aftereffects of such a parental lecture in an undated entry: "I am bored to extinction by nearly everything down here at Oyster Bay at home. I ought to take an interest in politics. I mean to, but I simply can't. I might if I were not always thinking about what I wish I could do, about what I would do if I have the wherewithal."[12] Or perhaps she commented on the coal strike because TR impressed upon her the seriousness of the problem. Either way, it warranted no further comment in her diary. Instead, the end of the month found her shopping and worried about lacking the "wherewithal."

In Chestnut Hill with the Lees, Alice's life accelerated as the fall social season opened. She attended parties, dinners, and balls. She bought a "pocket pistol" and "had great fun with it." Alice moved from house to house in Boston and New York, taking advantage of all invitations. Parental complaints mounted: "Family putting the hoof down about my staying at several very amusing places," Alice sniffed. She returned home, made up her accounts to Edith, and felt sorry for herself. On December 13, she had an "at home," but: "No one ever came to see me. What wouldn't I give to be a most marvelous belle and be more run after than any other girl."[13] Since Alice had a habit of seeing those whom she wanted to see, it is hard to tell whether complaints such as this were absolutely true. Did "no one" really visit or did only people for whom Alice didn't care appear?

December promised her first Christmas in the White House, but her diary suggests she felt thwarted in her current crush, ignored at Christmas parties and dances ("No one paid very much attention to poor Alice"), and grumpy about having to spend most of the month with relatives. On the twenty-fourth, she slept until 12:30 p.m., shopped until midafternoon, and stopped in at Auntie Bye's. After a family Christmas Eve dinner, Alice skipped church to play with "a most fascinating baby pistol," her Christmas present from TR.[14] On Christmas Day, the Roosevelts celebrated in their traditional manner, beginning with stockings and concluding with dancing. Alice did not share most of the rest of her day with the family. "Got up about quarter before seven," she recorded. "Archie had a surprise Christmas tree for the family. Then we had our stockings on the bed in Father and Mother's room. Breakfast at eight and then our big presents. $305.00 all together from Mother, Grandma and Grandpa. Most of my other things were stupid but I had great amusement... for the benefit of the family. Mr. [Robert Munro-] Ferguson gave me some very nice lace. Lunch at Auntie Bye's.... Called on Marjorie Nott and won fifteen dollars from Freddie Hale.... Of course we all danced afterwards in the East Room."[15] Her teenager's cynicism, coupled with a bad case of the doldrums, seemed to blight most of the holiday season. She left as soon as she could to see friends in New York City.

The 1903 winter weighed heavily upon Alice. For weeks in a row she was dejected and unable to enjoy her social rounds. She slept late almost every day. She compared herself unfavorably to other women. In mid-January, she revealed part of the source of her pain. She was trying to recover from her crush on Arthur Iselin, a process that took well into the spring.

She slept the days away, but nights were no better. At a dance at the Italian embassy, "No one paid any attention to me and I really am beginning to feel absolutely despondent about ever having a good time again." She was not meeting the men she found attractive, and she seemed to be without a best girlfriend as well. Alice missed the kind of friend in whom she could confide her feelings. After a series of unhappy days, Alice couldn't help comparing herself with two acquaintances: "They are both so attractive and everyone likes them so much. It is very hard to have friends like them and be one's self a perfectly nondescript sort of a person. I don't think I have made an impression on anybody, and no one really cares to play with me, or to dance with me. Oh *how* I wish I were a most marvelous belle."

Theodore, observing his eldest child, complained to Ted: "Sister continues to lead the life of social excitement, which is I think all right for a girl to lead for a year or two, but which upon my word I do not regard as healthy from the standpoint of permanence. I wish she had some pronounced serious taste. Perhaps she will develop one later."[16] Alice concluded her diary entry, written the same night TR wrote to Ted, in a way that would have given Roosevelt hope, had he known. "How I hate going out," she groused. "What is the good in it anyway. A crowd of vapid people almost all of them no good whatsoever in the world. I feel dead tired."[17]

Like the parents of many teenagers, Edith and TR approved of some of their daughter's friends, but not others. Alice was not allowed to accept invitations until Edith had sanctioned them. But there were many times that Edith herself organized Alice's schedule, presumably filling it with suitable associates. "I've arranged for you go from Phil. to Orange on the 2nd as there is a dance there that night. There is also one on the 3rd. Cousin Mamie...has asked you to dinner on Saturday night and I have accepted, and on Monday you can come home—I only hope you may have as good a time as I used to have," Edith concluded with a touch of wistfulness in a letter full to the margins with scheduling details.[18]

Alice consistently penned "no hope for Alice" in her diary, echoing Edith or Theodore, or both, and eventually Edith noticed her stepdaughter's depression. Beyond carping letters to Ted, Theodore made no attempt to address Alice's pain. Both TR and Edith attributed Alice's excessive sleeping and her unhappy moods to either an infelicitous social life or some sort of high dramatics. One Sunday evening in January, Alice wrote up a description of the mother-daughter talk that Edith, at least, seemed to find comforting: "This evening Mother said that she too had been noticing the queer worried expression that I have been acquiring by long months of patient practice in my eyes and my handsome carriage. The poor dear Lamb was afraid she had hurt my feelings and came back to my room and told me that she didn't want me to think that she thought that the expression came from worried feelings inside, because she knew that it didn't. My feelings hadn't of course been in the least hurt, but how little can she imagine what really naughty thoughts I have, and what fascinatingly 'darling' things I do, though these all are probably temporary, and only because I am so very youthful."[19] Edith did not take Alice seriously. The First Lady was preoccupied once again with becoming pregnant. Perhaps she was happiest with young children who loved her uncritically and could never talk back.

The holiday spate of White House receptions didn't particularly enliven Alice's downcast state. The Roosevelts held the big, traditional New Year's Day reception in the renovated White House, and Theodore and Edith stood to welcome the crowds of admirers. Alice found the Judicial reception "exactly like all the rest only queerer people if possible." But she was good at receiving lines and official dinner parties, and had become a practiced social chameleon. Alice could switch on her First Daughter bearing and manners whenever necessary. One European visitor commented that Alice had "a brilliant manner and a friendly conception of her duty to her father's guests…very competent, thoughtful, picturesque, with an inexhaustible stock of pleasant surprises." This is in direct opposition to Alice's own self-image: "I [stand] by, looking on with open mouth. I am a fool. I can't join in repartee of any kind." She told her diary that she didn't think she would go to New York for any of the social life at all in 1903.[20]

Alice's unhappiness reached a denouement at the end of January. She tried to explain her sense of desperation to Edith, but wound up in a deeper morass of sadness and self-pity:

Mother had early tea with the children and I went down and sat with her and wept madly all through it. Because I can't go abroad— because I can't go to Jamaica, because I can't do a great many very unimportant things that my own selfish self wants to do. I also said that Father doesn't care for me, that is to say one eighth as much as he does for the other children. It is perfectly true that he doesn't, and Lord, why should he. We are not in the least congenial, and if I don't care overmuch for him and don't take a bit of interest in the things he likes, why should he pay any attention to me or the things that I live for, except to look on them with disapproval. Of course he loves me in a way because I am one of his children, and he certainly does possess his much-prized "sense of duty." Heaven knows I am perfectly well aware [that I haven't] got it in my commonplace self to love anyone overmuch, except Alice, but I certainly do love him with all the love that I am so far capable of.[21]

Alice clearly signaled her estrangement from her family, her need for attention from Theodore, her desire from compassion from Edith, and her belief that her father loved her less than her siblings and then only out of a sense of duty. Are the words in Alice's diary her own, or are they Edith's? Did Edith say crushingly to Alice, "Well, Alice, what do you expect? You don't take an interest in your father's life. Why should he automatically take an interest in yours?" What did Edith respond when Alice accused her father of not loving her? Could Edith have said, "Of course he loves you Alice. You are his daughter." The ambivalence in Alice was profound.

Her position often forced Alice to endure such inconsistencies. In an interview at the time of her ninetieth birthday, Alice recalled that she thought she was "a rather pathetic creature, terribly homely and that they were just saying I was pretty because I was the President's daughter." "Sometimes," the nonagenarian continued, "I look at pictures of myself then, trying to see what they thought was pretty. But then I determined not to be a pathetic creature. I decided to defeat it so I became resistant, contrary and I tried to be conspicuous."[22] Alice had two choices. She could turn inward and be tractable, conformist, and "good." That is what her parents exhorted her to do, pointing out the model of cousin Eleanor Roosevelt. Or Alice could resist. She could make of the world what she wanted. This option had the advantages of going against her parents' wishes, and of guaranteeing attention—good or bad—for Alice, who never took attention for granted. Choosing at an early age to "be conspicuous" meant that she was ripe for the celebrity role. Alice Roosevelt became bigger than life—no matter how hollow or lonely she may have been—as a self-defense mechanism.[23]

Edith was unable to comprehend her stepdaughter. As a girl, Edith had

been serious minded and solemn. No doubt she believed that she was trying to help Alice shape up or grow up, or both. But the incongruity between Alice's needs and Edith's attempts to meet them frustrated both
women. "Alice," TR wrote to Ted not long after Edith's talk, "has been
just as good as gold of late."[24] Perhaps Edith's methods really were temporarily effective; arguments with her parents almost always preceded re-
morseful promises to change. Or perhaps Theodore had no idea of his
daughter's emotional state.

Travel was the remedy for Alice's depression, just as it had been for her
father's asthma, and her mood perked up in mid-February 1903, when she
was allowed to experience a New Orleans Mardi Gras. Edith Root, the
daughter of TR's secretary of war, accompanied her. En route to Louisiana
by rail, Alice noted that "reporters at all the stations were most skillfully
rushed off by the porters."[25] Newspapers announced Alice would be queen
of the Comus Ball, sponsored by New Orleans's oldest and most prestigious club. It was only a rumor—the local debutantes commanded all the
royal thrones—but she still had an excellent time. They stayed on Avery
Island with former Rough Rider and Tabasco sauce entrepreneur John Mc-
Ilhenny and his family, and "for a week we went nearly every evening to a
carnival ball, the Atlanteans, Momus, Proteus, and Comus, and to a small
dance, the Carnival German, and to a benefit opera as well!" She was welcomed by the king and queen of the Comus Ball in a tribute that brought
her a standing ovation. Alice also found time to bet money on a race of
some sort, where she "came out ten ahead." Alice worried, as usual, that
she was not as popular as her friends. "Edith Root is having a very swell
time, I am afraid better than me. Anyway she gives me the impression that
she is. . . . Oh why aren't people devoted to me?" Nevertheless, she wrote in
superlatives to thank Mrs. McIlhenney: "It was all *too* marvelous and I
don't ever expect to have quite such a good time again." To Alice's credit,
the New Orleans newspapers lavished a similar praise on her: "Never did
[a] young girl wear her honors more sweetly and with such unaffected
grace. . . ."[26]

Upon her return home in early March, Alice spent more time at Auntie
Bye's, her refuge after lectures from TR and Edith. Perhaps in response to

the publicity surrounding the Mardi Gras trip, Alice recorded that "Mother says it is unfortunate in my station in life that I am born with a [penchant] to make myself conspicuous and that I should have been an actress." Alice's response to Edith's criticism was deceptively jaunty: "Heigh Ho! Wait until I am 21!" However, that same day, in the most private back of her diary, Alice demonstrated that Edith's comment did hurt her: "All that I want is to have a large fortune, next to that to have a change of ideas. I can't force it to come but suppose I am merely passing through a phase."[27] "Passing through a phase" was Edith's phrase, echoed by the teenage Alice in sad parody.

An imminent trip to Puerto Rico also served to increase Alice's immunity to parental disapproval.[28] A gratifyingly large crowd gathered on March 14 in New York Harbor to see her off. Policemen, detectives, and Secret Service officers circulated among the hundreds of people who waved the First Daughter good-bye. Alice found the three weeks with Governor William H. Hunt's daughter Beth were great fun. She laid a cornerstone, reviewed the troops, stood in a receiving line for two hours, christened a fire engine, and visited an industrial school and a sugar plantation. She watched as WELCOME TO MISS ALICE ROOSEVELT was spelled out "in different colored fireworks ... going off with loud cracks" in the dark. She was on her "best official behavior." "I am really trying to be very good," she wrote Edith. "Every other word I say is 'me gusto mucho Puerto Rico' with a beautiful smile." Crowds gathered to cheer her. Her conduct made her presidential father happy. "I am very much pleased that you found the visit so interesting," TR wrote, "and it was a good thing in more ways than one. You were of real service down there because you made those people feel that you liked them and took an interest in them and your presence was accepted as a great compliment."[29] Although Alice in later life recalled that she did not often do "something in a public way" within the United States, where her father held the political limelight, she conceded that "it was a little different when I was overseas. In places such as the Philippines and in Puerto Rico and Cuba I was called upon to fill a far greater number of public engagements."[30]

Nothing she did escaped censure or comment. As a behavioral model

Alice was fair game, newspaper editors felt. In 1903, the First Daughter went as a guest of Mabel Gerry to the Chicago Horse Show "for a week of being stared at." John McCutcheon, of the *Chicago Tribune,* drew a cartoon—that Alice loved—in which spectators, judges, and horses all craned their necks upward to Alice's box. The center of attention was the First Daughter, and the band played "Alice, Where Art Thou?"—yet another song written in her honor.[31] But the gods of publicity take as well as give. About the same time as McCutcheon's cartoon, a rival Chicago paper printed a much less flattering editorial accusing her of "'chanking' vigorously" at the theater and elsewhere in public and warned "the soubrettish young women who copy the peculiar characteristics of the daughter of her strenuous sire" not to emulate her gum chewing. While Alice, "never pausing in her violent mastication," gambled at the racetrack, the "young horsemen" bet on whether she would "choke herself or fracture her jaw."[32]

In the spring and summer of 1903, Alice also began a new, headline-making friendship, and despite Edith's desire for a female support system in Alice's life, the thrill-seeking Russian countess Marguerite "Maggie" Cassini, was not the type of woman Edith had in mind. The friends became experts at escaping their chaperones. Alice's spending habits worsened as she tried to keep up with the seemingly unlimited budgets of Maggie and Cissy Patterson, who often joined the pair. Together, their audacity was compounded. Alice taught Maggie how to gamble. Maggie taught Alice how to smoke. Cissy taught them both to dance the newest, raciest dances. They all flirted with the same men and defied the same barriers of social etiquette.[33] The "Three Graces," as newspapers called them, scandalized New York and Washington with their disregard for proper behavior. "Our friendship," Maggie recalled in her memoirs, "had the violence of a bomb, the duration of a skyrocket." She and Alice shared "a common taste in fun and pranks, a delight in flouting the conventions, in mockery, in outrageous behavior generally." Maggie described her relationship with Alice as "two badly spoiled girls set only on their own pleasure," imposing "a veritable reign of terror." Theodore and Edith were certain they squandered their days and nights in frivolous pursuits and demoralizing pleasures.

When she was older, Alice contextualized her father's frustration: "Most of these society friends were the offspring of his own childhood friends, whom he had spurned. He was very self-conscious about it....My father was always taking me to task for gallivanting with 'society' and for not knowing more people like my cousin Eleanor." But even Eleanor was envious. "Alice was so much more sophisticated than *I* was," she admitted.[34]

But cousin Eleanor would never have behaved as badly as Alice and Marguerite did toward those who entertained them. George Westinghouse gave a ball for the pair and told the two friends to create the guest list. Their desired invitees numbered so many that Westinghouse had to build an annex to his ballroom. Even though the workers put in overtime, the extension was not completed by the day of the dance. "So," Maggie recalled, "the imaginative Mr. Westinghouse ordered orchids, carloads of orchids, and with these he completely blanketed the unfinished walls. On the night of the ball we seemed to be dancing in a room hung with exquisite velvet coverings of mauve and purple and violet. Such a prodigal and extravagant gesture!"

Unfortunately, as the orchids wilted, they reminded Alice of "a cemetery after a huge funeral." So Alice and Maggie left long before the ball was over. Another generous host, Knickerbocker James Hazen Hyde, also gave a ball in their honor. This, Alice and Maggie did not condescend even to attend. The day of the Hyde ball, they received an invitation to dine alone with the dashing bachelor Congressman Nicholas Longworth in his private club. The women cabled last-minute regrets to Mr. Hyde, who never forgave them.[35]

Alice's lifestyle as celebrity First Daughter annoyed Theodore when it became apparent that she could use her position to gain special treatment from people such as Westinghouse and Hyde. Alice was furious with her father when he put a stop to her traveling for free on the railroads, a traditional benefit of the presidency. "Horrid father won't let us travel anymore on the passes. I am so mad at him. My train bill so far this season has been $176.25!"[36] Roosevelt saw such opportunism as unfitting in a democratic society. On the other hand, the things he most abhorred caused the greatest admiration in young women around the globe. The *New York Tribune* reprinted an article entitled "Gleanings" from a British newspaper:

> Miss Alice Roosevelt, says an English society writer, seems to possess a good deal of the indefatigable spirit of her Presidential papa. Socially she is certainly one of the most strenuously active young women of her time. She is almost as much *en évidence* at fashionable functions in New York as she is in Washington, and thinks nothing of making the trip back and forth between the two cities (it takes five or six hours) simply to be present at the entertainment of some friend.... It would astonish English girls to see how this daughter of the ruler of the great republic makes these flying trips. She seldom travels with a maid, and when alone carries her own jewel case and dressing bag. When she reaches her destination she calls up her own cab and makes arrangements in regard to any luggage she may have. Miss Roosevelt is a remarkably healthy, bright looking girl, and does not show in the least the hard work that must be the result of being a belle in two cities. Late hours, six out of seven nights a week, combined with a series of receptions, luncheons and dinners, to say nothing of innumerable train journeyings, are apt to prove a bit fatiguing, but the indefatigable young woman from the White House shows no sign of flagging in her pursuit of pleasure, and is evidently enjoying herself enormously.[37]

President Roosevelt only slowly came to appreciate the importance of his eldest daughter as an image management tool. It was an opportunity lost; putting her to work cutting ribbons, laying cornerstones, or leading parades in the United States would have been a public relations asset for his administration. It would simultaneously have distanced her from the daughters of "the malefactors of great wealth" such as Grace Vanderbilt and Cissy Patterson or even unhealthier influences such as the countess Cassini. More important, Alice would have felt loved and needed by her father. If Roosevelt had somehow found a way to make his daughter more of a partner, capitalizing on her assets, both their relationship and his administration would have benefited.

Alice continued her rebellions. When Roosevelt said that no daughter of his would smoke under his roof, Alice climbed on top of the White House roof and smoked. "I smoked on the roof, outdoors, and in everyone else's house," she recalled. "I naturally...smoked to annoy the family." Alice was the first American woman to smoke openly in the nation's capital. She carried cigarettes in her compact and delighted to shock those around her by dropping it so that they would spill out. An uncle tried to cure her by making her smoke two big black cigars. "I smoked them both through with enjoyment," she said. "He was sure I'd be sick, but I wasn't."[38]

Cigarettes were occasionally found in the hands of "gentle and distinguished foreign women," but never American women, whose male relatives loathed the idea. Once again, the First Daughter changed the rules. The *Washington Mirror* blamed her for the increased use of cigarettes by women in public and suggested, "Probably if this habit of the Lofty were known to those in Parental Authority, there would be an exhibition of the strenuous life which has never found its way into the standard works of the Author." Parental Authority knew. By 1905, they had given up and could even joke about it. The remodeling of Sagamore Hill was nearly complete, but, Edith quipped, "We can't have a fire there because the chimney smokes like a daughter!" And Theodore drew a cartouche of cigarette-smoking Alice, the cloud of smoke reaching as high as her pompadour. Perhaps if they knew that Alice and young Kermit swapped tobacco and corncob pipes, they wouldn't have been so sanguine.[39]

Alice rebelled against the humiliation of her father's attitude toward, as she put it, "Large Families, the Purity of Womanhood, and the Sanctity of Marriage." She founded the Race Suicide Club, so named because of TR's speech condemning white Anglo-Saxon Protestant women who were derelict in their primary duty of producing sufficient numbers of children to keep America strong. Alice and three friends had great fun with this secret club, as a surviving letter attests. "In view of certain rumors which have reached me," the "Chairman of the Committee on Orthodoxy" wrote, "concerning a prominent member of the R.S.C. I feel it my bounden duty...to recall to your memory certain clauses of the catechism which I am afraid you may be in charge of forgetting at this crisis—viz: 'What is the object of the same'? (The question preceding this answer you may possibly recall?) Also—'What will thou submit to in return for the golden token'? If these two articles are faithfully adhered to you will still be considered an honorary member of the R.S.C." The answer to the second question was, "I will submit to all but the token will not be forthcoming." The Golden Token was Alice's idea, and the club and its meetings made, she admitted, "the rudest game" of TR, who would not have enjoyed the parody.[40]

Other peccadillos were more public. Alice was also known to slide miniature bottles of whiskey into her elbow-length gloves and smuggle them into teetotaling houses so she could present them to her male dinner partners. In her purse, she could be counted on to carry four essentials: cigarettes, a fertility image (no doubt sanctioned by the R.S.C.), her green snake named Emily Spinach (after her thin aunt), and a copy of the Constitution. Justification for her reputation as a wild thing mounted. She convinced the daughter of the secretary of the navy to duck out of an official troop review and gallop down the nearby dunes instead. She went aboard one of America's first submarines—and may have been the first woman to do so.[41] The German navy named a boat after her and requested her portrait as its eponym. The *New York Herald* calculated—only partially tongue-in-cheek—that in fifteen months Alice had graced 407 dinners, 350 balls, 300 parties, 680 teas, 1,706 social calls, and 32,000 people by shaking their hands. She had to ask Belle Hagner to order "two dozen more . . . photographs of that charming young creature Alice Lee Roosevelt," which, she figured, "had better all come to me first so I can put my spider tracks across them." Alice gambled at Newport, at the racetrack, and in foreign countries. Once a journalist snapped pictures of the First Daughter at Benning racetrack, outside of Washington, as she handed money to a "betting commissioner." Friends of the president suppressed the sale of the photographs to the newspapers, and Theodore had "a serious talk" with his daughter. That did not stop her.[42]

One of the most retold stories of the wayward First Daughter originated as family friend and western novelist Owen Wister tried to carry on a conversation with the president. Thrice a supremely unselfconscious teenager flung herself into their midst, burst out with a question, then receded. "Alice," her exasperated father threatened, "the next time you come in, I'll throw you out the window!" He turned to Wister and shrugged, "I can be President of the United States—or—I can attend to Alice. I cannot possibly do both!"[43] Continued diatribes from Edith on her "extravagance" and her "uselessness" made no headway. Grandma Lee's stern admonishments had little effect. "[I] trust you will profit by my lecture, and keep your good resolutions and be careful what you do when on your many visits, as reports get so exaggerated," the doughty woman cautioned.

Even warnings from her friends did not dissuade Alice once she had a taste of the freedom of behaving exactly the way she wanted. "Really, I envy you all the interesting side[s] of the life you lead, only...," a friend predicted, "you'll wake up some day and realize it all too late. Why not postpone some of the playing 'till later, and see now what you can make out of your position. Imagine having the entire world open to you—to be the girl in it so to speak. You ought to follow your Father's example—he leads the men of the country—you ought to [lead] the women."[44]

Alice sped toward the worst of her money woes after teaming up with Maggie, Cissy, and the other big spenders in their circle. Alice's allowance went to clothes and gambling debts. Ball gowns were very expensive, and Alice had rejected the earlier practice, enforced by Edith, of making over her dresses. In order to keep up with her new friends, she expended an increasing amount on a greater number of dresses. "I am in a pretty bad way," she confessed in October 1903. The next month, she had to ask her grandpa Lee for the thousand dollars she had run over budget. Her grandfather had a special place in his heart for Alice, and it was lucky that he did. His response makes one wonder what, precisely, she told him about her situation. "Under the terms of the trust, the trustees [Grandpa Lee and her uncle George Lee] are authorized to pay over to you, at any time, a portion of the income if in their opinion they think it is necessary to do so. Your uncle and I consider that it would be right and proper, under the circumstances, to pay you the money, therefore we send it." Further, Grandpa Lee admitted, "Your Uncle George and I are the only ones who know anything about this financial operation and we won't tell Grandma." Alice seems to have promised to change her ways in return for his assistance. Even so, he couldn't resist a mild lecture, but it was one of the more loving rebukes that Alice received from an adult: "You say that you don't really think that you are as bad as you seem. You are not bad at all in my estimation, but you lead such an exciting, undomestic life that you will come to grief, physically, before you are 21 years old. Of course it is all right 'to go it whilst you are young,' but I am afraid that you are overdoing it and will regret it later. You go with people who have money to burn and, I fear, lead you into extravagances. But as you are going to turn over a new leaf and reform I won't find any more fault with you now." Grandpa was concerned. The historical record suggests that he threatened to cut her off from free access to her funds should she prove unable to reform. To test her, he gave her a thousand dollars. He told TR and Edith that if she spent it in less than four weeks and came asking for more, he would put her on an allowance for the rest of her life, which is precisely what happened. As a consequence, Alice never had unlimited access to her inheritance, and to the day she died, she received a quarterly stipend.[45]

Alice spent most of 1904 in a perpetual whirl of parties and musicales at embassies, teas and receptions at friends' houses, and balls and dances. She attended the St. Louis World's Fair in late May and participated in official events. A group of "thousands" of women gathered around to see their idol arrive. Alice remembered "a tremendous crowd at the station rubbernecking quite a good deal," that followed her all around the fairgrounds. The *New York Times* corroborated her description, trumpeting that Alice was "fairly mobbed" by "an enthusiastic crowd" of five thousand women, all shrieking, "There she is!" and "Hurrah for Miss Roosevelt!" Ted was amused to note, when he visited the fair after his sister, that her "trail over the fair is still visible." He found a Ferris wheel car and a camel named for her. The press noted that three hundred women exactly copied the First Daughter's "dress and manners."[46]

Alice's increasing fame—and the sheer number of letters she received—prompted the family to deem it necessary for a White House secretary to open Alice's mail, read it, and then pass it on. This hampered Alice's flirtations. "Alice dear," wrote one male friend, "[I] didn't realize that Royalty underwent so many trials, at least that their friends did! I shudder to think my scrawl had been opened and perused by a masculine eye! and a strange one at that! Of course now I feel tongue-tied—what can you expect? Now that he finds I'm not begging for your money—or [angling] for your... handkerchiefs, perhaps he will [let] you read them first.... Can't I get up a signal with you—to write on the envelope and let me within the Golden Gates?" Another joked, "Hope the Secretary doesn't read all of this letter—or his hair will fall out."[47]

Alice's friends had to learn to cope with her celebrity status, and most did so cheerfully. Charles McCauley wrote, tongue-in-cheek, "I want you to have this little 'jewel' so that when the *N.Y. Herald* of Feb.18th appears the article will read something like this: From the King of England a diamond brooch; the German Emperor, a diamond and emerald necklace; [from] Mrs. Astor a diamond tiara; Miss Vanderbilt a turquoise and diamond bracelet; Major McCauley a pin of diamonds and rubies, etc." At least her fame allowed Alice's friends to monitor her doings: "I saw a *Paris Herald* and February 11th [sic] was recorded as Miss Alice Roosevelt's birthday." Another friend "saw in the paper that you were here to go to Chicago for the Horse Show." But sometimes even her hosts couldn't keep up with her: "Reporters of [Boston] *Transcript* just called to know when you are coming, where are you going to stay, and who is coming with you. I couldn't enlighten them," Grandpa Lee wrote in despair.[48]

Coming to terms with her fame was not easy for anyone connected to Alice, least of all the First Daughter herself. Less than a month after he assumed the presidency, Roosevelt wrote to Owen Wister: "[A]s for the children, we spend no small part of our time in doing our best to prevent them becoming self-conscious through being talked about. They lead exactly the lives led by any other six children who live in a roomy house with a garden and go to school, and are on the whole pretty good, and are not always good at all."[49] This attempt at normality obviously did not last long. Alice's debut began a process the end result of which no one could truly foresee. It became harder to control the media interest; "camera fiends" planted themselves expectantly at the front door of the White House.[50] If Edith and TR were committed to the ritual that launched their daughter into society, they were ambivalent about her propulsion into the hearts and drawing rooms of America—while still unmindful of her growing need for guidance and attention.

Chapter 5

"Frightfully Difficult Trying to Keep Up Appearances"

IN ONE SENSE, at least, Alice Roosevelt adhered to the conventions of her age. Her motives, though, differed from her peers'. Finding the perfect spouse was her top priority. While her friends desired the social approbation that came from being a wife, for Alice marriage meant—she hoped—independence and wealth. As with so much else, she inverted the expectations of the day, turning them to her own advantage. But courting was not easily accomplished in the public crucible of the White House.

When she was fourteen, she confessed that she was "planning hard about everyone in the matrimonial line of course!"[1] To this pursuit she devoted much of her time. To find a husband, a young Knickerbocker woman looked first within her own social circle, and second, if family ethics permitted, to titled Europeans. That avenue was not open to the First Daughter. Theodore Roosevelt thought it abominable to marry off the cream of America's women to foreign men. He was responding in part to the many daughters forced to marry against their wills by scheming parents who needed money or sought to improve their social status.

Alice was not opposed to marrying a rich man. In fact, she sincerely hoped she would. Given the elaborate social rules under which elite Progressive Era lovers labored, she was more likely to meet a man of substance than not. Conventions governed how and where and when one met a potential beau. The New York winter season began in November with the Madison Square Garden Horse Show, continued throughout the holidays, and ended with the approach of Lent. A few intimate parties and one or two larger affairs such as the Tuxedo Ball preceded it, but the first place to see and be seen was circulating among the boxes at the horse show. Dinners, receptions, dances, cotillions, suppers, plays, operas, and parties of all sizes and themes sustained the season. The Assembly Ball was the most important event of the winter. At this glamorous gathering of American elites, proud parents formally introduced their daughters to society. Usually held in mid-December, the Assembly Ball and its parties segued into the New Year's balls given by wealthy society leaders such as the Astors, the Millses, the Gerrys, the Reids, and the Goelets. These events began and ended with dancing, included a five-course supper and a cotillion, and stretched until the wee hours.

Wealthy New Englanders courted according to an elaborate and intricately prescribed system. Class absolutely dictated the social system, the social ladder, and the social season with its hierarchy of greater and lesser events, all of them exclusive. Alice Roosevelt, as the product of a marriage between the Brahmin Lees and the Knickerbocker Roosevelts, had entrée to the best parties and balls of both Boston and New York, including the gatherings of the Four Hundred. Ward McAllister coined this term in 1888 from the maximum number of people who could fit into the Astors' formal ballroom in their Fifth Avenue mansion. The Four Hundred differed from Knickerbockers and Brahmins; it included industrialists who had become rich virtually overnight. Because it was such a diverse group, these newly rich shared little but "social insecurity."[2]

Theodore Roosevelt cautioned his daughter that some captains of industry, such as Cornelius Vanderbilt and Edward H. Harriman, were really Robber Barons whose ostentatious wealth disguised the absence of business ethics and personal morals. Alice considered the Four Hundred a livelier group than the tradition-bound Knickerbockers, and therefore a great deal more fun. Theodore found such taste appalling. Alice's insistence upon including the sons of the Four Hundred among her circle of acquaintances (thus adding them to the pool of her potential husbands) was a continuing source of discord between Alice and her parents. "Got in a row with dear father this afternoon," Alice complained to her diary in 1904, "all about Maggie, my friends, my taste, etc." When Alice settled upon Nicholas

Longworth, TR's relief over the bridegroom's sterling midwestern lineage may have tipped the scale of parental approval, despite the incongruity of the First Daughter's choice. Nick had a sense of humor about the Four Hundred and as a student at Harvard, coauthored a stinging parody of McAllister: "Ward McAllister—Wow! Wow! Wow! Were hit not for that vulgar hupstart, George Washington, we might still be livin' under the rine of 'er grycious majesty Queen Victoria! Ward McAllister—Wow! Wow! Wow!"[3]

Nick was charming and funny but was neither Alice's first love nor her last. Alice had been smitten with a few other young men, but only two of them, Edward Carpenter and Arthur Iselin, were anything more than infatuations. Alice fell into and out of teenage crushes with the same frequency and intensity as the rest of her girlfriends. The status of their hearts was a popular topic of correspondence, and marriage the foremost occupation of Alice and her friends whenever they gathered. "If you can come [visit] we will try and get some men over for Sunday to captivate your fancy," promised one friend. The letters from Alice's women friends repeatedly mention affairs of the heart—speculations on engagements, commentaries on party guests, and knowing references to men who "send their love." Sometimes their letters had virtually one topic: "Write me a few times and tell me all about yourself and [your] lovers.... Is there any immediate chance of your becoming Mrs. John Greenway?" asked one friend. "I wonder how many dukes H.R.R. has in tow? Do write me if you know," a Newport girlfriend commanded. H.R.R. herself—Helen Rebecca Roosevelt, the daughter of Franklin's older half brother—queried Alice, "How's the handsome young doctor? You certainly are the very most fickle female I have ever known." Helen could accuse Alice of capriciousness because she had been stuck on the same beau, Douglas Robinson, for ages, and they would wed. Helen also didn't have newspapers reporting whatever they chose about her—if she had been as "fickle" as Alice, no one would have known. But if Alice danced twice with the same man, she would find her engagement announced in the next day's papers. The resulting storm of protest at home always exasperated Alice: "Had a foolish temper fit this morning with Mother. A newspaper paragraph saying... [Henry] Cushing is in love with me. I tell you, the papers can make [it] up absolutely out of the whole cloth."[4]

Discretion was a highly prized virtue. Edith Roosevelt, born as the Civil War began, deplored many modern trends. In her generation, courting happened in the drawing room under the watchful care of a chaperone. She and Theodore were so circumspect that they went abroad to marry, in deference to the memory of TR's first wife, and they stayed in separate hotels before their wedding.[5] Edith could not help that her stepdaughter was a celebrity, and both parents believed independence should be cultivated in children, but Edith lectured Alice on the impropriety of being too well known. Edith feared—justifiably—for Alice's reputation, as reporters trailed her and crowds congregated at the sight of her.

The most derogatory insinuations about Alice appeared in the slanderous paper *Town Topics*. Socialites paid to make sure it never published their names, and they certainly never admitted to reading it. Publisher William D'Alton Mann implied that the First Daughter's morals were suspect. "From wearing costly lingerie to indulging in fancy dances for the edification of men was only a step," Mann wrote. "However, it is admitted that she is a smart girl, and smart girls are supposed to be clever enough to take care of themselves without the aid of chaperones."[6] This item suggested four major missteps: expensive intimate wear, dancing for men, being clever, and going without a chaperone. These charges against the First Daughter were so serious that the publisher of the very respectable *Collier's Weekly* took Mann to court in protest.

Alice generally reveled in the (flattering) publicity, but her stepmother believed, with the etiquette arbiters, that "the very essence of good manners is self-possession, and self-possession is another name for self-forgetfulness."[7] This impasse between mother and daughter caused them both much anguish. As Alice's prominence grew, Edith approved less and less of what she did. The two did not discuss Alice's feelings about men as she entered marriageable age.

Alice's diaries and letters provide a sketchy but revealing chronicle of her "affairs," as she called them. In her strong and distinctive script, Alice recorded her attendance at lunches and balls and listed who "took her in" to dinner, the party favors she received, and sometimes the men with whom she danced. A large part of Alice's teenage journal consisted of a running tally of what she labeled her "crushes." She indicated these by drawing a thick heart in her customary black ink and usually inserting a number inside of it. Often she labeled the heart with a name. This was not her system alone, as certain friends' letters utilized the same shorthand. "Dear 76" is what Alice called Edward Carpenter on April 24, 1902. Eight days later, she penned, "Have broken 6 [hearts] now it reaches about 87. Daniel, Leonard, Nelson, Holden, Walker, and Pryor." When she reached her one-hundredth crush, William Burden, she added, "Last?" This was a triumphant fashion in which to consider men, suggesting a competition, serious or not, among Alice's circle as to how many hearts they could break. "How many little heartlets have you had since I last heard from you?" inquired Helen Roosevelt once.[8]

Deciphering the emotional code is not an easy task. Measuring her desirability to various suitors was surely akin to gauging her approval rating from her parents. Perhaps Alice simply relished her outward success at the game of romance, with its exhilarating exertion of command over the opposite sex. There were few other ways a woman's power could exceed a man's in the early twentieth century. Once married, she lost that power as the husband became the legal head of the household. Certainly Alice Roosevelt displayed the shifting passions that were often the hallmark of those newly entered into society. She understood the strict moral and social codes, but she also had the typical teenager's confusion when trying to understand herself in relation to men and to assess her talents in comparison to other women of her age.

Alice absorbed at least three different interpretations of the maxims governing courtship. Her earliest came from Edith's and Theodore's firm opinions on the place of young ladies in society. Edith had a reputation for intolerance toward people considered sexually promiscuous, and had been known to bar the White House door to anyone who did not measure up to her strict behavioral code. Theodore linked marriage and childbearing with the good of America, calling motherhood—strictly, of course, within the sacrament of marriage—a "primary duty of life."[9]

A second view came from the older and world-wise cousins and friends Alice met and overheard at Auntie Bye's sophisticated salon. Divorce was rare, but among elites nearly any conceivable accommodation between husband and wife was discussed. The third approach to courtship Alice read about in the popular novels and prescriptive literature of the times, such as *Godey's Lady's Book, Leslie's Illustrated Weekly,* and etiquette books. Such periodicals, often pocket size, advised young people on appropriate ways to greet, call on, and write to each other, and how to observe the traditions of christenings, debutante balls, weddings, receptions, teas, and funerals. Gender-specific duties were emphasized: how to take a man's arm and when, how to coordinate your menu with your ballroom decorations according to season, and what to do with your chaperone at a party. Weekly magazines filled their pages with serialized fiction moralizing on the perils of ignoring the rules. In these stories, good women fell because they had been seen alone with a man, or with too many men, or with the wrong man. The etiquette manuals provided delicate guidelines on courtship that were sometimes all the more confusing because of their vagueness. For instance, this sentiment sounds self-evident, until one tries to apply it: "No well-bred woman will receive a man's attentions, however acceptable, too eagerly; nor will she carry reserve so far as to be altogether discouraging."[10]

The proper age for marriage, according to contemporary authority Dr. Elizabeth Blackwell, was between twenty and twenty-three for men. The average age of marriage for women around this time was twenty-two. The idea that a woman's physical weakness indicated her spiritual superiority still lingered in the early 1900s, while health concerns for the childbearing woman dictated much thinking about the ideal marriage age. Contradictory notions of sexuality in the late nineteenth and early twentieth centuries were expressed in a dialogue among ministers, doctors, and social critics. Social-purity crusaders kept the issues—masturbation, prostitution, the duties of wives and husbands, age of consent laws, the white slave trade, family limitation, and pornography—alive. The one thing all three groups had in common was a dislike for society's "heartless discriminations in favor of the rich and the influential." Alice declared publicly that sex was never spoken about in her family. She claimed to have gleaned her information from the " 'begat' series" in the Hebrew Bible and observing the farm animals at Sagamore Hill, but she informed historian Elting Morison in the 1950s that her father "had told her the facts of life."[11]

Alice knew that for men part of her interest was that she purposefully broke some rules. Her devil-may-care attitude incited heated debate among family and friends, but they need not have feared. Though etiquette books warned "Those who defy the rules of the best society, and claim to be superior to them, are always coarse in their moral fibre, however strong they may be intellectually," Alice had an uncanny sense of how far she could push.[12] She had seen the punitive potential of society—she had to look only as far as her friend Marguerite Cassini's exile for an example of how quickly a person could be ostracized because of rumors. Alice remembered, too, the warning about a girlfriend who wore an embroidered dress that buttoned up the back to go driving with a group of friends. Upon their return, her buttons were askew. "I was told," Alice recalled later, "I wasn't to see her in certain houses after that."

The rules Alice broke were never the inflexible laws that would have meant her expulsion from society. They were not maxims dealing with sex or romance. Looking back on her youth, Alice once explained to an interviewer: "The restrictions came more from the social conventions of the day. One was never allowed out with a date and one had to go to a dance with a chaperone. One could never give a man a lift, not even a White House aide. There were always enough watchful eyes to check on one. Woe betide the girl who emerged from the conservatory at a dance with her hair slightly disheveled. As one's hair tended to fall down at the best of times it was frightfully difficult trying to keep up appearances."[13]

Alice suffered the wrath of Washington commentators who damned her for eating asparagus with her gloves on, jumping fully clothed into a swimming pool, betting in public, and shooting her pistol off the back platform of a train—all of which she did—but her joie de vivre was always carefully constrained within the most important societal boundaries. None of these misdemeanors was sufficiently serious to risk her position in society or with her parents. Alice's sharp sense of family loyalty would not allow her to incur her father's mistrust, and that is one reason that, as president, he could send this astute daughter overseas as his goodwill ambassador.[14]

Alice's ability to conduct herself with social ease was amazing when compared with that of her cousin Eleanor. In December 1902, at the prestigious Assembly Ball, Eleanor and Alice were two of the "Magic Five" Roosevelt cousins who made their collective debut. The eighteen-year-old Eleanor Roosevelt was nervous, fearful of not being asked to dance, and afraid of saying or doing something to embarrass herself or her family. Even years later she remembered that night with repugnance: "There was absolutely nothing about me to attract anybody's attention. I was tall, but I did not dance very well.... I do not think I quite realized beforehand what utter agony it was going to be or I would never had had the courage to go.... [B]y no stretch of the imagination could I fool myself into thinking that I was a popular debutante! I went home early, thankful to get away...."[15]

Making the social codes fit her, instead of the other way around, was both Alice's defense and her gift to other women. Theodore's early absence and Edith's ambivalent mothering resulted in one of Alice's greatest strengths: her sublime public self-confidence. Alice never forgot that she was a Roosevelt, and the longer she served as First Daughter, the more of an asset her aplomb, her certainty of place and of station, became. As a young woman, Alice learned the importance of having a protective mask to wear when necessary.

Just before Christmas 1902, Alice, then eighteen years old, confessed some of her goals to her diary: "I should like after going to New Orleans for Mardi Gras and Carnival, to travel South through Puerto Rico and Jamaica, come home about Easter and then go abroad [to] take in a London season...and the...Regatta. Come home for the house I have [built] at Newport and then have large parties on the *Mayflower* everyday for the international races [and] to have parties during the fall. Later in the [season attend the] Horse Show then...get proposed to by the only man I ever

loved and marry him. How's that for a programme?" she concluded jaun-
tily.[16] Missing is any interest beyond elite society, just as TR feared. Nelson
Aldrich called such casual poise part of "the values of belongingness and
order," and attributed it to "the haven of Old Money," which gives to its
members a lineage, a recognizable name, a destiny, a place in the world,
potentially boundless love, and social security, as well as a shortcut to identity. Alice's sense of belongingness allowed her to cultivate her insouciance.
Cousin Eleanor, by contrast, almost wholly absorbed the etiquette-book
standards. "I remember one afternoon rowing on the river at Farmington
with Eleanor," Alice told an interviewer later in life. "For some reason or
other she started lecturing me on the sort of presents one could receive
from gentlemen—flowers, books, cards, were all possible, I was assured,
but jewelry of any kind, absolutely not. I listened to her earnest discourse,
fingering all the while a modest string of seed pearls that an admirer had
given me the week before."[17]

When it came to finding a husband, Alice's consistent contravening of
the social code had side effects. Carrying a snake with her to parties—as
she frequently and gleefully did—distinguished her in an immediate and,
Alice hoped, fascinating way from other young women. This may have
been another attempt to define herself apart from the role of First Daughter, as well as to test her acquaintances to see if they really liked her. One,
she thought, was "awfully nice and I hope he won't dislike me anymore. It's
all about the difference between 'The President's Daughter' and 'Alice
Roosevelt,'" she fretted. A full two years after her father assumed the presidency, Alice wrote that "I am afraid the only attention I get is just out of
curiosity to see what I am like on account of my position." Whenever her
friends did something notable, Alice got top billing, and even when there
wasn't much newsworthy, their activities were still reported because of the
First Daughter's participation.[18]

Alice had girlfriends of every disposition, but she easily and rapidly
dismissed men who could not stand the test of public display as well as she
did. Caspar Milquetoasts were no match for Alice's quick wit or the Roosevelt family lifestyle. Only a man with Theodore Roosevelt's strength—as
defined by a daughter—would be a compatible life partner. "Why don't

you cultivate [Mr.] Hare?... Try him—he is fierce enough to suit even you," wrote a friend, only half in jest. Such men were less likely to conform to the moral codes and hence less likely to be immediately accepted by Mother and Father. Alice had long spurned the companionship of those her age, acknowledging that "attraction for me had very little to do with sex. It was more closely connected with a certain vitality, a sense of humor, and a mental affinity. That was when the mayhem started."[19] Mayhem is exactly what Edward Carpenter caused in Alice's teenage heart.

Alice met Carpenter, as she called him—defying convention—on her 1902 visit to Cuba. Between official duties, Alice and her women friends flirted with the men of the American military who had been invited to the balls as dance partners. Carpenter and his best friend, Frank R. McCoy, were career army officers serving as aides to Major General Leonard Wood. Alice liked Carpenter's sense of humor and his uniform. Her diary of the trip consists almost solely of the ups and downs of her relationship with Carpenter, and an ongoing log of how much money she won or lost betting on jai alai.

Alice and Carpenter had a stormy relationship. She related having "almost literally groveled in the dirt at his feet last night begging him to... send me a message by McCoy. I have never been so humiliated before and never intend to be so again. I suppose it is just good discipline but all the same it is uncomfortable and loathsome.... I shall never get over the turn down. It has been my first and I trust my last. I must... retaliate." This sentiment did not last long. The next day, she "[b]ought silly little charms for Carpenter.... He came to lunch and we 'had it out' afterwards. I really have a... temper." Apparently the reconciliation did not meet with success. Whether prompted by her temper or Janet Lee, Alice's competitor for Carpenter's heart, the next night, Alice scratched dolefully, "Carpenter has absolutely thrown poor Alice over."[20]

Things were looking up by the time Alice left Cuba two days later. A crowd of friends came to see her off, but Carpenter, she exulted, "stayed in the boat after the others left.... He gave me some photographs [of himself]...."[21] Upon her return to Washington, Alice happily carried on a regular exchange of letters and gifts with Carpenter for almost two months.

Carpenter began one lengthy letter without a salutation. Instead, in a manner that would have caused society arbiters to feel faint, he wrote, "Don't you DARE!!! to do it. If you do I'll haunt you, I swear I will. And when I get rigged up to haunt I'm a holy horror and no mistake." He recounted his invitation to a friend: "Do me the favor of punching my head three times," because he had been, in an attempt "to be funny, and to show off," foolish enough to suggest to Alice in his last letter that she take a photograph of herself with another man and put it in a locket. "And," Carpenter panted, "instead of saying 'Never!' or 'Not in a thousand years,' or some other comforting sentence, [you] had said instead that it was a charming suggestion which [you] would follow out at once and would give the locket to the man!... But oh, if you do! If you do! Well—you'll see me roused." Apparently Alice was not attempting to make him think that he was her only love interest, for he rather plaintively asked her, "What ever did you dance that cotillion with him for? In your heart I believe you are fond of him." He signed his letter FAITHFULLY, YOUR, L.A., shorthand for Alice's nickname for him: Lazy Ape.[22]

The two were reunited briefly when Carpenter and McCoy visited the First Daughter at the White House on May 27, 1902, but by that time Alice had turned her attentions to the Knickerbocker heir J. Van Ness Philips and a dashing relative of General Lafayette, Charles de Chambrun. Alice wrote on the twenty-third that she loved de Chambrun, her ninetieth crush, but this affair was short-lived. On May 28, during what must have been an uncomfortable, or perhaps titillating, dinner, Alice was seated between Van Ness and Carpenter: "J.V.N.P. took this occasion to tell me that the only way for me to cure him would be to marry him. I simply yelled and laughed so. Then we, Van Ness, McCoy, Carpenter and myself went down to Chase's.... Van Ness again made his remark to which it goes without saying I said no." Van Ness had the worst of it that night, because Carpenter and McCoy accompanied Alice and Edith Root home.[23]

Hearing Van Ness Philips's intention bothered Carpenter, who came to see Alice the next day. It took him two and one half hours to communicate what was on his mind to the by-then unreceptive Alice. "He started off by saying that he was in love with me and then he asked me to marry him. He said he would give me a year and a half to think about it for then he would be a captain of artillery and in command of a light battery. He wants to call me 'Alice' when we are alone together. On the whole, he behaved like two idiots.... I positively said no." The following day, Alice "received notes from Carpenter and Philips—It's very foolish."[24]

Alice took her first two marriage proposals in stride. Had Alice consulted the advice literature rather than her own sense of romance and fun, she would have been chastened. *Ladies' and Gentlemen's Etiquette* cautioned, "The prerogative of proposing lies with the man, but the prerogative of refusing lies with the woman; and this prerogative a lady of tact and kind heart will exercise before her suitor is brought to the humiliation of a direct offer. She should try, while discouraging him as a lover, to still retain him as a friend." Ward McAllister warned ominously that a woman should "be cautious how she refused the first offers of marriage made her, as they were generally the best." If Alice felt remorse at having received the proposals or regret at turning them down, she did not confide it to her diary.[25]

Although Alice did "retain them as friends," Carpenter and Philips virtually disappeared from her diary—and her heart. The latter wrote hopefully but unsuccessfully in July. Because they traveled in Alice's social circle, she was not overtly rude to Carpenter and Philips. *Practical Etiquette* warned, "A young lady ought to be very careful how she mentions offers of marriage that have been refused by her." Society expected a forward course for the man: "The duty of the rejected suitor is quite clear. Etiquette demands that he shall accept the lady's decision as final and retire from the field. He has no right to demand the reason of her refusal. If she assign it, he is bound to respect her secret, if it is one, and to hold it inviolable. To persist in urging his suit or to follow up the lady with marked attentions would be in the worst possible taste."[26] Alice thought both men ultimately foolish for their persistence—and looked on them both with disdain.

And, by midsummer, her heart was once again preoccupied. Alice fell for Arthur Iselin, a long-lasting infatuation that would eventually make her miserable enough to swear that she would never marry. In October 1903, Delancey Jay, the scion of one of America's oldest families, confessed to Alice that he thought of her often and "I . . . also find myself using your picture, barbarian that I am, like an idol—it hangs by my bed like an up to date Madonna or Saint of some kind! You really look quite serious and nice in it." But he knew that his suit was shaky for "I'm not Arthur Iselin!" By July 1902, four of Alice's friends cornered her at dinner and "gave me fearful lectures this evening because I like Arthur Iselin so much. They are trying to 'open my eyes as to his character.' "[27]

If Iselin's character aroused the suspicions of Alice's crowd, at least his lineage would have made her parents happy. In 1924, Mrs. John King Van Rensselaer approvingly described his family as one "whose ancestors have directed the social life of New York for ten or more generations [and who] still continue to entertain and be entertained without the blare of publicity."[28] As with Carpenter, Alice had a stormy and uncertain affair with Arthur, in spite of the fact that Alice seemed to care deeply for him. Initially, it appeared that the relationship would be reciprocal. Arthur wrote to her in April, when they were only beginning to enter the flirtation stage, "Dear Alice, I saw the enclosed in today's *Herald* and thought it might be from you—[signed] Arthur I." He had glued a clipping to the top of a page that read, "Sweetheart, I will call Saturday, 8:45 or 9; do not refuse me, darling. I love you, love you, love you." Arthur had underlined the last part and appended "Madly! Madly! Madly!" This was a sense of humor to compete with her own. Despite her diary entry of July 19, 1902, vowing, "I swear by all I believe in that if Arthur Iselin ever asks me to marry him I will," the coveted proposal never came.[29]

In early August, Arthur's affection showed signs of waning. Alice saw him at a party, "but it was very stupid. Arthur is very much in love and intends to marry a beautiful Southern girl . . ." Diary references to Arthur continued unabated throughout the month, sprinkled with examples of her frustration, such as "poor Alice" and "no hope for Alice."[30]

By late 1902, Alice's desire to marry had intensified. It had been a year since her debut, and as family troubles and budget woes worsened, the combination had an unfortunate influence on her self-esteem. Her diary for this period often alluded to how unattractive she was and how much nicer other women were. On November 18, as the social season began at the Madison Square Garden Horse Show, Alice made another promise to herself: "Saw Robert Goelet. They say he is engaged. If he is not I will try to love and marry him. I pray to God that he asks me to marry, cares for me and me alone love[s]." Three weeks later, Alice had dinner with friends and remarked that it was "frightfully rude" that "Arthur Iselin—the beast—never turned up." Arthur's lack of response saddened Alice. The next night found her making her second debut at the Assembly Ball. Arthur's absence was all she noted. After the ball she confessed her fear that "he will soon be engaged to someone or other and I don't know how I will stand it. I pray God make him love me." Then, seeking solace, she wrote his name over and over: "Oh Arthur, Arthur, Arthur, my love and my life." This Alice would do seriously with only one other man: Nick Longworth.[31]

Suitor Arthur Bredon was a brief distraction. But he did not compare with *her* Arthur. "I would be absolutely fascinated by him," Alice reflected, "if I allowed myself to be, but I have just gotten over my feelings for Arthur Iselin and I really believe I was rather in love with him. I don't want to go through another experience of the same kind, unrequited affection, etc., for it was really very unpleasant." In mid-January, Alice cast about for friends to divert her. She received a teasing and not very comforting letter from a girlfriend: "Are Arthur [Iselin]'s classic features still too much for your peace of mind[?] I hope you have recovered your sanity by this time." Even parties with the Four Hundred failed to help lift her sense of gloom. "Arthur Iselin simply hates me," she concluded sadly. She resolved, "I should never get married, anyway not for a long time and then only for love."[32] The desolation over Arthur caused the excessive sleeping and moping her parents had ignored.

Eventually, Alice felt more like herself. In one very full evening, she attended a reception at the British embassy and another at the Italian embassy. She "played madly round" with Arthur Bredon and Van Ness Philips and "had really quite a good time." Soon after, she danced a cotillion with Philips, admitting, "I led him on, so he proposed more or less all over again." Alice never enumerated his faults in her journal, but they were probably not connected with money. Marrying into the Philips family would have erased her financial woes. At any rate, Alice could never be happy with a man whom she could manipulate into a marriage proposal, refuse, and then remanipulate—regardless of his wealth.[33]

Her mind never strayed far from marriage, for the night before Philips's second proposal she had received important news from a friend: "Helen tells me that [illegible] told her this evening at dinner that he liked six girls very much and that he could fall in love with one of them and that one of them was me Alice Lee Roosevelt. Resolved: that I shall make him propose to me."[34] The name of the young man is illegible because Alice didn't want her maid to read it—she had once caught her maid reading her diary and ever after, in order to hide confidential information, Alice slanted her hand-writing to an extreme and unreadable degree. It didn't matter, in some respects, who the man was. It was important that he be wealthy, fun, of good family, and able to fall in love with her—soon. Alice's wording allows for some latitude in interpretation: did she intend to have him propose for the sake of keeping score, or because she really would have said yes despite her earlier vow to marry "not for a long time and then only for love"?

What she did want—and badly—was to escape the constraints of family life and to have more money. She imagined herself somewhere between Auntie Bye's popular political salon and her good friend Grace Vanderbilt's footloose, cosmopolitan, and unimaginably wealthy life. The most enticing characteristics of such an existence were heaps of money and immediate independence. Popularity was desirable, but ran a remote third. Alice knew she would have to depend upon her husband for riches, and that once she said "I do," she would at least be free of parental control. Popularity was something that any intelligent and witty woman could manage on her own in high society, especially given enough money. If Alice's husband-to-be was socially accepted in his own right, so much the better. As she reached the marriageable age of nineteen, she spent her birthday with a group of friends and noted, "After supper we all sang and Nick played. Nick Longworth [and] Bredon... were the stars. Perfect marvels." Congressman Nicholas Longworth—wealthy, sought after, and utterly charming—the bachelor representative from Cincinnati, would soon oust all thoughts of Arthur Iselin.[35]

In the White House, Alice Roosevelt was the First Daughter of the land: a role model, a symbol of the times, a source of national pride. It took her father a while to learn how to capitalize on Alice's "well-knownness," but once Alice stepped onto the foreign stage, Roosevelt saw his opportunity. By sending Alice overseas, he added to the prestige of his administration, kept his daughter and his wife happy, and reclaimed the limelight for himself. And so overseas is where Alice would go. The "perfect marvel," Nick Longworth, went, too.

Chapter 6

"He Never Grew Serious About Anything"

NATIONAL PREOCCUPATION with the First Daughter's unmarried state reflected Alice's pensive, private deliberations. Arthur Iselin's proposal eluded her, and she had turned down Edward Carpenter and J. Van Ness Philips. Time was growing short. Society's arbiters recommended that a woman marry within three years of her coming of age. Alice never evinced any real desire to remain single, never displayed a distaste for the institution of marriage or worried that being coupled would infringe upon her independence. In TR and Edith, she had a loving model. When she conceptualized marriage in her writings, she thought of it as a method of increasing her monthly stipend and allowing her to be with the man she loved. Her pragmatism precluded any dreamy thoughts about bridal showers, honeymoons, or walking down the aisle on her father's arm. Alice wanted to marry, sooner than later—but her problem was finding the right man. But then when she found him, she was never really sure of him.

The sons of diplomats, politicians, businessmen, and the idle rich constituted the large array of potential husbands from which Alice could draw. The president's eldest child might have married into the elite American military establishment, perhaps a graduate of West Point or nearby Annapolis, given TR's fondness for the navy. Alice could have followed the example of four of her relatives and married within the family.[1] No matter how large the theoretical pool, the actual pursuers for Miss Alice's hand had one thing in common: courage. The famous First Daughter scared away all but the most intrepid souls.

The paradox of Alice Roosevelt was that she should have been able to marry anyone. But because she was the president's daughter—with its visibility, political power, and her own attention-seeking, autonomous living—few men actually approached her. Edward Carpenter may have spoken for the many when he wrote to her: "Do you know I can't think of a blessed thing but the cold eye of your secretary reading this—it is enough to freeze the fingers off anybody."[2] Neither could Alice marry beneath her socially—and not only because she swore never to be poor. A titled European or a Democrat would not have gained the family's acceptance; the former because of her father's well-known aversion to marrying off Columbia's daughters to the sons of foreigners, and the latter because that would have been harboring the enemy. Nick Longworth's combination of bravery, political ambition, age, personality, and lineage thrust him to the forefront of her suitors.

The advice manuals warned women against men "much older than themselves, licentious men, drunkards, gamblers, cold-hearted tyrants, those whose work took them away from home frequently, and 'despisers of the Christian religion.' "[3] Alice chose a man who embodied at least five of these fatal flaws. Nick was much older, a womanizer, a lover of alcohol and gambling, and given to long hours on the floor of the House or on floors of houses other than his own. TR and Edith were conservative parents who believed that marriage was sacred, intended for procreation, and best done between a man and woman of similar backgrounds. Edith once warned Alice against Nick. "Your friend from Ohio," Edith told her, "drinks too much."[4]

By the turn of the nineteenth century, most Americans chose their own mates and married for love. The late 1800s saw a resurgence of the upperclass rage, begun in 1785, of marrying into aristocracy, one that did not taper off until after the 1956 union of Grace Kelly to Prince Rainier of Monaco.[5] While some people found the idea of an American girl becoming a real princess quite charming, others, especially Theodore Roosevelt, found the custom deplorable. "My father," Alice said, "wanted me to meet all sorts of people but not to marry them. A foreigner would have been bad, except perhaps an Englishman."[6] As long as his daughter married in the general realm of the society to which the family belonged, TR had no cause to fear the dissolution of Alice's inheritance through marriage. He knew the premium Alice placed on the things money could provide.

Plagued by mounting debts, Alice confided to her diary in 1902, "I swear to literally angle for an enormously rich man.... I cannot live without money." A year later, she pledged, "Vow. That I will accept the next man who proposes to me. I have run over a thousand over my allowance." More than enough money for the average American never stretched far in the company she kept. Love was most significant when she wished for reciprocity. "Please love me," she wrote over and over in secret diary letters to her various beaus. Alice implored Arthur Iselin, "Please, please love me.... Would you not love me enough and ask me to marry you?" And later she would write, "Nick love me be kind to me."[7]

How well did the twenty-year-old Alice understand love? Arguably, not at all. Much of love was a game of possession to her, even as late as the beginning of her relationship with Nick. After a date with a beau one evening in 1904, she wrote, "The moment he was gone I suddenly went crazy about him, about the same old feeling, and I treated him like a dog, that is to say I ignored him absolutely and I am sure he won't fall in love with me—and of course I want him to."[8] Despite the capriciousness of her youth, Alice had an internal scale of measurement that she called love, and this must be considered when evaluating the role it played in her decision to marry. Long after her husband's death, Alice said, "One of the reasons I married was because I felt I had to get away from the White House and my family. I didn't want to stay there. I wanted a place of my own...."[9]

These statements belie the intense feelings of love for Nick Longworth that Alice committed to her diary. She married him because he was much different from the Groton and Harvard "boys" she disparaged. His age— he was thirty-six years old in 1905—made him attractive, in part because of her own intellectual precocity and her admiration of the sophistication she saw at Newport. As Alice neared her twenties, her troubled relationship with her father stood as a poignant accent to the love she sought from her male friends. Edith and Theodore thought that a more mature man would settle their daughter down, so they fostered Alice's penchant for fatherlike figures. The press mirrored to Alice her place in society, and from it she received the approbation she rarely got from her father. Half of the clippings in her voluminous wedding scrapbook are about Theodore Roosevelt—having nothing whatsoever to do with Alice or her wedding—mute testimony to a daughter's admiration. Only there, in between its pages, could she fully capture her father's attention. She looked for a substitute in someone like Nick, fifteen years her senior, who would surely lavish her with unconditional love. How much of Nick's attraction for the First Daughter was based on age is hard to know, but that dynamic surely contributed to what even Alice later acknowledged as her "father complex."[10]

Alice also married Nick because he was a politician. She often castigated herself for not taking a serious interest in politics, but Alice underestimated her acumen. The political arena was the world she knew best. As a girl, Alice had met President Benjamin Harrison and decorated nursery chairs with flowers picked with British diplomat Cecil Spring-Rice. As a woman, she would thrive in the very middle of the national political scene from the Bull Moose years through Watergate. Nick spoke the language Alice had heard all her life, but this time, the mouthpiece was handsome and dashing. A eulogy for Nick summarized how Alice eventually came to feel about her husband: "He never grew serious about anything and his anger was only peevishness. He ate and drank abundantly and well, dressed in luxurious elegance, and viewed his political career as a source of amusement and a means of keeping himself occupied.... He was too intelligent and self-respecting to be blatant or hypocritical, or to have had any illusions about politics."[11]

This, however, was hindsight. Alice married Nick in part because of his derring-do, because he had lived his young life with a renegade spirit similar to Alice's, because it appealed to Alice's vanity to win the man who had unsuccessfully wooed her good friends Marguerite Cassini and Cissy Patterson, and because he was both wealthy and strong. Unlike the "Groton boys," Nick knew his way around politics, high society, and women. He stood up manfully under the derision of those members of the Fourth Estate who claimed he would always be Mr. Nicholas Roosevelt, playing second fiddle to his headstrong and famous wife. As many a younger competitor for Alice's favors had already discovered, her sharp tongue and disregard for social conventions augured poorly for a wife who should maintain and remain in her own separate sphere. Nick had the energy, intellect, and more than enough money to keep up with his intended.

Representative Longworth probably also had, as the press insinuated, a keen idea of the political mileage to be gained from marrying into the First Family. Alice enjoyed her position as First Daughter. There was no reason to believe she wouldn't also love being First Lady. In 1906, it was not a far-fetched idea that Nick might someday win the presidency, especially with the backing of his popular father-in-law. If Nick had to suffer through intimations that he only married Alice for her political worth, Alice, too, heard whispers that she wed Nick solely because he was the fastest ticket back into the White House.

Alice and Nick met, according to the most widely held story, about the time that Nick was introduced to Marguerite Cassini, probably during the winter season of 1903. Alice maintained that her father first told her about the "new congressman" from Ohio, who was "Harvard and the Porc," and who he thought "might amuse" her. Alice initially mentioned her future husband to her diary on her nineteenth birthday, in 1903, noting his presence at a dinner she attended. He became a permanent fixture in Alice's diary around her twentieth birthday.[12]

Nicholas Longworth was born November 5, 1869, in Cincinnati, Ohio, the eldest child and only son of Nicholas and Susan Walker Longworth. The Longworth family moved imperturbably and confidently among other leading citizens: the Wulsins, the Tafts, the Graydons, the Fleischmanns. These were the founding families of Cincinnati's art, music, and charitable institutions, and social clubs such as the Pillars and the Queen City Club. Nick's father, Judge Longworth, had served briefly on the Supreme Court of Ohio and loved all outdoor sports. He invested in the relatively new pastime of amateur photography and dabbled in writing. His novels, *Silas Jackson's Wrongs* and *The Marquis and the Moon*, if not best sellers, at least secured his place among Cincinnati's men of letters. After his death from pneumonia at age forty-seven, the elder Longworth was remembered as someone who would "literally take the fur coat off his back for a friend whom he thought was in need...."[13]

Nick was the fourth generation of Longworths in Cincinnati. The family fortune accrued through real estate, viniculture, and the law. Appropriate to his station, Colie—the name the family used to distinguish Nick from his father—attended the opera and the theater, learned to speak fluent French, and received tutoring in the classics. Rookwood, the family estate, offered skating and fishing ponds, a herd of cattle, and apple orchards alongside the riding stable. Nick did not come of age in cosmopolitan New York or Washington as did his bride-to-be, but his education lacked for little nonetheless. The Longworth family summered at Newport and toured Europe in the autumns. They created a stir when they installed the first indoor arc lights in the area. Nick enjoyed the best his family could provide, aided by his mother and sisters, whose lives revolved around his needs. His youngest sibling, Clara, who as an adult became an accomplished Shakespearean scholar, wrote that "all that was best in life must be reserved for Colie," to whom the family referred adoringly as "the first born of Israel."[14]

When he was five years old, Nick began to study the violin. It became his lifelong avocation, and he was widely recognized as a gifted violinist. Cincinnati prided itself on possessing the most sophisticated musical community in the Midwest. The annual Cincinnati May Festival, begun in 1873, continues today. The festival brought some of the world's best talent to the city—composers, musicians, and conductors—and many of them stayed for part of the summer to teach at the Cincinnati College of Music. Nick absorbed the cultural atmosphere and likely took lessons from visiting professors; Leopold Stokowski called music Nick's "natural element."[15] Nick also played the piano expertly, composed pieces for violin and piano, and sang—often with lyrics he made up on the spot. Nick loved classical music best, especially Mozart, Vivaldi, Beethoven, and Brahms, but also enjoyed contemporary popular songs. In later life, Nick served as president of the Washington, D.C., Chamber Music Society and founded the Friends of Music in the Library of Congress.[16]

After preparatory school, Nick entered Harvard and graduated in the class of 1891. Scholarship was not his strong suit. Alice admitted that Nick "didn't quite gobble books the way we did."[17] He made friends easily, and the Porcellian Club welcomed him, making him a brother "Porc" to his future father-in-law. Alice recalled the premium her father placed on this. As a brotherhood of patrician white men, the club offered its members entrée to social and business opportunities later in life. During the college years, the Porc was the unexcelled leader among Harvard's many clubs, and as such, acceptance was the measure of the man. As "legacies," TR's sons Ted Jr. and Kermit were admitted. The Brotherhood of the Porcellian rejected the lanky undergraduate Franklin Delano Roosevelt, despite the fact that FDR's own father was a member. FDR called this exclusion the "greatest disappointment of my life."[18] Even though Nick was a midwesterner, his charm and his wealth—not to mention his solid C average—made him Porcellian material. He was also a gentleman athlete—rowing, riding, fencing, and playing tennis.

Nick spent one more year in Boston, at Harvard's law school, but returned as all good Buckeye sons did, to earn his LLB from the College of Law of the University of Cincinnati. He gained admittance to the bar in 1894, at age twenty-two. Nick's first legal problem was attending to his father's tediously tangled estate, and he soon found the conviviality of politics more to his liking. His political career began in 1897, when he joined the Young Men's Blaine Club, under the tutelage of Cincinnati political boss George B. Cox. After serving on the Cincinnati school board and the Republican National Committee, he spent two terms in the Ohio House of Representatives and another two in the state senate. He won election to Congress in 1902 and took the oath as a member of the Fifty-eighth Congress on March 4, 1903, just as the famous Alice Roosevelt was returning from Mardi Gras. Unlike Alice, Nick seldom challenged the rules. As *Leslie's Illustrated Weekly* put it in 1906, "His path has been lined with roses because of his money and family influence.... He turned to politics for diversion."[19]

Alice was not initially struck by Representative Longworth; after all, meeting him was her father's idea. Or perhaps it was that Nick was engaged to a hometown girl. In fact, Nick seems to have been deeply involved with several different women before Alice. Nick's reputation as Cincinnati's Don Juan was so well known that the city's matrons were watchful. One of his flames warned Nick: "Oh Boy, you've got a horrid lot to live down—so don't lose a minute's time in denying it. I've been fighting four battles here at home for my mother has been informed by many 'well wishers' of your 'past' and she pleads with me to see you in your true light."[20]

Nick was simultaneously involved in a longer and more significant liaison with Miriam Bloomer, whom he called Little Hooty. Their connection involved a level of intimacy impossible for Alice, living as she was in the public eye. The usual meeting place for Nick and Miriam was the Pillars, another private Cincinnati club. Nick cared enough for her to be seen in public with her on his home turf—but also to be vulnerable with her, to care about having hurt her (he sent her roses in apology), to be jealous of her, and to confess that he was "thoroughly swizzled. I have no doubt but that this state of mind makes me seem very ridiculous in your eyes; but you must try to treat it with the same philosophy as the Frenchman who, being informed that an acquaintance was desperately in love with his own wife, said— '*Tiens—C'est bizarre mais ce n'est pas un crime.*'"[21]

Their relationship continued after Nick took up his place in the U.S. House of Representatives, and in the *New York Times* in 1907, she was described as "a former fiancé of Nicholas Longworth." "I'll come," Miriam promised Nick, "on the 4.30 train and you can meet me and we'll dine quietly any old place—for I'll have on a street dress and then if you like you can come out here with me and stay all night...." They remained friends even after Nick was married—Little Hooty was present at his White House wedding and the postnuptial dinner—but not long after she watched Nick marry Alice, Miriam suffered "a severe nervous collapse."[22] Habitual clandestine meetings in Washington and elsewhere put Nick in a league wholly apart from Alice. He had mastered the art of deception in relationships long before he knew the First Daughter.

The romance between Nick and Alice had to wait for both of them to fall in and out of love with other people. The 1903–1904 social season marked the creation of the Alice, Maggie, Charles, and Nick quartet. By January 1904, Alice had targeted a new crush in Charles de Chambrun. Unfortunately, so had Maggie Cassini. This ill-timed complication tried the friendship between the two women, which underwent further testing when Maggie swept Nick off his feet—after she was through with de

Chambrun. The society press and the Washington rumor mills made much of this intriguing set.

"Charly" de Chambrun was the new secretary at the French embassy. In her memoirs, Maggie painted a picture of the felicitous Frenchman: "He was the greatest fun...long as a rainy day and quite handsome except for an awkward walk. He had a crazy giggle which made you think him a fool till you discovered he was brilliant with an encyclopedic memory....When we danced he stepped on my toes. At tennis he never watched the ball, at bridge he failed to follow suit, always too busy laughing at some joke, his own or another's. And lazy! But he was charming, amusing, a promising diplomat, and soon was the center of our parties."[23] The four of them—the president's daughter and the Russian ambassador's daughter, the representative from Ohio and the French diplomat—made up a clique both powerful and exotic even for the capital city.

The month of January 1904 decided Alice's fate where the Frenchman was concerned. Even as she awarded him a heartlet in her journal, Alice watched as his relationship with Maggie deepened until she could not deny it. Her January 20 entry explains much about the state of her feelings:

Called on Mag Cassini and found her upstairs in a lightly scented bedroom in her wrapper, a gorgeous Chinese one. Dinner at Nick Longworth's. Mr. Aggasiz took me in. Nick Longworth on the other side. Chambrun talked to me afterwards. He doesn't feel a bit for me anymore—Not that he ever really did and when I am so devoted to him. John...and N.L. played and sang. We went on about 11:30 to the... dance. Auntie Bye receiving.... The men who were at dinner had a corking table.... I won fifty dollars from Nick whether Walter Luckerman had on a wig or not. He said I couldn't find out but I did. But the family heard and I got into hot water. Poor "lil" A. Danced madly until the finish. Really enjoyed myself. But I wish C de C would care for me. <u>dear</u> Charly.[24]

The next day's entry continues the tale. She had lunch with Nick at the House of Representatives then "went back to N.L.'s for an hour or so and then to tea at Mag Cassini's—great fun. . . . Had such a nice talk with C. de C [at a reception] . . . Mag sat next to N.L. at dinner and had talked to him afterwards until about 11:30. I am very much afraid he is quite devoted to her. And then she had nabbed C. de C. for a half hour conversation. He is so funny about her. Oh <u>dearest</u> Charly."[25]

There was still a bit of competition involved in her response to the situation, as though she were beginning to be torn between the men, or as though she were unhappy that either would be more interested in her girlfriend. Even as Charly held her interest, Nick spent an ever-increasing amount of time with them. Charly and Maggie quarreled when her father discovered the seriousness of Charly's intentions. Maggie then turned her gaze to Nick. At least Cissy was out of the picture, after her earlier flirtation with Nick. Cissy married the dashing womanizer Count Joseph Gizycki of Poland, thirty years her senior, in April 1904. The small wedding at her parents' Dupont Circle house was an indication of their disappointment in Cissy's choice.[26]

The trio of Alice, Nick, and Maggie beguiled the press and Washingtonians who enjoyed speculating which woman Nick would choose. They played together throughout the 1904 winter season, attending dinners, cotillions, skating and sleighing parties, taffy pulls, and sight-seeing trips to the House of Representatives, usually chaperoned by Nick's mother, Susan Longworth. By February, competition between the two young women for Nick's attention had intensified. "Once when within the same week," Maggie recalled, "we gave two dinners at the [Russian] Embassy with Nick at one and Mrs. Longworth, his mother, at another, the hullabaloo was really something. The papers rushed into stories about the marked devotion of 'the brilliant young Cincinnatian to the fascinating Countess Marguerite Cassini.' . . . Then Alice went out to Cincinnati for a visit and bang, around swung the weathervane again."[27]

In twos, threes, and fours they enjoyed great times through the spring of 1904. They spent many happy evenings about the town, ending often at Nick's Washington club, the Alibi, where, over the dinners he prepared, they dissected the evening's gossip. Nick's culinary specialty was "Toothsome Terrapin," and his hobby was wines—natural, given the Longworth family fame for the Catawba grape wines produced at Rookwood in his great-grandfather's time. The four of them developed their own private language, full of inside jokes and innuendoes. Nick and Alice, though, shared "a slashing wit," which bound them together appreciatively. In March, de Chambrun left for Paris. He wrote to Alice to remind her that the odds were uneven while he was gone. "Tell Nick, for goodness sake, to turn his attention to his Cincinnati constituents and that, when I come back in three weeks, I trust to find him exerting his energy and application to a closer attention to business." De Chambrun couldn't make up his mind about his favorite flirting partner: "Tell Mag she is a daisy, and please say many pleasant things to yourself from me," he encouraged Alice.[28]

The women quarreled before Alice's trip to Ohio. "I really like Margarite [*sic*] Cassini—but I don't think she knows what the words truth, honor and loyalty mean." Alice left out the details of the battle, but gave a hint of the cause in a later diary entry. "Why am I such a failure? I am not so much less attractive than many girls I know who have a very good time, and with my position as my father's daughter...I should have a more marvelous success but I certainly do not. Oh how I wish I did. Oh for money and self-assurance." Three days later, Alice was pining for something else. "How crazy I am about Nick," she wrote, putting words to the source of her altercation with Maggie. The Countess Cassini, for her part, explained, "It became more and more fun to tease my friends by trying to take their beaux away from them." Alice was falling in love with Nick, and Maggie failed to see or chose to not see. In her autobiography, the Russian attributed it to her penchant to view "only her own fun." Alice repeatedly asked Maggie whether or not Nick had proposed to her, and was placated in receiving a negative response from her friend. By May of 1904, though, the halcyon days were over: "Nick and Maggie out to Country Club again. She is going with him instead of riding with us....I am sure she has him. N.B. Revenge on her.... Oh nasty Maggie I'll get even yet, see if I don't."[29]

The picture became more and more bleak. "Maggie was to have come and seen me this evening. I telephoned for her. They said she was at the Boardmans and when I telephoned there Josephine said she was out walking with Nick. She had met him in some square or other. In the first place I think it is a very cheap thing to do: to go out walking at night with a man. In the second place she should have let me know she wasn't coming . . . and thirdly . . . and not least importantly, I am furious with him for having misled her." Then she closed by swearing the same oath against Nick that she had against Maggie: "Revenge, N.L. Retaliate."[30]

Alice hedged her bets. One of her friends had been untrue to her, but she was protective of both of them just in case—until the next day brought devastating news of what had transpired in that park. As they sat and smoked up on the roof of the White House, Maggie confided to Alice that Nick had proposed to her. Although Maggie rejected him, Alice was hurt but philosophical. "Heigh-ho. He is the second person (French Charlie was the first) that I have vowed to have and she has reft from me so I suppose there will be a third. . . . I don't think he should have been as nice to me as he has been, well, well, well." Theodore Roosevelt's daughter kept her sorrows to herself. No matter how deeply she felt her rejection and her sadness, she continued as though nothing had happened. The following day, she had lunch with Nick at the Alibi, and by the end of the month, the countess was stopping by for tea at the White House again. Maggie remembered that after her disclosure, "the inseparable twosome was no longer so inseparable. . . . We were still friendly, we still saw each other here and there. But the old intimacy disappeared."[31] Perhaps it is a measure of Alice's pain, or the revenge she swore, that she never once mentioned Marguerite Cassini in her own autobiography.

Alice tried to move on. Nick disappeared from her journal as she went about the business of being First Daughter, but she mentioned only one other, short-lived, crush. No other man caught her attention. Christmas Eve 1904 marked a turning point in their relationship. Nick telephoned the First Daughter, and they breakfasted together. Alice had "a delicious time" because "Nick . . . the liar said he loved me." The hopeful tone of her diary was justified, according to her chronicle of Boxing Day: "[H]ad a long talk with Nick . . . he made violent love [to me] all day long. Well! Well! Nick!" "Violent love" did not mean the same a hundred years ago as it does today, so it is difficult to know precisely what Alice meant, especially in light of a later—but suspect—statement that she had never kissed a man before she

Alice Hathaway Lee Roosevelt,
Alice's mother, near the time of her
engagement to Theodore Roosevelt

BELOW: Auntie Bye and her
"blue-eyed darling"

First Lady Edith Kermit Carow
Roosevelt, Alice's stepmother

Theodore Roosevelt, Alice's politician
father, in a characteristic pose for the
cameras and the crowds

The Roosevelt
family: Quentin,
TR, Ted, Archie,
Alice, Kermit, Edith,
Ethel, at Sagamore
Hill in 1903

Alice's bedroom at
the White House,
where she confided
her secrets to her
diary

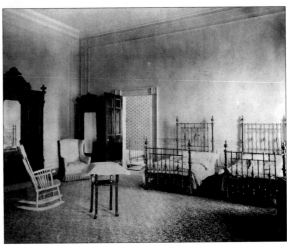

OPPOSITE: First Daughter
Alice Roosevelt

Prince Henry of Prussia and Alice
at the launching of the kaiser's yacht,
the *Meteor,* Washington, 1901

A popular figure on
sheet music, Alice appears
in this selection as a Gibson
girl; patriotically flanked by
Rough Rider-like buglers;
and sharing billing with
Marguerite Cassini

Alice's trademark large hat is just visible in the center of the cameras
in this newspaper cartoon.

A French chocolate card featuring
the American Princess

A hand-tinted postcard of the First
Daughter from 1904

Alice and Nick Longworth enjoying each other's
company on the Far Eastern trip

Watching the Sumo wrestling exhibition in Japan

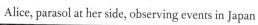

Alice, parasol at her side, observing events in Japan

Eligible bachelor Representative Nicholas Longworth

ABOVE: Rookwood,
the Longworth house
in Cincinnati—Alice
could never quite
call it home.

Willard Straight,
Alice's dear and
witty friend

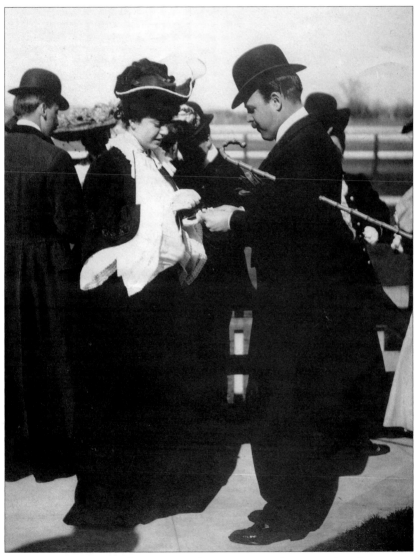

The First Daughter counting her winnings at the racetrack with
Representative Longworth, one of the series of photographs TR censored.

The White House bride with Manchu on her lap

ABOVE: The addictive excitement of the Chicago Coliseum during the 1908 Republican National Convention

Alice, age twenty-four, resisting the effort to start a draft for her father at the 1908 GOP convention

The Longworths keeping tabs
on the enemy at the Democratic
convention in Denver, 1908

BELOW: Alice and Nick in 1911,
stepping out as young swells
in the nation's capital

Purchasing war bonds from the Girl Scouts, 1917

＊◆＊

BELOW: Quentin Roosevelt posing with his airplane, before his death behind enemy lines in France during World War I

TR without his glasses, as his family would have seen him.

had married. A diary entry for January 19, 1905, read, "Nick had a supper at his Alibi.... Nick and I in a very dark corner afterwards. It was quite wonderful but I know that I will wish I hadn't. I know he doesn't <u>really</u> care for poor little me."[32] Like most women, Alice governed herself by an internal scale. If she knew he truly loved her, she could allow more physical intimacy.

After that, Alice expected their relationship to be different. A woman named Beatrice caught Nick's fancy—or so Alice thought—and this threw her into a depression. She worried he was only "trying to be nice" to her and that he didn't care for her anymore. On the last day of January 1905, Alice concluded: "I know that Nick does not love me anymore—if he ever did—which I am not sure of, and he has made me love him. Oh, I love him so much."Alice swore revenge on Beatrice, but the same day she "reverted" because her "dear lamb" had come to tea at Auntie Bye's and taken her for a drive to explain the misunderstanding.[33] Such an explosion of fear, followed by a reconciliation, would become the pattern for their courtship and marriage. Their wooing was dazzling, destructive, seductive, and not unlike a roller coaster in its giddy ascensions and conspicuous declines.

"Dearest Little Alice," Nick wrote as she turned twenty-one in February 1905, "May I be permitted to call you 'Little Alice' this last time, for tonight at twelve o clock you will become of age and be an heiress and then I suppose you won't be little anymore." He included a photograph of himself as a birthday present, "scarcely an 'objet d'art' and cavilers might say by no means an 'objet de vertu' but at least it may serve to remind you sometimes of your devoted Nick."[34] Soon the couple had quarreled again. Alice was no longer sure she wanted to marry him. Was there an understanding between them at this point? Her fears battled with her professions of love: "Oh Nick I love you passionately Nick—I want to see you—have you with me always for every moment of this day and night for ever and ever." For months, she filled her journal with page after page of unsent letters to her beloved, concluding them all with "My Nick."[35]

In the late spring they were apart, but Nick's letters were mostly reassuring. He wrote in April of the "so many things I want to tell you and so many things I want you to tell me" that were difficult to commit to paper.

He wrote, too, that he was "wild to know what the President said of me," which was worrying despite his disclaimer: "not perhaps so much because he is the biggest man in the world as because he is the father of the most charming girl in the world." Alice wanted details of his social life. "I have not amused myself very much," Nick wrote from Cincinnati, "principally because the person I want to see is not here." By the end of April, he swore he was "longing to see you, honey. I keep missing you more and more all the time."[36]

In early June, Alice went to stay with Nick and his family. Their glorious time together marked another turning point in their relationship, evident in Nick's prose:

> My darling girl: It is useless for me to try to tell you how I miss you. It really seems as though the light had gone out of the world. I am in the depths of despondency and if it was more than three weeks longer I don't know what I should do. As it is I can't pull myself together a bit. You were more charming than ever here. You were sweet to everybody and everybody was crazy about you. There wasn't a minute that we were together that I didn't wish was an hour and not an hour that I was away from you that I didn't wish was a minute. It was a beautiful world when you were here....[37]

"I love you and I always shall," he concluded, and three days later, Alice "practically told Charlie [McCauley] that I am engaged to Nick." Earlier in the week she began an entry noting that "Father is making peace between Russia and Japan," and then went to matters more pressing: "With Nick and [a friend] at dinner—after the people left as usual I put on another [illegible] my pink wrapper and Nick when he was kissing and feeling me did an evil thing—but it was my fault. I have let him do so much...But it was terrible. We are actually engaged though of course we have been for some time practically so, and I love him more than anything else in the world."[38] Was whatever he did terrible because it hurt her in some way, or did she mean that it flew in the face of convention? Was it terrible because it happened before they had an officially announced (and therefore less likely to be retracted) engagement? What was different this time, when her last no-tation called what they did in the dark corner "wonderful"?

Throughout her adult life, Alice Roosevelt Longworth maintained that she did not like to be touched, hated to be kissed, and didn't particularly enjoy dancing because it put human bodies in too-close proximity. Perhaps when she was young she did enjoy it. If so, then somewhere in her later life she had a change of heart. It is possible that Alice suffered from what so many late-Victorian physicians warned of: "the brutal and impulsive be-havior of husbands on their honeymoons."[39] If she built a resentment against Nick, borne of his selfishness, then this might explain some of the mistrust and unhappiness that would come to characterize their marriage.

Alice was sensitive enough to protocol that the terrible nature of the June event prompted her to write that she would regret it. Whatever they did was clearly not advocated by the social arbiters—mother and father uppermost—either because Nick would lose respect for her and then never marry her or because they were not properly engaged. Whatever it was, the evening of June 11, 1905, was a second instance of something physical be-tween them that escalated the stakes. After the first, six months earlier, Alice considered whether or not she could or should marry Nick. After this June night, she felt herself engaged to be married—and he must have actu-ally asked, and she must have responded positively, reading between the lines of his letter to her of June 20:

> My darling little girl: Your letter was the sweetest thing that ever came to me. I had been waiting for it so long that I almost feared it was not going to be like that.... But O Honey, when I did get it it made me feel prouder than anything in the world that you should say what you did, for it makes me think that I must be a pretty decent sort of a person when the most charming girl that ever lived really cares for me.... Alice, darling, I simply can't tell you in a letter what I want to. I am simply wrapped up in ... love of you....[40]

While President Roosevelt monitored the peace process between Rus-sia and Japan, his daughter kept a close watch on her fiancé as he went home to Cincinnati. "I am so desperately sorrowful—he is going to see all his old girls. I know [he] is—I can't bear it. He said he wouldn't the brute. . . . I can't live without him." To Alice's great relief, Nick returned to her without asking for a separation. They had much to discuss, for preparations for the East Asia trip had begun.

Alice wrote Auntie Bye all about her talk with the Tafts and their good advice as to what she ought to pack.[41] Her separation from the family began when Edith and TR left for Oyster Bay in late June. As she foundered in the unknown waters of emotional and physical love, and embarked upon a long, stressful tour halfway around the globe as her father's special emissary, Alice was without parental support. Because of her nervousness about Nick and the trip, she lost five pounds and suffered alternately from indigestion, toothache, and eczema. Nevertheless, Edith and TR went about their lives unconcerned: "My parting from my family…was really delicious," Alice wrote sardonically, "a casual peck on the cheek and a handshake, as if I was going to be gone six days. I wonder if they really care for me or I for them."[42] In Nick, Alice believed she had found someone who proved that he truly loved her, and gave her evidence of his affection. At least Auntie Bye seemed to approve of him, even if Edith did not.

Chapter 7

"When Alice Came to Plunderland"

THE TUMULTUOUS RELATIONSHIP between Alice and Nick took an unusual turn when President Roosevelt decided to take full advantage of his daughter's nascent diplomatic skills. In 1905, he was engaged in mediating peace between Russia and Japan, recently at war over lands they both claimed. The president wanted to send a high-level delegation to East Asia (the Far East, as it was then styled by Westerners), and decided to attach Alice as a goodwill ambassador. When Nick was chosen for the political junket, Alice readily consented. The trip would prove successful professionally—Alice charmed her hosts—and personally, for the trip cemented Alice and Nick's engagement. The last act of this journey was played out in the White House on February 17, 1906, with the wedding of Princess Alice to Congressman Longworth.

In 1905, President Theodore Roosevelt asked his daughter to be part of a multipurpose delegation from Washington to East Asia. Alice was thrilled.[1] Roosevelt wanted this mission to be part fact finding, part goodwill, and part saber rattling. Led by Secretary of War William Howard Taft, the assemblage left Washington with a large party of congressmen and their wives, newspaper reporters, and Alice. The group was bound ostensibly for an inspection tour of the Philippines but, because the trip coincided with Roosevelt's mediation of the Russo-Japanese war, Taft traveled to Japan to confer unofficially with Tokyo about the peace process.[2] TR directed Alice to continue to China in the midst of an anti-American economic boycott in order to reassure Peking personally of his goodwill. The First Daughter would have audiences with the mikado in Japan and the dowager empress in China. The delegation of seventy-five people included, among others, Senator Francis G. Newlands and Representatives Frederick H. Gillett, Herbert Parsons, Charles Curtis, Bourke Cochran, and most important of all for Alice, Nick Longworth.[3]

Alice spent all of 1904 in the United States, and so she looked forward to seeing new lands and being away from home for the four-month-long journey. Auntie Bye cautioned her before she left, "Don't just for the sake of a sensation carry your complications too far! There are plenty of excitements that will come to give interest and not leave regrets so be careful."[4] The admonition seems not to have been ignored, for Alice amazed everyone with her generally polite and considerate behavior on the trip.

Alice, her chaperone Mrs. Francis G. Newlands, Secretary Taft, her friends Mabel Boardman and Amy McMillan, and a few others left Washington early on July 1, 1905. They stopped first in Chicago, where they received the news of the death of the venerable secretary of state, John Hay. Alice worried the journey would be canceled because TR might need Taft back in Washington, but President Roosevelt assured Taft that the delegation must continue. The train rolled on toward the coast. It was the first time Alice had been west of the Mississippi.

Californians were interested in the First Daughter, and she was ready for adventure. She met influential San Franciscans and lunched under the giant redwoods as a guest of the Bohemian Club. Alice played poker in the evenings, and papers reported that she escaped her chaperone for a brief excursion through the fringes of infamous Chinatown—although she wrote to her father after sailing for Hawaii, "I did not go to Chinatown in San Francisco and treated with scorn all invitations to do so." She didn't need to go there to seek adventure because, as she told TR, there was "an opium den" and "a gambling place" on board ship. She promised him that she had frequented "neither one of them!" Taft seconded her good behavior, telling his wife, Helen, "Alice conducts herself very well. She is modest and girllike. I quite like her."[5]

Helen Taft was sharper-edged than her affable husband. She found his assessment difficult to take. Her hands were full journeying across Europe with their sick children rather than on the junket with her husband, where she would much rather have been. Adding insult to her daily lot of frustration was the time she tried to hold a train for the late arrival of her luggage and could not do it on her own. "I am Mrs. William Howard Taft of Washington.... My husband is the Secretary of War of the United States." The stationmaster only looked at her blankly. It was not until she said, "You must have heard of him. He's traveling now with Miss Alice Roosevelt," did the stationmaster spring to attention, hold the train, accompany her out, and carry her luggage aboard. Her friends teasingly referred to her afterward as "The Mrs. Taft whose husband was traveling with Miss Alice Roosevelt." From that moment on, the only references Helen Taft made to her husband about the First Daughter were derogatory.[6]

Elsie Clews Parsons, wife of Representative Herbert Parsons, shared Mrs. Taft's feelings about the delegation's most famous member. In her memoir, Parsons recalled "rubberneck" crowds anxious to see Alice. "We had a chance fully to appreciate for the first time what an attraction for the American public Alice, as everybody called her, was. To many, perhaps to most, Alice was the party. This was so outside as well as inside the country, before the trip, during the trip, and after the trip. Many times after our return, the only question that was asked me of experiences and impressions was 'How did you like Alice?' "[7]

After joining with the rest of the delegation, the party sailed on the *Manchuria* on July 8. Alice reported to her father that they had a "very cheerful time" on the way, with good companions at their table, including Nick Longworth. Alice gave the inside scoop to TR about her fellow passengers. She wrote him that she invited "the congressional dames" to tea in her room "to placate them and make them love the trip. They are pretty terrible, most of them," Alice confided, especially one woman "whose color comes in a box and she always wears a dainty ribbon tied here and there to match it."[8] After days, they docked at Honolulu and, Alice wrote Edith, were met by boats "with bands of such fascinating Hawaiian music." They toured a sugar plantation ("just like the ones I had seen in Cuba") and refinery, went sight-seeing, "swimming and surf riding" ("which was great fun"), and danced the hula. Alice loved the "strenuous day," despite being "nearly suffocated" in thirty to forty leis "reaching from my neck to almost my knees—and for politeness sake I couldn't take them off." Back on board the *Manchuria*, the delegation began the ten-day trip to Tokyo to pay their respects to the Japanese. On July 24, they docked in Yokohama, which was, Alice enthused, " *'banzai, banzai, banzai'* all the way."[9]

The American minister to Tokyo, Lloyd Griscom, met the excited travelers. He considered "the pick of Congress crossing the Pacific to survey our outlying possessions" astonishing. "Ten years ago," he mused, "this would have seemed a fairy tale."[10] Griscom, an able and tactful diplomat, intercepted the Japanese plan of having Alice stay at the Shiba Rikyu, one of the royal palaces, because "it might be embarrassing for the President of a democracy to have his daughter accorded the honors of a royal princess," and instead made sure that Alice stayed at the embassy. Griscom believed that "the Japanese were firmly convinced that Alice was the Princess Royal of America" and so, he wrote, "Our journey to Tokio was a triumph." The Japanese lined the roads, waving American flags and cheering for Alice, "while the women bowed double again and again. Alice clutched my arm," the minister recalled, "and exclaimed 'Lloyd, I love it! I love it!' " A host of Japanese officials met them in Tokyo, including Prince Tokugawa, and members of the war department. Taft wrote his wife that they dined that night with the prime minister at a banquet given by the Nagasakis "in honor of Alice and me."[11]

Alice enjoyed seeing the lands she had read about as a girl materialize before her eyes just as much as she liked the attention. She wrote her father that "we have seen Geisha dancing, wrestling, jiu jitsu, fencing, and acting—I don't think it would be possible to see more in six weeks than we put into six days!" In her memoirs, she described the cycle of diplomatic entertaining: lunch with Prince and Princess Fushimi, a reception for Count Matsukata and Count Inouye, a dinner given by the businessmen of Tokyo, lunch with the minister of war, standing in a reception line with Princess Nashimoto and Princess Higashi-Fushimi where the Japanese women filing past curtsied to her as well. Baron Albert d'Anethan, the Belgian dean of the diplomatic corps, recorded this incident: "At a garden party given at the American Legation, the daughter of the President was paid homage next to and on the same level as the Princesses Fushimi and Hashimi." At the same garden party, Alice presided over a table at which sat Prince Fushimi, Princess Higashi-Fushimi, Marquis Oyama, Count Inouye, and Baron d'Anethan. Regardless of the demands that leading such a gathering made on the twenty-one-year-old, in later years, Alice always remembered the amusing sight they made: "All the Japanese ladies wore big floppy hats and carried parasols.... We look[ed] like a slightly stoned version of the Ascot scene from *My Fair Lady*."[12]

Alice recognized that the ebullition of Japanese officials sprang from their high expectations of the peace talks: "Not only the Government, but the man in the street was interested in and friendly to the Americans as well. Crowds followed us everywhere.... They cheered when the American Secretary of War went out on the balcony to wave good-bye—they cheered the daughter of the American president when she appeared—and then they cheered us all over again." It was, for the Japanese, an "unparalleled opportunity to cultivate American good will," Griscom thought.[13] Japan counted on America to meet its demands for control over Korea, the Manchurian railways, and the island of Sakhalin. In early May, when Taft and TR cemented the itinerary, Roosevelt knew that the Russian ambassador to the United States, Count Arturo Cassini, was "having a fit about Taft stopping at Japan on his way to the Philippines."[14] Roosevelt hoped the peace settlement would gain a balance of power in East Asia, but his sympathies lay more with Japan than Russia.

The Americans met the mikado on July 26, the morning after they arrived in Tokyo. Presented to the emperor in groups, they bowed three times and repeated the procedure in another room, where the crown princess received them in place of the ailing empress. After a luncheon given by the emperor, Taft informed his wife that "Alice Roosevelt, Griscom and Mrs. Griscom and I went up and were received by the Emperor and the Princess, and the Emperor seemed to be in a very great good humor."[15] The emperor sought to influence the outcome of the peace treaty through his hospitality toward the American guests. He seated Alice on his right, "although, of course," Alice told her father, "the conversation was chiefly about you...." The emperor's desire to impress his important American guests explains the rare honor he accorded them by allowing them to see his private garden, "hitherto never exhibited to foreigners." It also explains why, according to Taft, "the Prime Minister said that he was very anxious to have an interview with me...." The unplanned meeting resulted in "virtually a secret treaty whereby Roosevelt agreed that Japan was to absorb Korea."[16]

Leaving Tokyo for Kyoto, the delegation enjoyed more admiring Japanese crowds. Taft recounted the scene for his wife: "I have never seen such a popular tumult and gathering.... Every member of the party was cheered to the echo, especially Alice... there were cheers and cheers and cheers... from Tokio to Yokohama... whenever we stopped at a provincial capital they brought in presents for Alice Roosevelt and me and that continued until 1:00 the next morning when we reached Kioto."[17] Alice was showered with so many gifts that her friend the interesting Willard D. Straight referred to her as "Alice in Plunderland."[18]

The importance the Japanese and Chinese placed on family and tradition made Alice a particularly effective goodwill ambassador. Griscom remembered the bouquets thrown to "the daughter of the Peacemaker," and he believed that "never had there been such a demonstration for foreigners." Other members of Griscom's staff wrote privately, "[T]he Japanese did wonders for them and the whole show was a very great success. Miss Roosevelt did her part very well and made a great big hit with both Japanese and foreigners. I never saw the Japanese crowds loosen the manner they did this time—wild cheers and great crowds everywhere." Alice conceded, "No people have ever been treated with greater consideration and kindliness than we were by the Japanese, not only Mr. Taft and myself, but the entire party." "I don't know what would be left of you," Alice wrote TR, "if you had come out here!"[19] The First Daughter wore "the Japanese national costume" on her visit to the wife of Marshal Oyama, further endearing her to her host country.

After the signing of the Treaty of Portsmouth on September 5, 1905, a Japanese newspaper commented on the significance of the trip to Japan: "Miss Alice Roosevelt, upon whose intelligence and resolute character the Americans pride themselves, frequently renders assistance to the President in delicate missions where tact and diplomacy are required. Some months ago Miss Roosevelt...was received in Tokio by the Emperor and Empress with the highest honors. This visit must be considered as one of the happy preliminaries of a peace so swiftly concluded."[20]

Amid more cheering crowds, the delegation left Japan for the Philippines—and Taft's real reason for the trip. His mission was an inspection tour of the Philippines, but he also hoped to influence the legislators who accompanied him. He had spent almost four years as the civilian governor of the islands and was consequently an advocate of Philippine advancement. Taft wanted to lower the 1902 Philippine tariff and grant a greater measure of self-governance to the American protectorate. To facilitate their education, the travelers listened to shipboard lectures on Filipino economy and history. Mr. Taft sincerely hoped to enlighten the congressmen so they would vote to "support measures of benefit to the archipelago." Taft realized that Roosevelt wanted to inspire the Filipinos by sending Alice, so "that he might show to the people of the islands his interest in them and his confidence in their hospitality and cordial reception of his daughter."[21] She won international praise for her conduct in the Philippines where, as a representative of the U.S. government, she spent most of her time in semiofficial tasks.

Alice and Taft spent much of their ten days in Manila on the familiar round of receptions, banquets, speeches, balls, and information-gathering side trips. For the people they met, though, their visit was something special. One American soldier stationed there wrote his mother that he was expecting "to have a swell time for a few days" because of the Taft party and "big naval parade" in their honor.[22] Ten thousand people marched past the reviewing stand and attended a reception at the Malacañan Palace where the First Daughter "stood for hours with the [Governor Luke E. and his wife] Wrights and Mr. Taft, all of us literally dripping, while we shook hands with the hundreds of guests."[23] Students at various schools showed off their accomplishments to President Roosevelt's daughter. With some of the women of the delegation, Alice sat in on a meeting of the island's women's club. Before they left Manila for a two-week tour of the other islands, the Filipinos hosted a ball for Alice. "The eyes of the whole world are upon her," according to the *Washington Post*, "representing as she does not only the Chief Executive of our nation, but the typical American girl." The *New York Times* confirmed that Alice wore a native gown to "the most elaborate affair in the city's history...which was presented to her by several Filipino women, who were occupied three months in making it."[24]

On August 14, Taft made mention to his wife of yet "another important entertainment," that he attended, "a dance and reception given by the Filipino ladies to Alice Roosevelt." Taft wrote that "Alice was promptly on time at nine o'clock and was gracious and courteous." Rear Admiral Enquist of the Russian navy and his staff made unusual and no doubt insistent guests at the ball. Enquist was there to lobby Taft concerning his ships, which were being forcibly held in Manila after a battle with Japan. The attention to the First Daughter caused the *Washington Post* to note slyly, "It is a little trying on the limelight artist to keep a focus on Oyster Bay and Manila at the same time."[25]

Alice spent the next fortnight spreading American goodwill around remote areas of the Philippine Islands. On Panay, the delegation toured a sugar mill and listened to appeals from the local populace to remove the high U.S. tariff on sugar. They dined in Iloilo and left the next day for Bacolod on the island of Negros. There, Alice and the other women brave enough to have traveled through the rough waters drove around the island with the local governor's wife. Sailing southward, the party reached Sulu, where it was rumored that the sultan proposed to Alice, declaring "that his people wished her to remain among them." As it meant joining his harem, Alice declined.[26] At Camp Keithly, Alice stayed with the officers' families in their bamboo houses before leaving at dawn the next morning to journey eighteen miles to Camp Overton in "mud to the horses' knees, ruts to the hubs of the wheels, and miles of bamboo corduroy that consisted mainly of holes."[27] After more island-hopping, the excursion returned to Manila, from there to sail for Hong Kong.

Episcopalian Bishop Charles H. Brent of the Philippines, who met with the Americans to discuss the fate of church lands and to argue for greater self-governance for the Filipinos, believed that Alice's visit helped to cement the ties between the two peoples: "The very fact that our democratic system forbids the transmission of hereditary glory, or the reflection of official character even from parent to child, made the incident even more striking in the minds of a people who hold domestic ties in high esteem, and who were ready to be influenced by the daughter of her father...."[28] Although the bishop appreciated the visitors' earnestness and their willingness to learn from and about the Filipinos, it was not enough to propel Congress into action on behalf of the islands.

The delegation left Manila on August 31 and disembarked to the cheers of crowds in Hong Kong three days later. While she visited the British colony, Alice decided that she wanted to see Canton, despite the Chinese boycott of American goods that threatened Sino-American relations. The embargo damaged U.S. trade and worried Washington. President Roosevelt attempted to mitigate the excesses of the American Immigration Bureau officials, as the Chinese blamed the unequal enforcement of U.S. immigration laws for their woes. The boycott had originated in that port city. Anti-American sentiment was violent in Canton at the time, and so the women of the party were prohibited from landing.[29]

It is unclear whether Alice actually ventured into Canton. In her autobiography she maintained that she coaxed an American gunboat captain to take them to the island of Shaneen, just across the narrow canal from Canton. There, she wrote, "only an occasional coolie on the opposite bank shook his fist at us." Her friend, actor and official photographer Burr McIntosh, recalled that the women were "strongly advised" to stay on British soil. "At Hongkong there were rumors of bitterness against the party at Canton, where already the city was placarded with signs bearing the Portrait of Miss Roosevelt in a sedan chair, being carried by four Turtles in place of coolies. This is a threatening insult...but Miss Alice wanted to see Canton and that settled it." According to Alice, she, Nick, and a few other intrepid travelers made it back from Canton unscathed.[30]

The poster was an attempt by the boycott organizers to convince the rickshaw drivers, who were of the coolie (or laboring) class, not to transport Alice. The turtles stood for henpecked husbands and were meant to shame the drivers into refusing to carry the Americans. Alice's visit had an important effect on the boycott, for it led to a split among the ranks of organizers. Some argued for increasing their visibility while the American press was present to report it. Others believed they would sooner win their demands if they ceased demonstrating in honor of the First Daughter. Their disagreement allowed American Foreign Minister W. W. Rockhill to win from Prince Ching an edict calling for an end to the boycott. The poster showed the strength of Alice's symbolism, for there was no doubt that the woman in the placard was Alice Roosevelt. Nothing daunted, Alice brought a copy home as a souvenir, after she intervened to save the lives of the poster artists for their ridicule of a foreign visitor.[31]

The delegation left Hong Kong safely. Taft and most of the party boarded a return ship to the United States. Alice, her chaperone and friends, Nick Longworth and a few other congressmen—with the inevitable reporters—continued on to China, where President Roosevelt calmed the diplomatic and economic waters by sending his daughter to visit Tz'u Hsi (Cixi), the formidable dowager empress of China. In Peking Alice stayed with the Rockhills for one night, then left the next afternoon for an audience with the dowager empress at her summer palace, followed by lunch featuring "Snow-flake Shark's Fins." Alice spent the night in Prince Ching's palace and had an entire hall to herself. The audience with the dowager empress occurred early the next morning. The rest of the delegation had to drive out from Peking at dawn, arrayed in their best clothes, and even then, only the highest ranking members of the group were allowed to see the aging and powerful Tz'u Hsi.[32]

Mrs. Rockhill presented Alice first. After she and the others had made their three curtsies (or bows), the women of the party left to dine with the Empress of the East and the Empress of the West. Tz'u Hsi joined them after lunch to distribute expensive presents. She spoke through an interpreter, Dr. Wu Ting Fang, the international attorney and scholar who served as foreign minister to the United States from 1897 to 1902 and 1907 to 1909.[33] Suddenly, Alice recalled, Wu "turned quite gray, and got down on all fours, his forehead touching the ground." He continued to interpret, lifting his head only to speak. Theodore Roosevelt, when questioned about it later by Alice, decided that Tz'u Hsi might have humiliated Wu "to show us that this man whom we accepted as an equal was to her no more than something to put her foot on—that it was a way of indicating that none of us either amounted to much more than that in her opinion."[34] After Tz'u Hsi left, the party strolled through her gardens. All except for Alice, who led the way seated in a royal sedan chair held aloft by eight bearers. She laughed as her friends teased her.

The American newspapermen showered the First Daughter with exorbitant praise, despite the perilous proximity to "undemocratic" behavior. The *New York Times* rhapsodized, "It is all very well to preserve the majesty of the law, which knows no distinction of persons; of the social conventions, which leave no room for an American Princess. But even among us there are public and private persons of both sexes and the President's daughter has an individual quality which the most rabid Americanism must recognize." The American Princess spent the rest of her time in China entertaining diplomats and high-ranking Chinese so that Alice's only complaint was the lack of time for sightseeing.[35]

Alice and her party traveled next to Korea on the battleship *Ohio*. The American minister, Edward Morgan, took them by special train from the coast to Seoul. Alice's memories were of a Korea "reluctant and helpless...[and] sliding into the grasp of Japan. The whole people looked sad and dejected, all strength seemed to have been drained from them." Alice lunched with the Korean emperor and the crown prince, received the Korean cabinet, and was entertained "industriously" by Korean and Japanese officials. According to her friend Willard Straight, vice consul and secretary to the American minister in Seoul, they "came, saw, and conquered.... [They] were treated with more consideration than has ever been shown visiting royalty before.... These people are looking for straws just now and the Roosevelt trip looked like a life preserver...." The Koreans hoped the United States would compel the Japanese to keep their promise of Korean independence. It was not to be. Alice stayed in the peninsula ten days and by the time she left was "more than fed up with official entertaining, with being treated, one may say, as a 'temporary royalty.' "[36]

Straight, a talented amateur artist, tried his hand at doggerel in an attempt to capture something of Alice's visit. The poem also conveyed his feelings of righteous fury as the Japanese "murdered" Korea, his simultaneous vexation at the Koreans' inability to overcome internal corruption enough to help themselves, and his conviction that Alice represented their last chance:

> When Alice came to Plunderland,
> The Crown Prince sought her lily hand,
> The Emperor had a pipe
> Dream that this was where his native land
> Could shake the Japs forever and
> Secure a friendship ripe
> With father.
>
> But now there's trouble brewing, for
> The Emperor doth reign no more,
> The Japanese are out for wealth,
> They're not in business for their health.
> The Koreans wail, "What can we do?
> Our clothes is picked, our watches, too
> Our country's in receivers' hands.
> We've neither graft nor fees,
> Since Alice came to Plunderland
> We've nothing left to 'squeeze'."[37]

Alice and her companions returned to Japan on September 28, 1905, three weeks after the Treaty of Portsmouth that ended the Russo-Japanese War had been signed. This time they stayed almost fifteen days, long enough to tour the national shrines and historic sites. Official entertaining decreased because the Japanese blamed President Roosevelt for the unsatisfactory conclusion of the peace treaty. While they retained control of Korea, the Japanese returned Sakhalin to Russia without receiving an indemnity. This, a colleague wrote to Straight, the Japanese blamed on the United States because "caricatures of Roosevelt were displayed in the street" and the anti-American sentiment exploded in a series of riots. There was "not a *banzai* to be heard. I have never seen a more complete change," Alice recalled. "We were told that if anyone asked, it would be advisable to say that we were English." Plainclothes policemen accompanied Alice and her friends during this return trip.[38]

Not everyone displayed anger, however. Alice shrewdly noted that the anti-American feeling was strongest with the Japanese people, not the government officials. And it wasn't universal. She received a reassuring note from a girls' school: "To our great regret, we have learned that during the recent riot in Tokyo some of your countrymen were insulted, and also some Christian churches were burned by the mob. But the fact is that they did not know what they were doing, and we sincerely hope that your countrymen will not misunderstand us on account of incidents of this nature." Certainly this letter represented the views of only some Japanese citizens. The writers made a comparison that other denizens of the Land of the Rising Sun would have found repulsive: "We all appreciate with gratitude what America has done for us since the coming of Commodore Perry. What your distinguished father has done at this time will be remembered forever in Japan."[39]

The letter she received from "Russian women" was more fervent. "We, Russians, love you dear Miss Alice, with all our heart, as the daughter of the one who does all his best to get peace and give us the peace of soul and of mind!" Patriotically, they asserted that "Russia is not exhausted and would find means to continue this war, but we are morally tired of this blood being shed on the fields of the far East." They wanted Alice to pass along their thanks for President Roosevelt's assistance. The Russians, who had lost militarily at Port Arthur and at Mukden, were aided in their peacemaking efforts by the fact that Roosevelt's overarching goal was a balance of power.[40]

Those observers not watching the foreign diplomacy were keeping an eye on a certain Ohio congressman. Nick, seeking privacy, was not always easy to find. At the first port of call—Hawaii—he and Alice, the Newlandses, and a few other junketeers lingered and had to scrounge a skiff to take them out to the *Manchuria* before they were left behind. Mr. Taft and Mrs. Newlands occupied an uncomfortable position. They were charged with looking after the President's daughter. Taft had the job because he was head of the delegation and because TR was a friend. Mrs. Newlands was an experienced chaperone, acceptable both to First Daughter and First Lady. The secretary of war also controlled, to the extent possible, the publicity surrounding the trip. Taft's longtime acquaintance with the Longworth family and his role of elder statesman made him further responsible to fellow Cincinnatian Susan Longworth, Nick's mother, for any potential shipboard scandal.

Alice knew that the East Asia congressional junket would serve as an alembic: so much time together in an unfamiliar setting would solidify her relationship with Nick or dissolve it. She worried about their behavior and was "terribly afraid that it will get out about my being too obviously with Nick." Nick was along because of his seat on the House Foreign Affairs Committee. He said he wanted a firsthand look at the tariff situation, the Hawaiian labor problem, and the U.S. occupation of the Philippines. The press and most of America were hoping to see Nick's commitment to a different sort of foreign affair. REPRESENTATIVE LONGWORTH TO GO ALONG— TROPICAL ROMANCE ANTICIPATED, one headline blared.[41]

International reporters chronicled all of her movements during the trip, but no journalist wrote as frankly about the relationship between the First Daughter and the congressman as William Taft did to his wife, Helen. No reporter had Taft's inside position, nor could anyone writing for the public allow themselves Taft's candor about the relationship between his two fellow travelers. Taft had a better news source than journalists: Alice's traveling companions Mabel Boardman and Amy McMillan. They gathered information on the indefatigable First Daughter's emotional state for the secretary. He then wrote to his wife: "Mabel Boardman told me that Alice told her sister that she and Nick were engaged; they are a great deal together but Nick impresses no one with his sincerity. I don't think the engagement is much more binding than a Kentucky engagement. I quite like Alice—she is . . . straightforward and does not appear to be spoiled. In certain respects she is younger than her years. She is quite amenable to suggestion and I have seen nothing about the girl to indicate conceit or a swelled head. A broader, better man than Nick could wield a very beneficial influence over her. Certainly his is not for her good."[42] As Taft noted, "Alice likes to smoke cigarettes—indeed she is quite nervous unless she has a chance after a meal. She likes strong drink occasionally and Nick always helps her, though such a habit ought not to be formed in one as highly strung as she is."[43]

Taft liked Alice, and she for her part was "really quite devoted" to "Uncle Will," at least then. He exercised very little discipline over her and was seldom out of sorts. She remembered never having "the least awe of him. I always felt that I could 'get away with' whatever it was he objected to." Taft did rein in Alice in protocol matters, insisting once that she host a ladies' luncheon for the congressional wives of the party. Taft also delivered one or two "curtain lectures" to the First Daughter, "more in sorrow than in anger," and only because he felt keenly his responsibility to the president.[44]

Alice lived a fine line between being consumed with (as yet unannounced) love and being the First Daughter. She still doubted Nick's constancy. Her worries about his behavior and about public and familial reaction, considering the rocky course of their courtship en route to Asia, were well founded. She faced the daily temptation to be alone with Nick, but then she would abrogate her duties as her father's ambassador. Because she was not a private person on the East Asia junket, it was doubly difficult to court and be courted. The intimate task of finding out whether or not she and Nick could make agreeable lifemates had to be conducted, out of necessity, under public scrutiny, which, given their status, may have been the best possible rehearsal. They spent a great deal of time together, but her journal does not specify how much of it was alone. They had Spanish lessons one day; the next, they and some other shipmates played cards before the evening dance; the following morning was filled with the official photograph shoot. The difficulty for Alice was clear to Taft, as he complained to his wife: "It has not always been easy to secure from Alice the graciousness that our treatment here deserves, because she seems to be so much taken up with Nick. She becomes absorbed in him and pays but little attention to anybody else. She is however amenable to persuasion and has quite winning ways when she devotes her attention."[45]

There were enough mornings and afternoons and evenings with Nick to make the secretary of war uneasy. Had they been aware of Taft's severe

misgivings, Edith and TR would have flinched. "Nick and Alice are doubtless engaged," the secretary wrote Helen Taft. "They occasionally quarrel—Alice enjoys the society of some college boys in the interval and then
they make up. Nick has much control over Alice but I can't think either is
so in love with the other that there is any assurance of their happiness in
married life. Alice is not a bad girl—she has good generous impulses but
she lacks discipline greatly."[46] If Alice portrayed the woman without a care
for Nick's sake, inside she felt melancholic. When the couple fought, Alice,
despite her outward appearance, had the worst of it, for she had the most
invested in the relationship.

Taft's astute comment on Nick's control over Alice was borne out by
her keening in late July: "Oh my heart, my heart, I can't bear it. I don't
know what is the matter with me. Nick... looked at me... as if he didn't
like me, and said he wouldn't play with me tomorrow morning and I feel as
if I might die. He will go off and do something with some horrible woman,
and it will kill me. It can't make any difference, I can forgive him anything,
anytime, but it hurts like it hurts. Nick, love me, be kind to me—I am crying—I am crazy with grief. Oh my blessed beloved one, my Nick." Alice,
stoic daughter of stoic parents, pushed aside her own grief in public to assuage Taft's fears that her divided attention would undermine the elaborate
protocol necessary to their endeavor. On her conduct in Japan, a Nagasaki
newspaper reported, "Miss Roosevelt charmed us all, as she seems to have
a way of doing wherever she goes; simple and unaffected in dress and manners, she reminds me of her father, and she has the same cordial handshake,
the same way of giving you her undivided attention for the time that you
are speaking with her."[47] What such a double existence cost Alice emotionally is impossible to measure.

By mid-August, there was nothing Taft could do. The engagement,
while not officially announced, was recognized by the congressional travelers as authentic. Taft still hoped it might be a short-lived tropical romance,
but, of course, the truth is that Alice had fallen for Nick months before the
ship set sail. Still, Taft maintained that Nick liked the "prestige" of being
coupled with the president's daughter more than anything else.[48] The press
speculated on the courtship, but wrote little, as it could secure no confirma-

tion. Instead—a picture being worth a thousand words—newspapers published photographs from the junket, always careful to print those in which both Nick and Alice appeared.

Alice's diary grew ever more sparse throughout the trip, until she stopped writing altogether. One more piece to the puzzle of their relationship exists, though—a letter from Alice to Nick while they stopped in Korea. Because neither left the delegation for any length of time, Alice probably wrote to Nick because they were not speaking. The letter, dated Thursday, September 1905, is on letterhead that reads AMERICAN LEGATION, SEOUL, KOREA.

Your losing your temper and getting these uncontrollable dislikes for me has got to stop. You say that it is because I get on your nerves by doing and saying foolish and rather conspicuously common things— if that is the case it is very decidedly the pot calling the kettle black as no one could accuse you of over-refinement in any direction—either in words or deeds. [When] you left this morning and I asked if you felt any better about me you said "no I do not" in a tone of such frank dislike and with an expression of such active disgust that if I did not love you so much would make me never wish to see you again. Indeed I can not help feeling hurt in what you are trying to bring about— trying...something which will give you an excuse to [get] out in as gentlemanly a manner as possible of what you consider a most unpleasant hole. I shall not give you that excuse unless you consider this...sufficient. But your behavior has been ridiculous and most contemptible—I am disappointed.[49]

This is a unique letter. Her rare display of force was in stark contrast to Nick's second thoughts. If Nick wanted to be released from the engagement, Alice was not ready to let him go regardless of the fact that she thought he disliked her and was disgusted by her. Perhaps the vision before her eyes was her stepmother's unmarried sister, Aunt Emily Carow, whom Alice called "a horrid old maid."[50] Maybe the immaturity of which Taft wrote met the specter of spinsterhood on that trip. For all his faults, Nick would save her from being an "old maid" and, if she gambled right, might return her to the White House as First Lady. Alice had told Griscom she wanted to marry a man who would be president and prominent politically for she hated to look forward to the obscurity into which she would fall after her father ceased to be president. But the content of the letter and the tone pervading it prove how deeply the wounds ran. In comparison to her parents, Alice feared she lacked the moral fiber to contribute to a marriage like theirs. Nick dominated Alice's emotions, unhealthily, Taft thought. He swore that he would "never believe that they are permanently engaged until I hear that they are married."[51]

The diplomatic mission of the trip had been a success in more ways than one, as had been Theodore Roosevelt's efforts to mediate peace between Russia and Japan. TR summed up his position on his handling of the Russo-Japanese War in a posterity letter sent to Alice in Tokyo on September 2, 1905, the day the peace treaty was signed. The president maintained he did not seek the prominence that came to him because of the settlement, but that in the end it was a good thing he had chosen to moderate the peace. Further, TR complained to Alice, "It is enough to give anyone a sense of sardonic amusement to see the way in which the people generally, not only in my country but elsewhere, gauge the work purely by the fact that it succeeded. If I had not brought about peace I should have been laughed at and condemned. Now I am over-praised." This letter foreshadows the role that Alice would play in her father's life after her marriage, when he increasingly sought her advice and discussed political situations with her. Edith, meanwhile, had been sending Alice letters full of political news ever since she stepped on board the *Manchuria*.[52]

The First Daughter and her entourage sailed for the United States from Yokohama on October 13, enduring "a rough passage." As the trip wound to its close, two stories inspired national gossip. Newspapers circulated a rumor that American railroad magnate E. H. Harriman had made a bet with millionaire Robert Goelet that he could beat the fastest recorded Japan-to-New York time.[53] Goelet took the bet. Harriman, his wife, their daughter Mary (a good friend of Alice's), and Robert Goelet had been visiting Japan to consider the possibility of rail lines through China, which is how they came to return on the *Siberia,* with Alice and her party. The *Siberia* was already ahead of schedule, so Harriman seemed to have the odds in his favor. When he summoned his private railway car to meet them in San Francisco, the junketeers lost no time embarking from boat to railroad. Harriman's train raced across the country until it was officially slowed by an urgent telegram from President Roosevelt. TR feared for his daughter's safety on the speeding train—and he was offended by her having accepted a ride from one of the "malefactors of great wealth" against whom he had spent a large part of his presidency railing. TR's brief order to Harriman to "slow down" succeeded, but it did not impede the free publicity that Harriman gained by chauffeuring the First Daughter. Indeed, when TR's telegram reached the newspapers, his fatherly concern for the speed at which Alice rocketed across the plains solidified in the popular mind that Harriman's railway was fast—and comfortable enough for a princess.[54]

While Taft may have had his own reasons for not wanting to hear of Nick and Alice's engagement while abroad, the rest of the nation was breathlessly waiting to learn of an Edenic conclusion. Furious speculation began as soon as the steamer docked in California. The *New York Times* suggested that Alice was "closely attended by Congressman Nicholas Longworth. Both she and Longworth laughingly declined to discuss their reported engagement, but she called him Nick."[55] Before any confirmation could be released to the press, however, the couple had to ask permission of the bride-to-be's parents. Alice put off this chore because she felt "shy and self-conscious" for fear that they might be " 'sentimental' about it." Finally, Alice cornered Edith in her bathroom "and told her the news while she was brushing her teeth, so that she should have a moment to think before she said anything." Meanwhile, Nick, "with great formality was announcing it to Father in the study."[56]

Alice did not record Edith's and TR's responses to the proclamation. Victorian etiquette had suggested that the suitor ask for his intended's hand in marriage—but in the twentieth century, securing the father's consent was not as crucial.[57] On the other hand, the father was the president of the United States. Nick and Alice informed her parents because they already had the eyes of the nation on them; parental disapproval would have come up against a storm of protest from a nation of romantics hungry for happy endings. But even if the Roosevelts had wanted to prevent their daughter from marrying Nick Longworth, they could not have. Years of controlling the nation rather than Alice meant they could not dictate, or even suggest, a more appropriate suitor. But perhaps Nick's flaws were not so evident at the time. The First Lady was "well satisfied" with the engagement, allowing her concerns about Nick's drinking and the age difference to be outweighed by his inheritance, intelligence, and obvious desire to succeed in politics.[58]

NASUM NANDA read Nick's mysterious cable to his sister Clara. In the siblings' special code NASUM meant an engagement was about to be announced. But NANDA was not in their lexicon. After applying "imagination and a small amount of concerted effort," Clara decoded NANDA as Nick and Alice. The bride-to-be was similarly busy trying to write her relatives before the journalists got wind of the news. Correspondents vied for the scoop, but it was the editor of the *Chicago Tribune* who, soon after the couple reached the capital, wired his Washington office asking whether or not they were engaged. "She went out driving with Nick Longworth this afternoon without a chaperone," came the reply. "If they are not engaged, they ought to be." The careful surveillance paid off. The *Tribune* divulged the engagement a half day before the family did. Then the floodgates opened. Alice's scrapbook contains more than two hundred clippings from papers across the United States and Europe announcing the engagement. Her celebrity status overshadowed the wedding details. She relished the publicity, while TR and Edith simply threw up their hands, powerless against the onslaught of demands for details of the engagement, the invitations, the wedding dress, the decorations, the music, the celebrant, and on and on. Alice called the two months between the engagement and the wedding "a turmoil."[59]

The newspapers first wanted to know when Nick had proposed. He told the *New York Evening World*: "I did not know officially that I was engaged until the announcement." This could not have thrilled his fiancée, who had already expressed fears about his complacency. One skeptical but enterprising journalist prodded the weary congressman—Was it on the steamer on the way back from the Philippines, he asked? "I don't really know," Nick responded. "I've been in what you might call a trance for so long that I am somewhat mixed as to dates." Another paper placed a premium on creativity: "Rumor says that the fateful question was put as they were entering the door of the Empress Dowager's palace in Peking, and that the affirmative came at the same spot as they emerged!" Burr McIntosh wrote in the *Literary Digest* that Alice's courage and pluck in the Philippines made Nick's heart "bump around at a rather lively rate." McIntosh speculated, "If anything was necessary to cement a love match already begun, those wild rides among the hills did it."[60] All of these stories are highly romantic and completely false. Alice never pinpointed a specific time, and neither she nor Nick ever released explicit details to the press. Their engagement grew out of their intellectual and physical passion until it was simply understood. Perhaps Alice, so desirous of the marriage, never pressed him for an actual proposal.

Americans expected a good marriage from Alice Roosevelt. The representative of American womanhood finally embarked upon her "destiny," with ambivalent feelings as her baggage. Alice went to great lengths to win and keep Nick. She compromised her heart, her integrity, and possibly her body to win him. The First Daughter never allowed her fans to see even one tiny glimpse of her confused emotions. She and Nick, used to standing consistently in the spotlight, presented a mostly united front to the world.

Alice had superstar status in an age before film stars. Her dash across the country was daring and exciting, and more than one young American must have sighed in disappointment to hear of the paternally enforced slowdown. As Alice passed through their hometowns, children lined the streets and waved the American flag. Women and men jostled one another at the stations to get a look at the First Daughter. Brass bands played in her honor from the Pacific to the Atlantic. Alice stepped off Harriman's train in New York at the height of her popular acclaim. She was "an American girl who has not been spoiled," despite her great successes overseas, according to the *Richmond Times-Dispatch*. Ordinary citizens agreed that the important thing about Miss Roosevelt was that she was emphatically American and truly her father's daughter. The *New York Times* remarked that she looked "as chic and as full of spirits as when she left several months ago with Secretary Taft. Homage she has received in the Orient apparently had not turned her head." The *Times* quoted Alice's brief speech to the reporters: "You may say for me, I am more than ever convinced there is no country like our own."[61] Alice understood politics.

One delicate question surfaced after the East Asia trip. Did the presents given her by foreign leaders—rolls of costly Chinese fabric, jewelry, expensive clothing, national works of art, even a little black dog named Manchu—legally belong to the federal government or to Alice? A Canadian newspaper suggested that foreign officials "looked upon Miss Alice as an American Princess, as a daughter of the Government, as a representative of the nation—or they never would have given her such presents. Mr. [William Jennings] Bryan is in the Orient, but it is not likely that he will be loaded down with any such shower of gifts." As she sailed home, reporters estimated their worth. Theodore and Edith heard bloated claims that MISS ROOSEVELT'S EMBARRASSING PRESENTS necessitated twenty-seven crates and a $60,000 duty. TR sent her a warning telegram: "Do not bring in any present that you do not really value, and if the presents are of much money value leave them in storage at Custom House until we can talk over method of paying duty. I know nothing about the presents excepting what I see in the papers which I take for granted is a wild exaggeration but I send this telegram by way of precaution."[62]

Alice was grateful her father had taken her side. Articles in her defense claimed she "was placed in a position where she could not decline any of the presents...without placing the Government in the attitude of rejecting friendly overtures." A *Times* editorial posited that if the Congress passed a bill exempting Alice from import duties, "we do not believe that there would be a score of Americans who would object." At a press corps interview in late October, Alice emphasized, "The gifts I received in the various places we visited I accepted as a compliment to my country and not in the nature of a personal tribute." Whether the gifts were for America, its president, or its First Daughter, most people felt that she deserved them, because as a Chicago daily claimed, "She did much to cement friendship between the United States and foreign countries." Alice eventually paid $1,026 in duties. While still a hefty sum, the outcome vindicated Alice. The press had exaggerated the number and the value of the gifts.[63]

Theodore Roosevelt's private diplomat had carried herself with aplomb overseas. She continued to receive interesting gifts—such as a "large brass shell which was used during the siege of Port Arthur last winter."[64] More important, tremendous praise came from her own family, including a precious note from Auntie Bye written after a fellow junketeer had told her approvingly about Alice's behavior; it concluded: "My little Alice that was really mine for four years. [H]ow perfect how dear you are to the old Aunt."[65]

Her trip resulted in the enrichment of the administration, the nation, the Roosevelt family name, and Alice's own character. Her visit spurred citizens to ask questions about the tariff situation in the Philippines, the Chinese exclusionary laws, and the future of Korea. After Alice's journeys, Roosevelt's admirers and his detractors tried to define the line between the nature of royalty and the nature of celebrity in a democracy. Alice's visits were looked upon as an honor by most of the people of Hawaii, the Philippines, Korea, Puerto Rico, Cuba, China, and Japan, and they hoped that Alice's goodwill missions would encourage stronger diplomatic ties with the United States.

Alice's ambassadorial spunk served as a role model for Progressive Era women, because of a fame rightfully earned. She was neither a Victorian woman nor a New Woman, but rather something else entirely: a modern celebrity. The First Daughter had the prestige of the White House attached to her and not the taint of the theater, from whence sprang the other legendary women of the day. President Roosevelt learned by the time he sent Alice to East Asia that her fame would increase with each stop on the itinerary. By 1905, TR knew both that his daughter's celebrity status was inevitable and that it could help his administration. As the newspapers noted, "There have been few young women in America, or for that matter in any other country, who have received so much newspaper attention as has Miss Alice Roosevelt."[66] TR might have worried privately about the effect of Alice's prominence on her own life, but he did not have to fear the results of her fame on his administration when she functioned as his good-will ambassador.

Chapter 8

"To Bask in the Rays of Your Reflected Glory"

A CONFUSING WELTER of details and decisions filled the two months of turmoil between the official announcement of the First Daughter's engagement on December 13, 1905, and the wedding, set for February 17, 1906. Congratulatory notes showered onto the White House staff. Wedding gifts began arriving shortly after the nuptial date was made public. The *New York Tribune* described Alice as "overwhelmed with congratulations," and "almost buried in flowers" from well-wishers around the world. The crew of the German "torpedoboat-destroyer" *Alice Roosevelt* sent their hopes for the future happiness of their "patroness." Many of the notes mentioned the months of publicity she and Nick had endured. Alice knew that the attendant hoopla had ended the American guessing game for, as she wrote to tell her cousin Eleanor, "I hope you are surprised but I am much afraid you are not!"[1]

Her wedding occasioned a national celebration. Alice represented the ideal of true American womanhood—she had grit, poise enough to keep up with Europeans, good breeding, unostentatious wealth, attractive looks, athletic ability, common sense unspoiled by too much education, and charitable impulses (if one looked hard enough). As Anne Ellis wrote in her memoir, aptly titled *The Life of an Ordinary Woman*, "We felt very near to her. You see, this was Romance, and having none of our own we took part of hers."[2] Americans from all walks of life sent Alice congratulations, written laboriously by hands not used to holding pens, hasty notes scrawled on postcards showcasing the bride and groom, letters from women and men sighing at the wonderful conclusion to the grand saga.

· · ·

After five years of continuous journalistic coverage, Americans had exempted Alice from the standard of female impropriety attached to having one's name in the newspapers more than thrice—especially since it now appeared she would follow the acceptable path to the altar. Alice Roosevelt personified the female side of her popular father: she led the strenuous life. If it was in a manner of which TR sometimes disapproved, what matter? Americans generally didn't. Seldom did newspapers criticize Alice by calling her or her actions unladylike. At the turn of the century, she was helping to change the definition of proper behavior for women. Newspapers attributed her hijinks to the exuberance of youth.

Being eldest daughter of a charismatic and much-loved president allowed her unmatched freedom—balanced by the drawbacks of public life. Alice joined no reform movements, unlike so many of her Progressive Era sisters. Women's clubs and benevolent societies, including the Junior League, taught elite women important lessons in how to maneuver through public spaces—whether legislative corridors, ethnic ghettos, or hometown battlegrounds—but Alice learned by living in public. Newspaper reporters and cameras taught her to act efficaciously and becomingly in the masculine public sphere. Her fame as First Daughter might have been a hindrance to participation in settlement homes, while her temperament kept her away from causes that TR, at least, labeled noble, such as the Newsboys' Lodging House of his own youth.

But now, Alice stood on the threshold of what most of the world at that time considered a woman's noblest calling. Marriage was right and good—and after her stormy public adolescence, Alice appeared finally to be settling into a seemly adulthood. The nation breathed a sigh of relief along with TR and Edith at the proper conclusion to Alice's youth. She had chosen, to all appearances, a creditable man—a politician like her father; a solid midwesterner. No effete easterner, no foreign royal would claim Princess Alice. With fondness, Americans set about commemorating her wedding. The Roosevelt-Longworth marriage became an emblem of national pride. One Californian encapsulated all the themes of Alice's time as First

Daughter: the worthy daughter of the worthy sire, the spirit of democracy, the importance of marrying an American, the subtle reminder that her fame eclipsed Nick's:

> Here's to Alice Roosevelt,
>   Who's won a home with Nick,—
> The lad who failed so many times,
>   But finally made it stick.
>
> We wish her health and pleasure
>   Throughout a long, good life,
> And we are glad no stranger
>   Has won her for a wife.
>
> 'Tis not that she is better
>   Than many a handsome maid;
> 'Tis not that she is brighter,
>   Or of a finer grade,—
>
> But just because she's Alice
>   Of strenuous, square-deal hue,—
> An ordinary mortal,—
>   (Although her blood is blue).
>
> We send this greeting, Alice,
>   From California state;
> And trust you'll long live happy,
>   And make a loving mate.[3]

As congratulations flowed in, Alice systematically pasted them into her scrapbook. They were happy reminders of the affection of friends, relatives, and anonymous well-wishers. TR's friend Owen Wister jokingly asked Alice "How could you increase your poor father's duties by adding to them the duty of being a father-in-law?"[4] The funniest and one of the most loving congratulations came from Alice's confidant, Grandpa Lee. He wrote that her Boston relatives were overjoyed at the news of her engagement to "Nick Longworth, 'Harvard, 1891.'" He continued in his kindly and prepossessing way:

> I was not surprised in the least as I had read of it for at least 365 days in the newspapers. You have raised the old nick for quite a long time and now you have decided to settle down for life with a young Nick. Good! I hope that he has a good, kindly disposition, but with sufficient strength of character to make you:
>
> 1st Get up in the morning and breathe the fresh air.
> 2nd Make your breakfast off something besides lemon juice.
> 3rd Leave off cigarettes, cigars and cocktails.
> 4th When traveling leave at home the dog and snakes.
> 5th Conduct yourself so as to be happy and make him happy too.
>
> But you are all right and I congratulate [you] again and feel that you have done the right thing. Uncle George has just been in here and says "That Nick is a first rate fellow." So that point is settled.[5]

Meanwhile, Nick's friend Julius Fleischmann sent the groom a note attesting to the change love made in him: "Your friends [in Cincinnati] now knew it all, when you were home this fall, they say now that you were not the Nick as of old but a very tame sort of 'eat out of your hand' individual. Well I did not know it but I hoped it for I felt that it was the goal you most deserved to reach...."[6]

Like her mementos from the East Asia trip, Alice's wedding gifts caused comment. In combination with her Asian loot, MISS ROOSEVELT COULD OPEN A MUSEUM WITH THESE PRESENTS, one journalist suggested. Alice groused that there was "fantastic exaggeration" about the number and type of gifts she received—but she cast doubt on her own statement by asserting, "I had about the sort of presents that any girl gets from her relatives and friends and friends of the family; with the exception of a few from foreign potentates." Indeed, she later chortled, "The one thing I really relished about my wedding was the presents." In 1900, the limited range of acceptable gifts included silver boxes, cloisonné, picture frames, hand mirrors, belt clasps, and "pins of every conceit for the hair." Usually wedding presents were for the bride specifically. The other option was gifts for the bride's new home. Appropriate here were vases, tea caddies, apostle spoons, "embroidered table-cloths, doyleys, and useful coverings for bureau and wash-stands."[7]

While Alice did receive conventional gifts, she also received heirlooms, such as the priceless memento from her uncle Francis H. Lee. Uncle Frank sent "a silver can belonging probably to your great great great grandfather Joseph Lee who was a privateersman in the Revolution [and] furnished models for the Navy of that period, was a partner and brother-in-law of George Cabot[,] President of the famous Hartford Convention, this can according to the hallmark was made in London in 1751." From the White House aides, Alice and Nick received a cut-glass cake dish, which she used every day. Their fellow congressional junketeers sent Alice an aquamarine and diamond pendant. John Greenway sent her a deer's head, "quite one of the nicest things that I got," Alice wrote to thank him.[8]

Among the most glamorous presents were an invaluable Gobelin tapestry from the French government, a mosaic from Pope Pius X, a bracelet with a diamond-ringed miniature of Kaiser Wilhelm of Germany to match the one he gave her when she christened the *Meteor,* and an enamel snuff box from King Edward of England, with his miniature on the lid, also set in diamonds. The king of Italy gave Alice what she described as a "rather hideous" inlaid mosaic table, too big ever to be used in any of her homes. Her very favorite present came from the Cuban government. Old friend Senator Henry Cabot Lodge suggested to the Cuban legislature that pearls might be rather more to the bride's taste than the bedroom suite inlaid with semiprecious stones upon which they had tentatively agreed. So, in grateful remembrance of Colonel Roosevelt's part in the 1898 war of liberation from Spain, Cuba presented the First Daughter with a string of pearls from Boucheron in Paris worth twenty-five thousand dollars. She wore those pearls the rest of her life, and had them on when she died. The Japanese government sent gold cloth embroidered with the royal kikumon—a stylized chrysanthemum pattern—the badge of the imperial family. The empress dowager and emperor of China gave Alice the most exorbitant gifts, including eight bolts of Chinese silk brocaded with gold, a jade "ornament," a "pair of gold earrings, set with pearls and precious stones," "one pair of bracelets, set with red and green jewels," and "a white fox robe." Monitoring the proceedings, one British foreign officer concluded that "no sovereign's daughter could have had more tremendous to-doings than this Republican young lady."[9]

Commemorating the wedding became a national pastime. "Just now the fashionable fad is the presentation of some kind of a wedding present to Miss Alice Roosevelt," the Medford *Patriot* affirmed. Westerner Anne Ellis and her friends, vicariously living the romance, all chipped in fifty cents apiece for a special-order centerpiece of Battenberg lace. "We inserted a paper—we had no cards—with all our names on, and sent it, then waited, reading the papers to see what other people had sent."[10] In the outpouring of popular affection, she received a number of unusual presents—hand-made and home-baked goods, feather dusters, washing machines, books, bales of hay, a hogshead of popcorn, live and stuffed animals of many sorts, and a "large linen centerpiece" from the children of the Colored Industrial Evening School, in thanks to the president for "his attitude toward ne-groes." The United Mine Workers of America gave Alice a railway car full of coal as a wedding present, in appreciation for the president's services in settling the anthracite coal strike of 1902. Because they "consider[ed] themselves children of the amiable President" the Abenaki tribe also sent a gift.[11] Many Americans wrote songs in their honor, for example, "Alice, the Bride of the White House," "Love's Happiness (A Wedding Song)," and "The Wooing of Alice and Nick," which concluded with a lullaby. Reporters meticulously listed the presents as the country took pride that a daughter of Columbia was worthy of such worldwide attention.[12]

Anyone could read about Princess Alice's wedding presents, but few were able to view the gifts. After the turn of the century, a bride decided whether or not to display the wedding presents, though the trend was away from displaying gifts. Instead, presents were shown to best friends only for the purpose of celebrating the love and good wishes of the bride's circle. Social arbiters warned women against parading their treasures for crassly comparing one giver's choice (and financial outlay) to another's. In the First Daughter's case, it would have been impractical to show the wedding presents to all visitors, because of the sheer numbers of people who could claim a right to view the gifts, and because of the incalculable worth of her presents. Alice enjoyed the ritual of the "excitement of gifts coming in, of opening them and then arranging them in the library over the blue room," where she let only her closest friends see them.[13]

Wedding etiquette further stipulated that the bride-to-be must recognize the graciousness of the giver by sending thank-you notes written in her own hand. This Alice did not do. She "skimmed unconcernedly along the surface," in her own words, writing only a few notes in between the congratulatory parties. Edith Roosevelt, who considered good manners the measure of a person, took it upon herself to marshal the forces of propriety. She and Belle Hagner, her social secretary, wrote many of Alice's thank-you notes, while Alice remembered that "even guests and younger members of the family were pressed into the service." There were so many gifts to be numbered and acknowledged that Edith had to cancel her usual luncheon with the cabinet wives in February.[14] Edith and Belle thus relieved Alice of one of the most onerous chores connected with the event.

While Alice enjoyed the prewedding whirl, Nick confronted unusual pressures. Two controversies erupted in his home state. First, the national Women's Christian Temperance Union was "up in arms" because the Ohio delegation wanted to give Nick and Alice a crystal punch bowl. Although the good women prayed for a change of heart, the delegates were not swayed. They sent an enormous punch bowl that stood—on its glittering pedestal—nearly two feet high, ornamented with pears and apples, and came with a dozen matching cups. The bowl was so large that its velvet-lined shipping box was the size of a writing desk. But not everyone caught wedding fever. Nick heard that half of the Ohio state senate balked at passing a House-authorized joint resolution of wedding congratulations. The fractious Buckeye senators declared the resolution "undignified" because "too much publicity had already been given to the coming nuptials." They defeated a motion to suspend the rules and vote on the resolution. The reason—a Midwestern condemnation of "too much publicity"—was likely of little consolation to the bridegroom in the face of the undeniably lukewarm support from his former colleagues.[15]

Just at that time, some of President Roosevelt's western friends arrived to comfort the beleaguered Nick. A group of ten Ponca Indians marched down Pennsylvania Avenue bearing a wedding gift of a buffalo skin for Nick, for they reasoned, "Can a man be boss of his own wigwam if it is so that all the ponies, the beads, the buffalo hides, belong to his wife?" Representative Longworth hid. The determined delegation proceeded to the White House, where they asked the president to present the skin to "Shining Top."[16]

The newspapers included everything but the buffalo skin as they calculated Nick's worth. Would Alice's money problems now be solved? Estimates of the Longworth fortune varied widely. One newspaper had him "heir to $300,000," while another stated that "the realty part of the estate alone will go to the $2,000,000 mark," and a third claimed that he was "worth about $15,000,000."[17] The Longworth family fortune accrued decades earlier when the first Nicholas Longworth accepted land in payment for his legal services. Eventually he invested in more land, and then in grapes and a winery, producing an average of 150,000 bottles of wine a year. He is often credited with beginning the wine industry in the United States and with having produced the first sparkling wines in the country. When the first Nicholas died in 1836, his fortune was estimated at $15 million. Whatever the exact figure in 1906, it was enough for Alice—who had already visited Rookwood and seen the Longworth holdings—and it was acceptable to Edith, who approved of Nick's "comfortable income according to our not over-ambitious ideas."[18] Nick was, however, never able to keep up with the friends from Alice's youth. Her dream of being "fabulously wealthy" eluded her.

Susan Longworth lunched at the White House on December 13, 1905, the day the engagement was formally announced. Traditionally at this meeting the families would have discussed the formalities of the match. Alice remembered Susan Longworth as "rather a formidable lady who was better dressed and straighter-backed than anyone in Cincinnati. . . . I enjoyed her in a way," she recalled, but "was never able to play the part of the dutiful daughter-in-law."[19] No doubt this was influenced by Alice's iconoclastic lifestyle. Mrs. Longworth, a traditional, conservative Ohioan who thought of herself first and foremost as Nicholas's mother, did not wholly approve of Alice—but it was the simple fact of Nick's marrying that put her off balance. Writing to her friend Katharine Wulsin, Nick's mother confessed:

> I was utterly unprepared for the announcement—having made up my mind (in the comfortable way that mothers have) that I knew more about my son than any one else did. The President has given a most cordial consent & seems very much pleased. Mrs. Roosevelt sent for me to come to see her a few days ago and she said Alice was the most charming person to live with on account of her sunny temperament and thoughtfulness for others—that in spite of her irresponsibility and impractical ways she was the most punctual person (in which she differed from the President who wasn't) and she said "When Nick tells her to be ready at a certain time she will never keep him waiting a minute."[20]

Another friend tried to comfort her by suggesting that the president's daughter might be the only young woman who could keep "Nicky's" interest, "for instance as we know that he was in deadly terror of getting sick of his wife at the breakfast table and that the *'stat d'aime'* involved in this fear would be apt to make him tire of any usual nice girl. In this case I really believe that the 'six white horses' as represented by the celebrity of the princess will do much to cast a glamour over the situation and create an illusion around his domestic life which he might not have in any other way...."[21]

At the time this letter was written, "Nicky" was already thirty-six years old. But the writer certainly had his measure. Alice knew she was marrying into a close family. Clara, her future sister-in-law, recollected, "The mutual and tender link which bound [mother and son] was at the base both of his ambitions and their fulfillment. Nothing could have been deeper or more complete than his filial veneration, but, aside from this essential fact, he treated her more as a sister than a parent...."[22]

Once Nick's engagement was announced, Susan Longworth receded to the background. Though she lived with him in Washington some part of the year, she was absent from journalistic and firsthand accounts of the wedding. In terms of public interest, the Roosevelts topped the dowager from Ohio, just as newspaper articles featuring the bride outnumbered those on the bridegroom. Susan, fiercely protective of her son and his career, could not have been unaware of the imbalance.

Approximately one thousand invitations were sent out, but this number excluded the majority of those who wanted to come. A longtime Washingtonian explained, "Social America was on tiptoe, hoping for an invitation. The Has-Beens tried resuscitation, and the Never-Wasers resorted to novel tricks to break in. Many people, quite unknown to the Roosevelts, sent expensive presents and then brazenly asked for invitations. Their gifts were promptly returned." Having the right connections in a political town like Washington meant that even private parties were only as private as the limits to one's social or political network. White House receptions could be crashed with relative ease. One insider wrote that "almost any well-mannered white person could still wangle an invitation to a White House reception except during the weeks of preparation for the marriage of 'Princess Alice' to . . . Nicholas Longworth." Lottie Strickland—one such well-mannered white person—made it all the way from New Orleans to Cincinnati before she was apprehended as a stowaway. Strickland and her friends had come to the momentous decision that she should represent the common folk at the White House wedding. "I hid in [railroad car] sleepers," she said, "but the passengers helped me. I started from home with ten cents. We thought that a working girl ought to be at the wedding, and I am sure if I get to see President Roosevelt and tell him what I want he will allow me to attend."[23]

Everybody wanted to go to the wedding. It was the biggest social event of the season, maybe of the Roosevelt presidency. Washington insiders' social standing was in jeopardy. "Such wire-pulling as is going on here fills even the oldest politicians with awe. . . . Some matrons are already negotiating with Florida hotel keepers," so that they could be out of town—a last-minute, face-saving excuse, according to the *Washington Post*. The *Times* suggested that requests for invitations were limited by neither class nor gender: "So widespread has been the interest in the marriage, and so prevalent the mistake as to its social and official significance, that Miss Isabelle

Hagner, Mrs. Roosevelt's secretary, and Mr. Loeb, private secretary to the President, have been sorely beset for the past two weeks with communications from men high in official circles all over the United States, with requests that are almost commands for invitations to the wedding."[24]

Despite the Roosevelts' disclaimer that the ceremony was a private function, one's proximity to the seat of power was measured by the receipt of the coveted invitation. One Washingtonian remembered that she and her family were lucky enough to be included, but after their invitation arrived they faced a different sort of problem: all of their friends begged them to "use their influence" with the Roosevelts to extract more tickets. Finally, the demands forced Theodore and Edith to issue a public statement explaining the criteria used in issuing invitations: "The capacity of the White House required that under existing circumstance invitations be limited to the closest kinsfolk, the personal friends of Miss Roosevelt and Mr. Longworth, and certain classes of officials in Washington. No friends of the President and Mrs. Roosevelt are being asked unless they also come within one of these classes, and even with these limitations the number of guests threatens to overtax the capacity of the White House." The invitation list redefined Alice's own group of peers. The *New York World-Telegram* reported the disappointing news that some of Alice's dearest friends could not secure an invitation.[25]

A colder cut awaited. Alice was interviewed just before the wedding, as reporters searched for clues as to the bride's plans. " 'Why aren't you having any bridesmaids?' they asked Alice. 'I'd love to. Yes, I'd just love to,' she replied, 'but I'd have to have at least 150 if I had any. It's too bad I can't have any, but I can't make my friends jealous, and how could I ever choose six bridesmaids from among them all? I'd want them all, and I must say,' with a bewitching smile, 'that I think they'd like it.' "[26] It is possible that Alice wanted to be the center of attention and so chose to have no competition from friends she feared were prettier than she. It is certainly true that Alice got to be a "most marvelous belle" on her wedding day. Perhaps this was her symbolic public revenge on those who had gossiped about Nick's prior womanizing. Many of her friends were already married, and hence could not serve as bridesmaids. However, it is worth noting that "the fashion of bridesmaids has gone out temporarily," the author of *Manners and Social Usage* asserted, while another etiquette guide took it for granted that the option of dispensing with bridesmaids existed: "In America, if there are no bridesmaids. . . ."[27] Further, not one of the many memoirs mentioning the wedding comment on Alice's decision to approach the altar unattended. If it had been truly unusual it would have drawn note, especially as many of them were written by women of her own class who would have recorded any exceptional circumstances.

In late January, Alice set about shopping for her married life. This task consisted of acquiring a trousseau, "a complete stock of apparel sufficient to last [the bride] during the first few years of her married life." New York thrilled that MISS ROOSEVELT TO BUY TROUSSEAU HERE, as the *New York Herald* proudly proclaimed on Christmas eve. Nick and Alice spent a week shopping—or trying to shop—but nothing, including "private" luncheons, escaped the notice of the press. Alice began at Kurzman's, a Fifth Avenue clothing importer frequented by elite New Yorkers (including Alice's grandmother Mittie). Well-wishers crowded the streets and surrounded their car as the couple, joined at times by Nick's sister Clara, went from store to store attempting to make their purchases. Alice recalled that she and her fiancé were "dogged by reporters, [with] inquisitive crowds following when I went shopping; to some extent [it was] the sort of thing a royalty or a move star endures, or enjoys." Alice and Nick stopped their car to run into a millinery shop, and as they did so, the long line of photographers and reporters that followed behind them blocked the street. "Traffic," the *New York Times* revealed, "came to a standstill until Roundsman Thompson of the mounted squad with the assistance of half a dozen hastily summoned policemen stepped in, cleared the crowd away, and established police lines on either side of the entrance to the store."[28] Alice, Nick, and Clara had difficulty getting to the boat that would ferry them to Long Island because of the crowds. Once aboard, they good-naturedly posed for pictures and waved good-bye to their fans.

Alice did enjoy the fuss. She accepted her role as America's First Daughter and understood that reports of her actions and words were likely to appear in the newspapers. The push-pull of being raised by Theodore and

Edith—who faced each other from opposite ends of the publicity spectrum—resulted in Alice's having few private days. By this time, Alice could joke easily with journalists. "[T]here is one secret you will not learn," she teased, "and that is where we are going immediately after we are married."[29] To a degree, Theodore reconciled himself to his daughter's fame. Edith never did. The First Daughter—caught in the middle—mostly did what she wanted to do, always conscious of whether her father was watching. When he was not, she filled in the sadness with cameras and reporters. Eventually, Alice would try to use Nick for the same ends.

Nick was ambivalent about how much he enjoyed being the companion of a woman whose very presence could draw a crowd of one thousand. Nick had luxuriated in Alice's limelight while they toured East Asia and could escape when necessary. But now he was firmly and officially part of her entourage. He wrote her in October that he was "snatching a few moments between newspaper reporters to tell you that I have gotten home alive and 'have nothing to say' from which you can see that being in love with a celebrity is not altogether a bed of roses." In another letter to her he confessed that he "simply love[d] to bask in the rays of your reflected glory."[30] The *Washington Mirror* had accurately predicted Nick's challenge, even before they left on the congressional junket: "Princess Alice will be in her glory in an Oriental environment, with bowing and salaaming at every turn. She has withstood more adulation, flattery, and throwing of bouquets than perhaps any woman in America. She will get all this to her heart's content, but what will she do when she gets back to the Land of the Free. 'Nick' had better learn a few steps, how to leave the room backwards and how to ko-tow... or he will find himself out in the cold when the Princess enters her Washington palace."[31]

Nick apparently knew how to "ko-tow." Alice remained the country's foremost female celebrity, the closest thing the nation had to royalty, and the typical young woman all at once—no doubt a trying combination in one's fiancée. He stood a distant second in media interest, but he did inspire curiosity. *Leslie's Illustrated Weekly* hastened to add, "It is no discredit to Mr. Longworth to say that he suddenly has become an important public personage by reason of the fact that he is the White House bridegroom and son-in-law of the President." Not discrediting perhaps, but embarrassing. Visitors to the House of Representatives viewing galleries pointed to Nick and whispered, "There's Alice's husband."[32] Nick must have been counting the days until Alice receded from public view and he could settle into married life with the certain knowledge that his bride's patrimony—and *past* fame—could assist his career.

At the time, however, Nick continued to send loving letters when they were apart, assuring Alice he was living "the life of an anchorite so far as food, drink and other alleged temptations of the flesh are concerned." He told her he was sad without her: "I don't like anybody here and its simply because a foolish (sometimes) little person called Baby Lee has wound herself into the very inmost convolutions of my soul and I can't get rid of her for a moment, even if I wanted to." "You are just a part of my life," he wrote passionately, "that nothing and nobody else can fill." In the midst of the wedding preparations, Nick also had to keep his constituents happy and pay attention to his House seat. Alice was learning about it all. "Far from being bored by your discussion of politics as she is played in Ohio," Nick wrote her with enthusiasm, "I love you all the more for taking an interest in it." He laid out his predictions for the upcoming electoral campaign and promised, "I will talk more about politics with you next month, and I would honestly rather have your advice about people and things than anybody's I know."[33]

When they were reunited, festivities continued apace at the White House. Two thousand guests attended the congressional reception on the first day of February 1906, where Alice and Nick were the center of attention. Her celebrity status intact, the First Daughter "was kept almost as busy bowing and smiling as was her father." On Sunday, February 11, the *New York Times* pointed out, Alice did not attend church, but stayed home to write thank-you notes before she and Nick dined with Susan Longworth. The next day, Alice's twenty-second birthday, TR and Edith gave a larger dinner at the White House, followed by a musicale in her honor.[34] Willard Straight was invited to both. Carpenter was in town, too, and Goelet—all three former flames attended the wedding.

Two days before the ceremony, Nick threw a party for his ushers at the

Alibi Club. Theodore Roosevelt attended the stag event but left before the merriment reached a level unseemly for a president.[35] One more congratulatory party was held that week—the night before the wedding—lending credence to White House usher Ike Hoover's observation that "for at least two years before her marriage there was never an evening when there was not some party being given in her honor."[36] Finally, Alice's dream was coming true: she had found a wealthy man, made him love her, fell for him in turn, and gloried in the culmination of her days as a single woman in the White House. Alice was toasted, congratulated, gifted with fabulous presents, remarked upon, photographed, followed by crowds, and almost entirely free from parental control.

Alice and Nick were seen alone every day when Alice drove Nick to work. The *Philadelphia Record* detailed the habits of the two they called "not coy lovers." "They drove to the Capitol this morning in the smart high trap the President gave his daughter a year ago, Miss Roosevelt holding the reins and wielding a whip like the clever horsewoman she is. At the House end of the Capitol she stopped for an instant to allow her fiancé to alight, then drove leisurely back to the White House."[37] Grandpa Lee would have been proud—Nick had the commendable effect of making Alice rise in the morning and breathe the fresh air. He would have looked askance, though, at the fact that it was she who held the reins. Another habit the couple had developed would upset him more: "The bride elect became the central figure [at White House functions], and so often after a brief appearance, she would quietly disappear—she and Nick."[38]

On the tenth, Nick came down with tonsillitis or the grippe.[39] Alice lost weight and suffered from another attack of eczema. The tensions normal to any wedding could have caused the couple to take to their respective beds, but the concentrated publicity was fierce and may have contributed to second thoughts. A series of letters written by Alice to Nick prior to their wedding helps to give some clue as to the couple's relations.

From these letters the capricious nature of their relationship is plain. They did love each other. To suggest otherwise is contradicted by the documents. "I ought to know it is too wonderful to last," Alice wrote Nick resignedly. "Don't lose your head about anyone please don't, Nick. Think of me. I love you so very much I am so jealous, my darling please." Her closing to that note was fatalistic: "No matter what happens I have been happier than I ever imagined anyone could be my darling."[40] In another letter she cried, "I didn't really think you would write to me, but oh why didn't you? I fear you care for someone else...." At times, Alice's worries about his constancy made her angry:

Nick—[Someone] has told me all sorts of things about you this evening that makes me fearfully unhappy. He says that Katherine Elkins means to have you before the winter is over, that she will marry you and that you will really want to marry her. You are a cur and a cad if this is so—now don't you really think you are. When you telephoned to me today your voice didn't have a very sincere ring when you talked about Monday night. Or does it only seem that way to me in the light of subsequent conversations. I have had letters from friends and then Josephine told me that she lunched with you on Tuesday and that you were very cross—evidently had a bad attack of remorse on account of the night before. Oh darling lamb, so you really regret it all so much. I am just more of a philosopher—What is done is—well, just done— a fact not to be gotten around, but at least not to be thought and worried about. I am afraid that I wish you [would] die, rather than marry anyone else but me.... Beloved—love me and marry me—Alice.[41]

This letter has the same protean tone that William Howard Taft attributed to Alice and Nick's shipboard romance. Her letter began in ire and ended in a plea. This time it appeared that Nick went off with other people to punish his fiancée after a tiff, whereas in East Asia Alice had gone elsewhere to console herself.

On the other hand, Alice did communicate to Nick her happiness in the relationship. "My own beloved Nick," she wrote once, "today has been very dull and tiresome because I haven't seen you once. And I haven't been able to think of anything else. Last night when...you kissed me, I was so happy, so wonderfully, marvelously happy. I love you darling...." Her letters speak often of missing him: "My darling, darling, darling Nick, if you don't come soon I shall go quite mad.... My own darling, I love you more every moment though I don't think it's possible to love any more than I do now already love."[42]

A letter from Nick to Alice is worth quoting in length in part because it is one of the very few of Nick's extant courtship letters, and because it gives a good sense of the workings of their relationship from his perspective. "My darling little girl," it began—a salutation suggesting both a cognizance of their age difference and a comfort with it:

It's no use. I simply can't stay away from you any longer and I am coming on Saturday night so that I shall be in Washington at 12:40 on the B&O on Sunday. Buck is coming with me but we can send him in another hack and you and I will drive back to my home for lunch, yes? Then if you like we will go to Nat's party at the Alibi and if we get tired we can adjourn to my well-furnished study. I think it would be nice to go to Mrs. Norman's for lunch on Tuesday so let's accept. Everything has come out nicely, even better than I expected so that I can come back to you conscientiously. I don't see any reason why you should not be the lady representative from the East half of Cincinnati for some years to come. I went out in Society last night and stayed up at a ball at the Country Club till 4:30 a.m. It wasn't so much the dancing that kept me there as it was listening to the thousands of nice things that were said about my Alice. You are really the most popular person in the world not even excepting my *"pere-au-loi perspective"* and I simply love to bask in the rays of your reflected glory and it isn't only the people in Society that say nice things about you but everybody including all my really toughest friends—perhaps that's the nicest thing about it.... We'll never be away from each other so long again. I can't and won't stand it so you will have to make up your mind to be right by my side from now until I become a senile and decrepit old man. But the last thing that will ever be left in me when everything else is gone will be the wholly absorbing love for you Alice....[43]

While Alice may have held the reins, Nick was firmly in control. He began with a possessive diminutive. By accepting the Norman invitation and assuming that Alice would want to retire to his study, he made up his mind and Alice's. He informed her that he stayed out until early in the morning, but sweetened that news with compliments. The relatively strict gender roles of the Progressive Era were mitigated by Alice's independent spirit and strong personality, but this letter suggests Nick was more patriarch than partner.

Alice was not a typical woman of the age. Once given a taste of the freedoms brought to her as First Daughter, she would have found it difficult to play the traditional wife. But at age twenty-two, Alice had neither the experience nor the desire to step far outside prescriptive norms. In fact, she actively sought a conventional path. Her overall lack of doubt concerning her own desire to marry Nick must have meant that she was comfortable with Nick's taking charge.

Finally all the wedding preparations were finished. The couple secured their wedding license. Edith released the wedding program to the newspapers on February 14. The invitation turmoil had died down. The majority of the presents had been received. Grandma and Grandpa Lee, Auntie Bye and Uncle Will, Auntie Corinne and Uncle Douglas had arrived, along with various cousins. Susan Longworth presided over the last days of her son's bachelorhood from their rental home on Eighteenth and I streets. Nellie Grant Sartoris, daughter of former president Ulysses S. Grant and a White House bride herself, was on hand for the festivities.[44]

At that time, Edith took Alice aside to have the traditional premarital mother-daughter talk. Alice remembered later, "Anything to do with sex or childbirth was just not discussed. Yet it was curious how much surreptitious attention was paid to the consequences of sex in those days. For instance, I never discussed such matters with my stepmother when I was a teenager, although she did come to me before I was married and said, 'You know, before you were born, your mother had to have a little something done in order to have you, so if you need anything, let me know.' "[45] Although Alice was not as naïve about sex as she would have later generations believe, her confusion at this announcement was understandable. There wasn't a lot to go on. Perhaps it was a surgery necessary for her mother to become pregnant. Edith did not habitually speak about sex—nor about Alice Lee. While she discharged a distasteful duty, she added to the overall edginess of the bride.

The day before the ceremony was filled with an East Room rehearsal, minus only the minister and the president, who was engaged in matters of state and could not be pulled away. Then all of the attendants followed Nick and Alice to the Alibi Club for an informal dinner hosted by Charles McCauley. As she wrote her name in the Club book, Alice grandly proclaimed "that hers should never again be written as Alice Lee Roosevelt." At 10:00 p.m., the party moved to the Keans, where they joined the large contingent of out-of-town guests staying at the senator's home.[46]

At last, the day of the wedding dawned. The morning of Saturday, February 17, 1906, started early for the White House staff, but the bride did not arise until 11:00 a.m. The father of the bride spent the morning writing letters about election fraud and the U.S. Naval Academy, while Edith knitted and chatted with Grandma Lee—to keep her mind off the chastisement she really wanted to give her dallying daughter.[47] At least the First Lady could remain calm in the knowledge that Ike Hoover had everything else under control. Out of curiosity, Grandpa Lee mingled in the assembling crowds of onlookers who gathered to get a glimpse of illustrious wedding guests.[48] Alice watched the throng as she dressed quickly. Her American-made gown was white satin, high-necked, and trimmed with point lace from Alice Lee's wedding. She wore elbow-length white kid gloves. The dress had a very long train of silver brocade woven especially for her in New Jersey. Alice adorned herself with the pearl necklace from the Cuban government, a diamond brooch from her parents, the kaiser's diamond bracelets, and Nick's wedding present to her, a diamond and pearl necklace. Her long hair was ordered with difficulty on top of her head in a pompadour. It held the lengthy tulle veil and traditional orange blossoms that completed her wedding ensemble.

At 11:30, the East Room was packed full of invitees. On a makeshift platform in front of the east window sat the altar, adorned with white Easter lilies. American Beauty roses, white rhododendrons, and pots of azaleas disguised the cavernous state room. Isabel Anderson watched as a "prominent society leader with a penchant for associating herself with the family at every wedding which she attended" tried to bully her way into the circle of relatives in the front rows. A White House aide barred her admittance "and the lady returned, baffled." Just before noon, Edith, wearing a russet brocade dress, entered on Ted's arm. They walked up the aisle, cordoned off from the guests, and sat down with the rest of the family. Nick waited at the altar with his best man, Nelson Perkins. Precisely at noon, under the direction of Lieutenant William Santelman, the United States Marine Band broke into the "Wedding March" from *Lohengrin*. Alice picked up her bouquet of white orchids. Father and daughter slowly progressed to the altar. As the bride met her intended, the Episcopal bishop of Washington, the Right Reverend Henry Yates Satterlee, intoned the marriage rite from the *Book of Common Prayer*.[49]

Clara Longworth de Chambrun felt the wedding "bristled with 'officialdom,'" since so many members of the Supreme Court, the Senate, the House of Representatives, and the senior officials of the diplomatic corps were in attendance. "My impression," Nick's sister recalled, was that everyone invited appeared, "also that whether those who came did so as a matter of duty, right or friendly inclination, each of the three categories appeared equally convinced of possessing a 'superior claim' over the rest." Sara Delano Roosevelt told her daughter-in-law Eleanor that "Alice looked remarkably pretty and her manner was very charming." Eleanor, who was pregnant then, could not accompany Sara and FDR since social morés dictated that she stay in confinement. Eleanor was probably relieved to avoid the White House, which at that time always made her "'rather nervous.'"[50]

The wedding service was over in fifteen minutes. Alice and Nick processed out to take the only photographs of the day. It was unusual—and Alice would say later, regrettable—that so few pictures were taken, but for once the newspaper reporters' cameras were not allowed in. Before the official photograph, cousin Franklin stepped forward to help adjust her veil, which had slipped because of the weight of her pompadour. The cameras clicked, gave off a puff of smoke, and recorded for posterity the fourth White House wedding of a president's daughter.[51] One photograph froze Alice in time between the two most important men in her life. She stood in the center, ramrod straight, hands at her sides. Her new husband was close to her on her right. To her left, Alice's father leaned away from the couple, jamming his hands into the pockets of his coat, unconnected from the event. Most photographs of the new bride showed her looking tired—her eyes are puffy—and just a tad overwhelmed by the morning's experiences. "I am told," Alice commented later, "I fluctuated between animation and grimness on my wedding day."[52]

After the picture taking, the parents of the newly married couple received guests in the Blue Room, as the bride and groom collected their intimate friends for a private wedding breakfast. The other invited guests gathered in the State Dining Room for a larger celebratory meal featuring heart- and wedding-bell-shaped sweets. The bride's cake was the source of one of the most talked-of episodes of the day. Finding that the knife provided by the caterer insufficient to cut the cake, Alice asked White House aide Major Charles McCauley if she might borrow his sword. Thus she cut the first piece with a flourish and handed it round.[53]

"The Brothers Immediate" of the Porcellian Club met in their time-honored send-off of one of their own to his married life. The other guests were startled to hear male voices singing the traditional club and school songs above the popping of champagne corks. The Porc allowed no one but members in good standing to enter the male sanctuary. While the Brothers toasted Nick and reminisced, Alice changed into her traveling dress and said private good-byes to her family. Edith's exhaustion showed. "Mother," Alice told her, "this has been quite the nicest wedding I'll ever have. I've never had so much fun." Edith leaned close to her and retorted, "I want you to know I am glad to see you leave. You have never been anything but trouble." Alice remembered that it was "quite fantastic. It just came out like that." She took it in stride. "'That's all right, Mother. I'll be back in a few weeks and you won't feel the same way.' And I was and she didn't. Well, I don't *think* she did." While it is true that Alice had been troublesome for

Edith, it is not true that she was only trouble. There was a great deal of warmth between the two women that would grow as Alice moved into adulthood. The tone is not unlike that used, even today, by many Eastern elites with their children in public. And, of course, Edith was exhausted. She confided to her diary that at the cabinet dinner three days later she was "so tired" she "nearly fainted."[54]

Nick and Alice began their secret exit around 4:00 p.m. Even though the day was chilly, hundreds of well-wishers remained on the White House grounds hoping to see the famous pair. The White House staff had planned the escape in elaborate detail. Rumors had been purposefully spread among the crowd as to which door the couple would use, and these were heightened when an automobile appeared at the West Gate on Executive Avenue. At the same time, another car drove up to the Southwest Gate. The anxious crowd divided in two, and as they were moving to surround the cars, a third auto slowed to a stop directly in front of the White House. Finally, completing the confusion, a fourth car appeared at the East Gate. Two of the four cars belonged to Nick. One at a time and in pairs the cars started their engines and honked to each other. Finally, Nick and Alice climbed out the window of the Red Room and onto the south portico of the White House, and one of the cars drove up to whisk the couple away. Friends and family members pelted Nick and Alice with rice (although Alice's youngest brothers switched to beans when they ran out of the traditional hymeneal token) as they raced away to their honeymoon. Their immediate destination was Friendship, the country estate of John R. McLean.

Alice Roosevelt became Mrs. Longworth on paper, but to journalists, photographers, and the average American citizen, she remained Princess Alice. Media coverage had extended to every facet of her life—clothing, schooling, friends, activities, family—and inevitably to the rite of passage that marked her adulthood. The last burst of media enthusiasm released Theodore and Edith from the compelling bonds of their daughter's turbulent lifestyle, just as it signaled Alice's final freedom from parental control. As Nick and Alice escaped to Friendship and their future, a journalist claimed the ultimate summation:

> After the wedding is over, Teddy
> And they sail on the honeymoon train,
> Then you can shoulder your big, big stick
> And get in the spotlight again.[55]

As a national event, the wedding of the First Daughter was a great success. The French, along with other nations, mused, "Doubtless our gallantry toward Miss Roosevelt will serve to knit closer the ties of friendship which unite us to the great republic." However, the *Journal des Debats* also recognized that while friends, the two countries still stood divided by cherished cultural norms. Jumping through a window was "novel...judged by French standards, for the irresolute women of our climate need under such circumstances the support of strong arms in which to be carried off. They do not know how to take themselves off...."[56] If Alice were irresolute, it was only about the quality of Nick's love. She might crave his attention, but Alice Lee Roosevelt Longworth possessed the inner strength to take herself off when Nick, in a sadly familiar and devastating move, would also abandon her.

Chapter 9

"Alice Is Married at Last"

THE PROMISE of spring in the air on their wedding day might have been an omen of good fortune for their marriage. It was too early to tell. The Roosevelt family prepared to enjoy life without the high-maintenance Princess Alice around while destitute Washington journalists cast about for a replacement for their best headline maker. The *New York Times* gave a weak effort with THE NEW BELLE OF THE WHITE HOUSE. Buried on page two of the magazine section, the article tried to drum up some interest in fourteen-year-old Ethel, an entirely nice girl who was celebrating, as younger sisters do, the fact that she could move into the big bedroom Alice vacated.

Ethel lacked Alice's penchant for notoriety, and the press, finding little newsworthy in the staid Cathedral School girl, soon returned to more fertile ground.

> Alice is married at last. The sod torn up in the scuffle has been replaced. The store teeth and suspender buttons and tufts of hair that marked the scene are gathered up.... The earth has resumed its course around the sun.... Ever since she debuted into society... there has been constant danger that she would stampede the cabinet with her poodle and pet garter snake or demoralize the senate with one of her skirt dances and acrobatic stunts. With proposals enough to paper her bedroom and suitors so thick on the steps that guests had to crawl in and out of the pantry window, she was fast becoming a menace to the Mormon church.... It rejoices me that Alice is wed. I trust it will settle her nerves.[1]

The editorial's epic tone was about right.

The *New York Evening Mail* theorized that "American men and women all look upon the President's daughter as in a sense their daughter, feeling 'a paternal solicitude for her future happiness.' " It had not been just a wedding, according to the *Philadelphia Press*. Alice and Nick did a national good deed: "The thoughts of countless young and single hearts have been turned toward the bliss of wedded life by this happy event.... For the number and kind of marriages in the land has more to do with the happiness and prosperity of the United States of America than the tariff, the Panama Canal, railway rate regulation or any other one of the big questions that engross the attention of the nation's lawmakers."

Others took a different tack. In the sensible heartland, the call was for normality. The *Springfield Republican* was glad that Alice was now "the wife of her husband," a fact rendering her "beyond the clutch of international diplomacy; the last camera shot is fired, and she becomes that finest of American figures... 'a regular woman.' "[2] Fans who had made her their hobby regretted the change in Alice's status. One wrote: "We who have watched Alice Roosevelt and learned to love her, think it as a great mistake in her leaving her Father until he was out of office, especially as there is no one left in the White House to take her place. How we shall miss her! Now she has dropped down the line into plain 'Mrs. Longworth.' "[3] That remained to be seen.

Meanwhile, the focus of this continuing attention had quietly slipped away to Friendship, the seventy-five-acre oasis of millionaires Ned and Evalyn Walsh McLean in northwest Washington. Secluded and luxurious, there were beautifully landscaped grounds for wandering, and a private golf course and swimming pool. This Eden served as Oyster Bay had for Alice Hathaway Lee and Theodore Roosevelt on their honeymoon. At Friendship the newlyweds could be alone together to discover the intimacies that chaperones and social conventions had postponed until the vows were exchanged. The kind McLeans took Bye's role and provided for the Longworths' every whim. Theodore Roosevelt had confided to his diary, of his 1880 honeymoon with Alice Lee, "our intense happiness is too sacred to be written about."[4] Their daughter likewise refused to divulge her thoughts on her own honeymoon, but she did save a letter she received at Friendship that must have desacralized their joy.

"You are without a doubt the happiest woman on earth today," the anonymous female writer began, continuing:

> I have thought so many times that I would not undeceive you....I believe you to be all that is honest and pure; therefore I do not believe that "Nick" told you before he led you to the altar that "he" is the "*Father* of a beautiful child, *our* child. *My* child." You are a wife but not a Mother, and could you know the intense love I bear the Father of my child you could not but know that it is *reciprocal*. Dear girl he *loves* me in a way in which he and you do not share that love, for *I* am the *Mother* of his child. Until three years ago he was contentent [*sic*] to remain away from everything pertaining to marriage, but Ambition seized him, he met you dear girl and decided to win you at any cost, for he had wealth a (small portion) and he desired "notoriety," which he has obtained at the sacrifice of his love. I lived in Washington where I frequently saw you together until he desired me to return to this city. He has made arrangements whereby I may travel and meet him when you start on your tour. He has liberally provided for us. I am not dependent. I have promised him not to reveal this for the love of him but think you should know the man you are to perhaps spend your young life with. Sometime *you* shall see *his* image and *likeness*— and then I will reveal to you *my* identity as I am far too heart-broken to say more.[5]

We can only speculate on the discussion that must have arisen in the wake of this shattering letter, and the hollowness Alice must have felt. No other such letter exists among Alice's papers. Why she saved this one is a mystery. Nick's Don Juan reputation was well known to Alice—and to everyone else in Washington—and so the letter may have been nothing more than the horrible act of an unbalanced mind. It is also possible that the author really was involved with Nick, and if so, her timing was cruel.

While the affair seems believable, one thing about it does not: the child. Rumors of Nick's philandering both before and after his marriage to Alice were regnant, but there was never a whisper of a child. Add to that the fact that Alice never became pregnant by Nick, and it is plausible to conclude that he was infertile. Of course, the tragedy for Alice is that she could not have realized that on her honeymoon when she was deeply in love with him. Unless Nick knew he was infertile because of some childhood illness or injury and told her so, that letter was a serpent in the garden. Whether this felt like abandonment or deceit, it planted more doubts in the very midst of what should have been a time of bliss. Alice thus never had Nick to lean upon, wholly and without reservation. If she somehow took the woman's allegations in stride, it was not long before Nick's attentions truly did stray, just as she had feared. In the same way that Eleanor Roosevelt had to depend upon her own strengths because of her parents' early deaths and her husband's infidelity, Alice was denied her last hope for a relationship based on unconditional love and shared trust. Mother, father, surrogate mother, and husband all abandoned her in real and profound ways. This last betrayal reinforced early lessons about self-reliance.

Alice could hardly have contemplated separation from Nick in the wake of the letter. What would her father, the president of the United States, have said, had his daughter backed out of the international event that was her wedding, only days after its conclusion? The wedding gifts weren't even all opened at that time. Alice had chosen her own bed, and in the stalwart Roosevelt tradition, she was doomed to lie in it. Or maybe she was so utterly in love with Nick that she, who herself had been the recipient of censure from the press and the public, convinced herself that the letter was a hoax. In this way Alice could preserve her sanity and allow her marriage to start off on the best possible footing.

Whichever it was, the Longworths carried on with their plans. They left amid the expected fanfare for the next phase of their honeymoon: a three-week trip to Cuba to see for themselves the site of TR's heroics during the 1898 Spanish-American War. The Cubans had presented Alice with her favorite wedding gift, her trademark pearl necklace, and she was delighted to say her thanks in person at the reception at Havana's Presidential Palace.[6] Support for America was strong but not shared by everyone. Nevertheless, the Longworths enjoyed the goodwill of all they encountered, especially "ancient Cuban Generals who came in with bouquets to tell the Lady that they had fought with her father," as Willard Straight observed.[7] He was there serving as secretary to their old friend Edward Morgan, then the U.S. minister to Cuba.

Straight had just been posted to Cuba and had the unenviable task of finding a suitable place for the Longworths to stay, once he discovered—in the week before they arrived—that no one had seen to it. Eventually, Straight located a house, but then had to equip it with everything from furniture to silverware and linens, hustling along those who told him, "*Mañana.*" Once the Longworths arrived there were "balls and many grand parties." "They killed off two on their first night here," Straight recounted to a friend, "one at the American Club and one at the Palace." He thought "it seemed to bore [Nick and Alice] to be by themselves for any length of time." Straight, always very affectionate toward Alice, may have seen what he wanted to see, or perhaps discord appeared because of Nick's roving eye or his trysts with the bottle.

In Cuba, the Longworths met the vacationing Florence and Warren Harding. Warren, the new lieutenant governor of Ohio, was a friend of Nick's, but the women did not know each other. It might have done Alice good to unburden herself to Mrs. Harding, who was the stoic victim of Warren's ongoing marital infidelity. Alice and Florence would be great friends for a time, both appreciating in the other their determined personalities, their mutual interest in astrology and the occult, and their shared position as political wives. While the friendship eventually unraveled, it began beside the blue Caribbean waters when both women were trying to relax, one after a wedding and the other after an electoral campaign.

En route to Santiago, the Longworths took "a nice leisurely train that stopped when Nick or Willard or Edward Morgan wanted to shave." On board, Straight noted, "we spent most of the day with our feet in the windows, Longworth and myself experimenting and attempting [creative concoctions] with whiskey, gin, vermouth and limes and sugar. It was a successful party." From there they took a boat trip to Daiquiri, where a ship's flags spelled out WELCOME HERE. It was, a military guide noted dryly, "a much more courteous reception than your father got when he landed there in 1898."[8] At Daiquiri, they mounted horses and rode along the "Rough Rider trail" to the site of TR's battlefield valor. Alice was unimpressed. The hills were "mildly sloping" and the whole scene seemed "on as small a scale as the war itself had been." The disappointment colored their trip back to Santiago and may have contributed to what Alice called a "heated argument" with Nick against the trunk of the Peace Tree that was, of course, captured by photographers.[9]

Alice was in for a cruel shock about her groom. Sometime during the honeymoon, she came upon Nick, "drunk and on the floor." She was "revolted." It was the first time she thought with any seriousness of Edith's warning about Nick, but by the time the two returned home the fight was forgotten, or at least put aside for the press.[10] The new husband called the trip "the most delightful I ever had . . . one of endless delight." The piece was notable less for Nick's superlatives than for the fact that Alice was not quoted (she "smiled her approval") and was referred to only as "Mrs. Longworth" or, by Nick, as "my wife."[11] Was her unusual reticence a result of travel weariness, Nick's dictum, or the work of a reporter schooled not to speak to wives when husbands were present? This curious silence began a pattern of Alice standing, or trying to stand, in Nick's shadow. It didn't last long. One journalist wondered whether "society is to have a princess royal" or whether "Mrs. Nicholas Longworth intend[s] to conform to the etiquette which applies to the wife of a junior member of Congress?"[12] Although she made a policy of not granting interviews, Alice's irrepressible nature and her wit—more brilliant than Nick's—made obscurity unthinkable.

First on her agenda, unpredictably, was family. "With the perversity of human nature," Alice recounted in her autobiography, "having become removed from them by marriage, I became aware of how delightful families are, of what good times they can have together. So, late every afternoon, I went over to see them for an hour or so between tea and dinner." She and Nick returned to Washington on March 4 and dined that noon with the president and the First Lady. Edith's diary that month is full of lunches with Alice, or Alice and Nick. Kermit joined them because, he acknowledged, "I can't imagine Sister as a stately married lady. . . ." Their father opined, "I think Sister is much improved by her marriage."[13]

Alice and Nick moved to 831 18th Street in Washington, which had been Susan Longworth's home.[14] Susan had taken up residence there with her son when he joined Congress so that she could be close to her darling "Nicky." She reluctantly returned to Rookwood in Cincinnati, loath to leave her son and her adopted city. A letter to her from a fan of her new daughter-in-law warned her against staying:

> We saw by the paper you were to make your home with her. This will be a great mistake as everyone likes to be head of the house, especially a bride likes to be alone with her husband without his mother. . . . More unhappy marriages have come from a man taking his wife to his mother's. It was bad enough for 'our Alice' to marry a man so much older than she without having an old lady always around.[15]

Susan's *harrumph* at the unsolicited polemic may be assumed.

Alice tried to settle into married life. This was not easy, as postwedding parties continued unabated, the desire to host gatherings of her own was strong, and tourists found their home an irresistible stop. "For awhile," Alice remembered, "I tried to have 'days at home,' but soon had to give them up, as they amounted to keeping open house for the passers-by. Sightseeing stages actually used to stop and let off their passengers, who would come in, wander around, have tea, and occasionally depart with a souvenir such as a doily or a small spoon."[16] Like Kermit, her friends wanted to see whether there were any changes in the new married Alice. One Sloper wrote, "You probably know all sorts of interesting things including 'how to be happy though married.' " Still, her friend charged, Alice had been seen at the horse races with a male friend. "Really Agile," ran the tongue-in-cheek sermon, "you are still as mad as ever I hear and bet quite recklessly. Don't you realize what a shocking example you are setting to your innocent little friends like me—and being at the races with Mr. Hitt! I was of course scandalized but have recovered in spite of the shock."[17]

Alice scandalized more than just old friends when she gave up the custom of calling. Calling was an institution in Washington where the roster of politicians and their wives changed every few years. Calling protocol was strict. Calls lasted usually less than thirty minutes. The one who was "at home" and receiving the calls ensconced herself in her drawing room and her butler or maid announced each new arrival. Callers sized each other up over their teacups and moved on. If someone was not at home, callers left their calling cards according to an elaborate system of particular corners folded down, which conveyed information about the caller. Given the central role of politics in daily life, social calls in the capital were unlike those anywhere else. Because politics is about power and calling is a custom in which the realities of power—social and political hierarchies, changing configurations of power, the identities of those with and those without political influence—are laid bare, the masks evident elsewhere are eliminated.[18]

"Virtuously," she thought, Alice began calling. But she came quickly to believe that "no sane human beings should let themselves in for" such an ordeal. This break with tradition caused gossip across the District. Cousin Eleanor was "appalled" by Alice's "independence and courage." One newspaper editorialized, "If young Mrs. Longworth takes the lead and flings these customs to the winds there will be great rejoicing in the Dupont circle contingent.... Hitherto in Washington officialdom has ruled with an iron rod.... Now, according to the dream of Mrs. Longworth, the statesmen must feel the power of social rank.... This will, of course, be an innovation and, no one except the daughter of the chief of the Executive would dare to start such an enterprise."[19]

Alice never looked back. One function of calling was to climb the social ladder. She was already at the top. Regardless of the job Nick held, Alice Roosevelt Longworth would always be a Roosevelt and the president's daughter (even when Theodore Roosevelt was no longer president; even when he was dead). She needed no acceptance from the cave dwellers (long-term residents in the capital city), for although she had not been born in Washington, she had lived there much of her life, and showed every sign of staying.

Alice was entering her political apprenticeship when discussions with her husband and her father gave her a serious interest in politics. Her desire for the story behind the political story, for the nuances of a political relationship, the journey of a bill in Congress, or the actions of a Supreme Court justice could not be satisfied by fifteen minutes of stilted and public conversation. Uniform calls failed to showcase her wit. She was the master of the personal. Time and time again acquaintances commented that she could best be understood in person, where the arched brow, the subtle display of the canine, the graceful motions of her hands, the trailing sentence, provided innuendo understood by an alert audience.

In May 1906, Alice had a chance to compare the Washington traditions she was overthrowing with Cincinnati's customs when she accompanied Nick to the music festival, "a somewhat formidable experience for one who is not musical," she recalled. Although she saw British composer Edward Elgar conduct his own work, she did not wax rhapsodic about the festival. She was pleased that she'd "weathered it fairly well." Nick took pity on her and whisked her away for a sanity break during an intermission. This backfired. They "returned very late," and, according to the *Cincinnati Enquirer,* the city's elite "frowned deeply."[20] It had not been her first trip to the Queen City, but it was her first time in Susan Longworth's home as the daughter-in-law. It was never an easy role for Alice. Nick's dutifully tender care of his mother made him into a different man in Cincinnati. Despite calling Susan "Mummy," he ruled the roost so sublimely that Alice referred to him as "the eagle." Her nickname for Susan—"Bromide"—encapsulated Alice's dismissal of her dull, conventional mother-in-law. "My conduct is pleasing in the eyes of the eagle," she penned sardonically. "Altogether thus far I have amused myself much for there is nothing like the joy of leading that little life of my own. . . . It is quite frantically entertaining—this business of getting both eagle and bromide to stand without twitching and feed from the hand. I fully expect them by the end of the week to be in strong leading string and quite house broken. The eagle suddenly became amenable (more so than the other—but it is more important that he should)."[21]

However, Alice's relationship with the Longworths would disintegrate until by 1912 they were barely speaking. Strongly held political differences, as well as more mundane disputes, would annihilate the initial sweetness of their encounters. Susan, at bottom, considered no woman good enough for her son. Alice accepted a fragment of the blame: "I was not...one who 'merged' with the family she married into; not by a long shot, I fear. Besides being an egotist, I was far too much one of my own family...."[22] But that was all in the future. By the end of the month, Alice and Nick were happily and haphazardly, Auntie Bye thought, embarking upon the final phase of their honeymoon.

Europe presented tremendous opportunities for the president's daughter and the Ohio representative. They were guests of Ambassador Whitelaw Reid at Dorchester House in London. "In confidence, strictly, [the Reids] told me," wrote Bye to Alice, "the King is to dine with them and when they spoke of your coming the King said he would come while you were there! He really is an old dear and how he would have loved you. It is well for Nick that he is old now," Bye said flatteringly.[23] The Reids planned for the Longworths to meet all the most brilliant people in Great Britain, and Alice looked forward to seeing family friends, too.

The European honeymoon was fraught with international implications. The same position of First Daughter that made King Edward VII want Alice for a dinner partner made her itinerary potential dynamite for U.S. foreign policy. President Roosevelt advised them that if they planned to visit Austria, they must also go to Budapest, "so that you shall not seem to ignore Hungary and pay heed only to Austria. If you go to Austria and Hungary I should avoid stopping either at Vienna or Budapest, or else I should stop at both; and if you do go...you and Nick listen smilingly to anything that any one from an Austrian archduke to a Hungarian count says about the politics of the dual empire, but, as I need hardly add, make no comment thereon yourselves."[24]

They sailed on June 1, 1906, on an American ship, the *St. Louis,* as "it was considered 'better politics,'" than sailing on a foreign-owned ship. Eight days later, they arrived at Victoria Station, London, to the acclaim of "a small crowd of well-behaved newspaper men." They were met by the Reids and taken to Dorchester House, where a much larger group and "a perfect battery of cameras" appeared. Then began a dizzying whirl of amusements among the British "smart set." Ambassador Reid wrote Edith in excruciating detail, including explanations of which princess was which and who the various duchesses and ladies "used to be."[25]

The long-awaited dinner with King Edward was on June 12 at the ambassador's residence. Alice was the first person presented to the king and made "her prettiest curtsey." She was seated by him at dinner and he "stayed much longer for the supper after the music than he had planned to do." The king was complimentary about Alice, who "enjoyed herself very much." The party was made up chiefly of Britons, "on the theory that Alice had come to England to see English people...." After this event, Roosevelt wrote his daughter, "I took sardonic pleasure in the fearful heartburnings caused the American colony in London, and especially among the American women who had married people of title, by the inability of the Reids to have everybody to everything. Nothing was more delightful than the fact that some of the people who were not asked to the dinner, but who were asked to the reception, hotly refused to attend the latter."[26] Cutting off one's nose to spite one's face elicited from TR, and from Alice, too, only the thinnest of sneers—especially when it concerned Americans who married into foreign aristocratic families.

The next night produced more evidence of Alice's celebrity. The Reids hosted a lavish reception—dinner and dancing—for eighteen hundred people at Dorchester House that Alice found "all so like the parties during the London season that one reads of...." America's Princess stood cheerfully in the receiving line. The ambassador and the king were pleased. An invitation to tea with the queen at Buckingham Palace arrived next. Alice remembered the occasion as "all very informal." Only the queen, Mrs. Reid, Alice, and a lady-in-waiting were present, until the queen of Greece arrived. Queen Alexandra was hard of hearing, but she carried on in a style any Roosevelt would admire, for "it didn't seem to worry her much. She kept up a fluttery irrelevant conversation." Alice, accustomed to fame, "felt very much at home with her...."[27]

Nick and Alice also found time to be tourists at Blenheim Palace and Covent Garden. They viewed a debate in the House of Lords and another in the House of Commons. Alice sat in the Speaker's gallery, and Nick saw the "procession with which the Speaker every day enters the House to open the proceedings." MP Sir John Henniker Heaton had them to tea on the terrace, a mixed blessing, Alice thought. "With the Houses of Parliament behind you and the Thames in front, and with half the men who govern England strolling about, it is a thing to remember. On this particular afternoon, however, it was as cold as Greenland. The tea was late in coming, we were all shivering, and would have given a good deal to be comfortably inside instead of romantically on the terrace."[28]

Because they were more than tourists, the Longworths also lunched with the Speaker of the House of Commons, had tea with the Duchess of Albany, and were the guests at a gathering where Lord Curzon spoke. George N. Curzon, author and statesman, had returned recently from India and his controversial partitioning of Bengal, and was about to become chancellor of Oxford University. Lady Curzon, whose Washington wedding had awed Alice as a child, glimmered in Alice's memory. One of the events Ambassador Reid tried to decline—the luncheon for three hundred members of the Society of American Women in London—turned out to be "really rather agreeable." Reid had been outmaneuvered by the society's president, who asked Nick to speak, which he did "with dignity and grace."

The remainder of the day would have tried the endurance of a professional athlete. From tea the ladies went to dinner, while Ambassador Reid and Representative Longworth attended the official Foreign Office dinner in honor of King Edward's birthday. The women intended to rejoin the men for the after-dinner reception, but were literally carried away by the crush. Finally, in "the small room where the supper for the Royalties and the Ambassadors was laid," they found each other again. After "a rather weary time struggling with the crowd to get hats and overcoats," they went on to "an early ball" at the home of the Duke and Duchess of Devonshire. This was to begin with a supper, but none of them could find room for it. Instead they left after thirty minutes for the Duchess of Westminster's. Alice danced at the insistence of her host, but she resisted the offer of yet another supper.

While Alice enjoyed mingling with so many different people, she was particularly thrilled by lunching with the king at his Ascot pavilion because she sat next to Archibald Phillip Primrose, the Fifth Earl of Rosebery. She thought him "one of the most brilliant and engaging figures in English political life." As she had read many of his books, mostly historical monographs, she was intensely interested in him. Lord Rosebery had been foreign secretary under Gladstone, whom he had replaced as prime minister. His service was short-lived, and his transformation from statesman to author was complete by the time the Longworths met him. But as an aristocrat of long bloodline, he commanded respect, and the luncheon was notable for the presence of "half a dozen Royalties."

Throughout the continuous rounds of official duties, Alice, according to Mrs. Reid, "has really had an enormous success and people everywhere have been charmed with her. Her natural frank manner and quickness of repartee please everyone." Nick also met with approval: "We all like Mr. Longworth so much too and the men feel he has such clear views about the questions at home and discusses them so well."[29]

The only unfavorable press came from American newspapers as they reported what can best be described as the knee-breeches flap. Some felt Representative Longworth had acted undemocratically when he wore knee breeches for his formal court presentation. The Longworths felt that wearing such attire was "of no more consequence" than "taking off one's shoes when one goes into a temple in Japan." In fact, they thought it "a mere matter of manners." And, as Alice pointed out, Nick had worn his breeches before the king at their first meeting, the dinner on the twelfth. Yet something about Americans bowing to the head of another country, especially the old Mother country, smacked of injudicious toadying. Alice, properly attired in her wedding dress, escaped journalistic censure. On every other subject, though, the American press praised the couple. "I don't care what the foreign papers say about Alice," Edith confided to Belle Hagner at home, "as long as the American papers continue to behave as they are doing."[30]

Among the private joys of their time in England was their introduction to English country life at Wrest Park, the Reids' country home in Bedfordshire. It was Alice's first encounter with the legendary peacefulness of the English countryside. A large number of congenial people gathered, including Delancey Jay, Katherine Barney, Ogden Mills, Gladys Vanderbilt, and the Reids' friend famous cricketer F. G. Menzies. The weekend whiled happily away in bridge, golf, lawn tennis, "automobiling," and some church-going on Sunday.

On the twenty-second, the Longworths moved on to Germany to pay their respects to King Edward's nephew, Kaiser Wilhelm, and to watch some yacht racing. The dinner on board the kaiser's ship, the *Hamburg*, was entertaining. The kaiser was a good host, asking many questions about their journeys and their concerns for the United States. Alice, an astute judge of character, drew a comparison between the two leaders: "King Edward had great dignity and impressed one as having reserves of strength that would always be there when the occasion called. The Kaiser, though one could not say that he was undignified, was restless, loquacious; he would take up a subject, rattle it about, express an arbitrary opinion that he appeared to think disposed of it, and then go on to something else. Yet it is stimulating and amusing to talk with that sort of character."[31]

The Longworths returned briefly to London for another ball before starting for Paris, where, according to the local newspapers, they were "everywhere welcomed with genuine sympathy. The congenial couple have elicited what in France is called excellent *'presse.'* Their portraits in straw hats and travelling attire are a feature of the front pages of over a dozen morning papers." Their hosts in France were Ambassador Robert McCormick and his wife, Katherine Medill McCormick. The McCormicks were great collectors of European art and first editions of French literature. They were also the parents of Medill and Robert. The former would go on to the U.S. Senate, while the latter would become the formidable "Colonel" McCormick, owner and publisher of the *Chicago Tribune*. Alice had once viewed Bert McCormick with an eye to engagement. All that was in the past, and as the ambassador and his wife met the Longworths, the newspapers raced to describe the visiting dignitary: "Mme. Longworth, with the grace of a true Parisienne, gave a nervous shake to her skirt, [and] adjusted her straw hat, tipped to the front according to the latest fashion.

There was no trace of fatigue on her bright, fresh face as she daintily alighted to the platform. She is exceedingly captivating," the *Petit Parisien* enthused. "Her countenance has an expression of graceful refinement, blended with shrewd, sly, good natured humor, and her attractive face finds a delightful framework in her luxurious locks of blonde hair."[32] And Monsieur Longworth? He was not mentioned.

Official gatherings were interspersed with visits to Nick's family in Paris, with dress shopping at Worth's and sightseeing at Versailles and Rochefort. Nick's sister Clara and brother-in-law Adelbert de Chambrun ("dear Charly's" brother) joined them for dinner at the Elysée Palace, hosted by French president Armand Fallieres. Alice sat between Fallieres and Georges Clemenceau, then minister of the interior. She enjoyed Clemenceau, who regaled her with stories of his youth in America. Clara remembered the couple being "taken up as the latest novelty by the 'Monde Chic,' just as they had been in London."[33]

There followed a leisurely trip to Bayreuth. This was Nick's week of the honeymoon, a pilgrimage stop for many music lovers then and now. Bayreuth, located in southeastern Germany, was the result of composer Richard Wagner's dream to unify Germany by showcasing its art. In the 1870s, Wagner oversaw the creation of a festival and the construction of a *festspielhaus* to replace the crumbling eighteenth-century baroque opera house built by German royalty. While Wagner's theater and its special effects were absorbing, the real draw was the music. It fed Nick's soul, but Alice found the sixteen-hour Ring Cycle "something in the nature of an endurance test." At least she could amuse herself with the many Americans present, some of whom were presumably just as bored as she.[34]

After viewing the medieval cities of Nuremberg and Munich, the Longworths returned to Paris to stay once more with Nick's sister Clara and her husband. Relations between the two couples would never be perfectly close, because Clara, like all the Longworth women, found Nick's marriage to Alice incomprehensible. No woman would be good enough for Nick, but the jejune First Daughter seemed an odd match for her distinguished brother. Impeccable manners triumphed on the honeymoon tour, however, and Alice and Nick contentedly played tourist in the Bois de Boulogne and the Champs-Elysée, seeing French theater and sampling local cuisine. At one café, Alice recalled, the patrons were engaged in the disconcerting pastime of "singing a song with rather ribald verses about the King of Spain's marriage and about ours."[35]

As July wound down, the two prepared to depart. Willard Straight wrote from Cuba asking Alice to meet him in New York, for fear he wouldn't see her for a long time. "The days of the Daiquiri are numbered and I am pulling out of this station very shortly," he informed her. President Roosevelt had helped transfer Straight to China, a larger field for his talents. Straight teased that he wanted to greet Alice upon her return "bearing liquor, lacquer and lunacy—which is an ode still incipient." He knew to make prior arrangements because "it would be a hopeless thing to try and break the cordon of secret police. I might simply want to offer you a nosegay and I'd be arrested as an anarchist with a little bunch of greenhouse bombs."[36] His charming offer was probably refused, if only because the Longworths were not lingering in New York City. They planned to collapse temporarily at Sagamore Hill for a debriefing from President Roosevelt.

The couple also needed time to sort out some problems. Perhaps Nick was bothered by the intimate nature of Straight's note or his wife's inability to appreciate Wagnerian opera. Maybe there had been a heated discussion about the fact that Alice was not pregnant, as so many Americans, the chief executive especially, hoped. Theodore Roosevelt had been "delighted" to learn of the birth of his niece Eleanor's baby, and shared the national disappointment over the absence of similar news from his daughter. Maybe Alice and Nick disagreed about his political future, as the headlines from home were reading LONGWORTH FOR GOVERNOR, a position Alice never really desired for him—or her.[37] Or more likely Nick had overindulged in alcohol or flirting—the two often went together with him—causing Alice's withdrawal.

Whatever its exact nature, some cloud had darkened their honeymoon sky, and the *St. Paul*'s passengers eagerly tattled about the couple's apparent estrangement to the ubiquitous journalists: LONGWORTHS IN SILENT MOOD ON VOYAGE HOME: DINED ALONE AND SPOKE TO ONLY THREE PERSONS the headline read. Their shipmates "confessed...that the President's daughter and her husband, who were naturally enough quite tired from the strain of nine steady weeks of going about, were somewhat of a social disappointment....Mrs. Longworth looked tired and even angry when she came aboard at Cherbourg....Mr. Longworth also participated in this silent mood, and for three days the bride and bridegroom were not seen or heard to address one word to each other. They sat on deck passing the time, each with a book." Only the steerage passengers, who presumably had not seen much of the Longworths, cheered when the couple disembarked.[38]

The Roosevelts met Alice and Nick at the docks nearest to Sagamore Hill. After a brief respite in the bosom of the family, the still-smarting Alice retreated to Newport, where she would often go for surcease from pain caused by Nick's drinking. Alice amused friends there with tales of her European exploits and willed away the hurt.[39] Nick went to his mother's home, ready to meet with labor leaders who were courting him.

Politics called. The Longworths needed to present a united front for the voters in Ohio, which is where the leader of the Republican Party suggested they go posthaste. "Tell Nick," TR wrote Alice in a letter full of fatherly advice, "I think his people will like to feel that you have a genuine interest in the city and come out there to make yourself one of Nick's people."[40] And eventually to Cincinnati went the president's daughter and her husband. Marriage and honeymoon had changed neither Nick nor Alice. He remained true to the bottle and happy in the company of other women, while she learned anew the virtues of self-reliance. Alice, at age twenty-three, loved Nick, but she wore her wariness like a protective shield.

Chapter 10

"Mighty Pleased with My Daughter and Her Husband"

WHEN ALICE AND NICK appeared at Oyster Bay "full of all sorts of amusing stories" from Europe, it was time to plot election strategy and for Nick and Alice to put their divisions aside. TR found no evidence that the glamorous European honeymoon had "hurt Nick at home," but warned them that Nick's opponents "will do all they can to make it injure him." Representative Longworth's first job was to reconnect with the Republican Party.[1]

Alice really wanted to return to Washington while she was still the president's daughter. But taking TR's advice, the Longworths made their obligatory trip to Nick's Ohio district, after visiting Sagamore for political and psychological sustenance. "Sister has improved an awful lot," Ethel confided to Belle after seeing Alice, "and I think that Nick has too. They are perfectly sweet together. Sister simply worships him."[2] The whole family agreed.

The Longworths were the picture of contentment upon their return to Rookwood. Met by reporters who wondered about Princess Alice's plans, she laughingly told them, "I would willingly try to assist my husband to return to Congress if he would allow me to do so." While Alice was young and devoted to Nick, she enjoyed Cincinnati—to a point. As Ethel put it, "Sister loves Cincinnati, but is a little ashamed to love it too much, I think." Alice herself allowed, "I never stayed very long at a time in Cincinnati in those days. I should say I went East on an average of two or three times a month, to stay at Sagamore, or at Newport with Grace Vanderbilt, and always to visit Auntie Bye at Farmington."[3] When she left, it was solo. Nick stayed at Rookwood with his mother. Alice was as ambivalent about Susan Longworth as she was about Cincinnati.

Bucolic and peaceful, the Queen City also had an unctuous side, covering the predictably vicious politics of an important town in an important state. In that year's election the labor vote was testy and demanding of both parties. Nick had told Alice about how he had been "made sick" in 1905 by the "nasty mud-slinging campaign in Ohio," and how "conditions were such that I couldn't bring myself to speak for the whole ticket." In that year, he was "heartily glad" to see that "the old order of things has definitely ceased and [political boss] George Cox has definitely retired from politics." Nick's assessment of Cox would prove to be premature. While it wasn't on a national scope like her father's political scene, Alice found that learning about the history of Ohio politics and who supported Nick and why could be moderately diverting.[4]

In September, the Longworths' visit to Columbus caused a stampede that nearly cost them their lives. Alice tried to unveil a statue of Ohio's martyred hero William McKinley on the Capitol grounds. Local authorities lost control of the crowd, numbering more than fifty thousand, and two people were taken away in an ambulance. Others fainted in the squeeze. In an effort to stave off pandemonium, Alice pulled the ribbons to unmask McKinley's statue early. As she did so, the streamers were quickly seized by souvenir seekers. The crowd dashed forward and the Longworths escaped through a window behind them into the governor's office. They tried to fight their way into a waiting car but failed, and bolted themselves behind the door of a nearby office building. There they stayed until the police came to extricate them. "It was the worst crush I ever witnessed," Alice said to reporters. She told them she had been "terrified" and had "seen nothing like it in my trip around the world." However, she confessed to her hosts privately that "it was the most exciting experience of my life," confirming that Alice knew precisely what the press wanted a well-brought-up young woman to feel in the middle of a raging crowd—and it wasn't excitement. After reading the frightening newspaper reports, Edith wrote her daughter that she "felt it was a bad day for Roosevelts when I saw that you had had to steal out of town as if you were escaping from a lynch mob."[5] That's one time it was a relief to board the train for Cincinnati.

It was an even greater relief to learn that Nick had been renominated for Congress without opposition, despite rumors of his break with the weakened but not powerless George Cox, and the frustration of labor union members who knew Nick was not their friend. Nick's acceptance speech made Alice happy. "Stripped of all unnecessary verbiage," Nick declared, putting the unions in their place, "the issue in this campaign is plain and clear—stick by Roosevelt.... Upon questions of party policy, I am first, last, and all the time a follower of President Roosevelt. Not because he is my friend and counselor in many things; not because we are of near family connection; not because of my admiration for him as a man, but because upon great, public questions I believe that he is right, and because I believe that by following his leadership I shall be doing that which is right."[6]

The campaign officially opened on October 7 in Cincinnati, and Alice arrived early to the kickoff. She was met with a standing ovation. She bowed and waved to Nick, who returned her smile from his place on the platform. Throughout the campaign season, her presence swelled the size of crowds that came to hear him and see her. Alice sat on platforms while Nick spoke; they shook hands all over the district. She opened the Cincinnati fall festival. In Marietta, she laid a cornerstone while her father's vice president, Charles Fairbanks, spoke. Alice left nothing to chance in the 1906 election, hiring a spiritualist to provide her with an "occult formula" to guarantee Nick's victory. It was her first campaign with Nick, his first attempt at reelection since their marriage. Her popularity was "Longworth's strength," and she wanted to be a useful campaigner.[7]

Their victory was sweet. The press recognized their partnership: "Mrs. Longworth is the great issue in her husband's campaign. She accompanies him to his political meetings, and probably makes more votes by her presence than he does by his oratory." Even Edith had to admit, "You must have enjoyed campaigning. I used to love to go with Father, and the papers have said such really nice things." Then, from her father, the note that crowned her efforts with glory: "Let me congratulate you and Nick with all my heart upon the successful way in which both of you have run your campaign. I tell you I felt mighty pleased with my daughter and her husband...." Edith, too, wrote with praise: "Last night they put on one of the bulletin boards here [at the White House] 'Alice and Nick have won' and the crowd called out 'Hurrah for them both.' "[8] Nineteen hundred six also propelled another interesting man into office: William E. Borah was elected to the U.S. Senate from Idaho.

After the victory parties were over, Alice and Nick, violin and the dog, Manchu, in tow, headed to Oldgate, Auntie Bye's Connecticut home. Although Bye worried about the dearth of excitement there, she had nonetheless pelted Alice with invitations in the weeks after the honeymoon. Bye hoped the visit would wash away the muck of the campaign, as they gave her all the latest election news. Of course, Bye was never really out of the loop. The more political of TR's sisters, Bye kept in close touch with him, even when she was away from D.C. It was to her house the president went to relax. Her circle of acquaintances was wide. She considered her friend (and nephew) Joseph W. Alsop's successful race for the Connecticut senate "preliminary steps" to national prominence. She placed great faith in Alsop's prediction that Nick's seat was secure because of Alice. "I cannot begin to say how empty the house seems without you and Nick," Bye wrote plaintively to her favorite niece after a November visit.[9]

In the middle of the campaign Alice had received, through a diplomatic pouch, a letter from Willard Straight. He wrote from Russia, where he was a warfront correspondent with Reuters and the Associated Press. Straight sent details about the events since Bloody Sunday, January 22, 1905, when the czar's troops had opened fire on starving workers protesting the despotism that caused their hunger. Straight chronicled a government attempting to implement civil reforms. The anger of the peasants still simmered, he wrote, and it was "open season for Czars and policemen." His letter described the terrible conditions of the peasantry, the amazing differences between Russia and the Europe of Alice's honeymoon, and some memorable characters he encountered. "You who are fond of the game would love it here. Servants are accepted universally as spies. At the Embassy they keep all secret codes...in a time lock safe...." Russia was quiet, and

"Warsaw is the storm center at present—but there are constant uprisings and burnings in the provinces." Straight was right; Alice was fond of the game—and fonder still of those who played it wittily and well. His conclusion and his postscript are intimate, suggestive, but inconclusive: "For the rest—all that need not be said—you know. Thief. For which I am very glad." A postscript introduced an acquaintance to her who was on his way to Washington: "I like that he will have a chance to see something of you. It is a very wonderful world this in which we live—isn't it?"[10] Alice's difficulties with Nick were tempered by a long-distance flirtation with the up-and-coming Straight.

Nick, meanwhile, was dealing with the effects of having wed a hobbled heiress. He learned that Alice, while moderately wealthy, did not have access to all of her mother's legacy. A series of letters from Grandpa Lee to Nick made plain the older man hoped Nick would oversee his willful granddaughter's finances. "There is not much use in writing to Alice about it, as her knowledge regarding money and property is limited to the quickest method of 'blowing' it in, so I leave it to you to talk the matter over with her." He suggested that her property be held in trust for her, realizing that "the income from this property, say $2500 more or less, and the $2000 which I allow her are all her present income...."[11]

Alice received a $500 allowance from Grandpa Lee quarterly, and occasional income from her Boston property. She never ceased wanting more, as her grandfather well knew. "I am," he wrote her sadly, "aware that if you have any monies...you are very uneasy till you start it into circulation." Alice grew increasingly conscious of her poverty compared with her wealthy friends, especially Evalyn Walsh McLean, eventual owner of the Hope diamond. Grandpa Lee also controlled stocks and bonds for Alice, but he called them "local securities." She asked him to send the "money" to her, which made Lee remonstrate with her. While he professed to be happy to be "relieved of all contingencies regarding the investments," he also wrote that neither she nor Nick "would know anything about them." "If you elect to have the money," he cautioned, "you must not invest it except with the sanction of Nick and under his advice. Don't undertake to speculate unless your advisor will assume all loss. Women generally lose every cent, playing that game. You let it alone." And, he commanded, "Show this to Nick." In the end, the decision was made to sell some of the stocks (Massachusetts Gas Company and American Telephone and Telegraph) in order to send her $8,000 in May, leaving $515.55 in her account.[12] It isn't clear what she wanted the $8,000 for, or exactly how much remained of the stocks, which Lee continued to oversee.

Since Alice's funds were so tightly controlled, very little went to charity. Alice frequently received letters asking for money from people from all over the world, and as the veracity of such cases was difficult to establish, she generally did not respond. Alice felt that she could ill afford to be lavish in her giving. Beyond Nick's salary as a representative he had his own dwindling fortune, which he spent lavishly on clothing, food, drink, and his club life. In 1906, there was still a certain amount of money. But already, as Alice noted, "Nick was not sufficiently well-off to keep up more than the house in Washington."[13] Worsening financial troubles were still in the future.

For the moment, there was the start of the new House session and the holiday with her family. Alice sat up in the executive gallery for the opening of the House of Representatives on December 3, taking it all in and watching Nick below her reacquaint himself with his colleagues. She received alongside Edith at the annual diplomatic reception. "I think that I saw more of the family during the three winters after I was married...than I did during the entire time that went before. During the five winters in Washington that I was grown up, I spent much time seeing my friends in less stiff surroundings than the White House provided. I had no sitting-room of my own....So I used to meet them at their own houses or at my aunt's....But as soon as I had a house of my own, I began to realize that I had a particularly pleasant family."[14] And her marriage to Nick was not the refuge she had hoped it would be.

The relationship between Alice and her parents improved. While visiting the White House, Alice holed up with Edith, the three youngest children popping in. Theodore Roosevelt joined them frequently to "talk about the people he had been seeing during the day, the public questions that were up, or [to] discuss...latest news of the boys from school...my activities in the world of 'society,' people and things generally." Alice usually stayed until "the last possible moment" and then rushed home to dress for dinner. At least the family no longer reproached her for ignoring them.[15]

Nick's first Christmas as a member of the family was "ideal," TR proclaimed to his sister Corinne. He "joined easily and naturally in every detail of the celebration," the president reported, including the traditional stocking opening in TR and Edith's bedroom. Alice, he thought, "enjoyed it... more than she has any Christmas since our last one at Sagamore six years ago—for this is our sixth Christmas in the White House." The holiday celebration continued as the entire family went to the German embassy to exchange presents with the Baroness and Ambassador Speck von Sternburg, old family friends.[16]

The question on everyone's mind that holiday was who would succeed TR when his term expired. Roosevelt desperately wanted to stay in office another four years, but he had announced at his 1904 election that he would serve only two terms—the remainder of McKinley's and his own. He regretted having made such a promise, but he had to keep it. The press considered Nick an inside source since he was both the son-in-law of the president and a good friend of Republican front-runner and fellow Buckeye William Taft. Nick took his cue from his father-in-law and reiterated to reporters that TR would not run again, no matter how much he might personally desire it.

While Alice stuck close to the family, Nick was glum about his failure in the House to procure higher pay for U.S. diplomats. Success in that endeavor was still some years in the future. In February, Nick had more bad news: Roosevelt was set to appoint an African-American man named Ralph Tyler to be customs surveyor at the Port of Cincinnati—a thing Nick's constituents told him in no uncertain terms that they deplored. Nick was "at the White House three times a day pleading desperately with an Exalted Personage to keep Ralph Tyler away from Cincinnati so that the son-in-law can continue to come from there." Some solace returned in the celebration of his first wedding anniversary, but even more when Roosevelt eventually selected someone other than Mr. Tyler.[17]

After Easter, the Longworths returned to Cincinnati. Alice interpreted the local scene for her father as the "Taft movement" got off the ground. Despite whispers of a third-term draft for TR, Nick publicly announced his support for his friend Taft. That instantly made him an enemy of Taft's opponent for the Republican presidential nomination, Joseph B. Foraker, and simultaneously angered Boss Cox by his coming out for Taft before Cox wanted him to. Nick was carefully quoted as saying, "Personally—and speaking only for myself—I am for Taft for president."[18] Alice was well-enough schooled in politics to know that an attempt by her father in 1908 was not in his best interests. At least she knew that intellectually.

Alice escaped to see her Lee grandparents in Boston and to visit everyone in Washington. That spring, she frequented Benning racetrack near Washington. She was the society headliner and often in the company of wealthy brothers Perry and August Belmont, the first a former Democratic congressman and the latter an investment banker and racehorse owner. The absence made Nick's heart grow fonder. "Darling little Bubby," he wrote in May: "I've just gotten back from the Pillars where I had a very quiet and respectable evening playing bridge. . . . And now I am about to go to my lonely beddy without my sweetest bubby to put her head on his shoulder. I've missed you all day my darling, and I'm going to miss you more tonight."[19]

Some Cincinnati friends joined the Longworths on a two-day drive to the Kentucky Derby, where the crowd greeted Alice with "an ovation of hand clapping, waving handkerchiefs and cheers." Local reporters were uncharacteristically sensitive: "It must be awful to be a President's daughter and not be able to draw a natural breath without an extra being published about it. And the great mass of people expect a celebrity to do something unusual every minute of her life, so the calm, 'jelly regular, splendidly null,' perfectly bred conduct of the lady of the day yesterday came as a great blow to the populace, who would have preferred having her do some interesting stunts."[20]

As the summer heated up, Nick and Alice returned to Hawaii. Their last visit had been in 1905 as part of the congressional junket. Then they had spent barely a day on the main island, "Just enough to whet my appetite," Alice recalled. On the way, the couple luxuriated in a five-week western holiday—after a setback. Alice fell headfirst into the red, oozing muck in Yellowstone. Nick, "instead of displaying his customary gallantry," doubled over in "a most provoking laugh." Friends took Alice to the hotel to wash off the sticky clay; Nick "preferred admiring the scenery to facing his wife's pique." After visiting San Francisco, the couple considered exploring Alaska. But the siren call of Honolulu could not be denied.[21]

They stayed in a cottage at Waikiki, swam daily, feasted on Hawaiian delicacies, and were shown the sights by friends and local elites. On Maui, the breathtakingly beautiful Haleakala, which rises straight out of the sea to jab upward toward the heavens, made her feel "like a rather vigorous lotus eater," right out of Tennyson's poem. They rode horseback up a volcanic mountain at midnight, reaching the edge of the crater just as the sun did. They spent the next two days ambling down the mountain and along the cliffs above the coastline, interrupted only by well-wishers who greeted them with leis. Their exploration ended with a luau in the Iao Valley, its lush vegetation and peaceful stream hiding the memory of the fierce battle won there by King Kamehameha.

Alice was enthralled by the entire Hawaiian experience, as she told a friend in a wistful letter: "We had the most delicious time this summer in Honolulu—Living in a frivolous cottage in a palm grove beside a marvelous ocean. Quantities of...human beings ready for anything at any moment and the most wonderful riding and bathing you can imagine. I hated to leave and I am homesick for it the whole time." It was not all sight-seeing, for they greeted five thousand people at a reception hosted by Governor George R. Carter. For that duty, they were reunited with the secretary of commerce and labor, Oscar Straus, who had sailed to Hawaii on their ship. Straus told reporters that Alice "charmed everyone who met her," and she was styled "Mrs. Longworth, Woman Diplomat."[22]

Election activities accelerated throughout the fall, as did election rumors. Nick was variously mentioned as Ohio's next governor and its next senator, as Cincinnati's next mayor, and as America's next ambassador to Germany. Meanwhile, TR embarked on a speaking campaign through the Midwest, down the Mississippi River, and then south through Tennessee, Louisiana, and Arkansas. Edith sent her daughter an advance copy of the president's schedule with instructions not to show it to anyone, so that Alice could plan to meet TR in Canton, Ohio.

President Roosevelt's popularity was so great that he was able to hand-pick his successor in the White House, and after some deliberation, chose William Howard Taft. Taft, from Nick's congressional district in Cincinnati, had been a family friend of both the Longworths and the Roosevelts for years. Taft had served in various capacities in TR's administration, including governor-general of the Philippines and secretary of war. Taft idolized Roosevelt but was not, as TR deluded himself, an exact political duplicate. On the eve of the 1908 presidential election, the two friends lived in a mutual admiration society. In fact, the only real critics of the transition from TR to Taft were Alice—who hated to see the family vacate the White House—and Helen Herron Taft. Mrs. Taft had an abiding suspicion of the charismatic Theodore Roosevelt, and found fault all through the 1908 campaign. She thought that TR should have announced for Taft earlier than he did and could be warmer in his public appeals. Helen Taft's misgivings began a sad series of events that led to the breakup of the Taft-Roosevelt friendship and TR's ultimate challenge of Taft's incumbency four years later.

Alice and Nick traveled between Washington and Cincinnati all fall, gathering information, tracking the campaign, and keeping an eye on Nick's district until Alice came down with appendicitis. For several months she had suffered mysterious on-again, off-again pains, the "mulligrubs," as she called them. At Nick's insistence, she reluctantly missed her grandparents' golden wedding anniversary. She had to have her "appendix plundered," as she put it to her friend Eleanora Sears. Assisting the physician on the appendectomy was Dr. Sophie Nordhoff-Jung, who would become Alice's most trusted doctor. Alice holed up in the White House for the surgery. The rooms were larger and more comfortable than any hospital. Edith could shield her from the prying eyes of the media. The chance to be within the circle of the family again was too much to pass up. Nick wrote his mother that during Alice's surgery "the President and I sat hand in hand, so to speak, in the library and heard the reports."[23]

Surgery was not taken lightly in 1907. Auntie Bye's tender letter from

Connecticut made clear her own feelings: "My darling big girl, I hate you to have had even a threatening of appendicitis and not to have been near to look in. Sweetheart you are so far from me that my heart often has a sore spot at not seeing you, and you never forget, do you dearie that the old Aunt is always ready to fly to you literally at any moment were you ailing and needing me."[24]

The greatest benefit of convalescing in the White House was being close to the hub of the political news. Alice cooked up a plan with her father to attempt to discover what the phlegmatic Mr. Taft intended for the subject of a critical speech, his first upon his return from the Philippines. Alice and the president hoped for a real curtain-raiser, a speech to galvanize and unify Republicans. The two men came to Alice's room, where Taft found TR's energy overwhelming. "Finally," Alice recalled, "I propounded my question. I can see the Secretary, perfectly enormous, sitting in a solid wing chair, his hands clasped on his middle, saying with a slow rumbling chuckle, 'Well, I thought I would talk about the Philippines,' whereat there was a roar of protest and ironic mirth from Father and me. Indeed I was so emphatic that one of the stitches in my scar broke."[25]

The Christmas holiday barely interrupted politics. Nick's best present came in mid-December from Speaker of the House Joseph Cannon: appointment to the powerful Ways and Means Committee. Nick wrote his "Dearest Mummy" that he had been "having a very busy time quite different from what I had expected after election when I thought I was entitled to a good loaf. But the Fates have decreed that I am to sit practically every day ... with the Ways and Means committee from 9:30 in the morning until 5:00 in the afternoon absorbing facts and figures about the most abstruse and difficult subjects before congress nevertheless it is most interesting and I am enjoying it."[26]

Amid the celebration, there was time to see to the important niceties of life that Alice often found so easy to ignore. "Thank you most deeply for your thought to send me the joyful tidings of the birth of your blessed Baby boy! ... and a very merry Christmas to you both and the two little ones" she wrote to Franklin and "Eleanor-dear."[27] Everyone enjoyed the traditional Christmas at the White House. Alice, Nick, and the other children came in to TR and Edith's room on Christmas morning and opened their stockings. After breakfast came a tableful of presents for each child, then a three-hour horseback ride for some members of the family—but not Alice, lest she pop another stitch.

That January was the start of the last full year of Roosevelt's presidency. He fought more and more frequently with congressmen who felt his protection of the "poor, ignorant, and turbulent" was at the expense of businesses he believed went too far in their search for profit. The beginning of a rift within the Republican Party could also be seen in debates over the tariff, a complicated bill guaranteed to alienate as many members as it would please. TR had managed to avoid it for seven years. By the time the GOP had committed itself to a review of the current tariff, the progressive half of the party favored increasing it, and the conservative half preferred the status quo. While the tariff would be left to TR's successor, other bills would be seen as anticorporation—such as the Pure Food and Drug Act and the meat inspection rider—and would push conservative Republicans to back Taft. The quarrelling in Congress occurred during a brief economic downturn that had all Americans, even wealthy bankers such as Grandpa Lee, "hoping for better times."[28]

Better times, for Alice and her family, were not on the immediate horizon. They shared an overwhelming sadness at leaving the White House. Fame was wearing but addictive. Even the youngest among them understood its value. Alice confessed that "no one will ever know how much I wished, in the black depths of my heart, that 'something would happen' and that Father would be renominated. It was against human nature, against mine anyway, not to feel that the prospect of all those great times coming to an end was something to be regretted, though most secretly." One of Franklin Roosevelt's favorite stories, told by his "Uncle Teddy," was TR's response when pressed to run for the third term: "They are sick of looking at my grin and they are sick of hearing what Alice had for breakfast."[29]

The winter provided political interest, but everyone agreed that Taft was certain to be nominated—unless TR changed his mind. In Taft's own state of Ohio, during a civic celebration in the tiny town of Norwood, the spontaneous applause at the mention of Roosevelt's name went on so long that it disrupted the speaker's address. Nick defended Theodore Roosevelt frequently and publicly. Thanks in part to his marriage to the First Daughter, he, too, seemed certain to maintain his House seat. He was rewarded when delegates to Ohio's Republican convention in early March lauded Roosevelt but voted for hometown favorite Will Taft as the party's next standard-bearer.[30]

Alice tried a different form of public activity that year when Ruth Hanna McCormick become the national director of the Women's Committee of the National Civic Federation (NCF) in May. Since TR had forced her to attend Ruth's wedding to Medill McCormick, Alice and Ruth had become lifelong best friends. Ruth's father was the first president of the NCF, founded by wealthy businessmen in 1900 to promote harmonious relations between labor and capital. Prominent women joined the cause. Because of Marcus Hanna's position, his daughter, who shared many of his views and was politically active in her own right, was the logical choice to head the Women's Committee.

Women's suffrage was emphatically not on the agenda, but there were early attempts to include working women on the committee. "The professional woman agitator has misrepresented her sex. Who ever heard of a mother with seven children wanting to vote? But who is more competent to suggest improvements in her own and her working husband's condition than such a mother?" asked one of the Women's Committee members. Daisy Harriman exhorted listeners at the organizational meeting to form a local chapter of a women's division in New York City by reminding them of the influence they have over the "owners and stockholders," and asserting that since they "spend the money which the employees help to provide," they should "take a special interest in their welfare, especially in that of the women wage earners."

In order to see for themselves, female elites such as J. P. Morgan's daughter Anne Morgan, Sarah Platt Decker, Corinne Roosevelt Robinson, Maude Adams, Daisy Harriman, Gertrude Vanderbilt Whitney, and Alice Longworth attended NCF meetings to hear working-class women, union representatives, and others speak about ameliorating the lives of the working poor. The May meeting delegates were welcomed to the White House by Theodore Roosevelt, and one can speculate on the role of Alice in this coup for Ruth's fledgling committee.[31]

Alice attended meetings and undoubtedly discussed labor problems with Ruth, but she never cared for working in a group. While Alice didn't mind lending her name to an organization whose goals she shared, *Robert's Rules of Order* and fund-raising were not her style. Those smacked too much of the earnest reformer whom one admired but didn't emulate. Alice preferred to be closer to the seat of power.

Alice attended her first national political convention that year when the Republicans met in Chicago. It gave her "a taste for that form of entertainment that I do not think I shall ever get over," she wrote in her memoir. In fact, from 1908 on, Alice went to the conventions of both parties. They were usually spellbinding, sometimes heartbreaking, almost always full of action. "The real fun," she knew, was "outside the convention hall—at the headquarters of the national committee and of the candidates—in the conferences that are peppered through the various hotels and are going on day and night—at the all-night sessions of the committee on resolutions which has the drafting of the platform." And there were festivities, including Julius Fleischmann's theater party where "we were cheered and made much of," many lunches and dinners out with friends, and all of Chicago to explore. Ruth and Medill—a local—were her guides around the Windy City. Auntie Corinne, Uncle Douglas, and cousin Corinne accompanied them. The French ambassador Jules Jusserand and his wife, and the British ambassador James Bryce and his wife, also made fascinating companions.[32]

The June convention was full of the hurly-burly that became so addictive for Alice. Nick and Alice, Ruth and Medill, and Auntie Corinne and Uncle Douglas monitored the events together. Setting a precedent that drew a standing ovation, Alice made sure that others could monitor events as well. With "a simple act of courtesy," Alice took off her trademark large hat. "Fancy women," she puzzled, "deliberately putting an obstacle in any one's way to the enjoyment of a thing so big and important." After her

thoughtful act, "There was a noticeable absence of large millinery crea-
tions in the house." The same held true four years later.[33]

Even though he wasn't there, Theodore Roosevelt's progressive ideas
infused the platform, and his name set off a fifty-minute cheer. Alice jeal-
ously counted the length of the Taft demonstration—twenty-five minutes,
half of her father's. She heard every speech and maintained the Roosevelt
family line on her father's third term. "I was given the usual amount of
publicity, which consisted largely in attributing to me many pert remarks
and actions of which I vow I was never guilty—such as . . . waving a fan
with 'Third Term for Teddy' on it, and being generally boisterous. I really
do not believe I was boisterous." "Keen, interested," she agreed, but not
boisterous.[34]

Surely part of the difficulty lay in defining *boisterous*—and in the continuing desire of her adoring public to see her misbehave. In May, for example, Alice had placed a tack on a chair in the diplomatic gallery in the
House of Representatives and watched, laughingly, as her dupe impaled
himself. This earned her some fan mail:

> Last week cute Alice Longworth
>   Placed a tack upon a chair
> In the gallery of Congress
>   And let some one sit down there.
> The victim muttered "I am stuck,"
>   And gave a little spring,
> Then used some pointed language
>   About the pointed thing.
> Of course, 't was only "just a joke"
>   (And not a tactless one),
> But it started a new fashion
>   For the dudes of Washington.
> Those who listen from the gall'ry
>   While some windy statesman rants
> Are wearing anti-puncture
>   Tire-protectors on their pants!

"I want to say," her pro–third term admirer wrote, "the world laughs with you and you become more popular than ever...." Mail like this Alice assiduously tucked away, as it balanced out continuing warnings from the family to avoid "too much newspaper notoriety."[35]

The 1908 convention did nominate Taft. New York congressman "Sunny Jim" Sherman got the vice presidential slot. Alice had tipped off reporter William Allen White with that insider news. The culmination of the convention for the president's daughter came when she held an "impromptu" reception for "hundreds" of convention goers. MRS. LONGWORTH WELCOMES CROWD: PRESIDENT HIMSELF COULD NOT SURPASS DAUGHTER'S HANDSHAKING ACHIEVEMENT blared the *Chicago Tribune*. A friend inadvertently started the reception by shaking Alice's hand good-bye, and suddenly a queue of strangers appeared behind her, hands out. One woman complimented her: "'Mrs. Longworth, you are the dearest girl in America,' to which she responded, 'I am glad to have you say that.'" The *Tribune* reported, "No one, not even Senator Lodge, has attracted the attention in the Coliseum that has been given Mrs. Longworth, and a queen could not have received it more modestly or more graciously. The oldest men, as well as the youngest, went much out of their way to see 'Teddie's' daughter, and she could have started a furious ovation at any time by simply rising and bowing to the public."[36] She also could have started a third-term stampede for her father.

After a brief holiday in a Chicago suburb, the Longworths and the McCormicks hopped the train to Denver to "see how the Democrats did it." There, in the heat of a Colorado summer, Alice also measured the demonstration for William Jennings Bryan, which aimed to top TR's in Chicago. "As yelling, sweating delegates tramped past our box, we noticed that they had watches in their hands and heard them occasionally inquire of one another if it had 'gone over the time yet.'" It was visibly difficult for Alice to hear the Democrats slander her father, but she generally maintained her composure.[37]

Alice did make an interesting acquaintance in Denver: Ruth Bryan Leavitt, Bryan's daughter, who would become the first woman elected to Congress from the South. Alice confessed to a "fellow feeling" for her. The three politicians' daughters found themselves "trotted out" from their unobtrusive box at a pro-suffrage rally. Alice was "unmistakably, distinctly, and undisguisedly bored," as "all the vice-presidential candidates in town," spoke earnestly on the necessity of women's suffrage, "and did not appear to observe that the subject was a rather dreary one as far as most of the listeners were concerned." Rather than being able to listen unobserved, an efficient soul—knowing trophies when she saw them—herded Alice and the two Ruths onto the stage quite against their wishes. "Nice, gentle quiet little Mrs. McCormick" gave a speech to promote her work with the National Civic Federation. Stirring music, with nearly everyone joining in, followed her talk, and through it all, "Mrs. Longworth sat, a monument of astonished and bewildered boredom." Of course, whether other women stifled yawns and shifted in their seats was not publicized. If the daughter of William Jennings Bryan—Bryan was fated yet again to be the Democratic Party's unsuccessful presidential nominee in 1908—were to fidget, the *Denver Post* could not allude to that, as that would have been impolite of the main journalistic organ of the town hosting the Democratic convention. To the attendees it didn't matter, as Alice "was crushed, torn, jammed, pushed and almost trampled to death" in admiration.[38]

In the early years of her marriage, Alice seemed to be trying out different roles for herself: involved political wife, NCF reformer, charter member of the Washington Congressional Club (for wives of congressmen), dutiful daughter (better late than never), style setter (she was on the best-dressed lists and famous for her "Alice Longworth picture hat"), and the irrepressible Princess Alice. Her sense of humor remained intact through it all. A carload of tourists looking for Sagamore Hill had their chauffer pull alongside Alice, Ethel, and Quentin, who were shopping. "I wonder," said one, "if the President's daughter, Mrs. Nick something or the other, is there and if we can get a peep at her and the other daughter, Miss Ethel." And Alice, "with features as immobile as a graven image," replied, "To the best of my knowledge they are not at home just now." A local Democratic Party leader overheard the exchange, flagged down the car full of disappointed celebrity hunters, and explained the joke.[39]

Nick and Alice appeared to be much in love. While Alice was mocking the sightseers, she received a touching note from Nick in mid-August:

"Manchu and I had a rather panting and fitful slumber. It having eschewed its basket for a distinguished and at times audible position beneath my bed whence I had not the heart to drive it because we both missed our Bubbie so much." Nick sent Alice two dozen red roses in Oyster Bay. Every day she was away from him, she told reporters, he sent her flowers. His devotion, she averred, was evidence of the happiness of their marriage. By month's end, Nick joined her for a fortnight at Sagamore.[40]

The Roosevelt family spent the fall beginning the sad task of packing up the White House. Edith longed for the quiet of Sagamore, but worried about her husband's transition to retirement. She confided in Cecil Spring-Rice, after the temptation of a third term had passed, that TR's "mind is full of his African trip. He is to start next April and take Kermit who will be nearing the end of his first year in college. They expect to be gone a year and Theodore has promised to write an account of his trip for *Scribner's,* and as this means a book afterwards I hope he may be busy and interested for the summer after he comes home."[41] Roosevelt's African safari was to be part scientific expedition, part spiritual renewal, and part a way to take himself out of the limelight so Taft could act without journalists claiming TR was the puppet master guiding hapless Will.

Alice alternated between distaff duties in Cincinnati and politics in Washington. Nick gave a "eulogy and a defense of the president's administration" in Rock Island, Illinois, wherein he proposed that Theodore Roosevelt should return to the presidency after two Taft terms. His idea was tremendously popular. Nick was the man in the middle that year, trying to celebrate his father-in-law, elect his constituent Taft, and keep the way open for his own advancement. His visibility increased as he rode the election trail with vice presidential candidate Sherman, giving speeches and riling up the crowds. While he was away, Alice told reporters that she would stay at the White House with her parents. "Then she added, with a sort of wistfulness that was never a part of the old Alice Roosevelt, 'the house is so big and I would be so lonesome by myself with Mr. Longworth away.'" When he worked for Taft inside Ohio, Alice campaigned with him, usually a silent but compelling draw on the platform. In Pittsburgh, she took part in a parade and a five-hundred-dollar fund-raising dinner in her honor, and led the applause later that night as the speeches began.[42]

Nick—in a statement about either his loyalties or his ambitions—made sure that he and Alice spent the election night at the Tafts' Cincinnati home. There, with the extended Herron and Taft families and Nick's sister Nan Wallingford, they waited to hear the results. The outcome for Taft was clear by midnight. Crowds gathered outside, bands played "Hail to the Chief," and the people's choice ambled from his easy chair to acknowledge his victory. Happily Nick's election had the same ending and, as Alice wrote John Greenway, "by a larger margin than was expected." Alice shared in the congratulations: "We are credibly informed [that] you largely contributed," wrote Edwin Morgan.[43]

While Alice anticipated it and had indirectly worked for Taft's victory, she resented the crowing of her in-laws. Their constant glorifying of Taft made Alice "indulge a proclivity toward malice that occasionally comes over me." Whenever the Longworths suggested they owed little to her father, Alice became furious. When the election details arrived, the Longworths "gloated" as they compared them with TR's 1904 returns. "The stage was set," Alice shrugged, "for the first steps that led to the 'breaking up of a beautiful friendship.' "[44]

More than one friendship disintegrated after 1908. Alice never quite felt the same about her in-laws, and Roosevelt and Taft experienced the dissolution of their comradeship as well. Taft was not another TR. His personality was cautious, judicious, and vapid. TR was the personification of energy.[45] Despite what the Roosevelt family considered his promise, Taft did not retain TR's cabinet. Nor did he continue Roosevelt's policies unbroken—any more than TR had carried on McKinley's policies. Helen Taft and Edith Roosevelt even clashed over the best way to run the White House.

As the end of her father's presidency became real, Alice herself "helped to make bad blood" by doing a scathing but hilarious impersonation of the new First Lady. She contorted her visage into what she called her "hippopotamus face" to sneer, "this, my darlings, is what is coming after you."

Receiving a ticket from Helen Taft to let her into the White House for the inaugural luncheon was the final straw: "Instead of taking it as obvious routine," Alice recollected, "I flew shouting to friends and relatives with the news that I was going to be allowed to have a *ticket* to permit *me* to enter the White House—I—a very large capital I—who had wandered in and out for eight happy winters! Indeed, I gave myself over to a pretty fair imitation of mischief-making."[46] There was no relief in sight for Nick. He remained the man in the middle.

Chapter 11

"Expelled from the Garden of Eden"

ALICE ROOSEVELT LONGWORTH closed out the election year of 1908 with an act of uncharacteristic sentimentality. She and TR's aide Archie Butt walked through the White House: "We went from room to room and each one had some sweet memory for this girl whose career in the White House has been the most dramatic of any in its history. 'Princess Alice,' she was called, and she ruled over her kingdom as no other woman has ever done there.... To me she is far more attractive now than she was as a young girl, for she has developed not only physically but mentally and in poise. She was sad this afternoon, for she seemed to realize just what the change would mean to her. She was not complaining, for she has too much of her father in her for that, but she did not hesitate to give voice to the note of sadness."[1]

Alice could not escape being changed by her time as First Daughter. As Archie Butt noticed, she grew up under the gaze of the public, just as Susan Ford, Amy Carter, and Chelsea Clinton would do at the end of the century. And like theirs, her blossoming was accompanied by moments of parental despair. But Alice remained utterly independent and protective of her inner self even as she gave generously of her public persona. If observers were correct, she enjoyed the status of her position enough to hope that Nick would carry her back into that historical house once again. Nineteen twenty-four, in fact, was the year suggested by some members of the GOP during the election: Taft for two terms, then TR back again for eight years, then a seasoned Nick Longworth ascending to the presidency in 1924.[2] That was a long time away.

Before any dreams of returning, there was the inexorable march of awful "lasts" to endure: the last Christmas, the last birthday celebrations, the last receptions, balls, and dinners, the last guests, the last day, the last night. "Nobody likes to leave the White House, whatever they say. We were no exception," Alice stated emphatically years later. Each member of the family marked the looming change in his or her own way. Alice found time to bury a voodoo figure in the White House garden, a hex on the next occupants.[3] Ethel prepared for her debut. Young Quentin led his "White House Gang" on merry chases and lived in the present. Edith packed systematically, hoping for a smidgen of normality to come. TR gave away mementos—White House china, photographs, trinkets.

Christmas at the White House was a large family affair. Nick and Alice plucked gifts from a Christmas tree burdened with surprises for sixty revelers. The Roosevelts wanted to make the holiday especially memorable. Try as they might to keep it at bay, melancholy lurked among the tinsel. Alice thought a photograph taken at the time showed the family looking "as if we are being expelled from the Garden of Eden."[4]

Ethel's debut returned effervescence to the winter social season. Wine, aging since the 1905 nuptials, buoyed the 440 guests, who danced continually on a floor so shiny that it reflected the chandeliers above. Even the "tottering ancient" older sister Alice found it "one of the prettiest parties I have ever seen at the White House." Butt oversaw the details of the ball, and wrote that the White House looked "far more beautiful than it was even at Alice's wedding."[5]

Alice had the hardest time keeping up a happy appearance. Eleanor and Franklin had been invited to the traditional January diplomatic reception at the White House. They saw cousin Alice only briefly. She had "a cold and a headache etc. but she looks lovely and very well and so quiet!" Eleanor reported. ER—who never knew quite how to approach her cousin—also mentioned cattily that Ethel didn't appear spoiled by her foray into adult socializing the way her older sister had, and pronounced Ethel "not along Alice's lines at all!"[6]

President Roosevelt warded off sadness by surrounding himself with congenial dinner guests. Nearly every night, Butt chronicled, "Mrs. Roosevelt starts out to have family dinner and by 1 o'clock the President has asked so many as to make it almost a state affair. He is certainly the soul of hospitality. He dearly loves a great number of people around his table. He is just as happy with a lot of schoolboys as he is with a lot of statesmen, a little bit happier, I often think."[7] At that particular time, the schoolboys were a useful antidote to the terrible daily feuds dished up by conservatives in the Republican Party, some of whom looked forward to March with a joy as intense as the family's sorrow.

Lively reports of the titanic clash of wills on Capitol Hill poured from reporters' pens: "The last annual message of President Roosevelt and the last session of the 60th Congress came together with a crash. It was not quite a case of an irresistible force and an immovable body, but it was near enough to make things interesting for awhile. Every session of this Congress has during the last two years furnished, at its opening, an exhibition of some such conflict with the President." By the time of his last annual address in 1909, Congress and the president had reached a parting of the ways. The final session was a battle about presidential power centered on the Secret Service, an ideological clash that eventually gave birth to the Federal Bureau of Investigation. Alice called it "one long lovely crackling row between the White House and the Capitol," but she had observer status.[8] For those involved, the price was dear.

Nick navigated the middle, fast becoming his chosen place. At the same diplomatic reception where Eleanor sized up Alice, Butt observed many absences among the congressmen who "showed their resentment toward the President by remaining away."[9] But "Old Nick," Butt thought, looked anxious about House matters. "He is very popular there and members tell me that he conducts himself with wonderful discretion. But to be a member of the body which feels itself insulted by the President, and yet retain his temper when that body attacks his father-in-law, is a difficult task, especially to one who is as devoted to Mr. Roosevelt as he is. As he said goodnight to the President last night, the President hit him on the back and said: 'Poor old Nick! What is he not suffering for love's sake these days!' Nick laughed and said, 'I think I am enjoying it about as much as you are, Mr. President.'"

Nick escaped to the Metropolitan Club. He skipped out on the House debate over the tone and the wording of Roosevelt's last message. He thought, for everyone's sake, he ought not participate in the conversations where he'd have to stick up for TR or defend himself. Nor did he want to "embarrass some [of his] personal friends there who may want to hit back for home consumption." Nick tried not to feel impatient. He hated sitting on the edge of his seat so he could "skin out of the House to prevent voting to censure [his] own father-in-law." Alice avidly followed the recalcitrant Congress, her husband's awkward position, and her father's "spanking" by the intractable politicians. While neither man in her life was particularly happy, she was thrilled to be at the center of things. "I suppose what you don't know about politics by this time is not worth knowing," her mother-in-law wrote her.[10]

On Alice's twenty-fifth birthday, the Longworths concentrated on politics in Grand Rapids, Michigan, where Nick gave a Lincoln's Day speech and Alice laid a cornerstone for a new federal building, "with all the solemn rites of the Masonic ceremony." Thousands cheered her as they sang one of her father's favorite hymns, "Onward Christian Soldiers."[11] The extravagant attentions paid them were a reminder that their lives would continue in the pattern imposed by Nick's service in the House and Alice's celebrity.

The family proudly circled round TR for a last moment of glory to watch the Great White Fleet make its magnificent return from around the world. The twenty-six white battleships sailed past slowly, each booming a twenty-one-gun salute. The president toured the flagship, greeted the officers, and basked in triumph. Roosevelt had sent the fleet out to exhibit American naval strength. It was the capstone of his efforts to build a more efficient navy and one of his greatest accomplishments.

Inevitably, the last evening in the White House arrived. The president and First Lady hosted a small dinner for the Tafts, who were staying overnight on the eve of the transfer of power. Alice and Nick, Auntie Bye and Uncle Will, Belle Hagner, Henry Cabot Lodge, Archie Butt, the Roots, and the Tafts' good friend Mabel Boardman took part in what Alice considered a "curious occasion." The Tafts, she recalled, were trying to stifle their "natural elation," while TR was already assailed by doubts concerning Taft's abilities to carry on the Rooseveltian vision. Butt "was frankly emotional," and the devoted Root dropped tears into his soup. Helen Taft's insistence on having things her way in the White House meant she was, in Edith's opinion, overly aggressive and unconscionably early in making hurtful changes. "It was," Alice wrote, "a singularly hushed and cheerless dinner." The only thing that made the night bearable for her was the roiling snowstorm that shook the shutters and kept the Tafts awake. It presaged a miserable inaugural. Her voodoo was working.[12]

Indeed, the snow continued unabated, temperatures dropped, and the sun shone the next day only long enough to create a "loathsome slush." Taft's well-wishers braved the storm, but futilely, as the administration of the oath of office took place in the Senate, out of public sight. Alice, Edith, Bye, Quentin, and Belle skipped the swearing-in and went instead to console themselves over lunch at the Longworth home. The other family members were at school or work, except for Quentin, who remained to sit in the president's box and watch the inaugural parade with his pal from the White House gang—the new presidential son, Charley Taft. TR exited immediately after the inaugural address, as audience members wept quietly.[13]

Edith's famous restraint finally gave way on the train. In her thank-you note to Belle for the thoughtful farewell gift of terrapin—TR loved it and ate "every last morsel"—Edith confessed that TR "did not get any sherry for I drank it all, and found it most comforting." Looking for the positive, Edith thought the flowers from well-wishers festooning their carriage made them "feel as if we were on a honeymoon journey." They were optimistic about their futures. Both said they longed for private life. While Edith had no real regrets at departing, she feared TR was conditioned to the publicity. She told his military aide that Roosevelt, despite his professed desire for it, had "forgotten" how to be "the simplest American alive." "My future is in the past, save as I may do the decent work that every private citizen can do," Roosevelt wrote stoically. Yet Edith knew that TR received letter after letter suggesting that 1908 was not the end of his political career. This is exactly the sort of idea Alice relished. A return of the Roosevelts to power was her ideal. Meanwhile, she didn't miss the chance to check out the new regime at the inaugural ball, where she was gratifyingly "gulped over." Archie Butt knew, if Alice couldn't admit it publicly, that the Princess wanted to maintain her distinctive place in Washington society.[14]

Taft's inauguration forced Alice into a different relationship with the new inhabitants of the White House. Alice survived the first visit to what had been her home, but not without bitterness. It was a small gathering of congressmen and their wives, and it ended early. Mary Borah, the wife of Senator William E. Borah of Idaho, recalled President Taft filling the room with his "hearty roar," as a result of something Alice said. But when Mrs. Taft loudly told a guest that she had "found the [White] [H]ouse in a very bad condition," Mary Borah looked sympathetically at Alice, who directed her attention elsewhere. "Your visit must have been trying poor child," Edith wrote, "though your account of it was most amusing. I don't think you need call [at the White House] again until next month, but you will surely be invited before then to some feast or function and remember for Nick's sake to be really careful what you say for people are only too ready to take up and repeat the most trivial remarks."[15]

As her father and Kermit departed for Africa, Alice embarked on her own journey—an intellectual journey. Officially without a title (beyond wife of a representative—and she was one among hundreds of those) and without the outsized presence of her father, Alice forged an identity differ-ent from the footloose First Daughter. Reading far into the night, she cul-tivated her wide-ranging interests. She began a lifelong and serious study of human evolutionary biology, a topic that also fascinated her father. She read about the latest developments in astronomy. The Philadelphia author Mary Cadwalader Jones gave Alice her first volume of the *Oxford Book of English Verse*, a book she consulted so regularly that it was held together with string by the end of her life.[16] Alice educated herself more systemati-cally about politics. Slowly but surely she laid the groundwork for the real presence she would become in Washington. Made from her father's mold, she could speak on nearly every subject and charm people from many dif-ferent backgrounds. She was charismatic, fun, daring, and fascinated by politics and politicians, by the ebbs and flows of Washington society, and by whatever was new or amusing. The few topics she found tedious, she sidestepped. The tariff was one such subject.

As the former president readied to depart "in a roar of cheers," the new president called Congress into special session on March 15, 1909, to address the tariff.[17] High protective tariffs had been a GOP cornerstone, but progressive Republicans advocated reform in light of the great profits made by barely regulated trusts and monopolies. With TR's approval, the 1908 Republican Party platform promised some action on the Dingley Tariff of 1897. The party was committed to revision, but the platform did not stipulate whether tariff rates would be revised up or down. Taft found, to his sorrow, that a unified Republican stance was a thing of the past. The tariff, and Taft's handling of it, exacerbated the fissure in the GOP ranks opened during TR's presidency.

In Taft's special session to address the tariff, the Republicans had a large congressional majority, but within the GOP there existed a progressive faction called the Insurgents. These men, led by George W. Norris of Nebraska, were generally supportive of Roosevelt's ideals, and they worked with Democrats to weaken the power of the office of Speaker Joseph G. Cannon, a Republican from Illinois. Cannon—so conservative that it was said of him that at the creation of the universe he'd have voted for chaos—led up the Progressive agenda in the House. "I am god-damned tired of listening to all this babble for reform," he raged.[18] The first salvo in the Insurgents' war against the broad and autocratic powers of the crusty House Speaker was the adoption of the Calendar Wednesday rule. It allowed committee heads to call up bills not passed by the Rules Committee, which was in the Speaker's control, thus sidestepping his power.

The House discussion on the tariff bill gave the Insurgents another chance to flex their muscles as they pushed toward the traditionally Democratic position of low tariffs. Nick Longworth championed high tariffs. He was from the home state of both Taft and William McKinley. Many Republicans thought of the high McKinley Tariff of 1890 as the acme of tariff legislation and anything connected to the name of the sainted McKinley was dear.

From the time of his appointment to the Ways and Means Committee,

Nick's intellectual absorption with the tariff had deepened. The representative felt "that no protective tariff law of itself, ever closed a factory, ever mortgaged a farm or caused an American working man to lose his job; and no free trade law failed to do all three."[19] Reflecting McKinley's influence, Nick worked to create a permanent tariff commission to remove politics altogether, and he was willing to use reciprocity—an agreement with foreign nations to lower the U.S. tariff if they lowered theirs—to make adjustments in tariff schedules. It was a stimulating subject for Nick, and he enjoyed the feinting and the sparring of the sprawling tariff bill.

The representative's wife believed "there is nothing I forget quite so quickly as details of a tariff bill, and even when one is up I enjoy it principally for the passions it arouses in the rate advocates and rate makers.... I spent hours listening to the [1909] debates, yet all recollection of them is as completely gone as if my ears had been stuffed with cotton-wool and my eyes blindfolded." What Alice did keenly note is how Insurgents were "making themselves felt"; more evidence of the strength of her father's vision.[20]

From the gallery, Alice happily followed the House battles. From his seat on the floor, Nick watched nervously. Only Theodore Roosevelt paid no attention at all. He resolutely ignored the political situation in the United States during his safari until, that is, the wounded and self-righteous Gifford Pinchot turned up bearing tales of Taft's betrayal. Pinchot, retained in Taft's administration as chief forester, had been fired for questioning the integrity of Taft's secretary of the interior. The seeds Pinchot planted then grew slowly but steadily to flower in 1912.

Taft's tariff bill was a contentious one, backed fully neither by the Democrats nor the Republicans. When he made support for the tariff a test of party loyalty, Taft increased the risks to his party. The Payne-Aldrich Tariff was bitterly fought and in the end made no one perfectly content. President Taft signed the bill in August 1909. The Insurgents became convinced that Roosevelt's handpicked successor was not made from the stern stuff of their standard-bearer. Taft's suspicions of the Insurgents deepened to a steely dislike. Meanwhile, dissatisfaction with Speaker Cannon seethed sub rosa.

While Nick toiled in this poisonous atmosphere, Alice escaped. Long captivated by the vision of air travel, Alice led the newest Washington craze. The first successful human flight had occurred in late 1903, at Kitty Hawk, North Carolina. In 1909, Orville and Wilbur Wright and their sister, Kathleen, appeared at Fort Myer to try to get their airplane into the air for sustained periods. Day after day for months, Alice and other Washingtonians went to learn about flying machines and were taught, she thought, with "unfailing patience" by the "modest, self-effacing" Wrights. Orville Wright spent half an hour one day showing Alice how the airplane worked from top to bottom. She was fascinated. She pleaded with him to take her flying, to no avail. From President Taft to cabinet members, congressmen to military observers, the grass filled with dreamers. "When the machine actually left the ground and circled the field, a hundred feet or so up, it gave us a thrill that no one in this generation will ever have," Alice recalled. Taft was there on July 27, to see Orville stay up in the air for a record-breaking seventy-three minutes. Even the slightest wind would ground the attempts and entail long periods of waiting for the propitious moment. Since Alice's boredom threshold was low, she took to entertaining the crowds by running "a most popular 'lunch wagon.'" From a dozen vacuum bottles she poured iced tea and the newly fashionable gin, club soda, and lemon juice concoction called a Tom Collins.[21]

Her curiosity about flight had been aroused in part by a frequent visitor to Sagamore Hill when she was a child, the aviation pioneer Samuel P. Langley, an astronomy professor, secretary of the Smithsonian Institution, and an airplane inventor. In the 1890s, Langley experimented on the banks of the Potomac with his "aerodromes." By the time Alice was watching the Wrights, Langley had been dead three years. He never achieved his goal of building a flying craft capable of carrying people, but Alice remembered his zeal as he spoke over dinners with the Roosevelts about the future of flight.

Busy with the tariff, Cannon, and the Wrights, neither Alice nor Nick found time to write to their mothers until August. "I always know in their case," Edith wrote Susan Longworth resignedly, "that the old proverb is true and I should be told any bad news very quickly." When she wasn't listening to the "boring" tariff debate, Alice was reading in the heat of the day, walking in Rock Creek Park in the late afternoon, playing cards with such friends as Ned and Evalyn Walsh McLean, and having dutiful dinners with the "political lights of Ohio and their wives." Between the Wrights' flights, she had been a patroness of a production of Oscar Wilde's controversial play *Salome*.[22]

Nick was troubled by stomach pains, probably brought on by stresses in the tariff battle, which was rapidly turning into a war, between Taft Republicans and Roosevelt Republicans. In such a conflict, Nick would always be trapped midway. As it was, he and Alice spent a good deal of time with President Taft that summer while the First Lady and the children were vacationing away from Washington. Alice was less than reverential. She arrived very late to one of his parties and made such an outrageous apology that "everyone laughed. The President took her hands in his and said: 'Alice, if you will only stop trying to be respectful to me, I believe you would become so.' 'And then I would bore you to death as the other women do,'" Alice countered. Nick was glad, he finally wrote his mother when the "agony" of the tariff bill was past, "that Alice has found diversion in the aeroplane flights—'Sans ca' she would indeed have had a dull summer."[23]

In late June, Edith, Ethel, Archie, and Quentin took a steamer to visit Edith's sister Emily Carow in Italy. Alice, staying behind, wrote Ethel that rather than going through the "unsatisfactory" ritual of waving a dockside good-bye, she'd prefer that the two of them "wilt in the hole of a fortune teller and then have nice cool drinks" as a farewell. Alice was not well while her family was away. Worse even than the month she spent exercising her restraint in Cincinnati was a flare-up of pain in her jaw from the old childhood injury that necessitated frequent trips to a specialist in Boston. Alice looked for sympathy from Edith, but it was not forthcoming. Edith's letter attests to her own difficulties: traveling with children, a good friend's death, six months away from TR. "It was very nice to get your letter and to hear about your successes even though it has not been an amusing one." After reminding her stepdaughter of her duties concerning Susan, Edith continued, "I do hope you can meet me when I land, and will have arranged to go wherever I am going."[24] It was always this way—Edith's love for her stepdaughter was real, but generally communicated with asperity.

While TR was a little out of the spotlight, in Africa, Alice jumped in. She participated in a fund-raiser for the Anti-Tuberculosis Society of Cincinnati. Still trying to figure out her post–First Daughter role, she agreed to sell flags on the society's behalf, and sold the most flags and the highest-priced flag. This was front-page news in the *New York Times,* especially as the paper could report some of the intimate details of the Longworth marriage: "Her first flag was bought by Thomas Pegan, a business man, who paid her with a $100 bill. The second one she took herself, emptying her purse of its $15. Congressman Longworth said his wife was receiving entirely too much attention, so he hunted out one of the society girls who was in an obscure doorway and gave her $50 for a little strip of white cloth. Mrs. Longworth did $1,000 worth of business in a half hour."[25]

If Nick felt it necessary in this case to squelch Alice's fame—which also nicely resulted in some publicity for him—he found himself defending her honor shortly afterward when a minor scandal erupted with the publication of Emma Kroebel's memoirs. Kroebel was Germany's "chief mistress of ceremonies" in Korea when Alice and Nick ventured there with the congressional junket in 1905. Kroebel told of behavior so shocking that few could believe it, even of Alice:

The emperor [of Korea] finally decided to bestow upon the daughter of the president of the United States the highest honor at his command, namely, a reception at the graveside of his departed consort, the empress. An imposing suite of dignitaries and flunkeys were accordingly dispatched to the grave in a picturesque and secluded spot a mile outside Seoul. . . . As the diners gathered, into their midst roared "a cavalcade of equestrians. . . ." At their head rode a dashing young horsewoman clad in a scarlet riding habit beneath the lower extremities of which peeped tight-fitting red riding breeches stuck into glittering boots. In her hand she brandished a riding whip and in her mouth was a cigar.

It was Miss Alice Roosevelt. We were flabbergasted....Every-
body was bowing and scraping in the most approved Corean court
fashion, but the rough rider's daughter seemed to think it all a joke.
As the mistress of ceremonies I stammered out a few words of greeting, and the guest of honor mumbled a word of thanks, but nothing
more. She was mainly interested in the colossal figures of gods and
the mammoth stone images of animals which hold watch over the
graves of the departed members of the Corean dynasty.

Spying a stone elephant which seemed to strike her fancy, Alice
hurtled off her horse and in a flash was astride the elephant, shouting
to Mr. Longworth to snapshot her. Our suite was paralyzed with horror and astonishment. Such a sacrilegious scene at so holy a spot was
without parallel.[26]

Kroebel charged that Alice was uninterested in all formal entertainments, and after this imbroglio at the tomb of the empress, never attended
another; instead, she forced Nick to attend in her place.

The next day's paper carried Nick's defense of his wife: "It was too
preposterous to be taken seriously, he snorted, as nothing of the kind took
place or could have taken place. He said he never knew or heard of the author of the story, but complimented her upon her vivid imagination and
said it had afforded the subject of it a great deal of amusement." Whether
Nick did not permit Alice to speak on her own behalf or whether she asked
him to respond to Kroebel is unclear. Perhaps, since one of Alice's credos
at the time was "there is nothing so satisfactory as a lie that is accepted immediately for the pure truth—but also nothing so barren as one that is
unbelieved," she could not respond for fear of that barrenness.[27]

As she herself admitted at the time, in Korea Alice had reached her sat-
uration point with official appearances. As Taft had suggested, she may
have been punishing Nick for any romantic slight by pairing up with Willard Straight. In 1905, just after the junket ended, Alice had penned a
thank-you to Straight: "Those photographs are excellent, but please oh
please don't ever let anyone see the one of 'Nick' in my nice but abbreviated
[illegible]. I don't think my family would ever forgive me if once they
learned the truth—and astride the guardian angel at a martyred Empress'

tomb—it would be almost too much!"[28] Straight kept her confidence. Nick upheld the Roosevelt name in print, and the story died down.

December brought some of the Roosevelts together for their first fractured Christmas. Alice was battling jaw pain, walking six miles a day, and leading "a most decorous existence," when she and Nick—who had turned forty in November—journeyed to Sagamore Hill. Ted was present for Christmas Day. TR was still abroad with Kermit, confessing in a letter to Arthur Lee that while the trip "has been a great success, I am now an elderly man, not fit for very hard exertion," and "only a fair shot." TR brooded in Africa and the others had "not much" of a Christmas. Edith decided to sail for Egypt in mid-February to rejoin TR. "I can scarcely wait and yet I am torn asunder to think of leaving three boys behind to say nothing of Alice," Edith acknowledged to a friend.[29]

She need not have worried about her stepdaughter. Part two of the battle to oust Speaker Cannon commenced while Edith was readying to leave, providing a handy distraction for Alice. Insurgent leader George Norris opened the winter session with a resolution to increase the size and the power of the Rules Committee, while simultaneously barring the Speaker of the House from membership. Democrats supported him and after "a continuous rough and tumble on the floor," involving a filibuster and every other possible ploy to delay the vote, the standpat Republicans lost. "Mr. Cannon," a progressive newspaper screamed in justification, "is personally opposed to every reform that is now being advocated by any political party." Nick, longing above all to see harmony prevail, regretfully joined the Insurgents. Cannon lost his position and his reputation and, Alice winced, "was greeted with jeers and cat-calls" instead of the "fear, respect, and even some degree of affection" that he had known before progressivism swept the land. The lesson of Joe Cannon's fall was not lost on Alice: Nick was considered for the new Rules Committee, but not ultimately selected because of his role in toppling Cannon and threatening the Old Guard Republicans.[30]

Alice's increasing dislike of the assertive and caustic First Lady, Helen Taft, did not help things. For her part, Helen, mirthless and unable to match Princess Alice for sheer dramatic appeal, found much to criticize in the other woman. Alice's blasé response to societal restrictions was well known to Helen Taft. She would have heard of Alice's demonstration of the new dance craze, the Turkey Trot, at a ball in Washington. As one observer put it, Alice lit a cigarette first, "to give zest to the performance." Her male partner was forgotten, but Alice "sailed down the middle of the room, puffing little jets of smoke at the ceiling, to the horror of the women." One of them thought "Alice looked like a steam engine coming down a crimped track."[31]

Events reached a climax for Helen Taft at the president's diplomatic reception in January 1910. Alice watched with interest the expressions on Washington faces as the wife of the Russian ambassador began to smoke. She joined in. The courtly Taft bent down to light Alice's cigarette. The other European women then took out their cigarette cases until the room was full of a sight few Americans had ever seen: a bevy of women smoking. The First Lady was not amused. Alice smirked. Taft's biographer considered this a terrible faux pas: "The only person [Alice] could not charm out of disapproval after one of her escapades was the President's wife and she underestimated Mrs. Taft's influence—or did not care. It was Nellie who kept Nicholas Longworth from being appointed minister to China, a post he coveted, because she thought that Alice might stir up storms in the Celestial Kingdom."[32]

Whether Alice would have liked the position of diplomat's wife, especially in a place as remote as China, was unlikely. She did enjoy her visit there in 1905, and there were friends of hers in different capacities in East Asia, but China wasn't exactly the Court of St. James's. Like Cincinnati, China was too far away from Washington. With her father about to return, and increasing numbers of people sharing her frustration with Taft's administration, the capital was more enticing. It was hard to remain angry at Taft. For Christmas that year, the president, who had a sense of humor, gave Alice Longworth a cigarette holder![33]

In May, Alice sailed alone for England to meet the rest of the family gathered around TR, fresh from his successful safari and an invigorating scuffle with Britain's protectorate Egypt, which he suggested was not fit to rule itself. The English gave him a warm welcome. Nick was chained to Congress that spring, but Alice amused herself shipboard with Harry Emery, then chairman of the tariff board. Emery was perfectly congenial: "an economist, a philosopher, and all-'round scholar and the most delightful companion for long stretches of cards, poetry, or general chatter." The two of them had lunch with Tammany boss Tim Sullivan. Alice saw right through him: "I think he was as straight and well-intentioned and genuinely sympathetic in his personal relations and humanitarian enterprises, as he was callous and corrupt politically."[34] She also met another Democrat: longtime TR foe William Randolph Hearst, the newspaper tycoon who had spent the last decade printing critical articles about Roosevelt.

Kermit, Ethel, and the faithful Willard Straight met Alice at the dock. That night she and TR and Kermit huddled together exchanging news. Alice analyzed the past year's political battles. TR, listening, became ever more certain that he could not campaign on behalf of Taft and his policies in the looming congressional elections. But first Roosevelt had other public duties. At President Taft's request he represented the United States at the funeral of Britain's King Edward. He gave a series of prestigious lectures, including the Romanes lecture at Oxford University. In that address, "Biological Analogies in History," Roosevelt distilled a lifetime's thoughts on human evolution and history. This particularly interested Alice. But so did the Derby—this year socialites were swathed in black mourning crepe. Alice amused herself with friends such as the Astors and the Arthur Lees in London, and "three days of plays, restaurants, and races" in Paris, where her luck held. She won enough on the horses to pay for her entire trip— including spending money.[35]

The trip home passed quickly because Ruth and Medill were on board to dissect the political situation in the United States. None of the party underestimated the meaning of the exuberant greeting awaiting TR. Alice stood beside her father as New Yorkers met him with a happy riot of noise and color from a flotilla of boats in the harbor and a dockside teeming with well-wishers. Nick came aboard the ship with the welcoming committee.

The reunited couple joined the Roosevelts trailing behind TR, who thoroughly enjoyed being the star of the confetti-sprinkled parade in his honor.

Duty beckoned:

> Teddy, come home and blow your horn,
> The sheep's in the meadow, the cow's in the corn.
> The boy you left to tend the sheep
> Is under the haystack fast asleep.[36]

The allusion in the newspaper doggerel to President Taft's frequent naps pointed to the larger problem of deteriorating relations within the Republican Party. Nick filled in TR on the House side of things. Roosevelt could no more stay away from the fracas than he could refrain from criticizing his former friend Taft who, he had decided, had "not proved a good leader, in spite of his having been a good first lieutenant...."[37]

In the spring of 1910, Alice turned twenty-six, Ted's marriage to the thoughtful and kind Eleanor Butler Alexander was announced, and Nick and Alice were leaders in a new society craze: roller skating from door to door picking up friends as they went and "winding up at somebody's house for supper."[38] Also that spring, Alice's good grandfather, George Lee, passed away. His death left her much sadder and a little wealthier. His bequest to her was $5,300 a year, the same amount that his children would receive. This made her happier than the recurring proposition that Nick might become governor of Ohio, an idea that bloomed with the Washington tulips.[39] Alice nixed it, but it was a difficult idea to kill.

It was unthinkable to live in Ohio, so far from the center of power. And the balance of that power kept shifting. The Republican split was on everyone's mind. TR's progressive legislative program—explained by him as the morally correct action of providing an equal playing field, or a "square deal," for all citizens—was interpreted by conservative Republicans as undue governmental shackling of corporate America. Because of the bumbling way Taft handled the Payne-Aldrich Tariff—for example, excluding progressive congressmen's states in his tour to drum up support for the bill—doubts about Taft increased. Meanwhile, Americans read the serialized epic of TR's gallant African expedition from his own pen. Then the newspapers filled with fulsome reports of Roosevelt's visits with the crowned heads of Europe. The average citizen had never stopped admiring the larger-than-life "Teddy," and the grand welcome he received made the contrast between the beleaguered Taft and the heroic Roosevelt even greater.

By 1910, the vise that squeezed Nick Longworth tightened. His friendship with Taft and other conservative Ohio politicians caused him much worry. His camaraderie with the Tafts predated his marriage. While Nick was not entirely a creature of Boss Cox, he still needed hometown support to stay in the House. Cincinnati had been the butt of a muckraker's sharp pen in 1905, when Lincoln Steffens denounced the powerful Cox and his Byzantine methods, which resulted in cries for reform in the widely read *Cincinnati Post*. Nick was not especially committed to reform, but not especially *not* committed to reform either. He was committed to retaining his seat in the House of Representatives.

Nick tried to make his position unambiguous to his volatile father-in-law, who saw Nick's dilemma clearly. Despite his disgust with Taft and his "lawyers' Administration," TR told Nick, "Of course you must stand straight by Taft and the Administration. He is your constituent, and, as you say, while the situation for you was awkward enough while I was President it [is] even more awkward under the actual conditions." Roosevelt lobbied gently: "But in standing straight for the President, do keep yourself clear to stand for progressive policies." TR was full of advice. He saw only "doubtful ... wisdom" in the governorship because it was unlikely to serve as a stepping-stone to the White House. But Taft thought it a good idea. In the "hot fight" at the 1910 Columbus convention, the Ohio GOP finally settled on Warren G. Harding as its gubernatorial candidate. Florence and Alice watched the proceedings together, with entirely different agendas for their husbands. Both women got their wish that July. In her autobiography, Alice claimed that Nick was relieved: "He enjoyed the work in Congress and year by year was gaining in experience and seniority. The governorship was not in line with his plans."[40]

It definitely wasn't in hers. Taft wrote to his wife in late September 1910 about an evening spent at the Longworths' with Archie Butt and some others. He noticed Alice "drawing away from" him because of the "situation between her father and me, though she professes to be very affectionate still. The whole evening," Taft mused, "was one suggestive of sadness in that there was little sympathy between Alice and her mother-in-law. She dislikes her mother-in-law extremely, and her mother-in-law dislikes her extremely . . . Clara and de Chambrun have very little to do with Alice, and form such a contrast that the mother sympathizes with them. Nannie, I believe, is the [sister-in-law] with whom Alice gets along the better. Alice is very unhappy here, calls it Cincin-nasty, and is only too delighted when she can get away."[41]

Theodore Roosevelt, meanwhile, had some difficult decisions to make. Still enormously popular, lobbied by those who felt Taft was not upholding progressivism, and uncertain that his original plan of spending a couple of years writing would sustain him financially and emotionally, TR felt compelled to help his party in the off-year congressional elections. While some Republicans were thrilled to have the charismatic Colonel Roosevelt beside them at the podium, others—the standpatters, Taft's men—searched for ways to avoid joint appearances in their hometowns. Roosevelt set off on an elder statesman's tour. In Osawatomie, Kansas, on August 31, 1910, Roosevelt gave a landmark talk. Labeled "The New Nationalism" by historians, and considered "the most radical speech ever given by an ex-president," it sounded suspiciously like a presidential platform. It presented a clear challenge to Taft's leadership. "The truth is," TR confided to Henry Cabot Lodge that August, "we have had no National leadership of any real kind since election day 1908." In the 1910 off-year election, Democrats took over the House of Representatives, which may have signified the electorate's impatience with the president, or it may have been a vote of support for TR's progressivism.[42]

Nick and Alice avidly followed Roosevelt's actions, even as they "slept, ate, and breathed Schedule K," of the Canadian reciprocity bill when the Sixty-first Congress reconvened on December 5, 1910. Alice remembered the last day especially, after Nick's bill to establish a permanent tariff commission failed. While Nick dealt with the sine die deluge, she couldn't keep away from the excitement. "I stayed up at the Capitol until I got hungry, when I would hop into the electric [automobile], taking one or two friends with me, others following, and go back to the house to cook eggs and drink buckets of coffee; then to the Capitol again; a few hours there, and back we would go to my house to the pantry. I claimed to have a record that averaged an egg an hour for twelve hours," she recalled.[43] The reciprocity bill passed in 1911 but failed when Canadian voters rejected it in their election shortly thereafter. By that time, it was just one more insult for Taft, amid mounting cries for Colonel Roosevelt to declare himself a candidate for the presidential nomination in 1912.

In late September 1911, the Longworths visited the Panama Canal, a project irrevocably linked with the man with the Big Stick—which is why Alice wanted to go. The *New York Times* announced, CONGRESSMAN SAYS TAFT IS DOING GREAT THINGS QUIETLY. But Nick adroitly hedged his bets. When the *Times* asked him about the presidential race, "It was pretty far ahead to guess, he said, but he conveyed the impression that in his opinion the best man to succeed Taft was Taft. As to insurgents, the Ohio Congressman thought a majority of them were actuated by patriotic motives, though some were no doubt playing politics." While Nick smoothly doled out compliments to both sides, his friendship with Taft had been deepening. That year Taft had celebrated his birthday over lunch with Nick—just Nick—at the White House.[44] One can only imagine the shipboard discussions that must have taken place as Nick and Alice examined all the potential scenarios for 1912.

As a break from the political worries, the Longworths enjoyed Panama. They accompanied Colonel George Goethals, the man in charge of building the canal. They met with the colonel's aide, West Point graduate Robert E. Wood, who was in the middle of his decade of service in Panama. Alice was fascinated by the "color and the atmosphere of those early mornings, those torrid days, which we spent watching the work at the locks and at the Gatun dam; the machinery, and the thousands of men digging the Culebra cut."[45] Breathtaking in size and scope, Alice never lost her enthusiasm for the project. She treated with disdain all later suggestions that

Panama be given control of the canal. It was TR and the United States who had brought to fruition the dream of a canal; it was the United States that should control it.

In October, Alice was an honored guest in Pittsburgh, where she christened a reproduction of the *New Orleans,* a steamboat built in 1811 by her ancestor Nicholas Roosevelt. Taft was there, too. Alice scrutinized him through narrowed eyes, "meditatively—speculatively," wondering about his likely moves.[46] Taft had always wanted a seat on the Supreme Court. He was not enjoying the presidency. A bare few months into his term, his beloved spouse had suffered a paralyzing stroke. Anguished about his wife's condition and deeply wounded by the animosity shown him by progressive Republicans, Taft was not a happy man. Might he, Alice wondered, step down after just four years?

The 1912 election was one of the most important in American history. Four strong candidates staked out very clear positions on issues that touched every voter. The outcome of the race, while wholly unsatisfactory to the Roosevelts, resulted in profound transitions in both major political parties and a sea change in national politics. And it culminated in betrayal for Alice: political abandonment by the husband who had promised to stand by her forever.

Chapter 12

"Quite Marked Schizophrenia"

THE 1912 ELECTION was a defining event in Alice's life. She watched angrily as her husband, whose loyalties were stretched to the breaking point, chose his friends over his wife and in-laws. In Alice's mind, he opted for expediency over integrity. Nick had every reason to be pragmatic about his career—third parties rarely won. But in pledging himself to William Taft rather than to Theodore Roosevelt, Nick Longworth underestimated his wife's devotion to her father and the Progressive cause. Alice's and Nick's assessments of the importance of progressive politics, of a united family front, and of what would be best for them as a couple clashed. In the end, the election was a disaster for everyone: Alice, Nick, TR, the Tafts, and the Republican Party.

Alice Longworth earnestly shared the convictions of her father's Bull Moose Party, including his support for women's suffrage, but not his controversial belief in judicial recall. The complicating factor, of course, was that also running for reelection in 1912, as a committed standpat Republican, was the husband she truly cherished. It was a very real contest with difficult personal consequences. Alice loved her husband, but she idolized her father. She knew "it was particularly hard on [Nick] that I was, of course, single-minded in enthusiasms for anything that Father decided to do."[1] While Alice managed to hold her marriage together despite the tempest of the election, the shock of Nick's betrayal drained her last reserve of trust. It was this political betrayal that drove them apart, rather than Nick's dalliances with other women. Unlike her cousin Eleanor, whose life shattered in 1918 with the knowledge of Franklin's adultery, Alice—the

politician—was devastated in 1912 by Nick's political infidelity. Like Eleanor, Alice would use this disappointment to build a stronger public self and
to go in a direction more independent of her husband, pursuing her own
ends.

In early 1912, Theodore Roosevelt stood poised on the brink of announcing that he would enter the Republican primary against incumbent William Howard Taft. He desperately wanted the presidency again. He longed
to complete some of his initiatives, undo a few of Taft's, and fulfill the
promises he made in the New Nationalism speech. But it would be risky.
While Theodore Roosevelt was an idol of many Americans, he lacked the
backing of the powerful Republican National Committee (RNC). TR
would be accused of hubris, of royal ambitions. He knew that he could not
be perceived as actively seeking the nomination; it had to fall to him as the
natural result of the voters' unhappiness with Taft. Roosevelt also knew
that should he win the nomination, he might lose the national election. He
understood the complications. As he wrote to his son Ted, "...I feel as
Nick Longworth strongly feels, and as most of my best friends feel, that for
me personally the nomination would be a veritable calamity, and I do not
want to take it if it can possibly be avoided."[2] Yet Roosevelt had a strong
sense of duty. He came to believe that Americans wanted him back in the
presidency to enact his progressive agenda. His political enemies called it
self-deception.

Yet it was clear that even in President Taft's home state, TR had supporters: OHIO LEADER WANTS ROOSEVELT IN 1912, read the headline in early
December 1911. Nick leaped into the fray. LONGWORTH SAYS FRIENDS WILL
OPPOSE ANY BOOM FOR PRESIDENT, the newspapers blared two days later.
Nick issued a statement saying he'd just returned from Oyster Bay and that
he, "like all of Mr. Roosevelt's real friends," was discouraging any TR
draft. Nick spoke with the authority of the insider—he was on his way to
open Christmas presents with the Roosevelts on TR and Edith's bed.[3]

Like Nick, Alice counseled her father against his seeking the Republican nomination:

Don't much like it. Hate to have him get it by a fight... [I]f he does declare himself a candidate he must make it clear that it is not because of a demand for him on the part of the many people to whom he makes a picturesque appeal. Nor to satisfy those also [who] are pretty dissatisfied with the present administration—nor must he be deceived by the clamor for him by those who are running for office and feel that with him at the head of the ticket they will pull through even though he is defeated. He must make it clear that he is a candidate because he considers his policies the right policies and his remedies the right remedies for existing wrong conditions. He should lay unmistakable emphasis on the difference in what he stands for and [what] Taft stands for.... It must be because he is convinced that the people wish his views carried out. His motives for being a candidate are his convictions. This must be clear to all.... It would be harmful to his party or country were he defeated for the nomination and more seriously harmful to party and country were he defeated for election.[4]

Ignoring both daughter and son-in-law, by mid-February 1912, TR had finagled an "extemporaneous" tide of support from the group of pro-Roosevelt governors who called for him to "put his hat in the ring." Just before TR went public, Nick wavered. TR assured him, "I think you are right as to your saying that you are for Taft. In my judgment, it would be a mistake for you not to say so. You have definitely declared yourself, and I think it was the only thing you could do." This assuaged Nick's fears temporarily, as did TR's promise to "soak it to 'any Roosevelt creature' who dared to worry him in Cincinnati."[5]

The object of this protection wasn't comforted for long. The next day, Alice wrote, "Nick feels it a tragedy. If I can only keep him cheerful, sober and moderately contented. I've begun to have a desperate feeling again. That lost feeling of being absolutely alone. Darling Nick, I love him so much." Later that night, she followed up with, "I have just been in Nick's room again talking with him. He says that if Father comes out he will probably declare that he will not run again. I can hardly bear it. I shall do my utmost to persuade him not to. I can see how he feels. He says he can 'wobble' no longer—if it came to choosing between Father and Taft—certainly he is for nearly all that Father stands for . . . [but] that poor fat man has been courting him. Only must [Nick] sacrifice us for that lump of flesh? It is Nick's district. . . . I can't decide whether Nick has the conviction or the morals. It is bitterly hard."[6]

Alice believed that Nick truly was on the progressive side of the Republican Party and so should follow his conscience and declare for TR. His idea of pulling out of his own House race would consign them to living at Rookwood, being "sacrificed" for Taft, who had come a-wooing. Her private anguish was trying to weigh his "convictions" and his "morals." Nick and Alice were troubled by the political possibilities long before TR announced that he would run. And as for her "lost feeling of being absolutely alone," that was the feeling of abandonment from her youth washing back over her when Nick drank and flirted with other women—or with other political beliefs.

Nick's inability or unwillingness to remain sober concerned Alice because she despised drunkenness. Alice especially detested sloppy drunks. The loss of control, the surrender of one's command over one's self, and the ugly personalities that alcohol could awaken repulsed her. Whispered conversations about her uncle Elliott's sad death and Grandfather Carow's alcoholism swirled around her childhood. Alice took on the stern disapproval of her parents on this subject. An inebriated man was by definition feeble, lacking self-discipline and drive. Alcohol weakened Nick's judgment and made him reckless in social situations. When he drank he was indiscreet with her female friends. Whether he meant it to or not, it hurt. The extent of his dalliances is impossible to recapture, but Washington rumors circulated consistently. In Nick's defense, if ever there was the temptation to seek an escape with alcohol, the 1912 campaign was it.

They had another "gloomy talk" the next day, February 17, 1912, but followed it with a "really splendid" conversation, she recorded. "He asked me to state my side. I think I made a very clear and serious presentation of my views. I can only pray that he is guided by what I say." The stakes were high. If Nick committed to the wrong campaign, he could jeopardize his political future. Roosevelt would not have disowned him for backing Taft, but it was likely that the party regulars would pull their support if he switched to the progressives. Alice left for Oyster Bay to speak directly with her father. "We talked the whole thing over," Alice enthused. "He says Taft's chances are 3 to 1 against him (F.) for the nomination. He was more wonderful than ever." Roosevelt was clear-eyed about the race. Huge crowds flocked to see him that spring, and he told a reporter, "It's my past that brings them; not my future—a trap for politicians like myself." The difficulty of combining progressive principles, victory at the polls, and family harmony vexed Alice daily. One morning she "had a talk with Nick and was a fool and wept. . . . If he will only have a serious talk with Father." Alice knew the persuasive power of TR, "such a persistent talker," as Taft put it cynically, "that he can keep up the courage of his followers far beyond any justification for it." The next day things were better again as she talked "on the telephone this morning with my darling Nick." "I love him so," she confided to her diary.[7]

Instead of joining her as she asked, Nick went to see Taft. Alice recounted what he said. Taft was sympathetic and told Nick to "do whatever he pleased. Rather hard to say anything else, it strikes me."[8] With Taft's reassurance secured first, Nick only then took the midnight train to Oyster Bay. TR promised there would be no pro-Roosevelt competitor in Nick's district. Alice was cautiously happy. Nick was miserable. Despite both TR's and Taft's approval of his course, Alice noted that "his nerves [were] on edge," he was "still gloomy and [had] a pain in his interior."[9]

On February 21, 1912, Roosevelt formally announced that he would be a contender for the Republican presidential nomination. The Longworth family was predictably furious. Alice joined Nick on March 8 in Cincinnati where Clara had been publicly excoriating Roosevelt. Alice was livid. "Clara said she was justified in her opinion of Father. Always has said he was a man of overweening personal ambition. I got furious and told her that Father was entering in it for the principle—Poor Nick angry—Says I must 'shut up.' I am not going to take any more than I have given but if anyone has the impertinence to cast doubt on Father's good faith before my face—I shall certainly hurl the truth at them. . . . I am in this fight for all I am worth and we must and will win." The relationship between Clara and Alice was permanently damaged. Not long after this Alice's diary fills with epithets such as "Those hateful people. How I dislike and despise them."[10]

As March wore on, and the primaries and state conventions began, Alice stepped up her study of the issues. She had to be armed with arguments from both sides. She was finding it difficult to maintain her composure. As TR wrote Kermit, "I think [Alice] felt she just had to see me because of course all respectable society is now apoplectic with rage over me." Auntie Bye understood, as she, too, found it "wearing to live in a non sympathetic atmosphere when most of one's so-called friends differ in public beliefs from oneself." Alice thought Ruth and Medill were "the only people I can 'rant and rave' and really talk to." Even Edith was sending Alice "strong and unsympathetic letter[s] about Father," cautioning her to consider Nick's position. "I don't care," Alice fumed.[11]

Meanwhile, her in-laws never paused in their jibes. Alice remembered the toll this took on her: "We all managed to keep the peace to a surprising extent, though I was so full of bottled-up savagery that I very nearly became ill. Food choked me and I existed principally on fruit and eggs and Vichy [water]. I had a chronic cold and cough, indigestion, colitis, anaemia, and low blood pressure—and quite marked schizophrenia."[12]

Political bulletins and exclamations of hope that she could not express to her husband tumbled together in Alice's diary. "How I want to sock it to the other side!"—for example. Sagamore Hill was awash in political advisers, congressional hopefuls, men and women lobbying for various favors. The Roosevelt home had always been swimming in political ideas: "A daily dish of the household," Alice called it. And there is no overestimating the influence of the one sitting at the head of the table, serving the main course. Alice spent her time at Sagamore Hill, in close contact with Roosevelt National Committee campaign leaders, especially Chairman Joseph M. Dixon and Vice Chairman Frank Knox. A great deal of her news came from other Roosevelt workers, particularly Ruth and Medill, John O'Laughlin, George Perkins, and Gifford Pinchot. Dixon and O'Laughlin were in the habit of telephoning her with early predictions and ultimate reports of the primary tabulations. This must not have been easy for Nick Longworth to stomach—made all the harder as evidence of TR's great popularity with the average voter was inescapable. As a couple they worked it out. "Nick pleased me so," Alice noted in her diary, "by saying... that he was pleased about Illinois," where TR swept the primaries.[13]

Nick worried about being tarred with his father-in-law's brush. He wondered whether to repair to his home state to campaign for the Ohio primary. "If he goes he probably will be asked... questions and if he stays he will be taunted with having preferred the flesh pots of Washington to his home town. Hard either way, dear lamb," Alice wrote.[14] They decided jointly that he should go to Cincinnati. The couple was close that spring, dining alone together often, discussing politics, dancing, enjoying Nick's violin and their friends. But politics eventually called him to Rookwood. Two weeks remained before the Ohio primary.

Alice missed her husband, but was thrilled with her father's important primary victory in California. Once TR announced, Alice never wavered in her loyalty. No real criticism of TR appears in her writings. Nick, knowing he could not ask her to be objective, suggested his wife not join him in Ohio, especially during the convention. He told her that "the feeling there was unbelievably bitter." Alice knew that he really meant "particularly in his own family." He also requested she not go to hear TR speak at the convention. "It would be sure to get in the papers," Nick warned, "and it would not appear well...." She did as he wished, but not joyfully. Instead she took herself off to Sagamore to find comfort with her clan. Meanwhile, the Rough Rider himself was predicting a victory on the first ballot to the cheering conventioneers. Despite the deep divisions in Ohio, Roosevelt added that state primary victory to his earlier wins. Luckily, Longworth also won his primary race. The papers described Nick as maintaining a "complacent, if not altogether pleasant neutrality."[15]

In early June, TR informed Alice that should he lose the Republican nomination, he would create his own political party and go toward the national election regardless. "Father and I walked around.... He is so adorable. I love him so very much that I don't see how I can bear it if all does not go well. I told him all I have heard—and he talked about everything in his own wonderful way...." The likelihood of the new party brought

Nick's simmering frustration to a boil. He "wished he had followed his instincts and withdrawn for then he could speak out freely." Alice tried to comfort him. "He will be a great man," she mused, "he is so really clear-headed and right minded, but so sensitive, my darling precious lamb."[16]

The great question prompting Roosevelt's decision and Nick's annoyance occurred because of the decision of the Rules Committee concerning contested delegates in the run-up to the national caucus. By the time the Republican convention began, Roosevelt had 411 committed votes, Taft had 201, and the fiery Wisconsin progressive, Senator Robert LaFollette, had 36. One hundred thirty-six delegates were coming to the convention "uninstructed" and could cast their vote in Chicago any way they pleased. There was a critical mass of 254 contested votes. The Rules Committee, packed with Taft's men, handed 235 to Taft and only 19 to Roosevelt. TR reacted with outrage. Flinging aside tradition, he vowed he would personally attend the convention and fight for the votes he considered stolen from him. The Roosevelts arrived in Chicago the night before the convention opened. TR put it succinctly to a friend: "The Republican Party [has] become pretty nearly hopeless. Either it had to be radically regenerated from within, or a new party had to be made. I attempted regeneration. By simple swindling, the party bosses (as I cannot help thinking, rather fatuously) defeated the attempt."[17]

The long-anticipated Republican convention convened on June 16 in Chicago with crowds of people pushing against one another to catch a glimpse of the Roosevelts and the Longworths. Alice was in the thick of things. She and Nick had separate rooms at the Blackstone Hotel because of their chaotic schedules. Alice tried to mill about to get a sense of the crowd, but was "besieged by cameras" and had to retire to TR's room. Her days consisted of viewing the proceedings at the convention and plotting strategy with the Roosevelt campaign leaders, including Ruth and Medill. Alice and Nick spent the morning of the seventeenth going over his speech, and she "marked what he might cut."[18] The eighteenth they were together all day again, while Nick went out at night.

On the nineteenth, Nick alternated between excitement and mournfulness. At his side, Alice was by turns elated by the enthusiasm shown for TR, worried about Nick, and angry at the "hoards of creatures taking [her] picture...." It was probably elation that induced her to try *again* to convince Nick to support Roosevelt. She really believed he was, in his heart of hearts, a progressive, but Nick could hardly retract his public vows of support for his fellow Ohioan.[19] Alice never stopped attempting to get her husband to see that his policies were more like Roosevelt's than Taft's—and she never lost the feeling that Nick was somehow wrong not to fall in line with the family, blood being thicker than water.

It was certainly her strong "tribal feeling" and her anger at the Republican regulars for depriving her father of the nomination that prompted Alice to reject their proposition of making Nick governor of Ohio. Warren G. Harding sidled up to the couple in the Chicago Coliseum and offered to support Nick in a run for the governorship. Alice's impatience with the Ohio GOP's "strong-arm tactics" got the better of her. Before Nick could answer, she shot back: "I [do] not believe that Nick would accept anything at the hands of the Columbus convention...one [can] not accept favors from crooks." Nick begged her to apologize. She never did.[20]

Ultimately, the president's control of the party machinery was too firm for Roosevelt to dislodge. On the twenty-second, as Nick and Alice sat together, stone-faced and unsmiling, Harding nominated Taft, calling him "the greatest progressive of the age." Taft supporters roared. Roosevelt branded the whole thing a sham and insisted it was "in no proper sense any longer a Republican convention."[21] On June 23 just before midnight, Theodore Roosevelt and his followers shook the rafters of nearby Orchestra Hall chanting, "Thou shalt not steal," as they announced the creation of the Progressive Party, soon dubbed the Bull Moose Party, to challenge both the Republicans and the Democrats for the presidency in 1912. "Such spirit, buoyancy, and enthusiasm," Alice noted to her diary. She was there, with Edith, Ethel, Kermit, and Archie, waving to the well-wishers. Nick was not at her side. He was off making celebratory toasts with the Ohio delegation. Hurt and saddened, Alice avoided him the next day. Reporters noted that Nick "wore a dejected look," while Alice "breathed defiance."

"He will do," Alice told reporters threateningly, "what he thinks is right, regardless of how it may affect his political career." And, she could have added, his marriage. Nick chose the Republicans over the Progressives. He chose alcohol over Alice. She wanted a divorce. At a hasty but firm family tribunal, her parents talked her out of it.[22]

The train to Washington was "crowded," Alice recalled, "with enemies and deserters." Alice lobbied for converts to the Progressive Party. She turned her charm and intelligence to Idaho's Senator William Borah. He had come to Washington, D.C., six years earlier, a handsome, TR-worshiping, maverick Republican. Borah listened as Alice tried every political inducement she knew. But in 1912, his conscience told him to stay with the GOP. He had attended the convention as a Roosevelt supporter and had wavered, believing the Republicans had unfairly chosen Taft. With unassailable logic, Alice reminded the senator that he had once before left the Republican Party, then to follow a lesser man than her father. But Borah's experience in the 1896 election and his support of silverite William Jennings Bryan had taught him the futility of third-party attempts. Across the aisle of the Pullman dining car, Alice Longworth and Bill Borah squared off. Her well-marshaled arguments, personal magnetism, and Roosevelt mystique did not prevail. The senator won. Borah kept TR on a pedestal but would vote for Taft in 1912. Next time they met, he would not be able to resist her.[23]

On the twenty-fifth, Nick and Alice traveled to Baltimore with the McLeans to take in the Democratic convention. It did not bring good news. As Alice sat near cousins Eleanor and Franklin, the Democrats nominated progressive New Jersey governor Woodrow Wilson. TR's supporters hoped the Democrats would put forward a right-leaning Democrat, leaving voters to choose from among TR and two conservatives. Eleanor told her friend Isabella Greenway that Alice was looking well and bubbling over about the "wonderful" Chicago convention. But Nick, Alice worried, was "gloomy" and "despairing," and she said she herself felt "so tired and depressed."[24] She was not close enough to Eleanor to confess the personal toll of the GOP decision.

Still, TR's speaking tours proved his popularity undimmed. As his fortunes eclipsed Taft's, Nick's fell. Progressives in Ohio threatened to "smoke out" Nick and work doubly hard for his defeat if he didn't declare for Roosevelt. "His wife is progressive," the Ohioans mused, "but every act he has ever done in Congress stamps him as a reactionary." Alice was sorry for him. "My darling helpless Nick ... I do love him so much," she wrote. The aftermath of the conventions and the realization that Wilson would probably take the presidency gave Alice another cold. Nick's turmoil made him reassess his course. After a consultation with President Taft, Alice recounted, Nick "talked, quite calmly; he said he had three choices—to withdraw and do nothing; stay in and be an active Republican; or stay in and do nothing except for himself—and if I can't see [it] I am lacking in sense and am a 'woman.' The latter anyway is true! But I will not betray him, darling Nick." Nick felt the best he could do was to "stay in and do nothing except for himself."[25]

Alice left for her annual summer visit to the Lee relatives in Boston, protesting that she hated to leave her precious Nick. They met up afterward at Sagamore Hill, where an important decision was made for her, against her will. On the wide veranda looking out over the bay, Theodore, Nick, and Alice sat rocking and strategizing. The men laid down the law: Alice could not attend the Progressive Party convention in Chicago. "I could scream," Alice stormed, "but if N. was defeated, as he probably will be, and I felt I have done anything he hadn't wanted in a political line I should feel frightfully." Her presence at the convention might cause Nick to lose votes, but it surely would have helped her father. In her autobiography, Alice described the depth of her unhappiness: "I used to have ignoble thoughts of goading Nick into doing something that would justify me in packing my bag and hopping a train to Chicago—something reprehensible, such as making a display of friendliness to the unfortunate Mr. Taft. That was the unattractive frame of mind that I was in for days at a time during those dementing months of the campaign!" She loyally but reluctantly stayed out of the spotlight. Her father approved of her resolution. He described Alice to a friend as "a most ardent, intelligent and uncompromising progressive."[26]

More than one thousand "serious, earnest, almost fanatical men and women" converged on the Windy City for the opening of the convention on August 5, but MRS. LONGWORTH NOT THERE, the papers noted. She was at home being "rather unpleasant this morning to Nick. It suddenly came over me in a rush what I was missing." To add insult to injury, her mother-in-law came for a visit. Alice could hardly remain civil. She was imagining an escape, to "Egypt and India and China and the Great West and South America and the South Seas. I felt as I could burst unless I went to one of my distant lands."[27]

The Progressive Party convention was, Edith thought, "like a great religious meeting with deep seriousness beneath all the enthusiasm." TR was in his element, greeting supporters, plotting strategy, exuding enthusiasm and confidence. His speech was apocryphal and stirring, repeating the famous closing of his Orchestra Hall oration: "We stand at Armageddon, and we battle for the Lord." His "confession of faith" sent legions of campaigners off to their home states on fire to spread the gospel of progressivism. Alice kept up through phone calls and telegrams, and kicked against the fate that denied her a front-row seat at that historic convention. To Auntie Bye she confided, "It was a bitter disappointment and I don't think I shall ever get over not having seen it. But poor Nick is having a dreadfully hard time and being such a dear about it all and he felt very strongly and was back[ed] up by Father."[28]

As the fall wore on, Alice consulted with headquarters and visited her father regularly. She heartily approved of the Bull Moose ideal: "The platform is the best thing I've read for ages. I in fact read it again and again today and am 'for it.' I am getting active pleasure out of it—not an atom too radical." Still, Alice hated to be sidelined by the combination of her own celebrity and by the expectation that she show outward loyalty to her husband's cause. In her autobiography she lamented how "my sister-in-law and everyone I knew were busy working for Taft." Auntie Bye expressed the same desire Alice had: to "help campaign for Father, or do any work for him." Everyone was feeling the strain. Her stepmother confessed to Belle Hagner, "There is such a hard time ahead that I can scarcely keep a stiff upper lip. I wish I could see you but Washington is the forbidden city for me."[29]

The subject of a three-day parley at Sagamore was whether or not to run a Progressive in Nick's Ohio district. Roosevelt had earlier ruled that the Progressive Party would support slates in every state possible while protecting Nick. By August, the matter was out of his hands. The Progressive Party in Ohio chose to run A. O. Zwick against Nick. Alice's anger was tinged with pragmatism. "I can see [both] sides and it won't do to talk. But I feel rather betrayed and as if it might easily go to the devil. My precious Nick. I am so homesick for him." Nick worried that what might happen in the national election—the Progressive Party would facilitate a Democratic victory—would now happen to his detriment in his own district. Alice summed up her fears for her husband's election and her loyalty to them both: "I am with Father heart and soul—and with Nick heart and body (I suppose that is about it) and altogether [it] is one of the most unpleasant situations conceivable and I have to face it and do *my* best to make the best of it."[30]

It was a terrible time for them both. Grace Vanderbilt invited her to a costume ball in Newport, the playground of the aristocracy. Nick forbade her. Alice escaped anyway. The ball would make the front pages, Nick seethed, and Alice's photo splashed across the country would provoke an outcry in his district. It didn't help that Grace contributed financially to TR's campaign. "I feel," Alice penned sullenly, "it would be ridiculous to stay away for political purposes. It is not going to be a debauch," she asserted to her diary, and she thought it crazy "to give up going" for fear of "what 'people' will say." She and Eleanor Sears left for the Vanderbilt "cottage," the Breakers, on the twenty-second and turned her attention to the rehearsal for the quadrille. After dinner with Senator Aldrich—she could not leave off politics for long—the ball opened. Alice and Grace "led the cotillion at 4:30 a.m. down around the ocean." She danced happily until breakfast at 7:00 a.m. and fell into bed an hour later.[31]

The next day, she received a telegram that made her furious. In a vengeful mood, Nick had gone to Ilesboro, Ohio, to play golf and see a woman of whom Alice disapproved. When the couple reunited, Alice wrote: "He hates me and I him—don't like his politics or his personality but I hate feeling as I do at the moment that our life together is...a failure and on the verge of breaking up." Alice's tone was ominous. "Things will never be the same again," she thundered. "He knows what I feel about his going to Iles-boro, unreasonable and unwarranted as it was." Nick took to drinking, and Alice didn't stop him. The tit-for-tat injuring "wounded [her] deeply."[32]

Things only very slowly returned to normal. Alice's commitment to the Progressive cause deepened. She promised to "get names for" the woman's finance committee to help with the fund-raising. Nick's position remained untenable. Newspapers made much of it. LONGWORTH STILL FOR TAFT, the headline read, followed by BUT DECLARES THAT ROOSEVELT POLICIES MUST BE CARRIED OUT. "I am what I have always been, a Republican," Nick repeated wearily, but, "at the same time I want it understood that as a Republican I am a Progressive." "There is much merit in 'but,'" one editor joked.[33]

In mid-September 1912, the Longworths went to "Nick's place"—in her anger disavowing all personal connections to Rookwood—to await the election. Cincinnati bored Alice, and the anti-Progressive sentiment there angered her. She took refuge in reading. She consumed *First and Second Maccabees* in the Apocrypha, biographies of Alexander the Great, and Os-car Wilde's poems, but continually interrupting her was the realization that TR "stands for everything that is upright and Progressive and inspired and how sad it will be for the people if he is not made president."[34] So strongly did she feel that she defied both her husband and her father to attend a Pro-gressive rally in Columbus, where TR's vice presidential nominee, Hiram Johnson, spoke. She was the focus of intense interest even though she tried to remain an onlooker. Buckeye Progressives made much of having lured Princess Alice out of hiding.

Nick faced a serious political crisis. He told his sister, "I would go down the street during the campaign and meet first one of my intimates and then another. The first would say 'I cannot vote for you Nick, because your father-in-law is running for President at the head of the Progressive Party and I am not a Progressive.' The next would say: 'I am sorry Nick, but since you are for William Howard Taft as President, I can't vote for you, I am for Roosevelt.'" Alice stayed off those Cincinnati streets, playing cards with Nick's sister Nan and reading until late the plays of Franz Wedekind and August Strindberg, and James Frazier's classic *The Golden Bough*. Alice longed to go to Washington, but decided against it as Nick "seems to want me very much here. He is so dear and nice now, but I always know something will happen, sooner or later and that it won't last."[35] They were living in a public pressure cooker.

Alice did go—alone—to Chicago on October 12 to hear TR's big speech at the Coliseum. Ever the politician's daughter, she circulated among the train conductors and porters, taking the pulse of the voters, and was thrilled to find them all avowed Progressives. Thousands more supporters gathered to meet TR with "the most wild enthusiasm." She, Medill, and a pregnant Ruth dined with TR afterward, when he was supposed to be resting his throat. While in Chicago, Alice did a little passive volunteer work for the campaign by watching the sales at the Bull Moose store. It was the last day to register to vote, and she drew attention to the cause by her presence. She wouldn't actually get behind the cash register to sell items, probably because she had "asked again if my doing any professional political work would be objectionable," and TR told her it would be. He had requested she not be present in Cincinnati when he gave a talk in Nick's backyard. Even her appearance at an event could be misconstrued, but she had to be in the thick of things at least sometimes. "It was torture," she wrote, "not to be doing something." She did give money: six hundred dollars to her father's campaign, and four hundred to her husband's.[36]

On October 14, Alice was interrupted at dinner by a terrifying telephone call from the *Philadelphia Inquirer*. In Milwaukee, her father had been shot. An unbalanced fanatic who claimed he was opposed to Roosevelt's having a third term in the presidency aimed at TR from six feet away. The bullet slowed on impact with the triple barrier of Roosevelt's heavy overcoat, his lengthy, folded speech, and his steel glasses case. But the bullet did not exit his body. That did not stop the Bull Moose. He gave his scheduled speech before going to the hospital. Ruth telephoned to confirm the details and reassure Alice that TR would be fine.

Alice left for Roosevelt's Chicago hospital room on the morning train. She joined the rest of her family already there, except for Kermit, who was in Brazil. Nick arrived on the sixteenth as the physicians were debating whether to remove the bullet, which had lodged close to his heart. Nick went to the hospital to see TR, but was, according to Alice, "a little intoxicated" at dinner. "Of course [he] was tired but it is discouraging," to have him yet again unavailable to support her in such an awful time. Nick left for Cincinnati on the midnight train. He was making several campaign speeches a day.[37]

TR's opponents (Taft, Wilson, and the Socialist Eugene Debs) graciously called a temporary halt to the mudslinging in the presidential campaign as he healed, but Bull Moose strategy making continued uninterrupted. Alice was thriving; in the thick of it, taking care of her father and plotting tactics with the campaign leaders. Ruth was her mainstay during these worrisome days. The McCormicks were staunch Progressives, and Ruth had added her pleas to Alice's, trying to persuade Nick to join them. Officially, Medill headed the Bull Moose campaign activities in the West, while Ruth chaired the Chicago Committee of 100. Ruth was "a cracking success" at her job, Alice thought, and as a friend she was "the good angel."[38]

Leaving TR in competent hands, Alice reluctantly returned to Cincinnati on the twenty-third. Energized from the time with her family, she was critical of Nick. She attended a rally and heard him speak on the tariff. "He still pulls his mouth down . . . and opens it so affectedly and with such terrible . . . sounds. Middle western to a degree," she wrote, dismissively. She stayed away from the big hometown celebration of Taft, where Nick gave a flattering address. "I am not for any more of such," she wrote from her bed.[39]

A week later, Alice attended TR's best speech of the year, at Madison Square Garden. She had helped him write it. Sitting together, "he would pass over the first draft of every sheet . . . as he finished writing it" to her. Despite the huge and adoring crowd, according to her autobiography, they had "no illusions. . . . It was depressing to realize that the spirit, the enthusiasm, and the conviction of the righteousness of our cause were about to go down before the vastly greater number who did not believe in the issues as we saw them or who did not care."[40] Nick was similarly downcast. "Not a spark of life in him," Alice wrote. Just two days before the election, Alice recounted the wages of stress:

> Nick and I had a tremendous row after lunch on account of me not being for him, not "standing by" him, and I am so hurt and angry. I had prided myself on my self control and what is the use? Talking about going to Ruth in Chicago [for the election night] brought matters to a climax.... He suggested that I should not be [in Ohio] this autumn but I thought he wanted me to come and he seemed to like my being here—and now when I have been away for five days he seems to resent my interest and hopes in and for the Progressive Party.... Of course I am disappointed [in] him infinitely more I fear than he is in me. He is so "sensitive" in his political feeling but also I am heartily proud of the campaign he has made. And of course earnestly desire his success—but we are surely drifting decidedly far apart.[41]

By the next day, they were "on better terms," but Nick was "fatigued" and Alice's "thoughts [were] very far away." She mused again at length in her diary, and her loyalty is clear: "As for Father and his Progressive Party, I don't dare hope.... Everything is against us, but his fight is the fight for all that is great and advanced and human...."[42]

Election day 1912 was stifling. The Democrats carried the presidency as progressive New Jersey governor Woodrow Wilson won. Alice tried to put a good spin on it, looking toward the future and marveling at Taft's paltry eight electoral college votes to her father's eighty-eight. She thought TR's concession statement was "wonderful" and although her "heart ache[d]," she vowed she would hold her "head high."[43]

At least Nick won. Or so it seemed. But two days later it became clear that Nick lost his House seat by ninety-seven votes to the Democratic contender. Were those ninety-seven votes lost when Alice defied her father and her husband to attend the Progressive rally in Columbus? In later life, Alice thought so. At the time, she knew it was "terribly hard on my poor Nick. He looks so crushed, and I know he feels bruised and betrayed. He is

so painfully sensitive about things that really matter to him and no one realizes it. He seems such a nice matter-of-fact object, but I know how deeply
hurt he feels, and it is desperately hard to have been buoyed by false
hopes....It is all hideous and if we can only keep happy together...."[44]

Ever the pragmatist, Alice closed her diary entry with: "Now Nick
must become a real Progressive. These are quickly moving times and one
must be not only alert, but have firmly rooted ambitions and resolve to
keep in the current." One wonders how sympathetic Nick found her. She
railed to herself about how awful it would be to live in Cincinnati with the
"dull little people." Her admitted self-absorption might have had something to do with Nick's big debauch, what Alice called one of the ten worst
days of her life: "We dined at the Crosstown...Nick got very drunk—we
stayed interminable hours and when we got home he completely broke
down. I have an infinite sorrow and pity for him which I tried to make him
feel, but it was very terrible. I want him to realize that I have the greatest
faith in him and that this is only a temporary setback and it leaves him the
most free to pursue his own line of action....It is desperate but unless I
go to the devil or go to pieces I will pull him through to a successful
ending."[45]

While Nick's banishment from the House of Representatives lasted
only one term, the effect of the divisive battle of 1912 on the Longworth
marriage would be more profound. Less than a month into her plan of pulling Nick through, Alice confessed to being "absolutely at sea as to the
course I should pursue," given the "rather derogatory thoughts" she felt
Nick was having about her. His mother and sisters apparently felt the same,
as they suggested that the couple ought to purchase their own house rather
than live at Rookwood. Nick would not hear of it. First electoral defeat,
then turned out of his own home by his own family. His reaction was evidence of his despair. "He says," Alice recounted in her diary, "it is a question of divorcing and that he chooses me over all the rest including politics.
He simply must not mean it. I try to make him feel that I am willing and
delighted to be anywhere he wants but it is decidedly discouraging and I so
dread his...breaking down again."[46] Susan Longworth and Alice Long-

worth were never close, and the thought of living with her for two years was shriveling. How his depression, and his "moments," which "exhausted" her, coupled with her general arrogance toward the Midwest would play out remained to be seen. Alice took refuge in Christmas at Sagamore Hill—but she knew the demons would be waiting when she returned.

Chapter 13

"Beating Against Bars"

ALICE HAD TO WILL HERSELF to call Cincinnati home. Small-town politics were of only middling interest to her. She had no real friends there. Ruth Hanna McCormick lived in Chicago, but that was as far away as Washington. Worse, Alice and Susan Longworth were forced into close, daily proximity at Rookwood. Nick, their buffer, returned to his law firm but was more interested in potential constituents than clients. For the first ten months of exile, Nick suffered, according to Alice, with not even one "unreservedly cheerful political moment."[1] He had every intention of being reelected in 1914—and that was the only game afoot for his wife. The Longworths' misery did not draw them closer. In fact, their marriage devolved into one of tolerant and usually amused—but distant—affection. It was characterized by lengthy separations, occasional jealous outbursts, and a joint commitment to keeping up appearances. Curiously loving letters held them together, as though they liked each other much better apart.

Alice found three ways to escape from Cincinnati: she left as often as she could for visits to Sagamore Hill; she went to parties; she devoured books and newspapers. For his part, Nick had his usual trio of diversions: wine, women, and song. A comfortable and liquid conviviality formed the backdrop for Nick's ongoing relationships with Ohio politicians, local women, and society friends. Cincinnati's biannual May music festival brought great artists to his doorstep, and he could indulge his love of music. Alice mistrusted the politicians and liked few of his friends. She ignored the women as much as she could, but sometimes she stumbled on them. Out walking one day, Alice came upon Nick and a young Cincinnatian curled about each other in the park. Looking up, the woman unblushingly called out, "Hullo, Mrs. Longworth."[2] At least the music was tolerable.

"I'm approaching my 29th birthday," Alice wrote to her sister. "I've added for you and me a verse of my own" to a poem Ethel had mentioned:

> For seven long years I've been wed
> I've had some assorted emotions,
> but frankly when all's done and said
> In spite of my fears which depress me,
> and in spite of the life that I've led
> I'd sooner have 'sparkling' occasions,
> than find my heart ruled by my head.

"Excellent sentiments, what!"[3] An excellent self-defense, as well.

Alice delayed the inevitable departure from Washington for as long as possible by staying on for the last months of the Taft administration. "Did you hear," she wrote to her sister, "that Mrs. Taft had a Turkey Trot class at the White House[?] To see her doing the Aviation Slide is said to be a very rare sight. I have made a beautiful imitation of it." Of course the best reason to linger was to see the change. "[I]t was almost impossible to believe that those odd beings called Democrats were actually there in the offing about to take things over.... It was not nearly so subduing as I thought it would be to be among the Lame Ducks," she recalled with glee. "We were busy with plans for a comeback." One who returned early was Belle Hagner. She had been asked by the new First Lady, Ellen Axson Wilson, to serve as her social secretary, and her continued employment made all the Roosevelts glad for her.[4]

Another interesting feature of the Wilson administration was the new assistant secretary of the navy, Franklin D. Roosevelt. TR wrote of his pleasure in the appointment: "It is interesting to see that you are in another place which I myself once held. I am sure you will enjoy yourself to the full...and...do capital work." But he promised to caution his niece to be "nice to the naval officers' wives. They have a pretty hard time, with very little money to get along on, and yet a position to keep up...."[5] Roosevelt knew the pity that his sister Bye, wife of Admiral William Sheffield Cowles, took on wives of men junior to her husband. Characteristically, this was only the *first* letter of unasked-for advice to reach the new secretary's desk from Uncle Ted.

Alice and Nick made sure to invite Eleanor and Franklin over. Never warm cousins, Eleanor and Alice had guardedly nice things to say about each other—despite the vast difference in their personalities and interests. Eleanor told her friend Isabella Ferguson about the Longworths' entertaining, where "one of the lady guests had a cocktail, 2 glasses of whiskey and liqueurs and 15 cigarettes before I left at 10:15. It was a funny party but I'm glad I'm not quite so fashionable! Alice looks fairly well though and is very nice." Even though it's a safe guess that the thirsty "lady guest" was Nick's friend, Alice nevertheless had a difficult time with the "rather fine and solemn little Sunday evenings" at her Democratic cousins' home, "where one was usually regaled with crown roast, very indifferent wine, and a good deal of knitting." Alice and Nick once took Susan Longworth with them. Susan knew that as Alice became bored, she "appeared to swell up" so that her "face becomes fat." That night she thought her daughter-in-law "was going to lose [her] eyes" altogether. Alice found her cousins hard to take and very tedious as a couple. But FDR on his own "asserted himself" and was much more fun.[6]

Franklin loved people and thrived on social interaction, but Eleanor was, she herself admitted, a "slave of the social system," making as many as thirty calls between lunch and teatime. ER's son believed that "tallying the number of calls she made and adhering to her rigid timetable were what counted with her, not the conversations she could have had with those she called on." Even Lucy Mercer's secretarial help didn't alleviate Eleanor's fears, which grew as she observed her cousin's seasoned socializing. Eleanor remembered Alice's as "a center of gaiety and of interesting gatherings. Everyone who came to Washington coveted an introduction to her and an invitation to her house." In 1913, Eleanor wanted most of all to blend in.[7] Such a timid response to the cosmopolitan and fascinating nation's center could only cause one cousin to look on with dismay and envy while the other peered back with disdain.

As the curtain rose on Wilson's term, Nick exited Washington first. Alice left her card at the White House with Belle, and "a day or so later went to a perfunctory and formal tea there." Nick wrote Alice newsy letters from Cincinnati with reassurances masking past troubles: "You may compose yourself in peace," Nick wrote, "with the knowledge that Margaret leaves on April 1. She is to marry a young doctor.... Possibly it will relieve your mind to know that Virgie and Hilda are in New York, and I haven't seen any women folk." Her response made no mention of the "women folk," but did make plain that she was "really slaving" at home packing up the house, taking "ammonia baths" for physical sustenance, and stepping out only to attend charity events and dine with Judge Learned Hand and writer Herbert Croly. "Good night my precious one," she concluded. "Your letter sounded cheerful and I am so glad."[8]

No other delaying tactic in sight, Alice eventually said her last good-byes. She hated to leave Washington—and would return only once while Nick was out of office—but upon reflection she was pragmatic: "It was an excellent thing for both of us to be out for a term. It gave him time in the district he had not had for many years, and it was most salutary for me to be removed for a while from the easy, agreeable existence that I was accustomed to in Washington." That was an echo of the Rooseveltian fear that an effortless life lacked the necessary character-forming challenges. And every now and then she could find something good about the peacefulness of Cincinnati. She once recorded pastorally that she "sat on the porch after dinner and said poetry and hymns and whistled and looked at the earth and the stars. Very blessed me."[9] Cincinnati was also good for walking. As she did throughout her life, Alice walked miles at a time for exercise and meditation.

In the spring, Edith and Ethel were busy planning the latter's wedding to Dr. Richard Derby, a surgeon friend of Kermit's. Theodore later called Dick "one of the most efficient, high-minded, loyal and fearless men I ever met." Nick and Alice arranged to meet up with each other at Sagamore Hill for the ceremony on April 4. Alice went on first, but then terrible rains drenched Cincinnati. Nick's first report was sobering. "The situation here is about as bad as it can be.... The center part of Ohio is a vast lake." He feared that Dayton would be entirely "wiped out" by floodwaters and uncontrollable fires, and thought "what may follow from disease and starvation is awful to contemplate." One can imagine Alice's reaction to such a missive, received while at the Ritz-Carlton hotel in New York City, where, with her maid, she was readying for the ride out to Oyster Bay. She had not seen Nick in weeks, and there were worries on her part about his straying. Now the rains brought these considerations to a halt while Nick responded as a leading politician from the stricken state. He had two boats out ferrying people and "helping wherever we can."[10]

Nick's next letter was less frightening—the loss of life was not as bad as he originally predicted. North of Cincinnati the floodwaters were retreating, but conditions were worsening in the Queen City, where "thousands of houses and factories are under water." "I am so thankful," Alice wrote, "that we live in a sort of Ararat." She wrote on the thirty-first, still thinking that he would be able to get to Sagamore for the wedding. In New York, she went to the opera, saw dressmakers, and dined with her aunts. At Sagamore, she caught up on family news. But these were diversions. "I hate not being in Ohio when there is so much to be done," she wrote Nick, "but I couldn't risk going out and not being able to get back in time for Ethel's wedding.... Darling precious Bubbet, I wish I could see you."[11]

The 1913 flood was one of the worst natural disasters in Ohio history. Governor James M. Cox declared martial law and called out the National Guard in the hardest hit areas around Columbus, Dayton, and Zanesville. Nick could not extract himself. Alice missed him: "It was the best wedding I've ever been to, at least when you weren't the bridegroom! For nothing can quite touch ours." Their letters professed sorrow at not seeing each other, and consistently used the nicknames they developed for each other, Bubbie for her, Bubby for him, with variations. "Precious Bubbet I do want to see you! I am pretty forlorn at times and your letters have been such a comfort," Alice wrote. Nick reciprocated. "I want my Bubbie back badly," he wrote twice in one letter that April.[12]

Despite her outward behavior, the family knew Alice's life with Nick was not ideal. Kermit, with troubles of his own in Brazil, wrote sensitively to Ethel: "I am feeling awfully depressed about Sister. Here's a hard outlook. She's tied down, and has most of the things which theoretically ought to make you happy, but which actually really have so very little to do with it." News of friends and family helped to divert Alice from the grind of Cincinnati, where she had gone once the waters receded. In March 1914 came the joyful tidings of the birth of Dick and Ethel's first baby, Richard Derby Jr. Travel always helped Alice, too. With Edith at Sagamore, the older woman observed how much Alice "enjoys a little change from family in law."[13]

A quarrel erupted in September, when Nick broke his foot doing the Turkey Trot in Cincinnati with someone not his wife. He was laid up on crutches for weeks. While he was hobbling around at the Myopia Hunt Club, watching golf tournaments and squiring about various women, Alice returned to her parents. "Tell me what the Puppuk thinks of the Maine election," Nick begged, but most of his letters were full of names that could only have made Alice unhappy. "Last night I had a dinner and a musical party here. Meyers, Ags, Shaws, Goodriches, Lucy, Mary, Amory, Betty Hig, Edith and her brother (Reynold with cold)."[14]

Willard Straight, who had married Dorothy Whitney in 1911, was one of the visitors to Sagamore Hill, but the distraction of an old friend was not enough to quench her desire for Nick, despite his wandering eye: "Darling Bubby. I love you so very much. You are so much nicer and more attractive and more everything than any one else in the world. . . . I'm getting a terrible longing to hear your voice so I may call you upon the telephone from town," Alice wrote feelingly. On the other hand, her letter outlined all the various obstacles to his joining her at Oyster Bay early—servants leaving, her planned visit to Auntie Bye, some shopping she had to do—despite Nick's desire to talk about the 1916 election with TR before he left the country. Alice's conflicted emotions disrupted the family. Edith wrote, adding with some aggravation, "This Sunday she spends with E. Ellis, a relief to the family for her temper is vile—no doubt she has trouble enough, poor soul, but not to be justly visited on us."[15]

Fretting about Nick's infidelities, Alice watched her parents wave good-bye to the large crowd gathered in their honor as they set sail for South America in early October 1913. TR had concocted a plan to explore an uncharted Brazilian river. He called it his "last chance to be a boy." Edith, a game traveler and a concerned wife, determined to go with him for the first two months as he made an elder-statesman's tour of Chile, Argentina, Uruguay, and Brazil. Edith insisted that Kermit postpone his planned wedding to Belle Willard to escort his father into the wilderness.[16] At fifty-four, Theodore's strenuous life had given him malaria, rheumatism, a blind left eye, and more. Charting the River of Doubt would very nearly finish him off.

Christmas 1913 thus found the Longworths apart again. Nick joined his mother in Cincinnati. Alice, Quentin, Ted and Eleanor, and Ethel, Dick, and their baby got together at Oyster Bay for part of the holidays. Alice spent Christmas eve with Ted and Eleanor—both of whom she always enjoyed—filling stockings, cooking eggs in the kitchen, and having "a nice, silly time." Christmas dinner was a prodigious affair. She ate, she told Nick, "five helpings of roast pig," after which "Ted and I went on, when the family left, to Birdie Vanderbilt's to a party—dozens of people there, who appeared glad to see me and bemoaned your absence." She had a marvelous time. The next days involved shopping, plays, a lunch where "all the ladies but me were ardent and active suffragists," and another where she met Giuseppe Garibaldi II. Alice found the son of the famous Italian nationalist-in-exile "a most perfect combination of both dreamer and fighter—very interesting about Mexico, but not the charmer I had been led to expect."

She told Nick that she was off to a New Year's celebration at the Long Island home of Willard and Dorothy Straight. "I love you very, very much," she assured Nick in closing. "Nice, snowy Cincinnati sounds very attractive, far more so than New York, which has a hard dry cast iron aspect and cold and blowy besides," she wrote before leaving for Long Island. More plays, *Der Rosenkavalier* ("nothing but German buffoonery on the stage, though some of the music was quite pretty"), and an interesting gathering where British suffragist Vera Laughton Mathews impressed her. She, Alice told Nick, "really knows quite a lot on the subject and expresses herself clearly and well." Alice concluded with a 1914 wish for her husband: "All I hope is that it will not be my fault if the New Year is not a happy one for you. Your devoted, Bubbie."[17]

The separations between the Longworths allowed Alice to play with her friends, who, unlike Nick's, were younger, uncritically fond of her father, and from the Eastern establishment. He had known his pals, especially the Cincinnati coterie, from his youth. They all grew up immersed in the Queen City's musical and political traditions. During Alice's absences Nick continued his philandering, which seems to have paused in the early days of their marriage and returned sometime after 1912. One longtime Cincinnati resident remembered that "Nick loved to kiss pretty ladies, which my mother was, and he loved to kiss her." Nick, she summed up, "could get away with anything."[18] Nick was generally discreet. Who knows but that, in certain quarters, it may have helped his political career to have been seen with local Cincinnati women—a sort of "take that, TR and Eastern progressives." In an era when one measure of a man's virility was his female conquests, Nick's womanizing, after his electoral loss, could offer constituents subtle but real proof of his prowess—and evidence that he was not under the thumb of his famous father-in-law, either.

Alice rejoiced when Nick pulled out of his depression to tell her in January 1914 that he would resume his political career. Perhaps the dissipation of her Newport parties was troubling her buried New England conscience: "You can't know how happy I am that you are going to run again— I suppose the governorship would be impossible to try for under the circumstances though how I should love to see you beat both Cox and Garfield—I am sure you have been able to decide all this much more easily without seeing me around and as you told me not to dodge any amusing things I am taking you at your word and staying until Tuesday or Wednesday—by that time I will be surfeited and I doubt if you will be able to force me away from Cincinnati again until the spring!" Politics were never far from Alice's mind. So anxious was she to see him reunited with his career that she wrote approvingly of the Ohio governorship. But Nick's situation would continue to be troubled by divided loyalties. As TR left to explore the River of Doubt in Brazil, his dedication to the Progressive Party had not wavered: "I am with you for this cause, to fight to the end," he vowed to his supporters.[19]

Before she and Nick could discuss matters in person, Alice had to attend the funeral of her grandmother Caroline Lee. It was a "very depressing" event, and Alice promptly came down with the mumps. Grandmother Lee's death was a break with her mother's side of the family. Alice felt extremely sad. She went to recuperate briefly at Auntie Bye's in Connecticut, so as not to "come home a green shadow to the arms of my Bubby." She thanked Bye for taking her in, writing, "My brief moment with you has the kind of joy that I can't even begin to tell you.... You don't know how hateful it is not to see you and have you near ... for there is no one in the world like my own Auntie Bye." Because of her grandmother's death, Alice was also "a little more prosperous."[20] Healed and a thousand dollars wealthier, she rejoined Nick in Cincinnati in mid-January 1914.

Rookwood seemed dreary and parochial. It was Susan's home, full of Longworth heirlooms and mementos of Nick's premarriage life. Because Nick was averse to the idea, the couple never established their own home in Cincinnati. Alice felt trapped. It reminded her of the First Daughter years when she had nowhere of her own to entertain. She went along to Nick's picnics, which gave him an excuse to "repair to the Shrine of the cellar and with appropriate ceremonies do Bacchic reverence...." As often as thrice weekly they hosted "musical parties" of trios or quartets. "[T]here never were more delightful evenings," Alice later reminisced. She learned to be a better listener, once even helping Nick edit an opera he composed.[21] Music never became her avocation but her diaries attest to her enjoyment.

While Alice joined in, these were really Nick's avocations. She kept from Nick knowledge of the one thing she really came to love in Cincinnati: Joseph S. Graydon. A tall, handsome, erudite attorney, Joe Graydon and Alice embarked upon what can best be termed an intellectual affair. Possibly, but probably not, consummated, their mutual affection is clear in his letters to her, and attested to in Graydon family stories.[22] Joe was eight years older than Alice, a Class of 1898 Harvard graduate who had attended Harvard Law and then the University of Cincinnati. His professional and civic careers were exemplary. He was a senior founding partner in Graydon, Head, and Ritchey, a member of the Cincinnati Bar Association, and a supporter of the fine arts in the Queen City. He was a horseman and a tennis player—but it was his mind Alice loved.

Joe Graydon was intoxicated with Immanuel Kant, René Descartes, Edward Gibbon, and William Shakespeare. His letters to her were liberally sprinkled with quotations. He cited long passages of Sir Thomas Browne. The windows in his home library were etched with figures from Geoffrey Chaucer's *The Canterbury Tales*. Though not an academic, he belonged to the Modern Languages Association of America, the Early English Text Society, the Medieval Society of America, Cincinnati's Classical Round Table, and the Historical and Philosophical Society of Ohio, among others. He owned a twelve-volume set of the 1911 *Oxford English Dictionary*. One of Graydon's heroes was Charles Russell, Lord Chief Justice of England. Alice asked him to send her Russell's writings; she wanted to know Graydon's mind.[23]

He called her Seraphina, "One beating against bars." That was rather more nicely than how Robert Louis Stevenson drew her in his novel *Prince Otto*, from whence the allusion came. The pet name was not an exact fit, but it pointed to Graydon's own intensive study of his new friend. Like Alice, Stevenson's Princess Seraphina was a politician. The fictional princess ably ran the country in the absence of her milquetoast husband. She was equally at ease commanding and philosophizing. By the end of the novel Prince Otto and Princess Seraphina have lost their country in a republican coup d'etat. They live out their lives happily if a bit aimlessly, united in love and writing their memoirs. But there was another side of the princess: "Chafing that she was not a man, and could not shine by action, she had conceived a woman's part, of answerable domination; she sought to subjugate for by-ends, to rain influence and be fancy free; and, while she loved not man, loved to see man obey her."[24]

Joe Graydon's nickname was probably a paean to Alice's political acuity. Yet which Princess Seraphina? The coldhearted, bloodless pawn of the prime minister or the exiled but sadder and wiser princess, penning "dull and conscientious" *poésies?*[25] Perhaps Graydon meant to convey that he understood Alice's frustration with her milksop husband, her banishment to Cincinnati, her unspoken ambitions for political influence and intellectual ferment. Maybe he saw himself as the prime minister: her motivator, her muse, but never quite her lover.

One reason that the literary friendship between Alice and Joe may have not crossed into physical realms was the existence of Mrs. Graydon. Marjorie Maxwell had married Joseph Graydon in 1901. They had two children. In his letters Joe never referred to his family by anything other than "madam and the two tall daughters." Alice could not have missed knowing the entire Graydon family, as their paths would have crossed at any number of important Cincinnati events. The Longworths and the Graydons were May Festival organizers and communicants of the Episcopal church; both Nick and Joe were members of the same bar and alumni associations, as well as the Pillars, the exclusive Cincinnati social club where Nick had been meeting women friends for decades. Auntie Bye knew and entertained Marjorie Graydon. Yet, according to her grandson, Graydon DeCamp, Marjorie was "the antithesis of Alice! As wide as the overstuffed chairs she sat in and not very charming or pleasant, by many accounts." In fact, Alice had helped Marjorie in some way with a favorite chair of hers. "Madam," Graydon noted sardonically, "sits and sits."[26]

Alice and Nick spent part of every summer in Cincinnati, and she usually joined Nick at Rookwood after Christmas at Sagamore. There would have been ample occasions for Joe and Alice to commune. Perhaps it was during a railway journey that they first discovered their common intellectual proclivities. Joe reminisced about a "trip to N.Y. via Washington... with cigarettes, stateroom and a taciturn Seraphina sitting on her feet in the corner."[27] The two tried to get together in Chicago, in New York, in Washington. When they were apart, they telephoned and wrote of books they had sent to each other, of poets they loved. Joe's letters show a man desirous of impressing Alice. "I would rather have you angry than uninterested," he emphasized.[28]

Joseph Graydon liked to portray himself as a simple Cincinnati attorney, the human antidote to the corruption and cynicism she complained of in Washington. "What you need," he told her, "is not Kant and the categories, nor Browne and incomprehensibles, but the association of people who are simple, child-like and free from guile—I was about to say—like me." But he was also a man of strong feelings, one who could match her passion. He loathed "statesmen who do not govern. Lawyers who have not the common law in their blood. Poets accentuating content, disregarding form. People who deny themselves that primary source of inspiration—their fellow man.... [It is i]n the minds of children and plain folk we are likeliest to find that spirit of truth and justice, which make us, not only as [Heinrick] Ibsen says 'Pillars of Society,' but possibly also members of that choir invisible that shall sing when human society is not."[29] The Bull Moose himself would have approved of such populist sentiments. Alice did.

Graydon saw the two of them as set apart and "refus[ing] to live in time and space...." He drew graphs for her to illustrate infinity. They took pleasure in differential calculus, Bishop Berkeley's "ghosts of departed quantities." They discussed Kant—and on that subject Graydon was the humble expert, she the willing student. Space, time, God, immortality, intellect, materialism, natural law—all topics of his penetrating mind. "Seraphina, I don't believe anybody but you would stand for this . . . it is because you have a catholicity of interest which is unique...."[30]

They shared a skepticism for traditional religion. Alice did not discuss her superstitions with most people, and the fact that she did with Joe Graydon speaks volumes about their intimacy. They enjoyed challenging each other. His letter to her in June 1918 began, "For clever Alice: In adopting free will as an acceptable item of table talk, why scoff at original sin?" He wrote four and a quarter pages on the topic, and then enclosed some of his philosophy, written a year earlier—another five legal pages' worth. Graydon's Episcopalian upbringing did not stop him from questioning the very fundamentals of Western religion, but he did so with a charity that Alice did not always share. This irritated him. Alice's diary in October 1915 found her musing, "Gnostics, their remains. Jewish life in [ancient] times. Must find if the difference between the Sephardim and Ashkenazim is not a difference in caste as well as ritual.... [S]urvival of life not being survival of memory. Return to the stream of life, having no recollection of 'ourselves' at age of two, yet nevertheless lived. Yet at age of two we have been so impressed subconsciously that it influenced our whole future life...."[31] Their relationship inspired Alice to reflection—always a satisfying exercise for her.

As his closing changed to "ever yours," his letters become more lover-like: "See that any attention you pay him remains vicarious—that adjective in your note, my dear Seraphina, was worth a great deal." He wondered whether her missing earring had been located, confessing that he "might be found hunting for it by night, to keep as a souvenir." Graydon could be vulnerable with her, admitting to depression ("a lapse into shadowland," he termed it), and "Machiavellian subterfuges, outbursts of simulated frankness, casuistical reticences; all the torturous devices denoting *not* an humble and contrite heart. Beware that man who with an owl-like countenance recounts old saws and modern instances to you, advising how you should order and direct your ways. He is not better than he should be, but a broken reed to hang upon."[32]

At one point, Joe could not see her as planned: "I have been forced to the conclusion that it were best I should not visit in Washington in absence of affairs requiring my presence there. Please do not think I should not like to—or that I am unappreciative of your asking me: nor must you think any other whatsoever suspicious or horrid things as the cause why I am, I hope, disappointing you."[33] A wife's distrust keeping him away Alice could forgive, but not his absence from the same political camp. In April 1916, Graydon's letter contained a warning for their relationship, had he but known it. Concerning the 1916 presidential race he wrote: "I want it thoroughly understood that I am not for T.R. from any consideration of principles, but only through the powerful not-to-be-denied influence of a member of his family. That is to say I am your personal convert."[34] But that was before the United States entered the Great War. Graydon was convinced of the righteousness of the Allied cause, and made plans to enter the army's intelligence branch. Alice was busy denigrating Woodrow Wilson and his handling of foreign affairs. Joe lashed out at Alice for her unpatriotic attitude. "I can find you at least 1000 ex or prospective Republican office holders who would be glad to get your news criticizing the Administration," he wrote. "Why, oh why, do you insist, at first insidiously and then more boldly, in venting it at me[?] You behaved very well about it when you were here, and, as I supposed, recognized the fact and my right to entirely disagree with you. But something has got you started again. Please refrain—I am backing the President and administration for the course of the war. Afterwards can take care of itself."[35]

He wrote next of his own attempts to join the military. At forty-one he was too old for officers' camp. Instead, he "negotiated for a commission in the Intelligence Branch" and was hoping to see it come through. Given the Roosevelt family's shared understanding of "the battlefield as a place of honor, fulfillment, and robust democracy," and Joe's clear sensitivity to his cerebral nature when compared to the model of her celebrity sportsman father ("You may think I never killed a lion or sat for a Sargent sketch, but the velocities of the banishing increments are mine"), Alice surely approved of Graydon's intended sacrifice, regardless of her fears for his welfare.[36]

Perhaps it was their still-diverging politics, or maybe it was the influence of "madam and the two tall daughters," but by late 1919 the affair was abating. While the philosophy nurtured her, the relationship could ultimately never satisfy her. Joseph Graydon did not share her passion for politics. Every time she tried to engage him on the subject, he begged off. His mind preferred to play with Kant's antinomies rather than with others' political destinies. Alice's true soul mate would be a man who combined Graydon's erudition with a political obsession. That man was still in her future. Nonetheless, when Joe was in his sixties and seventies, she was still sending him birthday remembrances—and Alice Longworth was not known for her sentimentality.[37]

Joe Graydon was Alice's first mature love. How much Nick knew is unclear. Alice's love for Graydon was based on an intellectual magnetism and a physical allure. If not sexually consummated, their relationship never-theless was Alice's first real independent step away from Nick and her father. After Joe, she would be able to envision a man who could match her intellect and share her love of politics, and a man with whom she could take the next physical step. Married to Nick out of habit and for appearance's sake, Alice lived ever more a life on her own terms—fond of her husband and at his side for important political events, and even free to play with him when it suited her, Alice could distance herself from his boozing and wom-anizing. And she could keep her eyes open for a man who appreciated the political game in all its nuances.

It was the war that came between Joe Graydon and Alice Longworth. Foreign news dominated the lives of all Americans, although most were not as ardent about foreign policy as Alice. The possibility of war against Mexico loomed in the autumn of 1913. Early in that year, military leader Victoriano Huerta's successful coup ended Mexican president Francisco Madero's administration and Wilson extended support to the constitution-alists, a faction committed to democratic policies and the overthrow of Huerta. Alice tracked the Wilson administration's handling of Mexican affairs. She read widely from several different newspaper subscriptions, dined with politicians, and quizzed Nick. Information came from Kermit in South America, who wrote to tell her that war with Mexico *and* Japan looked "pretty likely." It was the Mexican situation that caused Idaho's Senator William E. Borah to warm to foreign affairs.[38] Alice could not have helped noticing him as she read about the congressional debates every day. Ruggedly striking, Senator Borah already had a reputation as a rene-gade in the GOP. He was a man to watch.

Alice also had her inside sources such as George Goethals, director of the Panama Canal project. Together at a dinner at the Wilson White House, they perched "on the uncomfortable little gold chairs...muttering male-dictions on the Administration." Goethals wrote to her in March 1914 that Colonel Leonard Wood believed "intervention is a sure thing in Mexico." Thus it came as no surprise to her when, on Tuesday, April 21, 1914, Wil-son dramatically requested Congress to send the U.S. Navy to occupy Vera Cruz. "War is practically a fact today," Alice mused from Rookwood. She followed the turn of events closely, expressing her mistrust of Wilson and his motives. "His message was entirely against Huerta [seemingly] making his personality the issue. The resolution as passed didn't go quite his way.... I would wage a good deal that Wilson is privately communicating with [Pancho] Villa etc. and no wonder as he has given them the arms they will use against us. If Wilson puts this thing through on his own my hat is off to him—but if he fails his shortsightedness is murderously criminal."[39]

Two days later, she knew she was right: "12 Americans killed and 50 wounded at Vera Cruz.... [Wilson] has practically asked the constitutionals for approval of his message and the joint resolution.... At least they are stopping the arms from going across the border." The newspapers were full of the story, including Wilson's invitation to Argentina, Brazil, and Chile to mediate. For Alice this meant Wilson "has made us the laughing stock of the world and if this is true it is unbearably humiliating.... To have this whey blooded schoolmaster at the head is very bitter. I can only hope for some violent out break on the border which will make war imperative—and he will get into it and come out of it discredited."[40] War was an instrument of foreign policy for Alice, who seldom spared ink on its victims.

Another conflagration appeared on the horizon in early 1914. Ruth McCormick was hard at work on preparedness as head of the woman's section of the Navy League. Medill, recently returned from Europe, believed war there was looming. Like all the Roosevelt men, Medill felt that if peace were shattered, it would be his duty to fight. He was clear-eyed about it. He wrote his wife presciently that "while, in Mexico, there might be adventure out of proportion to agony, in Europe, the agony outweighs the adventure."[41]

The assassination of Archduke Franz Ferdinand was the catalyst for the war that Medill foresaw. As Alice drank Napoleonic brandy with Neil Primrose and the Rothschilds, her family raced toward the conflict. Dick Derby left in September 1914 to tend to the wounded in Europe, and Ethel accompanied him. Their five-month-old infant remained with his grandparents. The news from abroad was troubling. Nick's sister Nan Wallingford wrote from France to a Cincinnati friend about Italian workers who had cut telegraph wires to stop Parisians from communicating with anyone outside the city, about rampant fears that funds would become inaccessible, about horses and chauffeurs having been requisitioned for the military, and "hysterical women servants who have quite gone to pieces."[42]

When Alice visited Oyster Bay in mid-September, all the talk was of the future. "The war is so terrible that I can think of little else. All Europe seems to have returned to barbarism," Edith fretted. Ted was involved in establishing training centers for soldiers-to-be for the inevitable (as all Roosevelts believed) day that the United States would enter the war.[43] TR's family would be prepared despite President Wilson's insistence on Americans being "too proud to fight."

For Alice, the election of 1914 temporarily topped the war in Europe as it represented a chance for redemption and a return to Washington. She wrote in her diary for November 3, 1914, "It's not quite one this morning—and election day—hope he gets it. . . . It will be nice to be in Washington again—and an active part of the government again." But on the whole, Alice noted, the election seemed "trivial" compared to the war. Nick won back his seat easily and without much campaigning by Alice. They were both glad to return to D.C. in March 1915 for the Sixty-fourth Congress. Family and friends celebrated for them. When Alice and Nick dropped by Sagamore Hill before Thanksgiving, Edith thought they looked "well and happy." "Isn't it fine that Nick has got in again?" Kermit enthused. "It will make a lot of difference to Sister."[44]

Tempered by exile in Cincinnati, buoyed by her dalliance with Joe Graydon, Alice resolved to be her own person once again. She would stand separate from her husband's lack of self-discipline and her mother-in-law's disapproval. She was ready to be thoughtfully immersed in political debates in the midst of the international crisis. She tried to persuade Joe to visit her in Washington and, until the war interfered, she attempted to hold on to that most interesting piece of Cincinnati. Alice missed him. But, in the end, it was a relief to return to the capital city, to the life she had grown to love at the hub of the nation's political system. After the war, Alice Roosevelt Longworth would evolve into a Washington statesman. Not limited by a constituency as were elected politicians, she could go anywhere, talk with anyone. Her power came to be greater than any lobbyist's or social maven's because her home was the place to be, to see and be seen, to spill secrets, to meet people, and to broker deals that could not be made in Congress. Alice's drawing room became a required stop on the path to political prominence.

Chapter 14

"To Hate the Democrats So Wholeheartedly"

THE WORLD WAS AT WAR and the president of the United States did nothing, the Roosevelts fumed. When a German torpedo sank the British passenger liner *Lusitania* in May 1915, killing 128 U.S. citizens—not the first Americans to fall victim to German U-boats—Wilson and the Democrats made no military response. Nick's election returned the Longworths to a Washington on edge as the European conflict entered the bloody stalemate of trench warfare. Alice would come to feel that "all our lives before and after have just been bookends for the heroic, tragic volume of the Great War."[1]

Theodore Roosevelt led the charge against vacillating Democrats and called for military preparedness and, eventually, for U.S. involvement in the war. Alice was never more in accord with her father than over the issue of war in Europe. She thought about the U.S. situation this way: "To look always for the best yet to be alertly ready to deal with the worst in mankind is not a bad working scheme. Recognition of interdependence and mutual responsibility without losing individuality is crucial. Elevate the least without setting limitations to the total, and the only individual who can, who understands, is Father." She felt he was "the great personage of these times. Of all time for me."[2] Military preparedness and the election of 1916 dominated the headlines and family discussions. Alice assisted sporadically in the war effort, refined her political convictions, and sharpened her skills as a salon hostess. She and her father were close companions during the war years, though by the end, drastic changes had occurred: Quentin was dead, Theodore Roosevelt was mortally ailing, and Alice was falling in love.

·   ·   ·

Led by Theodore Roosevelt, the family advocated military preparedness. The United States should build up its armed forces and stay on the alert, because the conflagration overseas might require immediate involvement. After Germany invaded neutral Belgium on August 4, 1914, TR urged President Woodrow Wilson to commit American troops to stop Kaiser Wilhelm's immoral conquest. No one knew better than Roosevelt the German military capability, having seen it firsthand in 1910. He found the kaiser "an able and powerful man" with a "curious combination of power, energy, egotism, and restless desire to do, and to seem to do, things." But TR didn't trust the kaiser and suspected him then of promising peace while preparing for war.[3] His reservations proved correct.

As 1914 wore on, Alice and TR discussed Germany's relationship with England. Father and daughter conversed "steadily" on horseback for hours at a time. Roosevelt told Alice of his doubts about the kaiser. He believed the German atrocity stories flooding the American press and eventually abandoned his belief that the United States should remain prepared but neutral. Instead, TR supported American entry in the European war for two reasons: to check further German evils and to be a player in the postwar balance of power. As president, Roosevelt had seen "how far Germany is willing to go in doing what she believes her interest and her destiny demand, in disregard of her own engagements and of the equities of other peoples." When Ethel returned from the hospitals in France with somber accounts of German troops firing intentionally on the Red Cross and allied soldiers mutilated by their sadistic attacks, he sprang into action.[4]

TR spearheaded universal military training. To help move Americans off their neutral center point, he churned out didactic books and articles blasting Germany, President Wilson, and American pacifists. He worked with the National Security League, the American Defense Society, and the Army League. He wholeheartedly supported Leonard Wood's creation of the Plattsburg volunteer military training camp and reviewed the troops there, inspiring a martial spirit that the country's real commander in chief could not. Alice wondered how "anyone with common sense [could] hesitate to work for universal military training, far less talk of world disarmament. Poor oafs, poor fools, and Japan with her million men."[5]

A deep loathing for the administration ran through the Oyster Bay Roosevelts, who saw Wilson as idealistic, weak, and out of touch. TR did not mince words: "I despise Wilson," he told his sister. Alice called Wilson a "slimy hypocrite." Edith wrote furiously to a friend, "There is no mistake that could have been made that has been neglected in Washington. The veiled prophet of the White House cares only for his political future and is totally unconcerned as to the futures of the nation and the lives of those we love."[6] Sending one son after another off to fight, Edith felt she hated war as much as she loathed the commander in chief.

All the Roosevelts heard the call "to take their own part." Edith felt herself to be "a horrid example of the pariah woman, for I have not been able to take up any war work as yet. Quentin has his orders for active duty, and when he sails I will try to help the Oyster Bay Red Cross." Eventually she supported national "home charity work" through the Needlework Guild.[7] Richard Derby wrote to Belle and Kermit that they "talk of nothing but preparedness these days." His address to the Harvard Club was "a plea for national service. This morning's paper," he went on, "tells us that the House's bill contemplates a federalization of the National Guard and an increase in the army of up to only 135,000. They are so hopelessly on the wrong track, that it is discouraging. If they could only be made to see that universal service is the only rational and democratic method of defense." From Europe, Edith's sister Emily Carow, soon to be decorated with two Italian Red Cross medals, confessed, "I love my work and have been repaid a thousandfold by every soldier I have nursed." Women on the American homefront patriotically made clothing for soldiers. "No one moved," cousin Eleanor Roosevelt asserted, "without her knitting."[8] No one except Alice. She never knitted a stitch in her life.

Alice did, however, economize consciously during wartime in at least one characteristically outrageous way. She wore slacks in public. She was fifty years ahead of her time and pushing a firm social boundary. Men wore slacks. Women wore skirts. As the *Ladies' Home Journal* later asserted: "Without ever joining anything, she had a trick of doing things on her own account a year or so before other women would organize some sort of social crusade to enable them to do the same things without being talked about." Alice's action was another example of her insouciant independent streak where she pleased herself first. Despite the newspaper coverage, Alice was blasé. "I urge all the ladies to wear pantalettes," Alice said. "They're comfortable, economical and save considerable cloth."[9]

Nick was too old to be in uniform but was fighting the good fight in Congress. His "True Preparedness" speech appealed for federal support to the dye industry. He knew that the United States had only two dyestuff plants that could be converted into factories for high explosives. This was not enough. Readying other factories should begin immediately: "It can be done in the same plant, with the same machinery, and by the same men." He won House approval for the government to spend $180,000 on land to build a nitrate plant in Cincinnati. Despite calling himself a "militant" Republican, Nick was cautious. He and his father-in-law tempered their speeches during election season, going no further than criticizing Germany and calling for American entry in 1916. Nick limited his public excoriation of Wilson in deference to his large German-American constituency. Nonetheless, he warned Americans from the House floor that if war came, the country could not protect itself. Douglas Robinson called his speeches "a real service." "No one," cousin Douglas emphasized, who "has stood for adequate defense has committed political suicide...."[10]

In August 1915, Ted advocated a "comprehensive reserve system" and was among the first to join Wood at the Plattsburg camp. Archie signed up for Harvard's military training program. Sheffield Cowles, Auntie Bye's son, would join Princeton's military camp. The patriarch approved: TR eventually had four sons and one son-in-law fighting in the war, one son-in-law fighting Wilson in Congress, one daughter-in-law marshaling women's involvement in the preparedness campaign, one daughter serving beside her husband in Europe, and the other—Alice—by his side being "a real help to me politically." They were all, he crowed, possessed of "the dauntless spirit we ought all to have."[11]

As to traditional war work, Alice wrote in her autobiography that "one, of course, did that sort of thing too—washed dishes, scooped ice cream, cut pies, peddled Liberty Loan bonds, and made clumsy attempts at first aid." She posed in a Girl Scout uniform for wartime publicity. Her real contribution came from continuous entertaining. "I think," she recalled, "it pleased the Washington that went to and gave dinners, to feel that entertaining the representatives of the Allies had a recognized part in 'winning the war'!" It was for her, she readily conceded, "a far pleasanter form of 'war work' than canteens and Red Cross classes." This allowed her to "send...all the political news" when she wrote to soldiers.[12] It also perfected her considerable talents as a salon hostess.

Soldiering on among the "Washington that went to and gave dinners" was Alice's gift: bringing together those who planned strategy and made policy. Her home became TR's address whenever he traveled to the capital city. The Longworths socialized at this time with a combination of policy makers, the moneyed elite who backed the GOP, foreign dignitaries, and many out-of-town visitors. Mary Borah recalled that after Alice's guests strategized over soup and debated during dessert, she "always had lots of couches and...we'd settle ourselves on these and Nick would take out his violin and play for awhile." Sometimes virtuosi such as Jascha Heifetz and Efrem Zimbalist joined him.[13] Then "conversation would begin [again], usually about politics. Alice was intensely interested in politics." The political topics over teas and dinners and poker games were always the same that year: preparedness, party politics, and "what an ass Wilson is." By February 1916, Alice, Nick, and TR "had decided that there was nothing left for the President to do but resign." But Alice held out little hope for any sort of push from Congress. "On the whole they are such a stagnant lot, our 'statesmen,' that it is," she sighed, "pretty depressing."[14]

Acquaintances failed to notice the developing political concerns of the woman they still referred to as Princess Alice. Isabella Ferguson recounted to ER that she had met Alice in Cincinnati in 1916, where the latter was "filled with noisy exuberance [and] no reality—She was nevertheless refreshing [and] *un*changed (after not seeing her for eight years!). I had looked for strict dignity from numerous tales—but met old time lightness—She seemed to appreciate that you do your job in Washington a little bit better than anyone else."[15]

Turning aside the compliment, Eleanor passed judgment on her cousin:

Of course [Alice] isn't a bit changed [and] it is always entertaining to be with her but now that I am older [and] have my own values fixed a little I can only say that what little I saw of her…life gave me a feeling of dreariness and waste. Her house is charming, her entertainments delightful. She's a born hostess and has an extraordinary mind but as for real friendships and what it means she hasn't a conception of any depth in any feeling or so at least it seems. Life seems to be one long pursuit of pleasure and excitement and rather little real happiness either given or taken on the way, the 'blue bird' always to be searched for in some new and novel way.[16]

It was not Alice's modus vivendi to show a deeper side to her censorious cousin Eleanor.

In the midst of preparedness discussions, the 1916 election loomed. Contemptuous of the Democrats and still convinced that TR could make Americans see the light, Alice attended the Progressive Party convention in Chicago in June. TR instructed the delegates not to nominate him "unless the country has in its mood something of the heroic." He was the unanimous choice of the Progressive Party but gave them a "conditional refusal" as he waited to see what the Republicans did. Edith wrote a friend, "I cannot but feel that the Progressive Party has done great good in forcing its ideas of humanity and justice—that is really what it comes to—upon political machines. I must confess horror that in regard to its founders it has been a car of Juggernaut" under which she could see her husband being crushed.[17] Like her parents, Alice was ambivalent. She wanted her father back in the White House, but easily—cleanly. Instead of dragged along by the Progressive Party "juggernaut," she'd rather he be acclaimed by enthusiastic Republicans as he stood a better chance of victory with an established party.

At the Republican Party convention Alice's hopes dimmed as the GOP chose Charles Evans Hughes. She was devastated. She vowed she had "no feeling of personal chagrin at the result, only a sense of waste that the one man most qualified to cope with the intricate and appalling problems of this time, should have been refused the chance to serve, and what is more to lead, as only he can lead. This is no filial squeal, only my very sincere opinion. It is unnecessary to say how much I hope for the success of Mr. Hughes." TR believed the third party could not win. He withdrew his name, asking all Progressives to vote for the GOP, thus dooming the party he created.[18] One of Alice's friends ran on a state-level Progressive ticket. Alice wrote, "I was delighted to hear of your nomination.... Now go ahead and be elected and we will make things hum to a different tune in Washington," starting with "the impeachment of that white-livered coward in the White House." Whether the Republicans or the Progressives won was less important for all the Roosevelts than that someone defeat, as Edith put it, the "vile and hypocritical charlatan," Wilson.[19]

In the 1916 race Nick had to balance his zeal for military preparedness with his sensitivity toward the German-American voters in his district. Alice obliquely referred to the campaign as "unpleasant." For the November election, the two were in Nick's Cincinnati office, where Alice found listening to the returns a depressing business. "I became," she recounted, "increasingly a combination of Poe's Raven and Cassandra, with a dash of malevolent political observer." Nick went to bed, but she sat up alone all night, phoning her journalist friends to get the returns from the West Coast. With the wounds inflicted by her in-laws in 1912 still so raw, it was with "malicious pleasure" the next morning that she trumpeted the blow of Wilson's victory—even though she was fiercely disappointed in the outcome, too.[20] At least Nick's tactful campaign had worked. His constituents sent him back to the House of Representatives.

After repeated challenges to U.S. neutrality, Germany finally pushed President Wilson to a declaration of war on April 2, 1917. Alice was both triumphant and heartsick, as she knew "so well that we are on the edge of inevitable grief and tragedy." She followed war news avidly. She habitually spent afternoons in the House or Senate, listening to the debates and the speeches. The publisher of the *Washington Post* was so impressed with Alice's assessment of the European situation that he begged her to write a column on that topic. Though flattered, Alice professed herself "too aware of my quarter horse limitations."[21]

While Nick visited his mother, Alice read the rationalist writings of

British foreign secretary Arthur James Balfour. His Balfour Declaration of November 1917 gave hope to Zionists, calling for a Jewish homeland in British-held Palestine. Alice found Balfour so persuasive that she "got much excited and somewhat religious after an agnostic fashion." She chatted with him in April, when she also had met Joseph Joffre, the architect of the French war plan. By the spring of 1917, the latter was in Washington to request rapid mobilization of U.S. troops to France. Alice found Joffre likable and quick to confess France's dire position. By contrast, Balfour was "earnest" and charming. He loved to hear Nick play his violin, and she loved to talk foreign policy and philosophy with him. He became a friend to both Longworths.[22]

Spellbound by global events discussed around her table, in the middle of reading her father's latest contentious book, *The Foes of Our Own Household*, and helping Nick with his speeches, Alice felt moved to prophesy in October 1917: "The war will continue until sometime in April. Then Germany having arranged and maneuvered with Japan and Russia to consolidate her Russian gains and her Balkan conquests, will offer such terms that the allies cannot refuse... Belgium vacated. Alsace-Lorraine returned. Certain colonies to be self-governing. She will then set herself to the task of consolidating.... We meanwhile will have had men on the fighting front and will share in the face-saving 'victory.' Wilson will be a portentous and sorry fixture in the peace terms. And then when the war measures lapse, calamity and disintegration in this country. Mexico aflame once more. European influence threatens. The campaign of 1920 F. elected; appealing to all that is noblest.... Let us see. I have spoken."[23] Alice's prognostication on the foreign front were borne out with more accuracy than her domestic predictions. She was deeply concerned about the postwar situation, and continued to ruminate.

Alice took some friends to the newly established Camp Meade in Maryland to see her friend Ned McLean—by then Lieutenant Colonel McLean—in the 312th Artillery. It was her first look at "one of the immense conscript camps." The sight was riveting. She found the "streams" of men in khaki and all the bustle uplifting. Alice identified with the soldiers: "Am proud to be one of them," she penned. The stirring sights of Camp Meade redoubled her feeling that all men who avoided military service were "unalterably contemptible."[24]

She eventually made her way to Cincinnati to join Nick and left from there to travel to Oyster Bay for Thanksgiving. Ethel saw the toll that visiting Susan had taken on her sister: "She looks rather tired after a month in Cincinnati, but is as delightful as always. Much interested in the way political things are shaping themselves." TR reported to Ted, "As usual I talk politics at length with her." Alice had much to say about Wilson as she had been watching Senate Republicans introduce a series of investigations that she hoped would help unseat him.[25]

Alice followed international events closely. "[French prime minister Paul] Painlevé out, [Georges] Clemenceau in. [David] Lloyd George tottering. Everything is a mess. Perhaps, soon, Father will play the big part," she wrote. Contemplating TR as president in 1920 made Alice deliriously happy—so much so that she confessed to feeling "almost friendly to Harding" when he told her he'd overheard others saying "TR is the only man in sight for 1920." Whatever sort of scheming she and her father were doing about 1920, Alice wished she could spill the details to her best friend. After tea with Ruth McCormick, Alice recorded how "as soon as she knows as much as I do about plans for Father it will be easier talking. She is the best fun.... My father president again and my husband speaker would be absolutely satisfactory, even to me."[26]

But the immediacy of war interrupted dreams of 1920. Influenced by a patriotic desire to support the Allied effort, Alice participated in the democratic process to the extent that women were allowed in 1917. She voted. "My first vote cast against German in the public schools."[27] She was one of many Americans who succumbed to a jingoistic response to German militarism. While not as bad as those who called publicly for the elimination of German language programs or the curtailment of civil liberties for German Americans, Alice's sentiment was private, but clear. For the next several days, she dissected the elections in her diary: suffrage might have passed in New York, and Ohio would probably embrace prohibition, but these were "nothing of consequence in comparison to the fact that . . . Hylan elected" as mayor of New York City. She thought attorney John F. Hylan, a Tammany Hall insider, "the tool of the most corrupt and adroit creature in the country, the exposed candidate of the German propaganda.... There are no words to express my angry contempt for the [Wilson] administration in not supporting [reformer John Purroy] Mitchel.... It was a straight out issue between sedition and patriotism, and that cur in the White House took no part." She soon recorded how she awoke at 2:20 a.m. "consumed with political venom that endured until the clock struck 6." The following day, she "lost [her] temper with Nick" over whether the Red Cross or the YMCA was the more worthy recipient of their financial donation. Nick came down on the side of the Red Cross—an institution governed at that time by Cincinnati native and Taft confidante Mabel Boardman. But that fight was not about benevolence—Alice had spent part of the previous day making compresses for the Red Cross. It was caused by her continued rage against Wilson that sat like a thundercloud over their home.[28]

For distraction, she was staying up late "wallowing in" paleontologist Henry Fairfield Osborn's just-published *The Origin and Evolution of Life: On the Theory of Action, Reaction and Interaction of Energy*, which she found "thrilling."[29] The study of theories of evolution was a lifelong fascination for Alice. In 1917, Osborn was in the forefront of a movement referred to as "the New Biology," which called into question older ideas about the preeminence of environment in shaping human nature and actions. Experimental biology, based on laboratory observations and testing hypotheses, came to replace natural history during Alice's twenties and thirties, when she deepened her study of evolution and refined her ideas about social Darwinism.

One of the centers of the New Biology was the Station for Experimental Evolution, located in Cold Spring Harbor on Long Island, not far from Sagamore Hill. It was more than just a neighborly interest that kept Alice enthralled. She shared with her father a passion for biology; the sciences had been TR's first choice of study at Harvard. Theodore was writing a review of Osborn's book at the same time that Alice was reading it. Perhaps some of her absorption had an even more solipsistic source. To one who never knew her mother and admired her father, who grew up with stories of the heroic acts of ancestors, it seems logical that Alice might find the topic of heredity inherently engrossing. And the efficacy of either creating a better environment or in "breeding a better race" is one that engaged many Progressive Era reformers.[30]

Political activism retained its primacy in her life, however, and she rejoiced when her father announced he would visit Washington in January 1918, "as he alone can steer and eventually lead the Republicans." Alice had wanted to invite him herself, so that he could dole out advice on the congressional campaign in person, but she was relieved when other politicos prevailed upon the colonel to come. "He talks on nearly every side of the situation.... He can get the party [together] and crystallize their course of action, show up the present wrong doing as no one else can; and he must be in Washington to see certain people," Alice promised her diary.[31]

Over the early months of 1917, Theodore Roosevelt had hatched a plan to resurrect the Rough Riders to fight in France. He privately announced he stood ready to die in battle. His old friend Elihu Root gently teased that if he truly promised to die, President Wilson would doubtless agree to the plan. Nick tried to help the cause by sponsoring legislation empowering Wilson to create four special volunteer divisions just as TR described. But the president said no. The family was positive that "political considerations" were at the bottom of this "bitterest sort of blow" for TR.[32] More likely it was a combination of Roosevelt's poor health, his ongoing criticism of the head of state, and the fact that the weapons of war had changed since 1898.

His own soldiering prospects frustrated, TR looked to his sons as his surrogates. Writing to General John J. Pershing, the commander of the American Expeditionary Force (AEF) in Europe and a fellow veteran of the Spanish-American War, TR asked that Ted and Archie be allowed to serve. They duly embarked for France on June 20, 1917, when Alice was among the family massed to wave them good-bye. In July 1917, Ted took command of the First Battalion of the Twenty-sixth Infantry in the AEF's First Division. Archie, who left behind his new wife, Grace Lockwood Roosevelt, served under Ted. Also in July, Quentin embarked for Europe, a member of the Ninety-fifth aero squadron, the only pilot among the brothers. Kermit gained access to the front through contacts in the British foreign office. He was separated not just from his wife, Belle, but also from their young son, Kim. As a result, Kermit was the least gung ho of the brothers. Brother-in-law Dick arrived in France in November 1917 to join the American Medical Corps. He, too, left a family behind. But overcoming worries and fears was, as Alice recorded in her diary, the appropriate response for Roosevelt men: "I am certainly proud of the way our family has all stepped up to the fore. Without a thought, they were all in the trouble from the very first. Father backed all his sayings, and we have been able to show people that he meant what he said." The family "hung out our flag with four stars" to signal to the world that they had sent four sons off to combat.[33]

Another early entrant into the war effort from among the Roosevelt circle was George Goethals, recalled to active duty as quartermaster general in the army. And "Dear old Willard" Straight came to bid Alice farewell before sailing for battle in France. He left her with "shocking tales... of the incompetency and chaos at Camp Sill."[34] They didn't know it then, but it was their last meeting. Willard Straight fell victim to the terrible postwar influenza pandemic.

In the last months of 1917, American forces joined the Allies in hellish trench fighting as Lenin's socialist government seized power in Russia. Alice mulled this over. "It is desperately bad. The past turn of hideous war may seem merely the general run of things in comparison to what may come...." Christmas celebrations didn't even feel like Christmas. "Just [Father], Mother, Ethel, the Lloyd Derbys & me. A sadly reduced family. I cannot realize that next year the sadness of this may be a persistent and terrible grief," she worried. Nick was miserably stuck in bed fighting a cold, leaving Alice and her sister to put up a tree for the sake of Ethel's young son. On Christmas eve, Alice and TR stayed up late to talk politics. He read out loud to her from his correspondence. She "looked over" a speech he was to give at Princeton, went through his "goodly array of campaign documents," and his review of *Origin and Evolution of Life*. As Nick regained his health, Alice was gladdened that he and TR had many "long talks. They are very good for each other," Alice thought.[35]

The couple's return to Washington meant reimmersion in society. Alice recorded how she and Nick entertained one friend at lunch who "was so pompous about his European experience that I felt like a third rail, casting off sparks. Finally a certain aura emanating from Nick caused me to lapse into platitudinous civility." Nick could still exert some influence over his wife, and their thirteen years of marriage were not without fondness and good humor. The two were together as the new year dawned, part of the throng at Friendship, where they had spent their honeymoon. The McLeans' champagne flowed, but conversation stopped at midnight when a red, white, and blue sign spelling out GOOD LUCK TO THE ALLIES IN 1918 flashed on, amazing even those habituated to the McLeans' extravagance.[36]

Alice missed the joint session of Congress on January 8, when President Wilson laid out his plan for the postwar world. His Fourteen Points called for national sovereignty, a generous settlement of territorial boundaries, a decrease in the world's ability to create war, and, the fourteenth point: the establishment of a League of Nations. It was a noble and nonpunitive document upon which to base the terms of the peace. At its unveiling, even Alice had to "admit ungrudgingly that it is fine." This sentiment would not last. With her "Republican way of thinking," she soon rejected Wilson's idea as strangling the ability of the United States to act unilaterally when necessary in foreign policy.[37]

William E. Borah, powerful member of the Senate Foreign Relations Committee, feared an international peacekeeping league would commit the United States to a military defense of other nations—both unconstitutional and approaching "moral treason." Borah and "his dogged, studious, moralistic approach to political issues," would emerge as the leading isolationist in Congress.[38] Sharing his views, Alice worked for the defeat of Wilson's Fourteen Points—especially the clause to create a League of Nations—as passionately as she had ever done any political work. She was an integral part of a critical struggle that "defined the foreign policy positions of both parties for decades to come."[39]

By late January, TR's anger at Wilson's mismanagement of the country came to a head. The issue took on a decidedly partisan aspect for Alice. She left a House debate one day so inspired by a speech of Medill's that she penned, "It hurts, to hate the Democrats so wholeheartedly." Edith and

TR appeared at Nick and Alice's home "and began lobbying for the assembly of a War Cabinet" on the British model, "to take the management of the military out of the inept hands" of Woodrow Wilson. This was the opening volley against the Fourteen Points, and at the Longworth home Republicans and Democrats met to oppose Wilson and the League. Alice hosted a breakfast of nearly twenty men who had come to see TR, a press conference of thirty-three reporters, a "men's dinner" with a score of politicians who left with "stiffened backbones," and other luncheons, dinners, and receptions. It was a whirlwind of anti-Wilson, pro-Roosevelt activity, and Alice was the center.[40]

Beyond politics, Alice was swept up in the spirit of service as the war ground toward its conclusion. In December 1917, Ruth had asked her to serve on a committee for housing government employees in the District of Columbia. Alice solicited cousin Eleanor to serve with her. In April 1918, Eleanor, staffing a canteen, was surprised to see Alice "twice in two days" volunteering for Red Cross work. ER told a friend she was going to try to find a place for Alice, for, "it is a pity so much energy should go to waste!"[41]

A better line of war work soon beckoned invitingly: espionage. Alice had a small part in the Craufurd-Stuart affair, which changed Anglo-American relations. Motivated by patriotism, anti-German feelings, and love of intrigue, Alice was a willing participant in what became a social and diplomatic scandal with wider foreign policy implications. In the summer of July 1917, Alice met Brigadier General Marlborough Churchill at the McLeans' parties. By 1918, he had become chief of military intelligence in the U.S. War Department and recruited Alice to, in his words, "serve your country."[42]

Major Charles Kennedy Craufurd-Stuart of the British embassy was a bachelor with a variegated résumé of military and personal service. Socialite May Ladenburg, a friend of Alice's, had recently broken off her relationship with the droll major. Stung, Craufurd-Stuart suggested to military intelligence officials that Ladenburg was using her physical attributes to charm secrets out of her new lover, Bernard Baruch, the chair of the War Industries Board, to transmit them to the Germans. Churchill set out to see if the major's accusation were true. After conferring with Assistant Secretary of the Navy Franklin Roosevelt, Churchill sought Alice's help. He asked her to advise him as to the best locations for listening devices in May Ladenburg's home. Alice obliged, suggesting "an upper balcony with a large...kind of mattress on a swing....And then," Alice related, "I and three or four absolutely charming and practically *invisible* Secret Service men went over there and heard the most enchanting conversation between this lady and my old friend Bernie Baruch." May's questions about train movements were punctuated by kisses. "[N]o evidence ever emerged to indicate that Miss Ladenburg was a German spy. But the Baruch record, by later reports, contained almost ludicrous indiscretions...." Suspicions ran high in Washington. Ladenburg suffered social ostracism, and laid plans for revenge on her former lover Craufurd-Stuart. He became tangled in a web that spun far out beyond Alice Longworth and would poison Anglo-American diplomacy. The Craufurd-Stuart affair contributed to the U.S. failure to join the League of Nations—and had Alice known that, she'd have been doubly proud of her work. Eleanor disapproved of Alice's spying, but Alice thought "we were doing a *most* disgraceful thing in the name of looking after the affairs of our country, [and] it was sheer rapture!"[43]

Then in July 1918, the realities of war struck home. On Bastille Day, July 14, First Lieutenant Quentin Roosevelt died "in line of duty," behind enemy lines. The family heard that he had been "instantly killed by two bullet holes in the head...." Frank McCoy, family friend and a colonel with the 165th Infantry, wrote to the Roosevelts with the sad news. TR's response to McCoy epitomized the chin-up attitude of the family: "It was very dreadful to have Quentin die. All I can say is that it would have been worse if he had stayed at home." Privately, both Theodore and Edith were overwhelmed with grief. Adding to their worry was the news that Archie and Ted had been seriously wounded, although both would recover. Alice sought comfort from Joe Graydon. Despite their political disagreements, she asked him to visit her.[44]

Nick, made of different stuff and fighting a different war, was embroiled in congressional negotiations to locate funds to pay for the expensive conflict in Europe. Some of the methods Congress was considering, Nick informed his mother, would affect the Longworth family holdings. He suggested she transfer the title of their vacation home to her children to avoid the coming high taxes. Nick recommended foxily: "If you decide to transfer title it had better be done before the bill passes the House so that it may appear that it's not to avoid taxes, tho heaven knows the Longworth estate has paid its share...." His postscript reaffirmed the dubious legality of his advice: "I wouldn't speak of this to anyone except [our attorneys]."[45]

Alice was sojourning at Rookwood in Cincinnati when the anticipated news of the armistice came. She awoke very early in the morning and walked for an hour along Grandin Road. "There was no light or stir in any of the houses," she remembered. "I was alone in the November night—every whistle in the city five miles away was in full blast. The noise of the whistles was extraordinary—at first it seemed all dissonance, and then one would catch what seemed a wailing melody, or a crescendo of harsh harmonies. It was fantastic—but not ineffable. I recollect that I wanted to feel that the morning stars were singing together and the sons of God shouting for joy, but it was no use—I was sure they weren't."[46] Too many people dead. Too much destroyed. Too little stirring leadership in the country.

Alice and Nick returned to Washington that day, amid talk of Wilson's trip to Versailles to hash out a peace treaty. Harold Nicolson, a British delegate, saw the process as a quest: "We were preparing not Peace only, but Eternal Peace. There was about us the halo of some divine mission.... We were bent on doing great, permanent, noble things."[47] Woodrow Wilson also believed a League of Nations promised eternal peace. Not everyone was so sure. The day before he sailed for France, Henry White—the only Republican Wilson took with him—came to Alice's for tea. He assured her that "there would be no question of 'a League of Nations to enforce peace...A League of Nations perhaps, *en principe*, my dear,' but nothing that we should really have to worry about, he comfortingly insisted."[48] Alice was unconvinced.

Alice spent part of Christmas 1918 at Eleanor and Franklin's home, joined by Edward, Viscount Grey and Sir William Tyrrell, on break from their duties at the British embassy; Sara Delano Roosevelt; and a few friends of FDR's such as Louis Howe. Despite the armistice, it was a sad holiday.

Uncle Douglas Robinson had died of angina in September, Franklin was ill with the flu, and her father had been ailing for much of the fall. He spent forty-four days in the hospital that early winter, but came home on Christmas Day. Alice, Ethel, and Archie were among the family members there to greet him as he returned to Sagamore, the home he loved. After he was settled in, Alice returned to Washington, glad of the time with him. Then, on January 6, 1919, Theodore Roosevelt died peacefully, worn out by a life joyously and strenuously lived. THE OLD LION IS DEAD, Archie's telegram to his brothers in Europe read.[49] Alice's response is best gleaned from her autobiography: she could not bring herself to write about her father's death. It simply does not occur in her life story. She adopted her father's approach to her mother's death—curative, stoic silence.

That emptiness was filled to a degree as Alice continued in the cause to which she and her father were so committed. The emotional upheaval of his death and her own strong feelings against the League of Nations lent a zeal to her political work. That passion inclined her to another lion, Bill Borah, called "the Lion of Idaho" for his shock of thick hair. Although a Republican, Borah marched to his own drummer, and, as a contemporary put it, "hates anything that interferes with free scope for individuality." He was, as biographer Robert James Maddox noted, more like "Idaho's permanent ambassador to the outside world" than a typical senator. "Immune to most political pressures," Maddox concluded, "he cared nothing at all for party regularity and supported the national ticket only when the spirit moved him, which was seldom."[50] Iconoclasts both, Alice and Borah saw an echo of themselves in the other.

Alice was intrigued by the senator, with his "great leonine head" and his "fascinating" conversation—so good that he "could hold one spellbound for hours with tales of labor disputes in Illinois at the turn of the century."[51] Alice sat in the Senate gallery day after day, and soon found Borah's oratorical prowess only the first of many attributes she admired. The two powerful politicians were drawn to each other. They began by valuing each other as intellectual companions, comrades-in-arms, fellow progressive Republicans, and individuals devoted to shared causes. But before the League fight ended, they were lovers.

The first meeting between Alice and Bill Borah may have been during that heady time of the Progressive Party convention in 1912. Unlike Nick, who would not consider public support for Theodore Roosevelt, Bill, known even then for his individualistic approach to GOP tenets, seemed persuadable. He had bolted once before, in 1896, and he was a well-known supporter of TR who backed most progressive legislation. That's why Alice thought she could convince him to change parties in 1912, as she lobbied him on the eastbound train after the convention. Looking to make a convert, Alice "argued with him unavailingly." As he campaigned that memorable season, Borah widely condemned the Taft faction's theft of TR's nomination. But that was not enough for Alice. She would not move him out of her category of "enemies and deserters" because he did not join the Bull Moose Party—but she did respect his principles.[52]

The next time their paths crossed more than briefly, they were allies. The battle against the League brought out the anti-Wilsonian, isolationist side of Alice, who met with sympathetic assistance from the senator. The anti-League fight threw them together in an intense situation. She admired the fine figure Borah cut on the floor of the Senate, giving fiery speeches infused with the righteousness of their cause. For his part, Borah responded to Alice's commitment to their shared campaign, her own flashing mind at work on political strategy, and the way he saw himself mirrored in her appreciative eyes.

The seven years between the Bull Moose and the League controversies had seen a settling of the Longworths' marriage. Rumors of Nick's infidelities continued. Alice, thoroughly disgusted with his excessive drinking, lack of TR-like backbone, and amorous indiscretions, turned her copious talents to her first love: politics. She had forsaken her husband's House of Representatives for a seat in the Senate gallery. Like other political watchers, including her old rival Cissy Patterson, Alice had followed the unusual career of the distinguished and handsome Idahoan. Alice's intellectual affair with Joseph Graydon waned as her fascination with Senator Borah deepened.

In 1906, the year of Alice and Nick's celebrated wedding, an already-famous William Borah won election to the U.S. Senate. Born in Illinois and residing later in Kansas and Idaho, Borah early developed a westerner's anti-eastern sentiment. He lacked the social and academic pedigrees of men like Alice's father, husband, and Joe Graydon. Borah never completed college and read for the law in his brother-in-law's office. He was destined to be an outsider in the exclusive club that was the Senate, and what destiny didn't preclude, Borah's personal quirks confirmed. Forty-two years old in 1907, he arrived in D.C. with Mary McConnell Borah, his wife of twelve years, at the pinnacle of a successful career as a corporate attorney and criminal lawyer. Immediately preceding his swearing-in, Borah was involved in a sensational murder case against the illustrious Chicago barrister Clarence Darrow. Borah was special prosecutor in a trial that pitted him against the laboring men of the Western Federation of Miners, defended by Darrow. It was a difficult trial, for the man who had been murdered was Borah's close friend, former Idaho governor Frank Steunenberg. The accused killer was William D. Haywood, secretary-treasurer of the Western Federation of Miners. Borah lost the case, but Darrow thought Borah "the ablest man he ever faced."[53]

Overlapping the Steunenberg murder case was a potentially devastating lawsuit. Borah was indicted for fraud against the U.S. government. Essentially, he was accused of profiting on the land sales of the Barber Lumber Company whose interests he guarded as their attorney. This was not an auspicious prelude to his senatorial career. The indictment occurred just as the Haywood trial was opening, and the former governor, though deceased, was also indicted. This seemed more than simply bad timing to Borah and his supporters. They suspected a concerted effort by Borah's enemies to sully his political career, or an attempt to derail the murder case—or both. It became more complex when ex–Governor Steunenberg's ties to the mine owners came to light. If the indictment had gone to trial immediately, Borah might have been dropped as special prosecutor and the union men would have faced a less talented accuser. It appeared to be another round of the perennial western drama of mine owners against union men. In this case, the union men were aided by a small group of Borah's political opponents, including the district attorney and the man who had just lost the rancorous senatorial nomination to Borah.

Seeking to begin his Senate career rather than have it unscrupulously and prematurely ended, Borah called in favors from friends such as C. P. Connolly of *Collier's* magazine, Oscar King Davis of the *New York Times*, and his old school chum Kansas journalist and editor William Allen White. White shared Borah's idolization of President Roosevelt and his progressive politics. He also sympathized with Borah's plight: ready to serve in TR's "great administration" but unluckily caught in the land-deal quagmire. Borah asked his friend to intervene: "I feel that I cannot succeed in public life if I am to enter with [Roosevelt's] condemnation . . . upon me. . . . I feel if I cannot satisfy the President and the Attorney General of my absolute innocence that I must resign from the Senate." White sought an audience with TR at Oyster Bay. While President Roosevelt declined to pardon Borah for fear that it would lead to rumors of a cover-up, he did move to make certain the Idaho trial would be as clean as possible. The new senator was fully acquitted and took his seat with the Sixtieth Congress in 1907.[54]

Part of what Alice found fascinating about Borah, nineteen years her senior, were these ties to the romantic West of her father's youth. Borah migrated to Idaho in 1890, not long after TR had established his cattle business in the Badlands. Just as TR had to learn cowboy culture when he bought his Dakota ranch, Borah discerned that practicing law on the frontier demanded cunning, bravado, and original thinking to a degree he hadn't seen in relatively sedate, settled Kansas. Roosevelt reared his children on tales that exalted exactly those traits. It is easy to imagine Alice thrilling to Borah's saga of the 1896 conviction of "Diamondfield Jack" Davis, a hired gunman for a cattle company who killed two sheepherders.

Before the trial began, Borah went undercover (just as TR had done as New York police commissioner when Alice was a girl) and rode horseback across the rough terrain of Idaho and Nevada pretending to be a prospective rancher. He spent nights around the campfires with cowboys, swapping tales. Borah finally ran across a ranch foreman who told him of Diamondfield Jack's whereabouts on the night the sheepherders were killed. Other cowboys corroborated how Diamondfield Jack had gloated about the deaths. Satisfied with his fieldwork, Borah traded the cowboy hat for his attorney's chapeau and put the cowboys on the witness stand. Borah won the case. Diamondfield Jack was sentenced to be hanged, and the sheepherders rejoiced.[55]

Borah's bravery triumphed again when he put himself at personal risk in the case of the death of a strikebreaker in an 1899 Western Federation of Miners turnout against the Bunker Hill Mining Company. The man accused of killing the scab was Paul Corcoran, a local union man. Corcoran's friends testified that he was miles from the shooting when it occurred, but Borah had eyewitnesses who swore that they had seen Corcoran riding along on top of a railroad boxcar, carrying a rifle, and jumping to the station platform before the train came to a stop in the town where the scab was murdered. Corcoran's attorneys put railroad engineers on the stand who testified that Corcoran could not have stayed balanced on top of a boxcar through that serpentine stretch of line, nor could he have leaped to the platform unscathed. Borah decided to test the word of the railroad experts. He assembled the same train, packed it with witnesses, and clambered on top of the boxcar, rifle in hand. For six miles Borah rode the train around the curves and down into a canyon. When they reached the platform, Borah jumped off and hit the ground windswept and breathless, but with both legs intact. "It convinced the jury," Borah remembered. "They slept while the defense put forward its case."[56]

This was the stuff of legend. Theodore Roosevelt had fed his eager brood on such adventures, and Borah's past might have sprung from the pages of Alice's children's books. Physical daring, courage, battles of wit, justice triumphant—all set in the Wild West! How could she be immune? Few women were, if the rumors were true.[57] He was a politician cut from the same cloth as her father. Borah, the independent-minded senator with a talent for storytelling and a biography of blockbuster proportions—here was a man who brought to life the very qualities her father celebrated.

In reality, Borah was both more and less than the heroic lawyer driven by a moral vision of himself and the future. According to his wife, Bill Borah was "a very religious man and taught a Sunday school class in Washington year after year. . . . He never drank or smoked, but he would swear sometimes." He apparently loved horse racing, an enthusiasm shared by

Alice.[58] The contemporary sense of him was more akin to the portrait painted by the author of *The Mirrors of Washington*. This capitol insider suggested that Borah was melancholy, pessimistic, moody, emotional, impulsive, a loner wrapped in an "elusive charm." One could "imagine him as a...university professor, a moral crusader, even a poet...." "He is not a social being," in part because "he neither smokes, nor drinks, nor plays." Yet, despite himself, he was "too much of a personage to be ignored or suppressed, and manages to be a power in a party which has no love for him.... A report that Borah is on the rampage affects Republican leaders very much as a run on a bank affects financial leaders.... Borah knows that most of the men with whom he is dealing are clay and estimates with uncanny accuracy the degree to which he can compel them to meet his demands."[59]

Ohio politician James M. Cox, who lived in the Stoneleigh Court apartment building with Borah in the 1910s, came to understand him from their solitary evenings together. The "depth and quality" of the senator's mind "impressed" Cox, who believed Borah's great ambition was the Supreme Court, a better fit to the "lone wolf" Cox knew than the chummy Senate. Borah could be sociable, though, and enjoyed his afternoons with Idaho constituents at the regular gatherings of the round table at the Idana Hotel back home in Boise. Business and city leaders chewed the fat and solved the world's problems. Borah seldom agreed with everyone present, but he had the ability to remain friends and stay on pleasant terms with those of divergent views.[60]

A large part of Borah's charm for Alice was his love of literature. His formal educational background was as indifferent as hers, yet both autodidacts found solace and elevation in the written word. Their writings are rife with quotations from Shakespeare, Balzac, Kipling, Emerson, Beaumarchais, and Washington, Hamilton, Jefferson, Gladstone, and Pitt. Borah could quote long passages of Dante, Milton, Dickens, Thackeray, and Hawthorne. As a boy he loved recitation and used to make speeches to the mules on his father's farm as he plowed. Literature and history claimed his interest in school, but debate was his favorite pastime. Cox thought it "doubtful whether there was a more omnivorous reader in either branch of Congress."[61]

As a young man Borah had played the role of Mark Antony in *Julius Caesar* for a traveling Shakespearean company. The thespians chose him because he already knew the part by heart. When his father hauled him back to the plow, Bill's acting career ended. One scholar theorized that Mark Antony gave Borah two rules of life: "First, Borah had to assure himself that he was always acting from an unfettered conscience." This helps explain Borah's famous independence of action. "The second duty of the Mark Antony role was that Borah should pursue oratory as a high calling." Borah's father's prohibition against acting pushed him into law and politics, careers that valued an independent conscience and still let him emote.[62]

Bill Borah was recognized as the best orator in the Senate. He wrote his own talks and rehearsed them all carefully and aloud, but no longer to the mules. He read the addresses of Demosthenes, Cicero, Burke, Wendell Phillips, and Lincoln. He kept a notebook of quotes read and overheard so that he could work them into his orations. One friendly analyst concluded the senator's speeches "were not vacuous, and they were free from demagogy and partisan cant. Many of them were notable expositions on constitutional law or ardent declarations on liberty. . . . Borah did not offer oratory as substance; it was his tool."[63]

That tool helped unlock Alice Longworth's heart. "I enjoyed listening to Borah and [Senator James A.] Reed, too," she wrote. "Occasionally I did not entirely agree with what Borah said, or rather with the slant he gave some question, but he had a quality of earnest eloquence combined with a sort of smoldering benevolence, and knew so exactly how to manage his voice, that before he finished speaking I was always enthusiastic. He and Reed were decidedly the drawing cards from the gallery point of view." Daisy Harriman called Borah "a John the Baptist among legislators," who was "easily the most brilliant orator in the Senate . . . [with] a gift for promoting a number of things for which others take credit after he has originated them in his facile brain."[64] Borah studded his speeches with poetry, another passion he shared with Alice. To the day she died she could recite the works of poets from around the globe and across many centuries. Even among their erudite friends, the two were distinctive for the inspiration they received from the classics and the joy they took in wordplay.

They also had in common their adulation of Theodore Roosevelt. One contemporary observer speculated "that his one great desire was to be the successor of Roosevelt." This may explain the inconsistency that was known as Borah's chief failing. It is a fine line between maverick and contradictory behavior—and depends a good deal on the observer. For Alice, in the wake of Joe Graydon's betrayal—his unwillingness to demonize Woodrow Wilson and his inability to commit to a TR campaign in 1920— Borah's veneration of TR must have been balm. Pious, public canonization of her father she dismissed as excessive, but Borah communicated one thing over and over that must have pleased Alice at the most fundamental of all levels: his belief that she was made in her father's image. He told her often that he felt proud "to claim his wonderful daughter as a <u>dear</u> friend of long years."[65]

Alice's political beliefs found a champion in Senator Borah. Upon reaching Washington, he transcended his perceived antiunion stance and embraced a host of reforms including an eight-hour workday, the direct election of senators, and the creation of the Children's Bureau and the Department of Labor. Borah also fought for the 1916 Gore-McLemore Resolution warning Americans not to travel on belligerent ships, and against the espionage and conscription acts as violations of Americans' civil liberties. His resolutions led to the 1923 Dawes Plan to reschedule the German debt from World War I. He supported anti–child labor laws and giving women the vote, but only on the state level.

Alice and Borah did not concur on every issue. For example, Alice thought that the makeup of the Senate deteriorated after passage of the Seventeenth Amendment mandating the direct election of senators. This amendment was one of Borah's successes. Charles Merz, writing in the *New Republic*, characterized Borah as "a better states' rights man than most of his Democratic colleagues." In January 1922, House Republicans passed an antilynching bill that was blocked in the Senate under the leadership of Borah, who saw this as the top of a slippery slope of ever-increasing federal interference in states' rights. Summing up Borah's "maverick" status, Merz concluded, he was "a more liberal Democrat than Wilson" on some issues.[66] Further, Borah's voting record demonstrated a concern for farmers and laborers that Alice would have felt less and less keenly the farther the 1912 battle receded into the distance. Alice sat by Bill at a showing of a D. W. Griffith film, *Orphans of the Storm*, "a big spectacular performance with lurid scenes of the French Revolution...." The senator, she recalled, "behaved as if the scenes had been taken on the spot and became almost emotional about them, blazing with indignation at the cruel behavior of the French 'nobility,' fairly palpitating with sympathy at the vicissitudes of the populace and the heroines." Borah supported "world peace, limitation of armaments, justice for small nations, amnesty for political prisoners, honesty in government, economy, tax reduction, and the preservation of individual liberty."[67]

Borah's own political philosophy was unorthodox. This would not have distressed Alice. Neither of them could be classified as Republican regulars. A staunch defender of the Republican Party in her middle years, Alice nonetheless thought too independently to toe the party line. She had imbibed a heady dose of moral correctness in the 1912 campaign and afterward leaned toward her father's issues, such as conservation of the environment, protecting the rights of labor, and a strongly nationalistic foreign policy. Borah fought against high tariffs, while Nick Longworth championed them. Borah generally thought highly of Woodrow Wilson, and no Roosevelt or Longworth did.

Even when they disagreed they could do so amicably and openly. Borah regarded Alice as an intellectual equal—and he himself was considered an intellectual among senators, chiefly because of the breadth of the allusions in his speeches. But it was politics that bound them. A *Literary Digest* journalist suggested, "Those who love [Washington] are men like Senator Borah, who could hardly exist elsewhere than in the United States Senate; or, to go over to the other sex, women like Mrs. Alice Longworth...to whom it is breath in the nostrils."[68]

And it didn't hinder Alice's relationship with Bill that he was, continued the journalist, "an Apollo in appearance." An observer in the 1920s left some clues to the "real Senator Borah." In person, Borah was "far less austere, far less gloomy" than his photographs. He "frequently smiles and can tell a story gracefully." He had a "sardonic" sense of humor and, "in conversation, he is rarely discreet." He read "voluminously" and was popular because he could discuss "an extraordinary variety of matters." His mind was "alert and facile." Despite appearances, he was not truly a loner, but he did "find his own company excellent."[69] This, of course, could also precisely describe Alice Longworth. At bottom, she and Bill were kindred spirits.

They both believed Wilson's peace plan would compromise American autonomy in foreign affairs. The League of Nations was to be a multinational organization created to keep peace in the world by referring conflicts to its members. The League's Permanent Court of International Justice, known as the World Court, would rule on international disputes so that none would ever reach the battlefield. The League idea drew in many Americans who were tired of war. Roosevelt and other Republicans had initially been warm to the concept. But many people, including TR, Borah, and Alice, came to see the principle of collective action as counter to the tradition of American politics laid out in George Washington's admonition against "permanent alliances with any portion of the foreign world." Borah told TR in 1917 that "if [a league] would work at all it would simply be almost fiendish in its results." The Idahoan had been a member of the Senate Foreign Relations Committee since 1913 and thus was at the eye of the storm when Wilson vowed to make the League a central part of the peace treaty. Even before the details were made public in early 1919, Borah "espoused open warfare."[70]

In the face of the president's call to congressional unity on behalf of his peace treaty, the Republicans dissolved into two groups, varyingly opposed to the League idea. The "strong reservationists" followed Lodge's belief that with major changes a League might be acceptable. The "Irreconcilables," led by Borah, did not support any sort of league at all. On this, Alice was his intellectual twin. She felt they were trying to keep the United States "out of the internationalism that we felt menaced our very existence as an independent nation."[71] Glued to her seat in the Senate gallery, Alice listened to every speech she could. Ruth was right beside her, with the same firm resolve. The two friends worked together to stiffen the will of any politician giving the least sign of capitulating. Laying strategy was an ongoing affair, as the Irreconcilables traded ideas and reviewed one another's points. They met frequently at Alice's and gained the appellation the Battalion of Death for their ferocious tenacity against the League idea. For her leadership role, they christened Alice the "Colonel" of the Battalion of Death.

In early March 1919, Irreconcilables spearheaded the senatorial round robin statement to gather votes against the League of Nations as it was then drafted. They had more names than they needed. Lodge, chair of the Senate Foreign Relations Committee, conveyed the bad news to Wilson. The GOP would take control of the Senate after March 4, 1919, and thus Wilson would have to consult the upper house. Many Republican senators chafed at the section of the League covenant that gave Great Britain the equivalent of six votes to the one granted to the United States. Nor did they like the fact that small countries had the same vote as America. On March 3, Alice went to the Senate to hear the filibuster from Illinois' senior senator, the elderly and near-deaf Lawrence Y. Sherman. Sherman acknowledged that the League had put him in a "savage mood," and that he was "prepared to attack in 'meatax' fashion." He was "tacitly supported" by Wisconsin's Robert M. La Follette and others. After lunch, Sherman continued. Alice went home at 3:00 a.m. and returned "six hours later" to find the senator still on the offensive. He had begun at 8:00 a.m. and went on without interruption until noon, when the Senate adjourned. The filibuster forced Wilson to call the special session he swore he would not, and when the president denounced Sherman, the venerable senator dismissed Wilson as "a superfluous luxury." Alice then rushed to the House, which was full to bursting with spectators viewing "a rag bag of exhausted, frowzy legislators."[72]

While Congress was out of session, Medill, who had won election to the Senate in 1918, masterminded the speaking schedules of the Irreconcilables as they canvassed the nation in late April and spread the news of the destruction they believed the League of Nations would wreak upon the

United States. Alice and Nick went to Cincinnati for six weeks, time she thought "wasted." They arrived back in time for Nick—heretofore anti-suffrage—to vote for the woman's suffrage amendment, to Alice's "great pleasure."[73]

Upon her return, the Battalion of Death sent Alice on a mission to coax the "mild reservationists"—those who sought only minor changes to Wilson's League covenant—to join their side. It was difficult, but she kept at it, spending "more and more time at the Capitol." Meanwhile, Medill "was most amazingly resourceful in producing ideas calculated to annoy," while Bill Borah worked to stall matters by having a leaked version of the lengthy peace treaty read word for word into the record in the Senate. On July 8, the night Wilson returned from Paris, Alice had one of her mild reservationists in tow. She tossed him in her car and drove to the White House to calculate the size of the crowd and the intensity of its support. Needing help from all sources, Alice stood on the curb "fingers crossed, making the sign of the evil eye, and saying 'A murrain on him, a murrain on him, a murrain on him!'"[74] She did not relate whether the experience of hurling imprecations at the president won over her companion.

In an emotional plea before the Senate two days later, Wilson begged the intransigent politicians to pass his treaty so they did not "break the heart of the world." Alice, Frank Brandegee (a good friend and senator from Connecticut), and Medill went for a long drive that afternoon, angrily dissecting the speech and planning how best to invigorate the cause and "capture votes in the Senate." All summer and early fall the peace treaty sat before Lodge's Foreign Relations Committee, which finally released it to the full Senate in September. Seeking to get around the troublesome senators, President Wilson left on September 3 for his own speaking tour of the nation. Borah, Medill, and Hiram Johnson dogged his steps, patiently explaining to great crowds the fallacies in Wilson's logic. They kicked off their anti-League tour at Soldier Field in Chicago, which proved too small for the audience. Borah went on speaking to packed, cheering houses in Nebraska and Iowa.[75]

Meanwhile in Washington, at Lodge's suggestion, Alice wrote a letter to be made public that declared emphatically that TR had not supported the

League of Nations, as Wilson was telling crowds. Just as her stepmother and her brothers—recently returned from the war—were considering making a similar statement, Wilson suffered a paralyzing stroke. Alice's murrain had evidently worked. Her circle, she felt, was "noticeably lacking in the Greek quality of *Aidos*—the quality that deters one from defiling the body of a dead enemy."[76]

Wilson's illness meant no slowdown for the Battalion of Death. Debate over the treaty continued on Capitol Hill. Alice heard all the best speeches in the Senate. In between them she tried her persuasive powers on the un-decided and laid plans in the committee rooms and in senatorial offices with her comrades. So used was she to unrestricted access that Borah's secretary, Cora Rubin, remembered that Alice grew distressed the few times she couldn't get into Borah's office. Alice was so regularly in the senators' family gallery that the rules were changed to include "immediate members of ex-Presidents' families," so she wouldn't have to seek out a senator to gain access. On November 19, 1919, the Senate began voting on the Treaty of Versailles—with the reservations written in part by Borah and Lodge—including Article X that would create the League of Nations. Alice and Ruth were there for the ten-hour debate—breaking only to try to influence some reservationists, smoke a cigarette, or snatch a bite to eat.[77]

Bill Borah had the honor of the last speech. The Senate gallery was overflowing with the largest crowd Alice could recall. He was in top form. He charged the senators with nothing less than protecting democracy by voting against the treaty. Democracy, Borah thundered, was "vastly more than a mere form of government. . . . It is a moral entity, a spiritual force. . . ." And wedding democracy to "the discordant and destructive forces of the Old World" would cause democracy to "lose its soul." "Your treaty," Bo-rah warned, "does not mean peace," but war.[78] His gestures were sure, his voice resonant, his argument convincing. Even his sometime critic Hiram Johnson conceded that Borah had "excelled himself, and made the one great speech of the whole fight." The voting began at 5:30, and the treaty fell to defeat in the Senate, 39 to 55. It was called up again and defeated again, 41 to 51. A third vote, on the treaty without any resolutions, also failed. Finally, at 11:10 p.m., Congress adjourned. The jubilant celebratory dinner was held at Alice's house. Next to her as she drove home that extraordinary night was Bill Borah.[79] She was entranced.

The battle was not over, however. Lodge, the focus of pro-League criticism, decided to seek compromise by holding a conference of mild reservationists. Quite by accident Alice and Ruth discovered their secret meeting at Lodge's home. The Colonel was furious. She confronted Lodge. She made him explain himself. He wanted to try the treaty again, and pass it with his reservations. "I said to myself," recalled Alice, " 'He will have the Irreconcilables to deal with.' " She informed the rest of the Battalion of Death of Lodge's plans. She sympathized with the senator and understood that his job was to find the middle ground even though she believed he was as opposed to the League as she. Nevertheless, she called him Mr. Wobbly.[80]

Alice contributed to insider negotiations. She read unpublished correspondence concerning the resignation of Secretary of State Robert Lansing and had journalists at her door, informing her of scoops before they were printed. She and Frank Brandegee spent hours talking things over. Borah was often their subject. The Idahoan had a tendency to castigate GOP reservationists and to ridicule the very reservations he had helped Lodge to write. Historians, too, have criticized Borah for habitually charting his own course, changing that course unaccountably, and condemning Republicans as well as Democrats. One biographer suggested that "Borah approached true happiness when flagellating his own party."[81] Alice never shied from criticizing members of the GOP, but she had neither constituents nor bills requiring compromise.

When another vote was taken, on March 19, 1920, the Lodge reservations went down to defeat again. Irreconcilables and Democrats loyal to Wilson's version without the reservations teamed up to defeat the proposal. Then the treaty came up for a vote without the reservations. It failed a final time. The United States never joined the League of Nations. Senator Lodge blamed Borah, Alice, and Brandegee for having started the whole fight.[82] Alice's behind-the-scenes lobbying played an indisputable role in this key political event. She knew as much about the issue as diplomats and policy makers. Her knowledge, her presence, her pressure, and her influence over those men were real factors in the battle, and thus she, as Colonel of the Battalion of Death, helped to block U.S. entry into the League of Nations. Borah likened the death of the treaty to the surrender of Robert E. Lee.[83] The Battalion of Death adjourned to the Longworth home again for one more celebratory gathering. It felt somehow anticlimactic. She and the rest of the wary isolationists looked toward the Republican convention, ten months away, and feared a change of heart that would move the GOP to attempt a resurrection. But the gloom could not settle fully on Alice, for she was in love with the towering senator beside her, and carefully contemplating his future.

Chapter 15

"Hello, Hello, Hello"

THE 1920 ELECTION ushered in ten years of Republican supremacy and many political triumphs for Alice and those she loved. She continued to be, as the *New York Times* put it, "a leader in the capital's most exclusive circles, where her astute observance of political developments has made her a confidante of statesmen who value her opinion almost as much as they do her distinguished husband's."[1] The 1920s was also a very satisfying—if tumultuous—decade for Alice. She had fulfilling relationships with a large circle of friends, an ease with her husband borne of twenty years of marriage, a serious love affair with the most powerful man in Washington. And, at age forty-one, Alice Longworth became a mother.

Love cemented the bond that politics created. For their relationship, Bill Borah risked his marriage and his career—the latter based, ironically, on his oft-noted integrity—while Alice, presumably, risked Nick's career. Her code of ethics did not include cheating, but Nick had turned their marriage into an open one because of his years of infidelity. Alice and Borah did not flaunt their affair. They took pains to hide it, although rumors circulated through Washington nonetheless. When they were apart, hundreds of letters from Borah to Alice—spanning the eight years prior to Nick's death—attest to Bill's love for her. He showered her with almost daily notes, a correspondence mixing devotion, politics, appeals for her advice, and compliments on her political acumen. He thought Alice "the dearest one in the world," "instinctively wise," "a wonderful woman," "an inspiration," who helped him plan legislative and electoral strategies, to whom he confessed his melancholy, and who, in 1925, bore his only child. If Alice and Nick stumbled through the haze of an immature love and fatally tripped on the crags of ego, vanity, and unmet expectations, then Alice found a solid relationship based on mutual respect and shared passions with Bill. Her decision to carry their child to term spoke movingly of her love for Bill Borah.

With the defeat of the League of Nations behind them, Alice and her friends turned optimistically to the 1920 election. The 1918 off-year contest had gone their way, but Republicans lacked an obvious front-runner after Theodore Roosevelt's death. Among those names bruited about were Roosevelt family friend General Leonard Wood, Illinois governor Frank Lowden, the irascible Senator Hiram Johnson, and Ohio's Warren G. Harding. The Wilson years had reshaped the Grand Old Party. Gone were Roosevelt-era reforms. Instead the party took up the position of the right and held it solidly for the remainder of the century. During the 1920s, Republican ideals were much closer to Nick's than to Alice's, but she moved rightward, too, and the pair was always hopeful for Nick's advancement.

The Longworths were together for the opening of the Republican convention, held June 8 through 12, in the Chicago Coliseum. Alice and Nick, Ruth and Medill, Henry Cabot Lodge, Frank Brandegee, and Warren Harding took the train together. The conference was all the more interesting for leading up to the first presidential election in which women could vote. Congress had passed the Nineteenth Amendment in 1919, and by August 1920, enough states had ratified it to allow women full suffrage rights. Alice approved. She had "always believed that women should have the vote."[2]

Two days before the convention, Republican women met to lay strategy. Alice and Ruth were active in the Republican Women's National Committee (RWNC), a group with nationwide representation that worked on behalf of GOP causes and women's issues in particular. Alice listened as Auntie Corinne—a member of the RWNC executive committee—encouraged women to put aside personal preferences and work together for the good of the organization, which was in the middle of selecting a new chair. Alice supported Ruth's candidacy and lobbied women for their votes. After a fractious campaign, Ruth won the chair. She stood then on the brink of "the career she believed she was born to, electoral politics." Under Ruth's leadership, the RWNC focused on their real objective: "equal division of power and responsibility" for women in the Republican Party. It was an elusive goal. In 1920, only twenty-seven convention delegates were women. The RWNC began by organizing women in their geographic region. But the immediate task at the convention was women-friendly platform planks. Their cause was aided by Medill, Bill Borah, and a few other male progressives.[3]

At the convention, Alice and the rest of the Roosevelts worked for Leonard Wood, whom one contemporary described as "a big, well set-up man, approachable and with a fine presence."[4] Auntie Corinne gave the speech seconding his nomination. Nick was for fellow Buckeye Warren Harding. There was no love lost between Alice and Harding. She could not forget 1912. Harding wasn't even her second choice—Johnson was because of their shared fight against the League. She had little faith that either Wood or Johnson would win. Long before the convention, Alice and Congressman Bascom Slemp had put their heads together to figure out likely front-runners. That their prognostications were coming true was little consolation.

Alice's sidekicks in Chicago were Ruth and Medill, Borah, Wood, Brandegee, *North American Review* publisher Colonel George Harvey, and the rest of her "old birds" in Suite 404 of the Blackstone Hotel. She had arranged for those Republican power brokers to give her the slate of candidates before the convention opened. Suite 404 was the infamous "smoke-filled room" where Harding had been called before party leaders to confess any reason that he should not be made president. When, over breakfast, Harvey told Alice that her nemesis Harding had gotten the nod, she was furious. Why not some other, better qualified "dark horse," like Frank Knox? At least Harvey could assure her that Harding would "go along" with the anti-League position that he and Alice had hammered out before the convention opened. Alice reluctantly promised that the Roosevelt family would agree to "play ball" with this weak candidate whose best quality was that he could be controlled.[5]

Alice was in the thick of things in Chicago, and newspapers followed her movements. She was one of a small number of people, including the candidates and some lucky New Yorkers, who got hold of the third edition of the *Times* dated June 9 actually on the *ninth*. This made the news because the *Times* was flown to Chicago by airplane—a new, modern means of delivery. Alice was the only woman listed among the fortunate few, and it was clear that her status as an insider merited her the paper. Meanwhile, she must have cringed at the one mention of her husband by the mainstream press. A man from Kentucky, identified as a friend of Nick's, had missed the special delegation train and arrived late because, the *Times* reported, his "liquor had not been made in time."[6] Prohibition had gone into effect in January 1920, giving rise immediately to many alcohol jokes. Not that this troubled Nick. The wealthy in America found ways to slake their thirst for spirits unhindered by the technicalities of the Eighteenth Amendment.

The eventual Republican presidential candidate was among the capital's heaviest drinkers. That was but one reason Ohioans Harding and Nick got on so well. Like Nick, Harding was affable, friendly, and neither intellectually nor constitutionally suited to the nation's highest office. Alice thought Harding looked like "a decaying Roman emperor." Nick and Harding also had in common a penchant for extramarital affairs, a fondness for poker, and a love of golf. The times, Frank Brandegee famously scowled, did not require "first raters." As the GOP nominee, Harding was the compromise who "could carry Ohio... had no serious enemies within the party, and... made a winning figure on the stump." His running mate, Vermonter Calvin Coolidge—"a precise little object," Alice called him, "a little bit of whalebone, there"—was the exact opposite, in everything but his politics.[7]

Nick held on to Harding's coattails, and Alice understood the importance of pushing down past insults. They jointly signed a congratulatory telegram to the new nominee and were soon making pilgrimages to Marion, Ohio, home of Warren and Florence Harding.[8] A month after the convention Nick and Alice spent the night at the Hardings', talking late about the League of Nations specifically and "the campaign generally." Nick issued strongly supportive statements to the press, promising to deliver his district to Harding. He said that he and the presidential nominee "agree absolutely over the general situation and the issues. The Senator is growing in strength all the time." He promised to dedicate the last ten days of his own campaign to work in any way that Harding or the GOP needed. Before the Longworths left, they strolled along the streets of Marion so Nick could bask in Harding's reflected glory. Then Nick left for the hustings, stumping for Harding in Maine. In mid-August, the couple was back in Marion again, "calling on the senator," as he had decided to conduct a front-porch campaign as the great Republican William McKinley had done so successfully in 1896. Nick shared the porch with Harding, delivering a blistering speech against President Wilson's "reckless methods and [financial] extravagance" and the Democratic Party's ill-advised economic platform.[9]

Alice waved the flag, too: LOOKS LIKE GOOD G.O.P YEAR, SAYS MRS. LONGWORTH the *Chicago Tribune* headline blared. Because she was in the Windy City, the paper was certain she was "on a political mission." Alice demurred. She was in town only to visit Ruth, she maintained—but shortly after that the *Tribune* snapped a photo of her "conferring" at Republican headquarters.[10] Soon after, no doubt because of Ruth's influence, Alice became "one of the Republican leaders who will direct the fight for the capture of the state of Ohio," by joining the executive committee of the state's Republican campaign committee. Newspapers announced that she would "take the stump for the party when the big speaking campaign opens," as Ruth, Auntie Corinne, and brother Ted were doing. Alice never actually made a speech. She was supposed to have spoken in Jackson, Ohio, at a "barbecue and burgoo," along with Harding and Nick, but there's no evidence that she did. She was as shy before crowds as she was brilliant in small gatherings. The two venues take vastly different skills, and while Alice was glad to appear on podiums, she seldom opened her mouth. She understood the critical need for her presence and appeared at political events and TR memorials. For example, she went—right in the middle of campaign season—to dedicate Roosevelt Road in Wheaton, Illinois, west of Chicago. Like those of his sister, Ted's virtues as a speaker were not as useful as his physical recall of TR for adoring audiences.[11] The Republicans were glad to have Corinne, Alice, and Ted on their side, because the Democrats had their own Roosevelt: in San Francisco in late June, the Democratic delegates had chosen Franklin to be presidential nominee James M. Cox's running mate.

Franklin's last name caused confusion among Americans, and that confusion caused the hackles to rise in Oyster Bay. Too many voters assumed that Franklin was TR's son. To clarify, Republican Party leaders shooed Ted after Franklin on the campaign trail. Ted, using western metaphors, proclaimed FDR "a maverick. He does not have the brand of our family."[12] Speaking to a crowd of Rough Riders, Ted found a warm reception. Franklin and Eleanor were hurt. Alice thought they should have stood up for themselves at that point, but they didn't. This was the first crack in what would become a serious rift between the two Roosevelt branches.

Nick soldiered on with his speech making, through Maine—which the Republicans did win—and elsewhere.[13] Alice had her own part in the campaign. In Marion, she participated in a two-day conference of powerful, politically driven women that included Harriet Taylor Upton, a veteran of the suffrage battle in Harding's state; Margaret Drier Robins, president of the Women's Trade Union League and the International Congress of Working Women; and Auntie Corinne. They joined five thousand women across the nation who were observing Social Justice Day. Some of the women paraded to the Harding home to hear a lengthy speech about how the Republican Party would protect mothers, children, female farm workers, and the American family; support an eight-hour workday for women; speak out against lynching; and uphold Prohibition. Alice had spent much of August and September in Chicago, where party luminaries had gathered. One photographer there snapped pictures of two important politicians as they tried to learn HOW WILL THE LADIES, GOD BLESS 'EM, VOTE? The chair of the women's section of the Democratic National Committee enlightened Franklin Delano Roosevelt, while Senator Borah was double-teamed by Alice and Ruth.[14]

In the end, Alice was right: 1920 was a good GOP year. The presidential election was a landslide. The invalid President Wilson longed to run again and called for Americans to make their votes be "a solemn referendum" on the peace treaty and the work done at Versailles, but his party denied him the nomination. As Nick said smartly, "The President had his wish. A solemn referendum was had...and the League was repudiated." The Democrats were swept away by the tidal wave of discontent that Americans felt in the wake of the Great War, the bitter League battle, wartime incursions into Americans' civil rights, and the taxes levied to pay for World War I.

With a solid majority in the House and in the Senate, and with a Republican in the White House, Nick found himself considered for the speakership. The *New York Times* editorialized that "in spite of the handicaps of hereditary forehandedness and an overshadowingly illustrious father-in-law, he has worked himself up to a position of influence and authority in the House. He has wit, humor, industry, application, a good mind. In spite of a certain modesty, he has made his talents acknowledged. He studies public questions carefully. He can think on his feet as well as in a library," and— no small thing on Capitol Hill—Nick was popular. This was not to be his time, but Nick's day was approaching fast.[15]

Nick settled back to the House Ways and Means Committee where, since 1907, he had been devoting himself to the tariff that so absorbed his intellectual energies. Protectionism was Congress' first order of business. Republicans wanted to replace President Wilson's Underwood Tariff with one better suited to the postwar situation. By September 1922, they would succeed, when President Harding signed the controversially high Fordney-McCumber Act. Nick was of "the belief that the American market is primarily for the American producer" and that the high tariff would guarantee a bright postwar future for the United States. The only Republican in the Senate debate to vote against the tariff bill was Bill Borah. He feared the administration's handling of foreign affairs was "intolerant, shortsighted, [and] prejudiced" and would "keep closed the foreign markets."[16]

The final issue of World War I was settled when the United States concluded a peace with Germany in 1921. But two years later, people imprisoned as a result of Wilson's wartime Espionage Act were still in jail. This prompted Senator Borah to demand their immediate release. Supporting his call were the American Civil Liberties Union, the Women's Trade Union League, Jane Addams, and his old courtroom adversary Clarence Darrow, among others.[17] Some vestiges of war were slow to depart.

Another war-era bill, prohibition of alcohol, became law after the guns were silent. As soon as the Volstead Act passed Congress, lobbying began for its repeal. Alice marveled "that anyone ever thought it possible to legislate an appetite that is part of human nature out of existence." Nevertheless, Alice and Ruth, both plagued by their husbands' tendencies toward alcohol abuse, supported Prohibition. Among congressmen, Alice snorted, "the men who voted dry and drank wet were with us in large numbers." Alice never joined the women who crusaded against liquor and she was realistic about its use in her home. She continued to serve alcohol at dinner parties, as did most other Washington hostesses. Nick's Ohio constituents were "wets" and hoped for repeal, and Nick himself "had the deepest conviction of the folly, futility, and unfairness of trying to eradicate all drink." He also felt strongly that Prohibition was a "denial of the rights of the individual," as Congress should not be allowed to tell people what they could not do in their own homes. Alice and Nick gave their butler the creative task of replenishing their dwindling stock of alcohol. He became adept at making gin out of oranges with the small still they provided. In the Longworth tradition, the couple also tried their hand at wine making, but with less success than Nick's great-grandfather had enjoyed from his vineyards in Cincinnati. The pair proved better at brewing beer, and made a batch Lord Balfour loved.[18]

But Alice soon grew tired of seeing her "friends and acquaintances awash in bootleg liquor, from month to month thinking concentratedly on the next drink." She became a dry. Her decision was based less on a belief in the virtue of abstinence and more on the disgust she felt seeing the drunkenness around her. "If the people I knew got drunk," she averred, "I did not really mind, I merely did not wish to see them and associate with them when they were in that condition" because "tipsy people bored me, they irritated and exasperated me." Alice took to lecturing them on the inviolability of the Constitution and the evils of drink.[19]

Completely in character, though, she'd take the opposite position with any sanctimonious drys. "The fanatics on both sides were just about equally distasteful to me," Alice concluded. But Nick was the real concern. Ted and some of their friends believed that Nick's drinking had reached the stage where it would stop his career. New York congressman Jim Wadsworth told Ted "it would be a good idea for both of us to speak to Nick about his drinking, in view of the fact that he is a probable majority leader of the Republicans next year. Of course this is something that makes one feel like a prig to talk about to anyone, but I do think that Nick physically is going to suffer soon unless he cuts down considerably." Alice's repugnance reached new heights, especially when she contrasted him to that "sincere prohibitionist," Bill Borah.[20]

The *New York Times* front page proclaimed IDAHO LEADER NOW SEEN AS LEADER OF DRY FORCES, as Bill gave speech after speech criticizing the repeal effort. In every address he proudly called himself a teetotaler. Borah also became her champion as he led the opposition to Harding's plan to pay Colombia for the land on which her father built the Panama Canal. "Theodore Roosevelt was not a common adventurer," Borah proclaimed as he defended TR against the old charge of stealing Panama. Alice and Bill stood together against downsizing the navy, giving up too much American freedom of action overseas, making Europe pay its war debts, and remained firmly against continuing attempts to inveigle American entry into the League of Nations. Bill became friends with Ted, who had been rewarded for his campaign support with the post of assistant secretary of the navy. It was that same position that had helped launch TR to fame.[21]

Nick socialized with Alice but could just as often be found with Harding, playing poker in the White House. He was also keeping company throughout the decade with his "girls"—Alice Dows, Laura Curtis, Marie Beale, and Cornelia Mayo. Alice Dows and Nick shared a passion for music, and she could convince Nick to play his violin for her guests, bringing out in him, she felt, "a hidden shyness." But Nick, Ted, and Jim Wadsworth walked together frequently; daily, when bills were pressing. Once a week, they took lengthy hikes through Rock Creek Park and called it "the

Statesmen's Sunday Morning Marching Club." Borah, who rode alone at that time, often crossed their path and endured good-natured joshing about his horse's advanced case of "bog spavin."[22] In various configurations they spent countless hours dissecting the plans emanating from Capitol Hill and laying strategies.

The early years of the decade were absorbed by negotiations over the Washington naval disarmament conference. Borah believed passionately in the duty of the United States to maintain peace around the globe, and after the horrors of World War I, he wanted to assure peace through multilateral disarmament. Borah hated war and regretted voting for it as he had in April 1917. But the League of Nations—no matter how badly its supporters wanted the issue resurrected—was doomed to failure, Borah thought, and also unconstitutional.

Instead of the League, Borah felt the shared goal of decreasing tensions worldwide could be met by a formal agreement among powerful nations. He introduced the bill requesting President Harding to invite representatives from Great Britain and Japan to discuss a five-year plan of reduction of naval armaments. Eventually, nine nations sent delegates to Washington for the three-month-long conference. Borah believed that the naval buildup after the turn of the century had led to the horrible war just past, and without severe cuts in naval budgets across the globe, another conflagration would be upon the world in less than fifteen years. At the very least, he preached, working people would be bled of their paychecks because of the cost of the current naval arms race. The grand orator predicted "economic ruin...moral breakdown...industrial peonage for the masses...wounds and mangled bodies and shattered minds and millions dead...."[23]

The goal of the Washington Conference, which opened on Armistice Day 1921, was to slow the postwar naval race. Nick wrote his mother that during Secretary of State Charles Evans Hughes's opening speech "there weren't more than fifteen people in the audience of whom Alice and I were two, who knew how far the Administration were proposing in naval disarmament and the air was full of gasps."[24] Hughes stunned onlookers when he suggested that the United States should scrap tons of extant warships,

told the other nations what they should destroy, and proposed a morato-
rium on building certain types of ships.

While leaders needed convincing of the Hughes plan, the idea was so
popular in the national imagination that President Harding swallowed his
scruples and expressed his support. The program expanded to include Far
Eastern issues and land armaments. Although angered that the agenda had
strayed from his original idea, Borah worked for a positive outcome. He
made sure that newspaper reporters had free access to the conference debates and uncensored reporting. While Borah smoldered, more and more
topics were added. His research proved that the so-called treaties emerging
from the Washington conference were alliances cloaked as treaties, and he
could not vote for them. The Four Power Treaty, wherein nations promised to respect each other's Pacific holdings, the senator believed would
also bind the United States to defending Britain's island colonies. He and
his irreconcilable brothers went on the attack. As Democrats argued for
three hours on March 11, Borah, Johnson, and Reed assaulted their logic.
Their debate packed the Senate galleries, and Alice was riveted. Though
the Senate ratified all of the disarmament treaties to come from the Washington Conference, Borah opposed them on the grounds that the result
would give too much power to Japan in East Asia.[25]

After the conference ended, it fell to the new assistant secretary of the
navy, among others, to lobby for American adherence. Ted and Alice, who
felt similarly on most issues, were together many times a week throughout
the early 1920s. Alice was one of her brother's confidantes. He sent her letters marked CONFIDENTIAL and SECRET filled with their shared nicknames
for political players, and poetry to illustrate their prognostications. Weekends filled up with poker parties at the Longworths', dinners at the McCormicks', and luncheons at the McLeans'. The circle of friends expanded to
include Ethel Barrymore, Eleanora Sears, Lord Balfour, Charles Curtis,
and Bill—if not always Mary—Borah.[26]

In 1922, Nick and Ted worked together on the naval appropriations bill
wending its way through Congress. There was a move afoot in the House
to cut down the size of the navy to sixty-seven thousand men—which Al-

ice, Ted, and Nick opposed. They wanted eighty-six thousand, which conformed with the Four Power Treaty. Frequently, the two men discussed the plans and then, as Ted chronicled in his diary, "In the afternoon we got together and went over all phases of the situation from end to end." In a speech before the National Press Club, which Nick heard, Ted decried this manpower cut. Walking back to the Longworths' afterward, Nick strategized that it might be "a good play to have the entire Ohio delegation at his house on Wednesday where I could speak to them informally."[27]

Ted took up Nick's idea on the evening of April 11. "We had a meeting of the Ohio delegation at Nick's house," Ted wrote. "I brought down two bottles of whiskey to help their conversation, and Sister served them punch made with home made gin. I was in good form this evening and spoke well to them. Nick was much pleased with the results. He told me that there were only two men who were for the 86,000 amendment when they met, [including] himself.... When he left he said that with the possible exception of two men we had all those who had been there." That same day, Ted claimed the reduction would be a "national disaster" that would relegate the United States to a second-rate power able to exert "but little influence in the world for peace and justice."[28]

Nick talked Ted into trying to secure a letter of support from President Harding for the appropriations bill, which Harding duly wrote with their input. Ted had steered Harding into a higher dollar amount and away from phrase that suggested that "future international conventions might result in further reductions in naval armament." Nick read the letter in the House and, Ted thought, "made an excellent little speech at the same time. He conveyed just the right degree of solemnity and dignity. There is no question but that it had the right effect." Then, Nick, Medill, Ted, and some other "big navy men" all started calling folks to ascertain their upcoming vote. Eventually, they won "by a handsome majority against all odds and every prediction." House members broke into a spontaneous "Indian war dance" down the center aisle, accompanied by "loud cheers and wild whoops." Ted was ecstatic. He rounded up all "the young naval officers and our best friends" and took them to his home. They shared a bottle of champagne, a gift from family friend Arthur Lee. Ted thought, "It seemed rather appropriate to drink the success of our navy in champagne given to me by the First Lord of the British Admiralty."[29]

Later that summer, Susan Longworth died, on June 27, 1922, after a lengthy illness. Nick and his sister Nan were at their mother's bedside when the seventy-seven-year-old matriarch succumbed to pneumonia. He telephoned the news of his beloved "Mummy" to Alice in Washington, and she left the following morning for the funeral in Cincinnati. Susan and Alice were never close, but Alice knew her place was at her husband's side for the burial rites. The funeral was held at Rookwood, and among the pallbearers was Joe Graydon.[30]

While reconciled to a month in Ohio, Alice must have been of two minds about the letters she was receiving from Ted. "When are you coming back?" he wrote enticingly. "Washington is now the center of real activity and excitement. The railroad strike and the coal strike have pushed everything else into the back-ground." Ted had sought Bill Borah's views on the strike. "As usual, he has some good suggestions," Ted reported. Her brother promised to "go over [the political scene] in detail" when she returned to D.C., and give her the fine points from his dinner with President and Mrs. Harding.[31]

Tragedy visited the family again in October 1922, when Ethel's only son, eight-year-old Richard Derby, died very suddenly of blood poisoning. Christmas at Sagamore was a sad affair. Death continued to hound the Roosevelts. On May 1, 1923, Bye's husband, Will, passed away. The admiral and Bye had been married nearly thirty years. Edith wrote that his death had been "a long breathing away of life—no pain, but hard for Auntie Bye." Isabella Munro-Ferguson gave a heartrending description of Auntie Bye at this time. Her "superhuman courage" of the "great and lasting" kind held her upright, Isabella thought. "Nothing left but the ghost of her once big blue eyes and the defiant toss of her head—upon an entirely crumpled and wasted body—and a mind seemingly more vitally acute than ever before...." Bye suffered increasingly from disabling arthritis and deafness, compounded by worsening eyesight and circulatory problems. In the 1920s, she continued to entertain politicians and society leaders even as she surrounded herself with many lively members of younger generations.[32] Alice wrote loving letters and came to visit as often as she could, while Bye was stalwart in her pain and bore it uncomplainingly.

Then, in August 1923, Warren Harding died. Whispers of scandals had been circulating around the capital, and the president had taken himself off to Alaska and a western speaking tour to ponder his troubles. In California a heart attack killed him. Nick lost a powerful friend, but Alice had never cared for the Hardings. "When he came to Washington after his election," she recalled, "we saw him and discussed with him matters of policy and Cabinet prospects." She "was put up to tell him how ill-advised" Harry Daugherty would be as his attorney general. Harding ignored Alice—perhaps because of the contempt that showed whenever she spoke to him—but she and some of his "supporters" were proven right, as evidence of Daugherty's corruption mounted. Alice also had no patience with the "shocking" disregard in which Harding held the Constitution insofar as Prohibition was concerned. "No rumor could have exceeded the reality," she wrote, of the boozing upstairs in the Harding White House. The secret drinking spot was Harding's study, which had "air heavy with tobacco smoke, trays with bottles containing every imaginable brand of whisky...cards and poker chips ready at hand—a general atmosphere of waistcoat unbuttoned, feet on the desk, and the spittoon alongside." Alice's final words on Harding finished him off: "I think everyone must feel that the brevity of his tenure of office was a mercy to him and to the country. Harding was not a bad man. He was just a slob."[33]

Alice felt similarly about Florence Harding: not a bad woman, but a bit outré. She had known Mrs. Harding for years. Being First Lady had not improved her. Alice would have agreed with journalist Mark Sullivan's assessment of Florence. He found her insecure, jealous, incessantly chatting, and forever losing the battle to keep her unfaithful husband nearby. "In appearance," Sullivan wrote, "she was a little too mechanically marcelled, too shinily rouged and lipsticked, too trimly tailored. Towards her, Harding was always gravely deferential, and his men friends learned to be the same. They, and he always addressed her as 'Duchess' and gave her a deference and eminence appropriate to the fantastic title." Alice thought her "a nervous, rather excitable woman whose voice easily became a little high-pitched, strident."[34]

And yet, once Flo Harding became First Lady, Alice had to put aside her overt disdain. "There is no city in the world perhaps where political rank counts for so much socially" as Washington, and the First Lady was the highest-ranking woman, "shinily rouged" or not. Alice enjoyed having the White House open to her again and she did share at least one interest with the Duchess: the supernatural. Alice's fascination began as a girl after she and Kermit encountered gypsies. The two children visited them frequently enough to learn a certain amount of Romany.[35] She was attracted to the color and mystery of their lives—so very different from her own. As a young woman, she rejected traditional Christianity and refused to be baptized. She had her palm read and her fortune told at various points in her life. As an adult, Alice absorbed all she could find on Romany culture. At her death, those well-worn volumes still occupied an important place in her library. Alice and the Duchess, often accompanied by Evalyn McLean, indulged their interest in having their horoscopes read, but this threesome did not last long. Florence could be paranoid, and she bragged to Alice and Ruth about how she kept score of the slights against her and against Warren in a special little red book.

Thus, when the Coolidges moved into the White House, Alice was pleased. Under the Coolidges', "the atmosphere was as different as a New England front parlor is from a back room in a speakeasy." Grace Coolidge and Alice paired up often. They both loved acrostics, crossword puzzles, and other word games. They enjoyed watching the Senate. Alice often sat alongside the First Lady in the "President's pew" in the Senate chamber. Grace Coolidge had "a simplicity and charm...was amused by all the official functions and attentions, yet was always absolutely natural and unimpressed by it all," Alice thought. Though she liked Coolidge as a dinner guest, he could drive her to fury, for his taciturnity made him a social liability. Once she found him so "bad mannered" that she didn't speak to him for the rest of the evening. Nick had made a "felicitous" little speech—the sort of thing Nick did very well, she thought—and Coolidge, in response, "grunted." "*Poor* Mrs. Coolidge," Alice recalled, "*she* got up" to say a few words. When he wished he were elsewhere, he pursed his lips, folded his arms, and said nothing. He looked then precisely as though he had been weaned on a pickle. Alice gave currency to this phrase, which she said she wished she had originated, but thought that her dentist had.[36]

Nick would work very closely with President Coolidge, if his supporters had their way. As early as February 1923, they were proposing him for the authoritative position of House majority leader. But western congressmen, younger and less conservative in their thinking—those who, the *New York Times* pointed out, would never be caught dead in the spats worn by Longworth—withheld their support. Twenty-five "progressive" representatives assailed what they called the Millionaire Ways and Means Committee on which Nick had served for years, and suggested that the Old Guard controlling it wielded too much power. "Special privilege [has] entrenched itself in legislative power," just as it had during the Joe Cannon years—only back then, Nick had been the insurgent. Progressive congressmen called for a child labor amendment, assistance to farmers and veterans, "government control of necessities of life, when necessary, to prevent profiteering," excessive war profits, "uniform presidential primaries," and amendments to the Federal Reserve Act—but most of all they wanted promises of shared power in order to bring their bills to the floor.[37]

In November, Nick wrote to Republican members of the Sixty-eighth Congress about the possibility of becoming majority leader. Claiming that he did not seek the honor, and would be loathe to give up his place on the Ways and Means Committee, he asserted that "it was only after strong pressure and careful thought that I finally acceded and my candidacy was announced by my delegation. I have asked, and shall ask, no man to support me as a personal favor, and if the leadership comes to me I will undertake it with feelings far less of justification than of a stern sense of the seriousness of the responsibilities which it will involve." Nick, personally popular and backed by influential House members, was elected by voice vote. His task was to tack between the Republican conservatives and the progressive faction, keeping the former happy and the latter from bolting to join the Democrats and tip them the majority. He was an expert compromiser who could persuade without ruffling feelings. During Nick's two years as majority leader, the House "acted on 594 measures, nearly double the number passed in the same period of the previous Congress." Nick maintained that "the individual must sacrifice his own independence for the good of the whole." This belief would serve him well in the future— better than he might have ever guessed—for as Nick was scuffling with recalcitrant representatives, Alice reconnected with Senator Borah.[38]

The relationship between Alice Longworth and Bill Borah was the worst-kept secret in Washington. The two powerful, easily recognized individuals were seen riding in Rock Creek Park and whispering together in the halls of Congress. Borah, who seldom accepted dinner invitations, went frequently to Alice's. His attentions unleashed a side of her she generally kept hidden. Washingtonian Agnes Meyer recalled Alice about this time in a "very carnal sort of mood. She ate three chops, told shady stories and finally sang in a deep bass voice: Nobody cultivates me, I'm wild, I'm wild."[39]

Infrequently, rumors circulated about Borah. Some suggested his Lion of Idaho nickname referred to his record of sexual conquests, most of which occurred in his youth. There was evidence that his relationship with his wife was distant at best. There is little "passion, intimacy, or love" in the "business-like" letters to his wife the senator dictated to his secretary in the 1920s. Borah had been linked with Alice's longtime friend and sometime enemy Cissy Patterson—the same Cissy whom Alice had defeated in the battle for Nick twenty years earlier. At one party at the Longworths', Cissy and Borah supposedly disappeared. Alice, jealous of her rival, the next day sent Cissy some hairpins she said she'd found in the library. "I believe they are yours," Alice's note was purported to have said. "Alice, please look in the chandelier," Cissy retorted, "I think you will find my garter." Such rumors are impossible to substantiate—and Alice later denied that it ever happened—but Cissy moved on to another man and left the field open for Alice. It may or may not have comforted Alice to know that Cissy moved on to Nick. Alice apparently found them once, both drunk and making love on the floor of her bathroom; another time she thought she detected Nick hiding in Cissy's carriage. Later in life, Alice herself was known to recount the tale of how Cissy left her stockings "stuffed down the sofa and her chewing gum...parked under the mantel" at the Longworths'.[40]

Perhaps it was incidents such as that that caused Alice to "just let it happen" when she discovered in the early spring of 1924 that she was pregnant. Bringing the child to term and then giving it up for adoption would not have been done. Abortions were uncommon but possible to get for a woman of her background. They did not have wholly safe outcomes, and perhaps no one knew that better than Bill. One explanation for why he and Mary remained childless is that when he was a strapping youth, moving westward across the country to find a place to make his fortune, his money ran out in Boise, where he eventually became involved in politics. He took a job as secretary to Governor William J. McConnell and soon met the governor's daughter, Mary, "a vivacious, blue-eyed blonde, sociable and attractive, the prize catch in Boise's young social set." Rumor had it that Mary became pregnant, and because the governor couldn't stand the scandal of an illegitimate child—nor even of a child born less than nine months after the wedding ceremony—Mary sought an abortion. It was not performed well and resulted in Mary's inability to bear children. Bill, then, might have insisted that Alice not seek an abortion in 1924 because of the guilt and sorrow and fear attached to Mary's ordeal in 1892.[41]

Forty years old in February 1924, Alice was game to try motherhood. It certainly was a part of the human experience that she had not yet attempted. TR was known for his dire warnings against race suicide among white women, but as a young woman Alice had been the founder of the Race Suicide Club—its only goal to tweak her father's pomposity. Nevertheless, Nick's infertility kept Alice from doing her duty, as her father saw it, and producing scads of children. Even if TR's teachings had lost some of their grip on Alice, perhaps the deep pain caused by abandonment had not. A child of her own might finally be one human who would never abandon her. No matter what, this child would always be hers and, in the way children do, could fill an ancient void inside her. Whatever the reason—tradition, psychology, cultural mores—Alice decided to "let it happen."[42]

The historical record does not provide many clues about when Alice knew she was pregnant or what she told Nick. Alice's granddaughter, Joanna Sturm, believes that Alice never told Nick and managed to cover up Borah's paternity.[43] There is no evidence of what Bill told his wife, if anything. The human element of this pregnancy involved two powerful men, both old enough to be grandfathers. Nick was fifty-six when the child was born, and Bill was sixty. Mary Borah was fifty-five. All four of them must have come to the conclusion, decades earlier, that their marriages would not be favored with children. Although the 1920s was a time of liberation for women—suffrage, flappers, increasing educational and work opportunities—the centrality of marriage and children to a woman's life had not decreased.

If Alice conceived in April it was about the time Nick was being considered as keynote speaker for the GOP convention looming in June. Congress was working hard and Nick was legislating the Bonus Bill, tax cuts, the National Origins Quota Act, and farm relief measures. Business on Capitol Hill ended in June, and the Republican convention opened shortly thereafter, in Cleveland, Ohio. Alice, in what may have been a difficult first trimester, stayed home. She was in Chicago, Ruth noted, "not very well" and under the care of a physician. The last time Alice had missed a convention was 1912, when she had been forced to stay away from the jubilant Progressive Party gathering by her father and her husband. Bill Borah didn't go to Cleveland either.[44]

At least one national magazine had been promoting BORAH AS PRESIDENTIAL TIMBER, a pun on the natural resources of the Idaho senator's state. Borah supporters began a "literary bombardment" urging Borah for president, "which took the form of throwaways and endless chain post-cards," to be sent ideally to millions of voters. Borah said publicly and privately, "We are playing the game . . . far below the intelligence and character of the voter," and declined to run.[45] No matter how badly he might want the nation's highest office, had he run and somehow gained the Republican nod, he would never have been liberated from the fear that nosy journalists might discover his relationship with the majority leader's wife. And her pregnancy would be front-page news as soon as word got out.

At the Cleveland convention, Ted Roosevelt kept notes as he, Nick, and other leading Republicans gathered to hammer out the platform and settle on a vice president. For the latter position, the insiders discussed at least nine names, with no resolution at that first long meeting. The following day the platform was agreed upon, but the vice president was still up in the air. They mulled over the names of six more men, but reached no consensus. Then, Bill Borah's name surfaced, "but all of us," Ted wrote in his journal, "who knew Borah well were positive that he would not take it. Hour after hour passed.... The corridors were filled with newspaper men requesting information which we did not have to give them.... Longworth expressed a common view when he said he could not make out whether [President Coolidge's personal representative William M.] Butler had some deep laid scheme he was waiting to spring or whether he was simply a plain 'boob.' At shortly after midnight, with all as much at sea as ever, Butler came up to the room and said, 'It is settled. Borah is the Man.'... The conference adjourned at once to line their respective delegates up for Borah. We met the newspaper men in the hall and they turned hand-springs."

Ted had recently dined with Borah, who "definitely" said then he wouldn't agree to having his name put forward for vice president. But Butler told Ted that he had information from Washington that Borah would accept. Ted was dubious, but he knew exactly whom to contact for the straight scoop: "I put in a long distance call for sister.... I told her what happened. She told us just what we had expected—that Borah had talked to her at nine-thirty that evening on the telephone and would not take the vice presidency under any circumstances. Furthermore, he had not seen Coolidge since Monday. That left us bang up in the air. We did not feel we could tell Butler because that involved sister. We knew that the newspapermen would get hold of Borah at once and thought they would settle the matter."[46]

On the last day of the convention, President Coolidge sent for Senator Borah. Coolidge had been pursuing Borah for the second-place spot for months. On that day, Coolidge himself asked Borah if he would agree to have his name placed in nomination. "In which place?" Borah asked laconically. Coolidge told Borah that the convention would draft him for vice president anyway. Borah said he would decline the draft. Perhaps the president didn't believe him. He should have. The Cleveland convention—

which Ruth Hanna McCormick dismissed as "the dullest I have ever attended"—was enlivened only by the excitement of Senator Borah turning down the vice presidential spot. In the 1920s, the vice president was a nonentity, ignored by the press, party caucuses, and usually the president.[47] When Borah declared that he would be of better use to the country by remaining in the Senate, he was headed for greater things with his autonomy intact. The Republicans had to be content with Charles Dawes.

First, however, Borah had to win reelection in Idaho. Hindsight proves the senator had little to fear, but Borah was always skittish about campaigns. He had feuded so long with the Republican machine in his home state that had he been less popular with the voters and less well known nationally he might have had cause to worry. The campaign also meant his absence from Alice that fall. It could not have been the ideal situation for either of them. Bill and Mary Borah had not maintained a home in Idaho since 1907, and so, except for election years, the senator often remained in the District of Columbia when Congress was not in session. Unfortunately for Alice, her pregnancy coincided with a time of forced separation.

A torrent of letters flew between them. Brief and without context or preliminaries, they were part of a larger dialogue. Borah even wrote from his Senate office across town. The two augmented their notes with the telephone and frequent face-to-face visits, which made unnecessary traditional descriptions and details. Theirs was a correspondence in shorthand. The topics were almost entirely political. Alice saved Bill's several hundred letters to her, but he disposed of hers, despite the joy he took in them. She asked once whether she wrote him "too many letters." "No," Borah insisted. "No you do not—they are most welcome. Let them come in battalions!"[48] Beyond politics, their other favorite topic was themselves.

On the westbound *Portland Limited*, Bill muscled his way to the train's writing desk to reestablish their connection: "Wending my way slowly across the continent reflecting, dreaming, hoping, *believing*...." This was one of his first letters since the campaign had parted them. His tone, now that she was approximately four months' pregnant, was reminiscent of any father-to-be. "Be a good lady," he cautioned, "do not smoke too much—be careful of your eating—take lots of exercise and *remain* beautiful."[49]

Her first trimester over, Alice was then with Nick for part of the Democratic convention in New York. The lengthy contest took 103 ballots before the nominee emerged. Alice kept a gimlet eye on Franklin. He was working hard for presidential contender Al Smith, who eventually lost to John W. Davis. As always, reporters noted Alice's presence, and even they saw a changed woman: "She grows sedate—almost subdued, one would say.... She has been very intent upon the proceedings, following every maneuver with keen eyes—and silently." Of course they didn't know the real reason.[50]

Back in Cincinnati, Alice pored over the bulletins and newspaper clippings Bill sent outlining western thought and giving clues as to how Idaho voters might respond. She posted return envelopes full of her analyses of people and situations. They studied the restoration of the Progressive Party, as Robert La Follette and Burton K. Wheeler ran on that third-party ticket. "I guess your diagram of Wheeler is right and accurate," Borah responded to one such letter. "You are a wonder. I feel awfully proud of myself when I think of having passed safely under your keen analysis."[51]

By early September, the newspapers were announcing BORAH'S ELECTION DEEMED CERTAINTY, and even La Follette gave his support in a strongly worded telegram to Bill (which Bill proudly enclosed for Alice to see). Despite a resurgent Borah-for-president boom, Alice continued to worry about his reelection, and Borah fretted, too. His unease and the solitary traveling he undertook on the campaign made him ache for her: "'What will I do, what will I do with only a photograph to tell my troubles to.' I heard that song last night and thought it beautiful. I fear I am getting sentimental and I know how you dislike sentimentalists." That thought didn't stop him from posting very tender, secret notes: "My own sweetheart, I want to see you. It seems too long to wait but we will be inseparable, won't we. You can never know how dear you are to me."[52]

By the end of the month, things were looking up. Ted entered the race for New York's Republican gubernatorial spot and won the primary. Alice was overjoyed, and Borah "delighted." The West seemed likely to support Coolidge and Dawes, and Borah—with the combined support of Idaho Progressives and Republicans who preferred *him* in the White House—

wondered to Alice about his presidential chances in the wake of Teapot Dome and other misdeeds that shook the government. In the midst of those scandals, the *Literary Digest* championed Borah for the presidency, noting, "One can not talk with any group of Americans, whatever their situation in life, without finding how disgusted with current politics they are and how happy they would be to break away from their past allegiance." A candidate from outside the polluted mainstream was needed, leading this journal that echoed the *Boston Herald*, to conclude that the call " 'Borah for President' has considerable merit."[53]

Such sentiments had never really died down. While Borah was a fighter for clean government, and disgusted at the many outrageous failings of the Harding and Coolidge administrations, the conclusion of his September lament to her must have been extraordinary for Alice to read: "I have about reached my limit of endurance [for governmental scandal]: Lorimer, Stephenson, Newberry, Fall, Daugherty, now Dawes. If there was anyplace to take refuge where one could see a future I should hesitate no longer. But I can see something after next election—do not doubt it. These things, these fearful things feed my desire and enlarge my plans—and you will be there."[54] Bill in the White House! And Alice would be there with him—but how? The implications of the conversations that must have taken place in order for Borah to have written as he did are worth considering. Was this simply an idle lover's dream? Had they discussed divorcing their spouses and remarrying? If that were the case, surely as realists both knew that a divorced and remarried man would never be elected to the nation's highest office. If not marriage, then could Alice have been content with the position of backstage paramour?

Alice had long been used to the roles of president's daughter and congressman's wife, and she lived at a time when the social position for women was behind the throne. She was very good at analyzing people and events, exceptional at running a salon and bringing very different people together for extraordinary results. She had participated in a congressional junket and played a role in foreign policy. Alice Roosevelt Borah might have made the most politically savvy First Lady ever—but this could be only a reverie. Divorce would ruin careers—her husband's and her lover's, and possibly her brother's. But it is an astonishing thing that Alice and Bill must have spoken together of a shared future, and evidence of their ambition that this dream of a future included the White House. Of course, political considerations worked against the reality of Borah as president. His independent views made stalwart Republicans nervous. Idaho controlled too few electoral college votes to matter. But dreaming of happy futures is the lovers' prerogative.

"As the campaign draws to a close," Bill wrote to Alice from Idaho on November 3, "I am wishing a certain lovely lady with her radio were here to receive the returns as she entertained during the New York conventions. But I will be patient." They had managed to meet in Chicago.[55] Alice, approximately five months' pregnant, had the excuse of seeing her obstetrician Joseph DeLee of Chicago's Lying-In Hospital on East Fifty-first Street. Dr. DeLee had delivered Ruth's babies and was skilled in special-care obstetrical cases, and Ruth insisted that Alice allow herself the best physician in the field. Perhaps that September Alice and Bill discussed the timing of the announcement of her pregnancy, which came, not surprisingly, after the elections. Likely it was then that they evolved the secret code enabling them to write about their desire for each other and the awful, constraining reality of being married to others.

Chary of their spouses and anyone else into whose hands a letter might mistakenly fall, Alice and Bill used the innocuous word *hello* to mean all sorts of permutations of "I love you." *Hello* appeared with a purposeful regularity in his letters. Bill always closed with assurances such as "Hello, Hello, Alice, more than you know." The use of their code word was so apparent that even an artless spouse could have decoded the not-so-secret language: "I did enjoy your letters," he wrote in September, "you are a dear—hello. I am sending you some photos from the round up and some scenes—logging, hauling, and wheatfield scenes in my own state. These you are to see in person some time. Hello—again and again Hello." "But I do try to write and I do Hello all the time"; or "Hello every minute. I wish you understood fully how Hello." His usual closing was "Hello, Hello, Hello—Affectionately, Bill."[56]

Hello—even in its variations of meaning—could not convey all he felt for her, so Bill initiated a second clandestine system of expressing his suppressed feelings. He tucked copies of his speeches, newspaper articles, telegrams, and other printed materials pertaining to his career into the envelopes along with his notes to Alice. Then, in miniscule dashes, like sideways exclamation points, Bill underlined stray letters throughout the articles. When Alice put the underlined letters together they spelled out his secret messages. From a *New York Times* editorial entitled "How to Head Off a Third Party," Alice pieced together: "Darling, I am so lonesome. I want my own sweet girl. You are more to me than you have dreamed. I am counting the days until I shall see you." One week later, Borah signaled her, "My darling, I am more lonesome tonight than I can tell. Oh how I long for the dearest one in the world. Do you love me the same? Loved one, I kiss you goodnight." Before their rendezvous in Chicago, Alice read, "My dear, I am coming to see you soon and we will be happy again." Consoling her in their long autumn separation, Borah underlined, "My sweetheart, I love you above all earthly things."[57]

These touches of intimacy, tucked between political commentary, sustained the romance while they were apart. Borah, who was known far and wide as an inscrutable, pragmatic, reclusive, no-nonsense Westerner, sparkled in his secret musings to Alice. Their coded language explains part of her attraction to him. Nineteen twenty-four was the year they most frequently used their underlining code, when the emotional upheaval of pregnancy may have most called for the reassurance that the surreptitious but real reinforcement of their love brought. "Trust me to the end of my days," he willed her.[58]

In early October 1924, Alice, approximately six months' pregnant, left Cincinnati and Nick's reelection campaign to join a family conference in Oyster Bay about the New York governor's race and Ted's future. Bill waited impatiently for the news of her safe travel and for Alice's assessment of her brother's chances. Ted had offered to go west to campaign for Borah, who declined the proposal as it would take Ted away from his own fight, and Borah's victory looked secure anyway. While at Sagamore, Alice fell down the stairs. News of this pushed all thoughts of Ted out of Bill's mind: "I hardly know how to write. I am so uneasy and anxious lest your terrible accident cause you illness. Such falls sometimes injure internally.... About the best message I can hastily send is Hello Hello always and ever hello."[59] Her written assurance turned their attention back to the election.

Physically separated from her lover and emotionally removed from her husband, Alice confided in her best friend Ruth Hanna McCormick. McCormick's diary hints at discomforts and illnesses that Alice endured throughout the fall of 1924. Ruth could be counted on to understand fully the risks to all involved. From her comes evidence that Alice was not initially thrilled about the pregnancy. In early November, when Alice was three months from the birth, she wrote, "Alice arrived.... it has been decided that she tell everyone soon that she is going to have a baby. I haven't even dared to record it in my Diary. Poor Alice. She feels humiliated about the baby and dreads what people will say but I firmly believe she will be a different person after the baby comes and she holds it in her arms."[60] Ruth, the mother of three children, could empathize with at least some of Alice's feelings.

Election day 1924 brought good and bad news. Coolidge was elected. Nick and Bill won reelection, but Ted lost the governorship of New York to Al Smith. Only thirty-seven years old at the time of this defeat, Ted wasn't sure how to restart his political career. Elected to the New York assembly in 1919 and 1920, and appointed assistant secretary of the navy from 1921 until 1924, Ted's gubernatorial campaign was haunted by rumors of his involvement in the scandals that plagued Harding's administration, particularly the Teapot Dome debacle. Ted had weathered calls for him to quit his position at the navy because of his alleged involvement. Alice, protective of her favorite brother, tried to pull strings by asking Calvin Coolidge—unsuccessfully, as it turned out—to intercede on Ted's behalf with the Senate investigation. Nick had defended him on the floor of the House, saying he was "prepared to make a statement" as to Ted's blamelessness. Ted was innocent of any wrongdoing, but his high-profile campaigning for Harding and his past connection with the oil company involved in Teapot Dome made it easy for political enemies to link his name with the scandal. And for the Roosevelt family, one of those enemies was unexpected—and unpardonable. Cousin Eleanor, active as a Democratic organizer in New York State, built an enormous, steaming teapot, hoisted it on top of her car, and pursued Ted all across the Empire State. Her exploit did more damage without any words than did official calls for Ted's removal on the floor of Congress. ER later expressed regret at having played such a "rough stunt."[61] This worsened the bad feelings between the Sagamore Hill and the Hyde Park Roosevelts. Eleanor had violated the "tribal feeling" that Alice—Ted's loyal half sister, the outsider in the nursery—held to so closely all her life. Alice never forgave her.

Edith felt her eldest son had made "a good campaign," but in addition to the wisps of the scandal that clung to him, it appeared that Ted was wholly unacceptable to the temperance vote. As a fan of Alice's wrote to her a decade later, "If your brother Theodore were not an announced wet I would be glad to vote for him," for president.[62] But Ted, pulsing with the example of his father and the courage of his convictions, wouldn't hide his beliefs even if they were contrary to the majority of his constituency. He was one of those who voted wet *and* drank wet. It was morally commendable, but it cost him the governor's mansion.

Bill gloated to Alice, as he could to her and no one else, about his own landslide reelection: "I have a telegram before me which says that Coolidge vote in Ida[ho] was sixty four thousand... Borah eighty nine thousand—see how needless for my dear friend to have worried. Hello Hello. I wish very much I could have a long talk with you this evening. We will have many, many affairs of state to talk over in the coming months—and often I will be saying Hello—always saying Hello."[63]

Adding to their reasons to celebrate, Bill received the appointment he coveted and would occupy for the next nine years: chairman of the Senate Foreign Relations Committee. He took over from the redoubtable Henry Cabot Lodge, the Longworths' good friend and a colleague whose death in November 1924 they both mourned. Alice had known him literally her whole life. He first saw her in her cradle. One of her earliest childhood memories was the "rather special" congressman who was "mysterious, important, and powerful," and who defined for her how politicians differed from other men. Lodge reciprocated this affection, writing to Alice in 1921 in a plaintive letter, "I am fortunate in having so many good friends of whom I am very fond but the people I love are few. I do not have the faculty of dispensing my affections. You and yours have been a part of my inmost life and love for many years."[64]

With the elections behind them, Alice, and probably Bill, decided the time was ripe to announce the pregnancy to the family and to the press. It is not clear what role Nick played in any of these decisions, although Alice would have been sensitive to the effect of the publicity on his career. The last thing she would have wanted was for Nick to lose an election, as that would mean exile in Cincinnati—immeasurably worse this time, for it would also mean separation from Bill. So once both men were safely re-elected, and because the slender Alice was showing, it was time.

Alice had kept her stepmother in the dark. Edith's diary of November 12 contained a short, cryptic note: *"Bouleversé,"* which means "overthrown, upset, distressed." Edith elaborated slightly in a letter to her sister-in-law: "Alice's news was rather a blow...." Either Edith worried about Alice suffering the same fate as her mother in childbirth, or, like much of Washington society, she suspected the truth. Two weeks later, on November 29, Edith wrote to Belle Hagner, "The shock of Alice's news is still with me...."[65]

Kermit, touring Ohio with Nick, learned from his wife, Belle, who must have heard it through the women's side of the family grapevine—and heard that Alice characteristically downplayed the importance and her own happiness. "That is the most amazing news about Sister," Kermit replied. "No one here has told me yet, so in accordance with your instructions, I'm still supposedly in ignorance. I think that it's great...." He wrote to Belle the next day: "Yesterday Nick and I wandered around calling on his friends, political and otherwise. He finally told me about the expected arrival. He seems very much pleased about. I imagine Sister is doing a good deal of bluffing when she talks as she does."[66]

Tired of the rumors, an intrepid journalist finally telephoned Alice to verify. "Hell yes," Alice told him, "Isn't it wonderful?" The news was out. "One of the most original, interesting, and charming women in Washington official circles," would give birth in February, and "the country will await the event with scarcely less interest than the principals." First Lady Grace Coolidge passed along the bombshell to her husband. "Yes, I knew that," Cal drawled. "Alice told me a couple of months ago." Grace was stunned. "Imagine a man having a bit of gossip as choice as that and keeping it a secret!" she laughed to her friends. Ruth Hanna McCormick noted in her diary that day: "The morning paper announces that Alice Longworth is going to have a baby! So it is out at last! I have kept the secret so long it seems strange to hear [people] talking about it. Poor Nick will have a hard time of it for awhile and so will Alice. Everyone will gossip about it and then I hope it will be forgotten for awhile." Alice, being Alice, met the implied rumors head on. She told a journalist that she was "always ready to try anything once," and that—an allusion to her age—she was looking forward to the birth of her "gland baby."[67]

Most cave dwellers and politicians felt that the new Speaker of the House was not, could not possibly be, the father. Was it on purpose that the Chicago paper—run by the McCormick family who knew her well—announced that *"Mrs. Longworth"* was expecting the stork—not *"the Longworths"*? Nick's extramarital affairs were notorious to insiders. Fishbait Miller, the longtime doorkeeper for the House of Representatives, called Longworth "one of the greatest womanizers in history on Capitol Hill." One oft-told story happened, according to Miller, when a colleague wanted to have a bit of fun at the Speaker's expense. "Mr. Speaker," the congressman said. "Your pretty bald head reminds me of my wife's behind. Is it alright if I rub my hand across it? Then I'll know for sure." Nick considered this request, and then, hand on his own pate, retorted, "I'll be damned if it doesn't."[68]

Nick's reputation was infamous; but Alice was reputed to be untouchable, and Bill was aloof, serious, Christian, and so dedicated to matters of state that his life precluded mundane dalliances. Borah had a "reputation for integrity in public life," had fought for clean government, and publicly chastised members of his own party for corrupt practices.[69] While there were rumors about Borah's randy youth and Cissy Patterson's assertion that she and Borah were once lovers, no verifiable documentation exists to prove this. Cissy is hardly a credible source because she and Alice were once in competition for Nick—and Alice won—and because there was always a certain tension between the women that might explain Cissy's story of her encounter with Bill in Alice's living room.

Alice, Nick, and Bill were thrust into precarious positions with the announcement of the impending birth, but Ruth continued to worry about Nick. "It is ridiculous when you think of Nick. What will he do with it?" she mused to her diary.[70] No record exists of Nick's immediate response. It is possible that Alice never told him about Borah; and possible that Alice concocted to sleep with her husband around the time she knew she was pregnant in an effort to throw suspicion away from Borah.[71] Still, Alice was not prone to dissembling; she knew about Nick's cupidity; his drunkenness repelled her and precluded much intimacy between them; and despite rumors of many illicit affairs, not one woman ever charged Nick with a paternity suit. Either Nick was infertile or he was able to dissuade his lady friends from going public.[72]

When Alice's pregnancy was announced, she was in Chicago for an appointment with Dr. DeLee. Ruth McCormick was Alice's strength. She knew all about Alice's mother's complications and could talk with Alice to help allay her fears. It was Ruth who accompanied Alice to the hospital to see the doctor. She thought Alice appeared "more cheerful and more at ease about her situation." The physician agreed with her. DeLee, Ruth recounted, said Alice was "very well and in good condition and that she must come back here three weeks before the baby is due." Alice's Washington doctor gave his professional opinion that Alice should leave Washington sooner rather than later. "When do you advise her making the trip to Chicago? Make it early please!" he begged. "It is hard to keep her away from the Capitol and there are steps and psychic shocks!"[73]

One of the shocks was the suicide in October of Alice's very good friend Senator Frank Brandegee. His humor was acerbic, and his politics were very similar to hers. He appreciated her mind, and the two found each other absurdly funny. Brandegee was the only alcoholic Alice tolerated and even assisted when he was inebriated. In December, the opening day in the Senate was cut short out of respect for its deceased members, including

Lodge and Brandegee. After the solemn opening day, the Committee on Committees met and officially elevated Borah to chair of Foreign Relations. Then in the House, Alice watched the members applaud Nick, a perennial favorite among representatives. The drive for Nick as Speaker resurfaced. Borah had noted at election time, "I see the papers today are much about Nick being speaker and you being speakeress." Borah thought Nick "entitled to it." Alice agreed. The Speaker ranked fifth in Washington protocol, and wife of the Speaker of the House occupied a position with significant social clout. In December, Ohio Republicans unanimously endorsed him in a letter sent to all House Republicans. Nick had the assurance of his supporters that they commanded more than the necessary votes for the speakership, and this was borne out at a clandestine meeting in February 1925. At that conference, Republican leaders gave the nomination for Speaker to Nick an "unprecedented" nine months before the Congress was to assemble.[74]

YOU CAN'T HELP LIKING NICK went the title of a complimentary article in the *Literary Digest*. Nick won Speaker for three reasons: longevity, regularity, and personality. In office since 1902 with only one two-year lapse, he had piled up twenty years' experience. He never bolted the party, despite severe provocation in 1912—and in fact, his speakership would be known in part for his swift and stern punishment of the Republican Progressives who, as Nick put it in a Chicago speech, "under Wisconsin leadership showed their true colors at the election. They not only had their own Presidential candidate [La Follette], but worked harder against the Republican candidate than the Democrats did." And Nick was known far and wide as a good guy; a politician who didn't take politics too seriously, who could disagree with the Democrats and then drink with them, and who had as one of his closest friends his antithesis: rural Texas Democratic representative John Nance Garner. Nick was "a Republican during working hours, but he left his partisanship in his office."[75]

His drinking and the womanizing continued, despite cautions from worried friends and family. Auntie Bye's congratulatory note, which never exactly said congratulations, was a masterpiece of subtext: "to become a father and the Speaker of the House seems more than any one is entitled to, and if you could see your likeness in the *Hartford Courant* you would feel sure it had gone to your head. I would hardly like you in either position if it has given you this expression of dissipated good-fellowship."[76]

By the end of January 1925, Alice had settled into Chicago's Drake Hotel. Borah was more open about his concerns for her health in his letters, perhaps because he knew Nick could not be there with her and would not inadvertently intercept her mail. From Washington Bill wrote, "I am wondering how you are getting by with these first days. I am afraid you will be lonesome but you are so very wonderful—Mistress of all exigencies—that I am sure everything will come out fine."[77]

His letters arrived daily. He filled her in on political news and wished she could be with him to talk over topics such as his stance on the French World War I debt, hearings before the Judiciary Committee concerning the misdemeanors of two senators, and the status of various bills. Borah was full of anger toward President Coolidge, who had led him to believe he would act on the senator's suggestion of appointing Medill McCormick the new ambassador to Great Britain. But even as Borah was meeting with Coolidge on that subject, from London another man was named.[78] Bill received news of Alice through her letters, in telephone conversations, in phone calls from Ruth, and from the newspapers. He wanted to be with her. He shared Theodore Roosevelt's belief that motherhood was a woman's highest calling. A pent-up longing for progeny spilled out, and as the due date neared, he grew ever more rhapsodic about her condition:

I was delighted with your letter today—it seemed to me I could hear you speaking. But Alice the next four or five weeks are the most wonderful of your crowded and wonderful life. You will allow me to say won't you that it would have been truly a great wrong for you— so rich in personality—not to have had a child.

Now if you are going to have a child, you are going to pass through the miracle hour of giving a being life. Marvel of marvels—so you will be careful and listen to your Dr. won't you. I know you will for it is you and you are always true to the exigency.

You are not sentimental Alice but in your marvelous being is a profound and beautiful strain of the rarest and richest sentiment. Do not hesitate to cultivate it—do not disown it. It enriches your character and will enrich another life. I feel deeply about you these days and I am writing as a long long time friend—one who wants you to know how worthy you always are and how worthy you are going to be in your supremest days.[79]

Surely one of the points in her letters to which Bill responded was Alice's fear, shared by all first-time mothers, that she might not be up to the task of giving birth. In Alice's case delivery was complicated by the timing. February had been an important but not always happy month for the Roosevelt family. Her own birthday was February 12, but her mother and grandmother had died on February 14, and these dates loomed large in her imagination. Bill's letters of this time contained many more references to God and to his prayers for her, perhaps a response to her own worries. Auntie Bye, seasoned veteran that she was, betrayed no such worry to Alice when she wrote in early February of her longing "for a first glimpse of my second grandchild; you may like it or not," she chaffed, "but my grandchild it will be, though it is rather a horrid thought to be provided with a whole extra inexplicable grandmother."[80]

Edith arrived on the morning of the fourteenth, and learned from Ruth that she had taken Alice to the hospital—so Edith hurried to be by Alice's side. The six-and-one-half-pound baby girl was born, without complications, at 10:30 a.m. on the fourteenth, the very date on which Alice's mother and grandmother had died forty-one years earlier.[81] Ruth, Edith, and Kermit were with Alice, but Bill, like the rest of the world, read about the birth on the front page of every newspaper. He dashed off a letter:

Dear Alice: Just read the evening papers and we are happy beyond the power of words to tell. There are to be two Alice Longworths—did not believe such possible. It is wonderful! Most wonderful! We shall be impatient almost beyond endurance until we lay eyes on that baby girl. I can well understand the wise men from the east who impelled by I know not what sublime faith wandered on until they came to where the divine child was. Well we will be patient—as patient as possible. But I shall be disappointed if it does not talk—I think Alice's baby ought to be talking in one week at most! Isn't it wonderful. I know you must be very happy and proud—gratified that you have measured up to the noblest most divine exertion of women. Hello more than ever Hello. All the evening papers had an account of the coming of the baby. The first I knew of it was when I glanced down and saw your picture. I tremblingly reached for it—fearing that you might be very ill—but when I read the wonderful news I put that old paper in my desk as a memento. Hello Hello—yes Hello.[82]

A night's sleep did not diminish Bill's enthusiasm. He wrote to tell her the fate of a conference report in the Senate, but concluded by admitting that such matters of state were nothing "compared to the Alice Jr. that is now the most important fact in this great country of ours. I will guarantee more people are discussing the latter thing today than farm legislation."[83]

What Alice thought of comparing their baby to farm legislation isn't clear. It is intriguing, however, to speculate on her response to his letter, written upon news of the birth. The letter conveys his fear that she might be "very ill" and his pride that she had "measured up to the noblest most divine exertion of women." While this may be evidence of that deep streak of fatalism that animated the senator, missing from the letter are all of the tender endearments that a lover might whisper at this defining moment in their relationship—particularly one missing the birth of their child. Even though he believed Alice to be unsentimental, this was Bill's first experience of fatherhood. But his letter reads as though it were for public consumption. He used a plural pronoun—was Mary standing over his shoulder as he wrote?—and then switched to "I." He congratulated her for coming through the birth so well (and she had just turned forty-one). This letter was probably followed closely by a phone call in which the two parents could speak more confidentially about the birth experience, the baby, and their feelings.

Nick heard of the baby's birth thirty minutes before the members of the House of Representatives did. As floor leader, he had to stay in the capital. The announcement brought a spontaneous ovation from his peers. He met the infant the day after she was born and told the newspapers ironically that he was "a little bit jealous... because she looks so much more like a Roosevelt than a Longworth, but she's young yet." "Judging by the look on the baby's face," one paper crowed, "she is a true descendant of her famous granddaddy, Theodore Roosevelt." To which Borah wrote to Alice: "Good—like our Roosevelt."[84]

Photos of the infant also bear a distinctive resemblance to Bill Borah's flat, broad face. But by all accounts Nick Longworth took one look at the child thrust into his late midlife and fell irredeemably, irrevocably, head-over-heels in love with her. She, newspapers suggested, would be "the real speaker of the house so far as domination of the Longworth ménage is concerned."[85] And it was true. Nick and the baby became inseparable.

Alice said it was she who named the baby Paulina—pronounced with a long "i"—after her favorite apostle, a decidedly odd act for someone once referred to as "an aggressive atheist," unless she was swayed by the more spiritually inclined Borah.[86] The apostle Paul was credited with tremendous strength of character, a Jew who zealously persecuted Christians until his conversion. He left his philosophy in his letters to the churches he founded, and both Bill and Alice certainly read those that became part of the New Testament.

As a tradition in literature, the name Paulina has a more checkered cast. John Gower's *Confessio Amantis*, written around 1385, has a Paulina who is duped by the mendacity of her husband. In the sixteenth century, Montaigne mentioned a similar topic, with Paulina, the Roman wife who, because of the trickery of the temple priests, found herself lying not with the god Serapis but with "a wanton lover of hers." Gervase Markham's 1609 poem "The Lamentable Complaint of Paulina, the Famous Roman Curtezan" casts her in the role of the savvy courtesan, which was what Paulina referred to thereafter in literature. Fifty years later, Thomas Pecke's "Upon Paulina" has Paulina making a cuckold of her husband: "Paulina her first husband, made a Stag; / Nor had the last, any cause to brag. / She was as hard as horn, to first, and last." In that same year, Richard Lovelace's poem "Lucasta" makes reference to a woman who, like an unfaithful wife, appears to be one thing, but in reality is another. William Shakespeare, in *The Winter's Tale*, has Paulina standing up to the king's authority and defending her mistress from the fabricated allegation of adultery. Ultimately, Paulina emerges triumphantly, with a "behind-the-throne control" over the men in the play.[87] Alice and Bill, who read literature and poetry from all ages, likely knew that the unusual name Paulina was associated with adultery.

Whether Nick liked the name or not, he decided that this new addition to his life was a tremendous gift. There is no reason to think that Alice and Nick were not still fond of each other after their nineteen years of marriage, only that the romance had been long absent. At any rate, if Nick, the soon-to-be Speaker of the House, publicly voiced his suspicions as to Paulina's parentage, or gave a hint of his doubt publicly, he would bring down not just the chair of the Senate Foreign Relations Committee, but ruin his wife's reputation and destroy his own political career. In 1925, a man with several mistresses could be viewed with admiration for his prowess, but a man who was openly cuckolded was weak and foolish, clearly unfit to rule his house, let alone the House.

While Nick became accustomed to being a daddy, Bill kept up a steady stream of letters, professing his love, his desire to see Paulina, and his hope that he could soon talk politics with Alice in person again. Even with the interminable night sessions at the Senate preceding sine die that physically exhausted him, Borah wrote almost daily, if "only to say Hello." On Sunday, February 22, he penned another rhapsody in praise of her giving birth. "It is a beautiful day—one of those days which enriches the soul with aspirations beyond mortal attainment—one of the days which makes one wish for the company of dear friends—Hello yes today so much Hello that it all seems feeble when words alone must suffice.... Alice you are a very wonderful woman.... What a deep vein of true glorious sentiment in your marvelous being and now to be developed to its full bent. It is great but I expected it. I know down in your deepest feelings you must be very happy—Hello hello. And that will help a little won't it."[88]

While Alice had sent telegrams to inform people of the birth—for example, President Coolidge's secretary, Everett Sanders—the newspapers continued to provide intimate reports of Alice and Paulina. When they ran out of day-to-day news, the papers took to augury. A full-page article entitled "Science and the Longworth Baby" illuminated "Why a Brilliant Career Is Predicted for This New Descendent of King Robert Bruce, Ex-President Roosevelt and So Many Other Famous Ones." Even Edith Roosevelt, Ted told Borah, was "greatly elated over Paulina and thinks she is a wonder."[89] Ted was in the throes of assessing his political future after the gubernatorial loss, and Borah was providing advice.

Into the midst of the celebrations surrounding Paulina's birth came the shocking news of Medill McCormick's death. The coroner listed the cause as "myocarditis," but Medill had committed suicide, just as Frank Brandegee had. For Medill, it was the culmination of a difficult life marked by "self-destructive tendencies" and most recently by his electoral loss. His death devastated Ruth and their three children. Ruth had lingered in Chicago to help Alice through the first difficult month as a new mother, and Medill had purposefully gone away from his family to spare them. Edith found it "such a horrible blow" that she felt she "could not write to [Alice] or to Ruth.... So much of service and interest lay ahead" for Medill, she mourned. Soon after Medill's death, Ruth sought solace in her work. It was not an ideal time for her best friend to be wrapped up in a new baby, but it was Alice who pushed Ruth back into the fray. "When Senator McCormick died," Ruth told a reporter, "my thought was to give up politics myself. Alice knew what I needed better than I did. She told me that I must not only not give up but that I must not get out of politics even temporarily, not even for a day. She was right about it."[90] Work had saved TR upon his widowered state.

Perhaps Medill's death was a catalyst for Borah, a reminder that life is short, for immediately thereafter his letters brim with loving salutations toward Paulina. Even before he had seen her for the first time, he and Alice set aside a special place on Paulina's infant body where they could kiss but no one else would: "Give Paulina a kiss on the back of her little neck," he wrote a fortnight after she was born. "I know what Paulina will get on the neck," Bill crooned in the summer.[91]

In early March of 1925, Alice and Paulina returned to Washington, D.C., the latter clad "in garments of pink and white and blue, gifts of Mrs. Medill McCormick."[92] Bill was finally able to meet their daughter. There is no record of this moment, but it is clear that having the "two Alices" near to him was idyllic: "[A]s I wended my way home about 11:00 a.m. somewhat weary anyway, I looked out the window and as we passed 1733 and said Hello and was deeply thankful I could say hello and could hear the echo Hello. Oh I will certainly be glad to see Paulina and ———." He trailed off at the end of the sentence, as though it were too superficial to call Alice his "dear, dear friend" any longer. Alice, Bill, and Paulina were in Washington together from early March until May, when mother and daughter went to Cincinnati. Nick left on a two-month European trip on May 20 to assess the ramifications of tariffs and the Volstead Act. The 1920s were far removed from current fathering norms, and a two-month trip away from a newborn was entirely consistent with social expectations for the Longworths' class. Perhaps, though, Ruth's predictions of gossip were coming true. LONGWORTH POSES AS FOND FATHER, ran one sly headline in May.[93] And in some circles, Alice had been referred to as "Aurora Borah Alice," for a long time—a phrase that neatly captured Alice's incandescent personality as well as her love interest.

Mary Borah was one of the first people to meet Paulina in Washington. According to Mrs. Borah's memoir, Alice telephoned and said, "Mary, Paulina wants you to come over and have lunch with her." Mary recalled, "Paulina slept through most of my visit but woke up before I left and Alice let me hold her. She was a beautiful baby."[94] The reasons behind this extraordinary invitation are obscure. Assuming that Mary Borah did not fabricate the story, Alice may have been attempting to deflect suspicion caused by the rumors swirling around the capital—for surely not even Alice Roosevelt Longworth could be so brazen as to invite her lover's wife to see their child. On the other hand, it would be exactly the sort of action Alice would take to demonstrate conclusively that she cared not a whit about local gossip.

It is not clear whether either spouse knew for certain the identity of Paulina's biological father. Although long a senator's wife, Mary did not live in the nucleus of power as did the Longworths. "Little Borah," as she was called, had the reputation of being ditzy and scattered, and unable to formulate an original thought. "He never talks politics with me...I hint around a little, but I don't get much from him. I have to buy a paper to learn what he's going to do next," she told a reporter—who described her as "the good humored matron." James M. Cox remembered Mary as a woman who "chided the Senator a great deal about his carelessness in dress" and could tell a good story.[95]

Alice could be vengeful, as her childhood diaries show. She did not suffer fools gladly. She could gloat. But if Alice went to see Mary Borah in order to revel in her dual victory—stealing Borah's affections and bearing his only child—then it apparently went right over Mary's head. Alice was "a frequent morning caller" at the Borahs' apartment. Mary told a reporter that she and Bill became "close personal friends" with Alice and Nick. She accompanied Alice to hear speeches in both houses of Congress. In fact, on December 7, 1925, the day that Nick was elevated to Speaker of the House—and ten months after Paulina's birth—Alice watched from "the speaker's row of the gallery" with her two invited guests, one of whom was Mary Borah. Whether or not Little Borah knew the truth of Paulina's patrimony, she embraced the infant with a tenderness like Nick's, even carrying photos of Paulina and showing them off to friends.[96] Her memoir is full of complimentary references to Alice, from the time she first saw her as First Daughter past her becoming a mother. Its very tone gives rise to another interpretation: Mary, who may have had an abortion and who loved all children, was grateful to Alice for bearing Paulina, seeing her birth in some significant way as redemption.

To spare each others' feelings, or to preserve Bill's paternity from history, the adults involved never publicly confirmed the truth. But Bill could not hide his pride, and in a third code, initiated after Paulina's birth, he asserted his fatherhood. Unlike the previous codes, though, this one was more difficult to crack. On the tenth of July, Bill wrote to Alice from Boise, where he was in the middle of what he termed a "civil war" over water issues: "I know what those farmers and their families have suffered for the last five years and I feel deeply that they are being cruelly pushed by the

Gov. But I must not carry these things to P.F.P.—Hello." Three days later the abbreviation became more clear: "I feel very low in my mind today and thought I could gain advantage by communicating with P.F.P. and through her with P—How deeply I realize as to both—Hello Hello."[97] In the same letter, however, he concluded, "I love your notes about Paulina." This is a difficult point. Why write out Paulina if he was also abbreviating her name as "P"? He did both with no specific consistency or pattern, and often included Paulina in "Hello Hello."

By the end of the month, foreign events had superceded the local water war. Borah sent Alice a copy of a positive letter from a constituent because, "I always must have PFP hear the good news."[98] In August, tired of being away, Borah wrote, "I am getting quite homesick for PFP—Rock Creek Park, P—Jester, ect., ect. All because Hello." In September, he apologized for his monosyllabic responses to her phone call, but he had "three persons in committee" before him and couldn't talk. At least he had their photos: "PFP and daughter sitting here—hello hello." Even as Borah used PFP to refer to Alice and P for Paulina, he rendered the code much less mysterious when he changed one letter—the one letter that verified his role: "Dear Alice, I enjoyed your brief note this morning particularly how Paulina went after the visage of P.M.P. Anyway you must for me say Hello to her. She will in time think more favorably of her M.P."[99] Paulina's Male Parent—Borah's own hand provided the ultimate proof of his paternity—and Alice was P.F.P.: Paulina's Female Parent.

Possibly this cipher was to protect Nick and Mary. Possibly it was simply a generational code of ethics. Kiss, perhaps, but never tell. Paulina's Female Parent had as much to lose as Paulina's Male Parent, but their child would suffer most. There were rumors. Washingtonians shook their heads at the gossip that Alice would name her baby Deborah. A famous joke convulsed cave dwellers: "What do a new parquet floor and the Longworth baby have in common? There's not a bit of a 'nick' in either one." The senator's reputation as a loner helped them keep their secret. Ruth knew; perhaps Ted did. But even Borah's secretary, Cora Rubin—who had been with him since before he left Idaho—certified he had no real close friends.[100]

Alice never told Paulina about Bill Borah. Secure in Nick's love, Paulina found out only before she left for college when she overheard her governess, Dorothy Waldron, speaking with her mother.[101] It was unintentional. Perhaps Alice never meant to tell her daughter so as not to destroy Paulina's good memories. Mary, Bill, Alice, and, most important, Nick went on as though everything was normal, thus giving her the immeasurable gift of a stable childhood. What this cost the adults involved is unimaginable.

Chapter 16

"The Political Leader of the Family"

By 1926, ALICE LONGWORTH was referred to in print as "the political leader of the family." In 1927, her profile graced the cover of *Time* magazine, making her, Gore Vidal asserted, "a permanent, for good or ill, member of the world's grandest vanity fair."[1] Her power extended beyond the Roosevelt clan, and Paulina's birth had not slowed her down. She wielded quiet but real influence over two of the leading politicians of the day, the Speaker of the House and the chair of the Senate Foreign Relations Committee. Alice lived for politics. Her political acumen was so widely recognized that she was even briefly considered for the vice presidency on the Republican ticket at the 1928 convention.

Alice and Nick moved to 2009 Massachusetts Avenue on Dupont Circle after Paulina's birth. There, they played serious poker. Alice claimed to have cleared ten thousand dollars one winter—and that was after she paid Nick's debts.[2] They also threw impromptu lunches and hosted dinners attended by people from the upper echelons of the nation's capital, such as Secretary of the Treasury Andrew Mellon and Senate Majority Leader Charles Curtis.

The public gained a glimpse of Alice's private life when an acquaintance of hers, Nelle Scanlan, anonymously published *Boudoir Mirrors of Washington*, featuring the "singular" Alice Longworth. In an evocative and compelling word portrait, Scanlon insisted that "What she does, unconventional though it may be, is not inspired by a desire to shock, so much as an expression of self-determination, a vigorous protest against irksome customs and restrictions. Her attitude is one of supreme indifference to public opinion."[3]

The press predicted a similar future for Alice's daughter. "If Paulina is like her mother she will like the society of intellectual men; have an innate knowledge of politics and be deeply interested in world affairs. There is no woman in Washington who attends Congress more regularly and who wields a greater influence in official life than Mrs. Nicholas Longworth." The toddler accompanied her mother on social calls, enticed her father home from his Speaker's duties, and loved to hear the organ whenever Nick took her to church.[4] Paulina's first years were happily bounded by her family and her nursemaid.

"The daughter of T.R. is not submerged in the mother of Paulina," the *Ladies' Home Journal* noticed in the mid-1920s, a time of flappers, New Women, and sexual emancipation. In fact, Alice was "one of the most influential women in Washington," according to the *New Yorker*, which insisted that "an invitation to the Longworths is more prized by the discriminating than an invitation to the White House. Mrs. Longworth gives no guest lists to the papers.... Heavy politics are played at the Longworth house and Alice sits in.... She knows men, measures and motives; has an understanding grasp of their changes.... It is too bad for the Roosevelt political dynasty that Alice wasn't a boy. She is the smartest Roosevelt there is left—the old Colonel's daughter in more ways than one. She has a quick, inquiring, original and penetrating mind especially equipped to cope with political situations for which she has an instinctive liking." The *Ladies' Home Journal* interviewed both Alice and Ruth and concluded that both women "play politics for the love of politics, and they prefer to play them with men who run government rather than with women who seek to re-form government. Both are frankly and bitterly partisan. They are not without influence on national legislation concerning matters which interest them." Yet Paulina remained central to Alice's daily life. Ruth—well aware of what society expected of mothers—insisted Alice was "even more keen about the welfare and nourishment of Paulina than she was about the welfare and the nourishment of the Senate Battalion of Death that killed the League of Nations."[5]

Alice and Paulina regularly dropped in on the Borahs. By 1929, Little

Borah was spending her days caring for veterans of the Great War and for local boys and girls, some homeless, some orphans. She surrounded herself with neighborhood children, let them into her home, dried their tears, and helped them through their troubles. As a feature article put it dramatically, "Childless herself, [she] has offered herself as mother to the world's motherless."[6] The visits with Paulina must have brought Mary joy—she would have had the power to end them, otherwise. It is impossible to pin down Alice's reasons for taking Paulina to the Borahs, and interpreting this action would be easier if it were clear whether all four adults involved knew Paulina's parentage. The Longworths and the Borahs were friendly. Alice may have been thoughtfully calling on Mary with Paulina because she knew how much Mary enjoyed children. Or Alice might have found such visits darkly amusing. They gave Bill further access to Paulina, although he also saw her at the Longworths', where he could play informally and privately with the child. While Mary Borah had only praise for Alice, a real friendship between the two women seems implausible, given their disparate temperaments and their relationship to Bill. An acquaintanceship based on shared political beliefs, husbands whose work drew them together, and the delight they could take in Paulina is more likely.

Nick continued to take Paulina to the House of Representatives weekly. He indulged her. She played with his typewriter and wrote strings of nonsense letters that were fun to type—a child's love letter sent home in an official envelope marked TO MOT HER. Alice sentimentally preserved it. She worried about a case of trench mouth, which was "tiresome because I had to be very remote with Paulina. She is running all around. Seems fine. Has gained nearly ½ lb...." By the time Paulina was eighteen months old, Alice told Ethel, "I long, I really long to have" Paulina play with her Derby cousins.[7]

First Lady Grace Coolidge was especially fond of Paulina, perhaps because her own children were much older and because she had recently and suddenly lost her son Calvin Jr. to a relentless infection. Just after Christmas 1925, when Paulina was ten months old, she and Alice had called on the First Lady. After tea, the women were irresistibly pulled to the floor to play with the baby. Grace told a friend that Paulina resembled Alice and T.R., and "She seems to have the most real 'personality' of any child that I ever knew at her age. But that may be that she looks so much like her mother that I unavoidably see her mother's personality reflected in her."[8]

While Alice relished motherhood, her absorption in politics continued. Purely social events did not exist for Alice. "So many Congressmen's wives have gone to Washington expecting of course to become intimately acquainted with Mrs. 'Nick' Longworth," one newspaper article chirruped. "They had visions of playing bridge with her, drinking tea at her home and having her and her husband for dinner. But did they? No, indeed. The former Alice Roosevelt felt she had better uses for her time than gossiping with the average Congressman's wife. She would rather be in the Senate gallery listening to the discussion of subjects concerning which she frequently knows more than the speakers. She preferred reading philosophy and poetry to squandering hours at some dull tea table."[9]

Alice played the social game when necessary, releasing her eggplant recipe to the Congressional Club's fund-raising cookbook. Edith contributed her recipe for Indian pudding; Mary Borah gave hers for gingerbread and for marshmallow pudding; and Grace Coolidge's corn muffin recipe stood beside recipes from Helen Taft and Lou Henry Hoover. Alice had been a "charter member" when congressional wives formed the club in 1908 "to lighten the sorrows and increase the joys of official position." Famous for its cookbooks, music, and educational programs, its meetings were socially sanctioned distaff behavior and therefore a bit of a bore for Alice Longworth.[10]

More to her liking was a new adventure in May 1925: Alice posed for a Ponds cold cream advertisement. She sat for the painted portrait featured in the ad. She said she did this for the five thousand dollars to tuck away for Paulina's future. In her usual forthright fashion, Alice divulged the sum and its purpose, to the consternation of Ponds, which wanted customers to assume the ads were the spontaneous—and unpaid—endorsements of enthusiastic women. Alice was one of several famous smooth-skinned women who posed for Ponds: Queen Marie of Romania, Mrs. Marshall Field Sr.,

Anne Morgan, and Little Borah—which may or may not further explain Alice's involvement. After two decades of refusing to be formally interviewed by the press, Alice, by appearing in the cold cream ad, did give "official and social Washington another surprise."[11]

Alice was without peer in the capital city. When the celebrated Queen Marie of Romania visited the White House in October 1926, it was Alice she most wanted to see. The First Lady had been warned about the queen's impulsive nature and love of publicity and told not to leave Queen Marie alone at her reception. Concern for the ladies in waiting diverted Mrs. Coolidge for a moment. Immediately, Queen Marie summoned Alice. Wearing a simply cut dress made of Empress Tz'u Hsi's red silk, Alice sat by Queen Marie's side, who "from then on...paid no further attention to the waiting guests." Protocol dictated that the queen decided when the discussion was over, and Queen Marie's absorbed conversation with Alice derailed the White House plans. Bill and Mary Borah were present, and what Mary remembered of "the most important official function given at the White House during my 22 years in the capital" was Alice boldly offering a "cigarete" to the young Princess Ileana."[12]

Alice's unconventional behavior reached its acme at prizefights. "It indicates a primitive interest in a primitive affray," as one *Chicago Tribune* editor put it. "It represents interest in physical well being, skill, courage, and stamina." On Saturday nights, Alice liked to go to the fights with Ted. Nick went infrequently. Calvin Coolidge could also be convinced to accompany her. Alice's friend the fight promoter George "Tex" Rickard kept her apprised of the up-and-coming boxers and sent her tickets for the best fights. Tex orchestrated the celebrated 1921 "Battle of the Century" between U.S. heavyweight Jack Dempsey and French boxer Georges Carpentier. Alice was one of the few women crowded into Boyle's Thirty Acres in Jersey City, New Jersey, that night. Alice bet on the Manassa Mauler, because she thought it "a bit disloyal" to do otherwise. Her patriotism paid off. Dempsey dropped the Frenchman in the fourth round.[13]

While Alice enjoyed the nation's attention, her husband was entering the prime of his professional life. Well groomed and carefully dressed,

Nick cut a dapper figure. Legendarily cheerful, he could "find lovableness in his most pronounced political opponent." But there was more to him, for in Nick the House would have a new kind of Speaker, one who "will have to be reckoned with in his party councils. His is the gloved hand, but beneath the glove is an iron grip." His pride in the House bordered on the chauvinistic, and Washington watchers expected him to be a powerful Speaker.[14]

Nick had demonstrated his ability to play hardball in 1925 when he publicly repudiated thirteen GOP progressives and denied the La Follette supporters their committee seats. That fall, he and Alice traveled to Chicago, where in two different speeches he made clear that he would deal firmly with the "Radicals." "They have shown their colors...," he said, "and they are not entitled to important committee places or seats in the inner councils of the party they fought." Nick played on growing fears of Bolshevism in the wake of the Russian Revolution of 1917 by linking GOP reformers with extremism. When he had led the 1910 charge to defang Joe Cannon, the power shifted from the Speaker to the floor leader. Once elevated, though, Nick carried the power right back to the Speaker's rostrum. "Regardless of the rules," Nick told a reporter, "the Speakership always will be what the Speaker makes of it."[15]

Insiders believed Nick's success was not his alone: "In Alice Longworth he found a rarely accomplished political assistant, one who has been frequently described as the 'best man in the Roosevelt family,' and whose influence in public life, exerted through sheer political common sense, is not less than that of any woman who has ever lived in the capital." Still, marriage to her was not without its perils; the "distinction" of being the son-in-law of Theodore Roosevelt "was not entirely an asset, for there were those who looked upon him in the light of a social curiosity and even today, most of the visitors to the House ask to be shown Alice Longworth's husband." And, of course, Speaker of the House might not be "the final port in the ambitious political cruise of Nicholas Longworth...." Not everyone agreed. In his quarter century in the House, two journalists charged, Nick "never sponsored anything of the slightest importance, and until he was made Speaker in 1925 was known chiefly as the husband of Alice Roosevelt."[16]

Nick ascended to the speakership at the session of Congress that began on December 7, 1925. His opening words included a bit of flag-waving for the House, promising to make it "the great dominant legislative assembly of the World. Thus we may rest assured that the Republic of the United States shall forever live and that popular government shall never die...." And while Nick noted that the listening representatives were united in their hope to reduce taxes, he knew he faced challenges. He griped once that Congress is "always unpopular." Congress either "meddled" or "did nothing," in the public's perception. If Congress "follows a President it is likened to a flock of sheep.... On the other hand, if it defies the President then it becomes a bunch of factionists and demagogues." And, Nick insinuated, oftentimes when Congress did the hard work and hammered out a bill, the president reaped the praise. But Nick liked the challenge of bringing order through collaboration: "When Congress is making up its mind what to do there are 531 minds going through the process. In consequence there is much quibbling, and many poor arguments and foolish debates are heard by the country at large, for there is no secrecy about our deliberations.... In spite of all that I like my job. I know that without cooperation it could become the most unpleasant position in the world."[17]

Nick had the ease of manner that endeared him to everyone. He paused to shake hands and discuss a shared love of music with African-American House doorman Harry Parker. Ambassador Walter Evans Edge believed that "rich or poor, Jew or Gentile, Catholic or Protestant, presented no distinction to Nick." Nick saw the best in others, even Democrats. One of his best friends was his political enemy, John Nance Garner, a self-styled "plebian" who had served with Nick on the Foreign Affairs and the Ways and Means committees and rose to become House minority leader. "Cactus Jack" was not everyone's model legislator. One Senate insider called him "a chain drinker." Labor leader John L. Lewis memorably labeled Garner "a labor-baiting, poker-playing, whiskey-drinking, evil old man."[18]

But Nick and Garner understood each other. They shared the conviction that the Senate had nothing on the House. Cactus Jack and Nick used to linger long after the House adjourned, rehashing the day's business and strategizing for the morrow. They disagreed often and occasionally bitterly, but their friendship prevailed. "Keeping the Democratic leader informed, out of a true appreciation for his verve and his political acumen, was good leadership—but it went beyond that for Speaker Longworth," according to his House colleague Lewis W. Douglas. Douglas thought Nick an "excellent parliamentarian, and an able and colorful legislator," who got "high marks" from both sides of the aisle for his "impartial governance." Will Rogers made the Speaker's office his headquarters when he was in Washington because he knew that between Nick and Garner, he'd "get the real 'lowdown' on what the government wasn't doing."[19]

It was said of Nick that his aristocratic nature generally rubbed off on others. An editorial at the time of his death suggested that this happened in private, as part of the business of knitting together an obstreperous body of legislators. During World War I, Nick, Cactus Jack, and a few fellow collaborators, along with an occasional journalist friend, used to retire to sip a few companionable drinks. The "Board of Education," a room beneath the Capitol Dome, became their favorite haunt when Nick was Speaker. This space was stocked with illegal alcohol that greased the wheels of compromise. Garner said the room got its name because its use gave them an education: " 'Well . . . you get a couple of drinks in a young Congressman and then you know what he knows and what he can do. We pay the tuition by supplying the liquor.' " The Board of Education expedited legislative matters and smoothed over differences by coming to compromises in private, where misunderstandings could be avoided. Garner's access to Nick assured Democrats that they were being heard.[20]

In the Senate, Borah presented a marked contrast in his modus operandi. He often took the lead on an issue and, for opaque reasons, dropped it. One critical journalist described Borah as "individualism in all its glory and in all its futility," yet called him "without equal in the country to-day in arousing popular enthusiasm and delivering telling blows." Borah was condemned more each year for not living up to his leadership potential. His stubbornness got in the way, and he wore the "maverick" label with pride: once his ideas entered the mainstream, he often renounced them. Calvin Coolidge sized up Borah riding in Rock Creek Park one day and wondered "if it bothers the Senator to be going in the same direction as his horse."[21] Both those who loved him, such as Senate page Richard Riedel, and those who didn't, like journalist Drew Pearson, recognized his strengths. Pearson called him "the great advocate. Scintillating of thought, and enthralling of expression, he is without peer as the passionate pleader. He has raised his voice for many splendid causes, peace, disarmament, anti-imperialism, Russian recognition. He has stirringly denounced infamy, demagoguery, incompetence, and corruption in high and low places." Ultimately, he thought Borah was no organizer, no "commander, but a scholar."[22] Nick stood in the trenches; Bill dreamed from the mountaintop.

Alice knew that part of Bill's reluctance to fight every battle to the finish came from his ambivalence about politics. Time among his constituents always made Borah wistful. It is true the senator loved the adulation of Idahoans—he was always careful to send Alice laudatory editorials about himself. Yet the long bucolic drives, the days on horseback, the afternoons leaning on pasture fences listening to human stories made him rue the rural life he abandoned. On the campaign trail the rough but honest Idahoans gave it to Borah straight, and he admired them. He also felt for them. "I am moved to tears for these farmers," he confided to Alice. "After ten years of adversity, after the pledges of the last campaign, after six months of the farm board, after two years of Hoover, they are getting less for their wheat than it costs to harvest it. I could weep with them." After a hard day among the bitter yield, he wrote her, "It is h— to campaign with broken pledges scattered about you."[23]

Bill was also prone to bouts of depression. "I am very blue, no reason, just blue," he confessed to Alice soon after the 1930 election. His preferred remedy was a solitary horseback ride to "think out what it is all about." But when he was in Washington, in the thick of it and trading "spanks and spit" with senators and reporters, it was easier to summon the reasons he chose politics. "I wonder if God is going to be good to me," Borah mused to Alice, "answer my prayer and give us a real political upheaval, sweeping over party lines, over old traditions and recording for once the voice of an out-raged people." Borah's passion was most evident in such utopian plans as his attempt to banish warfare.[24]

The outlawry of war had been a topic of interest to the senator since the days of the League battle, and by 1927 it had the additionally interesting property of being the issue that could propel him into the White House. Borah never lost his mistrust of international organizations like the League, or his dislike of Europeans. Nevertheless, when, in April 1927—to mark ten years since U.S. involvement in World War I—French minister for foreign affairs Aristide Briand suggested that France and the United States join together "to outlaw war," Borah eventually made the issue his own. Lobbied hard by original members of the outlawry movement such as Chicago attorney Salmon O. Levinson, Borah conquered his suspicion of the French idea and modified it to suit his own purposes. It took the senator most of 1927 before he could find a way to back the plan fully.[25]

Taciturn President Coolidge made his famous, terse, and perplexing statement that he "did not choose to run" for reelection in 1928. Those who admired him put a favorable interpretation on this and stated boldly their champion was simply too modest to campaign but would accede to a draft. Those hoping for a change in the White House silently blessed Coolidge for his brevity and fought to bring their own men to the front. Bill, who seemed to want the presidency, but never quite enough, grabbed onto the outlawry issue as a campaign centerpiece. Earlier, he had made plain—in part to thwart the presidential aspirations of easterner Charles Evans Hughes—that the 1928 election could not neglect the farm problem and tougher Prohibition enforcement, two topics urbanites found uninspiring. Borah won a highly publicized debate on the question "Should the Republican National Platform of 1928 Advocate the Repeal of the Eighteenth Amendment?" He argued against Columbia University president Dr. Nicholas Murray Butler in front of more than three thousand listeners at the Roosevelt Club. A better rallying point than Prohibition for his rural base, he thought, was the outlawry of war. He hastened to spread the word. One Idaho newspaper duly explained: "If Europe spends a disproportionate share of its limited funds in military preparation it will have little left for

American wheat and corn."[26] Ultimately, Borah was wrong. The outlawry of war as the bridge between peace and prosperity never caught the imagination of westerners.

The presidential nod did not come his way in 1928, but he did play an important role in the Kellogg-Briand Pact, the idealistic treaty that made war illegal. In February 1928, Borah put forth Levinson's idea in a *New York Times* article—enlarging Briand's bipower treaty: *all nations* of the world should be invited to sign the pledge to outlaw war. This was swordplay with blunted tips. Borah had just cornered the French—whom he suspected of seeking special friend status with the United States through the originally conceived bipower treaty—while simultaneously evading the vexing diplomatic discussions of which types of war, exactly, were to be outlawed. Insisting that all nations promise to make all war illegal, Borah stood above the petty semantic squabbles of the diplomats, grandly offering a sweeping and simple solution, while capturing the moral high road. He became the "political mentor of the American peace movement."[27] Borah used the power of his position to promote the Kellogg-Briand Pact to his Foreign Relations Committee and to the country at large. Sixty-three nations ultimately signed. It was a brave and optimistic moment.

As history would prove, the treaty had one fatal defect: it contained no enforcement provisions. Whether it was realpolitik or inability to commit fully to a battle, Borah quit the fight before the critical enforcement provisions could be included. Proud to have foiled the French in their attempt to entangle the United States, Borah hoped the presidency would follow. Levinson and others saw the Kellogg-Briand Pact without the enforcement clause as only a beginning to their new world, but Borah saw it as an end. This was "gall and wormwood" to Levinson. Nevertheless, the attorney gratefully funded and chartered the William Edgar Borah Foundation for the Outlawry of War, still in existence today.[28]

Borah's supporters had been struggling for two years to make his case for the 1928 presidential race. Borah felt the GOP was controlled by harmful "industrial and financial combinations" that needed to be "purged." Maintaining his independence, Borah announced that this party reform could be done "under the auspices of any political body . . . [and] his speeches will be made in response to invitations of organizations willing to sponsor the reforms he will indicate." In part because he truly loathed the illegal activities of businessman Harry Sinclair and Secretary of the Interior Albert B. Fall in the Teapot Dome oil lease scandal, and perhaps because he had an eye to publicizing his moral credentials, Borah came up with the idea of soliciting donations to get the GOP out of debt. He sought to replace the $160,000 conscience money that Sinclair had given, earned out of the bribe he had taken from Standard Oil. Bill believed that once good Republicans understood that Sinclair's money was tainted, they would do the right thing. If not, "I know of no defense for Republican morality. For myself, I am not willing to sit quiet while this stigma remains upon the escutcheon of the party."[29]

At the same time that Borah was trying to find an issue for 1928, Ethel reported to Belle Hagner, "There is real talk—an undercurrent—of Nick as a Presidential possibility! Can you believe it?" Nick could attract bipartisan support. Reporter Frank B. Lord suggested in early 1927 that "if the Democrats of the House of Representatives were required to name the next Republican president of the United States, you would be perfectly safe in laying a wager of 100 to 1, which would be about the proportion in which they would vote, that Ohio would have another of her distinguished citizens in the White House...." But Nick was happy where he was. He told his sister that he had "realized *more* than I ever hoped for in the way of ambition. There was a time, I might have wanted to be in the Senate," but Speaker of the House "is much better and more in line with my aptitudes." Nick averred he had "a horror of the Presidential bee; I have seen it ruin too many good men."[30] He was content with the House and his daughter.

He suffered Paulina to make powdered sugar pies on top of his bald, indulgent head. He went to every French and piano lesson with her. She accompanied him to the Capitol Saturday afternoons and held court for the favored congressmen who came to spoil her. Alice thought taking her on to the floor of the House would "exploit" the child, so even though Nick wanted dearly to do so, he kept those chamber appearances to a minimum. Paulina concluded her Saturday ritual with a visit to Cactus Jack, who made much of her. Photographers loved to snap pictures of the Speaker and "Kitz," as Nick called her, who loved the attention. She was growing apace. Kermit told Ethel in January 1928: "I saw Sister in Washington, as much wrapped up in Paulina as ever. The latter was in good form. She is more advanced than [her cousin], indeed does not seem like a baby at all."[31]

In the end—and to Alice's great disappointment—neither Nick nor Bill earned the nod for 1928. The battle lines were drawn by the end of June. In Houston, Franklin Roosevelt walked to the podium leaning on his son Elliott to name "the happy warrior," Al Smith, the Democratic Party's choice. Two weeks earlier, the GOP convention had been held in steamy Kansas City, where Republicans selected Herbert Hoover on the first ballot. Bill Borah "delivered himself up, influence, statesmanlike presence, magnetic voice and all, to the nomination of the Great Engineer—much to the annoyance of some of his progressive friends." The platform contained strong planks on Prohibition, the outlawry of war, labor, and farm relief based upon Borah's ideas.[32]

As conventions go, this one lacked drama, though Alice's celebrity status drew attention. For a memorable few hours, her name was mentioned for the vice presidency. It was supposed to be a "hoax 'boom' " made by the editor-in-chief of the Western Newspaper Union, but it was taken seriously by some of the delegates present—evidence both that the significance of women's participation in politics had made such an idea possible and of Alice's own credentials as a canny, intelligent, and serious politician.[33]

Though Alice believed Herbert Hoover was not "politically seasoned," she nonetheless put party before persona and in 1928 took to the campaign trail. She liked Lou Henry Hoover, a Stanford geology graduate with a broad range of concerns. Herbert Hoover was an engineer by training, keyed to details and often seeing the big picture only at the last minute. For Alice, the real excitement in 1928 was Ruth Hanna McCormick's campaign for the U.S. Congress. She ran as a delegate at-large for a seat in the House of Representatives. Ruth undertook a sixteen-thousand-mile campaign across Illinois, speaking to farmers and miners of the economic assistance she would find for them if elected. She was a supporter of the outlawry of war and of Prohibition. The latter Ruth actually considered "a mistake, but it was the law and the government 'either ought to enforce it or repeal it.' "[34]

She beat her six opponents in April, campaigned all fall, and won more than one million votes to become "the first woman congressman from Illinois" and "the first woman elected state-wide to a national office." Alice was overjoyed. The two rented a house in Kansas City during the convention and even though Alice herself would never run for office, Ruth recognized Alice's talents. "Alice," she put it, "is a statesman and I am a politician.... She has no patience for the drudgery of details, but she has wonderful intuition as to where this or that tendency in politics is going to carry us, has an uncanny certainty in predicting results, and she dearly loves a fight." To Alice's delight, Ruth moved to Washington, D.C., to start work even before the special session of the Seventy-first Congress opened in April 1929.[35]

While Alice and Ruth worked hard for Hoover's election, one of Borah's biographers insisted that "no man did more than the Senator from Idaho to make Herbert Hoover President of the United States." It was Borah who saw to it that skittish middle western and far western voters cast their votes for the GOP. In return for Hoover's espousal of Borah's ideas in the platform, the new president expected Borah to orchestrate a compliant Senate into accepting the resultant legislation. Hoover underestimated Borah's independence. Over lunch on January 19, 1929, Hoover asked Borah if he would become his secretary of state. Borah declined, saying he had not campaigned for Hoover seeking a quid pro quo; nor did he have the financial wherewithal to move into the cabinet. And, Borah told the president, he prized his work in the Senate, especially his ability to disagree with Hoover—a liberty he would not enjoy as secretary of state.[36]

Just after Hoover's inaugural, politics took a backseat to the protocol war labeled the Alice Longworth–Dolly Gann affair. It set Washington abuzz. Dolly Gann was Vice President Charles Curtis's sister. Curtis had lived with his sister and brother-in-law since his wife had died in 1924, and Dolly had been his recognized hostess during his senatorial career. Large, blond, and assertive, she campaigned expertly for her brother, speaking to women's groups in particular. Mrs. Gann was well known to Washington society and could be found at all manner of parties and occasions. She was recognized as "having an excellent knowledge of national politics and the questions of the day."[37] The war began when her brother, Charles Curtis, became vice president.

In Washington society, protocol matters. "Protocol is the rule book by which international relations are conducted," asserted the chief of protocol during the Truman administration. One purpose of rules of protocol is "to create an atmosphere of friendliness in which the business of diplomacy can be transacted." In Washington protocol, the vice president—who also presided over the Senate when necessary—and his wife ranked second behind the president and the First Lady. Third ranking was the chief justice of the Supreme Court and his wife, then the Speaker of the House of Representatives and his wife followed by the ambassadors. Trying to ascertain the protocol for their functions, the august Senate Ladies Luncheon Club pondered the ramifications of an unmarried vice president. In February 1929, the Senate Ladies decreed that "an official hostess" could be only "the wife of the official." Thus, they chose the wife of the president pro tem of the Senate to be president of their organization—making her the second-ranking woman in the United States—and not Dolly Gann.[38]

Their opinion did not trouble Mrs. Gann, who played a major role in the Hoovers' inaugural ball. MRS. GANN ACTS AS 'FIRST LADY,' proclaimed the *New York Times*, and noted that the ball "formally opened with the arrival of Vice President Curtis and Mrs. Gann." But on March 30, outgoing Secretary Frank Kellogg at the State Department seconded the Senate wives' decision, stating "that in State social functions Mrs. Edward Gann . . . is to be seated after the wives of Ambassadors."[39] Secretary Kellogg made the clarification in response to Curtis's notification to the State Department that his sister would be his "official hostess." The vice president's response

was swift and furious. He swore he would not accept Kellogg's pronounce-
ment and made a formal and public statement requesting a reversal of the
decision—the first vice president ever to do so.

The newspaper coverage of this protocol question was serious and thorough. Page one of the *New York Times* gave the full text of Curtis's disputa-
tion. Trying to demystify the trouble, the *Times* explained that since the
president did not accept dinner invitations to private homes, the vice president was the nation's chief "diner out." If Kellogg's ruling were to remain
intact, it would mean that Helen Taft, wife of the chief justice, and Alice
Longworth, wife of the Speaker of the House, would both outrank Dolly
Gann, as would the wives of the ambassadors.[40]

After Kellogg's departure, Henry Stimson, the new secretary of state,
inherited the problem. He responded with dogged, official silence while
Washington hosts and hostesses clamored for an answer. Stimson's foot-
dragging obstructed the whole social season. Nothing daunted, the British
chimed in with their own tradition, where their Speaker of the House of
Commons had his sister as his official hostess. She sat "at the head of the
table in his household, but has no official precedence outside." In the mean-
time, the diplomatic corps spent two full hours considering the controversy.
No fools they, the diplomats said they would rely on the wisdom of the
"Ladies of the Senate," who had "refused to accept Mrs. Gann as ranking
with the wife of the Vice President."[41]

While Stimson stalled for time, opposition to the Kellogg decision mul-
tiplied. It became a mark of patriotism to support the vice president. Senator J. Thomas Heflin of Alabama proclaimed that he would fight on the
vice president's behalf because, "It's decidedly against American principles
to put Mrs. Gann off in a corner and make her step down for these foreigners." Senator Borah could not be drawn into the fray and refused to comment on Heflin's threat that the Senate should decide the whole matter.
Opinions came from around the country. Philadelphians saw it as a matter
of honor. Republican women there vowed that " 'no semblance of slight' to
the vice president should go 'unrebuked before the world,' " and they
chided Stimson for his "evasive position."[42]

Evasive or clever, Stimson ultimately decided not to decide. He said the State Department "would not rule on or arbitrate problems of official-social precedence." That sent the question right back to the dismayed diplomatic corps. A *New York Times* front-page article declared Dolly Gann a winner in the first round. And the next day's similarly placed story "scored a complete triumph" for Mrs. Gann when the dean of the diplomatic corps announced that she would be accorded the status Mr. Curtis requested "until we can obtain some definite ruling on this point from a constituted American authority." But this left a door open, and while some Washingtonians disliked the decision of the diplomatic corps—especially Washington's Old Guard—others didn't see any real loophole as there was no such "authority." So, as the spring social season began, Dolly Gann ranked second, in the place of the vice president's wife, a custom established in practice by an April 11, 1929, dinner given by the Chilean ambassador.[43]

Thanks to Alice, the calm did not last. GANN SOCIAL WAR REOPENS IN CAPITAL: ALICE ROOSEVELT LONGWORTH IS CREDITED WITH INITIATING NEW STAGE, read the headlines in early May. The Longworths refused to attend a dinner given by Agnes and Eugene Meyer, former chair of the Federal Farm Loan Bureau, because Dolly Gann was to be seated ahead of Alice. Mrs. Meyer had hoped to sidestep the controversy by having several round tables with a ranking host or hostess at each. Unfortunately for her, "Mrs. Meyer reckoned without Mrs. Longworth. The daughter of the late Theodore Roosevelt is undoubtedly the most popular lady in Washington. She not only dictates many of the political whims of 'Bill' Borah and other Senators, but when she takes the trouble she sets social precedent. Most of the time she is too busy either with politics or Paulina, but on this occasion Mrs. Gann apparently aroused her social ire."[44]

Editorial writers were quick to comment: "Precedents in official society have never meant anything to her. Details of etiquette which she ... found boring she rarely troubled to observe. ... A witty and forceful commentator on public affairs, Mrs. Longworth has for years made her own social laws; to challenge her freedom was to risk being barred from her brilliant salon. ... But before she is through with her campaign logic will have been forgotten in the play of tactics and the fire of repartee." Alice apparently suggested that during her father's administration she had inspired "Alice blue," but the contemporary administrative color seemed to be "Gann green."[45]

But both women always insisted that there was no "battle." Alice acknowledged that Nick cared about precedent, but she attributed their refusal to attend the Meyers' party to his fondness for alcohol. At lunch with Agnes Meyer the day before the Longworths were to dine at their house, Alice learned that their hosts had decided to seat Lady Isabella Howard, the British ambassador's wife, on Eugene Meyer's right, and Dolly Gann in the place of honor on his left. Alice told Agnes, "Ha, ha; you will be in trouble with Nick. I will tell him this thing, you see." Alice couldn't resist, as she said, "making trouble," which she wryly admitted later rebounded on her, because Nick said, "Don't want to go to dinner with Eugene anyway. Comes to my house and he drinks. I go to his house and I don't get a drink. He's obeying the law, and I'm disobeying the law, but he takes advantage of my disobeying the law and has plenty of drinks with us. I will not go to his house if he's going to put Dolly Gann ahead of the wife of the British ambassador." Alice phoned Agnes Meyer to say, "Nick won't go, but we all laughed about it. And we said he's using [the protocol issue] as an excuse...to avoid going to a dry dinner and having to drink heavily at home before and when he gets home afterwards." Alice insisted "it was a wet and dry row, really...."[46]

The following day, Alice recounted, Nick hosted a luncheon in the Speaker's dining room and "went around telling everyone how smart he was to get out of a dry dinner with his dear friend Eugene. They were all friendly about it. There was no bad feeling. But from then on they decided to pin it on Dolly Gann and myself." But, as she concluded, "Obviously, there never was any row; any one who knew me was aware that rank and conventionality were things I always fled from and shirked. I could not very well tell the true story—that Nick had seized a straw to avoid a dry dinner...." And when Alice and Dolly walked into the Senate gallery together, and sat in the same row—the vice presidential row—on May 14, they caused all heads to turn away from the speech on farm relief. The two women laughed and talked together, enjoying the disbelief etched in the faces around them.[47]

Yet, there are reasons to believe that Alice herself felt strongly that the sister of the vice president should not occupy the position of "second lady." Alice was untraditional. She did break rules. As she grew older, she became more conservative in some ways, and Nick certainly placed great importance on the traditions of his House—which would include the social rank of the wife of the Speaker. By fighting for the appropriate rank she would be "standing up for the dignities of the Speaker's office." And while her heart may have been in the Senate with the Lion of Idaho, outwardly she had a duty to support the House. The *New York Times* stated that "when she appears at any official function she is no more likely now [as wife of the Speaker] to allow herself to be outranked by those over whom she considers she has precedence than previously she would have dreamed of attempting to precede those who officially outranked her." Alice understood politics and respected the code, and while she later protested to an interviewer, "It had nothing to do with me," she amended her statement by noting, "Well I would come into it, you see because the wife of the speaker should go ahead of her...."[48]

It is also the case that Alice was not overly fond of the vice president. Charles Curtis cheated at poker. "We all said, 'Well we just don't come in when Charlie deals,'" Alice remarked once to an interviewer. "And Charlie would say to me 'Stay in, stay in,' when I said I was going to drop out, and then he would give me an ace to make me happy." To make matters worse, Curtis had a reputation as a political lightweight. One journalist at that time described him as "mediocre—a nice, genial, little fellow, but basically a run-of-the-mine Kansas politician."[49]

Alice did not change her ways when Nick became Speaker of the House. Averse to making official calls, a "penalty" of public life, as she called it, she refused to adhere to that social tradition. "He and I," Alice wrote, "had long before decided that I was more a liability than an asset to him along those lines, that if the wives of his fellow politicians were going to be affronted by my inactivity in assuming 'social obligations' he would have to make the best of it. He did not think, any more than I did, that a successful political career depended on such perfunctory and conventional activities."[50]

Dolly Gann gave an interview to the *New York Times* in July and suggested that as the vice president is a symbol of the nation, "it is his duty to see that both he and his official hostess are accorded 'every respect that the symbol of our government should receive from all right-minded people.'" Ultimately, Dolly Gann did gain her position as Washington's "second lady." Whether or not the January 1930 sacking of James C. Dunn, the chief of the protocol division at the State Department, was connected is not clear. The newspapers continued to report any sightings of Alice and Dolly Gann together. Their acquaintance lent credence to Alice's assertion that the Longworth-Gann feud was really about Nick's impatience with the Meyers' dry dinners. Dolly Gann went out of her way to pay tribute to Alice in her autobiography, writing that she admired Alice's independence, her ability to do "what she chooses and cares not a snap of her finger what anybody thinks of her." They were, after all, both Republican women working for GOP goals. Dolly thought that no one topped Alice for charm, erudition, or interesting experiences. "A law unto herself," she called Alice—apparently without irony—and thought she understood "how a woman of Alice's brilliancy might find it more satisfying to ignore less scintillating humans than to endure them."[51]

Profoundly absorbing at the time, the protocol episode passed into history and became a cultural reference point. Assistant Secretary of the Treasury Seymour Lowman had the best word on the affair. At a White House reception one night, President and Mrs. Hoover descended the stairs, followed by Vice President Curtis and his sister, then Secretary of State and Mrs. Stimson. At the bottom of the stairs, Mrs. Stimson inadvertently stepped on and ripped Mrs. Gann's train, causing Lowman's irreverent quip: "Now at last we will see where Dolly Gann sits."[52]

One story dated the end of the Alice Longworth–Dolly Gann feud to July 1950—twenty years later—at a political gathering at the home of

Peter and Ruth "Bazy" McCormick Miller. Bazy, the daughter of Ruth Hanna McCormick, was the editor of the *Washington Times-Herald*. Senator George W. Malone of Nevada brought Alice and Dolly to the front, and intoned, we "recognize no hostilities today, either of a political or private nature," at which time Alice and Dolly shook on it.[53]

Chapter 17

"An Irresistible Magnet"

By 1930, Nick and Alice occupied the center of Washington society, which, in that federal city, was generally synonymous with the political. "Society, in truth, came to them," the *New York Times* marveled, "the pick of anybody's party being likely to desert early and in considerable numbers to join any group assembled, however informally, at the Longworth home, or got up on the spur of the moment by Mrs. Longworth anywhere else." When British novelist Rebecca West sojourned in Washington in 1935, she noticed, "The city is dominated by the last good thing said by Alice Longworth...."[1]

Alice's significance for national governance resided in her ability to bridge the social and political. Henry James called the nation's capital " 'the City of Conversation,' " writing that "Washington presented two faces, 'the public and official' " and the inhabitants of the city spent their time talking, mostly about "Washington—almost nothing else." Even Nick's sister Clara, never fond of Alice, admitted that the Longworths' home "was always a center where personal friends and men of all parties met and mingled as they did nowhere else. Alice's vivid conversational talent made the dinner parties particularly memorable." The *Washington Times* asserted that "every man prominent in the politics of the last quarter century passed through the Longworth drawing rooms, irrespective of party. Nick's popularity and Alice's wit and charm combined to form an irresistible magnet."[2] A permanent fixture in Washington by then, Alice chose how to use her time, unconstrained—as much as she ever would be—by social expectations.

Nineteen thirty gave Alice an enormous political opportunity: Ruth Hanna McCormick was making a race for the U.S. Senate. Her delegate-at-large position was likely to be a victim of Illinois redistricting, and by May 1929, she had made up her mind to try for the Senate seat. It wasn't until September 22—a month and a week before the stock market crash—that Ruth formally announced. Alice and Bill were happy to have the publicity she brought to their continued noninterventionism as she campaigned against U.S. involvement in the League of Nations' Permanent Court of International Justice. All three saw it as a "back door" entrance to the League. The fact that such a position came from the first woman to make a "creditable attempt" at the Senate was all to the good. In April, Alice was with Ruth as Illinoisans cast their ballots in the primary. The grand tension of the vote counting made Alice shout, "Oh, I just can't stand it!" when an early prediction had Ruth winning by 175,000 votes.[3] Her victory was attributed to her World Court stance, though Ruth herself credited the support of female voters and the clean campaign she waged. Nick celebrated Ruth's nomination by handing her his gavel and inviting her to sit in his Speaker's chair. Next came the hard work of winning the general election.

By then, Cissy Patterson had become coeditor of Randolph Hearst's *Washington Herald*. Making her own kind of mischief, Cissy used her new platform to assail Alice. Bested in the competitions for Nick and for Bill, Cissy attacked with a page-one editorial. The opening salvo was entitled "Interesting But Not True":

Reports that Mrs. Alice Roosevelt Longworth will manage the Senate campaign of Mrs. Ruth Hanna McCormick are interesting, but not true.

Mrs. McCormick takes no advice, political or otherwise, from Mrs. Longworth.

Mrs. Longworth could not possibly manage anyone's campaign being too lofty to speak to newsmen and too aristocratic for public speaking.

Mrs. Longworth gives no interviews to the press.

Mrs. Longworth cannot utter in public.

Her assistance, therefore, will evolve itself as usual into posing for photographs.[4]

Alice called it "very amusing," but the rumor mills erupted, boosting sales of Cissy's paper considerably. That may be why she published a second editorial on the same topic entitled "Will She? Can She?"

> Some weeks ago, I wrote that Alice Longworth had no real gifts to bring to Ruth Hanna McCormick's campaign. Ruth McCormick is Alice Longworth's close friend.
>
> I was in error. I spoke hastily.
>
> Senator Borah, another *close* friend of Alice Longworth, has said that if Ruth McCormick is elected, he will vote to unseat her because of her excessive campaign expenditures. Mrs. Longworth may now present her real gifts. She may use her political influence, of which the country has for so long heard so much. She may soften this decision of the frugal gentleman from Idaho.
>
> But it is for Alice to come now bearing her offerings. Will she? Can she?[5]

This second editorial was brazen. Cissy, in the aftermath of her marital troubles, had published a novel in 1926 that her grandniece called "a deliberately bitchy book."[6] *Glass Houses* told the barely camouflaged story of Cissy's unrequited love for Bill Borah, and Alice's competition in the lists. The novel received good reviews, but her newspaper columns reached many more readers. Linking Alice and Bill so publicly and suggesting that Alice's only useful political service to her best friend was to influence Bill kindled more gossip. Cissy calculated none of it to assist the three principals, but to assuage her pain and sell her paper. It cost her something she really regretted, however: Nick's friendship. She wrote him a lengthy letter explaining, without details, that Alice had been "treacherous and vicious about me behind my back" and had struck first in the off-again, on-again relationship between them. Cissy blamed her column on the 102-degree weather, her loneliness, and the momentary loss of her "newspaper sense" that caused her not to see "that the story would burst like a bomb around the world." She told Nick that had she known, she might have hesitated—not with regard to Alice ("I haven't any"), but "on your account." Cissy told him sadly that she knew he'd have to stick by his wife and regretted that she had "lost your friendship." "But remember, my dear," she closed, "that if ever I can help you or your friends, or do anything for you, I'll be right there. You know that."[7]

Ruth was, as Cissy suggested, in the midst of tough times. Ruth's campaign expenditures were being publicly scrutinized by the Senate Campaign Fund Investigating Committee headed by Senator Gerald P. Nye. The impetus for this may have been nothing more than one senator's crusade to keep the Senate free of women. Nye wasn't the only man anxious to keep women out of the "most exclusive club," though. Hiram Johnson, their old friend from the League days, opined to his son that he had "mixed emotions" about how Ruth's opponent in the primary "had been outsmarted by a woman. . . ." Johnson thought the "thorough breakdown and demoralization [of the Senate] will come with the admission of the other sex." He found women politicians in general lacking in "patriotism, morality, altruism, and idealism." Alice could not help Ruth with the vindictive Nye Committee, which instigated a smear campaign that included a spy in her closet, wiretaps on her telephone line, and a break-in at her offices.[8] After surviving all that, Ruth—and the rest of the country—turned to the election in the fall.

Bill left Washington in September to rustle up Idaho votes, writing to Alice sometimes twice a day, enclosing clippings about their political friends and enemies. His campaign rolled along in its usual fashion. On the way west in early September, he was "holding levees on the train all day, everybody seems interested to get a close up. I could get along with less of it." Alice was traveling that fall—to Rhode Island and then to Cincinnati to enroll "Princess Paulina," as one newspaper called her, in a private school. Alice confessed she was "all of a twitter watching her learn to read." Between receptions and an unsuccessful attempt at a dude ranch vacation, the restless Borah confessed, "I wish I could have had a talk with you about politics. I should like to hear you 'illuminate' on some of the things now happening." He was feeling "so blue" that he was "afraid of" himself, while cogitating on the election in Germany: it "may mean much. Germany may present us some morning with a repudiated treaty."[9] Borah's prescience about the 1930 German election, which gave an alarming percentage of votes to Adolph Hitler's National Socialist German Workers Party, and his suspicion that Germany might repudiate the Versailles treaty, would prove to be true in three short years.

En route to yet another small campaign stop, Bill poured out his frustration with the platform adopted by eastern Republicans. "Is there no clear cut courage left?" he cried. "They sincerely do not stand up against the thirsty cry of the wets and dare not face the evils of repeal." He lamented again in early October: "Wish I had remained on the farm as father willed me to do." Part of his gloom came from his sympathy for his constituents, caught in the Great Depression. Yet he could still see humor—if a bit grim—around him. "Did you notice Coolidge in one of his essays suggest that the League of Nations take a hand in settling Brazil's internal war? My God, I think ours is the greatest gov. on earth, having survived certain presidents."[10]

Alice and Bill avidly followed Ruth's election fight in Illinois, where she was tangled up in the Prohibition quandary. The *St. Louis Post-Dispatch* poked fun at her dilemma: "And Ruth said to the dry voter and to the wet voter in Illinois, 'Entreat me not to leave either of thee or to return from following after either of thee: for howsoever thou believest, I will believe; and where thou markest thy ballots, there would I have my name; thy votes shall be my votes and thy office my office. When thou wouldst abstain or drink, then would I have thee do the same; the god of politicians help me if aught but death part thee and me.' " Ruth was a dry. Her opponent was a wet. Facing an Illinois referendum on the Eighteenth Amendment, Ruth promised to abide by the voters' wishes. This cost her support among the strong Prohibitionists, many of whom were women and her core of supporters.[11]

But it wasn't the World Court or Prohibition that counted most for

American voters in 1930; it was the Great Depression. Every week more banks closed, more people lost their jobs, homes, and farms, all while cheerful but hollow bulletins issued from the Hoover White House. The day before the election, Bill wrote to Alice, "I know how you are scanning the political horizon; bad year to bet." He was right. The Democrats routed the Republicans in 1930, and Ruth's attempt at the U.S. Senate failed. Bill loyally blamed the poor organization of the Illinois GOP. If she still "wants to do the big thing she still has a great chance to do so," he penned to Alice.[12] But he could afford to be generous—as he was only one of a handful of Republicans returned to office that Democratic fall. Nick was also re-elected, but it was clear he would lose his position as Speaker. Overall, eight new Democratic senators and fifty-one new representatives took their seats in Congress in 1930. Both Houses were almost exactly divided between the parties.

In the wake of the disaster, Alice mused to her sister, "What an election! I thought we'd have the House by 8 or 10—I never believed the reports from the headquarters that we'd have at least 25—or that there would be a real democratic sweep, giving it to them by 30 or more. We'd said piously all along, 'if there isn't an undercurrent.' There was one, but not a Simon-pure democratic one. So behold us, probably not sure of how long the House, or Senate, will organize until the next Congress meets! Isn't it fantastic, but it will be all kinds of fun—for anyone with a taste of chaos." Bill Borah's funk continued unabated. After the campaign, he stayed a week in Idaho giving speeches on foreign policy subjects. "I have literally," he complained, "never been so torn and driven. I am leaving now with a half dozen demands behind but I am more than weary, worse than the campaign." Alice sent him a long, typed discursive letter on the election, and some of Paulina's first attempts at writing, which Borah teased "looked better" than Alice's own handwriting.[13]

Unlike Borah, who, though prone to depression, was physically vigorous and politically powerful, the other man in Alice's life was in decline. Nick was losing his speakership. The end of the Seventy-first Congress had been a sentimental affair. Nick set the tone by playing reflective tunes on the piano in the House chamber. The representatives who lingered last sang "Carry Me Back to Old Virginny" in mournful harmony. Nick had made his good-bye earlier, saying, "Perhaps this is the last time I will address you from this rostrum.... If I am to retire from this office, I do so with profound gratitude to my colleagues ... for the esteem and confidence you have had in me." One of Nick's staff members, Lucile McArthur, cried as she watched the overwhelming display of fondness for Speaker Longworth on the part of his whooping and applauding colleagues. Members on both sides of the aisle gave Nick a standing ovation, and she remembered how Nick grew "redder and redder with pleasure and gratification."[14]

A group of people closest to Nick gathered for a private luncheon after adjournment. According to Nick's secretary, Alice, "the human dynamo," was present. "She was all over the place all the time; talking vivaciously to newspapermen who poked their heads in the door every once in a while and then oozed in to see what the party was about; to members who dropped in to say good-by to Nick ... and even to an occasional tourist who opened the door out of curiosity."[15]

But when the parties were over and the gavel banged down, Nick grew sad. He was suffering from a head cold he'd had for a fortnight and couldn't shake. Seeking congenial company, he made his fourth journey to Aiken, South Carolina, in as many years. He left Washington on March 30, 1931, to stay at the winter home of Laura and James F. Curtis. Though the Curtises had been described as "old and intimate friends" of Nick's, that was only half correct. *Laura* was his intimate friend. They shared, among other things, an ardor for music, high-stakes poker, and "wringing wet" parties.[16] At his mistress's home, weakened as he was by years of alcohol abuse, and worn out by the duties of the House, Nick's cold turned into pneumonia. The Curtises sent for Alice, who arrived on April 8—the first time she had been in Aiken since before her wedding. Alice allowed one of the attending physicians to release a confirmation of the pneumonia. When she heard, Cissy Patterson arranged for an oxygen tent to be flown to Aiken. President Hoover, also fretting about the health of his lieutenant, wrote

that day to Alice, saying, "We share your anxieties and your confidence...."[17]

Confidence faded as Nick took a sudden turn for the worse. Ever mind-
ful of the status of the Speaker, Alice kept the papers informed. The pneumonia overwhelmed Nick's worn body. He died that day, April 9, just
before 11:00 a.m., attended—as it turned out—neither by wife, lover, nor,
as he had desired, the transcendent measures of Beethoven's Seventh Symphony.[18]

Whatever mixture of grief or anger Alice was feeling, she turned not to
her hosts for solace, but to her family. Kermit and Archie flew to be with
her in South Carolina. Colonel Campbell Hodges, Hoover's military aide,
was personally sent by the president to help. Once in Aiken, Hodges reported back that the widow had everything under control. Mildred Reeves,
Nick's secretary, attested that in characteristic fashion, Alice had "retained
her self possession and was actively directing arrangements for the burial."[19]
Under Alice's direction, Reeves oversaw the competent staff that arranged
the special train to take Nick's body back to Ohio. Speakers of the House
were not entitled to lie in state; nor, since Nick was not a veteran, was he
permitted to be buried in Arlington Cemetery.

Perhaps as a last sign of respect for Nick and the independent but loving
life they had worked out, Alice invited Laura Curtis to accompany his body
on the train to Rookwood, which she duly did. James Curtis did not go to
Cincinnati nor was he one of the honorary pallbearers as the coffin was
carried from his home to the train station for a brief memorial by the citizens of Aiken. Alice Dows, another of Nick's mistresses, also accompanied
Nick's body to Ohio. She told Gore Vidal later that "we went in a private
train, like *two* widows." Alice Dows had poured out her love, presumably
for Nick, in reams of suggestive poetry. "Thy Gift" begins, "I love thee
with no vow or ring / Without an outward sign; / Yet I am chained by
everything / To keep me wholly thine." In 1927, she published her first
volume, replete with poems such as "When He Comes": "Flutters of expectancy / Fill the room— / Cries my soul in secrecy, / 'Will he come?'"
And when "he" does come, Dows concluded, "Then earth's transformed /
Into heaven."[20] Alice had entered her marriage to Nick without brides-

maids, but she was flanked by black-gowned grieving women at his funeral. Joe Graydon also was there, one of the honorary pallbearers.

Meanwhile, in the Capitol the Speaker's gavel lay draped in black and surrounded by lilies. This was the idea of doorman Harry Parker, who had especially fond memories of Longworth. A special service was conducted at Washington Cathedral, broadcast simultaneously on nationwide radio. The sympathy telegrams began arriving that day too. Among the first was a brief one that Alice kept all her life. Signed W E AND MARY BORAH, it read, "Our deepest sympathy." Secretary of War Patrick Hurley and others broadcast their tributes to Nick on NBC Radio. President Hoover eulogized his fallen Speaker in a statement issued to the national press: "Mr. Longworth served his fellow countrymen in state and nation for over thirty-three years—nearly the whole of his adult life. In his service he contributed greatly to the welfare of the American people. His happy character, his sterling honesty, his courage in public questions, endeared him and held the respect not alone of his myriad of friends but of the country at large. His passing is a loss to the Nation." Hoover's personal telegram to Alice echoed the same themes, that Nick was "entitled" to the "honors which he bore so modestly and yet so worthily."[21]

The president and the First Lady led the list of notables who trekked sadly to the Midwest, past the flags Hoover had ordered to fly at half-mast. Their nine-car presidential train followed that of Vice President Curtis and the congressional delegation. Eleven members of the Senate and a representative from every state came to pay their respects. First among them was Cactus Jack Garner, there to mourn the man he called "my closest and best-loved friend."[22]

The Right Rev. Henry Wise Hobson conducted the ceremony at Cincinnati's Christ Episcopal Church. In the front pews with Alice were Roosevelt women (Edith, Ethel, Belle, and Grace); her sister-in-law Nan Wallingford; Mildred Reeves; the despondent Laura Curtis; and presumably Alice Dows. Archie and Kermit were pallbearers. Six-year-old Paulina remained at Rookwood with her nanny. Thousands of mourners lined the streets of Cincinnati as a two-mile-long funeral procession made its way through Eden Park—a gift to the city by the Longworths—out to Spring

Grove Cemetery, Cincinnati's most prestigious burial ground.[23] Rt. Rev.
Henry Wise Hobson read the order for the burial of the dead as the flower-
draped coffin was lowered into the ground on the sunny, blue-skied day.

Alice's "boon companion," brother Ted, was serving as governor general of Puerto Rico. He and his wife, Eleanor, were too far away to make
the journey home. But the Roosevelt spirit came through clearly across the
distance in their notes of sympathy. "What a wonderful time for Nick to
go," Eleanor wrote characteristically, "at the height of his popularity...."
Ted enthused, in an otherwise loving letter, "It is a tragedy but it might
well have been worse." Perhaps he was thinking of their alcoholic uncle
Elliott, who had died scandalously in the home of his mistress. Ted was
glad that Kermit and Edith were with Alice. "Oddly enough," he mused, "I
should think K. and Mother would be the most comfort [to you]." Like the
rest of the family, Ted implored her to change her scenery and come visit
with Paulina.[24]

Newspaper columns swelled with quotes from friends about Nick's
leadership qualities, his sociability, his good humor, his steadfast conserva-
tism, and his effects on the House. Nick reestablished the power of the
Speaker and ruled just as firmly as Cannon, whom he had helped to unseat
in 1910. Longworth engineered several important innovations. He allowed
radio broadcasts of House debates—the quality of which had improved as
a result of the better work ethic and collegial tone he established. Speaker
Longworth, influenced no doubt by his friendship with Ruth Hanna Mc-
Cormick, did away with the trivializing term of address used to call upon
female representatives, "the gentle lady," and insisted that all members of
the House use the more acceptable "gentlewoman," the mirror of "gentleman." Further, Nick provided a rest room for the three female legislators in
the House, a welcome change that beat the Supreme Court's installation of
a lavatory for women attorneys by more than half a century.[25]

Longworth streamlined the functioning of the House. His reforms
made it more efficient than the Senate. The contradictions abounded: he
was Speaker of the House but referred to as Nick; he enjoyed the grubby
side of politics but saw true dignity in his calling; he loved Bach but could
play "The Pants of Queen Lil"; he wore spats but his good friend was a

Texas roustabout. Nick used his even temper, his amiability, and his wide friendships to lead by persuasion. Contemporary commentators realized that "even when he was bludgeoning the House he was never disagreeable about it." A "genial czar" was Nick—and it is perhaps the highest praise to recall that his passing was mourned by Democrats and Republicans alike. Will Rogers wrote that he'd "been told many times by Democrats that [Nick] was the most able and popular man in Congress." Nick summed up his approach in 1928 by saying, "I know of no nobler profession than the profession of politics, and by politics I mean the holding of office for the benefit, not of one's self, but of the public. Of course as a career it does seem precarious. Real success appears very remote. Moreover, there can be no hope of large money returned. No honest man has ever grown rich in the profession of politics. But there is another recompense which, to my mind, is the greatest of them all. I can think of no satisfaction greater than the knowledge that one has served one's country honorably and well."[26]

Alice did not grieve in public. Though sad, she was not debilitated by Nick's death, as Ruth Hanna McCormick's absence from his funeral suggests. If Alice had truly needed Ruth, she would have been there. While Alice wasn't mourning overtly, Laura Curtis was. Nick's lady friend looked to Lou Hoover for sympathetic understanding, "I know you realize how unhappy I have been," she wrote to the First Lady. Alice knew, too. She and Laura developed a close friendship in the wake of Nick's death.[27]

Ohio faced the pressing question of filling Nick's term. Several politicians thought it was time Alice evolved from a behind-the-scenes politician to an elected one. Representative John C. Schafer of Wisconsin stated publicly that Alice was "eminently qualified. She long has been interested in public affairs and knows intimately the problems which face Congress and the inside of legislations. . . ." He volunteered to campaign for her as "one of the best informed women in the country on politics and Congressional life."[28]

Ohio state senator Robert Taft felt only Alice could unite the two disparate factions in Cincinnati and actually get elected. Although Alice was "very reluctant," he believed he could persuade her. Taft told President Hoover that she would be "the strongest person" the GOP could snag, and "while she will not always be easy to handle...a strong personality like that who is regular would be far better than to run the risk of being defeated." A guaranteed Republican victory would be ideal, as Nick's death turned the House Democratic. The necessity for a stalwart Republican was critical, as the House stood at 216 Democrats, 215 Republicans, and 1 Farmer-Laborite. But Alice insisted she was too shy to campaign, and she did not want to be one of the women who, as she put it, used their husbands' coffins for a springboard. As a friend pointed out, Alice lacked the "faculty for suffering fools gladly, so essential in political life. Indeed, she did not possess the faculty for suffering them at all."[29] By December, the Republicans had lost the House, and Cactus Jack picked up the Speaker's gavel that Nick had laid down.

Nick provided for his family in his will, written nine months after Paulina's birth. He left his estate to Alice and made her his executrix. Original estimates placed his wealth at more than $16 million, which surely caused Alice to hope that the newspapers knew something she didn't. Nick, as one family member recalled, "had spent his money as though he owned the mint." His worth was eventually figured at $825,000 in personal property and $800,000 in real estate, mostly his share of Rookwood and the everdwindling surrounding lands. In December 1932, the Cincinnati probate court ordered Alice to pay a $25,919 inheritance tax—this after almost $200,000 went to pay Nick's debts.[30] Alice and Paulina were not left with a king's ransom, but then Nick said no honest man ever got rich in politics.

Alice did not linger at Rookwood. By the end of May, she had resumed life in Washington, where family visited in various configurations to check on her. Clara stayed with her into May, and the two reminisced with Lou Hoover at the White House. The First Lady had been especially considerate toward Alice during Nick's illness and death, and Alice truly appreciated her "rare and remarkable gift of sympathy." Ted and Eleanor left Puerto Rico to confer with President Hoover, stopping in to see Alice and Paulina. Of all her family, Ted understood the permutations of the Longworth marriage because brother and sister had been so close and so often together in the 1920s. "I know," Ted soothed, "just how hard it is for you under all the circumstances."[31]

America expected Alice to act the grieving widow—and in part, she was. She and Nick were longtime intimates and comfortable friends, and his death brought sorrow as well as release. Yet the routine of her days, the ebb and flow of her years, would have to be reconfigured. Their marriage had been so open for so long that Alice and Nick had come to an easy place. The baby brought them closer together. Nick really did love Paulina. If he had his suspicions about Borah, he adhered to the gentleman's code: he never cast aspersions; he never made insinuations. He stood up for his wife during the Dolly Gann flap and the Cissy Patterson newspaper editorials. The timbre of their conversations during the pregnancy is lost, but Nick's letters after the baby's birth included a resurgence in his use of their early-marriage nicknames. Jointly caring for the infant brought out a tenderness and a vulnerability that had not existed between them for years. After Nick's death, uppermost in Alice's mind was Paulina, and how much she would miss her father.

Alice, in the prime of life, was pragmatic, self-absorbed, and apparently happy without a husband. But her daughter was turning out to be as shy as her mother, yet without the gumption to push past it. A Cincinnati native, Angela Meeske, met Paulina at a debutante party and found her "a very *receding* person. . . . She was just—there. She never contributed very much." A close friend of the family sighed that "Alice doted on Paulina. But what I always thought was key was that she never let Paulina finish a sentence. She would feed her a line. Wanted her to learn repartee. . . . The pressure made her stammer."[32] Of course, finishing a sentence for a child who stutters is a counterproductive but natural impulse. Today, a parent might seek out a therapist for a child whose father had died when she was six and who later developed a stutter and a painful shyness. But at the time, therapy was not a common option.

Alice's role models for motherhood were Edith and Bye. Had Alice stayed with her outgoing and charismatic aunt rather than growing up with her introverted stepmother, she may have been a different parent to Paulina. Alice had the ideal of Bye—warm, engaged, and conspiratorial—but the reality of Edith. Bye could not give her much childrearing advice, because she died not long after Nick. In August 1931, Bye succumbed to the multiple physical troubles that assailed her. The blow was great to Alice. Bye's "blue-eyed darling," Alice was present at Bye's simple funeral service, along with brothers Kermit and Archie. Auntie Corinne was there with her son. Eleanor Roosevelt and her mother-in-law Sara Delano Roosevelt were also among the mourners.[33]

As the cherry trees blossomed in Washington a year later, Alice's dear friend Ruth Hanna McCormick married Representative Albert Gallatin Simms. Simms was a banker and a rancher and a former U.S. congressman from New Mexico. The wedding took place in Colorado Springs, but Alice did not attend, perhaps because she had rather a different take on Simms than did Ruth: "Marry Albert Simms!" Alice was dumbfounded. "Sleep with him—one thing. But never marry him—how could she have done it!"[34] Ruth moved into her new husband's home in Albuquerque, which was beyond the political pale. Between the Simmses' cattle business, and her involvement in local political and civic affairs, Ruth—and her advice—seemed far away.

Yet Alice needed her. Ruth had been described as a woman who "always had a solution for every problem," and she had once faced Alice's terrifying problem: a kidnap threat. In late March 1932, guards surrounded Alice's home to protect the seven-year-old Paulina.[35] She had received two different notes, two weeks apart, directing her to deliver fifteen hundred dollars or the child would be taken. The police believed the letters were inspired by the tragic kidnapping of Charles and Anne Morrow Lindbergh's son. The heartbreaking disappearance of the Lindbergh baby on March 1, 1932, was sensational news across the globe. Front-page updates appeared daily on the too-slim body of knowledge officials were compiling on the captors. Rumors circulated about a kidnapping ring eying high-profile children, including Alice's daughter.

The first note Alice received commanded her to take a taxi to a specific place in the country, then drive eighteen miles an hour to a spot where a signal would be given for her to place the money one foot from the edge of the road. Alice sent a go-between, and although they followed the directions, there was no signal and no one picked up the cash. Alice asked that the guards be removed from her home, and she and Paulina left for New

York. Two days later, guards were posted at Ruth's sister's home to protect her six-year-old niece.[36] Eventually, the scares passed, and life returned to normal despite the unanswered questions about the whole ordeal.

Memories crowded Alice's spring, as the House of Representatives paid tribute to its late Speaker and to all members of Congress who had died during the previous year. Alice was present on May 25, for the first time since the closing day when Nick brought down the gavel. She listened as Burton L. French, from Borah's state, eulogized Nick as a "man of ability," "a man of strength," a man who "commanded the attention of his colleagues." On the one-year anniversary of Nick's death, the House adjourned in remembrance. As a mark of their love for him, friends created the Nicholas Longworth Foundation of the Music Division of the Library of Congress. Many donors remained anonymous, which may mean that "Nick's girls" wanted to remember the evenings spent together with Nick serenading guests on his violin.[37]

His widow carried on. She continued to be involved in politics and reportedly had "forty lawmakers" to her home as an audience for the German ambassador. Her name appeared with regularity in the newspaper columns. Alice watched Bill's press coverage wax in the months leading up to the 1932 political season. Their correspondence continued, festooned still with "Hellos." *Collier's* magazine proclaimed Borah "Idaho's gift to America," a "legend," "something of a Paul Bunyan." To interviewer Beverly Smith of the *American Magazine*, Borah castigated critics who called him inconsistent and destructive. In spite of being "in an extreme minority," Borah countered, laying out his accomplishments for voters, "I have been able to help with work which I think is unquestionably constructive: The fight for the eight-hour day. The creation of the Department of Labor. The creation of the Children's Bureau. The amendment providing for the election of senators by popular vote. My resolution calling for a disarmament conference which resulted in the naval disarmament treaty. My resolution calling for an economic conference which led to the Dawes Plan. My resolution, as early as 1923, calling for the outlawry of war." Besides, Borah told Smith, "constructive and destructive" mean different things to different people. "Blocking the entry of the United States into the League may be called destructive. To my mind it was one of the most constructive victories in our history." And as for his having blocked anti–child labor and woman's suffrage bills, Borah reiterated that these were matters best left to the states—but that he had "always favored" such legislation.[38]

The Democratic Party caused Alice distress. That year brought the alarming possibility of Alice's feather-duster cousin attaining the Oval Office. Alice used all the weapons at her disposal—news media, the radio, dinner parties—to defeat FDR and reelect Hoover. Although she liked Franklin personally, she loathed his politics, especially his foreign policy. She believed that she "really could have had a lot of fun with Franklin if only the damned old presidency hadn't come between us." His ascension was an affront to family honor, dating back to the bad blood created when Franklin ran for vice president and Ted jeered that he didn't "wear the brand of our family." Alice thought Franklin should have snapped back, " 'I wear no man's brand, not even the brand of my cousin to whom I was devoted, for whom I once voted.' Instead of that, he took it seriously and was frightfully cross about it. It hurt, you see." In 1924, Eleanor had heated up the trouble with her steaming teakettle giving the false but unforgettable impression that Ted had participated in the Teapot Dome scandal. "It was a pretty base thing for her to do," Alice felt, that "not unnaturally continued the bad feeling." But she admitted that her branch of the family "behaved terribly. There we were—*the* Roosevelts—hubris up to the eyebrows, *beyond* the eyebrows, and then who should come sailing down the river but Nemesis in the person of Franklin."[39]

The thought of FDR in the White House so appalled Alice that she served on the board of directors of the women's division of the GOP in 1932. Lou Henry Hoover asked her to work in other ways, including on an advisory panel that boasted notable women such as Ruth Hanna McCormick Simms, tennis star Helen Wills Moody, three former First Ladies, and several college presidents.[40] Alice's friendship with the educated and multitalented First Lady had reached the point where the latter was sending floral remembrances of Paulina's birthday and presents for Christmas. Many of the leading Republican women were friends. Dolly Gann served as president of the Republican Women's League in 1932 and spent a cold January on a campaign speaking tour for Hoover. Her task was to defend him against charges that he had caused the economic crisis. Ruth was concentrating on her new marriage, but found a breathtaking two hundred thousand dollars to donate to Hoover's cause.[41]

Beginning on June 14, 1932, the Republicans gathered in Chicago—Alice's favorite convention city—in order to choose their presidential nominee. From her base at the Blackstone Hotel she was in her element. "Look, there's Alice," people called as she made the rounds of the Coliseum floor, assessing support for vice presidential hopefuls. Newspapers noted that Alice was the only dignitary sitting in reserved boxes "who dared leave the enclosure of the sacred elite and walk about with democracy."[42]

The prohibition amendment was a topic of great interest, as the rumor that the Democratic platform would commit to repeal made Republicans scramble for a middle ground. From the NBC studio Alice listened in to the radio debate between her journalist friend William Allen White and Columbia University president Nicholas Murray Butler on June 14. At the Republican convention headquarters, the resolutions committee was busy looking for the path congenial to the greatest number of voters.[43] Bill Borah did not tread it. The appellation Enigma stuck to Borah, a bundle of contradictions. "Whether I am a Republican or not... is an issue between myself and my constituents," he blustered. Public sentiments like that helped to seal his fate. The Republican Party passed him by in 1932—again. Herbert Hoover and Charlie Curtis were renominated without fuss on a platform that opposed direct handouts to counter the effects of the Depression, and put its faith in the tariff, federal belt tightening, and voluntary efforts to alleviate local financial distress.

Later that month, Alice returned to her Blackstone suite for the Democratic national convention. Because of her interest in conservationism, delegate Dudley Field Malone suggested that Alice should be appointed secretary of the interior, as flattering as it was unlikely. She found much to interest her, especially the moment when William Gibbs McAdoo released the California and Texas votes, putting Franklin Roosevelt over the top. Cactus Jack Garner won the second-place spot on the ticket. Alice and former New York governor Al Smith—who lost the presidential nomination to Roosevelt—shared a bitter, two-hour discussion about the outcome.[44]

The platform committed Democrats to the repeal of Prohibition, in a charge led—not surprisingly—by Garner. It also called for federal relief programs, help for farmers, an old-age pension, and a constricted tariff. But Democrats pledged themselves to more conservative measures: a balanced budget, "sound currency," "removal of government from all fields of private enterprise," and, like the Republicans, more federal budget cuts. FDR flew to Chicago to accept the nomination from convention delegates personally. He bucked the tradition that kept the nominees away to prove that, despite his polio, he was physically able to do the job. He walked laboriously but proudly to the podium on the arm of his son and promised all Americans "a new deal."[45]

After the Chicago hoopla was over, the Hoovers hosted a garden party for Republican leaders, prefatory to the official notification that Hoover had the GOP's backing. The First Lady invited the "real" Roosevelts to the White House garden party. Edith, Alice, and Ethel were the "center of interest." Alice, dressed in black and white—symbolic of the political differences between the two branches of the family—and Ethel held their own informal reception with the Marine Band for accompaniment. In the Blue Room, Edith stood supportively beside the presidential couple but wouldn't give a statement: "I haven't talked for the press, not in seventy-one years, and it's too late to begin now," she said mildly.[46]

The three Roosevelt women were near to President Hoover when he gave his acceptance speech that night in Constitution Hall. Edith sat on the platform, holding a bouquet of roses. Alice and Ethel sat in a box to her right. The speech opened the campaign season, and Alice threw herself into it. She joined Edith, Grace Coolidge, Helen Taft, Carrie Chapman Catt, and other notable women in signing an appeal to female voters, urging them to cast their ballots for Hoover in 1932. Alice published an article, "Some Reminiscences," in the widely read *Ladies' Home Journal,* explaining how her aid for Hoover did not come at the expense of "any personal feel-ing" against her fifth cousin FDR.[47]

Alice and the First Lady toured the Midwest, heading up parades in Indianapolis, where Alice was slated to speak, sharing platforms with state and local Republican leaders, catching bouquets, waving from the backs of trains, and greeting voters. "I'm glad to see my fellow buckeyes," Alice told an excited crowd in Cincinnati. In Columbus, she made a longer speech—thirty-one words. She explained that she had gotten "so carried away with the . . . spirit of the meeting that I just had to talk."[48]

That was a warm-up for her first real political speech, broadcast over national radio and given in Cincinnati. The importance of the battle was obvious, and family honor was at stake as well.[49] Alice's fear of speaking in public was legendary, yet she stood close to the microphone and let her cousin have it: "It seems to me that, regardless of the result, when we look back on this campaign, two things will stand out. The first of these is the extra-ordinary extent to which the Democratic party has based its fight upon the discontent of the people, bred of the world-wide depression. The calculated effort to capitalize on this condition without anything remotely resembling a sound plan for its relief, strikes me as an unusually ignoble policy for a great party and one of which its more high-minded members must, in their more candid moments, be completely ashamed." She found it particularly gruesome that Democratic propaganda suggested Hoover cre-ated and then prolonged the Great Depression, and stated that such efforts take "first rank among examples of conscious and unscrupulous partisan dishonesty." She charged that the record in the Democratic-controlled House was so bad that even they wouldn't talk about it:

> On the contrary, it muzzles those who were largely responsible for that record, tries to forget that the record was made, and its spokes-men denounce Mr. Hoover as preaching the doctrine of fear when he points out in detail what would have happened to the country had the Democratic proposals prevailed.

Why should we not shudder at the idea of putting the Democratic

party in complete control of the government in these critical times? I
hope those who are listening to me will let their memories go back to
the last session of Congress. The Democrats in the Senate, with no
program of their own, had to support Mr. Hoover's reconstruction
recommendations, which they now denounce. In the House the Democrats scuttled their own program in a way that alarmed and appalled
their own leaders, in and out of Congress. If not thwarted by the
President's vetoes, they would have plunged us into the chaos of national insolvency. When you consider this record, the promises and
pledges that they now make with such prodigal abandon for campaign
purposes, seem fantastic and absurd.

Her ringing conclusion was a small-*d* democratic one, suggesting that
voters should not be misled by their financial woes or the glamour of Franklin Roosevelt. "I do not believe in talking down to the voters. That is precisely what the Democrats do believe in doing. They belittle the intelligence
of the average citizen, and I, as an average citizen, resent it. There is no
more impressive sight than a great free people flocking to the polls. This
year we face a test. Are we truly free; free from prejudice, from resentment,
from blind bitterness, free within ourselves to cast our vote with patriotism, with intelligence, with faith? If we are we will vote for Herbert
Hoover."[50]

Edith applauded. The two saw eye to eye on this topic. "I suddenly
thought today," Edith wrote to Belle Hagner, "what Franklin D. stood for.
It is not Delano but Depression." Energized by her behind-the-scenes battles against FDR's presidential bid, septuagenarian Edith became the honorary chair of the F. Trubee Davison for Governor Women's Republican
Club in New York. Ethel agreed to serve as the active chair of the committee. Edith gave a Hoover campaign speech in Madison Square Garden. As
she complained to a friend, "These are trying times for us, and the confusion of names does not help. Continually letters [arrive] congratulating me
on my distinguished son the Democratic nominee. His line parted six generations ago from my husband's." Alice coped with the same confusion,
receiving letters about "her brother's nomination to the presidency."[51]

The Oyster Bay Roosevelts were disappointed in 1932. The Great Depression had ravaged Americans for nearly three years, and voters blamed the party in power. Anxious for change, they voted overwhelmingly for Franklin Roosevelt and the Democrats. Ted, who had been appointed governor-general of the Philippines in January 1932, took to telling those who asked about his relationship with the new president that he was FDR's "fifth cousin, about to be removed." Alice said often that she "wasn't so much for Hoover, than against Franklin, in a *nasty* way."[52]

Chapter 18

"The Washington Dictatorship"

IN JANUARY 1933, Alice Longworth had lunch with British diplomat Harold Nicolson. His subsequent description captured the essence of the mature, widowed Alice—in her prime and at her fighting best—nearly the age of fifty: "My word, how I like that woman!" he wrote to his wife, Vita Sackville-West. "There is a sense of freedom in her plus a sense of background. That, I feel, is what is missing in this country. Nobody seems to have anything behind their front.... But Alice Longworth has a world position, and it has left her simple and assured and human. It was a pleasant luncheon: you know, the sort of luncheon where one feels mentally comfortable and warm."[1]

About this time Alice's relative Joseph Alsop arrived in Washington. Joe was a sportswriter who moved on to news and became a syndicated columnist for the *New York Herald Tribune*. A pro–New Deal Republican, he amused Alice, and he regularly lunched at the F Street Club with her and the "then-famous, extremely conservative, and sharp-tongued" *Baltimore Sun* columnist Frank Kent, whom Alsop called "Mrs. L's admirer." "The object of these lunches," Alsop recalled, "was the destruction of political characters and political pretenses." Alice's impatience with pomposity was legendary, and government service, especially elected service, seemed to draw pretension like no other career.[2]

From Alsop's memoirs, a fuller picture of Alice in the 1930s emerges. Joe, nearly thirty years younger than Alice, described her as "very beautiful in a fine-boned way." He found her courageous, "witty, intelligent, and tough minded, [with] a mortal horror of anything or anyone with the least savor of gush or sentimentality, earnest dullness or overly ostentatious virtue. Such persons she enjoyed shocking, sometimes profoundly, as she had done to Eleanor Roosevelt since they were children together."Alsop, like so many others, enjoyed but had a hard time defining Alice's distinctive wit: "No one I have ever known had a wit like hers. It depended on extreme precision of language, combined with the wildest fancy which produced the most astonishing combinations. When [utilities executive and attorney] Wendell Willkie was nominated as the Republican presidential candidate at Philadelphia in 1940, I remember foolishly saying that the movement for Willkie came from the grassroots. Mrs. L gave a loud snort and said, 'Yes, from the grassroots of 10,000 country clubs.' "[3]

Alice Longworth did not confine herself to witticisms during the years of Democratic rule, for it was then that she really began looking on the world with detached malevolence.[4] The problem was, she cared too deeply about the future of the country to be entirely detached. But the malevolence she directed full force at her cousins. Attacking her archrivals was satisfying because she truly felt that the Democratic Roosevelts were making mistakes that carried profoundly disturbing political and global ramifications. Yet her malice was tempered by ambivalence. This is evident in the kinder things she said later, especially about Eleanor. During the 1930s and 1940s, though, Alice became known for the pitiless precision of the verbal daggers she could aim. When the New Deal years were over and the other Roosevelts gone, that reputation remained.

The day before Franklin Delano Roosevelt was inaugurated as president of the United States, Alice Longworth had taken her daughter to the White House to wish Herbert and Lou Hoover bon voyage. "Oh, it was grim," Alice recalled. The presidential couple "sat like waxworks, all stiff, bruised, and wounded." Those same words might have applied to her. FDR's ascension to the nation's highest office opened a new chapter for Alice. The previous decade of close ties to the party in power and easy access to the White House and the legislative halls ended. She continued to draw powerful policy makers to her, but in the 1930s, they were the outs. Instead, "hovering around" her, as she put it, were the "sufficient number of people who didn't like Franklin." That included her brother Ted. He tendered his resignation as governor-general of the Philippines to the new president and had it accepted. Borah retained his senatorial seat, but his was now the minority party. Alice was angry about the election results—she had worked hard to reelect Hoover, and FDR was in the place her brother ought eventually to have occupied—but she nonetheless watched the inaugural ceremonies from a ringside seat, thanks to the invitation sent her by cousin Eleanor. She then dined with the new First Family afterward.[5]

Friends occupied her days now that Paulina was eight years old and in school full time. Alice socialized with the Pinchots, whose presence brought back memories of her father, and with Sinclair Lewis and his wife, Dorothy Thompson, a fascinating couple whose writings she enjoyed. She was closest to columnist Frank Kent, humorist Will Rogers, and longtime Washington cronies like Evalyn McLean. In a gossipy 1931 book, society commentators characterized Alice as "brilliant if not gifted, who through the prestige of her position and the vitriol of her tongue dominates Washington's ultra-fashionable official group more completely than any other whip-cracker in the capital." Alice had a circle of friends in New York City centered around theater critic and raconteur Alexander Woollcott. Though not officially associated with his Algonquin Round Table, a group of luminaries from the worlds of arts and letters, Alice moved among the Algonquin members on her frequent visits to New York City.[6]

Friends such as these were invited to teas and dinners at her 2009 Massachusetts Avenue home. Joe Alsop described Alice's house in the mid-1930s as "a large, hospitable, remarkably ill-kept establishment." Mrs. L— as he and others called her—"stuck to the old way" of entertaining, especially concerning her table. He outlined a typical spring dinner: "The best creamed crab soup I have ever had or else a consommé so strong one felt one could skate on it. If the start was consommé, this was followed by soft-shell crabs, perfectly sautéed, without any of the carapace of crumbs that deviant chefs in those days had begun to give them. The accompanying salad contained tomatoes sliced paper thin and skinned, and cucumbers properly soaked in salt, and therefore, limp and less bitter to taste. The main course was usually a saddle of lamb—enough so that guests could eat as many slices as wanted—with glorious fresh vegetables. All this was followed by crème brulée, which her cook knew how to make better than any other in my experience."[7]

The talk was always political, and the tone grew increasingly intolerant of Democratic plans as President Roosevelt unveiled the package of legislation he hoped would heal America's domestic problems. In his first inaugural speech, Roosevelt famously told Americans that "the only thing we have to fear is fear itself." He quickly called Congress into session, and the "first hundred days" of legislation began. Bills for banking reform, agricultural assistance, and relief measures poured out. As FDR's New Deal programs attacked the financial problems most Americans faced, the Roosevelts, insulated from the worst of it by their wealth, attacked FDR. Edith had taken to referring to "the Republican Roosevelts" to differentiate her family from the Democrats in the White House. (Alex Woollcott called them the "out of season Roosevelts.") Archie's politics were moving further to the right than anyone else's in the family, and he could not even talk about the New Deal with some of his friends. "Shooting and fishing… seem to be the only pleasant things we can discuss together," he wrote grumpily to one New Deal administrator.[8]

Not all of the Democratic Roosevelts felt unalloyed happiness at FDR's election. Though in sympathy with her husband's policies, Eleanor nonetheless mourned the loss of privacy and the freedom of movement she feared would accompany her rise to First Lady. Her model for the position was Aunt Edith, who had treasured most the rare private times with her husband and family. But Eleanor would construct the role differently. In the crisis of the Depression, she soon picked up where she left off as First Lady of New York. There, she had taken leading positions in organizations such as the League of Women Voters, the National Consumers League, and the Democratic Party. In part, Eleanor had channeled the hurt and betrayal of FDR's extramarital affair with Lucy Mercer into a productive agenda, returning to the type of service she had performed in the Rivington Street settlement house and the Junior League at the time of her marriage. She worked with social activists such as Maud Schwartz, Rose Schneiderman, and Frances Perkins. Her circle in the 1920s and 1930s also came to include many women-identified women, like Elizabeth Lape and

Esther Read, Marion Dickerman and Nancy Cook, and Mary Dewson and Polly Porter—all but the last activists in related causes. Alice referred to them as Eleanor's "female impersonators," but Franklin could be just as cruel, joking about her " 'squaws' and 'she-men.' "[9]Alongside these reformers, Eleanor gained valuable experience that she put to use as she and Franklin evolved a working partnership. Eleanor became her husband's eyes, ears, legs—even a prototype spin doctor through her various published writings. Together the presidential couple assessed the impact of the Great Depression on the United States.

Republicans had been at a loss and uncertain about how to turn around an unemployment rate of nearly 25 percent and bank closures in every state. Roosevelt thus enjoyed a honeymoon period with some Republicans. Not Borah. Though in poor health, the senator managed to launch an attack on the National Industrial Recovery Act almost as soon as New York Senator Robert Wagner introduced it in June 1933. Borah played a very small role in the "first hundred days' " legislation of the New Deal because of painful "serious intermittent hemorrhages." Debate over the National Industrial Recovery Act went on without him. He was forced to enter Johns Hopkins Hospital for surgery. The cause of his pain was a significantly enlarged prostate, and while the operation was successful, the recuperation was slow, and he celebrated his sixty-eighth birthday from his hospital bed.[10]

Alice kept up the fight. She engaged in guerrilla warfare—stealthy, persistent, devastating. FDR announced that the United States should abandon the gold standard, and Alice was sitting in the Senate gallery next to Will Rogers as the bill passed. In "the Roosevelt tradition," Rogers reported, she "took it right on the chin and smiled." Behind the smile lurked anger. Like other Republicans, she saw this step as a foolhardy abandonment of sound money principles. Not long after the vote, Alice sauntered into a White House reception wearing her ideology. She was bedecked in gold: a golden pendant hanging on a gold necklace, a gold watch, gold hair combs. A crowd quickly gathered around her. Then, according to the *Chicago Tribune*, "she did her stunt" of "wiggling her ears in a truly professional way, causing the huge golden eardrops to dangle and jump." Alice made her point, and it was all the more striking because she seldom wore extravagant jewels. Humorist Cal Tinney joked, "If F.D.R. could have taken her to the Treasury and deposited her, the deficit would have turned into a surplus."[11]

At another White House reception President Roosevelt told Alice smugly that he was poised to sign a bill that would save the ailing country fifty million dollars. "That's a drop in the bucket," she leveled at him, "compared to what you are costing the country." Part of her calculated campaign was never to refer to Franklin as President Roosevelt. She enjoyed this, because it made him "wince."[12] Only in her published writings did she use his legal title, but in private it was always his first name.

Some of her most memorable one-liners were aimed at her cousins. She damned them both by suggesting that Franklin was "one-third mush and two-thirds Eleanor."[13] As the New Deal wore on and more and more legislation came pouring out of Washington, Alice huffed that the pants ought to come off Eleanor and go on Franklin. Since she believed that the New Deal was limiting the country, Alice drew an analogy: she said, "Nobody should ever underestimate the way he behaved when he had infantile paralysis, and how he had managed to adjust himself to a permanently crippled condition. I maintained that in the same way, he was trying to adjust this great lusty country into the same condition as his own." Even she admitted later that "that was pretty nasty." At a different time, she called Franklin a " 'Mollycoddle,' with a 'Mollycoddle Philosophy.' " These sorts of cuts went to the heart of her cousins' private weak spots: Franklin's paralysis and Eleanor's lesbian friends. It was humor of a sort only a relative could deliver.[14] Alice's "Eleanor face" was both a good likeness and very cruel. As she had with her "Mrs. Taft face," Alice did the Eleanor impersonation with the least encouragement. She contorted her mouth to mimic ER's prominent teeth, and copied Eleanor's high voice, ending her exclamations in a screech. Eleanor, who turned her pain inward—the opposite of her cousin—once asked Alice for a demonstration. It apparently hurt.

Alice might not actually have had the effect she intended, though. According to Eleanor's particular friend former journalist Lorena Hickok, Alice suffered some "discomfort" as she watched the effect of her Eleanor face on its inspiration. Mary Borah claimed that Eleanor "seemed to enjoy it.... [And a]fter that no one worried about their not getting along." The cousins could put aside their differences for the children; Henrietta Nesbitt, the Roosevelts' housekeeper, stated that Paulina "came over quite often to play with her White House cousins." ER generously offered to look after Paulina and included her in White House dinner invitations. She sent notes to Alice telling sweet stories about their young relatives. Both of them signed their letters "affectionately." Eleanor had lunch with Alice at Rookwood in 1938. "We never allow politics to come between us," Alice told a columnist. On more than one occasion a friend of Alice's heard her tell of how very beautiful she thought Eleanor was as a young woman, and how she admired her cousin for having overcome such a truly horrible childhood. Upon serialization of Eleanor's autobiography, *This Is My Story*, Alice exclaimed, "Did you realize Eleanor could write like that? It's perfect; it's marvelous...." One biographer asserted that Alice "could and did damn the new President, but let anyone outside the family say a single word against him and she would glare icily and remind the offending speaker that...members of her tribe were not to be spoken of in a derogatory manner." For example, Alice maintained that Franklin and his secretary, Missy LeHand, were not lovers, and did not hesitate to tell people that.[15]

Nevertheless, Alice's vituperation toward Franklin and Eleanor during the years they inhabited the White House, and even after, was relentless. Friends have suggested that Alice had been profoundly frustrated with Nick, because the apex of his ambition was only Speaker of the House; with Borah, who could not seem to curb his contrariness at those crucial four-year intervals; and with Ted, who failed to take her advice to return from Puerto Rico in time to resume his climb up the GOP ladder to the presidency.[16] Alice was a gambler used to winning, but she did not seem able to pick a man to whom she could hitch her star. Then, when Eleanor—she of little humor, grace, or wit—and Feather Duster Franklin made it to the White House instead of her, the reason behind the sharpness of the jabs at her cousins came into focus. If Alice was the smartest of TR's children, she was also stunted by her shyness and barred by her gender from the nation's highest office. "Nemesis in the person of Franklin," she said often. "We were out. Run over."[17]

The Roosevelts were not the only topic of interest to her. In the midst of the Great Depression, cave dwellers turned their energies to establishing the Washington National Symphony Orchestra. Alice sat on the national campaign committee and handwrote notes to potential subscribers.[18] She helped in an unusual way, too. Newly arrived Polish immigrant and virtuoso violinist Roman Totenberg made his American debut in November 1935 with the symphony. Before a glittering audience, Totenberg played Beethoven's Concerto in D minor on Nick's violin. One of Nick's former infatuations, poet and music patron Alice Dows, had convinced Alice that the young violinist would be worthy of the instrument. To keep it in good shape, and to help further the career of the already-decorated musician, Alice loaned the violin to Totenberg. Alice Dows paid the insurance "as long as Totenberg uses it," because, Dows told her, "You are doing a very generous and grand thing in letting him have it and I am eternally grateful." Two months after his debut, Totenberg played at the White House. The violinist recalled the president telling everyone, "That's the violin that [belonged to] old Nick," and joking, "I hope Mr. Totenberg plays it better than Nick did!" Alice was not invited that night, but Bill and Mary Borah were there to hear.[19]

Nick's violin was not, as was commonly assumed, a Stradivarius. Like nearly everyone else, Totenberg and Dows thought it was made by Antonio Stradivari, the seventeenth-century master violin maker. Around 1945, Totenberg queried a representative from London's W. E. Hill Company about the instrument. It was the Hill Company's opinion that Nick's violin "was a very good copy by [Giuseppe] Rocca," Totenberg recalled. Alice had the violin appraised by Rembert Wurlitzer in 1957 for tax purposes. Wurlitzer concluded that Nick's violin was "the work of some skilled copyist and is definitely not an original Stradivari." He placed its value at five hundred dollars. He thought it an excellent copy and felt it would have been hard for most people to tell it was a replica. Roman Totenberg's fame increased, and he eventually acquired a Stradivarius of his own in the early 1950s. At that time, he returned Nick's violin to Alice over a "very nice" tea at her home. Totenberg felt Alice expressed no more than an average interest in classical music. She was in the habit of attending the symphony in the afternoons in the 1930s and 1940s, and the popular riparian concerts along the Potomac. In 1957, Alice loaned Nick's violin to another violinist. The incomprehensible rumor that later emerged that Alice burned Nick's valuable Stradivarius is thus trebly incorrect.[20]

Alice was not immune to the economic downturn caused by the Great Depression, and no New Deal program existed for her. Nick's death had meant a substantial decrease in her income. Of course, poverty was relative. Like Alice, Evalyn McLean suffered from both the loss of her husband and the Depression. Looking one day for commiseration, Evalyn arrived on Alice's doorstep in tears and bearing her itemized budget. "Alice, what will I do?" Evalyn wailed, "I simply can't get my budget below $250,000 a year. Flowers, $40,000; household, $100,000; travel, $35,000. . . ." Past her initial shock, Alice, a good friend, "knew what was expected of her. 'Evalyn,' she said, 'you are quite right. You simply can't shave it one cent.' "[21]

Alice was never destitute, but she did take the advice of friends who suggested she capitalize on her continuing fame by writing a memoir. Alice embarked on the task in the fall of 1932, but soon found that writing bored her. Still, she managed to produce the required pages. She called it *Crowded Hours,* a title borrowed from her father's description of his exciting Rough Rider days. The book was published by Charles Scribner's Sons, which paid Alice a five-thousand-dollar advance. They promoted the book nationally with newspaper advertisements focused on the holiday gift-giving season. Parts of *Crowded Hours* were serialized in teasers for *Ladies' Home Journal.* Alice wrote as she liked, sparing no one, though the editors, she complained, took out the "hardest cracks." Alice enjoyed nothing about the book writing but the publicity. "By the time the proof reading was over," she told Belle Hagner, "on top of months of unaccustomed work, and that work writing—think of me writing, my angel!—I was so bored by it that I could see no shred of worth in it." She went to recuperate with Laura Curtis.[22]

The *Ladies' Home Journal* articles ran through the fall of 1932, while the presidential race was underway, which allowed her to use them as a way to puff Hoover. *Crowded Hours* was published in October 1933. Alice reveled in the revival of her fame. Like her cousin Eleanor, Alice received "a smattering" of votes in a magazine poll of the women who contributed to American progress in the past century. She even attended an Author's League fund-raiser for "needy authors," where she was embarrassed to find that she'd pulled her own name out of the hat for the prize of a first edition of Charles Dickens's *Pickwick Papers*. Her autobiography was on the bestseller list for weeks. ALICE ROOSEVELT SEARS NOTABLES OF FORMER DAYS, the *Chicago Tribune* headline read. "A sparkling flood of reminiscences," crowed a *New York Times* reviewer. Strangers and old friends—such as John McCutcheon, Frank Lowden, and Samuel McClure—sent congratulatory notes. Speaking requests poured in, most of which she declined. She gave a lecture entitled "I Believe in America" in Chicago in November 1938. The program chair from a Republican women's club pleaded for her to send "a short note, a challenge to inspire us...." The Dwinell-Wright Company asked Alice to update and complete *The Story of the White House and Its Home Life,* which she did. This was a fifteen-cent book, sixty-three pages long with her signature scrawled across page 61. She wrote the last eleven pages in first person, covering presidential families from her own to the Franklin Roosevelts. Charming and complimentary, her stories were calculated for the broadest possible audience and were not objective. The Hardings merited only one paragraph, while her friends the Coolidges were awarded seven. Even Mrs. Taft fared better than Florence Harding, who was dismissed in half of a sentence.[23]

To exploit her resurgent fame, Ponds cold cream reissued its previous advertisement. "Today Mrs. Longworth guards her skin's freshness with the same two creams she used and praised seven years ago," read the ad. It showed the photo of Alice in 1925 alongside a photo of "Mrs. Longworth today—fresher, more vital looking." "I never use makeup," Alice swore. "I never use anything on my face that I am not absolutely sure of." Ponds called her "one of the most vital figures in political and diplomatic circles in Washington."[24]

When Ted and his wife, Eleanor, returned home from the Philippines in early September 1933, Alice was thrilled to see them. It was not long before she and Ted launched their next project—one free of politics: a book of poetry that would be called *The Desk Drawer Anthology*. Alexander Woollcott was the inspiration. Sunning themselves at Woollcott's lakefront home in Vermont, Ted and Woollcott idly discussed all the poets whose works were good but "somehow escaped the accident of fame," and how most anthologies were little more than the favorite poems of the editor. They wondered whether an anthology could be created for which all of America did the selecting. If Ted and Alice would edit the entries, Woollcott promised to use his popular *Town Crier* radio show to ask listeners to send in their favorite poems for consideration—the ones they'd cut out and tucked in wallets or desk drawers so they'd have them to read again and again. More than forty thousand poems appeared as a result of his plea. It took Alice and Ted many months to read through and compile the poems, and the book was published by Doubleday, Doran just in time for Christmas 1937.[25]

Alice was also making a name for herself as a columnist. Although her policy was never to give interviews, she did feel free to express herself in print. "What Are the Women Up To?" she asked in a *Ladies' Home Journal* guest column in 1934. "Why haven't there been more than nineteen in Congress since they won the suffrage?" In this article the public glimpsed the political philosopher so well known to her friends. Alice wrote about the "unprecedented" women in government, such as "the best Secretary of Labor we have ever had," Democrat Frances Perkins; U.S. minister to Denmark Ruth Bryan Owen; and National Mint Director Nellie Tayloe Ross. "The fact remains, however," Alice mused, "that though women compose nearly half the vote, this is still a man's government...." She analyzed all the women in Congress, including Ruth Hanna McCormick and Isabella Greenway. She highlighted the role of women in the earlier temperance and suffrage battles. She suggested that "it took more power to achieve the suffrage than women have shown since the achievement," but that it would still take "a few more campaigns" until women's power was commensurate with their past successes. Alice noted that men generally called upon women as consumers and moral watchdogs of New Deal legislation. And she wondered slyly, why "as [women] are such an important part of domestic economics, more of their sex have not been sent to Congress to help frame and pass the measures which it is claimed so vitally concern them, and about which they are supposed to have such practical knowledge in their business as managers of the family's budget." Women's interest in politics, Alice concluded, "is undoubtedly more alert and intelligent than it has ever been before." It was an optimistic conclusion and a sophisticated read of the way male politicians were attempting to disenfranchise women since suffrage and to shift their power from the ballot and the statehouse to the home.[26]

The First Lady did not merit mention in Alice's article, presumably because she was not an elected official. Alice and Eleanor remained in contact, but temperamentally and politically they were no closer than they had been a decade earlier when ER was a shy political wife frustrated by the vexing tradition of calling. Eleanor once explained to Corinne her view of herself as First Lady: "I never think of myself as mistress of the White House with casual people, much less with my family." Her informality meant a more permeable barrier than the president desired with their cousin. Alice and her criticisms drove him to the breaking point. FDR told his son once, "I don't want anything to do with that woman!"[27]

In her autobiography, Eleanor insisted that "neither Franklin nor I ever minded the disagreeable things my cousin Alice Longworth used to say during the various campaigns. When the social season started after the third campaign, in which Alice had been particularly outspoken, she was invited as usual to the diplomatic reception." FDR, who should have known better, bet an aide that she wouldn't have the courage to appear after damning him every which way for the previous nine months. Alice did show up: politics was politics, family was family, and she was always game for a battle—or a party. Jim Farley, standing in the reception line with the President and the First Lady while Alice was making her way toward them, overhead FDR say, "Eleanor, *your* relative, not mine, is fast approaching." She set him off with public displays of her criticism. ALICE FAILS TO APPLAUD COUSIN FRANK, the headline read in January 1934, after Alice—prominent in the Speaker's gallery—never once clapped throughout Roosevelt's State of the Union address. Republican women stood up for their chief, stoutly maintaining that Alice could not clap because she had to hold her lorgnette so she could see.[28]

"Wary" would characterize the relationship between Alice and her presidential relatives. Alice enjoyed attending White House functions to get a view from within the enemy's camp. Eleanor was both driven by duty and in a highly conspicuous position. Not including Alice in White House functions would be an affront to ER's sense of family duty and would give reporters the satisfaction of confirming their suspicions about an undignified family feud. "We were going to see a lot of" her, Mrs. Nesbitt affirmed.[29]

It wasn't until late in the second term that the First Lady pushed aside her tribal feelings. As Alice told the story, a rumor circulated suggesting that she loathed going to the White House and attended only because a presidential invitation—from a relative or not—was a command. Eleanor thereupon wrote Alice saying that she and Franklin never wanted Alice to feel uncomfortable, and she should only come when she really wanted to. "How disagreeable people are, trying to make more trouble than there already is between us...." Alice fired back. "I *love* coming to the White House. It couldn't be more fun and I have always enjoyed myself immensely." Eleanor publicly denied such a letter: " 'There is nothing to that,' she said. 'Long ago I told all those, including Alice, to whom invitations to all White House functions go regularly as a matter of routine, that I wanted them all to feel under no compulsion to accept all of them. But this alleged conversation with, or note to, Alice simply never happened.' " Alice was still summoned to important, high-profile gatherings such as the visit of King George and Queen Elizabeth of Great Britain in 1939—where she wore a "beige lace gown," her "wide brimmed brown hat," and carried "a shooting stick." Nevertheless, she received fewer and fewer invitations on the recognizable heavy white card stock. Alice regretted this. "Perhaps it gave them pleasure not to have me," she said, "but they should have been better winners. They could have said, 'Look here, you miserable worm, of course you feel upset because you wanted this. You hoped your brother Ted would finally achieve this, and now he hasn't. But after all, here we are.

Just come if it amuses you.' But they took it all seriously. They took the meanness in the spirit in which it was meant."[30]

And it was mean-spirited. "Eleanor," Alice scowled, "is a Trojan mare." The double jab—the First Lady's popularity as a front for the nefarious New Deal legislation, and a poke at Eleanor's lack of beauty—was a palpable hit. New Dealer Harold Ickes thought that Alice's allusions to her cousin "would have been in better wit if they had been in better taste." He put it down to jealousy. Whatever it was, it was obvious. Alice appeared the day after Eleanor did at a crowded 1939 art exhibit for the benefit of Polish war refugees. She discovered that her cousin had posed in front of a Picasso. "Very well, then," Alice said as she moved to a Renoir, "I'll take this one."[31]

Perhaps the cruelest treatment of Eleanor was Alice's encouragement of FDR's relationship with Lucy Mercer Rutherfurd, ER's former social secretary whose love letters ER had found in 1918. As the responsibilities of governing took their toll, President Roosevelt reached out to his former mistress, whom Alice described as "beautiful, charming, and an absolutely delightful creature. I would see her out driving with Franklin," Alice recalled of their early days, "and I would say things like, 'I saw you out driving with someone very attractive indeed, Franklin. Your hands were on the wheel but your eyes were on her.' " FDR kept the relationship a strict secret from Eleanor—and he brought Lucy to dine at Alice's home at least once. Not until Franklin's death did ER learn of the liaison, from cousin Laura Delano. During the rapprochement between Lucy and FDR, Alice may have tried to warn Eleanor, but the latter wouldn't hear it, saying primly that she "did not believe in knowing" what one's husband did not want one to know. It is not clear when or if Eleanor ever learned of Alice's complicity. But Alice was unrepentant. She believed that Eleanor "had so little enjoyment, so little amusement" and "she always seemed to manage to hold Franklin back from having a good time." That was the context for her oft-quoted "Franklin deserved a good time. He was married to Eleanor."[32]

Yet Alice and Eleanor had much in common beyond their shared family ties. Both women married men who sought out other women. As it would turn out, both men had mistresses by their sides at their deathbeds. The shock, humiliation, anger, and sense of betrayal commonly felt by spouses so deceived might once have made for a bond between Alice and Eleanor. But Alice, as one interviewer suggested, was very prickly in public and very warm in person, while Eleanor was the opposite. Even for those closest to her, Eleanor couldn't be affectionate. Eleanor confessed that she suffered from "Griselda moods" during which she played the silent and sullen martyr, making living with her at these times very difficult. Michael Teague, a close friend of Alice's in her last decades, heard her acknowledge she knew "why Eleanor was the way she was, but her way of dealing with it didn't make it any easier for the rest of us."[33] The Rooseveltian ability to protect interior sorrows with a steel exterior was deep in both Alice and Eleanor. The wounds inflicted by Nick's drinking were painful, but Alice did not bleed in public. Alice and Eleanor had such different personalities that they could not help but respond to their situations differently—Alice by erecting a wall of witticisms and Eleanor by taking refuge in duty.

Another reason that their husbands' infidelity failed to make the cousins into confidantes was the era. Society rewarded men and punished women for engaging in the same behavior: a woman had to be "good" enough to keep her husband, but men were considered more virile if they had mistresses. A sort of mystery attached itself to men who attracted scores of women—film heroes Rudolph Valentino or Douglas Fairbanks, for instance. Men who had such an insatiable appetite seemed to draw women to them, and if that were the case, no real blame could be attached to the wife, because clearly, no one woman could keep such a man happy within the confines of their home. Still, because the initial assumption would be that there was a flaw in the wife, women did not confess their husband's infidelities—especially not to their peers. Such secrets were hidden; not at all the sort of thing made public, even among public men. If a vast segment of the American citizenry did not know about President Roosevelt's withered legs, even fewer knew about the lighthearted women who could revive his spirits despite the domestic and international troubles that plagued him.

So while Alice knew about—and probably abetted—Franklin's affair,

Eleanor would likely have heard only unconfirmed rumors about Nick's. But even had they known the details of each other's private lives, it is highly unlikely that they ever would have wept on each other's shoulders. Alice didn't weep. Just like her cousin, she found friends to sustain her and threw herself into political causes. While Alice lived with Nick's straying for many years, Eleanor did not know about FDR's reunion with Mrs. Rutherfurd until after his death. And for Alice, Nick's unforgivable sin was his drunkenness, not the other women. It was alcohol that damped his political ambitions. Temperamentally, the cousins were just too unalike to be drawn together, despite their similarities. Alice didn't care for what she saw as Eleanor's kind of preachy, saccharine, do-goodism. At the time, Alice was only one of Eleanor's critics. In the 1930s and 1940s, she didn't have the image of the heroic Eleanor that exists today. Nearer to the end of her life, Alice softened about Eleanor. She could comment for posterity on Eleanor's "really remarkable achievements," and how, "of all the Presidents' wives, none used her position in quite the same effective way that Eleanor did."[34]

Meanwhile, Alice was assisting Nick's former lover Laura Curtis. Laura's financial status was so precarious as a result of the Great Depression that she was on the verge of selling her house at 1925 F Street, NW. Friends decided that it would be a terrible waste to dismantle the home, sell the antiques, and dismiss the efficient staff, so they convinced Laura to convert her home into a social club. The F Street Club, as it became known, was created when Laura's friends, including Alice, contributed their money and bought a membership. Founded in April 1933, the F Street Club became the spot for wealthy Republicans to air their grievances over turtle soup, filet mignon, homemade biscuits, and dessert. Its membership broadened slightly in later decades, but it remained the place, as one newspaper put it, to "hob nob with the people who make the political wheels turn in Washington."[35] Alice frequented the F Street Club, as did Ruth, as would other luminaries such as author and politician Clare Boothe Luce.

The Roosevelts were effecting real change nationwide through their activist policies by 1935. Looking for a change of scenery, Alice took ten-year-old Paulina on an extended European trip, primarily to visit

Longworth relatives in France. Alice, recently named one of the twelve "great women of today" by columnist Elsa Maxwell, waved from the deck of the *Manhattan* to reporters and to her brother Kermit, who came to see them off. The trip did not ease her mind about the course on which Franklin had set the country. Upon her return, she continued to watch him closely. She sat in the Senate gallery monitoring debates. She maintained her broad reading of newspapers. She was present at events like presidential vetoes, even when they turned out to be Democratic victories. And she wrote about her observations. She thought the government itself was becoming a "menacing" trust, because "under the New Deal, the Government has moved to join hands with private monopoly to control the entire Nation.... That is the clear objective of a large part of all New Deal policy; control and regimentation of resources and individuals...." Events overseas added to her qualms. Benito Mussolini had been in control of a resurgent Italy since 1922. Adolph Hitler ascended to power in Germany a decade later. As fascism spread across Europe, militarism and fear trailed menacingly behind. On October 3, 1935, Mussolini invaded Abyssinia (now Ethiopia). Poet Ezra Pound wrote perversely, "7 million of subjected population in Abyssinia will be benefited," but Alice did not share Pound's fascist tendencies, and she knew that FDR's "moral embargo" was an insufficient response benefiting neither U.S. businesses nor Ethiopians.[36]

Alice's very real concerns with her cousin's policies (and her own financial worries) led her to take up journalism in a more consistent fashion. She began writing a daily column for the McNaught Syndicate in late 1935. Her column had various names: "The National Scene," "Capital Comment," "Alice Longworth Says," and "Alice in Blunderland," among others. It was carried by papers that included the *Washington Star*, the *Los Angeles Times*, the *Cincinnati Times-Star*, the *San Francisco Chronicle*, and the *Ft. Worth Star Telegram*, and read in cities from Honolulu to Boston. Alice's column was a shot glass–size comment on contemporary events intended to go straight to the bloodstream. The topics were wide ranging, from the evils of living under Hitler's tyranny to the abdication of Great Britain's Edward VIII, the U.S. Good Neighbor policy toward Central and South America, to the U.S. farm problem. The columns, one enthusiastic reader thought, would "do more to set the world straight than many political speeches."[37]

Alice had rich fodder in the 1936 election year. Her editors hoped that her political savvy and wit would create a readership on the right, or steal readers away from the sugary chat that passed for comment—especially in the early days—of cousin Eleanor's "My Day" column. Eleanor really did chronicle her day's doings, but Alice generally kept herself out of her writing. Both women occasionally exhorted their readers to action, and Alice was not above giving advice to politicians such as Alfred Landon, the Republican Party's lackluster 1936 presidential nominee. She also used the column to continue her digs at Franklin. "You can always tell," she wrote, "when Mr. Roosevelt is feeling at the top of his form by his tendency to identify himself with the great. Last January he completely identified himself with Andrew Jackson, and on occasions he has confused his personality with that of Thomas Jefferson." He would run for a third term, Alice predicted that year: voters must be wary.[38]

She maintained a critical watch over the White House. Following is a typical sort of censure from her pen:

The balanced budget plank in the Democratic platform, if any one has the nerve to propose one, is going to look fairly sick. Along comes [Secretary of the Treasury] Mr. Morgenthau asking for another two billion mortgage on the future, in addition to the hundreds of millions of current cash called for by the tax bill. On the theory that "there's gold in them thar hills" the administration evidently believes there is money to spare in "them thar taxpayers."

Mr. Roosevelt sees automobiles running, airplanes flying, relief checks fluttering to their recipients, people generally going about their usual avocations. He is apparently convinced that everything is lovely, so he still talks in financial hyperbole, and makes another peacetime record for the national debt.

Moreover, the one and a half billion dollar relief fund is now to be turned over to him, to be disbursed under his personal direction. That will keep the privy purse well lined and should enable him to satisfy his itch for spending for at least a few months longer.[39]

Like a dagger, "The National Scene" could inflict a rapid and telling wound. Roosevelt's court-packing scheme she called "a direct move to tighten the Washington dictatorship." On giveaways to farmers in the election year, she quipped, "American agriculture never faced a more promising season, so far as the political fruit crop is concerned." Alice warned about the "black soil magic" of the administration's attempt to evade the Supreme Court in the first Agricultural Adjustment Act by passing a second AAA after the first was ruled unconstitutional. In three swift sentences, Alice exposed Harold Ickes's lust for power while simultaneously condemning the totalitarian turn of the Revolutionary Party in Paraguay: "The Paraguayan 'liberators' have outlawed politics for a year. They have also put capital and labor under the jurisdiction of the secretary of the interior. That must make Mr. Ickes' mouth water." Ickes had been a Bull Mooser before becoming FDR's secretary of the interior.

Like Borah, Alice did not spare her own party. She could be critical of Republican National Committee decisions and chastise individual politicians, even, as it turned out, when she loved them. Of Borah, she wrote that he spoke "with a fevered vigor. But it was not the same voice that has crowded the Senate galleries for so many years. Possibly it suffers in radio transmission." She attended the 1936 Republican convention as a delegate, but sought to keep the feet of the faithful to the fire. Alice's columns called for responsible and moral conduct by politicians and urged a more forcible Republican challenge of the Democratic hegemony.

While Alice's columns were journalistic jabs—sharp, short, and to the point—Eleanor's began as diffuse peregrinations across the scenery of her life. Readers told Alice their preference: "As for Mrs. Roosevelt's pathetic attempts to write[,] what she writes and the way she writes it is an offense to any discriminating literary palate. Why occupancy of the White House warrants foisting that sort of tripe on the public is beyond my comprehension. I presume I am just one of the millions of Democrats who are literally fed up to the teeth with sanctimonious New Dealers all talking and acting like God." Margaret Cobb Ailshie, an old friend of Alice's, then publisher of the *Idaho Statesman*, vowed her paper would carry Alice's column despite the expense, because "with all due respect to your cousin, I think her column on 'coughing at concerts' is the Ne Plus Ultra of what not to write and how not to write it." A reader brainstormed, "We have been paying our farmers for not raising hogs, cotton, corn, etc. I wonder if... there is not some way of paying Mrs. Roosevelt for not writing...." One fan letter came from a man born in 1856 who commended her for her "keen and clear cut grasp... on our political and economic conditions and ability to put it on paper." Others made suggestions for columns, and one helpful reader, answering his own question, wrote, "Why am I writing you this legal treatise? Just because you have the ear of many who have influence...."[40]

Her columns moved some readers to civic involvement: "I can not afford to contribute money" to politics, one woman wrote, "but I am a good secretary and would be glad to give my services gratis after business hours if I could ally myself with a sane and just man or organization." She asked for Alice's suggestions. "The National Scene" prompted one reader to put aside a bit of his misogyny: "When I find myself liking a woman columnist better each day really, it shocks me.... You see, frankly speaking, my appreciation of what women can do and how well they do it, has been and is, in the majority of cases, very, very low. You bring it up a little bit for WOMEN...."[41]

She did receive many fan letters from female readers. They wrote to tell her how they admired her "courage" and her "use of the sacred market of free expression." One woman enthused, "I have always thought of you as: Being good for The United States of America." More than one fan suggested her father would be proud of her, as "a chip off the old block, alright, a living counterpart of our own beloved T.R." or one who was "hitting them 'between the eyes' just like your father." Several readers suggested that she become vice president or president of the United States. One booster was specific: "I have my candidates all picked out for the [1936] Cleveland convention. It is not Hoover or Borah, it is Gov. Landon for president and Alice Longworth for Vice President."[42]

Alice's columns were based on her intimate knowledge of Washington politics—but as one of FDR's most vocal critics, she was no longer a White

House insider. Nevertheless, at her parties and in her columns she gave currency to speculations and considerations that bespoke a wide range of sources. "Two dramatic possibilities were much discussed during the Winter and Spring," her column pointed out in June 1936: that the Republicans would choose a Democrat for their vice presidential candidate, and that the anti–New Deal Democrats would stage a walkout at the GOP convention.[43] In her own circle of friends, Alice kept up a spikier criticism. She had fun circulating this parody of Edgar Allan Poe:

> From the White House of the Nation
> Speaking without hesitation
> Comes the voice of unchecked knowledge
>   From the lady, Eleanor.
> In the limelight gaily basking
> Speaks the lady, without asking;
> Like the brook that rushed onward,
>   Ever onward, evermore.
> Speaks the expert on great problems:
> Home and children, love and war:
> Speaks the lady,
>   Eleanor
>
> And this expert ever flitting,
> Never sitting, never quitting,
> Gives her pills of fancied knowledge
>   Wisdom from her stock and store.
> And we hear the painful sighing,
> Hear a population crying
> For the stilling of the ringing
>   Sound of Eleanor.
> But the voice still keeps advising,
> Criticizing and chastising,
> Moralizing, patronizing, sermonizing,
>   EVERMORE.[44]

Columnist James Reston remembered Alice's "collection of anti-Roosevelt speeches, newspaper clippings, and jokes, which she read out to her guests with boisterous laughter and spiteful comments of her own." For example, among her papers was a cutting poem entitled "Rejected." It tells the story of the devil meeting FDR at the gates of hell and challenging the president's credentials to enter. Franklin replied with a long list of his misdeeds ("I paid them to let their farms lie still / And I imported stuffs from Brazil"), and his meanness ("I furnished money with government loans / When they missed a payment I took their homes"), and his enjoyment of it all ("When I wanted to punish the folks, you know / I put my wife on the radio"). At the end of this litany, the devil sent FDR away from hell, telling him firmly, "For once you mingle with this mob, I'll have to hunt another job."[45]

Alice certainly had her own critics. A representative of the Gannett newspapers wrote to Alice's publisher wondering how "so colorful an individual as...Mrs. Longworth...can produce such conventional and uninteresting copy."[46] That was the main complaint about *Crowded Hours* as well: that she didn't write as well as she spoke. Alice's columns started soundly, and the asperity was fun to read. Even cousin Eleanor could admit to a friend that Alice "certainly writes well. I wish I were as free as she, though I do not wish ever to be as bitter." But Alice's columns lost their sparkle, even as Eleanor's gained in depth of analysis and seriousness of purpose, and Alice's was discontinued while Eleanor's ran until 1962. An editorial entitled "Eleanor vs. Alice" was not particularly complimentary to either woman, but it condemned Alice for being "strictly a Tory in character" and having "all of her father's self-assurance, but little of his discernment." The irony is that she may well have had her father's discernment, but because of her father, what Alice lacked was precisely self-assurance. It is difficult to remember that despite the column, and regardless of her reputation as a wit, Alice was "terribly shy," as she put it, and supremely self-critical, too. All this she hid from the public that found her "so charming and so gloriously alive."[47]

Though unafraid to aid her friends and attack her enemies, Alice could only watch helplessly as the Republicans lost in 1936. That election represented Bill Borah's last chance at the presidency, but his candidacy was doomed from the outset. The senator had a dedicated but powerless following. As one observer wrote in 1936, "Borah's chief handicap is Borah, and a lifetime of non-allegiance to those groups which he now needs to make him President." His determination to follow his own course drew to him unusual supporters such as fellow Idahoan Ezra Pound. The poet wrote to Senator Borah from Italy with some frequency in an attempt to convert him to fascism for the moment that Borah would assume the presidency. While the poet's dislike for FDR and for England resonated, Borah was not tempted by Pound's cant and kept his replies noncommittal. "I suggest," Borah wrote Pound, "that you come back to Idaho and to the United States. . . . I can talk better than I can write. So drop in when you get home and see me."[48]

Many of Borah's backers saw him as Theodore Roosevelt's heir. In a 1936 word portrait, Bill Hard, a journalist friend, compared Borah to bedrock. The name called up the simplicity of western life and the red rock hills that helped create Borah, and the fact that he—unlike the effete easterner Franklin Roosevelt—knew how to get down to fundamentals. Hard came upon Borah sitting behind a newspaper, but surrounded by Mary Borah and her friends at luncheon:

> As usual, by himself. As usual, reading. As usual, making no festivity whatsoever of eating.
>
> And who, indeed, could possibly make any sort of festivity out of his sort of eating? Unaccompanied by any malt, vinous or spirituous liquors. Unaccompanied by tea or coffee. Unfinished by cigars or cigarettes or even a pipe. Just food. Consumed, apparently with the sole desire of acquiring enough strength to do some more reading.
>
> I am struck by his amazing withdraw-ness from other human beings, and by his equally amazing lack of upstage-ness in his dealings with them. He is both as "homey" as an old shoe, and as far away as the moon.[49]

Hardly the sort of thing to inspire the undecided voter.

As her column gained adherents, Alice could have used it to promote Borah's candidacy. She did not. Perhaps their relationship was cooling. Their letters taper off in the early 1930s, but they may simply have switched to the telephone with Nick gone. Other party members sought Alice's endorsement, and she received letters from elected officials such as Frederic C. Walcott of Connecticut, who wanted to "explain my vote to override the President's veto of the Independent Offices Appropriation bill." The Women's National Republican Club made her a guest of honor at their fifteenth anniversary celebration in January 1936 at the Hotel Astor. Senator Robert A. Taft and President Ulysses S. Grant's granddaughter, the Russian princess Julia Grant Cantacuzene, spoke before an audience of eighteen hundred stalwarts who craned their necks to see the famous Alice Longworth. Two weeks later, she attended the massive anti–New Deal Liberty League dinner, whose two thousand guests included a who's who of politics and business. Ohio Republicans were proud to have Alice sit on the State Central Committee to choose the slate and the voting agenda for the fifty-two Buckeye delegates to the national convention. In the end, Alice and the others chose Ohio's "favorite son" Robert A. Taft, rather than Borah, who was running his own full slate in Ohio.[50]

The campaign loomed. Alice went as a columnist and as a Cincinnati delegate to the GOP national convention to vote as instructed for the son of her former enemy, Taft, rather than for the father of her child. If she felt a moral quandary, she was publicly jaunty. She and Ruth were inseparable, two among nearly sixty female delegates in Cleveland and members of the preliminary platform committee as well. Ruth, able and prepared, told reporter Kathleen McLaughlin that she expected that three women were likely prospects for the GOP's committee on resolutions: Alice, Corinne, and herself. Alice was not chosen for that influential committee "for no reason," as veteran political reporter Arthur Krock put it, "that seemed significant in the larger convention sense." Instead, Mildred Reeves—Nick's former secretary—won that seat.[51]

The Cleveland convention turned out to be Borah's last stand. Seventy years old and fighting for the Republican nomination against Landon, Frank Knox, and Arthur H. Vandenberg, Borah never mustered the enthusiasm necessary to push him to the front. His support was confined to the western states and the party was trying desperately to seek voters nationwide as it faced the undeniable popularity of Franklin D. Roosevelt. Landon became the GOP's standard-bearer, with Knox as the vice presidential candidate. That "had a strong appeal," Alice told her readers, because Knox had been "with my father in the Rough Riders and followed him into the Progressive party in 1912."[52]

Alice and Corinne were two of the women the RNC called to serve that year on the recreated Women's Council of 100, whose job was tracking national electoral challenges. Alice asked novelist Mary Roberts Rinehart to join. Ethel Barrymore and other friends also added their names to the list.[53] The first incarnation had been organized in 1919 with the goal of returning a Republican to the White House. All of the original members were summoned back to "active duty." Their main job in 1936 was to get Alfred Landon elected.

Alice kept up the drumbeat in her columns as she surveyed the Democratic convention from her seat in the press section. She accused Senator Joe T. Robinson of alchemy when he told the faithful in Philadelphia that FDR had "complied with the spirit of" the 1932 Democratic Party platform. "If the spirit of black is white," Alice blasted, "if the spirit of sour is sweet, then the Senator is using his words correctly. But never, outside of metaphysical speculation, has the word spirit been called upon to bear such a burden." The Democratic Party could corrupt the English language, and Roosevelt could allow such chicanery. But that was mild compared to some of her charges: "The determination of Mr. Roosevelt," she wrote caustically of his acceptance speech, "to assume a leadership comparable to that of the Fuehrer in Germany and the Duce in Italy is more than ever revealed.... The intention of the Executive is clear: To continue to arrogate to himself the power that the Constitution distributes among the three branches of the government." She warned that Franklin was still laying the ground for an unparalleled third term and dared him to refute it. On June 30, she put it more succinctly by repeating what was being said "around Philadelphia": F.D.R. really stood for "Fuehrer, Duce, Roosevelt."[54]

Somehow putting politics aside, in July the family gathered to pay one last homage to Quentin Roosevelt with a memorial service and a dinner commemorating his life and career. Representing the Oyster Bay Roosevelts were Edith, Alice, Ted, Archie, and Kermit. President Roosevelt and his mother came from the Hyde Park side. Family friend Frank McCoy, New York City mayor Fiorello La Guardia, and General John J. Pershing, under whom Quentin had served in France in 1918, also attended. Kermit and Alice had grown apart, separated by their politics, as he leaned leftward. In 1921, Kermit had memorialized his brother with the publication of *Quentin Roosevelt: A Sketch with Letters*. Fifteen years later, Kermit had already passed the apex of his career. An adventurer at heart and an author like his father, Kermit lacked TR's moral fiber. His marriage to Belle seemed happy, but he increasingly found enjoyment in liquor and his mistress. The alcoholism that ran through the Roosevelt clan claimed Kermit: by the mid-1930s, "He was in the habit of having whiskey for breakfast."[55]

The Sagamore Hill Roosevelts also shared a soft spot for Alf Landon because he had backed TR in 1912. Landon was glad to claim that association. "As a mark of his enduring respect for the man on whose behalf he first entered active politics," Landon made a pilgrimage to Roosevelt's grave at Oyster Bay. He had a fifteen-minute, closed-door meeting with Ted before they set out to drive from New York City to Sagamore. Once there, Landon laid a chrysanthemum wreath on TR's grave, took tea with several Roosevelts, and then boarded a train for Topeka, where he would await the election results.[56] Landon's final campaign act was a radio address sponsored by the RNC. Also speaking on the hour-long program were representatives of various constituencies the GOP hoped to reach: African Americans, teachers, union members, and farmers. Alice Longworth spoke—for two minutes—to *her* constituency: all of America. On national hookup, Alice told listeners forcefully that her cousin's New Deal had "undermined civil service"—civil service reform was a goal of the League of Women Voters that year—and "that the merit system supported by her father [was] going through its 'darkest days.'" She urged Americans to turn away from irresponsible spending and put a "sane and orderly government" in the White House.[57]

Alice was so certain that Americans would not reelect a man she had been referring to as a dictator in her columns that she parlayed a hundred dollars with Woollcott on Landon's success. She lost. FDR achieved a landslide. The electoral college vote was 523 to 8. Alex Woollcott voted for FDR because, he gloated privately, "I want to disassociate myself from the swine who, almost in a body, are out for Landon." The Republican loss was so devastating "that there was talk of their imminent demise as a party."[58]

Two months after the election, Alice tried to bury the hatchet with the now-hundred-dollar-wealthier Woollcott at a fiftieth birthday party Joe Alsop threw for the theater critic. Woollcott told his radio audience, "The lovely Alice Longworth was so incautious as to make an election bet with me. Her check has just arrived with a suggestion that I give it to my favorite charity. I shall. It may console her to know that the entire sum will be devoted to providing food, clothing, shelter and medical attention for a poor broken-down old newspaperman named Alexander Woollcott." Humor patched up their friendship. They served together as two "book connoisseurs" who, for New York publishers, helped choose a list of five hundred indispensable books for every home library.[59]

It was probably her friendship with the radio star that led to one of the most unusual decisions of Alice's life—when she agreed to be part of a radio advertisement for Lucky Strike cigarettes. The "Lucky Strike Hit Parade" was a thirty-minute show that involved a sweepstakes. Listeners guessed which songs would be the "top ranking" songs on the program. The winner won "a prize of fifty fine-tasting Lucky Strike Cigarettes." As the musical countdown began, "With Plenty of Money and You," coming in at number three on February 3, 1937, the radio announcer broke in to introduce "its own 'Roll of Honour'—the men and women famous in many different fields who prefer Luckies over any other cigarette." Describing Alice as "one of the keenest observers of the political scene," the announcer and Alice had a scripted conversation that centered on her attendance at House and Senate debates ("Those . . . can get pretty heated, can't they?") and her absorption in the issues that kept her rooted in the building even during lunch in the Senate restaurant ("It's so convenient. They can have lunch and a cigarette and be back on the floor in no time."). Alice then explained why so many congressmen smoked Luckies: "All the speaking that goes with their careers means a continuous strain on their voices and throats—they really <u>need</u> a cigarette that is considerate of their throats—a light smoke." And, of course, for the finale, Alice herself admitted to using them, "off and on."[60] Her radio appearance was unusual, because Alice, though so voluble in private settings, still hated public speaking.

Smoking she did with greater ease. As a girl, it was a rebellion against her parents' rules and society's norms. Her example allowed other American women to light up. Alice Longworth contributed something else to the history of smoking, too. Ironically, it was she who gave Franklin Delano Roosevelt the long cigarette holder that became his trademark.[61]

Chapter 19

"I Believe in the Preservation of This Republic"

By 1940, when their daughter turned sixteen, Alice and Bill Borah were old friends. She had known him nearly half her life. He was seventy-four and she was fifty-six as the calendar turned to the new year—both of them old enough to have known great joy, made and lost friends, and contemplated their own mortality. They had had their squabbles and were no longer as close as they once had been, but Paulina remained their connection.[1] The senator, embarking upon his thirty-third year in Congress, missed the heady days of Republican rule when his words were scrutinized around the globe. Borah knew that the Supreme Court seat he desired would probably never come, but his doctor proclaimed him in excellent health and ready to remain a guardian of American democracy for years. Thus, his death, on January 19, came as a shock to everyone.

Borah's final battle had been to warn FDR against assuming the power to seize American businesses, war emergency or no. The senator lectured the president, invoking documents he believed were the basis for representative democracy. "The glory of the Bill of Rights," he stormed, "is that it is a restraint upon government as well as upon individuals." And if the United States were to abrogate its lofty position, countries trying to "fight their way back to civilization" from fascism and bolshevism and nazism would not be able to "look to this Bill of Rights as embodying their hopes and ideals."

Getting ready for work on Tuesday, January 16, Borah was stricken by a brain hemorrhage. He hung on to life for the next three days, coming out of his coma only briefly. The president was one of many who phoned to inquire about the senator's health. The physicians told reporters on the seventeenth, "There is no hope whatever." Bill Borah died, with his secretary and a nurse by his side, at 8:45 p.m. on the nineteenth. [2]

Newspaper boys from Washington to San Francisco hollered the news from street corners. The next day, Senator Arthur Vandenberg delivered his friend's eulogy by radio, a powerful tribute:

> He grew in stature with each succeeding year.... He grew in the talents which made him the greatest advocate and orator of his time. He became the Senate's dean—not alone in years of service, but equally in the personal prestige of a unique and mighty character which was worthy of the Senate in its richest tradition since this Government was born. He loved America and America loved him.... He believed in America with a passion that was the touchstone of his life. America—whether it always agreed with him or not—believed in him. It knew his courage. It knew his shining probity. It knew his soul-deep sympathy with human needs. It knew his deathless dedication to representative democracy. [3]

Seven years later, at the unveiling of a statue honoring Borah in the Rotunda, Vandenberg added, "Being human, he was not infallible. But he never hedged; he never was in doubt. He never sought the easiest way.... He wrote the honest verdict of his conscience upon every major issue that arose for nearly half a century, and...in every instance it had its powerful impact upon the affairs of men." Vandenberg drew a parallel with the first Republican president, noting of Borah that "there was something of Lincoln in him. He was the humanitarian who practiced what he preached." [4]

Franklin Roosevelt called Borah "a unique figure," "fair minded, firm in principle, and shrewd in judgment," a man who "sometimes gave and often received hard blows." These were softened by his "great personal charm and a courteous manner which had its source in a kind heart." Like many others who offered encomiums, Roosevelt praised Borah's mind, his integrity, his seriousness of purpose, and his commitment to Emersonian nonconformity during his thirty-three years in the Senate. [5]

Ruth McCormick Simms and cousin Eleanor flanked Alice during the funeral in the Senate. Ruth was one of the very few who understood Alice's grief. The First Lady represented her husband and the nation, but it was also a gracious family gesture to support Alice. They sat in the Senate gallery where Alice had so often cheered on Borah, where she had fully appreciated the nuances of his speeches, discussed in draft while they were alone together in Rock Creek Park or shoulder-to-shoulder in her sitting room. Few realized the truth of their connection. Friends who mentioned his passing in their letters could not know to offer her comfort, and commented on his death as just one more Washington event. It was Little Borah who accompanied the body on the funerary train to Idaho as crowds silently lined the track, who saw his body lie in state in the capital, and who attended the interment in Boise.[6]

The full contours of Bill Borah's love for Alice will always remain obscured by the clandestine nature of their relationship. Yet from the early 1920s until the day he died, Bill found in Alice a kindred spirit and a sympathetic sounding board. Her agile mind aided the formation of his political thoughts, and he found solace in the fact that a woman he held in such esteem returned his love. "I have a frightful struggle with the 'blues' on such a day," he wrote her once. "Actually my thoughts have been of you— one who is always an inspiration—who can dispel doubt and gloom and inspire hope and instill courage as no living creature can. I was thinking this morning if an aeroplane would unload you here the whole town would be different in an hour—you are a wonder." Alice took the edge off Borah's perpetual loneliness. She gave him political advice and worked on his behalf—a partner in his political career. Bill Borah never made it to the White House, and it isn't clear whether that highest position was Alice's hope for him. She swallowed her criticisms of Bill for the most part, and she understood his iconoclasm—she who had received such a large portion of that troublesome gift from her own father. In the end, to comprehend fully the relationship between Bill Borah and Alice Longworth, as political confidants, as lovers, and as parents of Paulina, one must, as Borah directed Alice, "read in my message much more than I have written."[7]

.   .   .

The 1940 presidential campaign was hard fought by Republicans, who assumed they would pick up Democratic voters made nervous by the thought of Roosevelt's controversial third term. "I am more interested in politics than ever," Alice told the newspapers, "because it is more necessary that people vote and vote intelligently today than it ever has been, because democracy is in such peril all over the world." Alice saw ominous international trends. Anti-Semitism and fascism were on the rise in Europe, and she believed demagoguery characterized the Roosevelt presidency. "We must get the power of decision in foreign affairs back into Congress. The power to make war back to the House, the power to make treaties—foreign agreements—back to the Senate.... Send warning that our government is a representative democracy, not only in form but in fact.... The center of our government has changed in 8 years to a hardly concealed authoritarianism," she mused.[8]

By late 1939, Alice thought that Ohio's Bob Taft was the Republican Party's best choice for a standard-bearer. One contemporary described Taft as "nothing less than a portable university. The campus was plain but the faculty first-rate. His exceptionally brilliant mind had the computerlike qualities of speed, accuracy, and utter thoroughness." Alice agreed. Flattered, Taft was "most anxious" for Alice to attend the convention as a delegate, as he knew that Ted had already come out for Thomas E. Dewey. Meanwhile, Republican nominee Wendell Willkie went after the Democrats from another angle: "Every time Mr. Roosevelt damns Hitler and says we ought to help the democracies in every way we can short of war, we ought to say: 'Mr. Roosevelt, we double-damn Hitler and we are all for helping the Allies, but what about the $60 billion you've spent and the 10 million persons that are still unemployed?'"[9]

But Alice was not a great fan of Wendell Willkie's. She threw her thoughts down on paper, contemplating the European situation and laying out her isolationism:

> The identical views of the 2 candidates have served to trick the people into believing that you can "aid Britain short of war"—and keep out of war. All out aid means war—is war—undeclared or declared. The

people had no choice. The Anglophiles—the Hitler haters—nominated their candidate Willkie— From that moment there was no choice—no alternative—to all the steps "short of war"—up to the brink—and over—in to war. So with regard [to] the scene...Japan is against us—Germany smashing Br. and Br. munitions transports and ours too. Smashing Suez—with the Spanish and French smashing Gibraltar. It ought to be a full...drawn war before many months have gone by—no "appeasing" by either side of the other—a fight to utter exhaustion. Administration has asserted that every measure that has been taken is for the purpose of national defense—to defend U.S.—to keep us out of war—the draft is...necessary to defend U.S.—IF ATTACKED— It is openly stated now that we are organizing an army for EVERY PURPOSE—for the purpose of defending Br because Britain is between U.S. and...German victory.... [This] year our...first line of defense...is the British navy.[10]

The summer of 1940 was a disquieting time. The news from Europe and Asia was relentlessly bad. After the German invasion of Poland on September 1, 1939, and the Allied declaration of war against Germany, Europe had settled into what Senator Borah labeled a "phony war." But that turned out to be a time of regrouping for Hitler, and in April 1940, the Nazi blitzkrieg began again. By the summer, Italy was in the war, and Germany had conquered France. England stood alone. Japan had announced the creation of the Greater East Asia Co-Prosperity Sphere, its term for the empire it wished to create across Asia. To protect this endeavor, Japan entered into the Tripartite Pact with Germany and Italy in the fall of 1940. This set the stage for the Japanese invasion of French Indochina. While some Americans believed that President Roosevelt should prepare for the inevitability of U.S. engagement, polls continued to show that the majority of citizens preferred not to get involved militarily.

Alice and other isolationists came to the same conclusion. They took a long view of history, noting that Europe had survived its battles for thousands of years. While even today we find Hitler and his campaign of genocide and enslavement incomprehensible, at the time most Americans did not understand the depth nor the breadth of evil in his plans. Consequently, isolationists believed the man in the White House seemed determined to bring the United States into a war of misguided nobility to protect the British. Alice feared this would bring political, social, and financial disaster to America. Worse, it would simultaneously increase the power of the president while providing a screen for the continuation of the New Deal programs she had been publicly criticizing. Alice had written to Ted in August of 1939, "I'm fascinated by Franklin's note to ... Hitler. To use the phraseology of the Covenant of the L[eague] of N[ations] to Hitler! Clanking the ball and chain of the Versailles treaty, which is Hitler's red rag, bloody shirt—the reason with a big R for everything he does. It can't have been inadvertent—mere stupidity. It must have been deliberate. 'Needling' the Führer. It's proof to me that Franklin's trite pieties mean nothing. That he wants war. That he realizes that war is the only way he can retrieve his power which has been slipping so rapidly—that only war can divert attention from his sweeping failures."[11]

Everyone had an opinion. Women and men of good heart disagreed about the best role for the United States, and argued endlessly the potential outcomes. Representative Hamilton Fish urged all candidates for the presidency to declare their stances on "collective security, entangling alliances, military and naval pacts, armed intervention, secret diplomacy, war commitments and delegating to the President discretionary war-making powers." Congress had outlawed certain types of assistance to belligerent nations in an effort to protect U.S. neutrality. President Roosevelt wanted to have the power to decide when and against which countries the acts would be used. This was unacceptable to isolationists and constituted a potential abuse of presidential power. Conversation grew heated in the capital city. Alice fueled the debate. After a dinner at the home of Senator Burton K. and Lulu Wheeler, Alice and the six other guests "rose to depart, determined to do whatever they could to avert involvement in war."[12]

Alice had studied George Washington's farewell address, and it became her starting point: "I know well that a prescription given to a small nation of three million people need not be the right direction for a world power.

But the lasting validity of Washington's exhortation would become apparent if people did not forget to remember how he qualified it: 'The nation which indulges towards another an habitual hatred or an habitual fondness is in some degree a slave.' This is my credo." Borah fervently shared that credo. He went to his grave regretting that he could neither stop Congress from repealing the arms embargo nor the president from wanting to cozy up to England.[13]

In November, voters responded to President Roosevelt's campaign promise that American "boys are not going to be sent into any foreign wars," although critics were quick to point out what he knew himself, that once the United States was involved, it would no longer be "a foreign war." The third-term issue turned out to be less important than Americans' desire to stay out of the tragedies unfolding overseas, and FDR's pledge soundly defeated Wendell Willkie in 1940.

It is worth remembering now the lack of public support for war that existed in this country until Pearl Harbor. In hindsight, and after more than fifty years' clarity about Japan's aggression in the Pacific and the atrocities in Hitler's Germany and Stalin's Russia, it is difficult to believe that people such as Herbert Hoover, Robert Taft, John L. Lewis, Lillian Gish, Charles A. Beard, Charles Lindbergh, Ted Roosevelt, Robert Frost, Charles Ives, John Dewey, Van Wyck Brooks, e. e. cummings, and Oswald Garrison Villard honestly felt that assisting the British-led Allies would threaten the very roots of democracy in the United States. The despair of the noninterventionists deepened as they felt President Roosevelt took step after unconstitutional step to drag the United States closer to military engagement and circumvent Congress's prerogative to make war.[14]

Kansas journalist William Allen White put together a group to encourage FDR's support for Great Britain: the Committee to Defend America by Aiding the Allies (CDAAA). White's committee was closely aligned with FDR's own outlook.[15] White intended to limit his support to lobbying for supplies and moral encouragement to the Allies, but he was forced to resign because he was outnumbered by more zealous members who felt that aid should involve full military commitment.

An organized opposition to the program of the CDAAA arose in the late summer of 1940, as Germany launched the Battle of Britain. Four Yale law students, including a young Gerald Ford and future Supreme Court justice Potter Stewart, wrote a petition they hoped would inspire other collegians to band together in a national, noninterventionist pressure group. This was the start of the America First Committee (AFC). "We demand that Congress refrain from war, even if England is on the verge of defeat," their petition declared. "But," as America First founder Robert Douglas Stuart Jr. put it, "it became pretty clear to all of us that we needed some heavies to make an impact." The four students sought these "heavies" at the Republican national convention. There sympathetic Senator Taft directed them to General Robert E. Wood. Later, at the Democratic national convention they picked up the support of noninterventionist senators Burton K. Wheeler and Champ Clark, who also suggested they contact Wood.[16]

Wood, born five years before Alice, is best remembered today for his long tenure as president of Sears & Roebuck. In 1940, he had just become chair of its board of directors. Wood was a West Point graduate, a veteran of the Philippine-American War, and an important aide to General Goethals in the Panama Canal building endeavor. In World War I, he rose to brigadier general and was a decorated acting quartermaster general of the army. Securing Wood was a coup.

The first executive committee meeting of the AFC occurred on September 21, 1940. Alice Longworth was a charter member of the national board of directors and of the Washington, D.C., chapter. In these capacities she accepted the AFC creed, which stated, in part, "I believe in an impregnable national defense....I believe in the preservation of this Republic. Embroiled again in European affairs, we shall lose it....Sympathetic as we all may be with unfortunate nations overseas, we must remember that we stand alone. Europe and Asia cannot be expected to fight our battles."[17] The organization stressed the protection of the American way of life by heeding the admonitions of Washington and Jefferson to avoid permanent or entangling alliances.

Support for the new organization poured in, from such young people as John F. Kennedy (who sent money and was a "chapter chairman" at Harvard) to farmers, celebrities, industrialists, former Populists, and Progressives. New members included Chester Bowles, Jay C. Hormel, Frank O. Lowden, Eddie Rickenbacker, and Lessing Rosenwald. The Amos Pinchots, former New Dealer Hugh S. Johnson, author John T. Flynn, journalist William H. Chamberlain, and Hoover's undersecretary of state William Castle joined the Washington branch, where Lulu Wheeler served as treasurer. Nonmembers like Senator Wheeler and socialist leader Norman Thomas gave speeches at AFC events. Songwriter "Reidy" Reid penned a ballad, "America First," which made clear that joining was a patriotic act: "The skies are bright, and we're all right / In our Yankee Doodle way / But it's up to us, every one of us / to stand right up and say / AMERICA FIRST! AMERICA FIRST! AMERICA FIRST, LAST AND ALWAYS!"[18] The AFC was the first major noninterventionist organization to oppose vocally the CDAAA. The AFC believed that the CDAAA had the advantages: President Roosevelt's actions were interventionist, the press was largely interventionist, the anti-Hitler emotional appeal was theirs. But the AFC had the majority of Americans believing as they did. That asset was one of only two things uniting the 850,000 individual America Firsters, that and their diversity—they shared no common "economic doctrines, social bases, or political affiliation."[19]

Any number of sympathies might have moved noninterventionists to join. For example, those with a profound abhorrence of war, including parents of potential soldiers and potential soldiers themselves, were likely to sign on. The AFC, however, generally distanced itself from radical pacifists. Those who mistrusted Great Britain—Alice, like many Roosevelts, had a case of this—and some Americans of German descent had an interest in America First. The belief that another world war threatened American democracy and capitalism motivated many members. They already worried, as Bob Taft did, about "the complete unsoundness of the New Deal theory of democracy." Taft particularly excoriated Roosevelt's Lend-Lease, destroyers-for-bases deal, and the methodical repeal of the cash-and-carry law, which pushed the United States closer to direct intervention. That alarm was sounded on all America First literature. " 'The path to war is a false path to freedom,' " was the first principle of the America First

Committee. The preamble to the organization's Statement of Principles and Objectives insisted that the freedoms guaranteed in the Bill of Rights "inevitably will be sacrificed if we enter this war."[20] The passionate belief that America stood most to lose should it enter the war was a consistent caution of America Firsters.

It proved, however, a difficult thing to keep AFC membership separated in the public mind from anti-Semites and fascists who supported Nazi ideology. "There is no room in our program," AFC bulletins insisted, "for persons with leanings that place the interests of any foreign country or ideology ahead of those of the United States. We do not countenance anti-Semitism nor political partisanship." The national committee dropped Henry Ford's membership because "the Committee could not be sure that . . . Mr. Ford's views were consistent with the official views of the committee."[21] Ford was known for having given credence to the fallacious *Protocols of the Elders of Zion,* and as General Wood readily admitted, they had made a mistake inviting him to serve in the first place.

Communists left the organization voluntarily as a result of the Nazi invasion of the Soviet Union in June 1941, which meant—for them—that American military efforts to help defeat the Germans and protect the Comintern became imperative. "Should America Fight to Make Europe Safe for Communism?" America First asked rhetorically. AFC literature insisted that "Communists who really desire to destroy our Government" were as unwelcome as fascists and "ultra-pacifists."[22]

Alice and other America Firsters watched in dismay as U.S. destroyers escorted British merchant ships carrying war materiel across the Atlantic after President Roosevelt repealed the "cash" and then the "carry" sections of the 1937 Neutrality Acts. They found FDR's definition of neutrality preposterous. Once Roosevelt used the loss of American lives from the unintentional German sinking of U.S. convoy ships to issue his "shoot on sight" directive of September 11, 1941, fifty-eight AFC members released a statement asserting that the president had usurped the powers of Congress. Among the signers were Alice and Ruth McCormick Simms, whose *Chicago Tribune* had been publishing anti-intervention editorials.[23]

Alice referred to herself as an "overage destroyer" in reference to yet another unconstitutional step of FDR's—the destroyers-for-bases deal of September 3, 1940, in which the United States traded "overage" U.S. destroyers for British naval bases. Many Americans shared her concerns. Just two months before Pearl Harbor, 80 percent of Americans polled rejected U.S. entry into the European war. These were the people the AFC lobbied, preaching nonintervention through speeches, letters to Congress, public debates, posters, press releases, newspaper advertisements, and rallies such as Women United, a "spontaneous nationwide expression from members of 54 cooperating women's organizations." Ted's wife, Eleanor, was "honorary chairman" of the event.[24]

The America First Committee canvassed celebrities to get the word out. Hollywood star Lillian Gish—who occasionally stayed with Alice on visits to Washington—was a popular AFC orator. By AFC count, thirty thousand people came to hear her speak in May 1941, and she reached larger audiences during a radio debate with a CDAAA representative. "Just a note of thanks for your valiant efforts to keep our flesh and blood from rotting in Europe, Africa, or Asia," wrote one man succinctly. But Hollywood bosses listened to fans who opposed Gish's view, and she resigned from the AFC rather than face unemployment. Alice was a comfort to Gish, who felt, in Alice's presence, that she could talk freely and in so doing, make sense of the political issues and her troubles. Lillian Gish thought Alice "much better than a dream come true. We regret," Gish wrote, "all the years we didn't know you."[25]

Charles Lindbergh, who knew Alice well enough to visit her home not long after his celebrated solo flight across the Atlantic, was another renowned America Firster. Lindbergh generated a massive backlash against the organization when he gave a speech many considered anti-Semitic in its message that Jews were calling for war with Germany. Speaking on September 11, 1941, in Des Moines, the aviator told Iowans that he understood why: "The persecution they suffered in Germany would be sufficient to make bitter enemies of any race. No person with a sense of the dignity of mankind can condone the persecution of the Jewish race in Germany. But no person of honesty and vision can look on their pro-war policy here today without seeing the dangers involved in such a policy, both for us and for them." Like other groups who called for war, Jews, Lindbergh cautioned, should fight to avoid it, "for they will be among the first to feel its consequences." While he stated he was not "attacking" Jews, he did single them out by suggesting that "their greatest danger to this country lies in their large ownership and influence in our motion pictures, our press, our radio, and our government."[26]

Despite Lucky Lindy's professed admiration for Jews, the response to his words was overwhelmingly negative. Revulsion, disbelief, and anger spilled across editorial pages nationwide. Alice Longworth was one of eleven members of the AFC national committee who met at the Chicago headquarters to assess the damage and consider a remedy. Six days later, to give time for absent committee members to vet the statement and to continue monitoring public response to Lindbergh's speech, the AFC released a one-page statement. It reiterated the national committee's concern that it was the interventionists who "sought to hide the real issue by flinging false charges" and "inject[ing] the race issue into the discussion of war or peace."[27] It stressed that neither Lindbergh nor the AFC was anti-Semitic.

The document did not censure Lindbergh. The organization did not force him to resign. The national committee did "condemn his speech and declare that 'his act must bring upon him the condemnation of all believers in democracy and peace.'" The committee maintained that its members were not in the habit of inspecting speeches before they were given, and the mail coming in to headquarters showed "89 percent supported Colonel Lindbergh's views and 11 percent were in disagreement." Included in the support was a strong letter from Hyman Lischner, who wrote to second the "farsighted words—aye, prophetic words of that courageous and robust American." Lindbergh had thought long about his speech, written six months before he gave it. A *Chicago Tribune* editorial emphasized that "it is better to handle the subject in public discussion than to leave it to the savagery of irresponsible private conversations." The America First Committee contained noninterventionist Jews among its members and leadership. While AFC directors felt Lindbergh's speech was "politically unwise" they nonetheless believed that American Jews were an important constituency to persuade, though difficult because of the rationale for their interventionism.[28]

The AFC used Alice's name as a guarantee that the group was neither anti-Semitic nor pro-fascist. When one interventionist called America First "the greatest Nazi propaganda movement that has ever flourished in this country," John T. Flynn of the AFC countered: "Does anyone believe General Robert E. Wood or... Alice Longworth or Governor Lowden... or any number of others are capable of representing the interest of so unspeakable a system as that of the Nazis?"[29]

Alice's friends and family were puzzled by her zealous noninterventionism. Kermit, who had briefly abandoned the bourbon for a commission in the British army and was fighting the Nazis in Norway, wrote to Ethel: "I can't quite make out what's the matter with Sister." He mused, "Of course she always is agin the Government and it may be that; but I wouldn't like having her mayhem fall into my hands in the fortunes of war, or perhaps I would." Kermit clearly understood the issue differently, and had congratulated Wendell Willkie for having made a "magnificent answer to Lindbergh." Alexander Woollcott wrote to a friend on February 25, 1941, "Alice Longworth has become such an isolationist that she no longer cares to meet me...." Donald Maclean, who worked for the British embassy and was secretly spying for the Soviet Union, accused Alice Longworth of being "fascist and right-wing... [and] everything that's awful." On the night of FDR's third inauguration, Joe and his mother, Corinne Roosevelt Alsop, were guests at Alice's dinner party. Among the isolationist guest list, Joe, an interventionist, "felt 'like a mongoose in a whole nest-full of cobras.'"[30]

Alice was not the lone Roosevelt in the AFC. Ted and his wife were active—attending an executive committee meeting on April 8, 1941, in New York City—although Ted did not share Alice's commitment. Getting tangled up in the world's wars did not appeal to him, but "if and when we are committed, then I feel that every last one of us have got to do all he can to bring the war to a successful conclusion." He took up command of his old WWI unit in early 1941 and was promoted shortly thereafter to brigadier general. Family friends also participated. Ruth joined the AFC national committee by November 1941, and had donated at least four thousand dollars to the cause. Ruth's daughter (Alice's goddaughter) Katrina McCormick Barnes was a financial backer of the AFC, as was cartoonist John R. McCutcheon.[31]

Was Alice's time wasted in such an effort? The AFC did not keep America out of World War II, but noninterventionists "definitely affected the strategy" of FDR's administration. They kept their position, which, they were proud of recalling, was the view of a large majority of the population, in front of the president—an important role in a democracy. Secretary of War Henry Stimson "felt that the non-interventionists had fought the President almost to a standstill near the end of 1941 when the Japanese attack on Pearl Harbor took the decision out of American hands."[32]

Alice followed her isolationist convictions, but the price for activism was high. The AFC never lost the taint of anti-Semitism. To an extent, all its members became tarred with that brush—despite their having joined for more than a dozen other reasons. Alice Longworth's own writings do not indict her as a virulent anti-Semite. Like most Americans of her class and time, she could display a complete lack of sensitivity toward Jews, while at the same time counting among her friends Jews both prominent and not so well known. "It is hardly fair," she wrote in a 1941 draft column, "to criticize Jews as a group. Persecution has been the difficult breath of their being for too many centuries to expect them to ignore their so-called racial sympathies and merge into the nations of which they are citizens. Their national citizenship is secondary to their age long blood ties." Even Belle Roosevelt, Kermit's wife and a friend of First Lady Eleanor Roosevelt's—and generally farther to the left of the political spectrum—could be insensitive, mourning "the note of bitterness" the narrators "injected" into the 1943 "Jewish Memorial and protest" she attended with ER.[33] Very, very few Americans were without prejudice.

The Japanese attack on American soil in the early morning hours of December 7, 1941, and the resultant deaths of 2,344 Americans extinguished the AFC. Just after Pearl Harbor, General Wood stated the case: "The principal purpose to which the AFC was dedicated and which bound together its members throughout the country no longer exists. As patriotic Americans, loyal to their government, the members of the AFC now have no alternative but to disband, cease their activities, and dedicate themselves to the job at hand—winning the war." Even the *New York Times*, no friend to the isolationists, could "salute the leaders of the America First Committee who have taken [this] patriotic action without a moment's loss of time."[34]

After the tragedy at Pearl Harbor, America Firsters became pariahs. Ted's wife, Eleanor, complained to Alice, "I went over to the Island last week for two nights and did they all walk round me like I was a swamp! I had told Alec [Woollcott] I would not come because it was nauseating to me to see people who screamed for war with no intention of interrupting their lives to take part in it." Eleanor felt she had a right to be angry, as she and Ted had been volunteering their time to assist Chinese refugees. Alice helped her by appearing at a charity sale in New York to benefit Madame Chiang Kai-shek's Fund for Chinese War Orphans.[35]

The war came closer when Alice's nephew Quentin, Ted's son, was wounded in Tunisia, North Africa. The newspapers gave the sanitized version, but from Ted—writing from the battlefront—came the real story of a bullet lodged forever between Quentin's kidney and liver. The promotion that followed was some solace, and Quentin was soon writing the family cheery missives again. Alice's brother Archie also joined the war effort. His service in World War I had earned him full disability, but that didn't stop him. Archie and his wife, Grace, stayed with Alice in Washington before he shipped out.[36]

Alice continued her denigration of FDR's administration. In April 1943, Kermit's wife, Belle, dined with Alice and Frank Kent. Alice was, Belle confided to her diary, "disarmingly loving to me, but my goodness, the accumulation of bitter criticism is hard to take, and Kent's antagonism (he was never, himself, an isolationist), I found intolerable—not one word of praise of anything or anybody." They talked politics, of course, and Alice's candidate at this early stage of the 1944 presidential election was Ohio's conservative governor John W. Bricker. Of the current crop in Washington, Belle reported, Alice and Kent "tore down everything and everybody.

Alice said she was sickened by the self-righteous attitude of those attempting to form a fine new world. I asked if she didn't think it a worthwhile objective, and she said frankly, no, it was impossible, and it was anyhow, only a cloak to throw over the desire and intent to remain in power."[37] Alice had watched efforts at innovation after World War I with the League of Nations and the World Court—and still thought she had been right about the futility of that task.

The two friends shared Alice's aversion to FDR. Kent was the well-known author of a syndicated daily column for the *Baltimore Sun* entitled *The Great Game of Politics*. It had been running since 1922, the year he went to London as a political correspondent. Joe Alsop thought him "by far the best of the vigorous political columnists in Washington." But his true calling was congressional muckraker. He wrote half a dozen books, most of them, such as *Political Behavior* (1928), exposing the customs—both conscientious and unsavory—of Washington politicians. Kent's letters to Alice demonstrate his infatuation with her. Kent, who was married, addressed Alice as "Darling," boasted to her of his successes, and professed his undying antipathy toward the New Deal.[38]

Another Roosevelt hater became even more important to her: president of the United Mine Workers John L. Lewis. Big, rugged, handsome—"a man of great physical presence," according to one who knew him.[39] Lewis was not, in fact, that different from Bill Borah, physically and temperamentally, Alice herself pointed out. She found them possessed of "the same large, shaggy heads and they both alternated between being very stimulating or very taciturn. They were *never* boring." Lewis was astute, powerful, recently widowed, and the preeminent domestic thorn in FDR's side, as he proudly led a controversial wartime coal strike. Journalist Elsa Maxwell wrote a flaming column in support of Lewis and the right of American workers to strike. Her paean to workers concluded with a characterization of Lewis as "that weird cross between William Jennings Bryan and Machiavelli, who was discoursing learnedly on Milton." She told him that at the cinema his picture was hissed more loudly than the pictures of Hitler or Hirohito. "Lewis' face grew solemn. 'Alas,' he said, 'the public forgets too quickly.'" "In my private opinion," the journalist confessed,

"John L. Lewis is the most fascinating, DANGEROUS, soft-voiced, gentle-mannered, blockbuster in the whole Labor Blitz." It's no wonder that Alice kept this column among her papers. And, as happened with Bill Borah, political sympathies couched in elegant language kindled the fires—and he amused her. "Humor was the great bond between us," she said.[40]

"Dear Aquarian," Lewis called Alice, in honor of their shared birth-days on February 12. The two exchanged books—it was she who had sent him the Milton—literary references, insider knowledge, and compliments. "Assuredly we should propitiate the gods," he wrote. "Verily, you have a deft touch with the Greeks. Perhaps I can aid with the Norse school and the Celtic spirits." She understood his cryptic messages: "Bread and butter, conceivably. The roses—the telephone—never! I vow it." And while he respected her boundaries, he found ways to insinuate: "I suspected the leaves would turn and secretly desired to remain and watch the event. [Yet] meek spirit and the conventions and duty prevented. A word, Alice, [about] these October nights. Beware of spells cast by the waxing hunters moon. If perchance you should become bespelled write me before you are dis-spelled. . . ." He let her know exactly where his mind was. He recounted a boring afternoon visit: "As my host droned on my roving literary eye was reading titles. It came to one and stopped. 'Crowded Hours.' The world he ees not too beeg, no."[41] From vacation he wrote, "You, compañero, have oft been in my mind. You have truly met your recent troubles bravely as I knew you ever would. Thanks for your superb letter from Grandin Road. Have read it oft—but shall burn it today. No other eye should ever see—. . . Later we will laugh again at many things, which only we can see." And his signature line for that letter: "The things unsaid. We know them. Juan."[42] He addressed her as ALL and signed himself JLL. "Dear friend," he also called her, and sometimes wrote letters with no content, perhaps for the sake of contact only, such as this one:

> Mon Ami: The night falls, the wayfarer needs must rest. 'Tis a cheer-ful inn at a crossing of the Camino Real. Mine host does one well, if one but carry a bulky purse that clanks anon. I supped well and was fain content save for one rude fellow to who I was sore put to be civil.

'Twas his head and not his heart. Albeit he should mend his manners, else he come afoul some gentleman less patient and more bold than this 'parfait gentil knight.' The elements weary the traveler but the inns refresh and help shorten the leagues that lie between. The Yuletide wanes and the old year with it. May the New Year be more to your wish, gentle lady, and all good fortune attend thee and thine."[43]

Alice enjoyed this wordplay. It was a language shared by few, and indulged in by even fewer.

Respecting her opinions, Lewis imparted Alice's "words" to a colleague, attributing them to "a well informed source."[44] She brought him into her inner circle of Washington politics and society, although he had already breached the walls of Washington's elite. Lewis, famous organizer of the working class, appeared in the *Washington Social List*. He was not, however, among the Harvard and Yale networks in D.C. Access to journalists and politicians in the informal venue of Alice's home was invaluable, as hers remained the hub of anti-administration gossip.

Alice and John Lewis had much in common. He became disenchanted with the New Deal and came to share her enmity toward Roosevelt. They had worked together on the America First agenda, and they shared a "love of strategy for its own sake." Even during the important 1941 strike, when the FDR White House favored the miners and convinced operators to negotiate with the union, Lewis, like Alice, had the gumption to "humiliate the president publicly for inept leadership." Lewis reported the progress of the strike to Alice. "The chess game which is coal is satisfactory at this exact moment of writing. I detect some signs of weakness in my noble opponent.... We can move either way we choose, later."[45] As war came, Lewis's reputation diminished. Americans desired unity—and Lewis did not obediently rally 'round the president. When Hitler invaded the Soviet Union in June and Stalin joined the Allies, Communist sympathizers in the labor movement shifted their support to Roosevelt. Always working the angle he thought best for labor, Lewis didn't care how people perceived him.

Alice and John L. Lewis also shared a horror of a fourth term for FDR.

Eleanor Roosevelt herself "doubted whether Franklin [could] be reelected" in 1944. ER saw only two likely candidates for the Democrats: John G. Winant and Henry A. Wallace, and she preferred the former. The president also preferred Winant, reported Belle Roosevelt after a forty-five-minute conversation with FDR. He said Winant "brushes aside all the inessentials with one gesture—and he can handle the English, which is a very important part of the set-up."[46] The ability to bring the war to a successful close, and to maintain the appropriate relationship with the British while doing so, was uppermost in Roosevelt's mind and a driving factor in his consideration of a fourth presidential term.

And then, in June 1943, came the sad news of Kermit's death. He had been stationed with the U.S. Army at Fort Richardson in Alaska, far from the battlefront and the glory. He was not well. Hard drinking and malaria had taken their toll. Unable to escape a series of personal failures, Kermit put a bullet through his head. Archie was philosophical about his brother's descent into liquor and aimlessness. "Of course, intellectually, I know it's the best thing that could happen," Archie wrote to Ethel, "but it is a real break with the past. Two of our generation have now gone, both in time of war." Archie's opinion was ultimately a cold one: that in dying when and where he did, Kermit "saved many a heart break and many an uncomfortable and a complicated time for those who were nearest and dearest to him."[47] Edith could not see it as Archie did. Kermit was always a happy and free spirit, the most like TR in many ways, and to know that he could not recover his joy and live a full life was a crushing realization for his mother.

Edith felt her age keenly. She had never stopped missing Theodore, and she longed for more time with her children. Her body showed signs of the years passing by, never so much as when she had fallen and broken her hip just before Thanksgiving in 1935.[48] She had been confined in a heavy brace, which helped the healing but made walking difficult. Heart trouble complicated her eighth decade. But it was Kermit's battle with alcoholism that hurt the most. World War II might have been Kermit's salvation—hard work and a noble cause—but his body was too far gone.

Ted, fifty-six years old, also had to overcome physical challenges to do his part in the war. A brigadier general with an arthritic hip who commanded his troops with the aid of a cane, Ted's career and his life ended in a blaze of glory. On June 6, 1944—D day—Ted led the U.S. Army Fourth Infantry Division from the first boat that went ashore on Utah Beach. Under enemy fire, he got them inland. Then he went back and did it again—leading wave after wave upon the beach. Three days later "the most decorated soldier to serve in World War II" died from a heart attack. He was awarded the Congressional Medal of Honor posthumously "for gallantry and intrepidity at the risk of his life above and beyond the call of duty" that "contributed substantially to the successful establishment of the beachhead in France." When a son dies a hero's death, the son dies nevertheless. Edith wept through the first church service she attended after she heard the news.[49]

Lieutenant Colonel Archie Roosevelt remained at his post, battalion commander with the 162nd Infantry in New Guinea, until a grenade and malaria sent him to a hospital stateside to recover. All of Theodore and Edith's boys had served in World War I. Quentin did not return. The remaining three served in World War II. Only one, Archie, came home to see his mother and his sisters and to try to pick up life as before.[50]

Chapter 20

"Full Sixty Years the World Has Been Her Trade"

Aₗᵢcₑ Lₒₙgwₒᵣₜₕ'ₛ public drubbing of the New Deal created her reputation as the leading political wit in Washington. Her epigrams encapsulated concerns some Americans felt about the Roosevelts' leadership. They were repeated endlessly. Alice became identified with her one-liners—so much so that her other contributions to American political discourse faded from public memory. People forgot that such wit is possible only when upheld by a broad intellect, insider status, and years of political and legislative expertise. For the two long decades of Democratic rule, Alice inspired the Republican troops with her constant barrage. She was part court jester, part Machiavelli. She had access and power and institutional memory. More and more the media referred to her as Princess Alice again (a title she thought "*too* utterly revolting" at that stage of her life).[1] Eventually, she embraced the celebrity role of acerbic political analyst. The general public paid her sustained attention; politicians could not ignore her, even though as the cold war began Alice was still an "out of season" Roosevelt.

Not until 1952 would Dwight D. Eisenhower's presidential victory shatter the Democratic hegemony. The World War II hero defeated Alice's candidate, Robert Taft, who had failed in his White House primary attempts in the 1940s, too. The cynical satisfaction of watching the man who defeated him, Thomas Dewey, lose to both Franklin Roosevelt (in 1944) and Harry S Truman (in 1948), hardly made up for Taft's losses. Though she was able to celebrate the emergence of a new champion in Richard Nixon's election to the House of Representatives in 1947 and to gain satisfaction from a groundswell of posthumous critical press for Franklin Roosevelt,

Alice Longworth remained largely isolated from the White House during the Truman years.

Mitigating her sense of being outside the center of power was the ongoing success of Alice's dinners. Alice's salon continued at the heart of Washington entertainment, helped by the fact that First Lady Bess Truman was not known for her brilliant diversions.[2] Darrah Wunder, longtime executive secretary of the Cincinnati League of Women Voters, wrote about Alice in her memoir. "I loved Alice Longworth's dinner parties, although one had to do detective work to find out who the guests were. Alice would say, 'Bob you know Darrah Wunder, or Bunny or Archie of course you know Darrah.' Of course they didn't, but I knew Bunny de Chambrun, married to [Pierre] Laval's daughter, and Archie Roosevelt, and I hunted up a good friend who briefed me on the ones I didn't know. It was at Alice's that I met John L. Lewis for she invited anyone that amused her." And everyone seems to have reciprocated, either by showing up or by inviting Alice to their parties. Wunder, who served as Martha Taft's private secretary, recalled how "Alice was wonderful to me and a great help, for when we were having some newly elected Senators and their wives to dinner and I feared the party wouldn't get off the ground quickly, I'd suggest we'd ask Alice and Bob would always agree."[3]

Personal losses continued in the 1940s. Her household and her circle of intimates would shrink when her daughter married and Ruth and Edith died. Union business and national politics frequently called John L. Lewis away from Washington. Alice turned sixty on February 12, 1944, without those closest to her. Joe Alsop remembered Alice caricaturing herself at that time as Atossa, from Alexander Pope's "An Epistle to a Lady" (1735). It was one of the countless bits of poetry Alice could recite from memory:

> But what are these to great Atossa's mind?
> Scarce once herself, by turns all womankind!
> Who, with herself, or others, from her birth
> Finds all her life one warfare upon earth:
> Shines, in exposing knaves, and painting fools,
> Yet is, whate'er she hates and ridicules.

No thought advances, but her eddy brain
Whisks it about, and down it goes again.
Full sixty years the world has been her trade,
The wisest fool much time has ever made.
From loveless youth to unrespected age,
No passion gratified except her rage.

Alsop thought that Alice's use of Pope's misogynistic writings to describe herself was evidence of an unhappy life, but she would hardly recite a positive poem about herself—that would be boasting—and to do so would elicit the fawning she so despised. Yet this poem reverberates with some of the criticism leveled at Alice, especially the indulgence in passionate rages. It held some bitter truth for her, too. "War is an inevitable thing," Alice philosophized, "peace is the interlude."[4] As a child she did feel "loveless"; as an adult she did enjoy exposing knaves and fools. "The world had been her trade" all her life. Alice had "gratified . . . her rage" against Franklin and Eleanor Roosevelt. In so doing, the reputation of her "eddy brain" had brought her new admirers and wider fame. As the cold war advanced, Alice Longworth retreated to the role of "the wisest fool." She was impatient with the Republican Party's inability to defeat Harry Truman in 1948, and less than thrilled about the anti-intellectual Dwight D. Eisenhower. In her sixties, Alice conformed—to the public, at least—to that sketch of Atossa.

But that mantle was not all that she wore. She often quoted another smidgen of "Epistle to a Lady:"

'Twas thus Calypso once each heart alarm'd
Aw'd without Virtue, without Beauty charmed;
Her tongue bewitch'd as oddly as her Eyes,
Less Wit than Mimic, more a Wit than wise.

Alice had not lost the ability to "alarm" men's hearts. John Lewis was a steady companion throughout the 1940s and 1950s. Her tongue certainly

"bewitched" legions of Americans, but she herself was often her own tar-
get. Though she might suggest she was "more a wit than wise," acquaintances and friends knew of her superior intelligence. She had stopped
keeping up with current fiction in the late 1930s. She concentrated instead
on contemporary history and current events, including the scientific news
that fascinated her, such as Edwin Hubble's discovery that the universe
contained more than one galaxy. During a trip to Pasadena, she, Paulina,
and two friends trekked up the San Gabriel mountains to the Mount Wilson Observatory. Alice spent the night listening to the lawyer-turned-
astronomer demonstrate the Hooker one-hundred-inch telescope. They
gazed into the depths of space, just as Alice had done so often as a girl at
Sagamore Hill. Hubble thought he'd "never spent a better night in a telescope" than he'd had with Alice, fueled as it was by her endless curiosity
and enthusiasm.[5]

Her fascination with biology continued as well. After all, she had studied social Darwinism for thirty years. She had watched as evolution had
been used by New Dealers who believed that some Americans were ge-
netically incapable of caring for themselves. Then Adolph Hitler viciously
twisted the field to justify his murder of those he deemed "sub-human." In
the postwar years, Alice followed the research being done at Cold Spring
Harbor Laboratory and studied the evolving field of molecular genetics.
She read avidly about the work of Linus Pauling, James Watson, and Francis Crick. She read paleontologist Louis B. Leakey and maintained her interest in primate behavior. Alice enjoyed *The Sea Around Us* so much that
she telephoned Rachel Carson to tell her so.[6] Politics and science were the
background for the rest of her reading, which included several newspapers
every day—always the *New York Times*, the *Washington Post*, and the New
York *Daily News*. Bill Walton, a *New Republic* journalist and Kennedy intimate, called her "one of the best read, best educated women I've ever come
across."[7]

Alice's schedule was idiosyncratic and structured by her reading habits.
Washington parties generally broke up early, as legislators had to be to
work in the mornings. After such gatherings, Alice retreated to her bedroom on the third floor of the Massachusetts Avenue house and read far

into the night—sometimes straight through until dawn. "It's intoxicating for me," Alice insisted. She read and reread books. She read book reviews. "I got no education and I'm rather glad I didn't," Mrs. L took to saying in the 1960s, "as it saved so much excitement for my antiquity."[8]

Alice's bedroom resembled a Dickensian shop, with books stacked upon books, spilling out of the revolving bookcase she kept by her bedside. When she wanted to look up a passage and could not locate the book she sought, she bought another copy. Proprietors knew her tastes and set aside volumes for her to consider. She frequented local bookstores, such as Olsson's on Dupont Circle, and the Saville in Georgetown, walking out briskly in the early afternoons. When she was forced to part with some of her books, one book buyer, novelist Larry McMurtry, described them as "excellent books, in several languages."[9] Friends learned not to telephone until after 1:00 p.m. Before then, a maid would answer and take a message. After 1:00, Alice would pick up herself and bark her fierce hello—more a statement than a question.

Such hours were difficult with a child, even one in her teens. Half a year after Alice's sixtieth birthday, and one month after Ted's death in France, nineteen-year-old Paulina announced her engagement to Alexander Sturm. Sturm was the son of Katherine McCormick Sturm, who was distantly related to the *Chicago Tribune* family, and businessman and artist Justin C. Sturm. Alex attended Yale, wrote and illustrated two books before he turned twenty, but was, Alice thought, not good enough for Paulina. She saw in him the thing she had most despised in her own husband: addiction to liquor. Paulina had mercifully grown up without the specter of alcoholism. While not a perfect childhood, at least it was free of alcohol-related traumas. She attended school in Cincinnati, and Alice took her to spend the summers in Wyoming at the Dewey Riddle Ranch. Paulina's debut was held at Cincinnati's exclusive Camargo Club, attended by hundreds of Washington and Ohio acquaintances.[10] Paulina had attempted Vassar College, which she disliked and from which she did not graduate.

Alice and Paulina did not have an idyllic relationship. Some friends suggested that Alice wanted her daughter to be just like her. Paulina was certainly as shy and as intelligent as Alice. But Alice grew up surrounded by half siblings, whereas Paulina was an only child with few playmates. Alice put her daughter on display, as doting parents do, but when Paulina resisted or withdrew, Alice finished her sentences and drew the spotlight back to herself. Kermit, who had good insight into Alice, once referred to Paulina as "Sister's competition." Paulina's stutter, fairly unusual in girls, may have been a result of anxiety or stress. For all her other talents, Alice was not an ideal mother. It's true that Edith's example of mothering was far from perfect, but Alice had also had her rambunctious and adoring, if distracted, father. Nick had died when Paulina was six, and all of the parenting duties then fell to Alice. She encouraged Paulina's horseback riding and even once fought Andrew D. Mellon's plan to raze Paulina's riding school. Alice was not demonstrative with Paulina, nor was she the sort of mother to whom a child readily went for comfort, physical or emotional. Paulina's nanny, Dorothy Waldron, did not wholly make up for it. She was strict and distant, a "dragon" to one friend's way of thinking, although another considered "Waldie" "a very nice person" who was close to Paulina."[11]

The difficult relationship with her mother may be what pushed Paulina toward Alex Sturm. After a brief courtship, they declared their intention to marry. As one of Alice's friends commiserated, she knew Alice would "be sad to lose her." And good Joe Graydon wrote at this juncture of Alice's life, offering solace about Ted's recent death and congratulations on Paulina's engagement. He "hope[d] not so much that she may have a happy life as that she may have a useful and interesting one which in the end is bound to be the most satisfactory." Was that a comment from an old friend who read in Alice's own choices "a useful and interesting" but not a happy life? Or was it a twinge of regret about his own choices?[12]

Paulina's wedding plans were made as the 1944 campaign unfolded. New York Governor Thomas E. Dewey was the Republican whipping boy, running against President Franklin Roosevelt's fourth-term attempt. Dewey, a dapper dresser, whom Alice found to be otherwise "incompetent" and "a frightful bore," looked "like the little man on the wedding cake." This dandy dismissal alone did not bring about Dewey's defeat at the polls, but some people gave it that much credit. From the vantage point of 1960, Clayton Fritchie wrote, "Politicians are agreed that such scornful quips hurt Dewey in the election."[13]

While the maxim was attributed to Alice, she regularly denied having formulated it. Not until 1968 was her confusion about how she came to be credited with it cleared up, when she received a letter revealing the true author. Isabel Kinnear Griffin wrote to say that twenty years earlier she was "working with Helen Essary Murphy on the *Democratic Digest*, [a] publication of the Democratic National Committee." An "unflattering picture" of Dewey that needed a caption prompted Murphy to pop out with, "He looks just like the little man on the wedding cake!" The two women loved the line so much they didn't want it to go unnoticed and felt the *Democratic Digest* was not a large enough forum. "We plotted," Griffin wrote Alice. "At the British embassy reception that afternoon we asked each person we met: 'Is it true Alice Longworth said Governor Dewey looks like the little man on the wedding cake?' As we had anticipated, it spread like wildfire, only now it had become: 'Have you heard Alice Longworth's description of Governor Dewey?'"[14] Such was a mark of Alice's stature as a wit.

The 1944 Republican convention was held in June in a swelteringly hot Chicago. Alice checked into the Blackstone with Paulina. The two watched the show with Ruth and her daughter Bazy. Unlike 1936 and 1940 when Alice was a delegate, in 1944, she had no official role. Paulina was a page and Ruth was a member of the resolutions committee from New Mexico. Ruth supported Dewey and as the owner of six thousand cattle and ten thousand sheep in Colorado, she told reporters she was "interested in the agricultural plank." Just for the record, she stated, "I was a member of America First, and I don't approve of alliance with Britain." Alice was hoping to see the GOP promise to provide "a big navy, and strong air power." The only public remark Alice would make about the contest that would pit the Republican nominee against cousin Franklin's fourth attempt was succinct and devastating: "The Republican party is here to elect a President and not retain a dictator." Privately, she thought sterner measures ought to be taken: "Amending the constitution to set a limit on presidential terms is long overdue."[15] Like many other Americans, she disliked any man's ability to serve in an unending presidency, too reminiscent of a dictatorship in those World War II days, and contrary to the aims of the founders, Alice thought.

Dewey won the GOP nomination, with John Bricker (whom Alice had damned with faint praise by calling him "an honest Harding") receiving the vice presidential nod. Taft was Alice's first choice in 1944, but the erudite Ohioan could never surmount his lack of charisma to win a nomination. Although "he could outthink almost everyone," Bob, unlike his genial father, hated to kiss babies and attend pancake suppers. Neatly nailing both Taft's personality and her loathing for FDR, Alice said, "Having the Senator replace FDR in the White House would be like a glass of milk after a slug of Benzedrine." Had Taft won in 1944, Alice's life would have been much different. He had called her "an intimate friend" since 1938. Alice truly liked Martha Taft, who was well educated, fun, and devoutly interested in politics. [16] Because of their friendship, Taft's election would have made Alice a political insider again.

Perhaps it was the disappointment of seeing Dewey triumph over Taft in the primary that gave impetus to the *Chicago Tribune* interview entitled "Politics Losing Hatred's Spice, Alice Laments." In 1944, the journalist wrote, "Everyone is so terribly amiable. No one really hates any one else.... Various combatants in the political arena today may think it pyramided with hate, but Mrs. Longworth scoffs at it...." Alice compared the "feeble" disagreements of the 1944 political scene to 1912 and found them "tepid." "'But then,'" Alice declared, "'then one really felt violent. I had heard of seeing red, but I didn't merely see red. Things danced redly before my eyes. O, it was wonderful.' Who hated? The other faction, she was asked. 'No, no, no,' [Alice] cried in excitement. 'We all hated! We hated. They hated. Everyone hated.' And you enjoyed yourself? 'A great many people didn't, but I did. It was a bath of hate and fury. There hasn't been anything like it since.' With that," the journalist concluded, "she sat back and smiled and smiled and smiled." Though Alice proclaimed it animated her, as one friend put it, "everyone always pretended to be nice and she pretended to be unpleasant."[17] Malevolence was becoming part of her persona.

The postconvention letdown was tempered that year by Paulina's wedding, which took place in Magnolia, Massachusetts, on August 26, 1944. Because Ted's wartime death had occurred only about a month earlier, the wedding was simple. Ethel Barrymore stood by Alice, and Ted's son, young Cornelius Roosevelt, gave the nineteen-year-old bride away before their two hundred guests. As her engagement photos attest, Paulina had grown into a beautiful young woman. She wore her mother's stunning pearl necklace, given to her by Cuba on the occasion of her own wedding, and a lace veil from Russia, a gift to Alice from the Romanovs. Justin Sturm played the organ for the seven-minute wedding ceremony led by the Right Reverend Oliver J. Hart. Paulina's grandmother Edith Roosevelt, her aunts and uncles, including Mrs. Ted, Ethel and Dick Derby, and Belle, were there to see her wed. Alex's mother was pleased with the event. She thanked Alice and called it "real perfection...all beautiful—well timed—well carried out and with great taste and charm!"[18] Alex and Paulina settled near his parents in Southport, Connecticut.

Ruth, suffering from pancreatitis, could not attend the wedding. Her health was failing, but surgeons delayed operating and her pancreas ruptured. Ruth had been in Chicago seeking votes for Dewey. She died there, with her daughters, Triny and Bazy, by her side. Alice's sorrow can only be imagined. Ruth had been her best friend since they were young women. She and Ruth had attended each other's weddings, buried husbands, raised children, plotted strategy, and fought side by side for shared causes. Alice had supported Ruth's career in electoral politics and allowed Ruth to cajole her into active work for which Alice frequently and fondly called her "B.D.—Benevolent Despot." With Ruth, Alice could be at her silliest and most playful. Ruth's family remembered the astonishing loud monkey impressions the two friends did, perching on the backs of the sofa, screeching, and picking imaginary lice off each other. The two could chitchat about "Freud and religion and sex...."[19] Mourning Ted and Ruth, whose deaths came so close together, must have taken an incalculable emotional toll on Alice.

Then, on April 12, 1945, she and a stunned world received news of the death of Franklin Roosevelt. Alice conveyed her sympathies to Eleanor.

The suddenly-former First Lady admitted to her that she was "shocked" by Franklin's death, but "grateful that Franklin suffered no pain and was spared a long illness." While Alice and Eleanor retained what Joe Alsop called the "suitable gestures of cousinhood," Franklin's death—with mistress Lucy Mercer Rutherfurd in the house—did not spur either woman to confessional confidences.[20] The spleen and duration of Alice's public condemnation of Roosevelt's New Deal had been too great.

Friends, lovers, family, enemies—all dying. The 1940s was a decade of loss. When death keeps such close company, the survivor's chill can spur some to work with renewed vigor, conscious of fleeting time, and others to sink into bitterness or melancholy. Alice kept in fighting trim, but just barely, if Isabella Greenway King's picture of Alice that August 1945 was true. "I had a marvelous time with Alice Longworth," she wrote to her son:

> Drove myself down to the Ritz...at 5:30 and remained till 10. We had a cozy dinner in her room. The visit will fill a whole letter. The high spots are that all is well with Paulina and Alex—but Alice's fingers are crossed and she knocks on wood as she speaks.... Alice is in bad shape with a deep rattling bronchitis which she can't shake and somewhat jolted from falling down her Washington stairs in the dark—and being generally battered and bruised and cutting her nostril open on the balustrade. She called the Dr who said he'd come in 3 hours. "If you can't come now don't come at all" was Alice's answer. So the cut healed of itself—when it should have been sewed—but doesn't show because as Alice says "It's in a wrinkle!"...A package was delivered during the evening. It was 2 detective stories ordered by Alice—for herself—there you have the picture except her extraordinary appearance which I felt—let her down rather shamefully.... She was charming, heart warming—and I do love her....[21]

Contemporary events soon replaced the detective stories. Alice had been paying attention to the "ceasefire reaction" in the press and the news from the Pacific as the atomic bombs brought an end to World War II. In the wake of the Allied liberation of Europe and the clear need for assistance to the war's survivors, Alice became an honorary chairman of Associated Relief for Austria (ARA). Its goal was "to distribute clothing, food and money to the peoples of that country 'who need it most, regardless of party affiliation, race or religion.' " Shoring up Austria with assistance from the non-Communist West to gain an ally in the upcoming cold war was a secondary but real goal.[22]

In the spring of 1946, Alice learned she would be a grandmother. What should have been unalloyed good news was tempered by her knowledge that her fears about Alex's drinking had been realized. Unable to assist her daughter or control her son-in-law, Alice continued to grow apart from Paulina. Alice was not close to Alex's family either. "The relationship between Mrs. Longworth and Mrs. Sturm," thought David Mitchell, a friend of the younger Sturms, "was very complicated and quite difficult at times...." It was to John Lewis that Alice confessed her concerns for the mother-to-be. "I know how hard it is to wait," Lewis reassured her.[23] A healthy granddaughter, named Joanna, arrived on July 9, 1946. Hers would be an unhappy and chaotic childhood, but Alice, kept at arm's length by her daughter, was unable to help for the first decade of Joanna's life.

Joanna was born a week before family matriarch Edith Kermit Carow Roosevelt turned eighty-five. Edith missed Alice. "It is so long," Edith sighed, "since we have had a family gossip...." After the deaths of Ted and Kermit, Edith had not often ventured far from Sagamore Hill. Age was telling on her, but she kept her sense of humor. She called herself "a battered old Mother, but still on deck!"[24] When Paulina was at Vassar, Alice had seen more of Edith. In Washington, Alice became a magnet for another generation of Roosevelts, as Bye had been earlier. Alice's nieces and nephews sought her out as their studies or jobs took them to D.C. Nephew Archie Roosevelt wrote in August 1950 to tell her about his upcoming marriage to Selwa Showker ("I know you will like her," he promised). One niece found Alice "a relation who is a real and understanding friend," while her new husband was "appreciative" of "the warmth of your welcome to us in Washington—and he does not say these things easily." And this particular relation was something unusual, as the niece, Edith, had married Alexander Barmine, described in the gossip columns as a "former Red

Army General," and by his wife as one who "incidentally happens to belong to a family of Russian nobility that dates only five hundred or so years
back!" Alice bucked cold war convention and made a point of dining with
them, signaling, according to journalist Cholly Knickerbocker, that the
couple was "not only socially acceptable, but are always welcome in her
home," and as a result, in others. Archie and Selwa ("Lucky") Roosevelt
echoed this, because they knew Alice's "stamp of approval meant that [we]
were also *persona grata* in the salons of the 'three Bs'—Mrs. Robert Woods
Bliss, Mrs. Robert Low Bacon, and Mrs. Truxton Beale."[25]

Alice didn't just introduce young relatives around, she folded them in
with an extraordinary group of friends. Her poker parties, which were
good sources of news, included, over the years, people as diverse as film
star Constance Bennett and her husband, Brigadier General John Theron
Coulter; Lawrence Spivak; Secretary of the Treasury Ogden L. Mills;
Mary Brooks, assistant chair of the RNC; "Wild Bill" Donovan, head of
the Office of Strategic Services; Maryland GOP powerhouse Louise Gore;
and Bazy and her husband, Peter Miller. Other friends, like philosopher
Isaiah Berlin, attended luncheons, teas, or dinners. In between visits, So-
licitor General Philip B. Perlman kept Alice apprised of interesting proceedings in court by "preparing a schedule of cases for your, well, if not
edification, certainly for your amusement during the fall and winter. For
instance, the Supreme Court willing, there will be two cases involving the
famed [alleged Soviet spy] Judy Coplon. . . ." He filled his letter with Justice
Department news written "very, very confidentially." With another frequent luncheon guest, Supreme Court Justice Felix Frankfurter, Alice discussed Benjamin Franklin, the U.S. Constitution, and the books they sent
each other. Chief Justice Charles Evans Hughes was a special friend, as was
Justice William O. Douglas. A profile in the November 1950 *American
Weekly*, when she was sixty-six, depicted Alice as "a living, vital legend in
a city where famous figures are legion. People still turned to look at her
erect, almost military bearing as she walked the streets—to gossip of
her headstrong actions, her famous feuds. Beneath the picture hat which
she almost invariably wore, her gray-blue eyes were still level and direct.
Her hair, once a light brown, was peppered with gray, but her posture made

her seem taller than her five feet, three inches and belied her age."[26] New hostesses made their appearance in the cold war years—like Perle Mesta and Gwen Cafritz, for example, but Alice's house remained the destination of choice for journalists and policy makers.

Alice ran "a political drawing-room" and like a diplomat, brought leaders from many different fields to her home on Massachusetts Avenue. She could be, as *Die Weltwoche* put it, "just as benevolent as malevolent." Trying to capture the essence of Alice for his readers, the columnist described her "tremendous influence by the subtle means which are only at the disposal of intelligent women. . . . However large a party, Alice Longworth is its natural center. This is due to her inexhaustible vivacity, her great art of imitation, the grace of her attitude and movements, but first of all to her ruthless intellectual honesty. She gives lavishly without stint, and does exactly the same without an audience. A stupendous memory enables her to recite, like Winston Churchill, not only Keats and Milton and the *Nibelungenlied*, but also the most exotic modern poetry. She is very angry with her compatriots because they have lost the habit of reading, and lives with her books until three o'clock in the morning. They, she says, are my best company."[27]

That company always included journalists and authors. She received a copy of Sir Richard Burton's *The Kasidah*, from C. D. Batchelor, a political cartoonist. Batchelor was the creator of one of Alice's favorite cartoons: "All this and Truman, too," which showed great, looming heads of ER and FDR, and down below, a miniscule Harry Truman. Intrepid travel writer and photographer Freya Stark came, as did Walter Trohan, conservative journalist and chief of the *Chicago Tribune* Washington bureau from 1949 to 1969. He and Alice shared strong opinions about U.S. foreign policy. They were both furious when President Truman relieved General Douglas MacArthur of his command in Korea. Trohan had the additional lure of being one of Truman's poker buddies, and so could bring back insider dirt. With journalist Malcolm Muggeridge, Alice exchanged views of his *Winter in Moscow*. "One or two chapters are amusing, I think," he wrote her modestly, "but I blush for some of it."[28]

While most of Alice's friends were men, she did have many women in

The dazzling Colonel of the Battalion of Death

ABOVE: The erudite Cincinnati attorney, Joseph Graydon, whose mind delighted Alice

⊷◆⊶

LEFT: The Lion of Idaho, Senator Bill Borah

⊷◆⊶

OPPOSITE: Alice with her infant daughter, Paulina, born in 1925

ABOVE: Nick and baby Paulina

❖

Alice appeared in a Pond's
cold cream advertisement as
an investment for her
daughter's future

MRS. NICHOLAS LONGWORTH
on keeping one's appearance up to the mark

Ruth Hanna McCormick shaking hands with a constituent, while Alice looks on

Nick Longworth throwing out the first ball of the baseball season in 1928

Ted and Alice sharing a laugh during the 1920s

Alice on the cover
of *Time* magazine
in 1927

⊶◆⊷

A dapper
Nick Longworth,
c. 1925

A formal photo of Nick
and Paulina

—◆—

Alice and Paulina and
their shared love
of reading

Alice Roosevelt Longworth

tells how Senators choose a light smoke...
considerate of their throats

"I often lunch in the Senate restaurant at the Capitol. Nearly every Senator and Representative there smokes, and the number I see take out a package of Luckies is quite surprising. Perhaps surprising is not the word. Because off and on, ever since 1917, I myself have used Luckies for this sound reason: They really are a light smoke—kind to the throat. It's simply common sense that these Senators and Representatives, whose voices must meet the continuous strain of public speaking, should also need a cigarette that is considerate of their throats . . . a light smoke."

Alice Roosevelt Longworth

In a recent independent survey, an overwhelming majority of lawyers, doctors, lecturers, scientists, etc., who said they smoked cigarettes, expressed their personal preference for a light smoke.

Mrs. Longworth's statement verifies the wisdom of this preference and so do leading artists of radio, stage, screen and opera, whose voices are their fortunes, and who choose Luckies, a light smoke. You, too, can have the throat protection of Luckies— a light smoke, free of certain harsh irritants removed by the exclusive process "It's Toasted". Luckies are gentle on your throat.

THE FINEST TOBACCOS— "THE CREAM OF THE CROP"

A Light Smoke
"It's Toasted"–Your Throat Protection
AGAINST IRRITATION–AGAINST COUGH

ABOVE: Mary Borah (second from left) and Alice (third from left), spectators at the Capitol while Native Americans perform a snake dance, May 1926

⁃◆⁃

Attesting to senators' smoking habits

ABOVE: A smiling Alice (back row, second from left) and a pensive Paulina (front row, third from left), with Vice President Charles Curtis

—◆—

Labor leader John L. Lewis, testifying at a public hearing about the 1943 miners' strike

Bride Paulina Longworth and groom Alexander Sturm take center stage for a day

Alice with her
infant granddaughter,
Joanna Sturm

BELOW *(left to right)*:
Katharine Graham,
Felix and
Marion Frankfurter,
Joe Alsop, and
Alice Longworth

The famous pillow, at her home in Dupont Circle

⋙◆⋘

BELOW: Charming Robert Kennedy who, Mrs. L thought, could have been "a revolutionary priest"

Making a point
to Richard Nixon

◆

BELOW: The "elbow-
in-the-soup"
concentration on
cellist Pablo Casals's
return to the
White House

Joanna Sturm with her grandmother—two women with lightning-quick
and curious intellects who loved and respected each other.

A family favorite photograph of Mrs. L, paused in her reading,
sitting by the phone she always answered herself

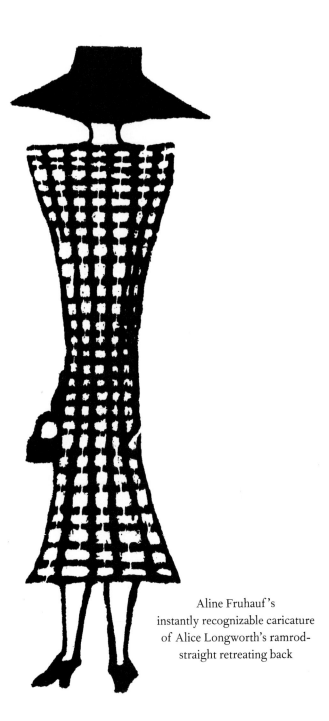

Aline Fruhauf's
instantly recognizable caricature
of Alice Longworth's ramrod-
straight retreating back

her circle, too. Nick's former lover Laura Curtis Gross was a longtime pal. There had been an attempt at a rapprochement with Cissy Patterson before the latter died.[29] Alice was close to Evangeline Bruce, Tish Alsop, former Office of Secret Services operative and columnist Kay Halle, and *Vogue* columnist Susan Mary Patten. A frequent visitor for poker and tea was the intelligent, straight-talking Bazy. She and her husband, Peter Miller, had purchased the LaSalle, Illinois, *News-Tribune* in 1946. In 1949, she took over the editorship of the *Washington Times-Herald*. Shortly thereafter Bazy and Miller divorced and she wed *Times-Herald* city editor Garvin E. Tankersley. Divorce was so uncommon in 1951 that the couple could hardly find a minister to marry them. Disregarding social custom, Alice attended their wedding and often invited Bazy and "Tank" to her home, shocking Washingtonians. After the sale of the *Times-Herald* to the *Washington Post*, Bazy became a successful columnist for the *Chicago Tribune*, writing "Sidelights from the Nation's Capital," for almost twenty years. She shared Alice's conservative political views and was very fond of the older woman.[30]

Edith Hamilton, the popular historian of the ancient world, traded books with Alice, who also sponsored a friend of Hamilton's for membership in the F Street Club. Alice became very good friends with the multi-talented and erudite Huntington Cairns and his wife. Hamilton and Cairns worked together to edit and publish Plato's *Dialogues*, and Cairns was also the editor of one of the most dog-eared books in Alice's library, *The Limits of Art: Poetry and Prose Chosen by Ancient and Modern Critics*. He was an attorney with the U.S. Treasury who, during WWII, had an engrossing position on the U.S. Commission for Protection and Salvage of Artistic and Historic Monuments in War Areas. Cairns was connected to the new National Gallery of Art in Washington. He also, for more than two decades, advised the federal government on censorship issues. He knew as many people as Alice did, in as many fields. Through contacts such as these, in 1947, Alice was able to help John Lewis locate a publisher for one of his books.[31]

That year, Alice assisted the career of another author. Her broad reading brought her into contact with a book she thought worthy of the Pulitzer Prize. She put *Tales of the South Pacific* by a then-unheard-of author named

James A. Michener into the hands of her friend *New York Times* columnist Arthur Krock, who was on the prize committee. *Tales of the South Pacific* was an "unusual" book, she averred, and very unlike Krock's own choice—which Alice felt had "no vitality!" The committee agreed with Alice. She congratulated Michener years later when she met him, saying, "I'm proud of the fact, Michener, that you didn't let us down." The Pulitzer helped to launch James Michener's career. He went on to write more than forty best-selling books, run (unsuccessfully) for Congress, and earn many other awards, including the Medal of Freedom in 1977.[32]

At her home and at the F Street Club, Alice entertained these and other writers. One political spouse emphasized how such parties were "an essential means of communication." David Mitchell experienced this firsthand. Mitchell came to dinner as a friend of Paulina and Alex's. He was a young banker, just stepping into his career. Thinking of his interests, Alice told him, "We must get a banker for you!" Mitchell was grateful at her considerate gesture, but later stunned when he found the other "banker" was Bill Martin, the head of the Federal Reserve Board![33]

But politicians were the mainstays of her get-togethers. Because "she could draw people out masterfully and she was interested in nearly everything," as one guest said, almost anyone could turn up for dinner. In the 1940s, if they were politicians they were usually fellow conservatives such as the Robert Tafts and the Richard Nixons. In later years she would enjoy inviting guests with diametrically opposed viewpoints and seating them next to each other—just because it was fun.[34] She was not the only hostess who did that, but in the immediate aftermath of the Franklin Roosevelt years, as her political leanings then were decidedly rightward, she preferred the company of kindred spirits.

Dean Acheson was one such. The son of an Episcopal bishop, an author, attorney, and secretary of state in the Truman administration, Acheson once resigned as undersecretary of the Treasury under Franklin Roosevelt. He objected to the president's decision to take the United States off the gold standard—the same thing Alice had protested when she draped herself in gold at the White House reception. Acheson was Alice's powerful contact in the State Department. He enjoyed her teas and found her difficult to resist. Acheson confessed to Joe Alsop once, Alice "tempts me to spice my talk." Alice was fond of pointing out to sundry visitors her five-foot-tall wall hanging of a prowling tiger that she thought looked just like the stylish and well-groomed secretary of state. The painting especially captured the subtle menace of his mien—right down to the eyebrows. Acheson's had "a prowling quality" and were "just like a cat's whiskers," Alice said; they "reacted involuntarily."[35] The secretary of state had the cold war to battle and was one of the authors of the U.S. policy of containment toward Communism. Alice shared Acheson's anxieties about the Soviet Union, and for her there was a historical continuum that explained the position of the United States in 1946:

> I think history has borne out my conviction that the first World War should have ended without victors and vanquished. Today it seems that even a German victory early in 1914 or 1915 would have been better than what we got eventually. At least there would not have been a Hitler and not a Russian frontier on the River Elbe. I have often wondered what would have happened to the German character if the Germans had had less misfortune in their past. But that's merely conjectural. Let us speak of the last war. People call me anti-British. That's absurd. I only insist that our relations with the British must not be ruled by a "habitual fondness." Our own interests first, and if they coincide with British interests, all the better. Franklin just as Wilson mismanaged our diplomacy. Of course, Britain's defeat would have imperiled our own security, but as the price of our assistance we should have imposed upon Churchill the spirit of compromise—not with Hitler and his fellows, but with the German opposition. To help Stalin unconditionally was sheer lunacy. What's the use of having Russian imperialism as the successor of both German and Japanese [imperialism]?[36]

Alice honed her opinions by talking with people such as Secretary Acheson, reading methodically, and attending congressional sessions. She was still one of the "regulars" who "habitually frequent every klieg-lighted congressional hearing." Alice was "on hand" for hearings on topics as diverse as candidates for the position of undersecretary of the navy (for which she was spotted wearing black and "daintily waving a long, red cigarette holder"), hearings on "Greek-Turkish loans," and the improprieties in government contracts during the war in the Senate War Investigative Committee.[37]

She herself became a topic in a Senate investigative committee in 1946. In a pamphlet written as part of a "smear campaign" to defeat Alice's friend Senator Burton Wheeler, Alice was accused of unduly influencing senators' votes as the leader of a powerful interest group, the so-called "social lobby." The acrimonious congressional debate began with Senator Wheeler denying that he knew the social lobby. "Well," the *New York Times* reported his interrogator as charging, "I saw the Senator dining with it in the restaurant of the Senate." "What silly nonsense," the Montana senator retorted. "To show the Senators the type of mind that is speaking I will say I had lunch, yes, with Alice Longworth, and I am proud of the fact that she asked me to go to lunch.... She never mentioned this bill. That is the social lobby." Wheeler was an old friend who would not have considered Alice's interest in legislation as *necessarily* lobbying for one outcome or another—and he was a canny politician who wouldn't have admitted it had it occurred. The whole notion would have caused Alice great amusement, but her power did not go unnoticed.[38]

In 1947, she had personal reasons for attending Senate Committee on Labor and Public Welfare hearings. Bob Taft—"Mr. Republican"—was the powerhouse in the GOP-controlled Eightieth Congress that opened on January 6. He and his colleagues set about undoing entrenched New Deal legislation, with varying degrees of success. They wanted to "restore those principles of freedom which had been the foundation stone of America's historical development," as Taft put it.[39] Leading the charge were young conservative legislators, like Ohio's John Bricker, Wisconsin's Joseph McCarthy, South Dakota's Karl Mundt, and California's Richard Nixon. Taft cosponsored the Taft-Hartley Act, designed to replace important sections of the New Deal pro-labor bill, the Wagner Act. For ninety minutes in the Committee on Labor and Public Welfare, Taft led the grilling of John L. Lewis. The labor leader was getting the better of the senator, and applause and laughter greeted some of Lewis's "sallies," the *New York Times* reported:

> "You think you are an average man, Mr. Lewis," remarked Mr. Taft. "It is practically up to you to decide what your union does." "I wonder why you make such an inaccurate statement, Mr. Senator," remarked Mr. Lewis in a drawling voice as he smiled. The chamber echoed to laughter. Mr. Taft persisted. He said the union was run by "powerful" men, not "average men." "I, too, have read in the papers that you are pushing the Republican party around and making the decisions," commented the witness. Quickly Mr. Taft replied that "in this Congress nobody can boss anybody else." "Methinks the Senator doth protest too much," parried Mr. Lewis. The audience tittered.

Alice listened to this wordplay sitting "behind the committee members." After Lewis made clear his opposition to "any amendment of the Wagner Act," he gallantly "extended his hand to her across the table as he left the witness chair."[40]

Family and friends wondered about John Lewis and Alice. The two depended upon telephone calls and visits when they were both in Washington, but their summertime and holiday correspondence gives a sense of their affinity. They exchanged Christmas presents and books; Alice gave him the edited volumes of her father's papers, which John professed he would "treasure." He read them with his daughter, Kathryn, both of whom had admired TR. John's notes echoed her concerns, chiefly Paulina. He worried about Alice's health. He devoted four pages in one note to ideas about when and where they could meet. Her letters, he assured her, "gave a lift to a tired man." The pair were co-conspirators when John Chamberlain of *Time* magazine begged Alice to use her influence over Lewis in the selection of a leader for the United Mine Workers fund: "We know that John Lewis has a great respect for your political acumen." Alice sent Chamberlain's letter on to Lewis, who gave her instructions as to what to say back and how to phrase it.[41] In the 1970s, Alice told a reporter she felt "lucky in my middle age, to find a new delightful companion." When the journalist asked whether they had discussed marriage, she admitted, "I think it was in the wind. But I didn't take it seriously. I wouldn't have married anybody. Once is enough, but, for me, he was the best company there ever was." Like Borah, John was a Renaissance man. He could discuss politics and poetry and family and foreign affairs spiritedly while making her feel she was the only one in the room. And she liked his philosophy for dealing with obstreperous elected officials: "Be subtle. Lure him with the rapier and then cleave him with the axe."[42]

The old causes had new incarnations. In 1947, her isolationism led her to unite with eighty other "prominent Americans" to champion a United States of Europe. She joined an appeal to all Americans for their support. It read, in part, "Twice within our lifetime...the national interest of this country demanded that we participate actively in wars resulting mainly from Europe's disunion. A third World War, springing from the same causes, lies as a threat to our peace and prosperity as long as Europe remains split up into isolated national units." The signers called for an economic union "dedicated to liberty and peace," governed by a "federal police force" that would "release the nations of Europe from the crushing burden of competitive armament." The American group was headed by Arkansas Senator William J. Fulbright and based on the pan-European ideas of Count Richard N. Coudenhove-Kalergi. Alice became a member of the national board, which included Herbert Hoover, Louisiana Democratic representative Hale Boggs, Clare Boothe Luce, James Farley, Allen Dulles, and Norman Thomas. They hoped to support "a common foreign, economic, and military policy and a common 'bill of rights.'" In fact, the organization they wanted sounded very much like the European Economic Community initiated in 1957. This project had something of the outlawry of war in it—a chief concern of Borah's, and perhaps for Alice a way to carry on in his memory. It also was an alternative to the United Nations, a brainchild of Franklin Roosevelt that held its first meeting in 1945. The United Nations involved the United States, but the United States of Europe would not similarly entangle America.[43]

Such foreign policy concerns dominated the 1948 presidential election.

As the cold war unfolded and the iron curtain divided Communist from non-Communist Europe, Republicans applauded President Truman's containment policy and his loyalty programs to locate and purge "subversives" from the civil service. The GOP hit hard at Truman's domestic agenda, suggesting that New Deal–type reforms such as a minimum wage and farm support had outlived their usefulness. Then the Democratic Party, with "one foot in the grave and the other on a banana peel," according to New Dealer Harold L. Ickes, split three ways.[44] President Truman gained a reluctant nod from the Democratic regulars. Southerners opposed to his civil rights initiatives offered their own candidate, South Carolina governor J. Strom Thurmond, on their own ticket, the States' Rights, or Dixiecrat, Party. Iowan Henry A. Wallace, one of FDR's former vice presidents, made a bid with his Progressive Party.

Republicans thus seemed likely to capture the presidency regardless of whom they selected. Alice was one of many celebrities actively working for Bob Taft. She was joined by film star Gary Cooper, poet John Dos Passos, humorist Dorothy Thompson, and columnist and Soviet expert Freda Utley, among others. And it wasn't just celebrities who came out for Taft in 1948. Paulina Longworth Sturm and Bazy McCormick Miller, "two young women, girlhood friends, whose grandfathers made political history," as the *New York Times* described them, founded Twenties-for-Taft. This organization began when the pair gathered twenty-five hundred names of women between the ages of twenty and twenty-nine who pledged to work on behalf of Taft's nomination. It was to no avail. The convention in June passed by Taft again and settled on Thomas E. Dewey, again. Alice was not surprised at Dewey's subsequent defeat. She didn't even vote for him. "You can't," she sniffed, "make a soufflé rise twice."[45]

On September 30, 1948, as the maples at Sagamore Hill dressed themselves in orange and red, Edith died. The end of the former First Lady's life was bitter. "I don't at all like living in this world," she wrote to Alice in 1944—as WWII raged, Franklin still held the presidency, and TR had been gone for twenty-five years. Survived by Alice, Ethel, Archie, and many grandchildren and great-grandchildren, Edith had seen too many years pass in conflict. The recent deaths of Kermit and Ted deepened her sorrow. She had traveled widely as a widow, and had lived a life rich with literature, friends, and family. She never lost her interest in politics. But at the end of her life the normally busy Edith had few plans. "Indeed," she wrote, "my strength is to sit still." But one of the last letters she penned was a thank-you to Alice in a hand shaky with her eighty-seven years. It contained a palliative—straight from the heart of a strong and complex woman seasoned but not broken by life's vicissitudes. "Dearest Alice," she began. "You came to me as a little child and have been a good daughter and I have many happy memories." Alice must have been touched. "Do come to see me when the first trees are blooming and Long Island at its best," Edith urged, "and I shall refuse to let the family sit upon our backs!"[46] It was a tender conclusion to their long relationship.

After Edith's death and with the continued political failings of the Republican Party, Alice found solace in the poetry of Ezra Pound. On her sixty-fourth birthday, she claimed a new "fitting" poem for herself: a stanza of Pound's "The Return":

> SEE, they return; ah, see the tentative
> Movements, and the slow feet,
> The trouble in the pace and the uncertain
> Wavering!
> See, they return, one by one,
> With fear, as half-awakened;
> As if the snow should hesitate
> And murmur in the wind,
> and half turn back;
> These were the "Wing'd-with-Awe,"
> Inviolable.
> Gods of the Wingèd shoe!
> With them the silver hounds,
> sniffing the trace of air!
> Haie! Haie!

These were the swift to harry;
These the keen-scented;
These were the souls of blood.
Slow on the leash,
pallid the leash-men![47]

In 1949, Huntington Cairns took Alice to visit Pound in St. Elizabeth's Mental Hospital in Washington, D.C. They met his wife, Dorothy Pound, "who really took care of him," Alice thought. Joe Alsop, Edith Hamilton, Robert Lowell, and Alice's friend painter Marcella Comes Winslow went to visit the poet. They remembered how his "beard was divided into three parts" and how Pound "used to wear three hats piled on top of each other. Alice thought "At the time it seemed quite natural...."[48]

Ezra Pound fascinated Alice. She owned several inscribed volumes of his poetry. But in Italy he had grown increasingly anti-Semitic. Pound made radio broadcasts condemning the United States as "illegally at war," because of FDR's "criminal acts." When the Allies conquered Italy, American forces jailed Pound, returned him to the United States, and indicted him on several counts of treason against America. When he was found mentally incompetent to stand trial, he was sent to St. Elizabeths.[49]

The mental hospital, one of its physicians averred, "had become a sacrarium for savants," and by the 1950s, visiting Pound "became a status symbol among some circles...a sort of conservative chic." While Alice may have gone for that reason, there were additional attractions: they could bash FDR together, she liked iconoclasts, Pound was a TR fan, and the poet may have reminded her of her days with Bill Borah. In short, as her granddaughter put it, "She had fun with him." Alice and Pound planned to coedit an anthology of poetry from around the world.[50]

A compassionate recognition of Pound's genius and artistic courage made it easier to overlook the fascism and the anti-Semitism and what poet Charles Olson called "the vomit of his conclusions." In 1949, a stellar list of poets saw past Pound's prejudices and awarded him the Library of Congress Bollingen Prize for the *Pisan Cantos*, written during Pound's incarceration in Italy. Established with Cairns's help (Cairns was a trustee of the Bollingen Foundation), the award brought tremendous controversy to the poet, but not freedom.[51] That took another nine years. In 1958, Pound's friends brought about his discharge from St. Elizabeths. Ernest Hemingway, Robert Frost, and T. S. Eliot organized the effort. Alice gave credit to Archibald MacLeish. They won their case in part because they charged that Pound's hospitalization was "intellectually damaging" to the United States, and in the cold war era such a suggestion carried weight. Pound was released into the care of his wife, who returned with him to Italy. The extent of Alice's influence is not clear. She was friendly with those who spearheaded the movement, and it's conceivable that she talked up the cause of his release to politicians and members of the Justice Department at her dinners. She thought Pound was mentally disturbed, but "not a danger to the country" and thus should not be locked up.[52]

One man whom she concluded *was* a true danger to the country was Alger Hiss. Hiss graduated from Harvard Law School and became a model New Dealer, devoting his professional life to governmental service in the Justice and State Departments. In 1947, he was president of the Carnegie Endowment for Peace. His impeccable career made it very hard for most Americans to believe the sensational charge leveled at him in 1948 by Whittaker Chambers, a confessed former Soviet spy. In front of the House Un-American Activities Committee (HUAC), Chambers accused Hiss of being a Russian agent who had worked with him in the 1930s—precisely the years he had served in Roosevelt's administration. Hiss denied it, and he denied knowing Chambers. Representative Richard Nixon, a member of HUAC, was one of the very few who took Chambers's allegation seriously. When Hiss and Chambers both came before the House committee, Alice was there. The case was thrilling and convoluted, and it had everything—duplicity, denials, wild goose chases, microfilm hidden in pumpkins, handwriting analyses, psychological profiling, and allegations of homosexuality. Nixon looked to be a strong cold warrior whose intellect and determination helped him unravel the threads of deception between Hiss and Chambers. After the HUAC hearings, in New York City, Hiss— to protect his name—sued Chambers for slander. He continued to deny that he was a Communist spy, and claimed that he was only a casual acquaintance of Chambers's.

Her friends at the Justice Department sent Alice an "unrestricted pass" for that dramatic case. She was fascinated, and could "hardly bear to leave New York and the trial," when she had to make a trip to Washington. She and her sister-in-law Eleanor were both absorbed in the whole process. Eleanor was reading *The Art of Cross-Examination*, and both of them felt "that any time we spend talking to people about other subjects is wasted!" Eventually, Hiss was sentenced to five years in jail. The public was divided as to Hiss's guilt, but the trial did convince most Americans that Franklin Roosevelt and the Democrats had not been vigilant enough about Communist espionage. When Klaus Fuchs, a Manhattan Project scientist, was found to have given the Communists secret information from the atomic bomb project, Nixon and other hard-liners appeared more reliable than those who advocated a dovish line on the U.S.S.R. After the Hiss trial ended, Alice sent around copies of Victor Lasky's *The Seeds of Treason*. One friend wrote gratefully, "I'm completely satisfied at last that [Hiss] and [his wife] Priscilla are guilty as Hell—and perhaps of a great deal more than has been revealed. Tell Mr. Nixon that he's my new hero—a stunning job he did. Wish they could send <u>him</u> to be your beau on the next big party instead of the infamous Mr. McCarthy."[53]

"The infamous Mr. McCarthy" was Wisconsin's Senator Joseph McCarthy, who capitalized on the fears of Communist infiltration to get himself reelected. In the 1950 campaign, McCarthy intimated that he knew of hundreds of current employees of the federal government who were Communists—and worse, that Secretary of State Dean Acheson knew who they were and allowed them to continue in their positions. Initially, McCarthy looked like an honest crusader. His anti-Communist rhetoric was not unlike Nixon's. Taft and other leading Republicans encouraged McCarthy or copied his talking points in their campaigns.[54]

It was a tense time. China had just "fallen" to Communism. The Soviet Union had recently exploded its first atomic bomb, ending the U.S. monopoly on atomic power. Events in Korea would erupt into a civil war in June, with U.S. soldiers involved there in the United Nations' first ground war. A reporter asked Alice's opinion of the Korean conflict as the U.N. forces were having little success stopping the Communist North Korean advance. "Maybe this will wake people up," Alice commented sharply, "and make them realize how they were sold out" by FDR's wartime diplomacy."[55] Her statement was both a slam at FDR's leadership and evidence of the way she thought of the world.

McCarthy's language influenced the 1952 election as Republicans and Democrats scrambled to prove their anti-Communism. According to Taft's election committee, Taft would "turn our country away from socialistic trends and will restore the free competitive economic system which made America great." Taft's campaign literature in the 1952 election listed Alice Longworth as 1 of 101 names of "The Citizens Crusade for TAFT." Alice continued fund-raising for Taft through the summer, right up to the eve of the 1952 convention in Chicago. She enjoyed her usual suite at the Blackstone Hotel and her usual publicity at the convention. She broke away from the Taft boosting to note that press appreciation of her clothing "will bring cheers" from Paulina, "who insisted upon and selected the wardrobe...."[56] Even Paulina's approval could not compensate for her disappointment that Taft quickly lost his position as front-runner and was denied the nomination yet again.

"Eisenhower was a pleasantly avuncular figure, ideal, I suppose, for the times, but there were certainly no sparks there," Alice said once, but that didn't stop her from being delighted to have a Republican back in the White House. She had worked for the GOP victory, made all the more exciting because her friend Nixon wound up in the vice presidential slot. He claimed that he never really considered seriously the possibility of his nomination for the second spot on the ticket until one of those "behind the scenes conversations" with Alice. She scolded him and told him to discuss it with his wife. "For the good of the party," Alice urged Nixon, "you should take it if you have the chance."[57] When he did, she was pleased. Alice handed out absentee ballots at the Eisenhower-Nixon headquarters in Washington, and donated money to the campaign to help spread, in Eisenhower's words, "the message of our Crusade." Alice must have cackled a bit to learn that John A. Roosevelt, Eleanor and Franklin's son, had crossed the party line and was also out campaigning for Eisenhower and Nixon. She urged her sister, Ethel, to come visit her in Washington and "take a look at Our Side as soon as they move in. Ike is doing well, don't you think?"[58]

She was moved to excesses of praise for Eisenhower: "Today for the first time since 1909," Alice wrote him after the State of the Union address, "I glowed with pride and enthusiasm for a speech by a president not only for what you said but for how you said it. I've looked at politics and government for a long time (it's 63 years this winter that I first came to Washington) and I want to tell you it's mighty pleasant to feel pride and confidence in the leadership which you have shown you possess." Alice was also pleased that the Eisenhowers reestablished the OLD SOCIAL WHIRL, as Bess Furman headlined in the *New York Times*, and Republicans were happy to showcase TR's daughter. Eisenhower told Alice that her favorite John Singer Sargent portrait of TR "occupies the dominant spot in the Cabinet Room these days."[59] The fact that a Republican was back in the White House also facilitated a resurgence in the Theodore Roosevelt industry.

Alice was very involved in the monuments established to honor her father. While the three remaining Roosevelt children did not always agree among themselves on the details, overall the siblings shared a vision of apposite memorializing. In 1919, the Theodore Roosevelt Memorial Association (TRMA) had been born to preserve the memory of the president. After Edith's death, the TRMA purchased Sagamore Hill and turned it into a "presidential shrine." President Eisenhower opened Sagamore Hill to the public in 1953 with a live national radio speech. On the veranda where the Roosevelts had spent so many happy summers were twenty of TR and Edith's grandchildren, wiggling loose teeth, coloring pictures, and waving to the visitors.[60]

Several books had marked the ongoing interest in the nation's twenty-sixth president, spurred by Harvard University Press's eight volumes of the *Letters of Theodore Roosevelt*. In the early 1950s, they were edited by Elting E. Morison and a young historian named John Morton Blum, author of the influential biography *The Republican Roosevelt*. The TRMA threw a party to launch the *Letters*, held at the TR birthplace in New York City. Blum recalled evocatively: "We had all assembled for cocktails when Mrs.

Longworth appeared in the archway...A hush fell as she stood there, a cigarette holder in her mouth, exactly like the holder Franklin Roosevelt had so often used and at exactly the same angle. She had on her head a diamond tiara and she wore a shimmering evening gown of 'Alice blue.' Mrs. Longworth was about seventy then and I was thirty, but I had never seen a sexier woman." She "projected," Blum felt, "the charisma attributed to her father...."[61]

The Republican landslide of 1952 made Bob Taft Senate majority leader, but he did not live long enough to enjoy it. Senator Taft died in July 1953 after a brief but devastating bout with cancer. He was sixty-four. In his memory, friends established the Robert A. Taft Memorial Foundation "to promote the advancement and diffusion of knowledge and understanding." Alice agreed to serve as a trustee, as did Bazy Tankersley and a number of senators who had worked closely with Taft. Had he lived, Taft would have supported another of Alice's causes that year: an alternative to "United Nations Day" called "United States Day." Governor J. Bracken Lee of Utah boycotted, for the second year in a row, United Nations Day. Backed by Alice, General Mark Clark and *Chicago Tribune* publisher Colonel Robert McCormick—members of the advisory committee to "United States Day"—the governor objected to the inclusion of the Soviet Union in the U.N.[62]

Communist Russia's insidious infiltration of American institutions, especially the federal government and even the U.S. military, was the "red flag" Senator Joe McCarthy waved before voters in 1952. His constituents reelected him handily in the Republican rout that year, which served to encourage him to heights of extremism. In his investigations—which ranged broadly across education, media, and government—McCarthy alleged that such men as Secretary of State Dean Acheson and Secretary of Defense George C. Marshall were soft on Communism. When McCarthy accused the U.S. Army of harboring Communists, the army struck back. In the televised Army-McCarthy hearings that spring and summer of 1954, it became clear that there was no low to which the senator would not stoop. His badgering provoked attorney Joseph N. Welch to ask, "Have you no sense of decency, sir?'" as Americans watched on new television sets a man who seemed to be without scruples or morals.

Alice attended the Army-McCarthy hearings, sitting sometimes with wife of the vice president, Pat Nixon. When asked by a reporter who saw her there for the third time what side she was on, "She replied: 'I maintain my usual viewpoint of detached malevolence.'" Alice's lifelong isolationism made her inclined to worry about Soviet infiltration, and McCarthy fed her love of spectacle and appreciation for political drama. But Alice saw a side of the senator she did not like at all. As her friends attested, she was a good judge of people and could see right through them. While she had initially enjoyed him "because he was so wicked," the moment McCarthy slid into alcoholism, "that ruled him out," stressed Bill Walton. "Now *there*," Alice said about Joe McCarthy, "was a cheap creature. He had the easy manners of a perfect jay." One friend remembered that Alice "hated" McCarthy and displayed on her mantel a devastating cartoon that made fun of him. At a party in 1950, while at the height of his notoriety, McCarthy draped his arm around Mrs. Longworth. "With a kind of yokel jocularity, he brayed, 'Ah, here is my blind date. I'm going to call you Alice.' She leveled her gaze at him and said, 'No, Senator McCarthy, you are *not* going to call me Alice. The truckman, the trashman, and the policemen on the block may call me Alice but you may not.'"[63]

Nixon's stature grew among conservatives, and Alice found him very interesting. He was "competent," and she liked him. Before and during Senator McCarthy's "sin of pride," as he called it, Nixon came often to her salon. He told stories from inside the battle, like the time he broke up a fight between McCarthy and Drew Pearson, just after the senator slapped the journalist in the cloakroom of the Sulgrave Club. "When Nixon sought your company he probably thought that it was a political advantage," one interviewer suggested to Alice. "I'm certain that he did," she responded. "We took it for granted that it probably was." As she championed him, he became something of a champion to her. A loyal supporter from his earliest days in the House, Alice swept up Nixon, his wife, and their two daughters. Their friendship was well known, and others went to her asking for her help in securing the Nixons for dinner parties. In 1955, papers noted that the vice president "took time off for a long private luncheon at the home of Mrs. Alice Longworth...." In 1959, Nixon appeared on her appointment calendar for at least eight tête-à-têtes. Her friendship lent both social and political cachet. Invitations to her dinners would have been very useful to him, as "political 'inside-dope' stories, rumors, tips, reports of personal feuds, and party intrigue are ... favorite topics of conversation."[64]

As Nixon toiled in President Eisenhower's shadow, the U.S. economy roared. The baby boom was at its height—Alice's own granddaughter was a part of that demographic phenomenon—and the first strums of bubble-gum rock were being played. The modern civil rights movement began as Barbara Johns and Linda Brown called the country to task for an unjustifiable system of separate but equal education. Eisenhower personally went to Korea to end the Korean conflict, as he had promised. While there was no real victor in that war, no atomic weapons were used, and the cold war remained the backdrop against which legislative decisions were made. Overall, the country was happy with Eisenhower's administration. When he announced his bid for renomination by the GOP in 1956, Alice cracked, "Well, I see he's thrown his halo in the ring again." She wrote to congratulate President Eisenhower on his reelection, and told him in person at the inauguration festivities. One week later, Alice's world shattered when her daughter died.[65]

Paulina's marriage had been brief and rocky. Alex never really found his stride as a writer, but in 1949, he and his friend William B. Ruger founded Sturm, Ruger & Company. Alex's fifty thousand dollars and Ruger's tool-making skills created what would become "the largest firearms company in the United States." Ruger had "perfected a design for a .22-caliber automatic pistol," which was their starting point. Paulina and Katherine Sturm's secretarial abilities helped launch the company. It was an optimistic time in the family, and Joanna was thriving. According to her grandmother, at three she could "talk glibly on every conceivable subject and she never forgets anything she is told. She adores Paulina and I think tries to be especially good on that account—Her father and his factory are also pretty grand." But two years later, when his daughter was only five years old, alcohol-related hepatitis killed Alex.[66]

Paulina turned to the Roman Catholic Church for solace. Encouraged by friends who thought that the stability and ritual of the mass and the church year would help her, Paulina took to her new religion with zeal. After Alex's death, Paulina and Joanna had moved back to Washington, D.C. She bought a small house at 1220 Twenty-eighth Street, about a mile from Alice's home. Paulina volunteered with Dorothy Day's Catholic Worker social justice organization, but she was plagued by persistent migraine headaches, and the grief caused by Alex's death would not lift. Paulina took nightly refuge in alcohol. Her physician prescribed sleeping pills and pain killers, and on January 27, 1957, an overdose of the medicines, coupled with alcohol, led to her death. Day wrote a poignant panegyric for Paulina, about whom she suggested "there was always something child-like and shy" but "she was valiant, too."[67]

Alice believed that the overdose was unintentional. Paulina had Joanna to live for. Just as important, a newly converted Catholic would never succumb to suicide, given the church's teachings. The church's official position was that suicide was "unlawful," a "most atrocious crime" wherein a human took to himself God's "dominion over life." Some friends expressed a different opinion about Paulina. Bill Walton thought that such accidents occur only when one is "wooing death." He admired Alice for her tenacious crusade to make sure that her daughter was not deprived of the ecclesiastical burial that she would have been denied had her death been ruled a suicide. Other friends blamed the doctor for prescribing the sleeping pills, because in combination with the other drugs, they were lethal. On the day of her death, Paulina's neighbors recalled that she had been in very good spirits and looking forward to an upcoming trip. They saw no reason for concern.[68]

As usual, Alice kept her deepest sorrows to herself. No matter how poor a mother she may have been, Alice did love Paulina very much. Her nickname for her daughter was "Presh," short for Precious. One note from Alice to "Presh my darling," scribbled in pencil and in haste, concluded,

"Remember only that I love you—my darling Presh. I love you. Mother."
Janie McLaughlin, who worked for Alice from 1958 until 1980, recalled
that Alice always kept photographs of Paulina in her bedroom. Alice, at age
seventy-four—and recovering then from a radical mastectomy—took in
her ten-year-old granddaughter. Even though there were others who
wanted Joanna to live with them, Alice stood firm. Paulina had left Joanna
in her care, and Alice wanted to honor that. Alice told Bazy, in an unusually
emotional exchange, that she felt she had "been given a second chance."[69]

At her Dupont Circle home, Alice created for Joanna "an aerie on the
fourth floor" and said the two would live as " 'free spirits' together." Looking for playmates for Joanna and support in the raising of her granddaughter, Alice reached out to her sisters-in-law and other family members. She
wrote to cousin Eleanor in July 1957, and ER promised to visit her and Joanna in Washington. Alice turned most of all to Ruth's daughter Bazy
Tankersley, who had a daughter, Kristie Miller, almost Joanna's age. The
two became close friends. Joanna would come to call Kristie her "pseudo-
sister." Both girls—especially Joanna—loved horses, and the Tankersleys
owned a horse farm in Maryland where Bazy bred and sold Arabians. After
school, Joanna frequently went to their Al-Marah Farm to ride.[70]

Joanna reaped the benefits of being Alice Longworth's granddaughter—such as having tea at the Eisenhower White House—but Alice and
Bazy also worked hard to provide stability and a life with routines and
schedules that had been missing. Every summer, for example, Alice
and Joanna returned to Wyoming, where Alice had taken Paulina as a girl.
Grandmother and granddaughter rode together at the Sunlight Ranch and
relaxed. The rest of the year, Joanna attended school, went riding at Al-
Marah, returned home for dinner with "Grammy," did her homework, and
went to bed. Alice and Joanna would find they were kindred spirits, and
their relationship would become extremely close.

But in the aftermath of Paulina's death, Ethel worried about her sister.
Ethel wrote eight months after the tragedy: "Is it all as beautiful and satisfying as ever? And do you listen to the wind and watch the shadows and
love it all? I am sure Joanna is busy and happy, which ... [is] ... good ... for
grandparents. ... Are you yet able to sing on your charred limb? I keep

thinking about you and yr agony of spirit over what is past and gone—and I hope that it is lessening. Such terrible blows take time to bud up the wound—it never heals of course. But some people's bandages seem wonderfully durable. Mine aren't." Then she quoted Yeats, from "The Ballad of Father Gilligan":

> He Who hath made the night of stars
> For souls who tire and bleed
> Sent one of His great angels down
> To help me in my need.

Ethel, always gracious, used Yeats as a bridge to connect Alice's sorrows with hers—both their souls tired and bled, but they could be "great angels" to each other. Her husband, Dick, was not well, and, as she told Alice gently, "I don't agree with you about not telling the bad things to the special ones, so I tell you all this."[71]

Chapter 21

"The Most Fascinating Conversationalist of Our Time"

THE 1960S OPENED with a thrilling presidential race. Alice Longworth was personally fond of both contenders, so she could not have been happier. She preferred Richard Nixon's Republican politics, but the whole Kennedy clan delighted her. Either outcome augured well for the upcoming four years. Nixon thought Mrs. Longworth "the most fascinating conversationalist of our time." Both he and his opponent, John F. Kennedy, pronounced Alice their favorite dinner partner. Mrs. L, as she was generally called then, was in her seventies and a recognized Washington icon. Should anyone outside the new Capital Beltway have forgotten, her national reputation was solidified by media coverage of her eighty-fifth and ninetieth birthday parties and the trip she and her granddaughter took to Asia, where she hadn't been for sixty years. Admirers there recognized her as "Alice Blue Gown." At home, her teas, like the hostess herself, had a legendary quality, and journalists, friends, politicians, and family came to entertain and be entertained as they had for the past fifty years. Katharine "Kay" Graham watched Alice for a model of aging gracefully. "Read a lot and not drink" was her summation of Alice's secret.[1] Even as Dupont Circle filled with multistory buildings and amusing hippies, Theodore Roosevelt's daughter remained engaged in current events and opinionated about the passing political scene, as feisty and independent a celebrity as ever.

The Eisenhowers had been good to Alice Longworth, but they were not dear friends. Nor, as it turned out, was President Eisenhower particularly close to his vice president. During the 1960 presidential race, Eisenhower informed reporters he could not think of a single instance when Nixon's ideas had been so compelling that he had adopted them. Alice had a higher opinion of Dick Nixon. She stood by him throughout his phoenixlike career, losing patience only at the bitter end of Watergate. She emphasized frequently to reporters that Nixon was "exceedingly level-headed," a man who "knows what goes on in the world."[2]

Alice avidly watched Nixon's performance in America's first televised presidential debate. Joe Alsop phoned Alice for her opinion. He considered her a brilliant "political handicapper" ever since she had told him, on election eve in 1948, that she didn't think Truman was beaten. "Well, Joe," Alice told him glumly in 1960, "your man's in, my man's finished. I don't see why they bother to go on with the election. Dick has finished himself off." Even though Alsop believed, like Alice, that "the real Nixon was vastly more interesting, impressive, and formidable than his popular image," he lost the election by less than one percentage point—a 118,000 popular vote difference—in one of the closest presidential races in U.S. history. The Nixons retreated to California. Dick and Alice kept up a running exchange of books, and Pat lamented the absence of their "famous 'sessions' which were always so stimulating." When Nixon ran for the California governor's seat, Alice sent him what he considered a "more than generous" financial contribution, but he lost and seemed destined for obscurity. However, she vowed publicly that Nixon would "continue to have my company, because this is a real personal friendship."[3]

As the Nixons left, the charismatic Kennedys moved to the center of Washington politics and society. "I like *all* Kennedys. I've a real feeling for them," Alice said. She called President Kennedy a "literate man of action," just like her father. While she thought that President Kennedy had a fine mind, she saw a kind of fire in Attorney General Robert "Bobby" Kennedy and felt he could have been "a revolutionary priest, a member of Sinn Fein." She also thought that Bobby would have made an excellent president or elder statesman. She told an interviewer in 1967 that Nixon and Bobby were "two of the trickiest politicians I've known—and I like tricks." Bobby had a sense of humor, which Alice appreciated. "I liked Bobby," she affirmed; they shared "a real feeling of amusement and empathy." Alice swore that, when together, they never discussed politics, but that they "would gossip about things." "We strive to amuse the other," she said, "as scrupulous and splendid guests—both of us . . . a hostess's delight!"[4]

As a friend of the Kennedys since the president's senatorial days, Mrs. L attended the inauguration. John Kennedy's address centered on foreign policy, warning that the United States was willing "to pay any price, bear any burden" to fight the threat of Communism. Alice, who was always more attuned to foreign policy than domestic, approved of his hard line on Communism, and she enjoyed all of the vivacious, optimistic, intelligent, passionate young people clustered around his family. She had been to "oh, lots" of the seminars at Hickory Hill, the estate of Robert and Ethel Kennedy. Home to a large and loving clan, Hickory Hill reminded Alice happily of Sagamore Hill, with its children and animals and air of informality. But Alice felt the Hickory Hill seminars were unique. Those invited to "Hickory Hill U." came to eat, drink, and discuss current events— from politics to psychology—under the leadership of experts such as Harvard historian Arthur Schlesinger Jr. and MIT economist Walter Rostow. Philosopher Mortimer Adler cotaught a session in 1962, for example, with Notre Dame's Father John J. Cavanaugh on "whether the Declaration of Independence makes America a Christian country." While this could have been intellectuals trotting out their pie-in-the-sky notions to show off, Alice concluded, "There was nothing precious" about the Hickory Hill gatherings; it was "not snobbery." She thought Schlesinger was "*so* good; he really was a pleasure to listen to." In turn, he found Alice "really quite witty and entertaining," which he didn't expect, as he had supported FDR. Other guests might include Secretary of Defense Robert S. McNamara, United States Information Agency head Edward R. Murrow, Secretary of the Treasury Douglas Dillon, economist John Kenneth Galbraith, Secretary of the Interior Stewart Udall, Ambassador Averell Harriman, and White House press secretary Pierre Salinger. Alice, with her typical modesty about her intellect, claimed she was "too self-conscious" ever to ask a question and usually sat "looking, listening, delighted to be there." Kennedy chronicler David Halberstam reported that at the Hickory Hill seminars, "the women had to be either very pretty, or Mrs. Longworth."[5]

Kay Graham, who became the influential publisher of the *Washington Post* after her husband Phil's death in 1963, described Mrs. Longworth during the Kennedy era as occupying "an established position in Washington as an older prominent figure whom we all adored. She was so established that she was known as 'Washington's other monument.'...Mrs. L had a distinguished aquiline face and long hair tucked up somehow, but not neatly. She was highly intelligent, witty, sharp, and irreverent. She had a caustic and quick wit....She was everybody's favorite dinner guest." In February 1963, British socialite Lady Diana Cooper, visiting Joe and Susan Mary Alsop, was the honoree at a party with a guest list that included Robert and Ethel Kennedy, Edward and Joan Kennedy, Douglas Dillon, Senator John Sherman Cooper, Ambassador David Bruce, and Alice Longworth. The "singular focus of the conversation," Lady Diana remembered, was "politics, politics."[6] And that remained Mrs. L's avocation.

Alice was in her element during the Kennedy era, as the president and First Lady sparked a renaissance of gracious entertaining. Invitations to her salon had always been "a passport to the President's ear" and, as one hostess noted, "Even presidents came to her parties." One analyst's opinion was that Alice's "flattery prompted politicians to repay her graciousness by taking her aside and divulging juicy classified tidbits." On the other hand, old friend Justice Felix Frankfurter was always glad to give her his opinions because, he told her, "you use your tongue for truth-speaking and not for blarney." In 1966, Robert E. Kintner, powerful president of NBC, rated Alice "a fund of accurate information...." Part of the appeal of dining at the Longworth table was a guarantee of confidentiality for all those present. For example, Alice's niece Lucky Roosevelt, then a *Washington Star* journalist, remembered, "We had a tacit understanding that I would never report anything about Mrs. Longworth's dinners, but thanks to her I came to know the Washington establishment."[7]

Alice Longworth's dinners were unaffected by the fads of younger hostesses. Lucky Roosevelt recalled, "We must have dined with Mrs. Longworth dozens of times, and the menu was always the same—crab soup, roast filet of beef with tiny potatoes and a vegetable or two, miniature biscuits, salad and cheese, and the best crème brûlée in the world. Delicious

French wines always accompanied the meal, and the long table was laid with a lace cloth, enough silver to stock Tiffany's and the finest Baccarat glasses." Alice's sister, Ethel, complimented her: "I don't think anyone entertains as well as you do. Everything about it is perfect—food and flowers and silver and china as well as the people you have." Alice Longworth's dinners were such an institution that she apparently didn't even alter her menu for the Catholic Kennedys. "You are a temptress—our Eve of the New Frontier," Ethel Kennedy wrote impishly. "It's always jolly eating meat on Friday." Alice also resisted the social innovation called the cocktail party, which she dismissed as "a Shriner's convention," where the liquor interfered with business.[8]

Her afternoon teas were traditional, too. They involved "tea from a small Dutch silver caddy; a shallow kettle bought half a century ago in London at the Army and Navy stores." Alice lit the burner herself and served Earl Grey tea from the venerable firm Jacksons of Piccadilly. Mrs. L preferred her tea Russian style—sweetened strongly with brown sugar and served in a tall glass that sat in a silver holder. The kettle on the table boiled loudly, but hostess and guests ignored it if the conversation was engrossing. With the tea, Alice served crisp homemade sugar cookies—sometimes with cinnamon—chocolate cake, and bread and butter. Alice Longworth had tea every afternoon, by herself on occasion, more often with one to a dozen other people. Generally, Alice phoned to invite friends, but every now and then people simply dropped in, as her name was in the local phone book.[9]

Those who gathered around her commented on how attractive Mrs. Longworth was. "Her face is mobile, always registering thought and emotion," one interviewer observed. Many friends praised her striking bone structure and the clear blue of her eyes, but Alice had grown very thin. Still lithe and flexible enough to put her toes behind her ears or stand on her head—both of which she did frequently—she was diagnosed with emphysema around 1960, the result of decades of smoking. She had quit by the time Janie McLaughlin came to work for her in 1958, but the illness left her short of breath and made her cough. Alice's greatest fear was that the emphysema would force her to slow the rapid pace of her conversation, which would be "absolute hell on earth." In the Roosevelt tradition, few people knew about the emphysema—but her sister did. "What a nice visit," Ethel wrote in 1962. "I feel all caught up and as ever, enchanted and bemused by you.... You have what is very rare—a way of disregarding, never mentioning, troubles and doubts and pains and aches—which surround us— you down them in a way that is an example."[10]

Even though she was frailer, Alice commanded center stage. John L. Lewis remained part of her life until his death in 1969. Austrian actor Oskar Werner, Johnson adviser Jack Valenti, producer of *Meet the Press* Larry Spivak, and Ambassador Sol Linowitz found their way to her table—her poker table, in the cases of Spivak and Linowitz—and the artist "Andy" (as he signed himself in cards to her) Wyeth and his wife, Betsy. Otto von Habsburg, legatee of the Habsburg dynasty, thanked her for the "charming luncheon." MacGeorge Bundy claimed Alice had overcome his "extremely strong prejudice against Sunday brunch," because hers was "sheer fun."[11]

Alice recalled the long-ago lessons from Auntie Bye. Bye was remembered not for her debilitating arthritis or her deafness, but for her ability to bring together all sorts of people, "all ages...and all kinds." A friend asserted that Bye had "a great gift for mixing people up and yet making everything go perfectly well. She had, in the finest meaning of the expression, a perfectly wonderful, extraordinary social sense." At Bye's home in Connecticut, "there were piles of books on tables and chairs—she read everything in the world—and her comments were extraordinary about all topics of the day."[12] That precisely described Alice as well. As television made inroads, Alice used it as another news source. She watched an occasional television drama like *Ben-Hur*. Her scientific, philosophical, political, and poetical reading continued.

Mrs. L earned her reputation for a caustic and quick wit, but she was also charming and full of good stories. She went out of her way to include bashful guests and to set them at ease. And she was a Roosevelt. This sense of self, and sense of self-in-history, was part of it. She was mellowing, but as Joanna's friend Kristie Miller asserted, Mrs. L still "did not suffer fools lightly. If you crossed her of course you were going to feel the lash." She could be impatient. Bill Walton called her "wicked," and "naughty," but Robert Hellman, who styled himself "Joanna's close friend and male alter ego," said he'd never seen Alice be cruel to anyone who was defenseless. More than anything, Alice was interesting and fun to be with, especially because of her mordant humor and her comprehensive intellect. Mrs. L was a polymath, able to discuss nearly any topic with more than passing knowledge. Walton remembered how entertaining it was to hear her quote great passages from various authors. "It would be something apropos, politically, that she thought fitted. And she'd just *rip* through it. She had," Walton summed up, "the goddamnedest memory of anyone I've ever run across." She could also laugh at herself. Once a dinner partner stopped her short with, "Alice, you say things with more finality to less foundation than anyone I know." She hooted "harder than he did."[13]

Alice thought no one had "a drier, more delightful, humorous, ironic view of life" than President Kennedy and she regularly enjoyed his company. She found him "an engaging character of great ability who needed no window dressing." She respected his mind, what she called "his natural bent for knowledge." She applauded First Lady Jacqueline Kennedy's attempts to restore the White House and support the fine arts. Alice was present in November 1961 when Spain's virtuoso cellist Pablo Casals played for the second time in the White House. The first appearance had been in 1904, when Alice was First Daughter. After the hour-long concert, in front of the other 152 guests, the president presented Mrs. Longworth to Casals. Mrs. L dined with the first family before the pre-Broadway opening of Irving Berlin's musical *Mr. President*, which she viewed from the presidential box—along with Kennedy matriarch Rose Kennedy and Bill Walton—at the National Theatre. The same summer of 1962, Alice, looking "spry and chic in a wide-brimmed, black straw hat," stood by the Kennedys in the White House at the unveiling of the restored "bison mantel," a TR era adornment. Alice was pleased when Kennedy signed a bill to name the Longworth House Office Building after Nick. In October 1963, she dined with the president and the First Lady at the White House as preparations for the 1964 presidential campaign were being laid.[14]

One month later, John F. Kennedy was assassinated in Dallas. Joe Alsop took it very hard, "sobbing uncontrollably" at the confirmation of Kennedy's death. Alice was not shocked—her own father had been shot by a madman—but she was deeply saddened. She thought Joe was being too "boy stood-on-the-burning-deckish." Alice especially decried any attempt to turn Kennedy into a martyr. The potential for assassination, she believed, came with the job of president, and she found it rather pathetic that Americans needed to deify Kennedy. "The moment he died," she mused, "the desire to have a god to worship was extraordinary."[15]

This is not to say she didn't mourn Jack Kennedy. She attended the funeral mass at Saint Matthew's Cathedral with the Alsops, and Ted Kennedy telegraphed to ask her to the East Room of the White House to "join in paying him respects." Alice's condolence letters were heartfelt. To Jackie, she wrote: "Your fortitude through those cruel hours in Dallas and after is unforgettable. I think you know my affection for you and Jack and how I appreciate the unique luster of intelligence, of beauty, of gayety you two imparted to the Presidency. Should you sometime care to see me you need only say so. Love from your affectionate old friend." And to Bobby she asserted: "You Kennedys have an epic quality, of the sort that legends are made of. I don't believe that any family has [ever] taken a brutal tragedy of personal loss with such unflinching courage. Especially you. Because I've always thought that you and Jack had a kinship, a like sense of purpose, beyond the fact of being brothers. I want you to know how truly sorry I am. Love to Ethel and to you."[16]

Alice knew what it was to lose a beloved brother. She was still mourning hers. Ethel Roosevelt Derby wrote in 1964, twenty years after their eldest brother's death: "Dearest Sister:—The Ted. I never forget when you called me the day we heard nor do I ever forget how brave you are, in more ways perhaps than anyone now, but I know." Ethel felt that "the years would not have brought him great satisfaction. What would he have done—," she asked rhetorically.[17] Thoughts such as that didn't much decrease the pain of the living.

When Senator Robert Kennedy was assassinated in June 1968, in the midst of the presidential nomination season, Alice had no public reaction. But she grieved Bobby's death as keenly as she had his brother's. At the time, she was having her portrait painted by Marcella Comes Winslow. Winslow remembered how pictures of Bobby decorated Alice's house and asked compassionately whether she wanted to pose that day, Alice replied, " 'Well, yes, what's wrong with you?' She liked to put on that nothing could really bother her," Winslow thought.[18] Alice was invited to the requiem mass at Saint Patrick's Cathedral in New York City and to the funeral train that took mourners to the interment in Arlington National Cemetery. But she passed up the offer to contribute to *That Shining Hour,* a book of recollections about Senator Kennedy put together by his sister Patricia Kennedy Lawford. Alice abhorred the public need to enshrine either Kennedy after death.

Alice supported former First Lady Jacqueline Kennedy's remarriage to Greek shipping magnate Aristotle Onassis. Not all Americans were pleased to see the iconic First Lady remarry. Alice knew what life on the pedestal felt like and congratulated Jackie for doing just as she pleased: "I've always thought that the delightful damsel at the right on the bull leaping frescos at the [Palace at] Knossos was a Minoan YOU—so now you are returning to the lands and seas of your forebears and Mr. Onassis' names should be Minos and Odysseus instead of those overworked classicals, inappropriate for the Mycenaen he most surely is. This is just a line to tell you what a great pleasure you are and to wish you happiness. . . ." In her return note Jackie "marvel[ed]" at Alice's "original and penetrating way" of seeing and sensing things. "I always did want to live in the Minoan Age," Jackie confirmed. And she closed with her hope that Alice would someday soon meet "Ari."[19]

By the time Jackie Kennedy was planning her wedding, Lyndon Johnson's presidency was winding down. Vice President Johnson had assumed the office in 1963 upon Kennedy's death. Alice thought highly of the whole Johnson family, and they treated her as a national treasure. President Johnson used to introduce her as "the closest thing we have to royalty." She considered him "a lovely rogue elephant," with whom she "had great fun." Alice felt "Lyndon had real flavor. He was not all tight and buttoned up." LBJ may have reminded Alice of Nick's old partner in the House, another Democratic Texan, Cactus Jack Garner, or it may have been Johnson's policy on Vietnam, but his wife, Lady Bird, thought that "they both recognize[d] in each other a strong untamed spirit." For whatever combination of reasons, in 1964, Alice crossed party lines and voted for Johnson. She had taken to calling herself a Bull Moose, not a Republican.[20]

During the Johnson administration, Mrs. L received invitations to banner White House events such as the large musicale in honor of Italy's prime minister Aldo Moro, where American opera diva Leontyne Price sang. The First Lady enjoyed Mrs L. After a lengthy tea, Lady Bird wrote in her diary that "one of the main things I like about Alice Longworth is her spirit and vitality at seventy-nine or thereabouts." Mrs. Johnson encouraged Alice to reminisce about her days as First Daughter once when daughter Lynda joined them for tea. Alice thought Lynda "a nice, serious creature," which was high praise. Lynda and Mrs. L continued their conversation at Alice's home, where they agreed that as a First Daughter "you were damned if you do and damned if you don't." A year later, Alice returned with Joanna for another tea with Lynda and Lady Bird. The First Lady found Alice, age eighty-one, "fiercely undaunted by old age, bristling with the quality of aliveness," telling stories about how she had to escape the White House for Auntie Bye's if she wanted gentlemen callers.[21] Lynda was probably sympathetic, given media interest in her and her sister, Luci.

As the Johnson daughters announced their engagements, that attention reached frenzied proportions. Lady Bird wanted to bring about "a meeting of the bride of half a century ago with the bride of 1966," and so she invited Alice—"an explosion of vitality and interest"—to tell Luci about her escapades. Lynda was also present to hear Mrs. L discuss how much less invasive the press was then, and how she and Nick were never bothered on their honeymoon by inquisitive journalists.[22]

Lady Bird Johnson was an activist First Lady whose cause, environmentalism, was called "beautification" then. Her interests resonated in Alice, who had inherited her father's concern for environmental conservation. Alice told an interviewer that the First Lady "was working so hard to make things better and pleasanter for people; she has unfailing good humor and knows what goes on with politics...." Mrs. L called on Lady Bird to give her tickets to a movie premiere to support the World Wildlife Fund. Alice's philanthropy was nearly always done quietly, and was frequently on behalf of environmental causes. One regular visitor to her home in her later decades was British naturalist Gerald Durrell, author of *My Family and Other Animals*, whose brother, novelist Lawrence Durrell, came occasionally as well. Alice often sent Gerald Durrell away fortified with a donation for the Wildlife Preservation Trust, which he founded.[23]

The Johnsons also had an admiration for Theodore Roosevelt in common with Alice. In January 1965, President Johnson hand delivered to Alice's door a remembrance of the forty-sixth anniversary of TR's death. "Yours is a proud heritage," LBJ wrote in a letter released to the public, "and I would like on this day to express to you something of the gratitude which our nation feels for the wise and vigorous leadership into the twentieth century which President Roosevelt gave us." Alice, giving credit where she thought credit was due, wrote to her friend MacGeorge Bundy to thank him for putting LBJ up to it. Bundy denied it, and suggested kindly that LBJ himself wrote the letter "because it so precisely reflects his own feeling about your father and about you." Regardless of its origin, Alice was "profoundly touched," she wrote to Johnson, "by your knowledge and estimate of what he was." Two years later, Alice helped President Johnson dedicate the giant statue of TR on Roosevelt Island in Washington, D.C. Alice seldom turned away an opportunity to showcase her father and his legacy. She and her sister, Ethel, took Lady Bird and Lynda on a personalized one-hour tour of Sagamore Hill, and one of the gifts Alice presented to LBJ was a biography of her father.[24]

Mrs. L also appreciated the Johnsons' concerns about the preservation of national history. She was a guest of honor at Mrs. Johnson's luncheon for "prime movers in historic preservation projects." Since she was not a member of the National Trust for Historic Preservation, Alice laughed to reporters that she must have been invited because they were interested in the "preservation of a national s-i-g-h-t." By then, Alice herself was regularly called "more of a landmark than the Washington monument."[25]

When Lyndon Johnson declined to run for reelection in 1968, Alice sent him a letter of support: "I want you to know how grateful I am for your splendid, faultless stand on Vietnam." By 1967, before the North Vietnamese Tet offensive, which halved U.S. public support for the war, Alice had begun to lose faith in the war effort. "We have not rushed into this god damned thing. We've taken a long time to get where we are and apparently we're going to take a long time to get away from it...," she complained to a friend privately.[26]

Events in Vietnam neither dampened Alice's enthusiasm for the Johnsons nor quenched her desire to revisit Asia when the chance presented itself in 1965. Alice decided to return to the sites she had visited in 1905 when, as she put it, "China was still Cathay" and she "saw it with the eyes of Kipling and Conrad."[27] Accompanying her was her granddaughter, Joanna, in college then, and her good friend Joan Braden. The three went by way of Honolulu, just as Alice had done sixty years earlier. Joanna's friend Kristie Miller joined them in Japan. Mrs. L's companions were amazed at her recall of the details of locales that she hadn't seen in more than half a century.

The highlights of the 1965 trip for Alice included a visit with her old friend Charles Lee, who owned a hotel in Hong Kong, and an interesting time at the Japan Monkey Center. There she indulged her lifelong fascination with primate evolution and was given a special tour of the center's extensive facilities. The Monkey Center had opened less than a decade earlier and had already established an excellent reputation as a research facility. Mrs. L found the many different monkeys more interesting than the current emperor and empress of Japan, having, she said, "met the Emperor the last time I was here." Nevertheless, Miller remembered, the Japanese people "liked her very much and were flattered by her having made the trip."[28]

In between excursions, Alice visited with Dorothy Emmerson, wife of the Charge d'affaires at the American Embassy in Tokyo. Emmerson recalled the eighty-one-year-old Alice sitting in the lotus position—taught to her, along with other yoga positions, by TR—on the veranda of one of the temples they visited. Mrs. L much preferred the temple architecture to the peaceful swept sand of the famous Tokyo rock gardens. The latter was Alice's "idea of hell." She "hated it, just hated it.... She said, 'That's my idea of nothing at all.' She got very angry. She got very passionate about

how sterile and boring [it was], and she really liked lots of stimulation....
Meditation was not her strong point."[29]

Just as in 1905, Alice was the center of attention wherever she went.
Kristie and Joanna remembered Alice's characteristic ability to transcend
hunger, weariness, and her desire for privacy. She was, Joanna described,
"a fire horse falling into harness." Anytime anyone "staggered up and said,
'Aren't you Alice Blue Gown?' she very graciously pulled herself together
and was so nice...she just made [people's] day." Apparently, Alice's age
was not a predictor of her energy level for, as Joan Braden remembered,
"Mrs. L was up every morning at the crack of down, rearing to go. I was a
python by comparison." Alice enthused, "We had such fun," and contemplated a trip to Moscow.[30]

New York called first. In 1966, Truman Capote threw his famous Black
and White Ball at the Plaza Hotel for his friend Kay Graham. The event
generated excessive publicity. Alice, Lynda Bird Johnson Robb, and Margaret Truman Daniel—three former First Daughters—converged and
chatted. Hollywood fixtures such as Frank Sinatra, Mia Farrow, Anita
Loos, Claudette Colbert, and Lauren Bacall attended the masquerade.
Partygoers spent magnificent sums on their designer attire—but Alice's
stole the show: a simple black dime-store mask held on by elastic. Alice
characterized the ball as "the most exquisite of spectator sports," a line the
New York Times borrowed for its headline.[31]

As Capote's ball unfolded in New York, a burglar was vandalizing Alice's home in Washington. The guest list had been published, so he knew
the house would be empty. He took mostly jewels, many of which had been
wedding presents. They were so distinctive that they were recovered
quickly from a Chicago smelting firm. Authorities had been alerted by
Windy City jewelers who were offered pieces engraved with Alice's name.
Alice received a box of "gold scraps" that turned out to be the "historic
mementos" she had gathered over seven decades. Most of the gemstones—
such as the diamonds set in the bracelets from Kaiser Wilhelm—were
gone. The one piece left whole was a locket that contained a snip of her father's hair.[32]

Social divisions in the 1960s ran deep. The rise of the counterculture, the African-American civil rights movement, and increasing unhappiness with American involvement in Vietnam generated a response from conservatives who Nixon, campaigning in 1968, would call the "silent majority." Alice Longworth straddled the divide. *Boston Sunday Herald* readers learned of a woman who "likes the Beatles, 5 o'clock tea, Theodore Roosevelt, Republicans." "I'm glad," Alice said, "to have had a taste of the Edwardian, but I like it now. It's exciting."[33]

She hung an "African tribal mask" on the small bronze Statue of Liberty that had been a wedding gift from the sculptor's family. "I hang this mask right on the Goddess of Liberty," Alice told an interviewer. "It symbolizes black power in a free land. America's black citizens are not only winning liberty; they're discovering a wonderful heritage in art such as this. Don't you find that exciting?" she asked. Among Alice's acquaintances was Portia Washington Pittman. The two women saw each other "quite often," Alice told another interviewer in 1968. "She's my contemporary, Booker Washington's daughter. She brings her grandchildren here." As she watched the changes around her—including Washington, D.C.'s first elected mayor, African-American Walter E. Washington—she said, "If I were younger I'd be delighted to run for vice-mayor of a ticket with a black mayor." Mrs. L had been attending prizefights with her chauffeur Richard Turner ever since he began to work for her in the 1950s. The two shared an appreciation for the local pugilists. Once when Turner was taking her somewhere in her ancient limousine, a car sideswiped them. The other driver then had the temerity to yell out his window, "Watch where you're going, you black bastard." Whereupon Alice rolled down her window and spoke precisely: "Shut up, you white son-of-a-bitch."[34]

As an octogenarian, she claimed Gloria Steinem as "one of my heroines," and feminist congresswoman Bella Abzug asked Alice to serve as "one of the Honorary 'Chairpeople'" for a fund-raising event. At age ninety, Alice told a reporter that her lifelong preference as a nonjoiner kept her away from the women's liberation movement—and the fact that she "feels she has been treated by men as an equal." But Alice had "followed women's movements all her adult life." "I'm enormously interested and wish them well. I think it's high time women are getting somewhere." In

1977, one month before the National Women's Conference was held in Houston, Joanna said that her grandmother "certainly is a feminist. But she'd never admit it. She feels it's tacky to identify yourself with a group, and to become overemotional. It's a question of esthetics." Guided by her "extremely feminist convictions," Joanna joined the National Women's Political Caucus, sought out a female stockbroker, and shunned marriage as "a sexist institution." Alice wanted it made clear that her own interest in feminism wasn't "borrowed from her granddaughter."[35]

Alice was very sympathetic toward the gay liberation movement. "I'm amused that some people are so shocked, as if they thought homosexuals and lesbians never before existed. That has never bothered me." Her insouciance in the face of the rest of the nation's anger and fear moved one gay rights group in Washington to make her an "honorary homosexual," which pleased her enormously. She attained cult status among some populations of gay men.[36]

Mrs. L enjoyed Joanna and her acquaintances, especially Robert Hellman, who spent considerable time with Mrs. L in her last decade. One friend of theirs who had tea with them on several occasions thought that Mrs. Longworth "had a keen sense of Washington fraudulence and enjoyed the company of young people who were fairly free from those pretensions. . . ." Another loved Mrs. L's "fantastic imagination," and approved of how her conversations didn't "move in a straight line. . . . Almost like someone flipping out on drugs." Alice thought this idea was "too much fun" and wondered whether after she "outgrew her hormones," she "started manufacturing LSD." She said frequently that "the secret of eternal youth is arrested development." When the tear gas from protest marches came through her windows, she joked that it "cleared my sinuses." She took to referring to herself as "a withered Twiggy," a reference to the era's slim superstar model.[37]

In an interview at the time of her ninetieth birthday, television commentator Eric Sevareid told her of the newest movement: "to liberate the old." "That *is* fun!" Alice interjected. Its purpose, Sevareid continued, was "to make people understand that old people have feelings, and that they even have sexual passion. . . . Are you for all that?" She smilingly shot back, paraphrasing Queen Victoria, "Well, as long as they don't do it in the streets." At another time, when asked her opinion of the sexual revolution, she said she'd always lived by the adage "Fill what's empty, empty what's full, and scratch where it itches."[38]

At the height of the counterculture revolution came the 1968 election, pitting Lyndon Johnson's vice president, Hubert Humphrey, against Richard Nixon. George Wallace of Alabama ran on a third-party segregationist platform. With Joanna, Alice attended the GOP convention in Miami that year, but found it "the dullest thing I've ever seen." The Republican Party stressed the orderliness of their gathering compared to the fisticuffs outside and inside the Democratic convention in Chicago. Alice reverted to her Republican roots. She spent the election eve phoning friends to remind them to vote for Nixon and sent him an encouraging telegram: "Here is to simply overwhelming returns tomorrow! It was such fun seeing Pat and the girls for a moment at Miami. Love to them and many recollections of earlier days."[39] His success almost didn't happen. Democrats held the House and the Senate.

Alice loaned her name to local charities. She had served as a member of the opening night committee for the six-day-long Washington International Horse Show at the D.C. Armory in 1965 and held the same position in 1968. She gave "one of the first top level dinners following the election," just before a fund-raiser for the John F. Kennedy Center. The best party of all, though, occurred after the inauguration, and she was the star. On February 12, 1969, Alice Longworth turned eighty-five. Guests included dignitaries of all sorts. President Nixon came and reminisced for forty-five minutes. Throughout the evening, a recent interview conducted for British television by Jonathan Aitken blazed. The interview showed Alice at her best—smart, funny, with a wide-ranging repertoire of topics. For Aitken, she did her celebrated mimicry of cousin Eleanor and showed off the Chinese tiger wall hanging that looked like Dean Acheson. Alice's birthday cake was topped by a confectionary replica of her trademark hat.[40]

President Nixon had earlier sent her a greeting, declaring, "Your valor has always been an inspiration, and your infectious good humor has given even the most serious of men and women the ability and courage to laugh at their foibles and appreciate the lighter side of life." His was one of many felicitations she received. Perhaps the most interesting began thus: "I think it 'fitting and proper' that you have a note from one of the members of the Borah tribe on the anniversary of your 89th [*sic*] birthday." From Texas, Lyndon Johnson saluted her: "Happy birthday from a long-time admirer. I don't know if there is such a thing as a social lioness, but all of us cubs think you're the best. One thing I want from history is for tomorrow's generation to regard Lynda and Luci with the same affection all Americans hold for you. And Lady Bird and I hope they'll be as beautiful." The Eisenhowers' telegram wished a happy birthday to "the youngest 85 year old we have ever known." With self-deprecating humor, she called herself "a loathsome combination of Marie Dressler and Phyllis Diller," but no one would have agreed with her comparison to the two disheveled celebrities.[41]

At this time in her life, Alice acquired yet another admirer—another man gifted with words and a sublime intellect: scientist, philosopher, and dreamer Buckminster Fuller. "At age 73," he wrote her, "the frequency at which one falls in love with other than one's grandchildren approaches zero. Therefore, I was astonished to find myself 'knocked for a loop' by you. So I hasten to send to you my abstract bouquet." This literary posy consisted of three of his books, *No More Second Hand God*, *Education Automation*, and *The Unfinished Epic of Industrialization*, as well as offprints from his articles on topics from computers to women's status. Borah-like, Fuller also included testimony from *Saturday Review* editor Norman Cousins praising Fuller as one of the "ten or twelve men in the world . . . whose influence transcends geography and language. Among these men are Albert Schweitzer, Bertrand Russell, E. M. Forster, Paul Tillich, and you."[42]

Many men appreciated Alice Longworth's amazing mind. Among her devotees was the "father of the nuclear navy," Hyman Rickover, who called her an "outstanding female scientist." He and Alice had one conversation that prompted him to send her a letter distinguishing the specifics of parsecs and astronomical units, and attaching some illustrations of measurement. Bazy Tankersley knew her to be a self-taught expert on nuclear fission. After one White House dinner the other guests wanted to know what topic had she broached that so intensely interested the royal visitor with whom she had been absorbedly speaking. "Astronomy," she told them. "Stars, galaxies, and where we are in the little corner of the galaxy." After that their discussion moved to "genes and the chromosomes.... Then," she said, "we branched into molecular genetics and things of that sort. He couldn't have been more fun." The study of quasars and quarks was "intoxicating for me," she told an interviewer happily. When good friend Harvard professor, attorney, author, and Supreme Court Justice Felix Frankfurter died, Alice was one of the few friends to attend his private memorial service. Frankfurter was a Democrat who helped start up the *New Republic* and assisted Zionist causes.[43]

Alice's bookshelf was filled with many tomes from Princeton University's prestigious Bollingen Series, launched in 1943, particularly on scientific and philosophical subjects. She read and reread books, "to fix them in my head," she said. Journalist Betty Beale found Alice in her mid-eighties reading Mario Puzo's novel *The Godfather,* John Birmingham's *Our Time Is Now—Notes from the High School Underground, The Treasure of Sutton Hoo—Ship Burial for an Anglo-Saxon King,* Nigel Calder's *Violent Universe, The World of Bats,* a book about Trinidad called *The Loss of El Dorado, Nixon* by Earl Mazo, as well as Voltaire (in French), Kipling, Pindar, Homer, Pope, Hawthorne, Whitman, and "dictionaries like Fowler's *Modern English Usage* because she 'loves words.'"[44]

Robert Hellman seldom found a subject on which Mrs. L was not conversant, and in many cases, an adept. He spent a great deal of time with her while finishing his doctoral degree in modern German intellectual history from Columbia University. They frequently discussed his topic, the left-wing pupils of Hegel and their scientific examination of the four gospels. Hellman attested to the fact that Alice had read Arthur Schopenhauer's *On the Four-Fold Root of the Principle of Sufficient Reason.* There was nothing an intellectual historian could teach her, he said, about Schopenhauer, Nietzsche, or Kant. She'd been studying them all her life. According to Hellman, "The most salient thing about her was her intellect."[45] Yet what most Americans saw was the wit.

The Nixons, like the Johnsons and Kennedys before them, were generous with their invitations. Alice went frequently to the Nixon White House to meet important guests such as the Shah of Iran, the Duke and Duchess of Windsor, and British Prime Minister Edward Heath. She attended a black-tie dinner given by the Brazilian ambassador in honor of her acquaintance Mauricio Nabuco, Brazil's ambassador to the United States from 1948 to 1951. Richard Nixon's favorite minister was the Reverend Billy Graham, and Alice could not help but encounter him at the White House. A dinnertime conversation once prompted her to send the cleric a book entitled *The Steel Bonnets,* which Graham, no more immune to Alice's sparkle than anyone else, promised to "always treasure." "What a marvelous woman you are," Graham gushed, "even if you don't believe."[46]

During the summer of 1970, Alice Longworth had a second mastectomy, prompting her to call herself "Washington's topless octogenarian." Generally, however, she preferred to keep quiet about the surgery. Later, when First Lady Betty Ford suffered from her historically public battle with breast cancer, Alice cheered her on with get-well wishes. When Alice felt up to hosting again, Henry Cabot Lodge Jr. exclaimed afterward, "The company and the food were, of course, superlative, but what made it so unique was you—as you have always been. Notwithstanding the vicissitudes of which you told me, you look marvelous—vivid and beautiful. Through the years you have generously extended your hospitality to Emily and me and it has always been something to look forward to and to look back on with joy. . . . You will always be for me the most stimulating, witty, and utterly delightful of companions."[47]

In 1971, according to journalist Dorothy Marks, Alice's social life had not let up much. Describing what Marks called a usual week, she said the eighty-seven-year-old began with service as the honorary chair of a charity ball celebrating the District of Columbia's "Age of Innocence, 1900–1910," the era when she was First Daughter. She attended the Washington Press Club's dinner welcoming new members of Congress, and stopped by a ball at the Spanish embassy for Prince Juan Carlos and Princess Sophia of Spain. "Two nights later she joined in the singing to help Soviet Ambassador Dobrynin and his wife harmonize '*Que Sera, Sera*'" at a private dinner party.[48]

The wedding of Patricia Nixon and Edward Cox on June 12, 1972, meant another opportunity for the nation to recall Princess Alice's nuptials. Later that year at a White House dinner honoring Presidential Medal of Freedom winners, she sat between conservationist Horace M. Albright and Bob Hope. "Conversation," Albright remembered, "was on many subjects and, at times, hilarious, mainly initiated by Mrs. Longworth and Hope." The topic turned to current fears about the overpopulation of the planet, and Alice reminded the dinner guests that when she was young, large families were praised. "She quoted her father's favorite lines which, in turn, created quite an uproar at our table:

> Teddy, Teddy, Rough and Ready,
> Hear his battle cry!
> Get the habit.
> Be a rabbit.
> Multiply!"[49]

During the summer of 1972, Alice attended the Republican Party convention, but it's not likely she knew how desperately and illegally President Nixon was scrambling to win reelection with the big margin of victory that had eluded him in 1968. She did know how he agonized about the election, and was fascinated by the contour of his career: "It's really amazing to see what has happened to Dick. There he was defeated by Kennedy and then by Pat Brown for Governor of California and he made that whin[ing], snarling speech. He's come through all that. . . . I didn't think that it was the end of him at the time and that he would get back, but I was one of the few who did. I <u>knew</u> that he would try again because he has that great quality of persistence. I'm not so sure though about his judgment, but I don't think he's ruthless," she mused. She thought Nixon's biggest handicap in the 1972 campaign was that he "is apt to bore people."[50]

Americans did "mind" Nixon personally, but his campaign tapped into the conservative backlash, and Nixon achieved the landslide he craved, although the Democrats maintained their congressional majority. Alice was invited to several inaugural festivities for President Nixon; however, she did not attend because she was under the weather. Nixon, who knew that she "could never resist anything political," sent her a handwritten note of concern.[51]

A distracting flurry of press interest in Alice's past occurred when *Washington Post* journalist Maxine Cheshire broke a story that horrified Mrs. L: "Was Alice Roosevelt in Love with FDR?" Eleanor Roosevelt's biographer, Joseph Lash, had interviewed a Roosevelt relative who swore that Alice had set her hat for Franklin. Alice adamantly protested to Lash. To ensure her denial would endure for posterity, she tape-recorded it—a tape, Cheshire wrote, "punctured frequently by outbursts of laughter." Alice feared that "her decades of outspoken disdain for FDR's New Deal politics may be interpreted as the pique of a jealous woman." In a later interview, Alice said, "I was no more likely to marry Franklin than I was someone's second footman." She meant every word, even though she had a sense of humor about it. When replying to the letter sent by a teenaged admirer of TR in the mid-1960s, for example, she used the stamp sold at that time—with Franklin's face on it—but she "placed the stamp upside down, so that Franklin was, in effect, standing on his head." And she told interviewer Jean Vanden Heuvel, "Franklin was great fun. I used to see him when he was a boy, always liked Franklin, was amused by him." Alice, who knew good politicians from bad, characterized Franklin as "an able politician...and...an engaging character!"[52] Her ambivalence toward Eleanor was well-known, and after ER's death in 1962, Alice got tremendous currency from repeating Eleanor imitations and quips.

But even the sardonic joy of reliving the Hyde Park Roosevelt years had to halt as Dick Nixon's administration crumbled under the weight of Watergate. At first Alice took the scandal in stride: "Everyone is hypnotized by Watergate. One hangs on the boob tube all day long. But depressed? I'm not depressed at all. . . . I don't think in those terms." Alice had seen scandal. She had lived through false accusations toward her father, she had watched Teapot Dome unfairly taint Ted's career. But Capitol Hill denizens lacking Alice's longer view were troubled. "The future of the Nixon administration dominates conversations. No dinner party is complete without a resident Watergate expert," noted one social-pages reporter. When the ad hominum attacks on Nixon started, Alice compared his attackers to Rudyard Kipling's Bandar-logs, the Monkey People who kidnap Mowgli in *The Jungle Book*. Kipling described how "they boast and chatter and pretend that they are a great people about to do great affairs in the jungle, but the falling of a nut turns their minds to laughter and all is forgotten."[53]

But as Watergate discoveries mounted, Alice found it difficult to countenance Nixon's actions. Still, she telephoned him in June—about the time the televised Watergate hearings led to the startling discovery of the secret tapes of Oval Office conversations—to assure him, as he put it gratefully, "of your continuing friendship and support. It has always been my experience in my political career," Nixon continued stentoriously, "that you learn who your real friends are—not when the road is smooth but when it is sometimes rocky. That is why Pat and I are so deeply grateful to be able to include you in our list of oldest and dearest friends." When Nixon refused to hand over the tapes to the Senate investigative committee and did away with the office of the special prosecutor, Alice remarked memorably, "My shoulders are in a constant state of shrug." That fall, after Nixon's declaration that he was "not a crook," Alice had to admit that while she had " 'known and liked Dick Nixon for years,' . . . he has done 'some asinine things.' " She told another reporter, "He's an old friend and I'm sorry he's having a hard time. Of course, there are things we disagree about." She said archly that Nixon's "potential clock keeps dick, dick, dicking away."[54]

Because of Watergate, one of the last times Alice saw the Nixons was at her ninetieth birthday party in February 1974. " 'So, the old crone had a birthday!' she chortled." The party at her house was front-page news, and guests came from all walks of life. Her sister, Ethel, helped her celebrate. They had become great friends in their old age, exchanging frequent phone calls and visits. "I think about solitary pleasures," Ethel wrote once, "and how you and I like them." She knew a different side of her sister than did others, and shared a similar love of and knack for poetry. Ethel took no joy from the limelight, whereas Alice reveled in her party. The long list of guests included old friends and newer acquaintances from political Washington: Mayor Walter E. Washington, Henry Kissinger, broadcasters David Brinkley and John Chancellor, S. Dillon Ripley of the Smithsonian, Art Buchwald, Sargent Shriver. She served champagne and rum cake. The Nixons gave her Iranian caviar, which she loved and ate with a spoon right out of the jar. "I'll wallow in it...let others wallow in Watergate," she said puckishly. So many reporters clamored for interviews that she took to calling it her "goddamned birthday." One cajoled her into reminiscing: "I loved [politics] around me, but had no temptation to run for office. I was too shy, that's the uncomfortable thing—I was always hideously shy, and I still have spurts of it. I'm not one for causes particularly...I was for the cause when my father was running—he was a cause for me. I'm very old fashioned, essentially, I'm for fun, a good old hedonist—interested, very interested in politics, and I like a lot of things."[55]

Many of the stories written about her featured a pillow Alice had been given earlier by Bazy Tankersley. Alice was very fond of it, and said laughingly, "It can be taken as nasty as you want!" The pillow read "If you haven't got anything good to say about anyone come and sit by me." She adopted it as her signature statement—not one most people could get away with, but as William Wright wrote in his study of Washington, "People who are spontaneous, uninhibited, and oblivious to their surroundings are not greatly admired in Washington, unless they have the enormous clout of an Alice Roosevelt Longworth...."[56]

Six months after that happy occasion, Nixon was forced to resign. He and Alice remained friends. She did not think much of his farewell speech, in which he quoted from Theodore Roosevelt's diary at the time that her mother, Alice Hathaway Lee, died. TR wrote, "When my heart's dearest died, the light went from my heart forever." Nixon used that, and a much longer passage preceding it, to suggest, as he said, that Roosevelt "only thought the light had gone from his life forever—but he went on. And he not only became President but, as an ex-president, he served his country always in the arena, tempestuous, strong, sometimes wrong, sometimes right, but he was a man." It was "not particularly pertinent," Alice snorted. The validity of comparing a grieving widower in his twenties with his life ahead of him and a man in his sixties with a career clearly behind him escaped her. At that stage, Alice felt "the Watergate story 'had gone on long enough.' It was getting to the point where it was about to become very boring. . . . I feel sorry for the people involved," she said. Alice was clearly conflicted about Nixon and Watergate. She called it "good, unclean fun" just as often as she expressed support for the outgoing president.[57]

Bill Walton summed up Alice's later years by saying that "her dotage wasn't like others." She wanted an "outrageous old age," and he could "never think of her as an unhappy widow." Alice, he emphasized, "*loved* her life."[58] She shared her home at this time with Cat, a large Siamese who kept her company when she read and who amused her with its haughty, feline demeanor. "Darling Puss-Cat, every gesture a small reproof," she said ruefully to it once. Kristie Miller and her husband, William Twaddell; Larry Spivak; Tish Alsop; Susan Mary Alsop; Evangeline Bruce; Michael Teague; Susan Weld; Sandy Roosevelt; Teddy Weintal; Lynn Magruder; Robin Roosevelt; and Lucky Roosevelt continued to see her frequently. Out-of-town friends called. No one wrote much, because Mrs. L seldom opened letters—or bills—which would accumulate among the books.

The greatest happiness of her old age was her granddaughter. Joanna and she had a relationship so close it defied description. Author Michael Teague thought they "were very good friends [with] a healthy respect for each other's independence and idiosyncrasies." Robert Hellman recalled that the two were very affectionate and "touching." He meant that Mrs. L, who was well known for not liking physical contact, touched and let herself be touched by Joanna. Bazy Tankersley felt that they had overcome much to reach a relationship of deep devotion to each other. Alice's niece Alexandra Roosevelt Dworkin thought Alice and Joanna were "perfectly evenly balanced."[59]

Poetry remained a great source of comfort and intellectual engagement, a shared joy between grandmother and granddaughter. The two recited reams of poetry together from memory. The amount of poetry Mrs. L knew and loved cannot be overstated. G. K. Chesterton's "Lepanto" was a favorite. Its subject is the 1571 battle between Don John of Austria's Catholic forces and Ali Pasha's Ottoman Turks in the Gulf of Lepanto. The poem is martial and full of brilliant imagery, and reads beautifully aloud because of Chesterton's musical cadences. Alice and Joanna could recite all nine stanzas at a rapid clip. One memorable night, Hellman brought his friend James K. Galbraith to visit Mrs. L. Galbraith, whose father had been ambassador to India, loved Kipling's poem "Christmas in India." To Alice's enthusiastic delight, Galbraith recited the entire poem from memory and the three had a glorious evening talking poetry and politics. Poetry "was the operative currency of Mrs. L's world" with guests, but especially with Joanna.[60]

When Nixon left for California and Vice President Gerald Ford assumed the presidency, Alice's political interests flagged. President Ford was a longtime member of Congress, but not an acquaintance of hers. Still, he invited her to the crowning social event of his administration: the visit of Britain's Queen Elizabeth II to Washington, D.C., during the American bicentennial. When Mrs. L received an invitation to the State Dinner, to be held on the White House grounds, Lynn Magruder encouraged Mrs. L to go, suggesting that Joanna's friend Robert Hellman escort her. After he scrambled all over town for a tuxedo, the two set off. A very professional, young female Marine assigned to Mrs. Longworth swept her right to the front of the line to meet the queen and Prince Philip. They exchanged pleasantries about the diamond-rimmed purse that Mrs. L carried, which had been a wedding gift from King Edward VII in 1906. After chatting with the Fords, Alice moved on. When Lady Bird Johnson came their way, Mrs. L inquired of Hellman, "Shall I ask her how Lyndon is?" "You can't do that," he whispered, "because he's dead." "Oh"—she glanced at him, not missing a beat—"then I shall ask her how Lyndon *was*."

Not far away from the festivities, in his Georgetown home, Joe Alsop was pouring cocktails for Mrs. Longworth's friend the young British editor of the *Economist*, Dudley Fishburn. Alsop was bemoaning the fact that Alice Longworth was in her nineties and just not getting out much anymore. Fishburn pointed silently at the television. There was Mrs. L on the lawn of the White House, surrounded by Cary Grant, Bob Hope, and Senator Fulbright.

When dinner was over and the toasts had been made, Mrs. L and Hellman made their way to the limousine. A White House employee tapped him on the shoulder. "We have someone," he said, "who worked in the

White House when Mrs. Longworth lived here." Hearing this, Alice turned to greet a tall, distinguished, silver-haired African-American man who asked if she remembered him. She did. They launched into tales of White House life "when all the world was young." She responded to his laughter with peals of her own. And when they were through, he inquired gravely if he might escort her to her car. She gave him her elbow, and the two walked slowly away.[61] It was Alice Roosevelt Longworth's last visit to the White House.

Epilogue

ALICE ROOSEVELT LONGWORTH died peacefully at home on February 20, 1980, after a brief bout with pneumonia. Joanna and Robert were by her side. Cat kept a vigil beside her on the bed. True to form, Mrs. L's last action was to stick out her tongue playfully at Robert. "I'm an old fossil, a cheerful fossil," she had said not long before. "I have no contemporaries."[1] Nor did she have an equal.

Fittingly, Alice Roosevelt Longworth came into the world in an election year and went out in one, too. She was not the only First Daughter to die in 1980. Esther Cleveland Bosanquet was born in the White House and married spectacularly in Westminster Abbey, but her death failed to make the same headlines. Alice was the first born and the last to die of Theodore Roosevelt's children—and she is the longest lived of all presidential children.[2] But her fame was never merely that of having been First Daughter. While those 1,616 days in the White House placed her in a rare position, she used it to become an American icon. She remains one to this day.

Few First Daughters stay in the limelight after they leave the White House, but Alice Longworth did. She went from feeling like "an extra piece of baggage in relation to the family" to the nation's most-watched female, and she colluded in the creation of that role.[3] It fed her desire to stand out among the growing Roosevelt brood and catch her father's attention. Launching the *Meteor*, releasing Emily Spinach past unsuspecting diners, racing the red touring car, or shooting off her "cunning" little pistol helped her to be noticed—gratifyingly—beyond the circle of the family. International recognition came after the 1905 Asian congressional junket. The Roosevelt-Longworth "wedding of the century" might have led right up the aisle to wifely obscurity, but she was already too famous. Instead, Alice shaped the female ideal of the era. Unaffected yet dignified, lively and unspoiled, Alice was the personification of the American girl at the opening of the twentieth century.

The men in her family helped keep the Roosevelt name before the public after her marriage. In 1912, her dilemma as Nick Longworth's wife and TR's daughter shone a sympathetic spotlight her way. While she began her resistance to Woodrow Wilson's League of Nations as a partner with her father, she ended by making a name for herself among Washington politicians quite apart from his. Her quick mind, her endless curiosity, her love of the game were assets to powerful men—and women, especially Representative Ruth Hanna McCormick—seeking passage of legislation and elected office. Until she was ninety, Alice Longworth cultivated politicians just as they courted her.

Her animus to Franklin Roosevelt's New Deal, coupled with her tribal fury that he had gained the nation's highest office instead of her brother or her husband, put her at the center of Republican detractors. It was less a reinvention of herself than an embracing of the inevitable that occurred somewhere in the post-FDR years. Alice saved her severest scorn for Franklin and Eleanor. She could criticize them as no one else could, for she was family, and no matter what she said, she would always be family. Franklin was a powerful president whose many years in office gave Alice time to build a comprehensive stock of scorn and consolidate her position as gadfly-in-chief. Newspapers played up their rivalry because it made good copy and boosted circulation. Alice knew the most powerful members of the fourth estate. She had learned from her father the importance of press control. Journalists had always mingled with politicians at her house. She appreciated those who made a profession of ferreting out and selectively making public the inner workings of the government. Alice Longworth was a passionate believer in democracy, including freedom of the press. As democracy's detectives, journalists protected the country. She found journalists entertaining and joined their number briefly. They shared secrets with her and kept her name before the public. Even as she hated to see Richard Nixon fall from grace, she could not help but admire the role played by her friend Kay Graham's reporters—so like the muckrakers of her father's era.

Columnists from Will Rogers in the 1930s to Sally Quinn half a century later printed Alice's pithy comments. And the more her verbal conceits were repeated, the more her reputation as a wit spread. The more it spread, the more people sought her out for her comments. Lady Bird Johnson knew that "in any gathering where she is present, Alice Roosevelt Longworth was one of the stars of the occasion, a natural magnet for everybody hoping to hear something spicy. . . ."[4] And that particular talent relegated all of her accomplishments to the background. It did so at the culmination of a series of blows during the Roosevelt and Truman years that would have crushed a lesser spirit: the deaths of her lover, two brothers, stepmother, and best friend. When emphysema and a mastectomy bracketed her daughter's death, it is perhaps no wonder that, thus reminded of her own mortality and in her seventies, Alice refortified the protective wall of "detached malevolence." It was a tactic similar to the one she had used to turn her youthful rebellion into a barricade to avoid further abandonment. That she could allow her granddaughter to breach that wall is a poignant reminder that Alice Longworth was a complex and intelligent woman. Had she been less, she would not have drawn people to her for eight decades. "Tell, tell!" she would demand of those who came to see her. "Tell" of other worlds, of privileged information, of governmental plans, of news of loved ones, of battles, of catastrophes, of scientific discoveries. It is ironic that Alice Longworth really couldn't pick a presidential winner. On Nick, Ted, Borah, and Bob Taft she bet and lost. By the time her betting finally paid off, in the election of Richard Nixon to the nation's highest office, Mrs. L was eighty-four and rather blasé. In the end, he let her down—twice, first by his underhanded dealings in Watergate and second by the sloppy way he dealt with defeat.

Alice made a career out of being Theodore Roosevelt's daughter. But she was no more bound by tradition than he. Eschewing her stepmother's early-to-bed early-to-rise sensibility, Alice stayed awake until the wee hours, reading, studying, prowling the house—she called it "kicking the tentpegs"—in search of more books, her main source of nutrition in her last decade. She opened her home to the city's School Without Walls, where Kristie Miller taught writing classes. One of the students, Glenn Kowalski, wrote a song about the rather surreal experience of analyzing the plot development of literature while sitting in "Alice Roosevelt's House." Another young Washington resident, Anita Wilburn, remembered how in the 1960s she would "hang out around Dupont Circle hoping to get a glimpse of her." Wilburn thought of Alice Longworth as "history on the hoof."[5]

Like an actor, Alice was adept at telling important stories for the umpteenth time as though they were new. She was frequently interviewed in the 1960s and 1970s by historians and other writers seeking to understand the changes in the nation's capital throughout the twentieth century. "Shall I tell that one again?" she would ask, and interviewers always said yes. Mrs. L could recall the time of gaslights and phaetons. She remembered presidents Benjamin Harrison and Calvin Coolidge. When she was First Daughter, there were only a handful of embassies in Washington, D.C. She was around when the Panama Canal was dug and before Mount Rushmore was carved. She could reduce interviewers to fits of laughter when she told about sneaking into the White House or jumping into the ship's pool fully clothed. They wanted to know if she, like Luci and Lynda Johnson or Tricia and Julie Nixon, had dated as First Daughter. Only kitchen maids went on dates then, Mrs. L said archly, and it was called "walking out."

Presidential children are inspected and judged today just as she was a century ago. But Alice expanded the sphere of activities for young women by choosing to ignore codes of behavior that had been standard for those of her background. Half of America was appalled, but the other half applauded as she smoked, bet, drove unchaperoned, played poker, and shunned organized charity work. As a young wife, the scrutiny continued when she gave up the custom of calling, wore slacks, and decided not to play the victim when Nick retreated to alcohol and other women. Dropping out of sight as some presidential children did was never a real option for Princess Alice. Therefore, better to make the best of it, to be amused by it. When even her meanest thoughts were counted as marks of her cleverness, she learned that if you can't say something nice, say it wittily.

"I can be serious, but I can't be solemn," she declared. That's why she could get away with popularizing a wincing put-down of President Truman's nemesis, General Douglas MacArthur: "Never trust a man who combs his hair straight from his left armpit." Or saying of childbirth—at a time when motherhood was near to sainthood—that "having a baby is like trying to push a grand piano through a transom." She claimed of the oversized purse she carried that it was "half filing cabinet, half psychosis." Near the end of her life, she allowed poison ivy to take over her front yard because she found it rather funny. Upon watching President Johnson bare his stomach on television to show off the scar from his gall bladder surgery, she deadpanned, "Thank God it wasn't a prostate operation."[6]

As a celebrity, Alice Roosevelt Longworth had a unique style. To the public, she was Princess Alice, or Mrs. L, or just Alice. No less than her father's, hers was an instantly identifiable "look." The rolls and rolls of gold-threaded cloth given her by the empress dowager of China in 1905 lasted until the end of her life. They became distinctive gowns cut from a similar pattern—unfitted, long-sleeved A-lines that allowed her maximum freedom of movement and showed off the fabric to perfection. Everyday dresses featured the same silhouette. She topped these off with her signature hat. She had worn hats ever since she was First Daughter and had made large-brimmed hats fashionable. They bothered LBJ, who complained he couldn't kiss her because of the brims. "That, Mr. President," she told him drily, "is why I wear them." Even after such habiliment had declined in popularity, Mrs. L maintained the custom.

Hers were wide-brimmed black or brown hats made for her by Washington milliners. This was the look that artist and caricaturist Aline Fruhauf captured so perfectly in 1971: the hat, the silhouette, and the ramrod-straight posture, hands jammed into the pockets of her dress. The image would have been instantly recognizable to most Americans, in and out of Washington.[7]

Alice, like Bill Borah, was sometimes accused of inconsistency, yet much was constant throughout her life: books; her intellectual curiosity; the need to be at the center; her conviction that the United States should not become entangled in the business of foreign countries; her dismissal of whiners, complainers, and those who indulged in regrets; her belief that what a later generation would call self-fulfillment, and what she called "an appetite for being entertained," was just as viable a path as "do-gooderism"; her support for conservative national fiscal policy; her loyalty to her friends; her shyness; her loathing of drunkenness; her fear of losing control; her commitment to independence. Being contrasted to her cousin Eleanor bothered her not one bit. Robert Hellman said Alice liked being "the un-Eleanor." There was—there is—no valid comparison with the longest-serving First Lady and the enormously powerful national platform that accompanies that position. Alice and Eleanor were friends, after all, and more than that, they were of the same tribe.[8]

One interviewer quipped that Alice Longworth had "a low boring point." She came by it honestly. Theodore Roosevelt once complained to his sister about a dinner companion: "I hated myself for being so bored to extinction by him. But there are very many honest people whom one sincerely respects but cannot associate with. I never can like, and never will like, to be intimate with that enormous proportion of sentient beings who are respectable but dull. It is a waste of time. I will work with them, or for them; but for pleasure and instruction I go elsewhere." Alice Longworth was lucky and intrepid enough to be able to choose from among the world's most talented citizens for dinner companions. Alexandra Roosevelt Dworkin remembered her great-aunt as "very outspoken—and on a basis of equality with presidents and authors, and so the communication was direct—the dialogue may have been beneficial to them. There was no kowtowing or dissembling to presidents and politicians because they were equals."[9]

Alice Longworth's life can tell us much about the Roosevelt presidency, the larger Roosevelt family, the role of women in nonelective politics, conservative politics in the twentieth century, even Senator Borah. But at the end of the day, Alice Longworth herself doesn't fit into any neat category. Progressive, New Woman, politician, political organizer, Washington insider—she was all of these but more. Perhaps statesman is closest to her role. Just as a diplomat studies the issues, gathers information, carries it to lawmakers, brings together important constituents so that they can create legislative change, and does so with tact, discipline, gravitas, and savoir faire, Alice was a statesman. Her close friend Bazy Tankersley affirmed that Mrs. L "always made you feel important and was interested in what you had to say. This was the secret of her great social success."[10] Because Alice was so avidly interested in politics and foreign policy, her role transcended that of the social hostess. She was interested in power, hers and others', and at ease with it as well. She had more power in her dining room than the one vote suffrage gave her. Politics was a deadly serious game, played at a time when manners mattered and statesmen were integral to the governmental process.

Alice did not take the world on its own terms. It wasn't all under her control, nor did everything work out as she would have liked, but she made of it what she wanted. That was part of the appeal of the prizefights—the blood, the gore, the strenuous athleticism, but also the fighter uncomplainingly getting up again and again. In 1955, a fractured hip didn't keep her from going with Turner to see an important boxing match.[11] She fed off the spectacle.

Alice Roosevelt Longworth was one of a kind: an autodidact known for her wit, an iconoclast who valued tradition, a celebrity whose influence was often private, a conservative who started and ended her life as a progressive (or at least a Bull Moose). For all her "detachment," no politician was more connected; for all her "malevolence," no hostess had a larger circle of friends or a more-sought-after salon. She didn't call herself a feminist, but no life could have been more dedicated to freedom of choice and individual empowerment. She never lost the rebellious streak that she nurtured in her youth and that propelled her to international fame. As one reporter summed up, "Mrs. Longworth has gone thru life doing what struck her fancy, leaving the conformists awash in her wake."[12]

Acknowledgments

Writing a biography is an impertinent task. It takes a certain audacity to believe that one can come to know another human being well enough to commit their life to the historical record. Luckily, over the many years of this project, I have been the grateful recipient of wisdom and encouragement from many wonderful people who have given me the courage to see this task through. To thank them publicly is a joy.

My work and my thinking have been molded by professors at the University of Texas: Robert Abzug, Oscar Brockett, John Brokaw, Robert Divine, Hafaz Farmayan, Peter Jelevich, Patricia Kruppa, Amarante Lucero, Richard Pells, Thomas Philpott, and Philip White.

Colleagues beyond Texas have contributed to my understanding of Alice Longworth through their writings and their conversations: Thomas H. Appleton Jr., Charles Calhoun, Willard Gatewood, Sandra Harmon, Richard Jensen, Theresa Kaminski, Karen Leroux, Kris Lindenmeyer, Judy MacArthur, Deborah McGregor, April Shultz, Amanda Smith, John Weaver, and Elliott West.

I am conscious always that I stand on the shoulders of giants—Roosevelt biographers and historians on whose fine scholarship my work leans: John Morton Blum, James Brough, Betty Boyd Caroli, Blanche Wiesen Cook, John Milton Cooper, Kathleen Dalton, John Allen Gable, Lewis L. Gould, Joseph Ornig, Edmund Morris, Sylvia Jukes Morris, Edward Renehan, Michael Teague, Howard Teichmann, and Geoffrey Ward.

A special word of thanks to the Borah scholars who kindly assisted me with interpretive issues: LeRoy Ashby, John Milton Cooper, Marian McKenna, Robert James Maddox, and Keith Miller. In addition, Professor Ashby located a critical document for me in the Claudius O. Johnson Papers.

I have been fortunate in my Monmouth College colleagues who possess specialized and extremely helpful knowledge that enabled me to solve various intellectual and technical mysteries: Dan Barclay, Marcie Beintema, Marlo Belschner, Daryl Carr, Ken Cramer, Rob Hale, Petra Kuppinger, Steve Price, Jeff Rankin, Anne Sienkewicz, Ira Smolensky, Shawn Perry-Giles, Douglas Spitz, William Urban, Mark Willhardt, and especially Bev Scott. With uncomplaining good humor scads of Monmouth College students have heard about Alice Longworth in classrooms, hallways, and my office. To all of you who keep asking, "how's Alice?"—and you know who you are—thanks a million.

Friends and colleagues have munificently shared their ideas, their expertise, or sources with me: Samuel Brylawski, Daniel Byrne, Aaron Cluka, Judi Doyle, Glen Elsasser, Jennifer Goedke, Sarah (Sally) Hunter Graham, Robert T. Grimm Jr., William H. Leckie, Nick Miller, John Milton, Stefan Rinke, Emily Roane, Michael H. Rubin, Larry Rudiger, Lisa Smith, Roger Smith, Henry Tsai, and Nancy Beck Young, I am indebted to Jerome Klena and Phillip Saeli for help with document retrieval and to Alexis Zanis for superlative organizing of the Borah letters.

This book, like all others, owes much to the unselfish assistance of archivists, curators, and librarians whose knowledge of their institution's holdings often results in the gift of hidden gems of information: Lenora M. Henson, Theodore Roosevelt Inaugural National Historic Site; David C. Alan, Lauinger Library, Georgetown University; Dennis Northcott of the St. Louis Historical Society; Tina Bamert and Margaret Yax of the Cincinnati Historical Society; Evelyn M. Cherpak of the Naval War College Library; Joseph R. O'Neill of the Joseph Cardinal Bernardin Archives and Records Center, Archdiocese of Chicago; Jane Keskar of the Kipling Society, London; Carol A. Leadenham and Ronald M. Bulatoff at the Hoover Institution Archives, Stanford University; Lesley Martin of the Chicago Historical Society; Andrea Cantrell, Special Collections, University of Arkansas Libraries; Darryl I. Baker and Sue Lemmon of the Mare Island Naval Shipyard; Michael Mohl of Navsource.org; Tomas Jaehn of the Fray Angélico Chávez History Library, Santa Fe; Troy Reeves at the Idaho State Historical Society, Boise; Jewell Fenzi of the Foreign Service Spouse Oral History Project; and the staffs at Churchill Archives Center, Churchill College, Cambridge; the Courtauld Institute, London; the Indiana Historical Society; the Newberry Library, Chicago; the Southern Historical Collection, University of North Carolina at

Chapel Hill; the University of Chicago Special Collections; the University of Vermont Special Collections; the Franklin D. Roosevelt Presidential Library; the Herbert Hoover Presidential Library; the Abraham Lincoln Presidential Library, Springfield; National Archives, London; and the Library of Congress. Especial thanks to two people whose passion for and knowledge of their subjects and their collections are unsurpassed: Anne B. Shepherd of the Cincinnati Historical Society and the peerless Wallace Finley Dailey, Curator of the Theodore Roosevelt Collection at Harvard University's Houghton Library.

Closer to home, the Monmouth College Library staff, past and present, has cheerfully fulfilled interlibrary loan requests and helped with arcana: Matthew Antoline, Elizabeth Cox, Lynn Daw, Sarah Henderson, Irene Herald, Lauren Jensen, Patricia Pepmeyer Launer, Rita Schnass, Sue Stevenson, and particularly Rick Sayre.

To have been taken under the wing of the ever-gracious Sterling Lord is surely some sort of miracle. He and Robert Guinsler at Sterling Lord Literistic have proven patient and kind beyond expectation. At Viking, executive editor Wendy Wolf has made what should have been a painful process of paring down the manuscript an interesting and shared intellectual puzzle. I am very grateful to Maggie Payette for the stunning cover design, to Francesca Belanger for the text and interior layout, to production editor Noirin Lucas and to publicist Sonya Cheuse for their dedication to this project.

My sincere gratitude to those who shared their memories or stories of Alice Longworth with me. They played an integral role in my learning about Mrs. Longworth: Susan Mary Alsop, Stephen Benn, John Morton Blum, Ann Catt, Gary Clinton, Anita Wilburn Darras, Sherrie DeCamp, Alexandra Roosevelt Dworkin, James K. Galbraith, Robert Hellman, Glenn Kowalski, Lynn Macgruder, Janie McLaughlin, Angela Meeske, Kristie Miller, Frances Mitchell, David Mitchell, John Pope, Mary Reed, Robin Roosevelt, Selwa Roosevelt, Alice Sturm, Joanna Sturm, Michael Teague, Jeanne Tomb, Roman Totenberg, and William Walton. Graydon DeCamp responded to my inquiry about his grandfather with enthusiasm while David Mitchell kindly helped me understand the Sturm family. Bazy Tankersley spent hours recalling critical details about her friend Alice Longworth, gave me valuable insight into Washington society, and magnanimously provided all manner of other support as well.

So many friends and acquaintances have been generous in their encouragement and support over the years: Rajkumar Ambrose, George Arnold, Margaret McAndrew Beasley, Steve Buban, Katie Cogswell, Hillary Lee Dickenson, Laura Duncan, Kathleen Fannin, Gayle Fischer, Richard Giese, Virginia Hellenga, Susan Holm, Doug Jansen, Pat Joe, William Julian, Sandy Kyrish, Peter Linder, Linsey McDanel, Bev McGuire, Leah McLaren, Paula Nuckles, Mary Helen Quinn, Steven Reschly, Alisa Roost, Hannah Schell, Salise Shuttlesworth, Thomas J. Sienkewicz, N. J. Stanley, Jacqueline Urban, William Wallace, and Andrew Weiss.

Karen Cates, Simon Cordery, Lewis L. Gould, and Kristie Miller went above and beyond by reading the manuscript in an *extremely* long draft form. Their suggestions and criticisms materially improved the book.

Thanks are just not enough for the crucial support that took the form of continuous chocolate, champagne, and cheerleading from Paula Barnes, Brad Brown, Karen Cates, Simon Cordery, Karen Gould, Krissi Jimroglou, Evelina Lipecka, Kristie Miller, Danielle Nierenberg, Mary Lou Pease, and Stacey Robertson.

There are some people to whom my debts are so profound that they can never be fully repaid. This project began under the tutelage of Lewis L. Gould at the University of Texas. He first suggested that I think like a historian and set me on the road to my future. Lew Gould's professionalism is threaded through with such generosity of spirit. He continues to personify for me the ideal scholar, teacher, and mentor.

Kristie Miller's cheerful and sociable self led me to the enormous cache of primary documents held by Alice's granddaughter. The real treasure, though, was Kristie. I remain grateful for her tangible and intangible support. She shared her sources with me, allowed me to use her grandmother's diary, introduced me to the people and places in Mrs. L's world, and most of all kept faith that the book would do Alice Longworth justice.

Joanna Sturm made this book possible by allowing me free and unfettered access to the documents that helped to tell the story of her grandmother's life. This book would have been very different if not for her multifaceted generosity. Like Joanna Sturm, Robert Hellman answered countless questions and challenged me to seek a more nuanced view of Mrs. L. His tour of Alice Longworth's library proved vital to my interpretation.

Every author must feel helpless contemplating how to thank one's family for the magnitude of their contributions. I do. For every good thing, thank you: James and Agnes Rozek, Ned and Mary Cordery, Doug and Larissa Rozek, Stuart and Annie Rumens, Adam Dix and Sara Rumens. In his autobiography, Theodore Roosevelt wrote that children are better than books. He was right. Gareth Cordery's lovely distractions have made it all worthwhile. Finally, I am blessed in my partnership to an extremely patient man who is also a brilliant historian. Simon Cordery's unflagging support was always at the center. But really, for Simon, there are no sufficient words. I hope the celebrations have outweighed the sacrifices.

Notes

Abbreviations

ARLC   Alice Roosevelt Longworth Collection, Library of Congress

ARLD   Alice Roosevelt Longworth Diary, Library of Congress

ARL Diary   Alice Roosevelt Longworth Diary, Joanna Sturm Papers

ARL Har   Alice Roosevelt Longworth Family Papers, Theodore Roosevelt Collection. Houghton Library, Harvard University

ARLPF   Alice Roosevelt Longworth Princeton File, Cincinnati Historical Society

ARP   Amos R. Pinchot Papers, Library of Congress

CH   Alice Roosevelt Longworth, *Crowded Hours* (New York: Charles Scribner's Sons, 1933).

CHS   Cincinnati Historical Society

EKR Diaries   Edith Kermit Roosevelt Diaries, Theodore Roosevelt Collection, Houghton Library, Harvard University

ERDP   Ethel Roosevelt Derby Papers, Theodore Roosevelt Collection, Houghton Library, Harvard University

FDRL   Franklin Delano Roosevelt Presidential Library

Greenway AHS   Greenway Collection, Arizona Historical Society

HHPL   Herbert Hoover Presidential Library

JSAP   Joseph and Stewart Alsop Papers, Library of Congress

JSP   Joanna Sturm Papers, privately held

KBR   Kermit and Belle Roosevelt Family Papers, Library of Congress

LC   Library of Congress

LHHP   Lou Henry Hoover Papers, Herbert Hoover Presidential Library

LLF   Lord Lee of Fareham Papers, Cortauldt Institute, London

Morison, *Letters*   Elting E. Morison, *The Letters of Theodore Roosevelt*, 8 vols. (Boston: Harvard University Press, 1951–1954).

NLIII   Papers of Nicholas Longworth III, Cincinnati Historical Society

NLP   Nicholas Longworth Papers, Library of Congress

NLPF   Nicholas Longworth Princeton File, Cincinnati Historical Society

NYT   *New York Times*

PHP   Peter Hagner Papers, Southern Historical Collection, University of North Carolina at Chapel Hill

RFPH   Roosevelt Family Papers, Theodore Roosevelt Collection, Houghton Library, Harvard University

RHMcC   Ruth Hanna McCormick Papers, Library of Congress

TR Diary   Transcript of Theodore Roosevelt Diary, Joanna Sturm Papers

TRJR Diary   Theodore Roosevelt Jr. Diary, Library of Congress

TRJRP   Theodore Roosevelt Jr. Papers, Library of Congress

TRP   Presidential Papers of Theodore Roosevelt on microfilm

WEBID   William E. Borah Papers, Idaho State Historical Society

WEBLC   William E. Borah Papers, Library of Congress

WHTP   William H. Taft Papers, Manuscript Division, microfilm edition, Library of Congress

WSP   Williard Straight Papers on microfilm, reel 1, Cornell University Library

Abbreviations of personal names in the notes

AHL   Alice Hathaway Lee

AHLR   Alice Hathaway Lee Roosevelt

ALR   Alice Lee Roosevelt

ARC   Anna Roosevelt Cowles

ARL   Alice Roosevelt Longworth

EKR   Edith Kermit Roosevelt

ER   Anna Eleanor Roosevelt

HHT   Helen Herron Taft

JLL   John L. Lewis

JSG   Joseph S. Graydon

LHH   Lou Henry Hoover

NL   Nicholas Longworth

RHMcC   Ruth Hanna McCormick (Simms)

TR   Theodore Roosevelt

TRJR   Theodore Roosevelt Jr.

WEB   William E. Borah

WHT   William H. Taft

Preface

1. Alice Longworth said Joseph Alsop gave her that appellation: "Princess Alice Is 90," *60 Minutes* transcript, 17 February 1974, Papers of Eric Sevareid, LC. See also "Alice Roosevelt Longworth," *Theodore Roosevelt Journal* 6, 2 (Spring 1980): 6.

2. Michael Teague, *Mrs. L* (Garden City, N.Y.: Doubleday, 1981), xviii.

3. Paul Horgan, *Tracings* (New York:

Farrar, Straus, and Giroux, 1993), 172; ER to Isabella Ferguson, 21 June [1916], Greenway AHS.

4. Mary Hagedorn interview with Mrs. Richard Aldrich, 30 March 1955, Hermann Hagedorn. Interviews relating to Roosevelt women, Harvard University.

5. Author's interview with William Walton, 27 May 1994.

6. Winifred Mallon, "Mrs. Longworth

Sets Tongues Wagging," *NYT*, 26 May 1929, 15.

7. Author's interview with Lynn Magruder, 14 October 2001.

8. Kristie Miller to author, 1 March 2001.

Chapter 1: **"It Was Awfully Bad Psychologically"**

1. Alexandra Roosevelt Dworkin feels strongly that the Roosevelts were not "aristocracy." "We're all," Dworkin explained, "just part of a large amorphous bourgeoisie, which is very different from the aristocracy." Author's interview with Alexandra Roosevelt Dworkin, 7 October 2001.

2. Michael Teague, *Mrs. L* (Garden City, N.Y.: Doubleday, 1981), 19.

3. For a comparison, consider Cornelius van Schaak Roosevelt's investment in the Illinois Central Railroad (ICRR): he loaned more than $2,000 to the ICRR in the form of a bond. In 1888, the railroad paid him back $450 plus $34.08 interest— nearly the average annual wage earned by a laborer. See C. V. S. Roosevelt's note in the Papers of the Illinois Central Railroad Company, N 1.5, 1856–1888, Newberry Library, Chicago.

4. Gore Vidal, "Theodore Roosevelt: An American Sissy," Random House Web site: http://www.randomhouse.com/boldtype/0501/vidal/essay_us.html

5. TR Diary, 30 June 1878.

6. Michael Teague, "Theodore Roosevelt and Alice Hathaway Lee," *Harvard Library Bulletin* 33, 3 (Summer 1985): 230 (Hereafter cited as "TR and AHL).

7. TR Diary, 18 April 1878.

8. TR Diary, 1 January 1878.

9. TR Diary, 21 August 1878.

10. Sylvia Jukes Morris, *Edith Kermit Roosevelt* (New York: Coward, McCann & Geoghegan, 1980), 58.

11. "Summer house," TR Diary, 22 August 1878; "dog," 24 August 1878.

12. Except for "I met Miss Lee Barry," in early September.

13. Typescript of letter from TR to "Old John," 25 February 1880, JSP.

14. TR Diary, for the old school, 27 November 1878; for the theater party, 30 April; for the walk, 4 May 1879.

15. TR Diary, 13 May 1879.

16. TR Diary, for pretty girls, 24 June 1879; for Edith, 16 November 1879.

17. TR Diary, 31 December 1879 and 1 January 1880.

18. TR Diary, for happy, 25 January 1880; for first love, 30 January 1880.

19. Anna Roosevelt to AHL, 1 February 1880, ARLHar.

20. AHL to TR, 13 July 1880, and TR to AHL, 15 August 1880, both ARLHar.

21. AHL to TR, 10 October 1880, ARLHar.

22. For 79 presents, AHL to TR, 10 October 1880; for ring, AHL to TR, 16 October 1880, both ARLHar.

23. Sarah Booth Conroy, "Rough Rider's Romantic Side," *Washington Post*, 10 May 1995.

24. AHLR to Anna Roosevelt, 3 November 1880, ARLHar.

25. AHLR to TR, 5 April [1881], ARLHar.

26. For "so kind to me," AHLR to TR, [4?] April 1881; for "at night, AHLR to TR, [30?] March 1881, both ARLHar.

27. Vidal, "Theodore Roosevelt."

28. Theodore Roosevelt, *An Autobiography* (New York: Charles Scribner's Sons, 1926), 80.

29. AHLR to Anna Roosevelt, 22 July 1883, ARLHar.

30. Teague, "TR and AHL," 236.

31. Teague, "TR and AHL," 237–38.

32. The doctor did not diagnose her with Bright's disease until just before she

gave birth. Anna Bulloch Gracie, "Account of the Birth of Alice Roosevelt and Death of Alice Hathaway Lee Roosevelt," 25 March 1884, ARLHar.

33. Edmund Morris, *The Rise of Theodore Roosevelt* (New York: Coward, McCann & Geoghegan, 1979), 240. See especially footnote 69. Also, Wallace Finley Dailey, curator, TR Collection at Harvard, e-mail to author, 10 September 2001.

34. For "go mad," David McCullough, *Mornings on Horseback* (New York: Simon & Schuster, 1982), 286; for "more we work," Lillian Rixey, *Bamie* (New York: David McKay, 1963), 50.

35. Rixey, 54.

36. Gracie, "Account of the Birth of Alice Roosevelt."

37. TR, *In Memory of My Darling Wife Alice Hathaway Roosevelt and of My Beloved Mother Martha Bulloch Roosevelt...* (New York: G. P. Putnam's Sons, 1884).

38. TR to "Dear Sir," 1 May 1884, TR 1858–1919 Collection, Chicago Historical Society.

39. S. J. Morris, 77.

40. Rixey, v.

41. Teague, *Mrs. L*, 12 and 10.

42. For bread, Betty Boyd Caroli, *The Roosevelt Women* (New York: Basic Books, 1998), 392; for warmth, Teague, *Mrs. L,* 28; for "wonderful feeling," Caroli, 392.

43. Teague, *Mrs. L*, 4–5.

44. Caroli, 62.

Chapter 2: **"Sissy Had a Sweat Nurse!"**

1. For "come between," Michael Teague, *Mrs. L* (Garden City, N.Y.: Doubleday, 1981), 36; for Baby Lee, Sylvia Jukes Morris, *Edith Kermit Roosevelt* (New York: Coward, McCann & Geoghegan, 1980), 91.

2. For "love once," Teague, 5; for "his fault," Betty Boyd Caroli, *The Roosevelt Women* (New York: Basic Books, 1998), 81.

3. For honeymoon, Sarah Booth Conroy, "Rough Rider's Romantic Side," *Washington Post,* 10 May 1905; for "Edith feels more strongly," Morris, 102.

4. See, for example, Elliott Roosevelt to Anna Roosevelt, 22 March 1886, Papers of Elliott Roosevelt Sr., FDRL.

5. For "one's daughter," ARC to Belle Willard, January 10, 1914, KBR; for "a terrible wrong," Caroli, 84.

6. Teague, 12.

7. Teague, 13 (emphasis in original).

8. Mary Lee, *A History of Chestnut Hill Chapel* (Chestnut Hill, Mass.: The History Committee of the First Church in Chestnut Hill, 1937), 35.

9. Teague, 16, 18 (emphasis in original).

10. For "gold beads," EKR to ARC, n.d.; for "no object," EKR to ARC, Thursday [1890?], both from RFPH.

11. Caroline Lee to ALR, n.d., 1906, ARLC.

12. For "eats mamma," Morris, 112–13; for "take baby brother," EKR to ARL, n.d. [1948], JSP.

13. EKR to TR, 15 August 1889; for Alice's being "distressed," see EKR to TR, 31 August 1889, both ERDP.

14. For "Papa's sister," Morris, 133; for "sensitive," Sally Quinn, "Alice Roosevelt Longworth at 90," *Washington Post,* 12 February 1974, B3; for "sweat nurse," Teague, 18.

15. Teague, 36–37.

16. Teague, 18.

17. Teague, 30, 36, 37. In *Crowded Hours* (New York: Charles Scriber's Sons, 1933) written while Edith was alive, Alice treats her stepmother more kindly than in her interviews with Teague. Alice most often

affirmed Edith's version of Alice Lee; see, for example, Dorothy McCardle, "Comparison with Teddy Puzzles Mrs. Longworth," *New York Post*, 10 August 1974, ARL Clipping File, Harvard University. See also Teague, 30. Alice does not mention Edith and Theodore's youthful romance in her autobiography.

18. EKR to ARC, fragment, n.d., RFPH.

19. Nicholas Roosevelt, *Theodore Roosevelt* (New York: Dodd, Mead, 1967), 24–25.

20. TR to Anna Roosevelt, 18 November 1895, in Anna Roosevelt Cowles, *Letters from Theodore Roosevelt to Anna Roosevelt Cowles* (New York: Charles Scribner's Sons, 1924),163.

21. Quinn, B3; Charles Selden, "The Father Complex of Alice Roosevelt Longworth and Ruth Hanna McCormick," *Ladies' Home Journal*, March 1927, 6. For the denial, see Henry Brandon, "A Talk with an 83-Year-Old Enfant Terrible," *NYT Magazine* 6 (6 August 1967): 8. Ruth Hanna McCormick, daughter of powerful Senator Marcus Hanna, would become an elected politician in her own right.

22. Teague, 36.

23. *CH*, 4.

24. For "tenement child," Quinn, B3; for "two iron bars," EKR to ARC, [26 January 1893?], RFPH; for "Alice suffers," EKR to ARC, 3 February [1893?], RFPH.

25. For "lock up," *CH*, 18; for "she does not mind," EKR to ARC, 25 February [1893?], RFPH; for "asthma," David McCullough, *Mornings on Horseback* (New York: Simon & Schuster, 1982), 106–7.

26. *CH*, 3.

27. For "Buffalo Hunt," EKR to ARC, n.d., 1891, RFPH; for sunset, ARL preservation tape, ICD 16021, 21 June 1967, JSP.

28. For "the children," EKR to ARC, 30 September 1890, RFPH; for "yesterday morning," ALR to EKR, 12 May 1893, JSP; for "the afternoon," EKR to ARC, 2 July 1891, RFPH; for "she knocked," ALR to EKR, 3 July 1896, JSP.

29. For "Andrew Lang," "Education," unidentified typescript (ts), JSP; for Theodore, *CH*, 29–30. See also TR to ARC, 26 April 1891, RFPH; for library, John Morton Blum to author, 2 April 2005.

30. For Latin and Greek, Unidentified ts, JSP, and Teague, 46; for history, ALR to TR, 10 August 1898, JSP.

31. Patty [?] to ALR, [February 1898?], ARLC.

32. For other letters, see, for example, Edith A. Clark to ALR, 14 February 1898, JSP; for Miss Spence, *CH*, 26.

33. See *CH*, 18; Lillian Rixey, *Bamie* (New York: David McKay, 1963), 113–14. See also Theodore Douglas Robinson to ALR, 9 March 1898, JSP.

34. Helen R. Roosevelt and ALR to FDR, 10 September 1897, Roosevelt Family Papers, FDRL.

35. ALR to TR, August 1897, JSP.

36. ARC to ALR, 21 August 1897, JSP.

37. ARC to ALR, 27 July 1897, JSP.

38. For "running riot," TR to ARC, 23 February 1898, Morison, *Letters*, 1:783; for "done by Helen," EKR to ALR, 14 April [1898], JSP.

39. For talk of war, EKR to ALR, 14 April [1898], JSP; for "bark," TR to Douglas Robinson, 2 April 1898, Morison, *Letters*, 2:809.

40. For "sick of," ALR to TR, 10 August 1898; for posterity correspondence, ALR to TR, 12 July 1898; TR to ALR, 19 July 1898, all JSP.

41. *CH*, 24–25.

42. ALR Diary fragment, 28–29 September 1898, JSP.

43. EKR to Mrs. William Dudley Foulke, n.d., 1898, Papers of William Dudley Foulke, LC.

44. For "gone to hell," V. C. Jones, "Before the Colors Fade: Last of the Rough Riders," *American Heritage* 20, 5 (August 1969): 95; for "signature," ALR to Carolyn Postlethwaite, fragment [1898] letter and Carolyn T. Postlethwaite to ALR, 16 October 1898, both JSP; "Gov.," Christine K. Roosevelt to ARL, 8 October 1900, JSP.

45. EKR to Cecil Spring-Rice, 15 December 1899, F.O. 800/241-242/9/1, National Archive, London; TR to Martha Selmes, 10 October 1899, Greenway AHS; EKR to Cecil Spring Rice, [c. 1899], F.O. 800/241-242/9/1, National Archive, London.

46. For basketball, see ALR to John Greenway, 14 April 1900; for ice skating, see ALR to John Greenaway, 11 March 1900, both ALR Folder, Greenway AHS; for the opera, ALR Diary Fragment, 14 October 1898; for the play, 15 October 1898, both JSP.

47. For one example of Ted's letters to Alice, see the "hollerday" letter: n.d.; for "thumb," ALR to EKR, 10 March 1900; for tea and cakes, ALR Diary Fragment, 18 October 1898, all JSP.

48. For "farmers," TR to ALR, 14 September 1900, JSP; for "bear," TR to Cecil Spring-Rice, 19 November 1900, Morison and Blum, eds., 2:1424; for "empty position," Morris, 206.

49. *CH*, 36–37. See Morris, 207–209 for the family and the inaugural.

50. *CH*, 41–42.

51. For "at the request," clipping included in William K. Verner to ARL, 28 February 1974, JSP; for response to news, "The Reporters: Jonathan Aitken Interview with Alice Roosevelt Longworth," Yorkshire Television, [January 1969].

Chapter 3: "Something More Than a Plain American Girl"

1. "Mrs. Roosevelt Moves Into the White House," *NYT*, 26 September 1901, 6; for "I can do much for you," EKR to ALR, 17 September 1901, ARLC.

2. *CH*, 43.

3. EKR to ALR, n.d. [1901], JSP; see Sylvia Jokes, Edith, Kermit Roosevelt (New York: Coward, McCann, and Geoghegan, 1980), 222–23, for the configuration of the second floor; for Alice's remarks about the interior design, see *CH*, 44–45.

4. William Wright, *The Washington Game* (New York: E. P. Dutton, 1974), 19.

5. EKR to Cecil Spring-Rice, 27 January 1902, Churchill Archives Center, Papers of Sir Cecil Spring-Rice, CASR, Churchill College, Cambridge, England.

6. The phrase is Ellen Maury Slayden's in her *Washington Wife* (New York: Harper & Row, 1962), 46. On the renovation, see EKR to Charles McKim, 9 September 1902; William Loeb to McKim, 13 September 1902; EKR to McKim, 15 September 1902; "Questions Referred to Mrs. Roosevelt," by McKim, n.d.; EKR to McKim, *n.d.* [Sunday]; EKR to McKim, 5 October 1902; all JSP.

7. Richard Derby to ALR, 1 October 1902, JSP.

8. "May" to ALR, 19 October 1902, JSP.

9. "Miss Alice Roosevelt Introduced to Society," *NYT*, 4 January 1902, 1; "White House Ball," *Washington Post*, 4 January 1902, 1.

10. For "planning for months," EKR to ALR, n.d. [1901], JSP; for "enchanted," *CH*, 47; Truman L. Elton, "Daughter of the President and Her Reputed Fiancé," *Richmond Times-Dispatch*, n.d., reel 461, TRP.

11. Stephen Birmingham, *The Right People* (Boston: Little, Brown, 1968), 123–124.

12. Carl Sferrazza Anthony, *First Ladies* (New York: Morrow, 1990), 296, 298.

13. Ward McAllister, *Society As I Have Found It* (New York: Cassell, 1890), 243.

14. For "elbow-in-the-soup," Michael Teague, *Mrs. L* (Garden City, NY: Doubleday, 1981), 76; for crash, *CH*, 47.

15. ER, *This Is My Story* (New York: Harper & Brothers, 1937), 37; EKR to ALR, n.d. [1901], JSP.

16. "Carloads" is Alice's description of how many of her friends attended (CH, 47). The *New York Tribune* reported 370 people, while Wilbur Cross and Ann Novotny (*White House Weddings* [New York: David McKay, 1967], 136), and Marie Smith (*Entertaining in the White House* [Washington, D.C.: Acropolis Books, 1967], 150) both stated there were "some seven hundred" guests in all. The *NYT* suggested that three hundred young women attended and nearly as many young men. See "Miss Alice Roosevelt Introduced Into Society," *NYT*, 4 January 1902, 1.

17. Mary Randolph, *Presidents and First Ladies* (New York: D. Appleton, 1936), 187; Marguerite Cassini, *Never a Dull Moment* (New York: Harper Brothers, 1956), 166; "Miss Roosevelt a Debutante," *New York Tribune*, 4 January 1902, 10.

18. Charles Seldon, "The Father Complex of Alice Roosevelt Longworth and Ruth Hanna McCormick," *Ladies' Home Journal*, March 1927, 72; Randolph, 190; Lillian Rixey, *Bamie* (New York: David McKay, 1963), 187; Ted Morgan, *F.D.R.* (New York: Simon & Schuster, 1985), 81.

19. *CH*, 47.

20. "Miss Alice Roosevelt Introduced to Society," *NYT*, 4 January 1902, 1; "Miss Roosevelt a Debutante," *New York Tribune*, 4 January 1902, 1.

21. Teague, 76.

22. Irving J. Rein, Philip Kotler, and Martin R. Stoller, *High Visibility* (New York: Dodd, Mead, 1987), 15.

23. Walton and Cripe, "Alice Roosevelt March" (Chicago: Victor Kremer, 1902); Harold L. Frankensteen, "The American Girl" (Detroit: H. A. Sage, 1905).

24. Teague, 70, 72 emphasis added by Teague. She did not destroy the letter. In it TR accused her of "courting notoriety," with "bizarre actions" that were "underbred and unladylike," TR to ALR, 28 August 1904, JSP.

25. Morris, 268.

26. Quentin Roosevelt to ALR, 14 December 1909, RFPH.

27. TR to ALR, telegram, 19 November 1903, TRP.

28. Teague, 108.

29. For Edward VII, 27 January 1902, ARLD; for card reception, 4 February 1902, ARLD; "Named by Miss Roosevelt: Benefit of Pascal Institute," *New York Tribune*, 5 February 1902, 7.

30. For "Sissie," EKR to ALR, 10 February 1902; for birthday, EKR to ALR, n.d. [1902], both JSP; "Groton Boys Gaining," *New York Tribune*, 16 February 1902, 9; *CH*, 47–48; for "love that boy," 15 February 1902, ARLD.

31. Andrew D. White to TR, 4 January 1902, TRP.

32. Cambon to Delcasse, 15 January 1902, in *Documents Diplomatiques Francais* II (Paris: Imprimerie Nationale, 1931), 32–33.

33. Christening practice, 23 February 1902; appraisal of the prince, 24 February 1902, ARLD.

34. Smith, 153–54; Morris, 234; Ona Griffin Jeffries, *In and Out of the White House* (New York: Wilfred Funk, 1960), 276–80.

35. 25 February 1902, ARLD.

36. "The Kaiser and Miss Roosevelt," *New York Times*, 26 February 1901, 1.

37. Worthington Ford, ed., *The Letters of Henry Adams* (New York: Houghton Mifflin, 1938), 375.

38. For the *Tribune* quote, see "Kaiser's Compliment to American Women through Miss Roosevelt," 26 February 1902, 2:4; "The 'Miss Roosevelt' Wrap," *New York Herald, Paris Edition*, 14 September 1902, 11; enclosed in Edith [Root] to ALR, 14 September 1902, JSP; Cassini, 169.

39. Clara Parrish to ALR, 6 February 1902, ARLC.

40. Whitelaw Reid to TR, 12 March 1902, TRP.

41. TR to Joseph H. Choate, 3 February 1902, Joseph H. Choate Papers, LC; "The 'Fuss' Over Miss Roosevelt," *Literary Digest* 24, 15 (12 April 1902), 509–510.

42. Selden, 72.

43. "Miss Roosevelt Will Not See Coronation," *NYT*, 8 March 1902, 8; *CH*, 50; TR to Joseph H. Choate, 3 March 1902, Choate Papers, LC; Whitelaw Reid to TR, 12 March 1902, TRP.

44. 21 June 1902, (written on inside back cover of diary); 27 January 1903, ARLD.

45. "The 'Fuss' Over Miss Roosevelt," 509–510.

46. Isabel Anderson, *Presidents and Pies* (New York: Houghton Mifflin, 1920), 68; 26 March 1902, ARLD.

47. *CH*, 52; "Miss Roosevelt Starts for Cuba," *New York Tribune*, 10 March 1902, 2; 13 March–7 April 1902, ARLD.

48. 6 March 1902, ARLD; "Appeal to Miss Roosevelt," *NYT*, 13 March 1902, 1; Alejandro Mendez Plasencia to ALR, 22 March 1902, JSP.

49. Clifford Howard, "The President's Daughter," *Ladies' Home Journal* 19, 5, (April 1902), 5.

50. 13 April 1902, ARLD (emphasis in original).

Chapter 4: **"I Tried to Be Conspicuous"**

1. For Highland fling, Martha Selmes to Julia Dinsmore, 10 January 1902, Dinsmore Family Papers, AHS; 25 April–11 May 1902, ARLD. For the miscarriage, see also Sylvia Jukes Morris, *Edith Kermit Roosevelt* (New York: Coward, McCann & Geoghegan, 1980), 237.

2. For "help me," EKR to ALR, n.d., JSP; for "toughs," Edmund Morris, *Theodore Rex* (New York: Random House, 2001), 108; for Edith's indisposition, 22–23 May 1902, ARLD, and *CH*, 53.

3. 30 June 1902, ARLD.

4. 28 and 31 October 1902, ARLD. "I pray for money!" 26 October 1902, ARLD (emphasis in original). See also 21 December and the undated entries at the end of the 1902 diary.

5. Manhanset House (Shelter Island, New York) program, 4 July 1902, JSP.

6. "Mr. and Mrs. Roosevelt Enjoy an Outing," *NYT*, 19 July 1902, 8; ALR to John Greenway, 29 December 1902, Greenway AHS; for "Got a talking to," 20 July 1902, ARLD.

7. 2–18 August ARLD; "Alice Roosevelt Loses a Game of Tag with the Camera," *New York Journal*, 17 August 1902, n.p., TRP; "Miss Roosevelt's Hand Read," *Philadelphia Press*, 19 August 1902, TRP; "Miss Roosevelt Loses Her Way," *New York Tribune*, 19 August 1902, 1.

8. Unidentified, clipping n.d. ("Miss Alice Roosevelt, who will soon summer at the Summer White House...."); Corinne Roosevelt Robinson to ALR, 25 May 1903, both from JSP; Luellen Cass Teters, "Fair Woman as Motorist," *Motor* magazine, January 1907, 19, quoted in Virginia Scharff, *Taking the Wheel* (New York: Free Press, 1991), 71–73.

9. For "coffee," 6 September 1902; for accident, 4 September 1902 and *CH*, 54;

for not loving, 1–17 September 1902, all ARLD.

10. For poker, see 17, 18 and 22 September 1902, ARLD; Henry Brandon, "A Talk with an 83-Year-Old Enfant Terrible," *NYT*, 6 August 1967, 69; and *CH*, 169–170.

11. 23 and 30 September 1902, ARLD.

12. N.d., at the back of the 1902 diary. See also 1 October 1902, ARLD.

13. "Hoof," 30 November 1902; "no one ever came," 13 December 1902, ARLD.

14. 23–24 December 1902, ARLD.

15. 25 December 1902, ARLD.

16. For the embassy dance 8 January; for "both so attractive," 11 January 1903, ARLD; TR to TRJR, 20 January 1903, reel 330, TRP. See also TRJR to ALR, 3 February 1903, JSP.

17. 20 January 1903, ARLD.

18. For Edith's sanctions, EKR to ALR, 9 November 1902; for scheduling, EKR to ALR, undated, both JSP.

19. 18 January 1903, ARLD.

20. For Judicial reception, 12 January 1903, ARLD; for European visitor, S. J. Morris, 273; for "I am a fool," 30 January 1903, ARLD. On 23 and 25 January Alice vowed not to go to New York anymore.

21. 27 January 1903, ARLD.

22. Sally Quinn, "Alice Roosevelt at 90," *Washington Post*, 12 February 1974, B3.

23. Author's interview with Joanna Sturm, 25 April 2005.

24. TR to TRJR, 9 February 1903, reel 330, TRP.

25. 16 February 1903, ARLD.

26. *CH*, 55. See also "Chosen Queen of Comus Ball," *New York Tribune*, 1 February 1903, 2; "Welcome to Miss Roosevelt," *NYT*, 1 February 1903, 1; "Miss Roosevelt Honored," *NYT*, 18 February 1903, 1; "Miss Roosevelt Charmed," *NYT*, 19 February 1903, 1; "Alice Roosevelt's Debut in Carnival Wonderland," *New Orleans Daily Picayune*, n.d. [1903], JSP; for betting and Root, 21 February 1903, ARLD; ALR to Mary E. McIlhenny, n.d. [1903] JSP; for "wear her honors," untitled article, *New Orleans Daily Picayune*, n.d. [1903], JSP.

27. 8 March 1903, ARLD.

28. ALR to EKR, 24 March 1903, JSP.

29. For "official behavior," *CH*, 56; for "very good," ALR to EKR, 20 March 1903; for "fireworks and gusto mucho," ALR to EKR, 24 March 1903, both JSP; "Miss Roosevelt's Ovation," *New York Tribune*, 4 April 1903, 5; TR to ALR, 27 May 1903, TRP.

30. Michael Teague, *Mrs. L* (Garden City, N.Y.: Doubleday, 1981), 73.

31. For "stared at," *CH*, 59; ALR to John McCutcheon, 29 November 1903, John McCutcheon Papers, Newberry Library, Chicago.

32. Helen Rebecca Roosevelt to ALR, n.d., ARLC. Helen pasted the unidentified clipping to her note. See also 24 October 1903, ARLD; "Miss Roosevelt Eager to See Horses Start," *NYT*, 4 April 1905, 9.

33. See Ethel Barrymore's *Memories* (New York: Harper & Brothers, 1955), 131, for an example of Maggie and Alice in competition over Nick. See also Ira R. T. Smith, *Dear Mr. President* (New York: Julian Messner, 1949), 60–61.

34. Marguerite Cassini, *Never a Dull Moment* (New York: Harper & Brothers, 1956), 188; for "gallivanting," Teague, 77; for ER quote, Geoffrey Ward, *A First-Class Temperament* (New York: Harper & Row, 1989), 45n7.

35. Cassini, 189.

36. 16 February 1904, ARLD.

37. "Gleanings," *New York Tribune*, 9 March 1903, 5.

38. Frances Spatz and David Camelon, "Legendary Ladies: Rebellious 'Princess Alice,'" *American Weekly*, 12 November 1950, 24–25. "To annoy the family," ARL preservation tape, ICD 16037, n.d., JSE.

39. "Smoking in Public," *Washington Mirror*, 3 June 1905, JSP; EKR to ALR, n.d. [1905], JSP ("I am distressed to hear..."); TR to ALR, 21 July 1905, RFPH; Kermit Roosevelt to ALR, 15 November 1905, JSP.

40. "S. Shakespeare" to "the Chairman of the 'More-Light-in-the-Darkness' Committee," 15 December 1905, JSP, and Teague, 82.

41. For purse, Sarah Booth Conroy, "Rough Rider's Romantic Side," *Washington Post*, 10 May 1995; for troop review, Walter Evans Edge, *A Jerseyman's Journal* (Princeton: Princeton University Press, 1948), 64; and "Mrs. Goelet in Submarine," *NYT*, 27 July 1911, 2. Alice wrote to journalist Samuel McClure two decades after the event to clear the record. She was usually credited with having gone to the bottom of the sea in the submarine. Not so, she told McClure. At Newport she "did go aboard a submarine." But, "it was hitched to the dock the whole time, obviously. I have a dim recollection that we were told we were a couple of feet underwater, if that is possible with the boat tied to the dock." She was happy to set the facts straight: "I don't in the least mind a 'story' on myself, when it is a true one, but this most certainly is not!" ARL to Samuel McClure, 18 June [c. 1925], McClure Manuscript, Manuscripts Department, Lilly Library, Indiana University, Bloomington, Indiana.

42. *CH*, 59–63; "Miss Roosevelt's Exciting Ride, " *New York Tribune*, 30 May 1903, 9; "Miss Roosevelt at York Harbor," *New York Tribune*, 29 July 1903, 8; "Miss Roosevelt Sinks in the Boat," *New York Tribune*, 11 September 1903, 9; "Miss Roosevelt's Photograph: Presented to Officers of Dispatch Boat Named for Her," *New York Tribune*, 4 November 1903, 6; "White House Brides," *New York Herald*, 5 January 1906, TRP; ALR to Belle Hagner, 23 July 1903, PHP; "Miss Roosevelt at Races," *NYT*, 12 April 1904.

43. Owen Wister, *Roosevelt* (New York: Macmillan, 1930), 87.

44. For examples of Edith's lectures, see 10 January 1904 and 10 May 1904, ARLD. This lecture from Grandma Lee is from Caroline Lee to ALR, 20 July 1903, ARLC. Unidentified author [signed "E———" to ALR, n.d., ARLD.

45. 8 October 1903, ARLD; George C. Lee to ALR, 5 November 1903, ARLC; Quarterly stipend: George C. Lee to ALR, 1 January 1904, JSP.

46. 26–31 May 1904, ARLD; *CH*, 64–65; "Women Mob Miss Roosevelt," *NYT*, 27 May 1904, 1; "Miss Alice Roosevelt," *World's Fair Bulletin*, June 1904, 34; July 1904, 40; TRJR to ALR, *n.d.*, JSP; copied the First Daughter, "Miss Roosevelt Gives Up Pike Trip," *St. Louis Republican*, 2 June 1904, 1, Francis Collection, St. Louis Historical Society.

47. For "Alice dear," unidentified author [signed "E———"] to ALR, n.d.; "Hair will fall out," Libby Lawrence to ALR, n.d., both ARLC.

48. Charles McCauley to ALR, 12 February [n.d.]; for *Paris Herald*, Gwendolyn [unknown] to ALR, n.d.; for Horse Show, Unidentified author, n.d.; George C. Lee to ALR, 20 June 1904, all ARLC.

49. TR to Owen Wister, 2 November 1901, TRP.

50. EKR to ALR, n.d., JSP.

Chapter 5: **"Frightfully Difficult Trying to Keep Up Appearances"**

1. ALR Diary, fragment, 14 October 1898, JSP.

2. Ward McAllister, *Society As I Have Found It* (New York: Cassell, 1890); "social insecurity" Kathleen Dalton, from "Theodore Roosevelt: Knickerbocker Aristocrat," *New York History* 67, 1 (January 1986), 46.

3. 20 May 1904, ARLD; Joseph Alsop, *I've Seen the Best of It* (New York: W. W. Norton, 1992), 33.

4. For "captivate your fancy," Margaret [unknown]to ALR, n.d.; for "Mrs. John Greenway," Gwendolyn [unknown] to ALR, n.d.; for dukes, Helen [Douglas] to ALR, n.d.; and Helen R. Roosevelt to ALR, n.d.; all ARLC; for "temper fit," 8 May 1902, ARLD.

5. Sylvia Jukes Morris, *Edith Kermit Roosevelt* (New York: Coward, McCann & Geoghegan, 1980), 98.

6. Mark Sullivan, *The Education of an American* (New York: Doubleday, Doran, 1938), 211.

7. Nora C. Klein, *Practical Etiquette* (Chicago: Flanagan, 1888), 8 and 61.

8. Number 76 was 24 April, 87 was 2 May, and 100 was 26 September, all 1902, ARLD. Helen R. Roosevelt to ARL, n.d., ARLC.

9. Carl Sferrazza Anthony, *First Ladies* (New York: William Morrow, 1990), 1:305–306. The TR quote is from "Message of the President of the United States Communicated to the Two Houses of Congress at the Beginning of the Second Session of the 59th Congress," *Congressional Record* (Washington, D.C.: Government Printing Office, 1906), 29, reel 427, TRP.

10. Klein, 21.

11. For men, Ronald G. Walters, ed., *Primers for Prudery* (Baltimore: Johns Hopkins University Press, 2000), 95; for women, Harvey Green, *The Light of the Home* (New York: Pantheon, 1983), 21; "heartless discriminations," Sondra R. Herman, "Loving Courtship or the Marriage Market? The Ideal and Its Critics 1871–1911," *American Quarterly*, 25, 2 (May 1973), 242; "begat series," Michael Teague, *Mrs. L* (Garden City, N.Y.: Doubleday, 1981), 57; John Morton Blum to author, 2 April 2005.

12. Abbey B. Longstreet, *Social Etiquette of New York* (New York: D. Appleton, 1887), 9.

13. Buttons askew and restriction quotes, Teague, 66.

14. For the asparagus, see Dabney Taylor, "Idaho's 'Little Borah' Looks Back on Her First 99 Years," *Idaho Statesman*, 19 October 1969, 14. Asparagus may be eaten with ungloved fingers. For overseas trips, see Chapter 7, below.

15. ER, *This Is My Story* (New York: Harper & Brothers, 1937), 37. Alfreda, Christine, and Dorothy Roosevelt rounded out the Magic Five.

16. 21 December 1902, ARLD.

17. Teague, 151.

18. "Awfully nice," 12 January 1903 and "I am afraid," 8 November 1903, ARLD; for top billing see, for example, "Led Newport Dance with Alice Roosevelt," *Washington Post*, 14 August 1902, and "Miss Roosevelt's Hand Read," *Philadelphia Press*, 19 August 1902; both TRP.

19. "Fierce enough," Libby Lawrence to ALR, n.d., ARLC; "attraction for me," Teague, 77.

20. ARL wrote about Carpenter every night in her diary from the first through the seventh of April 1902. The retaliation quote is from the third, the charms quote from the fourth, and the "poor Alice" quote from the fifth.

21. 7 April 1902, ARLD.

22. Edward Carpenter to ARL, 3 May 1902; and n.d., both ARLC.

23. 23–28 May 1902, ARLD.

24. Carpenter proposed on 29 May, and ARL received their notes on 30 May, according to her diary.

25. Eliza Bisbee Duffey, *Ladies' and Gentlemen's Etiquette* (Philadelphia: Porter & Coates, 1887), 125–26; McAllister, 242.

26. J. Van Ness Philips to ALR, 22 July

1902, ARLC; "A young lady," Klein, 18; "rejected suitor," Duffey, 135–136.

27. Delancey Jay to ALR, 29 October 1903, ALRC; 9 July 1902, ARLD.

28. Mrs. John King Van Rensselaer, *Social Ladder* (New York: Holt, 1924), 33. By 1924, when Mrs. Van Rensselaer wrote, the Mrs. Arthur Iselin to whom she referred was the former Eleanor Jay, sister of Delancey Jay.

29. Arthur Iselin to ALR, 16 April [1902], ARLC.

30. "Very stupid," 8 August 1902; "poor Alice, 3 August 1902; "no hope," 7 August 1902, ARLD.

31. "Me alone loves," 18 November 1902; "the beast," 10 December 1902; "oh Arthur," 11 December 1902, ARLD.

32. "I would be," 10 January 1903, ARLD; Margaret [unknown] to ARL, n.d., ARLC; "Arthur...hates me," 20 January 1903; "never get married," 21 January 1903; both ARLD.

33. Receptions, 26 January 1903; cotillion, 28 January 1903; "I led him on," 10 February 1903, all ARLD.

34. 9 February 1903, ARLD.

35. 12 February 1903, ARLD.

Chapter 6: "He Never Grew Serious About Anything"

1. Helen R. Roosevelt married her sixth cousin Theodore Douglas Roosevelt in 1904. ER married her fifth cousin once removed, FDR, in 1905.

2. Edward Carpenter to ARL, n.d. 1902, ARLC.

3. Sondra R. Herman, "Loving Courtship or the Marriage Market?" *American Quarterly*, 25 (May 1973), 239.

4. Karl Fleming and Anne Taylor Fleming, *The First Time* (New York: Simon & Schuster, 1975), 181.

5. Cleveland Amory, *Who Killed Society?* (New York: Harper, 1960), 227–46. Amory maintained that by 1900 "no less than 500 of America's '400'" had married foreign titles (229).

6. Michael Teague, *Mrs. L* (Garden City, N.Y.: Doubleday, 1981), 129.

7. "I swear," ARLD back of the 1902 diary; "vow," 3 October 1903, ARLD. To Iselin, n.d., ARLD, from the back of the 1902 diary; to Nick, 27 July 1905, ARLD.

8. 7 February 1904, ARLD.

9. Teague, 129.

10. Fleming and Fleming, 177 and 183.

11. Drew Pearson and Robert S. Allen, *The Washington Merry-Go-Round* (New York: H. Liveright, 1931), 230–31.

12. "'Tis True That They Are to Wed," *Cincinnati Enquirer*, 12 December 1905, clipping, ARL Scrapbook, LC; Marguerite Cassini, *Never a Dull Moment* (New York: Harper & Brothers, 1956), 190; "new congressman," Teague, 129; 14 and 17 February 1904, ARLD.

13. On Nicholas Longworth Sr., see his obituary, 1890 and "50 Years Ago in Cincinnati," *Cincinnati Enquirer*, 19 January 1940, in the Judge Nicholas Longworth Princeton File, CHS; and "Nicholas Longworth, Esq., of Cincinnati, and the Vineyards of Ohio," *Harper's Weekly*, 2, 82 (24 July 1858), 472–74.

14. Clara Longworth de Chambrun, *The Making of Nicholas Longworth* (New York: Ray Long & Richard Smith, 1933), 115.

15. De Chambrun, 222.

16. Constance McLaughlin Green, *Washington* (Princeton: Princeton University Press, 1963), 301.

17. Teague, 137.

18. Geoffrey Ward, *Before the Trumpet* (New York: Harper & Row, 1989), 236.

19. Llewellyn Thayer, "The White House Bridegroom," *Leslie's Illustrated Weekly*, 1 March 1906, 174.

20. Helen Hay to NL, n.d., NLIII.

21. NL to "My Darling" [Miriam Bloomer], n.d., NLIII. Miriam Bloomer lived in the Hotel Alms with her family. See *Mrs. Devereux's Blue Book of Cincinnati Society*, 1906, CHS.

22. "Former fiancé," "Miss Bloomer Not Burned," *NYT*, 29 September 1907, 2; "I'll come," Miriam Bloomer to NL, n.d., NLIII; at the wedding, Eleanor Adams, "Chit and Chat About This 'n That," *Cincinnati Enquirer*, 19 January 1964, ARLPF. See also Wilbur Cross and Ann Novotny, *White House Weddings* (New York: McKay, 1967), 139; "collapse," "Miss Bloomer Not Burned," *NYT*, 29 September 1907, 2.

23. Cassini, 180–81.

24. 20 January 1904, ARLD (emphasis in original).

25. 21 January 1904, ARLD (emphasis in original).

26. "American Bride for Count," *NYT*, 15 April 1904, 5; "Count Gizycki Hastens Wedding Preparations," *NYT*, 7 April 1904, 9.

27. Cassini, 199. See also "Mr. Longworth to Marry Miss Alice Next February," n.d., unidentified clipping, ARLPF.

28. Charles de Chambrun to ALR, 25 March 1904, ARLC.

29. "I really like," 27 January 1904; "Why am I," 12 March 1904, ARLD; "tease my friends," Cassini, 181; "only her own fun," Cassini, 200; "Nick and Maggie," 1 May 1904, ARLD.

30. 2 May 1904, ARLD.

31. 3 May 1904, ARLD. In Cassini's memoir, the story is different—so different, in fact, that it is likely that Nick proposed to Maggie twice (Cassini, 200).

32. "Had a long talk," 26 December 1904; "Nick had a supper," 19 January 1905, ARLD (emphasis in original).

33. 29–31 January 1905, ARLD.

34. NL to ALR, [11 February 1905], JSP.

35. From 15 January through 21 April, every entry ends with "My Nick."

36. "So many things," NL to ALR, 8 April 1905; "I have not," NL to ALR, 19 April 1905; "Longing to see you," NL to ALR, 25 April 1905; all JSP.

37. NL to ALR, 14 June 1905, JSP.

38. "Practically told Charlie," 17 June 1905; "Father is making peace," 11 June 1905, ARLD.

39. Charles E. Rosenberg, "Sexuality, Class and Role in 19th-Century America," *American Quarterly*, 25, 2 (May 1973), 140.

40. NL to ALR 20 June 1905, JSP.

41. "Desperately sorrowful," 1 June 1905, ARLD; ALR to ARC, n.d. [1905], ARLHar.

42. Lost five pounds, Sylvia Jukes Morris, *Edith Kermit Roosevelt* (New York: Coward, McCann, & Geoghegan, 1980), 297; "parting," 26 June 1905, ARLD.

Chapter 7: **"When Alice Came to Plunderland"**

1. WHT to Luke E. Wright, 17 March 1905, WHTP.

2. Henry F. Pringle, *The Life and Times of William Howard Taft* (New York: Farrar and Reinhart, 1939) 1:297–98.

3. Complete list of junketeers in "Personnel of Secretary Taft's Party," Mabel T. Boardman Papers, LC. See also "Taft and His Party Start," *NYT*, 1 July 1905, 1

4. ARC to ALR, 20 June 1905, JSP.

5. ALR to TR, n.d. [1905], JSP; WHT to HHT, 10 July 1905,WHTP.

6. HT, *Reflections of Full Years* (New York: Dodd, Mead, 1914), 292–94.

7. Elsie Clews Parsons, "Congressional Junket in Japan," *New-York Historical*

Society Quarterly, XLQ, 4 (October 1957), 338 (emphasis in original).

8. ALR to TR, n.d. [1905], JSP.

9. ALR to EKR, n.d. [1905], JSP; for "banzai," Michael Teague, *Mrs. L* (Garden City, N.Y.: Doubleday, 1981), 84.

10. Lloyd Griscom to Willard Straight, 21 April 1905, WSP.

11. Lloyd C. Griscom, *Diplomatically Speaking* (Boston: Little, Brown, 1940), 257–58; WHT to HHT, 26 July 1905, WHTP.

12. ALR to TR, 30 July 1905, JSP; George A. Lensen, ed., *The d'Anethan Dispatches from Japan, 1894–1910* (Tallahassee: Diplomatic Press, 1967), 206; Teague, 87; and *CH*, 84, for Alice's more contemporary and irreverent recollection of the event.

13. *CH*, 85 and Griscom, 257.

14. TR to John Hay, in Elting E. Morison and John Morton Blum, eds. *The Letters of Theodore Roosevelt* (Cambridge, Mass.: Harvard University Press, 1951–1954) 4:1168.

15. WHT to HHT, 31 July, WHTP; The newspapers claimed the empress was ill. ALR thought her "out of town" (*CH*, 80).

16. ALR to TR, 30 July 1905, JSP; WHT to HHT, 31 July 1905, WHTP; Parsons, 402; Griscom, 258 and 298.

17. WHT to HHT, 31 July 1905, WHTP.

18. Teague, 91.

19. Bouquets, Griscom, 260; "The Japanese did wonders," Martin Egan to Willard Straight, 14 August 1905, WSP; "No people," *CH*, 86; "I don't know," ALR to TR, 30 July 1905, JSP.

20. ARLC, undated and unsigned letter file; "national costume" from the same source.

21. WHT to Luke E. Wright, 17 March 1905, WHTP.

22. Fred Leith to his mother, 4 August 1905, Fred Leith Ms. Coll. 89, Naval Historical Collection, Naval War College, Newport, Rhode Island.

23. *CH*, 87; "Pageant for Taft,' *Washington Post*, 5 August 1905, 1. See also "How Miss Roosevelt was Greeted by the Little Brown Filipino," *Brooklyn Daily Eagle*, 3 September 1905, TRP, reel 461.

24. Mabel T. Boardman, "A Woman's Impressions of the Philippines," *Outlook*, 82 (24 February 1906), 435–46; "Miss Roosevelt's Reception in the Philippines," *Washington Post*, 6 August 1905, sec. 4, 6; "Miss Roosevelt's Ball Closes Manila Visit," *NYT*, 13 August 1905, 4.

25. WHT to HHT, 14 August 1905, WHTP; The Oyster Bay quote is from an untitled blurb in the *Washington Post*, 6 August 1905, sec. II, 4.

26. "Sultan of Sulu Offers to Wed Miss Roosevelt," *NYT*, 22 August 1905, 7. See also "Taft Party at Iloilo," *Washington Post*, 15 August 1905, 1. For an assertion that the sultan never proposed, see "Miss Roosevelt's Embarrassing Presents," *Literary Digest*, 4 November 1905, 644.

27. Boardman, 444.

28. Charles H. Brent, "The Visit to the Philippines of Secretary Taft and His Party," *Outlook*, 81 (14 October 1905), 371.

29. "Miss Roosevelt's Plans," *Washington Post*, 16 August 1905, 2; "Taft Party at Hong Kong," *NYT*, 3 September 1905, 1; TR to Victor H. Metcalf, 16 June 1905, in Morison and Blum, eds., 4:1235; TR to Herbert H. D. Peirce, 24 June 1905, in Morison and Blum, eds., 4:1251; "Boycotters Heavy Losers," *Washington Post*, 6 August 1905, 1; and "Extends the Boycott," *Washington Post*, 11 August 1905, 4.

30. *CH*, 91; McIntosh, "Mrs. Longworth's Pluck in the Face of Peril," *Literary Digest*, 32.9 (3 March 1906), 346; and

"Alice Roosevelt Defies Chinese," *Washington Globe*, 4 September 1905, reel 461, TRP.

31. CH, 92; "Gunboat for Miss Roosevelt," *NYT*, 4 September 1905, 1.

32. Menu, JSP; *CH*, 95–99.

33. Henry Tsai, *China and the Overseas Chinese* (Fayetteville: University of Arkansas Press, 1983), 100–103.

34. *CH*, 99–100; Paul A. Varg, *Open Door Diplomat* (Urbana: University of Illinois Press, 1952), 59–60.

35. "The Young Lady of the White House," *NYT*, 19 October 1905, 8; for part of the extensive media coverage of Alice in China, see "Miss Roosevelt at Peking," *NYT*, 13 September 1905, 4; "Miss Roosevelt Visits Empress," *New York Tribune*, 16 September 1905, 2; "Guests of Dowager Empress," *Washington Post*, 16 September 1905, reel 461, TRP. "Rides on Royal Palanquin," *NYT*, 20 September 1905, 1; "Empress Dowager and President's Daughter," *New York Herald*, 24 September 1905, magazine, 1.

36. *CH*, 103 and 104; "come, saw," Willard Straight to Frederick Palmer, 3 October 1905, WSP.

37. "To Miss Roosevelt," reel 1, WSP, #1260, Division of Rare and Manuscript Collections, Cornell University Library.

38. Frederick Palmer to Willard Straight, 24 September 1905, WSP; "not a banzai," Teague, 87; "if anyone asked," *CH*, 106; policemen, Lloyd Griscom to ALR, 19 September 1905, JSP.

39. The Girls of the Kamibe Higher Elementary School to ALR, 6 October 1905, ARLC.

40. "Russian women" to ALR, 14 August [1905], JSP; Lewis L. Gould, *The Presidency of Theodore Roosevelt* (Lawrence: University Press of Kansas, 1991), 181.

41. 29 June 1905, ARLD; headline, *CH*, 71.

42. WHT to HHT, 10 July 1905, WHTP. On Mabel Boardman and Amy McMillan, see WHT to HHT, 31 July 1905, WHTP. According to Kentucky historian Thomas H. Appleton Jr., a Kentucky engagement is a May–December romance. Appleton Jr. to the author, 8 December 1991.

43. WHT to HHT, 1 August 1905, WHTP.

44. "Congressional wives' luncheon," 71, the "curtain" (or private) lectures, 69, *CH*. For ALR's assessment of the luncheon, see ARLD, 3 July 1905.

45. 9–11 July 1905, ARLD; WHT to HHT, 3 July 1905, WHTP.

46. WHT to HHT, 25 July 1905, WHTP.

47. 27 July 1905, ARLD; Nagasaki newspaper quoted in "Miss Roosevelt in Japan," *New York Tribune*, 28 September 1905, 5.

48. WHT to HHT, 14 August 1905, WHTP.

49. ARL to NL, n.d., September 1905, ARLC. It is impossible to know whether or not Alice ever gave this letter to Nick.

50. ARL to NL, n.d. [1905], JSP.

51. Alice had told Griscom, WHT to HHT, 26 July 1905; "never believe," WHT to HHT, 31 July 1905, both WHTP.

52. TR to ALR, 2 September 1905, ARLHar; for example, EKR to ALR, 10 September 1905, JSP.

53. For the "rough passage" and the bet, see F. Palmer to Willard Straight, 20 November 1905, WSP.

54. *CH*, 106–7; "To Break All Records," *New York Tribune*, 24 October 1905, 1; "Miss Roosevelt Lands," *NYT*, 24 October 1905, 1; "Harriman's Race Stopped," *NYT*, 25 October 1905, 1; "Miss Roosevelt Here from Eastern Trip," *NYT*, 27 October 1905, 1; Harriman won the bet when the *Siberia* beat the *Korea*'s record by 27 minutes.

55. "Miss Roosevelt Lands," *NYT*, 24 October 1905, 1.

56. *CH*, 108–9.

57. Mary Elizabeth W. Sherwood, *Manners and Social Usages* (New York: Harper, 1897), 96–98.

58. Morris, 303.

59. De Chambrun, 193; "Alice Roosevelt to Become Mrs. Longworth," *Chicago Tribune*, 13 December 1905, 1; *CH*, 109.

60. "Longworth Didn't Know He'd Won," *New York Evening World*, 15 December 1905, and "Longworth Says He's in a Trance," *Brooklyn Times*, 14 December 1905, both from the ARL Scrapbook, LC; "rumor says," Thayer, 174; McIntosh, 346.

61. Truman L. Elton, "Daughter of the President and Her Reputed Fiancé," *Richmond Times-Dispatch*, n.d. 1905, reel 461. TRP; "Miss Roosevelt Lands," *NYT*, 24 October 1905, 1.

62. Untitled clipping, *Montreal Daily Star*, 18 October 1905, reel 461, TRP; TR telegram to ARL, 17 October 1905, JSP. See also "Miss Roosevelt's Embarrassing Presents," *Literary Digest*, XXXI, 19 (4 November 1905), 643.

63. "Six Months in the Strenuous Life of Miss Roosevelt," *Indianapolis Sunday Star*, 1 October 1905; and "Miss Roosevelt to Pay $25,000 Duty on Gifts," *NYT*, 18 October 1905, from reel 461, TRP. *NYT* editorial, 21 October 1905, 8, was entitled "Miss Roosevelt's Presents." ARL's quote to the press is from "The President's Daughter," *Indianapolis Morning Star*, 31 October 1905, reel 461, TRP; *Chicago Record Herald*, 17 October 1905, n.p., reel 461, TRP; "1,026 on Oriental Gifts," *NYT*, 17 December 1905, 1.

64. Thomas Sammons to ARL, 14 September 1905, JSP.

65. ARC to ARL, 31 October 1905, JSP.

66. Elton, "Daughter of the President," reel 461, TRP.

Chapter 8: "To Bask in the Rays of Your Reflected Glory"

1. "At the White House," *New York Tribune*, 14 December 1905, 16; Robert Toapp to ARL, 13 January 1906, JSP; ARL to ER, 8 December 1905, ER Papers, FDRL.

2. Anne Ellis, *The Life of an Ordinary Woman* (Boston: Houghton Mifflin, 1999 [1929]), 241.

3. V. V. Pittman to ARL, 17 February 1906, JSP.

4. Owen Wister to ARL, 17 December 1905, JSP.

5. George Lee to ARL, 7 December 1905, ARLC.

6. Julius Fleischmann to NL, n.d. [1905], NLIII.

7. "Miss Roosevelt Could Open a Museum with These Presents," unidentified clipping, n.d., reel 461,TRP; "I had about the sort," *CH*, 109–110; "the one thing," Michael Teague, *Mrs. L* (Garden City, N.Y.: Doubleday, 1981), 128–29; Mary Elizabeth W. Sherwood, *Manners and Social Usages* (New York: Harper, 1897), 197 and 118.

8. Francis H. Lee to ARL, 30 January 1906; ARL to John Greenway, n.d., [1906], both JSP. For the junketeers' gift, see "The President a Guest at Longworth Dinner," *NYT*, 16 February 1906, 1. Alice expressed her gratitude for the cake plate in *CH*, 111.

9. "Cubans Love Mr. Roosevelt," *Kansas City Star*, 6 February 1906, JSP; Thomas Henry Sanderson to Cecil Spring-Rice, 20 February 1906, FO 800/241, microfilm, National Archive, London. For the gifts from China, see the letter from the Chinese legation, Washington, to ARL, 27 January 1906, JSP.

10. "Gift from Negro Children," *NYT*, 15 February 1906, 2; [untitled] *Medford Patriot*, 8 February 1906, JSP; Ellis, 242.

11. Joseph de Gonzague to TR, 14 February 1906, JSP.

12. Anita Comfort-Brooks, "Alice the Bride of the White House" (New York: N. Weinstein, 1906); "Wooing of Miss Alice," *Washington Post*, 8 February 1906, JSP; for presents, see Nelle Scanlan, *Boudoir Mirrors of Washington* (Philadelphia: John C. Winston, 1923), 32–33; *CH*, 109–111; Irwin Hood Hoover, *Forty-Two Years in the White House* (New York: Houghton Mifflin, 1934), 34–35; Mary Randolph, *Presidents and First Ladies* (New York: D. Appleton-Century, 1936), 187–91; "A Car of Coal as a Present," *New York Tribune*, 28 December 1905, 1; "Gowns and Gifts for Miss Alice," *Philadelphia Press*, 29 December 1905, reel 471, TRP; "Beautiful Presents for Miss Roosevelt," *NYT*, 11 February 1906, 1; "Dowry Chest of Empress for Miss Roosevelt," *NYT*, 15 February 1906, 1.

13. For gift display traditions, Sherwood, 118 and 126; *CH*, 111.

14. *CH*, 111; 12 and 13 February 1906, EKR Diaries.

15. "W.C.T.U. Up in Arms," *NYT*, 11 February 1906, 1; "Ohio Senate Divided," *NYT*, 16 February 1906, 2.

16. "A Gift for Mr. Longworth," *NYT*, 16 February 1906, 2.

17. The $300,000 estimate is from "Miss Roosevelt's Wedding on February 14," *Brooklyn Times*, n.d. The $2 million estimate is from "Transferring Realty Estate of Longworths," unidentified typescript, n.d. The $15 million estimate is from "Longworth Didn't Know He'd Won," *New York Evening World*, 15 December 1905; all ARL Scrapbook, LC.

18. Gustavus Myers, *History of the Great American Fortunes* (New York: Random House, 1936), 186; Sylvia Jukes Morris, *Edith Kermit Roosevelt* (New York: Coward, McCann, & Geoghegan, 1980), 302.

19. Morris, 302. See also Sherwood, 125; "rather a formidable," Teague, 138.

20. Susan Longworth to Katharine Wulsin, 9 December [1905], Wulsin Family Papers, Mss844, CHS.

21. "Wigeon" to Susan Longworth, n.d., JSP.

22. Clara Longworth de Chambrun, *The Making of Nicholas Longworth* (New York: Ray Long & Richard R. Smith, 1933), 154.

23. The number of reported or remembered invitations ranges from seven hundred to eleven hundred. "Social America," Scanlan, 31; "almost any well-mannered," Constance McLaughlin Green, *Washington* (Princeton, NJ: Princeton University Press, 1963), 191; Lottie Strickland, "Tramping to the Wedding," *NYT*, 7 February 1906, 1.

24. "White House Their Goal," *Washington Post*, 22 January 1906, reel 462, TRP; "Longworth Ill Abed," *NYT*, 10 February 1906, 1.

25. "Use their influence," Randolph, 204; "capacity of the White House" from "Longworth Ill Abed"; "Close Friends of Miss Alice Not Invited," *New York World Telegram*, 14 February 1906, reel 461, TRP.

26. "Miss Alice Buys a Gown," *New York Post*, 2 February 1906, reel 461, TRP; and Wilbur Cross and Ann Novotny, *White House Weddings* (New York: McKay, 1967), 154.

27. Sherwood, 119.

28. Trousseau, Eliza B. Duffey, *The Ladies' and Gentlemen's Etiquette* (Philadelphia: Porter & Coates, 1877), 193, 292–294; "Miss Roosevelt to Buy Trousseau Here," *New York Herald*, 24 December 1905, reel 471, TRP; "Kurzman's Is Bought by Arnold, Constable," *NYT*, 8 May 1932, 4; "dogged by reporters," *CH*, 109; "traffic," "Miss Roosevelt Goes

Back to Washington," *NYT,* 1 February 1906, 9.

29. "Miss Roosevelt Goes Back to Washington," *NYT,* 1 February 1906, 9.

30. NL to ARL, 26 October 1905, JSP; NL to ARL, n.d., ALRC.

31. "Miss Alice Roosevelt Will Leave Washington," *Washington Mirror,* 3 June 1905, JSP.

32. Llewellyn Thayer, "The White House Bridegroom," *Leslie's Illustrated Weekly,* 1 March 1906, 174; Ellen Maury Slayden, *Washington Wife* (New York: Harper & Row, 1962), 90.

33. "Anchorite," NL to ARL, 23 November 1905, JSP; "far from being bored," NL to ARL, 5 November 1905, JSP.

34. "Bowing and smiling," "Reception to Congress at White House," *NYT,* 2 February 1906, 1; "Miss Roosevelt's Quiet Day," *NYT,* 12 February 1906, 1; "Miss Alice Is 22 Today," *New York World,* 12 February 1906, ARL Scrapbook.

35. Alice remembered this party happening at the Alibi Club (*CH,* 112), and Nick's sister recalled the same party occurring at "his mother's house" (de Chambrun, 195). Nick had eight ushers: Ted Jr; his brothers-in-law Buckner Wallingford and the Viscount Charles de Chambrun; a cousin, Larz Anderson; Guy Norman; Quincy Adams Shaw Jr.; Francis R. Bangs; and Frederick Winthrop. Nick's best man was Harvard classmate Thomas Nelson Perkins. See Cross and Novotny, 155–156; and "The President a Guest at Longworth Dinner," *NYT,* 16 February 1906, 1.

36. Hoover, 34.

37. "Gems for Miss Alice," *Philadelphia Record,* 15 December 1905, ARL Scrapbook.

38. Scanlan, 31.

39. "Longworth Ill Abed," *NYT,* 10 February 1906, 1.

40. ARL to NL, n.d., RFPH.

41. ARL to NL, n.d., RFPH.

42. "My own beloved Nick," ARL to NL, 15 February 1905, RFPH; "My darling, darling, darling," ARL to NL, n.d., JSP.

43. NL to ARL, n.d., ARLC.

44. "All in Readiness for the White House Wedding," *Washington Post,* 17 February 1906, ARL Scrapbook; Nellie Grant married Algernon Charles Frederick Sartoris on 21 May 1874.

45. Teague, 55 and 57.

46. "Wedding Eve Party for Miss Roosevelt," *NYT,* 17 February 1906, 1.

47. Lady Bird Johnson, *A White House Diary* (New York: Holt, Rinehart and Winston, 1970), 65.

48. Corinne Roosevelt Robinson, *My Brother Theodore Roosevelt* (New York: Charles Scribner's Sons, 1921), 238–39; and Morris, 304.

49. Isabel Anderson, *Presidents and Pies* (Boston: Houghton Mifflin, 1920), 33–34. For a few of the primary sources on the wedding, see "Miss Roosevelt's Wedding Plans," *New York Herald,* 13 December 1905; "Miss Roosevelt Weds in February," *New York Herald,* 14 December 1905; "A White House Wedding," *Middletown* (New York) *Daily Times,* [n.d.] 1905; all reel 471, TRP. See also "All in Readiness for the White House Wedding," *Washington Post,* 17 February 1906, 1; "The White House Wedding," *New York World,* 17 February 1906, 1, JSP.

50. De Chambrun, 196; "Alice looked," Joseph Lash, *Eleanor and Franklin* (New York: W. W. Norton, 1971), 221; "rather nervous," Geoffrey C. Ward, *A First-Class Temperament* (New York: Harper & Row, 1989), 45n7.

51. Preceding Alice Roosevelt were Maria Monroe in 1820, Elizabeth Tyler in 1842, and Nellie Grant in 1874. The latter

two, like Alice, were married in the East Room.

52. Teague, 123.

53. Ona Griffin Jeffries, *In and Out of the White House* (New York: W. Funk, 1960), 281–82; *CH*, 113.

54. "Mother," Teague, 128; "nearly fainted," EKR Diary, 20 February 1906. Kristie Miller, a friend of Alice Longworth's, believes that the public denigration of elite children by parents "counterbalances the swell-headedness that can come with being a Roosevelt," and that it further helps not to tempt fate. "If you compliment, the gods will smite you." Miller emphasized that such parents absolutely love their children, despite the language that is culturally specific.

Joanna Sturm, Alice Longworth's granddaughter, however, believes that Edith Roosevelt really meant what she said, and that this was an example of Edith's meanness, probably exacerbated by her exhaustion. (Author interviews with Kristie Miller, 17 August 1989 and with Joanna Sturm, 11 April 2006.)

55. Unidentified newspaper clipping, n.d., ARL Scrapbook.

56. "A Princess of America," *Literary Digest*, XXXII, 11 (17 March 1906), 414.

Chapter 9: **"Alice Is Married at Last"**

1. Unidentified clipping, n.d., JSP.

2. All newspaper quotes from "Post-Nuptial," *Literary Digest*, 3 March 1906, 310.

3. Unidentified author to Susan Longworth, 28 February 1906, JSP.

4. 27 October 1880, TR Diary.

5. Anonymous letter to ARL, 19 February 1906, JSP.

6. Invitation from President Estrada Palma to the Longworths, 22 February 1906, JSP.

7. Straight's observations in the following four paragraphs are from Willard Straight to "Paddock," 31 March 1906, WSP.

8. Jennings Stockton Coxby to ARL, 13 March [1906], JSP.

9. *CH*, 115–16. The quotes are from page 115.

10. The information about the honeymoon comes from the author's interview with Joanna Sturm, 11 June 2006. Her memory is that the incident with Nick drunk on the floor was on board a ship.

11. "A Delight, Says Longworth," *NYT*, 4 March 1906, 1.

12. "Mrs. Longworth on Social Etiquette," *China Times*, 7 September 1906; clipping included in Mary Harriman to ARL, 27 January 1907, JSP.

13. "With the perversity," *CH*, 137; March 1906, EKR Diary; Kermit Roosevelt to Belle Hagner, 18 March 1906, PHP; "Sister is much improved," James Brough, *Princess Alice* (Boston: Little, Brown, 1975), 198.

14. For photographs of the home as Susan Longworth decorated it, see "Miss Roosevelt's Future Home at the Nation's Capital," *Leslie's Illustrated Weekly*, 15 February 1906, JSP.

15. Unknown author to Susan Longworth, 28 February 1906, JSP.

16. *CH*, 116.

17. "Maggie" to ARL, 8 April 1906, JSP.

18. Catherine Allgor, *Parlor Politics* (Charlottesville: University Press of Virginia, 2000), 121.

19. "Virtuously," *CH*, 116; "appalled," ER, *This Is My Story* (New York: Harper & Brothers, 1937), 206; "Mrs. Longworth on Social Etiquette," *China Times*, 7 September 1906, clipping included in Mary Harriman to ARL, 27 January 1907, JSP.

20. "Formidable experience," *CH*, 116;

"returned very late," Eleanor Adams, "Tea with Washington's Grande Dame," *Cincinnati Enquirer*, 2 January 197[?], ARLPF.

21. ARL to Marjorie [Ide], n.d. [1906], JSP.

22. *CH*, 134.

23. ARC to ARL, 28 May 1906, JSP.

24. TR to ARL, 24 June 1906, reel 342, TRP.

25. "Better politics," *CH*, 117; Whitelaw Reid to EKR, 17 August 1906, ALRC. All unattributed quotes on the honeymoon come from this lengthy letter.

26. "Curtsey," Elisabeth Mills Reid to ARC, 29 June 1906, JSP; "enjoyed herself," *CH*, 119; TR to ARL, 24 June 1906, reel 342, TRP.

27. "So like the parties," *CH*, 120; "very informal," Teague, 142; "didn't seem to worry," Teague 150; "felt very much at home," *CH*, 123.

28. "The Longworths at Blenheim," *NYT*, 3 July 1906, 4.

29. Elisabeth Mills Reid to ARC, 29 June 1906, JSP.

30. "Of no more consequence," *CH*, 123; "I don't care," EKR to Belle Hagner, [19 July 1906], PHP.

31. *CH*, 122.

32. "French Opinion of Mrs. Longworth," newspaper clipping, 7 July 1906, from Herman Hagedorn, interviews relating to Roosevelt Women, Harvard University.

33. Clara Longworth de Chambrun, *The Making of Nicholas Longworth* (New York: Ray Long & Richard R. Smith, 1933), 197.

34. *CH*, 127. See also "Longworths Go to Bayreuth," 17 July 1906, 2; "Longworth Auto Accident," 24 July 1906, 1; "The Longworths at Carlsbad," 25 July 1906, 1; all *NYT*.

35. *CH*, 128.

36. Willard Straight to ARL, 28 June 1906, JSP.

37. TR to FDR, 7 May 1906, reel 341, TRP; "Longworth for Governor," *NYT*, 11 July 1906, 1.

38. "Longworths in Silent Mood on Voyage Home," *New York World*, 12 August 1906, clipping in JSP; steerage passengers, "The Longworths Home," *NYT*, 12 August 1906, 1.

39. EKR to Belle Hagner, 12 August [1906], PHP. See "Longworths Leave Oyster Bay," *NYT*, 18 August 1906, 1; and "Longworth at Home Again," *NYT*, 19 August, 1. Both suggest that the Longworths together stayed at Oyster Bay for three days and then they traveled together to Cincinnati.

40. TR to ARL, 24 June 1906, reel 342, TRP.

Chapter 10: **"Mighty Pleased with My Daughter and Her Husband"**

1. "Full of all sorts." EKR to Belle Hagner, 15 August 1906, PHP; "hurt Nick," TR to ARL, 24 June 1906, reel 342, TRP; "injure him."

2. Ethel Roosevelt to Belle Hagner, [17 August 1906], PHP.

3. "Longworths at Home Again," *NYT*, 19 August 1906, 9; Ethel Roosevelt to Isabella Ferguson, n.d. 1907, Greenway AHS; *CH*, 154.

4. NL to ARL, 31 October 1905 and 9 November 1905, JSP.

5. Betsy Greiner, "The Day Alice Came to Town," *Timeline* 4, 1 (February–March 1987), 16–25; EKR to ARL, 18 September [1906], ARLHar; "Mrs. Longworth Is Cause of Panic," *Chicago Tribune*, 15 September 1906, 1; "Mrs. Longworth Mobbed," *NYT*, 15 September 1906, 1.

6. "Longworth Renominated," *NYT*, 16 September 1906, 1.

7. "She bowed and waved," "Ovation to Mrs. Longworth," *NYT*, 7 October 1906, 1; "occult formula," [Illegible; last

name maybe Fife?] to ARL, 17 August 1906, JSP; "M" to ARL, 30 October 1906, JSP; "Longworth's strength," "Unions Against Longworth," *NYT*, 26 September 1906, 1.

8. "The great issue," "Longworth off Blacklist," *NYT*, 21 October 1906, 1; "enjoyed campaigning." EKR to ARL, 24 October 1906, JSP; "Let me congratulate," TR to ARL, 7 November 1906, in Morison and Blum, eds., 5: 488; "Last night," EKR to ARL, 8 November 1906, JSP.

9. Alsop's prediction, ARC to ARL, 29 October 1906, JSP. Joseph W. Alsop was the father of columnists Stewart and Joseph Alsop; "how empty the house," ARC to ARL, 22 November 1906, JSP.

10. Willard Straight to ARL, 13 September 1906, JSP. An earlier letter (28 June 1906, JSP) alludes to a "Thieves Guild."

11. George Cabot Lee to NL, 15 March 1906, JSP.

12. "Uneasy till you start," George Cabot Lee to ARL, 8 October 1907; "show this to Nick," George Cabot Lee to ARL, 30 March 1906; stock sales, George Cabot Lee to ARL, 13 September 1906, all JSP.

13. See, for one example of a charity letter, Bela Horvatz to ARL, 12 January 1907, JSP; "Nick was not," *CH*, 134.

14. "Uproar in the House," *NYT*, 4 December 1906, 2; diplomatic reception, "In the Society World," *NYT*, 13 December 1906, 11; "saw more of the family," *CH*, 136–137.

15. *CH*, 137–38.

16. TR to Corinne Roosevelt Robinson, 26 December 1906, Theodore Roosevelt Papers, American Antiquarian Society, Boston, Mass.; "Roosevelt Family at German Embassy," *NYT*, 27 December 1906, 2.

17. "Longworth's Plan Fails," *NYT*, 23 January 1907, 6; "Roosevelt May Cost

Longworth His Seat," *NYT*, 5 February 1907, 4. "Longworths a Year Wedded," *NYT*, 18 February 1907, 1; "Roosevelt Names Foraker's Choice," *NYT*, 1 March 1907, 3.

18. TR to ARL, 10 November 1907, in Morison and Blum, eds., 5: 836–37. "Longworth Is for Taft," *Chicago Tribune*, 11 April 1907, 5; and "Longworth for Taft," *NYT*, 11 April 1907, 5.

19. "Steel Millionaire Ross Must Pay for Banquet," *Chicago Tribune*, 31 March 1907, A1; "Society Stake is Won by Ardette," *Chicago Tribune*, 7 April 1907, A1; NL to ARL, 20 May 1907, JSP.

20. Jean Howerton Coady, "Alice's Derby: 1907 Winner Lost to Mrs. Longworth," *Louisville Courier-Journal*, n.d., clipping in JSP.

21. "Just enough," *CH*, 141; "Wife's pique," "Mrs. Longworth in Accident," *Chicago Tribune*, 15 August 1907, 4; "Longworths to See Hawaii," *NYT*, 9 July 1907, 1.

22. "Lotus eater," *CH*, 142; "Most delicious time," ARL to Beatrice [Bond], 8 November 1907, JSP; Carter reception, No title, *NYT*, 5 August 1907, 4; "Mrs. Longworth, Woman Diplomat," *Chicago Tribune*, 7 September 1907, 4.

23. "Mulligrubs," *CH*, 146; "appendix plundered," ARL to Eleanora Sears, 31 December 1907, ARLC; "hand in hand," NL to Susan Longworth, 13 December 1907, JSP.

24. ARC to ARL, 15 November 1907, JSP. See also "Mrs. Longworth Under the Knife," 12 December 1907, 1; "Operate on Mrs. Longworth," 13 December 1907, 1; "Mrs. Longworth Is Better," 14 December 1907, 9; all *NYT*.

25. *CH*, 147–48.

26. The *NYT* asserted that Cannon had to put Nick there because TR leaned on him. See "Longworth Placed on Ways and Means," 17 December 1907, 3. The

article also suggested that Alice and Nick's "teas" helped to reconcile the Ohio delegation with Cannon's choice. NL to Susan Longworth, 1 November 1908, NLIII.

27. ARL to ER and FDR, 23 December 1907, ER Papers, FDRL.

28. George Cabot Lee to ARL, 19 February 1908, JSP. See also *CH*, 146.

29. "No one will ever know," *CH*, 148; "sick of hearing," Kristie Miller to the author, 6 September 1989.

30. Spontaneous applause, "Fighting Spirit Was Aroused," unidentified clipping, 1 September 1908, JSP. The man speaking was TR's rival, Senator Joseph B. Foraker. For Nick's defense, see for example, "Defends Roosevelt's Acts," *NYT*, 23 February 1908, 10; Ohio convention, "Ohio Republicans Instruct for Taft," *NYT*, 5 March 1908, 4.

31. "Women in Society Unite to Help Labor," *NYT*, n.d. For ARL's presence, see "Women's Department of the Civic Federation," *NCF Review*, September 1908, 7–8, both RHMcC Papers, LC; "White House meeting, "Women in a Secret Crusade for Labor," *NYT*, 6 May 1908, 7; Ruth's role, author's interview with Ruth "Bazy" McCormick Miller Tankersley, 31 May 2006.

32. *CH*, 149 and 151.

33. "'No Millinery,' Convention Rule," *Chicago Tribune*, 6 June 1912, 3; and "Patriots Feel Hunger's Pains," *Chicago Tribune*, 20 June 1912, 7.

34. *CH*, 151–52.

35. "Meddlings," by Howard Saxby Jr, otherwise unidentified newspaper clipping enclosed in A. E. Robinson to ARL, 12 May 1908, JSP. See also "Mrs. Longworth's Joke," *NYT*, 12 May 1908, 1. For family warning, see George Cabot Lee to ARL, 21 May 1908, JSP.

36. William A. White, *The Autobiography of William Allen White* (New York:

Macmillan, 1946), 401; "Mrs. Longworth Welcomes Crowd," *Chicago Tribune*, 20 June 1908.

37. "How the Democrats did it," *CH*, 152; "Mrs. Longworth in Denver," *Chicago Tribune*, 7 July 1908, 5; "yelling, sweating delegates," *CH*, 152; "Mrs. Longworth Lost Temper," *Chicago Tribune*, 10 July 1908, 9; see "Alice and Ruth Described," *Chicago Tribune*, 8 July 1908, 9, for a gentler treatment of both women.

38. "Princess Alice Bored at Reception," *Denver Post*, 8 July 1908, 3.

39. "Hats Are Nearly as Big as Cartwheels and Grow More Freakish in Style," *Chicago Tribune*, 5 July 1908, E-1. She also made the list of "loveliest-dressed" women: "Loveliest Gowns in the World Worn by Women of America," *Chicago Tribune*, 5 July 1908, E-1. On the Congressional Club, see "Congressmen's Wives Clubs," *NYT*, 15 March 1908, 9; "No Clubhouse Yet for 'Congressionals,'" *NYT*, 6 April 1908, 7; for joke, "Mrs. Longworth's Joke," *NYT*, 22 August 1908, 1.

40. "Manchu and I," NL to ARL, 18 August 1908, JSP; roses, "Entertain Mrs. Longworth," *NYT*, 20 August 1908, 7; fortnight at Sagamore, "Longworths at Oyster Bay," *NYT*, 25 August 1908, 7.

41. EKR to Cecil Spring-Rice, 13 July [1908], F.O. 800/241-242/9/1, National Archive, London.

42. Distaff duties, Ethel Roosevelt to ARL, 30 September [1908], JSP; "eulogy," "Views of Congressman Longworth," clipping with a Rock Island dateline, 2 October 1908, Hermann Hagedorn. Interviews relating to Roosevelt Women, Harvard University; election trail, "Sherman's Western Tour," *NYT*, 20 September 1908, 3; "Sunny Jim Comes to Aid Uncle Joe," *Chicago Tribune*, 28 September 1908, 3; "house is so big,"

"Drops Politics for Styles, *Chicago Tribune*, 29 September 1908, 6; fund-raiser, "Honor Mrs. Longworth," *NYT*, 7 October 1908, 1. The five-hundred-dollar tab caused trouble for the local Republicans later. See "Longworth Dinner Costly," *Chicago Tribune*, 27 November 1909, 2.

43. ARL to John Greenway, 27 November [1908], Greenway AHS; Edwin Morgan to ARL, 9 November 1909, JSP.

44. *CH*, 156.

45. Archibald Butt to his mother, 19 June 1908, in Lawrence F. Abbott, ed., *The Letters of Archie Butt* (Garden City, N.Y.: Doubleday, Page, 1924), 43.

46. *CH*, 159 (emphasis added).

Chapter 11: **"Expelled from the Garden of Eden"**

1. Archibald Butt to Clara Butt, 28 December 1908, in Lawrence F. Abbott, ed., *The Letters of Archie Butt* (Garden City, N.Y.: Doubleday, Page, 1924), 258.

2. "President Singed By Abbot's Irony," *Chicago Tribune*, 7 October 1908, 4; "Abbot Skeptic on Longworth Story," *Chicago Tribune*, 10 October 1908, 4.

3. Michael Teague, *Mrs. L* (Garden City, N.Y.: Doubleday, 1981), 140.

4. Memorable holiday, Archibald Butt to Clara Butt, 26 December 1908, in Abbott, ed., 254; "expelled," Teague, 140.

5. "Tottering ancient," *CH*, 161; the details of Ethel Roosevelt's debut can be found in the series of letters from Archibald Butt to Clara Butt (26 December, 28 December, and 29 December 1909) in Abbott, ed., 254–261; "Miss Roosevelt's Debut," *NYT*, 28 October 1908, 1.

6. Eleanor Roosevelt to Isabella Ferguson, 8 January 1909, Greenway AHS.

7. Archibald Butt to Clara Butt, 29 December 1908, in Abbott, ed., 261–62.

8. Annual message, *Current Literature*, XLVI, 1 (January 1909), 12–13; "crackling row," *CH*, 160.

9. For Butt quotes in next two paragraphs, see Archibald Butt to Clara Butt, 8 February 1909, in Abbott, ed., 277–78.

10. "Spanking," *CH*, 162; Susan Longworth to ARL, 31 December 1908, JSP.

11. "Mrs. Longworth at Cornerstone Laying," *NYT*, 13 February 1909, 6; "Mrs. Longworth, Bricklayer," *Chicago Tribune*, 12 February 1909, 2.

12. *CH*, 164–65; "Tafts as Guests in White House," *Chicago Tribune*, 4 March 1909, 3.

13. "Loathsome slush," *CH*, 165; inaugural, Sylvia Jukes Morris, *Edith Kermit Roosevelt* (New York: Coward, McCann & Geoghegan, 1980), 343–44.

14. Terrapin, EKR to Belle Hagner, 4 March 1909, PHP; "simplest American," Archibald Butt to Clara Butt, 1 February 1909, in Abbott, ed., 323; "future is in the past," TR to Paul Morton, 2 March 1909, in Morison and Blum, eds., 6: 1541; "gulped over," *CH*, 166; distinctive place, Archibald Butt to Clara Butt, 1 February 1909, in Abbott, ed., 322–23.

15. Mary E. Borah, *Elephants and Donkeys* (Moscow: The University Press of Idaho, 1976), 49; EKR to ARL, n.d. [1909], ARLHar.

16. ARL preservation tapes, ICD 16022, 28 June 1967, JSP.

17. "Roosevelt Sails in Roar of Cheers," *NYT*, 24 March 1909, 1.

18. Lewis L. Gould, *Grand Old Party* (New York: Random House, 2003), 157.

19. Clara Longworth de Chambrun, *The Making of Nicholas Longworth* (New York: Ray Long & Richard R. Smith, 1933), 200.

20. *CH*, 166.

21. Ishbell Ross, *The Tafts* (New York: World Publishing, 1964), 225; "Officer's

Wife Flies with Wilbur Wright," *NYT*, 28 October 1909, 4; "Wright Sets New American Record," *NYT*, 21 July 1909, 1–2; "lunch wagon," *CH*, 167–69.

22. EKR to Susan Longworth, 14 June 1909, JSP; for Alice's days, *CH*, 169–72; "'Salome' at Magnolia," *NYT*, 25 July 1909, 7.

23. For Nick's stomach trouble, see EKR to Belle Hagner, 22 June 1909, PHP; "bore you," Ross, 225; "Alice has found diversion," NL to Susan Longworth, 1 August [1909], ARLC.

24. ARL to Ethel Roosevelt, 24 June 1909, ERDP; EKR to ARL, [September 1909], ARLHar.

25. "Mrs. Longworth Is First," *NYT*, 17 October 1909, 1.

26. "Book Hits Alice Roosevelt" *Chicago Tribune*, 17 November 1909, 1. See Emma Kroebel, *Wie ich an den Koreanischen Kaiserhof kam* (Berlin: Verlag von R. Jacobsthal, 1909), 162–67.

27. "Longworth Denies His Wife Insulted Ruler of Corea," *Chicago Tribune*, 18 November 1909, 5; Alice's credo, ARL to Ethel Roosevelt, 13 December 1909, ERDP.

28. ALR to Willard Straight, 12 October 1905, WSP.

29. "Decorous existence," ARL to Ethel Roosevelt, 13 December 1909, ERDP; "an elderly man," TR to Arthur Lee, 6 October 1909, LLF; "not much" of a Christmas, *CH*, 173; EKR to Mark Sullivan, 14 December 1909, Mark Sullivan Papers, LC, states that Edith will sail in mid-March. EKR to Belle Hagner, 13 December 1909, PHP, states that she will sail mid-February to meet TR in Khartoum on 15 March, as does EKR to Cecil Spring-Rice, 17 December 1909, F.O. 800/241-242/9/1, National Archive, London; for "I can scarcely wait," see EKR to Cecil Spring-Rice, 17 December 1909, F.O. 800/241-242/9/1, National Archive, London.

30. Newspaper clipping, Cannon Scrapbook, Joseph Cannon Papers, Abraham Lincoln Presidential Library, Springfield, Illinois; Nick joined the insurgents, Joseph Cannon to Edward Denby, 5 October 1910, Box 8, Cannon Papers; "jeers and cat-calls," *CH*, 174; Nick not selected, "Longworth Not Snubbed," *NYT*, 27 March 1910, 16.

31. Nelle Scanlan, *Boudoir Mirrors of Washington* (Philadelphia: John C. Winston, 1923), 22.

32. Ross, 236–37.

33. Ross, 246.

34. "Mrs. Nicholas Longworth Sails," *NYT*, 12 May 1910, 16; Tim Sullivan, *CH*, 176.

35. *CH*, 178.

36. Poem from *Life*, in Nathan Miller, *Theodore Roosevelt* (New York: William Morrow, 1992), 511.

37. TR to Gifford Pinchot, 28 June 1910, in Morison and Blum, eds., 7:95.

38. "Roosevelt, Jr., to Wed Miss Alexander," *NYT*, 11 February 1910, 1; Ted and Eleanor (whom the family called "our Eleanor" or "Mrs. Ted") were wed on 20 June 1910. Roller-skating, "Society at the Nation's Capitol," *Chicago Tribune*, 5 May 1910, 8.

39. "Bequest to Mrs. Longworth," *NYT*, 29 March 1910, 1, suggested Alice would inherit $10,000; "Alice Longworth an Heiress," *Chicago Tribune*, 28 May 1910, 12. The latter article states that she was to inherit one twelfth of $975,500. Finally, the reports settled on $5,300: "Mrs. Longworth's Legacy," *NYT*, 27 July 1910, 1. For governor idea, see "A New Longworth Boom," *NYT*, 9 May 1910, 18.

40. "Lawyers' Administration," from TR to Henry Cabot Lodge, 11 April 1910, in Morison and Blum, eds., 7:74; "of course you must" from TR to NL, 11 July 1910, in Morison and Blum, eds., 7:101; for Taft's idea, see "Taft Said to Favor Long-

worth in Ohio," *NYT*, 26 June 1910, 4; Ohio convention, "Ohio Convention Faces Hot Fight," *Chicago Tribune*, 26 July 1910, 5; Nick's relief, *CH*, 180.

41. WHT to HHT, 24 September 1910, WHTP.

42. New Nationalism, George E. Mowry, *Theodore Roosevelt and the Progressive Movement* (Madison: University of Wisconsin Press, 1946), 144; TR to Henry Cabot Lodge, 17 August 1910, in Morison and Blum, eds., 7: 117; 1910 election, Hoyt Landon Warner, *Progessivism in Ohio* (Columbus: Ohio State University Press, 1964), 262.

43. *CH*, 181.

44. "Longworths Off to Panama," *NYT*, 22 September 1911, 7; "Taft Begins Trip on 54th Birthday," *NYT*, 16 September 1911, 12.

45. *CH*, 183.

46. *CH*, 184. See also "A Roosevelt Pilot on Ohio," *NYT*, 9 October 1911, 1.

Chapter 12: "Quite Marked Schizophrenia"

1. Women's suffrage, *CH*, 282 and 339; Elaine L. Silverman, "Theodore Roosevelt and Women" unpub. Ph.D. diss., UCLA, 1973, 73; judicial recall, "Roosevelt Answers Cry of Revolution," *NYT*, 27 February 1912, 1; "hard on Nick," *CH*, 186.

2. TR quoted in James Brough, *Princess Alice* (Boston: Little, Brown, 1975), 215.

3. "Ohio Leader Wants Roosevelt in 1912," *NYT*, 3 December 1911, 16; for Nick's statement, John Callan O'Laughlin, "Politics Leading Issue in Capitol," *Chicago Tribune*, 5 December 1911, 5; for Nick's authority, see "Longworth Cheers Taft," *NYT*, 27 January 1912, 2.

4. 13 February 1912, ARLD.

5. TR to NL, 7 February 1912, in Morison and Blum, eds., 7:497; "soak it," 15 February 1912, ARLD.

6. 16 February 1912, ARLD.

7. "Gloomy talk," 17 February 1912, ARLD; "talked the whole thing over," 19 February 1912, ARLD; "my past," Lewis L. Gould, "The Price of Fame," *Lamar Journal of the Humanities*, X, 2 (Fall 1984), 14; "was a fool and wept," 21 February 1912, ARLD; Taft's sentiment from WHT to HHT, 20 July 1912, WHTP.

8. 22 February 1912, ARLD.

9. Longworth's meeting with TR was on 26 February. Nick's gloominess and "pain" from 27 and 28 February 1912, ARLD.

10. "Clara said," 8 March 1912, ARLD. When Clara de Chambrun wrote her biography of her brother, Alice received barely a mention—not even a photograph. See *The Making of Nicholas Longworth* (New York: Ray Long & Richard R. Smith, 1933), 203; 31 May 1912, ARLD.

11. Both sides, Augustus P. Gardner to ARL, 1 March 1912, JSP; "apoplectic with rage," in Brough, 216; "wearing to live," ARC to ARL, 11 July 1912, JSP; "rant and rave," 15 March 1912, ARLD.

12. *CH*, 192.

13. "Sock it," 17 March 1912, ARLD; "daily dish," ARL, "Some Reminiscences," *Ladies' Home Journal*, November 1932, 3; "Nick pleased me," 10 April 1912, ARLD.

14. 1 May 1912, ARLD.

15. "Feeling...bitter," 15 May 1912, ARLD; "to get in the papers," *CH*, 194; "Victory Surely His, Roosevelt Boasts," *NYT*, 16 May 1912, 1.

16. "Father and I walked," 8 June 1912, ARLD; "followed his instincts," 4 June 1912, ARLD.

17. TR to Arthur Lee, 14 August 1912, LLF.

18. 17 June 1912, ARLD.

19. "Hoards of creatures," 18 and 19

June 1912, ARLD; Nick really a progressive, 13 August 1912, ARLD.

20. "Longworth for Governor," *NYT*, 29 May 1912, 4; "strong-arm tactics," *CH*, 202–203.

21. Lewis L. Gould, *Grand Old Party* (New York: Random House, 2003), 189. For Nick and Alice, see "The Day's Sessions" and "Harding Nominates Taft," both *NYT*, 23 June 1912, 2.

22. "Such spirit," 22 June 1912, ARLD; "Roosevelt Delegates Go from the Regular to Rump Convention," *NYT*, 23 June 1912, 1; "Longworth in Trouble," *NYT*, 24 June 1912, 6; divorce, Michael Teague, *Mrs. L* (Garden City, N.Y.: Doubleday, 1981), 158, and author's interview with Michael Teague, 3 August 1989.

23. Arguing with Borah, *CH*, 204; "Borah Refuses to Join the Third Party," *La Follette's Weekly Magazine*, 28 September 1912, 8, 14, 15. For a sense of Borah's role in TR's inner circle at Chicago, see Nicholas Roosevelt's "Account of the Republican National Convention at Chicago, June 1912," compiled from notes taken on the spot, 93M-11, Harvard University.

24. "Delegates Storm Baltimore," *Chicago Tribune*, 24 June 1912, 5; the cousins together, ER to Isabella Greenway, 8 July [1912] and ER to Isabella Greenway, 9 July [1912], both Greenway AHS; Nick "gloomy," 25 and 26 June 1912, ARLD.

25. "To Smoke Out Longworth," *NYT*, 25 June 1912, 6; 8 July 1912, ARLD.

26. "I could scream," 28 August 1912, ARLD; "ignoble thoughts," *CH*, 212; TR to Robert Ferguson, n.d., Greenway AHS.

27. "Hail New Party in Fervent Song," *NYT*, 6 August 1912, 1; 6 August 1912; 7 August 1912, ARLD.

28. EKR to Belle Hagner, 9 August [1912], PHP; ARL to ARC, 10 August 1912, RFPH.

29. "The platform," 8 August 1912,

ARLD; "my sister-in-law," *CH*, 214–215; "help campaign," ARC to ARL, 11 July 1912, JSP. See also 27 March 1912, ARLD: "Only wish I could do anything to help along the work"; "stiff upper lip," EKR to Belle Hagner, 10 March [1912], PHP.

30. "Both sides," 19 August 1912, ARLD; "heart and soul," 20 August 1912, ARLD.

31. 14–25 August 1912, ARLD. For Grace Vanderbilt's contribution, see 1 November 1912.

32. 26 August 1912, ARLD. For Nick's drinking, see 1 September 1912. Alice recorded that he "behaved disgustingly."

33. "Get names," 8 September 1912, ARLD; "Longworth Still for Taft," *NYT*, 19 September 1912, 11; "Humors of the Campaign," *NYT*, 20 September 1912, 10.

34. 10 October 1912, ARLD. For Alice's reading, see 14, 15, and 16 September 1912.

35. "I cannot vote for you," de Chambrun, 204; Nick "seems to want me," 2 October 1912, ARLD. The titles of what she's reading are sprinkled throughout the Cincinnati days in her diary.

36. "Wild enthusiasm," 12 October 1912, ARLD; Bull Moose store, "Mrs. Longworth at Store," *Chicago Tribune*, 14 October 1912, 2; "asked again," 12 October 1912, ARLD; "torture," 4 October 1912, ARLD; campaign donations, 10 October 1912, ARLD.

37. 16 October 1912, ARLD.

38. Kristie Miller, *Ruth Hanna McCormick* (Albuquerque: University of New Mexico Press, 1992), 53; "good angel," 14 October 1912; "cracking," 19 October 1912; both ARLD.

39. "Middle western," 23 October 1912, ARLD; "I am not for," 26 October 1912, ARLD; see also "With Torches Honor Taft," *NYT*, 27 October 1912, 4.

40. "First draft," Teague, 112; "no illusions," *CH*, 221.

41. 3 November 1912, ARLD.

42. 4 November 1912, ARLD.

43. 5 November 1912, ARLD.

44. "'Nick' Longworth Beaten in Ohio?" *Chicago Tribune*, 8 November 1912, 5; "Longworth Is Beaten," *NYT*, 8 November 1912, 1; Jean Vanden Heuvel, "The Sharpest Wit in Washington," *Saturday Evening Post*, 238, 24 (4 December 1965), 32; "terribly hard," 7 November 1912, ARLD.

45. "A real progressive," 7 November 1912; "dull little people," 9 November 1912; "dined at the Crosstown," 13 November 1912. For Alice's self-absorption, see 10 November 1912, all ARLD.

46. "At sea," 5 December 1912, ARLD; "a question of divorcing," 17 December 1912, ARLD.

Chapter 13: **"Beating Against Bars"**

1. To will herself, ARL to NL, 31 March [1913], JSP; "unreservedly cheerful," *CH*, 223.

2. This story appears in many places. See, for example, Howard Teichmann, *Alice* (Englewood Cliffs, N.J.: Prentice Hall, 1979), 96.

3. ARL to Ethel Roosevelt, 30 January 1913, RFPH.

4. Turkey trot, ARL to Ethel Roosevelt, 30 January 1913, RFPH; "odd beings called Democrats," *CH*, 225; Belle's job, EKR to Belle Hagner, 5 March 1913, PHP.

5. TR to FDR, 18 March 1913, TRP.

6. ER to Isabella Ferguson, 12 December [1915], Greenway AHS; evenings at the FDR's, Michael Teague, *Mrs. L* (Garden City, N.Y.: Doubleday, 1981), 156–157.

7. Elliott Roosevelt and James Brough, *An Untold Story* (New York: G. P. Put-nam's Sons, 1973), 69; "a slave," and blend in, from ER, *This Is My Story* (New York: Harper & Brothers, 1937), 206.

8. "Perfunctory...tea," *CH*, 226; NL to ARL, 24 March 1913; ARL to NL, [25 March 1913], both JSP.

9. "An excellent thing," *CH*, 223; "sat on the porch," ARL Diary, 10 September 1917, JSP.

10. Richard Derby, TR to William Crawford Gorgas, 11 September 1917, in Morison and Blum, eds., 8:1238; "Ohio is a vast lake," NL to ARL, 27 March 1913, JSP.

11. NL to ARL, 31 March 1913; ARL to NL, 31 March [1913], both JSP.

12. ARL to NL, 4 April 1913, and NL to ARL, 5 April 1913, JSP.

13. Kermit Roosevelt to Ethel Roosevelt Derby, 2 June 1913, RFPH. EKR to Belle Hagner, 24 March 1914, PHP.

14. "The Puppuk," NL to ARL, n.d. [1913]; "dinner and a musical party," NL to ARL, 22 September 1913, both JSP.

15. ARL to NL; undated, JSP; EKR to Belle Hagner, 14 September 1913, PHP.

16. Joseph R. Ornig, *My Last Chance to Be a Boy* (Baton Rouge: Louisiana University Press, 1994), 37; Kermit Roosevelt to Ethel Roosevelt Derby, November 1913, ERDP.

17. ARL to NL, 27 December 1913, JSP.

18. Author's interview with Angela Meeske, 19 April 2004. Meeske was born in 1923, and her mother would have been nearer to a contemporary of Nick Longworth's.

19. ARL to NL, fragment, 8 January 1914, JSP; TR quote, Ornig, 39.

20. "Very depressing," EKR to Belle Hagner, 17 January 1914, PHP; recuperate, ARL to ARC, 31 January 1914, Anna Roosevelt Cowles Papers, Harvard

University; "a green shadow," ARL to NL, 16 January 1914, JSP; "my brief moment," ARL to ARC, 31 January 1914, RFPH. "More prosperous," ARL to NL, 16 January 1914, JSP.

21. "Shrine," *CH*, 230; "delightful evenings," ARL Diary, 24 April [1914], JSP.

22. Joseph S. Graydon's grandson, Graydon DeCamp, attests that "considerable family lore and speculation surrounds Joe Graydon's 'friendship' with Alice Longworth. We grandchildren have long suspected that they were something more than just friends. Or at least that they wished that were so. The only time I ever met Alice, at her house on Massachusetts Avenue in 1969, she welcomed me with a warmth that quite took me aback. I felt instantly like family, and was right at home in that big old house hidden behind a two-story tangle of massive honeysuckles. I am not only Joe Graydon's only grandson, I also resemble him [physically]." DeCamp, e-mail to author, 29 March 2004.

23. Graydon DeCamp to author, 2 April 2004; JSG to ARL, 23 November 1915, JSP, and Lewis Alexander Leonard, ed., *Greater Cincinnati and Its People* (Chicago: Lewis Historical Publishing, 1927), 4: 425–26; "Rites Wednesday for J. S. Graydon," *Cincinnati Post and Times-Star*, 25 February 1963; and "Graydon Will Is Filed," *Cincinnati Enquirer*, 14 March 1962, clippings in Joseph S. Graydon Princeton File, CHS; W. T. Semple to Mr. Greve, 22 April 1924, Classical Round Table, MssVF2434, CHS.

24. "Seraphina," JSG to ARL, 9 December 1915, JSP; Robert Louis Stevenson, *Prince Otto: A Romance* (New York: Charles Scribner's Sons, 1925 [1905]), 80–81.

25. Stevenson, 224.

26. Graydon DeCamp to author, 2 April 2004; JSG to ARL, 4 January 1917, JSP. See also ARL to ARC, 17 January 1917,

Anna Roosevelt Cowles Papers, Harvard University, for Alice's handwritten postscript, thanking her aunt for "being so kind to Marjorie Graydon."

27. JSG to ARL, 6 March 1916, JSP. ARL told Graydon's great-grandson, Stephen Benn, that she and Graydon went to New York together. Author telephone interview with Stephen Benn, 2 August 2004.

28. JSG to ARL, 29 July 1916, JSP.

29. JSG to ARL, 16 March 1916, JSP.

30. "Time and space," JSG to ARL, 6 March 1916; "departed quantities," JSG to ARL, 16 March 1916; "catholicity of interest," JSG to ARL, 25 April 1916, all JSP.

31. JSG to ARL, 14 June 1918; ARL Diary, 29 October 1917, both JSP.

32. "That adjective," JSG to ARL, 15 April 1916; "souvenier," JSG to ARL, 7 July 1916; "a broken reed," JSG to ARL, 25 March [1916], JSP (emphasis in original). The "shadowland" quote is from his letter to her of 7 July 1916.

33. JSG to ARL, 19 January [1918], JSP.

34. JSG to ARL, 15 April 1916, JSP.

35. JSG to ARL, 7 June 1918, JSP.

36. "Intelligence Branch," JSG to ARL, 23 August 1918, JSP; "honor, fulfillment," Edward J. Renehan, *The Lion's Pride* (New York: Oxford University Press, 1998), 4; "banishing increments," JSG to ARL, 29 July 1916, JSP.

37. JSG to ARL, 21 October 1943 and 23 October 1946; both JSP. JSG's birthday was 19 October.

38. Kermit Roosevelt to Richard Derby, 31 August 1913, RFPH. Robert E. Osgood, *Ideals and Self-Interest in America's Foreign Policy* (Chicago: University of Chicago Press, 1953), 250.

39. Goethels, *CH*, 226; "War is practically a fact," ARL Diary, 21 April 1914, JSP.

40. "12 Americans," ARL Diary, 23 April 1914; "laughing stock," ARL Diary, 25 April 1914, both JSP.

41. Kristie Miller, *Ruth Hanna McCormick* (Albuquerque: University of New Mexico Press, 1992), 103.

42. Nan Wallingford to Katherine Wulsin, 1 August 1914, Katherine Elizabeth (Roelker) Wulsin Correspondence, CHS.

43. EKR to Belle Hagner, 10 September 1914, PHP; military training centers, TRJR to John McCutcheon, 2 August 1915, Papers of John McCutcheon, Newberry Library, Chicago.

44. EKR to Belle Hagner, 20 November 1914; Kermit Roosevelt to Belle Hagner, 3 December 1914, both PHP.

Chapter 14: "To Hate the Democrats So Wholeheartedly"

1. Edward J. Renehan Jr., *The Lion's Pride* (New York: Oxford University Press, 1998), 5.

2. "To look always," ARL Diary, 1 November 1915; "great personage," ARL Diary, 3 October 1915, both JSP.

3. Elting E. Morison and John Morton Blum, eds. *The Letters of Theodore Roosevelt* (Cambridge, Mass.: Harvard University Press), 7:394, 397. See also Lawrence F. Abbott, ed., *Taft and Roosevelt* (Garden City, N.Y.: Doubleday, Doran, 1930), 1: 421–23.

4. Kathleen Dalton, *Theodore Roosevelt* (New York: Alfred A. Knopf, 2002), 443–45; TR's attachment to his letter to Lyman Abbot, 3 April 1910, in Morison and Blum, 7:358–399. The quote is found on page 396.

5. ARL Diary, 29 July 1917, JSP.

6. TR to ARC, 23 July 1916, in ARC, *Letters from Theodore Roosevelt to Anna Roosevelt Cowles, 1870–1918* (New York: Charles Scribner's Sons, 1924); ARL Diary, 9 October 1917, JSP; EKR to Mrs.

James Garfield, n.d., James R. Garfield Papers, LC.

7. "Pariah woman," EKR to Mrs. Garfield, 2 July [1916?], James R. Garfield Papers, LC; Needlework Guild, see EKR to Edith Wilson, 4 March 1918, Harold Ickes Papers, LC; EKR to Daniel Beard, n.d., Daniel C. Beard Papers, LC.

8. Richard Derby to Belle and Kermit Roosevelt, 22 February 1916, KBR; Emily Carow to Belle Roosevelt, 7 January 1918, KBR; ER, *The Autobiography of Eleanor Roosevelt* (New York: Harper & Row, 1978), 89.

9. Charles Selden, "The Father Complex of Alice Roosevelt Longworth and Ruth Hanna McCormick," *Ladies' Home Journal*, March 1927, 74; for Alice's quote, see Howard Teichmann, *Alice* (Englewood Cliffs, N.J.: Prentice-Hall, 1979), 100. See also "Her Pantalette Gown," *NYT*, 25 September 1915, 11.

10. Speech of Hon. NL, "True Preparedness," n.d., NLP; "Tie Vote on Buying Big Wright Plant, *NYT,*, 13 November 1919, 2; Douglas Robinson to NL, n.d., JSP.

11. "Comprehensive reserve," TRJR to John McCutcheon, 2 August 1915, McCutcheon Papers, Newberry Library, Chicago; ARC to Belle Roosevelt, 10 July 1917, KBR; "A real help to me," quoted in Dalton, 463; "dauntless spirit," TR to Edith Franklin Wyatt, 5 December 1917, Edith Franklin Wyatt Papers, Newberry Library, Chicago.

12. *CH*, 258. For the Girl Scout publicity photographs and more "war work" by Alice, see also James Brough, *Princess Alice* (Boston: Little, Brown, 1975), 246; "All the political news," Joseph J. Kerrigan to ARL, 1 October 1919, JSP.

13. *CH*, 258; ARL Diary 16 July 1917; 29 July 1917; ARL Diary, 31 October 1917, JSP. See also Gladys Brooks, *Boston and Return* (New York: Athenaeum, 1962), 193.

14. "Conversation would begin," Mary Borah, *Elephants and Donkeys* (Moscow: University Press of Idaho, 1976), 67; see ARL Diary for 1917; Wilson "an ass," 3 August 1917, JSP; "President...resign," ER to Isabella Ferguson, 24 February [1916], Greenway AHS; "a stagnant lot," ARL to ARC, 17 January 1917, RFPH.

15. Isabella Ferguson to ER, [late spring 1916], ER Papers, FDRL.

16. ER to Isabella Ferguson, 21 June [1916], Greenway AHS.

17. Patricia O'Toole, *When Trumpets Call* (New York: Simon & Schuster, 2005), 291; EKR to Mrs. Garfield, 2 July [1916], James R. Garfield Papers, LC.

18. "No feeling of...chagrin," ARL to Fred [?], 22 June 1916, JSP. When TR withdrew his name it was "committing infanticide" according to John Milton Cooper in "If TR Had Gone Down with the *Titanic*," in *Theodore Roosevelt: Many-Sided American*, Natalie A. Naylor, Douglas Brinkley, and John Allen Gable, eds. (Interlaken, N.Y.: Heart of the Lakes Publishing, 1992), 507.

19. ARL to Fred [?], 22 June 1916, JSP; "vile and hypocritical," Lewis L. Gould, *Grand Old Party* (New York: Random House, 2003), 209.

20. *CH*, 241–42.

21. "Grief and tragedy," ARL Diary, 1 July 1917; "quarter-horse limitations," ARL Diary, 15 July 1917 and 23 September 1917, JSP. The *Washington Post* editor was Ned McLean.

22. "Agnostic fashion," ARL Diary, 13 September 1917, JSP; Balfour as friend, *CH*, 249–50.

23. ARL Diary, 1 October 1917, JSP.

24. ARL Diary, 23 September 1917, JSP.

25. Ethel Roosevelt Derby to Belle Roosevelt, 29 November 1917, KBR; TR to TRJR, 29 November 1917, in Morison and Blum, 8:1257; ARL Diary, 11 December 1917, JSP; and *CH*, 264.

26. "Father will play the big part," ARL Diary, 16 November 1917; "almost friendly," ARL Diary, 19 October 1917; "as soon as she knows," ARL Diary, 7 December 1917, all JSP.

27. ARL Diary, 5 November, 1917, JSP.

28. ARL Diary, 7 and 8 November 1917, JSP.

29. ARL Diary, 18 November 1917, JSP.

30. Hamilton Cravens, *The Triumph of Evolution* (Baltimore: Johns Hopkins Press, 1988), 19.

31. ARL Diary, 28 November 1917, JSP.

32. *CH*, 246.

33. Ted and Archie, Renehan, 132; Kermit, Cecil Spring-Rice to TR, 19 April 1917, F.O. 800/241-242/9/1, National Archive, London; ARL Diary, 11 August 1917, JSP; "flag with four stars," TR to Archibald Roosevelt, 8 September 1917, in Morison and Blum, 8:1237.

34. ARL Diary, 1 November 1917, JSP.

35. "Desperately bad," ARL Diary, 12 December 1917; Christmas, ARL Diary, 24 December 1917, both JSP.

36. Pompous friend, ARL Diary, 5 January 1918, JSP; McLeans' party, *CH*, 266.

37. ARL Diary, 8 January 1918, JSP, and *CH*, 267–68.

38. John Milton Cooper, *Breaking the Heart of the World* (Cambridge: Cambridge University Press, 2001), 19.

39. Gould, 216.

40. "It hurts," ARL Diary, 7 January 1918, JSP; "War Cabinet," Renehan, 171; gatherings at Longworths' home, *CH*, 268.

41. Housing committee, ARL Diary, 21 December 1917, JSP; to serve with her, or perhaps to ask Eleanor to take her place on the committee—the document isn't clear, ARL Diary, 22 December 1917, JSP; ER to Isabella Ferguson, 2 April 1918, Greenway AHS.

42. George Egerton, "Diplomacy, Scandal and Military Intelligence: The Craufurd-Stuart Affair and Anglo-American Relations, 1918–1920," *Intelligence and National Security* 2, 4 (October 1987): 110–134; meeting Churchill, ARL Diary, 1 July 1917, JSP; "serve your country," Michael Teague, *Mrs. L* (Garden City, N.Y.: Doubleday, 1981), 162.

43. "Upper balcony," Teague, 162; "no evidence," Egerton, 113; "Ladenburg suffered, Egerton," 127; "sheer rapture," Teague, 162. For ER's disapproval, see Teague, 163.

44. "In line of duty," "Record of Transfers and Changes, Quentin Roosevelt," JSP; "instantly killed," ER to Isabella Munro-Ferguson, 28 June 1918, Greenway AHS; TR to Frank McCoy, 12 September 1918, copy in JSP; JSG to ARL, 31 August 1918, JSP.

45. NL to Susan Longworth, 22 August 1918, NLIII.

46. *CH*, 275.

47. Barbara W. Tuchman, "Woodrow Wilson on Freud's Couch," in *Practicing History* (New York: Knopf, 1981), 147.

48. *CH*, 277.

49. Renehan, 217–22.

50. Robert James Maddox, *William E. Borah and American Foreign Policy* (Baton Rouge: Louisiana State University Press, 1969), xiii, xiv. The contemporary's account is Clinton W. Gilbert, *"You Takes Your Choice"* (New York: G. P. Putnam's Sons, 1924), 192.

51. Teague, 179, 187.

52. *CH*, 204.

53. Beverly Smith, "The Lone Rider from Idaho," *American Magazine*, March 1932, 96. Smith is probably quoting from Oscar King Davis, "Borah Insists on Conspiracy," *NYT*, 27 July 1907, 3.

54. "I feel that I cannot succeed," Marian C. McKenna, *Borah* (Ann Arbor: University of Michigan Press, 1961), 73; *The*

Autobiography of William Allen White (New York: Macmillan, 1946), 374–75.

55. Dave Grover, "Diamondfield Jack," *Idaho Yesterdays* 7, 2 (1963): 8–14. See also McKenna, 24–27.

56. Quoted in McKenna, 30.

57. See Claudius O. Johnson, "Very Personal Notes on Senator William E. Borah," April 1939, cage 214, Claudius Osborne Johnson Papers; Washington State University Libraries.

58. Doug Baker, "Oregon Writer Visits with Mrs. W. E. Borah," [1966], clipping, WEBID; horse racing, McKenna, 9.

59. Gilbert Clinton, *The Mirrors of Washington* (New York: G. P. Putnam's Sons, 1921), 251.

60. James M. Cox, *Journey Through My Years* (New York: Simon & Schuster, 1946), 100; transcript of Westerman Whillock interview by Jeffery G. Seward, Boise: Idaho State Historical Society, 8 January 1974, 21.

61. Smith, 40. For the list of politicians quoted, see Henry F. Pringle, "The Real Senator Borah," *The World's Work* 57 (December 1928): 135; Cox, 100.

62. John Milton Cooper, "William E. Borah, Political Thespian," *Pacific Northwest Quarterly*, October 1965, 146–48.

63. Claudius O. Johnson, "Comment," *Pacific Northwest Quarterly*, October 1965, 145.

64. "I enjoyed listening," *CH*, 300; Daisy Harriman, *From Pinafores to Politics* (New York: Henry Holt, 1923), 359, 358.

65. "One great desire," Clinton, 255; "to claim his wonderful daughter," WEB to ARL, 24 September 1924, JSP (emphasis in original).

66. Alice and Seventeenth Amendment, *CH*, 338–339; Charles Merz, "The Idaho Minority of One," *New Republic* 43 (3 June 1925): 39, 40; "Borah as Presidential Timber," *Literary Digest*, 7 April 1923, 11.

67. *CH*, 319; "world peace," Pringle, "The Real Senator Borah," 134.

68. "Current Magazines," *NYT*, 8 March 1925, 25.

69. "Apollo," "Borah as Presidential Timber," *Literary Digest*, 7 April 1923, 11; Pringle, "The Real Senator Borah," 138–140. "Variety of matters" on page 144.

70. George Washington's Farewell Address, 17 September 1796, in Henry Steele Commanger, ed., *Documents of American History*, 4th ed. (New York: Appleton-Century-Croft, 1948), 174; Borah quotes from Maddox, 51 and 55.

71. *CH*, 277. The other Irreconcilables were Medill McCormick (who entered the Senate in May 1919), Robert M. La Follette of Wisconsin, California's Hiram Johnson, Frank Brandegee of Connecticut, Philander Chase Knox from Pennsylvania, George Moses of New Hampshire, former Progressive Miles Poindexter of Washington, and James A. Reed, Democrat from Missouri.

72. Ralph Stone, "Two Illinois Senators Among the Irreconcilables," *Mississippi Valley Historical Review* 50, 3 (December 1963): 451 and 454; "rag bag" *CH*, 281.

73. *CH*, 282.

74. *CH*, 285.

75. *CH*, 286, 287; Cooper, *Breaking the Heart of the World*, 167, 168.

76. *CH*, 288.

77. Transcript of Cora Rubin Lane interview by Jackie Day-Ames, Boise: Idaho State Historical Society, 25 May 1976, 19; "immediate members," *CH*, 296; 19 November, Maddox, 67; Alice & Ruth's presence, "Humor, Satire, Wit, and Spoofing Help to Kill the Treaty," *Chicago Tribune*, 20 November 1919, 2.

78. Cooper, *Breaking the Heart of the World*, 265. All the words in quotes are Borah's, except for "lose its soul"—that phrase is Cooper's.

79. Hiram Johnson to Hiram Jr. and Arch Johnson, 21 November 1919, in Burke, ed., *The Diary Letters of Hiram Johnson*, vol. 3; next to her was Borah, *CH*, 292.

80. *CH*, 295; Mr. Wobbly, Brough, 262.

81. Maddox, 67.

82. *CH*, 309.

83. Maddox, 68.

Chapter 15: "Hello, Hello, Hello"

1. "Longworths Await Stork," *NYT*, 20 November 1924, 19.

2. GOP convention, Kristie Miller, *Ruth Hanna McCormick* (Albuquerque: University of New Mexico Press, 1992), 124–25; "always believed," *CH*, 339.

3. Leola Allard, "Women Want Friend as Head of Convention," *Chicago Tribune*, 8 June 1920, 4; "the career...born to," Miller, 123. For Ruth McCormick as chair of the committee, Miller, 125; RWNC objective, "Seek Successor to Miss Hay," *NYT*, 8 June 1920, 4; cause was aided, Miller, 125–26.

4. Harold L. Ickes, *The Autobiography of a Curmudgeon* (New York: Reynal & Hitchcock, 1943), 226.

5. *CH*, 311; "Republicans Confer on Chicago Planks," *NYT*, 19 May 1920, 2.

6. "Chicago Sidelights on Day of Oratory," *NYT*, 12 June 1920, 3; "*Times* in Chicago on Day of Issue," *NYT*, 10 June 1920, 1; "New York Crowds Cool Toward the Ticket," *NYT*, 13 June 1920, 6.

7. "Decaying Roman emperor," "The Reporters: Jonathan Aitken interview with Alice Roosevelt Longworth," Yorkshire Television [January 1969]. "First raters," William E. Leuchtenburg, *The Perils of Prosperity* (Chicago: University of Chicago Press, 1958), 86; Harding as compromise, Lewis L. Gould, *Grand Old Party* (New York: Random House, 2003),

222; "precise little object," ARL preservation tape, ICD 16025, 20 September 1967, JSP.

8. "Callers Flood Harding," *NYT*, 15 June 1920, 1.

9. "Harding Accepts League as Issue," *NYT*, 14 July 1920, 1; "Longworth to Stump in Maine Campaign," *NYT*, 6 August 1920, 3; "calling on the Senator," Philip Kinsley, "G.O.P. Majority in Congress to Grow, Fess Says," *Chicago Tribune*, 15 August 1920, 5; "reckless methods," "Harding to Speak at Minnesota Fair," *NYT*, 15 August 1920, 3.

10. "Looks Like Good G.O.P Year, Says Mrs. Longworth," *Chicago Tribune*, 17 August 1920, 19; "T.R.'s Daughter at G.O.P. Headquarters," *Chicago Tribune*, 25 August 1920, 7.

11. "Mrs. Longworth to Help," *NYT*, 26 August 1920, 3; "Mrs. Longworth Enters Campaign," *NYT*, 27 August 1920, 4; "T.R. Jr. Cancels Talk," *Chicago Tribune*, 5 September 1920, 1; "Harding Goes South on Speaking Tour," *NYT*, 13 October 1920, 3, states that Alice was going to be a speaker; "Harding Demands Proof He Changed," *NYT*, 21 October 1920, 3, covers the Jackson rally, but doesn't list Alice among the speakers; "T.R.'s Daughter Helps Dedicate Roosevelt Road," *Chicago Tribune*, 3 October 1920, 3; "Republicans Count on Maine Victory," *NYT*, 9 September 1920, 3.

12. Charles W. Snyder, "An American Original: Theodore Roosevelt, Jr.," in *Theodore Roosevelt: Many Sided American*, Natalie A. Naylor, Douglas Brinkley, and John Allen Gable, eds. (Interlaken, N.Y.: Heart of the Lakes Publishing, 1992), 97.

13. "Cox Coming East for Final Appeal," *NYT*, 18 October 1920, 2; "Houston's Plans on Tax Changes Anger Kitchin," *Chicago Tribune*, 10 December 1920, 11.

14. "Harding Proposes a New Department," *NYT*, 2 October 1920, 2. "How Will the Ladies, God Bless 'Em, Vote?," *Chicago Tribune*, 26 September 1920, C-7.

15. "President had his wish," "White Undismayed by Result in Maine," *NYT*, 15 September 1920, 4; "The Next Speakership," *NYT* editorial, 15 January 1919, 10; "Turn to Longworth in Speakership Fight," *NYT*, 13 January 1919, 6; "Mann Opposition Gaining Strength," *NYT*, 19 January 1919, 6; and "Longworth for Gillette," *NYT*, 28 January 1919, 8.

16. NL, "Traffic and Trade Agreements Speech" to the House of Representatives, 21 December 1920, made just before the tariff came up for revision in January 1921, NLP; Marian C. McKenna, *Borah* (Ann Arbor: The University of Michigan Press, 1961), 191–93; "intolerant, shortsighted," WEB to RHMcC, 28 July 1923, Hanna-McCormick Papers, LC.

17. Francis Ralston Welsh, "Truth Versus Treachery: Senator William E. Borah," [1923], Commerce Papers, HHPL.

18. *CH*, 314 and 315.

19. *CH*, 316.

20. "Fanatics on both sides," *CH*, 316; Wadsworth's view, 7 May 1922, TRJR Diary; "Sincere prohibitionist," Thomas L. Stokes, *Chip Off My Shoulder* (Princeton: Princeton University Press, 1940), 228.

21. "Not a common adventurer," McKenna, 175; "tee totalar," Richard V. Oulahan; "Address Stirs the Capital," *NYT*, 31 May 1926, 1.

22. "Girls," Robert Allen and Drew Pearson, *Washington Merry-Go-Round* (New York: Blue Ribbon Books, 1931), 24; Music, "Washington Society," *Chicago Tribune*, 3 March 1927, 27. Dows is quoted in Clara Longworth de Chambrun, *The Making of Nicholas Longworth* (New York: Richard R. Long & Ray Smith, 1933),

220; "Marching Club," De Chambrun, 286–87.

23. "Borah Amendment Adopted by Senate," *NYT*, 26 May 1921, 1; "economic ruin," "Open Arms Parley Is Borah's Demand," *NYT*, 30 August 1921, 13.

24. NL to Susan Longworth, 13 December [1921], NLIII.

25. McKenna, 179. Evans C. Johnson, *Oscar W. Underwood* (Baton Rouge: Louisiana State University Press, 1980), 319–20; Robert K. Murray, *The Politics of Normalcy* (New York: W. W. Norton, 1973), 61.

26. TRJR to ARL, 21 July 1923, JSP; for their friends see TRJR Diary, entries for spring and summer 1922; Charles Curtis was no relation to Laura Curtis.

27. "In the afternoon," TRJR Diary, 9 April 1922; a good play, TRJR Diary, 10 April 1922.

28. TRJR Diary, 11 April 1922; Arthur Sears Henning, "Battle to Save Navy for U.S. Is Begun in House," *Chicago Tribune*, 11 April 1922, 1.

29. TRJR Diary, 13–16 April 1922; "Harding Wins Fight Against 'Pygmy' Navy," *Chicago Tribune*, 16 April 1922, 1; for Nick's letter, see "86,000 Adopted as House Passes Bill," *NYT*, 16 April 1922, 1.

30. "Pneumonia Victim," *Chicago Tribune*, 28 June 1922, 10; "Mrs. Nicholas Longworth," *NYT*, 28 June 1922, 12; "Mrs. Longworth Died After a Long Illness," *Cincinnati Times-Star*, 27 June 1922; "Simple Service for Funeral of Mrs. Longworth," *Cincinnati Times-Star*, 29 June 1922, both Susan Longworth Princeton File, CHS; De Chambrun, 268.

31. "When are you coming," TRJR to ARL, 26 July 1922; "go over…in detail," TRJR to ARL, 31 July 1922, both JSP.

32. EKR to Belle Roosevelt, 1 May 1923, KBR; "Admiral Cowles Dies in 77th Year," *NYT*, 2 May 1923, 19; Isabella

Munro-Ferguson to John Campbell Greenway, 11 August 1923, Greenway AHS; on Bye's infirmities, see Betty Boyd Caroli, *The Roosevelt Women* (New York: Basic Books, 1998), 128–131.

33. "When he came," 322; Alice's contempt, 323; "shocking" disregard, 324; "Everyone must feel," 325, all *CH*.

34. Mark Sullivan, *Our Times: The Twenties* (New York: Charles Scribner's Sons, 1935), 6:97–98; *CH*, 323.

35. "There is no city," Maurice Francis Egan, "Washington, Past and Present," *NYT*, 15 August 1920, 38; Romany interest, Teague, 43.

36. "Atmosphere was as different," and "a simplicity and charm," *CH*, 326; for the dinner party, see ARL preservation tape, ICD 16025, 20 September 1967, JSP; for the dentist, see Teague, xiv.

37. "Fight on Longworth Angers Penna. Drys," clipping in a letter from Ethel Roosevelt Derby to Belle and Kermit Roosevelt, 4 February 1923, KBR; Western congressmen, "Diplomacy of Organization," *NYT*, 30 November 1923, 14; "Progressives Call for Radical Laws," *NYT*, 1 December 1923, 1.

38. NL to Republican members of the Sixty-eighth Congress, 24 November 1923, NLP; "acted on 594 measures," Donald C. Bacon, "Nicholas Longworth: The Genial Czar," in *Masters of the House*, Roger H. Davidson, Susan Webb Hammond, and Raymond W. Smock, eds. (Boulder, Colo.: Westview Press, 1998), 130.

39. Katharine Graham, *Personal History* (New York: Knopf, 1997), 27.

40. Sexual conquests, Claudius O. Johnson, "Very Personal Notes on Senator William E. Borah," April 1939, cage 214, Claudius Osborne Johnson Papers; Washington State University Libraries; "passion, intimacy, or love," LeRoy Ashby, e-mail to author, 23 May 2006; for two versions of this Cissy story, see Alice

Albright Hoge, *Cissy Patterson* (New York: Random House, 1966), 72; Ralph G. Martin, *Cissy* (New York: Simon & Schuster, 1979), 189; for Alice denying it ever happened, see Paul F. Healy, *Cissy* (Garden City, N.Y.: Doubleday, 1966), 9; for the bathroom incident, see Martin, 190; for the carriage, Kristie Miller, e-mail to author, 19 October 1999; for the stocking and chewing gum, see Alsop, *"I've Seen the Best of It,"* 92.

41. "Vivacious, blue-eyed blonde," McKenna, 23; pregnancy rumor, Johnson, "Very Private Notes." Marian McKenna, author of *Borah* (Ann Arbor: University of Michigan Press, 1961), interviewed Mary Borah's personal physician, Dr. Ralph Falk. During one of their lengthy conversations, Professor McKenna asked Dr. Falk why the Borahs never had children, and asked specifically about the abortion rumor. Dr. Falk cited "doctor-patient privilege" and said that he "could neither confirm nor deny the fact of the alleged abortion." McKenna believed "it was a weak assertion." Had there been no abortion, it is reasonable to assume that Dr. Falk would have said so, especially as he was a good friend of the Borahs and because Mrs. Borah was still living. Marian McKenna, e-mails to author, 26 and 29 May 2006.

For Mary Borah's story of her earliest days with Bill Borah, see the transcript of her oral history at the Idaho Historical Society. (Mary McConnell Borah, interviewed by Rosita Artis, Boise: Idaho State Historical Society [OH #0013], 18 October 1969.) She tells the tale of a very brief courtship, truncated when Borah had to go to Washington for a case. They married instead of being separated, according to Mrs. Borah. For another version of how Mary met and married Bill Borah, see the transcript of Mary McConnell Borah, interview by Maureen Bassett, 15 October 1971, Oral History Project, Latah County Museum Society, Moscow, Idaho.

There is another piece of evidence to support the abortion theory. Ann Catt, curator of the Latah County Historical Society and Mary Reed, former curator at the McConnell Mansion Museum, both in Moscow, Idaho, where Mary McConnell was born, pointed out that there is very little in Mary McConnell Borah's memoir, *Elephants and Donkeys*, about her family. Her Moscow years are virtually ignored. Both Catt and Reed suggested separately how odd it is that Governor McConnell's daughter would fail to elaborate on her father, also one of the most prominent men in Idaho. His virtual absence from Mrs. Borah's memoir made them suspect some sort of falling-out. As Ms. Catt said, though, after Senator Borah's death, Mary Borah went to live with her sister in California—so any hard feelings didn't seem to have been directed at her sibling. (Author's telephone interview with Mary Reed, 30 May 2006; author's telephone interview with Ann Catt, 30 May 2006.)

42. In response to my question about why Alice allowed herself to get pregnant, Alice Longworth's granddaughter said she "just let it happen." Joanna Sturm believes emphatically that Alice Longworth would never have had an abortion. (Author's interview with Joanna Sturm, 12 June 2005.)

43. Robert Hellman, e-mails to author, 21 and 22 May 2006.

44. Alice stayed home, "Old Party Leaders Take Back Seats," *NYT,* 11 June 1924, 4; RHMcC Diary, 21 August 1924, courtesy of Kristie Miller; Borah not at Cleveland, McKenna, 208.

45. "Borah as Presidential Timber," *Literary Digest,* 7 April 1923, 11; WEB to RHMcC, 28 July 1923, Hanna-McCormick Papers, LC.

46. Ted's memories from his "Summary

of Republican National Convention, Cleveland, Ohio, June 10, 11, 12, 1924," TRJRP.

47. "In which place?" Charles Merz, "Borah's One-Man Party," *New Republic* 43 (10 June 1925): 67; "dullest," Miller, 145; vice-president, Richard Langham Riedel, *Halls of the Mighty* (New York: Robert B. Luce, 1969), 189.

48. WEB to ARL, 28 September 1924, JSP.

49. WEB to ARL, 11 July 1924, JSP.

50. "Roosevelt Is Happy as Smith Passes McAdoo," *Chicago Daily Tribune*, 8 July 1924, 2.

51. WEB to ARL, 25 September 1924, JSP.

52. "What will I do?" WEB to ARL, 16 September 1924; "My own sweetheart," Underlined in "The Neglected Farmer," clipping in WEB to ARL, 25 September 1924, both JSP.

53. "Borah and a Third Party," *Literary Digest*, 26 August 1922, 14.

54. WEB to ARL, 26 September 1924, JSP.

55. WEB to ARL, 3 November 1924, JSP; meet in Chicago, RHMcC Diary, 5 September 1924, courtesy of Kristie Miller.

56. "I did enjoy your letters," WEB to ARL, 23 September 1924, JSP; Hellos, WEB to ARL, 25 October 1924, 7 November 1925, and 4 October 1924, all JSP.

57. *NYT* editorial (14 September 1924) enclosed in WEB to ARL, 18 September 1924, JSP; "my darling," "At the Mercy of Congress," clipping, n.d., in WEB to ARL, 26 September 1924, JSP; "My dear," "Pot and Kettle Politics," *New York Journal of Commerce*, 18 August 1924, unattached clipping, JSP; "My sweetheart," "The Magic Power of Campaign Words and Phrases," clipping, n.d., in WEB to ARL, 23 September 1924, JSP.

58. Secret message in "Speaker Scores Party Leaders in Bad Faith," in WEB to ARL, 5 August 1924, JSP.

59. WEB to ARL, 8 October 1924, JSP.

60. RHMcC Diary, 6 November 1924, courtesy of Kristie Miller.

61. Uncertain future, "Roosevelt Rests," *NYT*, 6 November 1924, 3; Alice's intercession, William Allen White, *A Puritan in Babylon* (New York: Macmillan, 1958), 270n18; "prepared to make a statement," "T.R. Should Quit Navy, Democrat Says in Hot Row," *Chicago Tribune*, 16 March 1924, 3; "Demands TR Shall Leave Navy," *NYT*, 16 March 1924, 1; "rough stunt," ER, *This I Remember* (New York: Harper & Brothers, 1949), 32.

62. EKR to James R. Garfield, 15 October 1924, James R. Garfield Papers, LC; Katherine Edmondson Callaway to ARL, 20 January 1936, ARLC.

63. WEB to ARL, 6 November 1924, JSP.

64. "Rather special," *CH*, 1; Henry Cabot Lodge to ARL, 24 April 1921, JSP.

65. EKR Diary, Wednesday, 12 November 1924. Definition from *Cassell's Dictionary* (1971), 104; "Alice's news," Sylvia Jukes Morris, *Edith Kermit Roosevelt* (New York: Coward, McCann & Geoghegan, 1980), 462–63; "the shock," EKR to Belle Hagner, 29 November 1924, PHP.

66. Kermit Roosevelt to Belle Roosevelt, KBR. Both letters are dated 14 November 1924. The first was from Rookwood, the second from Zanesville.

67. The journalist was Robert Bender from the United Press bureau, James Brough, *Princess Alice* (Boston: Little, Brown, 1975), 275; "One of the most original," "Longworths Await Stork," *NYT*, 21 November 1924, 19; Coolidges, Brough, 274, 275. RHMcC Diary, 21 November 1924, courtesy of Kristie Miller; "Mrs. Longworth Expecting Stork," *Chicago Tribune*, 21 November 1924, 1; "gland

baby," "Princess Alice," *New Yorker,* 28 February 1925, 9.

68. William "Fishbait" Miller and Frances Spatz Leighton, *Fishbait* (Englewood Cliffs, N.J.: Prentice Hall, 1977), 103–4.

69. Robert James Maddox, "Keeping Cool with Coolidge," *Journal of American History* 53, 4 (March 1967): 776.

70. RHMcC Diary, 6 November 1924, courtesy of Kristie Miller.

71. Joanna Sturm, Alice Longworth's granddaughter, and Robert Hellman, Sturm's partner, feel very strongly that Alice "duped" Nick. "A woman as smart as Mrs. L. could have finessed that with a fellow who drank as much as Longworth," Hellman wrote. (Robert Hellman, e-mail to author, 22 and 21 May 2006.) Mrs. Longworth disclosed the truth about Joanna's grandfather when Joanna was an adult, and when all the other principals were dead.

72. Angela Meeske, a lifelong resident of Cincinnati, maintains that Nick Longworth was the father of a son, the result of an affair with a Cincinnati woman. The son, according to Mrs. Meeske, never tried to hide his connection—in fact, sitting by his chair in his living room was "an oversized portrait" of Nick. (Author interview with Angela Meeske, 19 April 2004.) This is the only rumor I've ever heard of Nick's fathering a child, except for the malicious letter Alice received while on her honeymoon.

73. RHMcC Diary, 24 November 1924 ("more cheerful") and 7 November 1924 ("Dr. DeLee"), courtesy of Kristie Miller; "When do you advise," Morris Fishbein, *Joseph Bolivar DeLee* (New York: E. P. Dutton, 1949), 156.

74. "Congress Begins Its Final Session in a Cheerful Mood," *NYT,* 2 December 1924, 1; WEB to ARL, 6 November 1924, JSP; "Longworth Campaign Started by Ohioans," *NYT,* 17 December 1924, 44.

See also "Wants Longworth in Chair," *NYT,* 20 December 1924, 17; "Longworth Is Confident," *NYT,* 24 December 1924, 5; Bacon, 131.

75. "You Can't Help Liking Nick," *Literary Digest* 87, 8 (21 November 1925), 46; "Flags at Capital at Half-staff," *Washington Times,* 9 April 1931, 2.

76. ARC to NL, 28 February 1925, JSP.

77. WEB to ARL, 23 January 1925, JSP.

78. RHMcC Diary, 27 January 1925.

79. WEB to ARL, 2 February 1925, JSP.

80. ARC to ARL, 3 February 1925, JSP; Caroli, 414.

81. See "Daughter Is Born to the Longworths," *NYT,* 15 February 1925, 1; "Longworth Cheered in the House," *NYT,* 15 February 1925, 1.

82. WEB to ARL, 14 February 1925. Borah usually did not use a plural pronoun. Either Mary Borah was reading over his shoulder or he wanted to make sure that his note was suitable should Nick read it. However, the transparent Hello, Hello code makes it likely that Borah was simply too transported by the news to be thinking clearly.

83. WEB to ARL, 15 February 1925, JSP.

84. "A little bit jealous," "Longworth Meets Infant Daughter," *NYT,* 16 February 1925, 5; "Miss Paulina Has Real Roosevelt Face" and "A Chip Off the Old Block," newspaper clippings, n.d., JSP. The quote is from the latter. WEB to ARL, 16 February 1925, JSP.

85. Untitled clipping from [*Chicago*] *Tribune,* 15 March 1925, JSP.

86. Alsop, 91.

87. Elizabeth Brunner, "The Battle for Feminist Approval: Paulina in Shakespeare's *The Winter's Tale,*" 1995, (http://members.tripod.com/~ElizBrunner/Scholar/PaulinaWinters.html).

88. WEB to ARL, 22 February 1925, JSP.

89. ARL, telegram to Everett Sanders; Everett Sanders, telegram to ARL, both 14 February 1925, Everett Sanders Papers, LC; "Science and the Longworth Baby," newspaper clipping, n.d., JSP; WEB to ARL, 24 February 1925.

90. "Self-destructive tendencies," Miller, 151, 152; EKR to ARL, 27 February 1925, JSP; "when Senator McCormick died," Selden, 76; "Mrs. Longworth Leaves Hospital," *NYT,* 28 February 1925, 2.

91. WEB to ARL, 28 February and 1 July 1925, JSP.

92. Untitled clipping, [*Chicago*] *Tribune,* 15 March 1925, JSP. See also "Longworth Baby Quits Chicago Today," *NYT,* 6 March 1925, 23; and "Paulina Visits Father," *NYT,* 8 March 1925, 2.

93. WEB to ARL, 1 March 1925, JSP; "Longworth Poses as Fond Father," *NYT,* 16 May 1925, 21.

94. Mary Borah, *Elephants and Donkeys* (Moscow: University Press of Idaho, 1976), 113.

95. " 'Little Borah' Has to Read the Papers to Keep Track of Noted Husband," *Lewiston Tribune,* 3 August 1936, WEBID; James M. Cox, *Journey Through My Years* (New York: Simon & Schuster, 1946), 100.

96. "Frequent morning caller," "Little Borah is Confidant of Ex-Servicemen," *Capital News,* May 1929, WEBID; "close personal friends," Suzanne Dabney Taylor, "Little Borah at 101," newspaper clipping, 29 October 1971, WEBID; Mrs. Borah as guest, "Washington Society," *Chicago Tribune,* 8 December 1925, 25; photos of Paulina, WEB to ARL, 18 July and 10 July 1925, both JSP.

97. WEB to ARL, 10 July 1925; WEB to ARL, 13 July 1925, both JSP.

98. WEB to ARL, 28 July 1925, JSP.

Sometimes Bill Borah used periods (P.F.P.) and sometimes he did not (PFP).

99. WEB to ARL, 5 August 1925, JSP. WEB to ARL, 17 September 1925, JSP. P.M.P. WEB to ARL, 16 October 1925, JSP. Alice herself referred to her father as "my parent," and this can be heard throughout the ARL preservation tapes.

100. Cora Rubin Lane, interviewed by Jackie Day-Ames, Boise: Idaho State Historical Society, 25 May 1976. See especially page 20 of the transcript.

101. Robert Hellman, e-mail to author, 20 May 2006.

Chapter 16: **"The Political Leader of the Family"**

1. "The 'Battalion of Death' in New Onslaughts," *Kansas City Star,* 24 January 1926, C-1; *Time* magazine, 7 February 1927, cover; Gore Vidal, "The Woman Behind *The Women,*" *New Yorker,* 26 May 1997, 73.

2. Henry Brandon, "A Talk with an 83-Year-Old Enfant Terrible," *NYT,* 6 August 1967, 69.

3. Nelle Scanlan, *Boudoir Mirrors of Washington* (Philadelphia: John C. Winston, 1923), 17.

4. "Little Miss Paulina Longworth," *Louisville Courier-Journal,* 19 September 1926, 9; JSP; Clara Longworth de Chambrun, *The Making of Nicholas Longworth* (Ray Long & Richard R. Smith, 1933), 283.

5. Charles A. Selden, "The Father Complex of ARL and RHMcC," *Ladies' Home Journal,* March 1927, 6; "Princess Alice," *New Yorker,* 28 February 1925.

6. "Little Borah Is Confidant of Ex-Servicemen," *Capital News,* May 1929, undated clipping, WEBID. For Mary Borah's explanation of her involvement with veterans, see her oral history at the Idaho

Oral History Center, pages 6 and 7 of the transcript, tape 2.

7. Letter to "mot her," n.d., JSP. The only other legible word is *Paulina;* ARL to Ethel Roosevelt Derby, postmarked 14 August 1926, RFPH.

8. Grace Goodhue Coolidge to Mrs. Dwight Morrow, 28 December 1925, quoted in Ishbel Ross, *Grace Coolidge and Her Era* (New York: Dodd, Mead, 1962), 168. Or, the timing may have been just before Christmas: see "Longworth Baby at White House," *NYT,* 16 December 1925, 52.

9. "Little Miss Paulina Longworth," 9.

10. "Mrs. Coolidge Writes Cook Book Recipes for Congressional Club's Favorite Dishes," *NYT,* 16 September 1927, 25; "Kitchen Secrets in New Cookbook," *NYT,* 20 November 1927, 22; for Alice as charter member, see "Congressmen's Wives Club," *NYT,* 15 March 1908, 9, and *The Congressional Club Cookbook* (Washington, D.C.: Congressional Club, 1927), 428, 437.

11. "Mrs. Longworth's Portrait to Advertise Beauty Cream," *NYT,* 1 June 1925, 1; Cornelia Bryce Pinchot to Bessie Dobson Altemus, 7 April 1927, Papers of Cornelia Bryce Pinchot, LC; for other women who posed, see Stanley Walker, *Mrs. Astor's Horse* (New York: Frederick A. Stokes, 1935), 93–94; "official and social Washington," "Mrs. Longworth Joins Royalty in Beauty Ads," *Chicago Tribune,* 1 June 1925, 9.

12. "From then on," Ross, *Grace Coolidge,* 199; Mary McConnell Borah, "Entertaining Royalty," clipping, n.d., WEBID.

13. "Who Goes to Prize Fights—And Why?," *Chicago Tribune,* 1 July 1921, 8; ARL preservation tape, ICD 16025, 20 September 1967, JSP. See also "Notables to See the Title Match," *NYT,* 14 September 1923, 14.

14. George Authier, "The New Speaker of the House," *National Republic,* January 1926, NLP.

15. Nick quoted in "You Can't Help Liking Nick," *Literary Digest* 87, 8 (21 November 1925), 46; "regardless of the rules, Authier, NLP.

16. "In Alice Longworth," Authier, NLP; "never sponsored anything," Robert S. Allen and Drew Pearson, *Washington Merry-Go-Round* (New York: Blue Ribbon Books, 1931), 230.

17. Nick's opening speech in de Chambrun, 293; Congress, "is always unpopular," S. J. Woolf, "Speaker of the House and Proud to Be," *NYT Magazine,* 12 February 1928, 3.

18. Harry Parker, "Recalls Longworth Smile," *NYT,* 10 April 1931, 18; Edge, De Chambrun, 285; "chain drinker," Richard Langham Riedel, *Halls of the Mighty* (New York: Robert B. Luce, 1969), 192. Riedel made this observation of Garner when Cactus Jack had become vice president. John L. Lewis quote from Anthony Champagne, "John Nance Garner," in *Masters of the House,* Roger H. Davidson, Susan Webb Hammond, and Raymond W. Smock, eds. (Boulder, Colo.: Westview Press, 1998), 146.

19. Robert Paul Browder and Thomas G. Smith, *Independent* (New York: Knopf, 1986), 52; "Will Rogers Says Longworth Was Both Able and Popular," *NYT,* 11 April 1931, 18.

20. Garner quote from Neil MacNeil, *Forge of Democracy* (New York: David McKay, 1963), 82; for more on Board of Education, see Champagne, in Davison, Hammond, and Smocks, 162; and MacNeil, 81–84.

21. Jules Abels, *In the Time of Silent Cal* (New York: G. P. Putnam's Sons, 1969), 36.

22. Allen and Pearson, 211–214. For

Richard Riedel's loving treatment, see *Halls of the Mighty,* especially pages 272–82.

23. WEB to ARL, 9 October 1930, JSP.

24. "I am very blue," WEB to ARL, 10 November 1930, JSP; "I wonder," WEB to ARL, n.d. [1930], JSP; banish warfare, Lewis L. Gould, *The Most Exclusive Club* (New York: Basic Books, 2005), 101.

25. For Salmon O. Levinson and Robins and their interests in having Borah as their spokesperson for the outlawry movement, see especially Robert James Maddox, "William E. Borah and the Crusade to Outlaw War," *Historian,* 29 (2), 1967: 200–220.

26. "The Roosevelt Club Borah-Butler Debate" (Boston: The Roosevelt Club, 1927); Idaho newspaper quoted in Charles DeBenedetti, "Borah and the Kellogg-Briand Pact," *Pacific Northwest Quarterly* 63(1), January 1972: 24.

27. DeBenedetti, 28.

28. Maddox, 220; Claudius O. Johnson, *Borah of Idaho* (Seattle: University of Washington Press, 1936), 405–406; "Idaho Varsity Takes Levinson $55,000 as Giving Honor to Borah," *Chicago Tribune,* 12 April 1929, 41.

29. "Borah Will Start Two-Year Campaign for New Party Deal," *NYT,* 12 June 1926; "Whooping It Up for Borah in Idaho," *Spokane Review,* 15 September 1927, JSP; WEB to Evan Evans, 21 March 1928, WEBID.

30. Ethel Roosevelt Derby to Belle Roosevelt, 14 January 1926, KBR; Frank B. Lord, "A 'Close Up' of Longworth," [*Movie* magazine] draft, spring 1927, NLP; Nick quoted in de Chambrun, 289.

31. Lucile McArthur, "Idle Moments of a Lady in Waiting," *Saturday Evening Post* 204, 12 (19 September 1931), 5; Kermit Roosevelt to Ethel Roosevelt Derby, 3 January 1928, ERDP.

32. "Delivered himself up," Thomas L. Stokes, *Chip Off My Shoulder* (Princeton: Princeton University Press, 1940), 228; platform, Johnson, 421.

33. Vice-presidency, Edward Anthony oral interview transcript, 12 July 1970, 35–36; hoax boom, Gene Dulin to Herbert Hoover, 8 August 1928, Campaign and Transition Files, both HHPL.

34. Preston Wolfe oral interview transcript, 18 August 1967, 14, HHPL; Robert Silvercruys oral interview transcript, 9, HHPL; "a mistake," Miller, 187, 191. For McCormick's campaign, see Miller, chap. 7.

35. "First woman," Miller, 196; "Alice is a statesman," Miller, 192.

36. "No man did more," Johnson, 408; lunch with Hoover, Johnson, 432–33.

37. "Senator Curtis Aided by Sister in Capital," *NYT,* 16 June 1928, 5; "Sister Speaks for Curtis," *NYT,* 8 August 1928, 3; "Mrs. Gann Is Hostess," *NYT,* 4 March 1929, 2.

38. Stanley Woodward, "Protocol: What It Is and What It Does," *Department of State Bulletin* reprint, 3 October 1949, 501; "Mrs. Moses Heads Senate Ladies' Club," *NYT,* 6 February 1929, 11.

39. "Inaugural Ball Largest Ever Held," *NYT,* 5 March 1928, 2; Kellogg's quote from "Mrs. Gann's Social Rank," *NYT,* 30 March 1929, 22.

40. "Curtis Protests on Social Ranking," *NYT,* 4 April 1929, 1 and 14. See also "A Man Who Must Dine for His Country," *NYT,* 15 March 1931, 81.

41. "At the head of the table," "Silence Enjoined on Curtis Status," *NYT,* 5 April 1929, 4; "Diplomats Confer on Curtis Hostess, But Refuse to Act," *NYT,* 9 April 1929, 1; "Stimson Won't Rule on Mrs. Gann's Case," *NYT,* 10 April 1929, 4; "Diplomats Accord Rank to Mrs. Gann as Curtis Hostess," *NYT,* 11 April 1929, 18.

42. Heflin quote from "Diplomats Confer on Curtis Hostess, But Refuse to Act,"

12; "Protest in Philadelphia," *NYT*, 10 April 1929, 4.

43. Stimson quote from "Stimson Won't Rule on Mrs. Gann's Case," 1; "scored a complete triumph," "Diplomats Accord Rank to Mrs. Gann as Curtis Hostess," 1; Chilean ambassador's dinner, "Mrs. Gann as Guest Has Honor Place," *NYT*, 12 April 1929, 1.

44. "Gann Social War Reopens in Capital," *NYT*, 5 May 1929, 23.

45. "Social War at the Capital," *NYT*, 8 May 1929, 25.

46. ARL preservation tape, ICD 16024, 20 September 1967, JSP.

47. ARL preservation tape, ICD 16024, 20 September 1967, JSP; see Jonathan Daniels, *Washington Quadrille* (Garden City, N.Y.: Doubleday, 1968), 233–35, which has a story that matches best with Alice's interpretation. "Obviously, there never was any row," *CH*, 32; "Mrs. Gann and Alice Longworth Sit Together in Senate Gallery and Chat in Friendly Vein," *NYT*, 14 May 1929, 2.

48. Winifred Mallon, "Social Battle Rages Anew in the Capital," *NYT*, 12 May 1929, 22; ARL preservation tape, ICD 16024, 20 September 1967, JSP.

49. Curtis cheating, ARL, "Of Politics and Politicians," n.d., JSP; "mediocre—" Robert S. Allen interview, 1970, 3, HHPL. But Curtis did love his sister. When he died, Charlie Curtis left her $25,000. See "Footnotes on Headliners," *NYT*, 23 February 1936, E2.

50. *CH*, 329.

51. "Mrs. Gann Defends Right to Social Precedence as Hostess to 'Symbol of Our Government,'" *NYT*, 31 July 1929, 24; "White House Changes Master of Ceremonies," *NYT*, 10 January 1930, 29; "Curtis and Speaker Guests in Box Party," *NYT*, 14 February 1930, 25; "'Alice' Greets 'Dolly' at White House Fete," *NYT*, 9 December 1930, 36; Dolly Gann, *Dolly Gann's Book* (Garden City, N.Y.: Doubleday, 1933), 121–22.

52. Addenda to Transcript of F. Trubee Davison, Oral Interview with F. Trubee Davison, 14 September 1969, 14, HHPL.

53. Frances Spatz and David Camelon, "Legendary Ladies: Rebellious 'Princess Alice,'" *American Weekly*, 12 November 1950, 25.

Chapter 17: **"An Irresistible Magnet"**

1. Winifred Mallon, "Mrs. Longworth Sets Tongues Wagging," *NYT*, 26 May 1929, 5; Rebecca West, "The Kaleidoscope That Is Washington," *NYT*, 12 May 1935, SM3.

2. James quoted in Constance McLaughlin Green, *Washington* (Princeton: Princeton University Press, 1963), 190; Clara Longworth de Chambrun, *The Making of Nicholas Longworth* (New York: Ray Long & Richard R. Smith, 1933), 283–84; "Nick Longworth's Political Career Colorful," *Washington Times*, 9 April 1931, 3.

3. Kristie Miller, *Ruth Hanna McCormick* (Albuquerque: University of New Mexico Press, 1992), 203. For the "back door," see John Milton Cooper Jr., *Breaking the Heart of the World* (New York: Cambridge University Press, 2001), especially 399–401; "I just can't stand it," Miller, 218.

4. Ralph G. Martin, *Cissy* (New York: Simon & Schuster, 1979), 275. See also Robert Allen and Drew Pearson, *Washington Merry-Go-Round* (New York: Blue Ribbon Books, 1931), 14–15.

5. Alice Albright Hoge, *Cissy Patterson* (New York: Random House, 1966); Martin, 276.

6. Hoge, 73.

7. Cissy Patterson to Nick Longworth, n.d., JSP. For the end of the feud between

Cissy and Alice, see Paul F. Healy, *Cissy* (New York: Doubleday, 1966), 238–239.

8. Hiram Johnson to Archibald M. Johnson, 9 April 1930, *The Diary Letters of Hiram Johnson*, vol. 5 (New York: Garland Publishing, 1983); Miller, 228–29.

9. "Holding levees," WEB to ARL, 5 September 1930, JSP; "Princess Paulina Takes Up the Three R's," clipping, n.d., in WEB to ARL, 17 October 1930, JSP; "all of a twitter," ARL to Ethel Roosevelt Derby, 23 December 1930, ERDP; "I wish I could have had," WEB to ARL, 19 September 1930, JSP; "so blue," WEB to ARL, 23 September 1930, JSP.

10. "No…courage," WEB to ARL, 27 September 1930; "remained on the farm," WEB to ARL, 3 October 1930; "Brazil's…war," WEB to ARL, 10 October 1930, all JSP. Emphasis in original.

11. "Whither Thou Goest I Will Go," clipping enclosed in WEB to ARL, 23 September 1930, JSP; Miller, 229–30.

12. "I know how you are scanning," WEB to ARL, 1 November 1930; "wants to do the big thing," WEB to ARL, 5 November 1930, both JSP. Ruth's loss, Miller, 233–34.

13. ARL to Ethel Roosevelt Derby, 23 December 1930, RFPH; WEB to ARL, 10 and 11 November 1930, JSP. For the long letter, see WEB to ARL, 12 November 1930. For "Presh's figuring," see 24 November 1930, JSP.

14. Donald C. Bacon, "Nicholas Longworth," in Roger H. Davidson, Susan Webb Hammond, and Raymond W. Smock, eds., *Masters of the House* (Boulder, Colo.: Westview Press, 1998), 139; de Chambrun, 317–18.

15. Lucile McArthur, "Idle Moments of a Lady in Waiting," *Saturday Evening Post* 204, 12 (19 September 1931):142.

16. Allen and Pearson, 24; Jonathan Daniels, *Washington Quadrille* (Garden City, N.Y.: Doubleday, 1968), 235–38.

17. Alice's confirmation, "Rep. Longworth's Right Lung Infected," *Washington Times*, 8 April 1931, 1; Cissy Patterson to Laura Curtis, n.d., JSP. "When I heard that Nick probably had pneumonia I instantly telephoned your house," Cissy wrote—but not Alice's home. See also "Death of a Speaker," *Time*, 20 April 1931, from their online archive: http://time-proxy.yaga.com/time/archive/printout/0,23657,741406,00.html. It attests to the fact that the oxygen tent arrived. Herbert Hoover to ARL, 8 April 1931, LHHP.

18. "Longworth Sinking," *NYT*, 9 April 1931, 1; "Death Ends Career of Speaker Longworth," *Cincinnati Times-Star*, 9 April 1931, 1, states that both Alice and Laura were at his bedside. See also "Longworth Is Dead," *NYT*, 10 April 1931, 1.

19. "Rites Will Be at Rookwood at 2 P.M. Saturday," *Cincinnati Times-Star*, 10 April 1931, NLPF.

20. "Longworth's Body Starts Back to Ohio for Funeral Today," *NYT*, 11 April 1931, 1; Gore Vidal, *Palimpsest* (New York: Penguin Books, 1995), 263; "The Gift," Alice Dows, *Illusions* (Philadelphia: Dorrance Publishers, 1931), 50; "When He Comes," Alice Dows, *Idle Hours* (Philadelphia: Dorrance Publishers, 1927), 55.

21. "Speaker's Gavel Draped," *NYT*, 12 April 1931, 24; see also "Recalls Longworth Smile," *NYT*, 10 April 1931, 18; W[illiam] E. and Mary Borah, telegram to ARL, 9 April 1931, JSP; Herbert Hoover, Executive Order, 9 April 1931, President's Personal File, HHPL; "Hurley Pays Tribute Over Radio to Speaker," *NYT*, 10 April 1931, 19; Herbert Hoover to ARL, 9 April 1931, President's Personal File, HHPL. See also "President Lauds Long-

worth for Service to His Country," *NYT*, 10 April 1931, 1.

22. "Cincinnati Grieves for 'Man of the People,'" *NYT*, 10 April 1931, 18; for the list of the pallbearers, see "Funeral Rites to Be Simple," *NYT*, 11 April 1931, 12; "Garner Mourns for Friendly Foe," *NYT*, 10 April 1931, 18.

23. Graydon DeCamp, *The Grand Old Lady of Vine Street* (Cincinnati: Cincinnati Enquirer, 1991), 87.

24. Eleanor Butler Roosevelt to ARL, 10 April 1931; TRJR to ARL, n.d., [1931], JSP; "oddly enough" TRJR to ARL, 12 April 1931, JSP.

25. See, for example, "Curtis and Cabinet Eulogize Speaker," *NYT*, 10 April 1931, 18; "Loss of Longworth Stirs Sorrow Here," *NYT*, 10 April 1931, 18; Arthur Krock, "The Week in America," *NYT*, 12 April 1931, E5; Longworth's career is assessed by Donald C. Bacon, "Nicholas Longworth," in *Masters of the House*, Roger H. Davidson, Susan Webb Hammond, and Raymond W. Smock, eds. (Boulder, Colo.: Westview Press, 1998).

26. John Q. Tilson, "The Late Hon. Nicholas Longworth, of Ohio, Memorial Address," *Congressional Record*, May 1932, NLPF; *NYT* editorial, "Speaker of the House," 12 April 1931, E1; and "Curtis and Cabinet Eulogize Speaker," *NYT*, 10 April 1931, 18; "bludgeoning the House," Allen and Pearson, 231; the term "genial czar" is Donald C. Bacon's; "Will Rogers Says Longworth Was Both Able and Popular," *NYT*, 11 April 1931, 18; for Nick's interview, see S. J. Woolf, "Speaker of the House and Proud to Be," *NYT Magazine*, 12 February 1928, 23.

27. Laura M. Curtis to LHH, 27 April 1931, LHHP; Kristie Miller, e-mail to author, 18 April 2004, quoting Ruth's daughter Bazy Tankersely.

28. "Mrs. Longworth Is Urged to Run for Congress," *Washington Times*, 10 April 1931, 3; see also "Death of Longworth Gives House to Democrats," *Washington Times*, 9 April 1931, 2.

29. Memorandum of Lewis Strauss's telephone report of Robert Taft's conversation, 28 April 1931, Lewis L. Strauss Papers, HHPL; "Republican Majority Narrowed by Death," *Cincinnati Times-Star*, 10 April 1931, NLPF; Frances Parkinson Keyes, *Capital Kaleidoscope* (New York: Harper & Brothers, 1937), 24.

30. "As though he owned the mint," Joseph Alsop, unpublished draft of his memoirs, 127 (in the author's possession); for assessments, see "Longworth's Estate All Left to Widow," 17 April 1931, 28; "Longworth's Estate Is Put at $825,000," 23 April 1931, 18; "Longworth Inheritance Tax $25,919," 8 December 1932, 15, all *NYT*.

31. ARL to LHH, 20 May 1931, LHHP; Mildred Hale to ARL, 15 May 1931, JSP; "rare and remarkable gift," ARL to LHH, 14 April 1931, LHHP; for Ted's return, see "Plans to Aid Porto Rico," *NYT*, 26 May 1931, 19. See also TRJR to LHH, 20 April 1931, LHHP; TRJR to ARL, n.d., JSP; "I know just how hard," TRJR to ARL, n.d., JSP.

32. Author interview with Angela Meeske, 19 April 2004; Kristie Miller's interview with Bazy Tankersley, 17 August 2004, in e-mail to author. Paulina Longworth was forced to use her right hand, even though she was left-handed. Some theories suggest that this forced right-handedness contributes to stammering.

33. "Mrs. Cowles Buried after Simple Service," *NYT*, 28 August 1931, 11. See also "Mrs. W. S. Cowles Dies at Age of 76," *NYT*, 26 August 1931, 16; Caroli, 130–31.

34. Miller, 238.

35. Kristie Miller, e-mail to author, 17

August 2004. Miller wrote that her father so characterized Ruth Hanna McCormick Simms, who was Miller's grandmother. "Alice Longworth Home Is Guarded," *Morning News* [Danville, Pennsylvania], 25 March 1932, 1; Genevieve Forbes Herrick, "Mrs. Longworth Reveals Threat to Seize Paulina," *Chicago Tribune*, 25 March 1932, 3.

36. "Longworth Home Guarded by Police," *NYT*, 25 March 1932, 3; "Kidnapping Threat Again Stirs Capital," *NYT*, 28 March 1932, 3.

37. "Late Speaker," *Cincinnati Enquirer*, 25 May 1932, NLPF; Memorial Address of Hon. Burton L. French, 25 May 1932, clipping from *Congressional Record*, NLIII; "House Mourns Longworth," *NYT*, 10 April 1932, 2; Friends' tribute, "Washington Society," *Chicago Tribune*, 4 April 1932, 19.

38. "Friends of the German People to Organize New Chicago Group," *Chicago Tribune*, 3 April 1932, G1; Walter Davenport, "The Man Who Grew Up," *Collier's*, 10 September 1932, 10, 11; Beverly Smith, "The Lone Rider from Idaho," *American Magazine*, March 1932, 100.

39. "Had a lot of fun," Teague, 159; "I wear no man's brand," Jean Vanden Heuvel, "The Sharpest Wit in Washington," *Saturday Evening Post* 238, 24 (4 December 1965):33; "Nemesis," Teague, 159.

40. ARL telegram to LHH, 24 October 1932, LHHP; "Noted Women Are Active in G.O.P. Campaign," *Chicago Tribune*, 12 October 1932, 6.

41. ARL telegram to LHH, 17 February [1932?], LHHP; for the Christmas present, see ARL to LHH, n.d., LHHP; "Mrs. Dolly Gann to Take Stump," 23 January 1932, 2; "Mrs. Gann Praises Hoover in Omaha Talk," 27 January 1932, 8; both *NYT*; Ruth's donation, Miller, 239.

42. "Look, there's Alice," "Women Delegates Noisier than Men," *NYT*, 15 June 1932, 13; "dared leave enclosure," "Keynoter Gives Women a Place—in Nine Words," *Chicago Tribune*, 15 June 1932, 3.

43. "Butler and White Debate Prohibition," *NYT*, 15 June 1932, 14.

44. "Two Feminine Notables Here Offer Contrast," *Chicago Tribune*, 27 June 1932, 3; "Society Draws No Party Lines When It Comes to Conventions," *Chicago Tribune*, 29 June 1932, 3; "Young for Nominee Is Urged by Malone," *NYT*, 11 April 1932, 3; "Mrs. Longworth and Smith Meet for First Time," *NYT*, 23 July 1932, 2.

45. Arthur M. Schlesinger Jr., *The Crisis of the Old Order* (Boston: Houghton Mifflin, 1957), chap. 28; Geoffrey Ward, *A First-Class Temperament* (New York: Harper & Row, 1989), 784–85.

46. EKR to LHH, 6 August 1932, LHHP; "Notification Made a Social Occasion," *NYT*, 12 August 1932, 1; "700 Dine with Hoover on Lawn at White House," *Chicago Tribune*, 12 August 1932, 8.

47. "President's Speech Is Cheered Wildly," *NYT*, 12 August 1932, 5; "69 Women Appeal in Hoover's Behalf," *NYT*, 26 October 1932, 13; "Mrs. Longworth for Hoover, She Says in Article," 14 October 1932, *NYT*, 4; "Nemi Tale Recalled by Alice Longworth," *NYT*, 14 October 1932, 14.

48. "Republicans Poised for Intensive Drive," *NYT*, 30 September 1932, 11; Genevieve Forbes Herrick, "Women's Angle in Politics Is Amusing, Original, and Quixotic," *Chicago Tribune*, 9 October 1932, G1; "fellow Buck-eyes," "Mrs. Hoover Hailed by Mid-West Crowds," *NYT*, 29 October 1932, 9; "Makes 31-Word Speech," *NYT*, 2 November 1932, 13.

49. "Here's a Sample of Conscious and Unscrupulous Dishonesty," *Cincinnati*

Times-Star, 4 November 1932, clipping from NLPF; see also "Republicans Fight to Hold Woman Vote," 3 November 1932, 17; "Democrats Scored by Mrs. Longworth," 4 November 1932, 10; both *NYT*.

50. "Here's a Sample of Conscious and Unscrupulous Dishonesty," NLPF.

51. EKR to Belle Hagner, 8 August [1933], PHP. In 1932, Edith told Belle, "I feel as she does...." EKR to Belle Hagner, 26 August 1932, PHP. "Women to Aid Davison," *NYT*, 30 August 1932, 4. EKR to Alice French, 6 July 1932, Alice French Papers, Newberry Library, Chicago. For a record of Edith's speech, see Caroli, 206. "Headline Footnotes," *NYT*, 23 October 1932, XX2.

52. "Fifth cousin," Ethel Roosevelt Derby to LHH, undated [1933], LHHP; "The Reporters: Jonathan Aitken Interview with Alice Roosevelt Longworth," [January 1969], Yorkshire Television; "against Franklin," ARL preservation tape, ICD 16024, 20 September 1967, JSP. Alice recalled on this tape that Edith went on to the White House to stay with the Hoovers, to make clear she was for Hoover and not for Franklin Roosevelt. Later in her life, Edith would soften about Franklin.

Chapter 18: "The Washington Dictatorship"

1. Harold Nicolson to Vita Sackville-West, 16 February 1933, in Harold Nicolson, *Diaries and Letters, 1930–1939*, Nigel Nicolson, ed. (New York: Athenaeum, 1966), 137.

2. Joseph Alsop, *I've Seen the Best of It* (New York: W. W. Norton, 1992), 91.

3. "Very beautiful," Alsop, 91; "a wit like hers," Alsop, 93.

4. She frequently used "detached malevolence" to describe herself. For an early use of it, see Franz Klein, "Alice Roosevelt

Longworth," 12 June 1946 Draft, for *Die Weltwoche*, 1, JSP.

5. "Oh, it was grim," ARL preservation tape, ICD 16025, 20 September 1967, JSP; Michael Teague, *Mrs. L* (Garden City, N.Y.: Doubleday, 1981), 170–71. "Hovering around," James Brough, *Princess Alice* (Boston: Little, Brown, 1975), 295; TRJR to FDR, 4 March 1933, TRJRP; Inaugural invitation, 4 March 1933, JSP.

6. Drew Pearson and Richard S. Allen, *Washington Merry-Go-Round* (New York: Blue Ribbon Books, 1931), 11; Samuel Hopkins Adams, *A. Woollcott* (New York: Reynal & Hitchcock, 1945), 176.

7. Alsop, 93.

8. EKR to LHH, 12 August 1933, LHHP; Archibald Roosevelt to Carter Harrison, 8 November 1933, Carter H. Harrison Papers, Newberry Library, Chicago. Harrison was on the New York State advisory board of the Federal Emergency Administration of Public Works.

9. See Peter Collier, *The Roosevelts* (New York: Simon & Schuster, 1994), 271, for "female impersonators"; Doris Kearns Goodwin, *No Ordinary Time* (New York: Simon & Schuster, 1994), 208, for "squaws and she-men." Both authors insist that FDR was fond of these friends of Eleanor's, and Collier drives home the point that they could be "resources" for his career.

10. Marian C. McKenna, *Borah* (Ann Arbor: University of Michigan Press, 1961), 306–307. See also the following *NYT* articles: "Senator Borah Goes Under Knife," 27 June 1933, 19; "Borah Reported Better," 28 June 1933, 23; "Borah Out of Hospital," 30 July 1933, 8. During the fall of 1932, Mary Borah had been seriously ill with "parrot fever," which she was said to have caught from one of the many birds that flew freely around their Washington apartment. See "Mrs. Borah

Afflicted with Parrot Fever," *NYT*, 22 September 1932, 12; "Mrs. Borah Improves After Getting Serum," *NYT*, 25 September 1932, 3.

11. The analogy to guerrilla war is from Brough, 292. "Mr. Rogers Finds Senate 'Fine Bunch of Fellows,'" *NYT*, 29 January 1934, 17. Alice liked Will Rogers. When he died, she agreed to be on a memorial commission to help establish a monument to him in Oklahoma. See "Organize to Build Rogers Memorial," *NYT*, 23 September 1935, 19; Alice's "stunt," "Bureau Chiefs Are Received at White House," *Chicago Tribune*, 2 February 1934, 19; Tinney quoted in Howard Teichmann, *Alice* (Englewood Cliffs, N.J.: Prentice Hall, 1979), 163.

12. "Drop in the bucket," Teague, 161; "wince," Henry Brandon, "A Talk with an 83-Year-Old Enfant Terrible," *NYT*, 6 August 1967, JSP.

13. Brough credits the phrase to EKR not ARL; see his biography, 290. Most other sources credit Alice with it. The percentages vary depending upon the source—but in a backhanded way (because of the era), this is a sort of compliment to ER.

14. These are famous stories, and they appear many places. See, for example, Collier, 345, 387–388; and Teichmann, 156. Brough, 200–298, also contains many of these tales. The first-person quote is from Teague, 161. For the "Mollycoddle" source and ER's response, see Blanche Wiesen Cook, *Eleanor Roosevelt* (New York: Viking, 1999), 2:385–386.

15. Hickock tale from Belle Roosevelt Diaries, 16 April 1943, KBR; Mary Borah, *Elephants and Donkeys* (Moscow, University Press of Idaho, 1976), 141; Henrietta Nesbitt, *White House Diary* (New York: Doubleday, 1949), 172; dinner invitation example, ER to ARL, 7 December 1934, JSP; see also Alice's letter to ER, dated

from the New Deal years, in which Alice thanks ER for volunteering to "look out for Paulina" while Alice was not in Washington (25 October, [?], JSP); "never allow politics," "First Lady Hits Hatreds," *NYT*, 15 November 1938, 12; horrible childhood, author's interview with Kristie Miller, 21 July 1996; "Did you realize," Brough, 298; "could and did damn," Teichmann, 156. If Missy LeHand and FDR were lovers, Alice "insisted" that she "would have heard about it," Brough, 308. Historians have come to different conclusions as to the specifics of an FDR-LeHand relationship.

16. For this last idea, see Collier, 331, 333.

17. Teague, 159.

18. See the handwritten note to "Alma" by ARL at bottom of I. J. Roberts to Alma Zimbalist, 9 March 1936, ARLC, for an example of her symphony work.

19. "Totenberg Hailed in Capital Debut," *NYT*, 8 November 1935, 18. In this article, the violin is identified as a Stradivarius. Alice Dows to ARL, n.d., JSP ("Here is the insurance for a year on the violin...."); "That's the violin," Author's interview with Roman Totenberg, 24 March 2005. Borah's presence, "Garners Honored at White House," *NYT*, 3 January 1936, 22. The occasion was the president's dinner in honor of the vice president, Nick's old friend Cactus Jack Garner.

20. Author's interview with Roman Totenberg; "the work of some skilled copyist," Rembert Wurlitzer to ARL, 31 May 1957, JSP. See also Scott Simon's interview with Roman Totenberg, 22 June 1996, www.npr.org/news/specials/fatherday/. Alice at concerts, Brough, 289. See also Blair Bolles, "Symphony on Potomac," *NYT*, 30 July 1939, X5. Alice did not "hate" Nick, nor was she "hurt" by him at the time of his death (Carol Felsenthal, *Alice Roosevelt Longworth* [New York: G. P.

Putnam's Sons, 1988], 168). Loaning the violin to a protégé of Nick's former lover is more her style. The name of the violinist who borrowed the violin is Charles Tuger or Luger (?). See his thank-you letter to ARL, 17 June 1957, JSP.

21. J. Timberlake Gibson, "The Million Dollar Drop-Out," *Washingtonian*, April 1976, 43.

22. "Book Notes," *NYT*, 23 September 1932, 20; Teague, xvi; Charles Scribner's Sons to ARL, 9 December 1932, JSP. See Loring A. Schuler to ARL, 15 March 1935, for the column ideas; 22 June 1934 for the editing, both ARLC; ARL to Belle Hagner, 6 December 1933, PHP.

23. "Mary B. Eddy Voted 'Greatest Woman,'" *NYT*, 21 December 1932, 21; "Mrs. Longworth Wins Prize Drawn by Her," *NYT*, 18 December 1933, 17; "Alice Roosevelt Sears Notables of Former Days," *Chicago Tribune*, 28 October 1933, 3; Robert Van Gelder, "Books of the Times," *NYT*, 28 October 1933, 13; Edward M. Kingsbury, "Alice Longworth's Vivid Story," *NYT*, 5 November 1933, BR 1; ARL to John T. McCutcheon, 6 December 1933, John T. McCutcheon Papers; Newberry Library, Chicago. Lowden thought the book "full of interest and charm from cover to cover." Frank O. Lowden to ARL, 17 October 1940, Papers of Frank O. Lowden, Special Collections Library, University of Chicago. McClure, founder of the magazine that bore his name, said that he "enjoyed the book very much." Further, he thought her articles "could render a very great service to the country." Samuel McClure to ARL, 3 February 1936, McClure Manuscripts, Manuscripts Department, Lilly Library, Indiana University, Bloomington. See the scanned flyer on http://sdrc.lib.uiowa.edu/traveling-culture/chaul/jpg/longworth/1/1.jpg, courtesy of the Special Collections Department, University of

Iowa Libraries; GOP women, May S. Baldwin to ARL, 21 January 1933, ARLC; Mayme C. Althouse to ARL, 21 January 1936, ARLC; Wayne Whipple and ARL, *The Story of the White House and Its Home Life* (Boston: Dwinell-Wright, 1937).

24. The advertisement can be found on page D7, 16 October 1932, *Chicago Tribune*, and on X8 of the same day's *NYT*.

25. TRJR, "Foreword," in *Desk Drawer Anthology*, Alice Roosevelt Longworth and Theodore Roosevelt Jr., eds. (New York: Doubleday, Doran, 1938), xiii–xix.

26. ARL, "What Are the Women Up To?," *Ladies' Home Journal*, 51 (March 1934): 9, 120, 122. ARL's journalist writings pale in comparison to the hundreds of articles her cousin Eleanor wrote.

27. ER to Corinne Alsop, 15 January 1936, reel 1, ER Papers on microfilm; "I don't want anything," Brough, 292.

28. ER, *This I Remember* (New York: Harper & Brothers, 1949), 219–220. See also Cook, 2:416. James A. Farley to ARL, 15 February 1974, JSP; Genevieve Forbes Herrick, "Alice Fails to Applaud Cousin Frank," *Chicago Tribune*, 7 January 1934, E3.

29. Nesbitt, 29.

30. "How disagreeable," ARL preservation tape, ICD 16020, JSP; "There is nothing to that," "First Lady Tells of Joining Guild," *NYT*, 6 January 1937, 16; royal visit, "Simplicity Marks the Garden Party," *NYT*, 9 June 1939, 1; "miserable worm," Brough, 292.

31. Harold L. Ickes, *The Autobiography of a Curmudgeon* (New York: Reynal & Hitchcock, 1943), 244; art exhibit, undated, untitled clipping, JSP.

32. "Beautiful, charming," Teague, 157–58; "did not believe in knowing," Brough, 247; "had so little enjoyment," Teague, 160; for Laura Delano, see Goodwin, 611; "The Reporters: Jonathan Aitken Interview with Alice Roosevelt

Longworth," Yorkshire Television, [January 1969]. In this interview, ARL recalls FDR and Lucy at her home.

33. ER could not be affectionate, author interview with Michael Teague, 3 August 1989. Teague thought that "Mrs. L understood Eleanor better than ER understood herself—or cared to understand herself." For Griselda moods, see ER, *The Autobiography of Eleanor Roosevelt* (New York: Harper & Row, 1978), 59–60. Kenneth S. Davis's description is useful here: "Her tendency to withdraw wholly into herself when hurt, assuming the role of martyr as she raised a wall of silence against those she thought responsible, refusing all their efforts to communicate. She called it her 'Griselda mood.' It was cruelly vengeful. For all its seeming passivity, it was the most devastating kind of psychological aggression when focused upon people of sensitive conscience who deeply cared for her." Kenneth S. Davis, *FDR: Into the Storm, 1937–1940* (New York: Random House, 1993), 303.

34. Teague, 160.

35. Robert L. Mason, "Capital Club Welcomes Chosen Few," *Bethlehem (Penn.) Globe-Times*, n.p., from the George Washington University Alumni Web site, http://www.gwu.edu/~alumni/images/photo/retro. See also "Mrs. J. F. Curtis to Become Club Hostess in F St. Home," 9 April 1933; and Mary Van Rensselaer Thayer, "Though Cozy, It Is Important," *Washington Post and Times Herald*, 2 March 1955, from the same Web site; see also "The F Street Club, 'a Nice Quiet Place,'" *NYT*, 26 April 1983, B6.

36. "Alice Longworth Sails for Europe," *NYT*, 18 July 1935, 21; "Thousands in Rush to Hear Roosevelt," *NYT*, 23 May 1935, 2. ARL, "The National Scene," unidentified newspaper, 4 June 1936, JSP. Ezra Pound to WEB, 10 October 1935, in Sarah C. Holmes, ed. *The Correspondence*

of Ezra Pound and Senator William Borah (Chicago: University of Illinois Press, 2001), 42.

37. Fred W. Carpenter to ARL, 9 January 1936, ARLC.

38. "You can always tell," ARL, "The National Scene," unidentified newspaper, 11 June 1936, JSP.

39. ARL, "The National Scene," unidentified newspaper, 28 May 1936, JSP. For quotes in the following two paragraphs: "a direct move," 15 February 1936; "American agriculture," 9 January 1936; "black soil magic," 11 January 1936; Paraguay, 13 March 1936, all JSP.

40. "As for Mrs Roosevelt's," Edith Dickey Moses to ARL, 10 January 1936, ARLC; Margaret Cobb Ailshie to ARL, 21 January 1936, ARLC. Idahoan Ailshie was a friend of Alice's from the First Daughter days. "We have been paying," James Telfer, letter to the editor, undated and unidentified; attached to Paul Block to ARL, 23 January 1936, ARLC. This document was also attached to E. C. Vandyke to ARL and identified by Vandyke as being from the *Milwaukee Journal*, 22 January 1936, ARLC; "keen and clear cut," A. H. Clambrey to ARL, 24 January 1935, ARLC; "why am I," William D. Sohier to ARL, 23 January 1936, ARLC.

41. "I cannot afford," Elizabeth T. Cedergren to ARL, 20 January 1936, ARLC; "woman columnist," James E. Coleman to ARL, 22 January 1926, ARLC.

42. Several letters remark upon Alice's courage. See, for example, Catherine Burton Spenser to ARL, 16 January 1936, ARLC; for "good for" the U.S.A., Laura Winans McDaniel, 31 January 1936, ARLC. For comparisons to TR, see Fred B. Jacobs to ARL, 29 January 1936; Arthur R. Atkinson to ARL, 22 January 1936; J. T. McGuire to ARL, 18 January 1936; all ARLC; "candidates picked out," James H. Throop to ARL, 30 January 1936, ARLC.

43. ARL, "The National Scene," 18 June 1936, unidentified newspaper, JSP.

44. Unidentified poem, sent to ARL from "R.C.," 20 November 1943, JSP.

45. James Reston, *Deadline: A Memoir* (New York: Random House, 1991), 104; the poem "Rejected" was attributed to James Knupp, n.d., JSP.

46. M. V. Atwood to V. V. McNitt, 19 February 1936. See also George Fergus Kelley to ARL, 16 April 1936. Kelley wanted to see her "get more punch" in her articles. "This seems to be the universal criticism," he wrote. Both letters are in the ARLC.

47. "Certainly writes well," Cook, 2:433; "Eleanor vs. Alice," unidentified clipping, n.d., NLP; "terribly shy" is from ARL preservation tape, ICD 16022, 28 June 1967, JSP; Elise French Linn to ARL, n.d., ARLC (emphasis in original).

48. Jonathan Mitchell, "Borah Knows Best," *New Republic*, 29 January 1936, 334; WEB to Ezra Pound, 3 January 1934, in Holmes, ed., 4; Tim Redman, *Ezra Pound and Italian Fascism* (Cambridge: Cambridge University Press, 1991), 89.

49. For Borah as TR's heir, see, for example, the poem written by Joe Butin, 25 February 1936, WEBLC; William Hard, "Foreword" in William E. Borah, *Bedrock: Views on Basic National Problems* (Washington, D.C.: National Home Library Foundation, 1936), 5, 6.

50. Frederic C. Walcott to ARL, 6 April 1934, JSP; "15th Anniversary to Be Marked Saturday By Women's National Republican Club," *NYT,* 12 January 1936, N8. See also Kathleen McLaughlin, "New Year Finds Women's Organizations Planning Many New Activities," *NYT,* 5 January 1936, N7. For Liberty League dinner, "National Figures Among the Guests," *NYT,* 26 January 1936, 37. "R. A. Taft Is Named Ohio 'Favorite Son,'" *NYT,* 28 February 1936, 2.

51. "Mrs. Longworth a Delegate," *NYT,* 14 May 1936, 6; " 'Princess Alice' Arrives and Doubles in Brass as Delegate and Writer," unidentified clipping, 5 June 1936, JSP; Kathleen McLaughlin, "Women Outnumber Men at Roll-Call," *NYT,* 7 June 1936, 33; Arthur Krock, "Steiwer Avoids Rifts," *NYT,* 10 June 1936, 1; for Reeves, see Kathleen McLaughlin, "Women Maintain Leading Roles in Many Phases of the Convention Activities," *NYT,* 11 June 1936, 16.

52. ARL, "The National Scene," unidentified newspaper, 15 June 1936, JSP.

53. Mary Roberts Rinehart to ARL, 5 April 1936, ARLC; "Republicans Summon Women's 1919 Council," *NYT,* 19 August 1936, 13.

54. "Spirit of black," ARL, "The National Scene," unidentified newspaper, 26 June 1936, JSP; "to assume a leadership," and "Fuehrer, Duce, Roosevelt," ARL, "The National Scene," unidentified newspaper, 30 June 1936, JSP; dare, ARL, "The National Scene," unidentified newspaper, 25 June 1936, JSP.

55. "Services Here Honor Quentin Roosevelt," *NYT,* 15 July 1936, 21; "whiskey for breakfast," Edward J. Renehan, Jr., *The Lion's Pride* (New York: Oxford University Press, 1998), 229.

56. "Oyster Bay Shrine Visited by Landon," *NYT,* 30 October 1936, 17. At tea were Edith; Ethel and Dick and their daughter Edith; Belle; and Ted and Eleanor.

57. "Citizens Join Broadcast," *NYT,* 3 November 1936, 14.

58. Alexander Woollcott to Ralph Hates, 28 September 1936, in Woollcott's *The Letters of Alexander Woollcott* (New York: Viking, 1944), 171. For the gloating, see his letter to Stephen Early, 20 October 1936, 172. "Imminent demise," Lewis L. Gould, *Grand Old Party* (New York: Random House, 2003), 274.

59. Edwin P. Hoyt, *Alexander Woollcott* (New York: Abelard-Schuman, 1968), 283. "Notes of the Fair," *NYT*, 18 November 1937, 21.

60. American Tobacco Company: Your Hit Parade and Sweepstakes, 3 February 1937, JSP.

61. June Bingham, "Before the Colors Fade," *American Heritage*, February 1969, 76.

Chapter 19: **"I Believe in the Preservation of This Republic"**

1. Alice was unable to forget the role she thought Borah played in bringing Harding to power in 1920. See ARL, "The National Scene," unidentified newspaper, 3 June 1936, JSP.

2. Borah's speech appears in Marian C. McKenna, *Borah* (Ann Arbor: University of Michigan Press, 1961), 370. The rest of the information here comes from McKenna, 370–372. See also "Borah Dies," *Chicago Tribune*, 20 January 1940, 1; "William E. Borah, Senator 33 Years, Is Dead in Capital," *NYT*, 20 January 1940, 1.

3. *Acceptance of the Statue of William Edgar Borah Presented by the State of Idaho* (Washington, D.C.: Government Printing Office, 1948), 25.

4. *Acceptance of the Statue*, 26, 27.

5. "President Pays Tribute to Dean of U.S. Senate," *Chicago Tribune*, 20 January 1940, 12.

6. Mary Borah, of course, received all the formal sympathy notes, such as the one from former First Lady LHH, n.d., LHHP; for funeral train, see "Idaho Plans Day of Mourning," *NYT*, 23 January 1940, 12.

7. "Frightful struggle," WEB to ARL, n.d., JSP; "read in my message," WEB to ARL, n.d., JSP.

8. "Alice Roosevelt Longworth's Political Intensity Grows," unidentified clipping, n.d., JSP; ARL, pencil fragment, n.d. ("We must get the power of decision…"), JSP.

9. "Portable university," Richard Langham Riedel, *Halls of the Mighty* (New York: Robert B. Luce, 1969), 149; Robert A. Taft to ARL, 7 December 1939, in Clarence E. Wunderlin Jr., ed., *The Papers of Robert A. Taft, 1939–1944* (Kent, Ohio: Kent State University Press, 2001), 2:95; Willkie quote from Lewis L. Gould, *Grand Old Party* (New York: Random House, 2003), 280.

10. ARL, pencil fragment, n.d., JSP.

11. ARL to TRJR, 26 August 1939, TRJRP.

12. Fish quote from Harold B. Hinton, "Borah Declares Real Neutrality Impossible for Us," *NYT*, 22 April 1939, 1; Elizabeth Wheeler Colman, *Mrs. Wheeler Goes to Washington* (Helena, Mont.: Falcon Press, 1989), 177.

13. Robert Ingrim, "Alice Roosevelt Longworth," draft, 12 June 1946, for *Die Weltwoche*, 3, JSP; Robert James Maddox, *William E. Borah and American Foreign Policy* (Baton Rouge: Louisiana State University Press, 1969), 226.

14. Arthur Schlesinger Jr., *A Life in the Twentieth Century* (New York: Houghton Mifflin, 2000), 238.

15. Wayne S. Cole, *America First* (New York: Octagon Books, 1971), 7–8.

16. "We demand that Congress," Justus D. Doenecke, ed., *In Danger Undaunted* (Stanford, Calif.: Hoover Institution Press, 1990), 7; Bill Kauffman interview with Robert Douglas Stuart Jr. in Ruth Sarles, *A Story of America First* (Westport, Conn.: Praeger, 2003), 208; see also Colman, 193–96.

17. "America First Creed," in Sarles, lv–lvi.

18. Robert Douglas Stuart Jr. interview in Sarles, 211; for members, see "Contribution Card" and 1940 stationery in the

Papers of Frank O. Lowden, Special Collections Library, University of Chicago and Colman, 194; Bernard K. Johnpoll, *Pacifist's Progress* (Chicago: Quadrangle Books, 1970), 228–31; "Reidy" Reid, "America First" (New York: Dixie Music Publishing, c. 1941), Papers of Frank O. Lowden, Special Collections Library University of Chicago.

19. Sarles, 4; Doenecke, xii. For the number of members, see Wayne S. Cole, "The America First Committee," *Journal of the Illinois State Historical Society* XLIV, 1 (Spring 1951): 312.

20. Robert A. Taft to Robert Hunter, 20 November 1940, Robert Hunter Papers, Indiana Historical Society, Indianapolis; "America First Committee: Aims and Activities," ARP; Robert L. Bliss, America First Cmmittee [hereafter AFC] Bulletin #281, Robert E. Wood Papers, HHPL.

21. "How to Organize Chapters of the AFC," 4, ARP; the 3 December 1940 resolution concerning Ford can be found in Sarles, 65.

22. "How to Organize Chapters of the AFC," 1.

23. R. E. Wood, America First press release, n.d., Robert E. Wood Papers, HHPL. In fact, the AFC felt so indebted to the *Tribune* that Stuart wrote to Lillian Gish suggesting that she write a letter of thanks to Colonel Robert McCormick. See Robert Douglas Stuart Jr. to Lillian Gish, 22 July 1941, Papers of Lillian Gish, LC.

24. James Reston, *Deadline* (New York: Random House, 1991), 103–104; see AFC Bulletin #190, 9 April 1941, AFC; Geraldine Buchanan Parker to "Dear Fellow Citizen," n.d., Robert E. Wood Papers, HHPL.

25. J. H. Reis, M.D., to Lillian Gish, 30 March 1941, Lillian Gish Papers, LC. See Lillian Gish's thank-you to ARL, n.d., JSP.

26. Lindberg at the Longworths, Betty Beale, "Mrs. Longworth Can No Longer Resist the Temptation!" clipping, n.d., JSP; Charles Lindbergh's speech is printed in full in Sarles, 65–69. The quote begins on page 67.

27. The meeting was held on 18 September. Lindbergh was also present. Sarles, 56. ARL appeared to have missed more National Committee meetings than she attended. She was not present at the March 1941 meeting, the 28 November 1941 meeting, or the 11 December 1941 meeting. See Frank O. Lowden Papers, Special Collections Library, University of Chicago. News release, "Chapters Please Release Immediately," 24 September 1941, Robert E. Wood Papers, HHPL.

28. "Condemn his speech," quoted in Johnpoll, 231; "89%" Sarles, 56; Hyman Lischner's letter is printed in full in Sarles, 64–65. On page 49, Lischner is described as a "physician of Los Angeles and former president of B'nai B'rith at San Diego." Lindbergh's speech written six months earlier, Sarles, 57; "Lindbergh, Willkie, and the Jews," *Chicago Tribune*, n.d.; text in Robert E. Wood Papers, HHPL; For a list of noninterventionist Jews see Sarles, 49–50; "politically unwise" Cole, "The America First Committee," 321.

29. "Lindbergh Views Hotly Assailed," *NYT*, 31 August 1941, 18.

30. Kermit Roosevelt to Ethel Roosevelt Derby, 7 February 1941, RFPH; Kermit Roosevelt to Wendell K. Willkie, 3 May 1941, KBR; Alexander Woollcott, *The Letters of Alexander Woollcott* (New York: Viking, 1944), 275; Maclean story from Katharine Graham, *Personal History* (New York: Knopf, 1997), 156; Alsop quote from Robert W. Merry, *Taking on the World* (New York: Viking, 1996), 90.

31. For Ted and Eleanor, see "Minutes of a Meeting of Executive Committee of New York Chapter America First, 8 April

1941," ARP; Ted and WWII, Edward J. Renehan, Jr., *The Lion's Pride* (New York: Oxford University Press, 1998), 228–29; for Ruth's involvement, see AFC Bulletin #691, 19 November 1941, Robert E. Wood Papers, HHPL. For Ruth's donation, see Cole, "The America First Committee," 315. "America First Group Names Some Donors," *New York Herald Tribune*, 12 March 1941; clipping in the Robert E. Wood Papers, HHPL, lists Barnes and McCutcheon.

32. Henry L. Stimson and McGeorge Bundy, *On Active Service in Peace and War* (New York: Harper & Brothers, 1947–1948), 375; Cole, "The America First Committee," 305.

33. "It is hardly fair," typed fragment, n.d. ("The result of the election last November..."), JSP. Belle Roosevelt Diaries, 16 April 1943, KBR.

34. Robert E. Wood to John T. Flynn, 12 December 1941, ARP; "The Debate Is Over," *NYT*, 13 December 1941, ARP.

35. Eleanor Butler Roosevelt to ARL, 2 August [?], JSP; Eleanor Butler Roosevelt, *Day Before Yesterday* (Garden City, N.Y.: Doubleday, 1959), 399–400.

36. Harold V. Boyle, "Lt. Quentin Roosevelt Wounded in Action on Tunisian Front," unidentified clipping, JSP. For the bullet story from the family, TRJR to Richard and Ethel Roosevelt Derby, 29 March 1943; TRJR to Ethel Roosevelt Derby, [?] March 1943; both RFPH; TRJR to Ethel Roosevelt Derby, 10 February 1943, ERDP, for the promotion. For a cheery letter to Alice, see Quentin Roosevelt to ARL, 29 March 1943, JSP; Grace Stackpole Roosevelt to EKR, 25 January 1943, Archibald Bulloch Roosevelt Family Papers, Harvard University.

37. Belle Roosevelt Diaries, 16 April 1943, KBR.

38. Joseph W. Alsop, *"I've Seen the Best of It"* (New York: W. W. Norton, 1992),

120; Frank Kent to ARL, 21 October 1944, and 9 July 1944 JSP; "Frank R. Kent, 80, Columnist, Dead," *NYT*, 15 April 1958, 33.

39. Bill Walton knew John L. Lewis and said this about him. Author's interview with Walton, 27 May 1994.

40. See Michael Teague, *Mrs. L.* (Garden City, N.Y.: Doubleday, 1981) 187, for Alice's quotes in this paragraph; Elsa Maxwell, "Elsa Maxwell's Party Line," *New York Post*, 21 January 1944, 12, JSP.

41. All quotes from JLL to ARL, 8 October 1943, JSP. The "Dear Aquarian" salutation is 17 July 1943, JSP.

42. JLL to ARL, [n.d. 1944], JSP.

43. JLL to ARL, 26 December 1944, JSP. Lewis was in a high-rise hotel in Indianapolis; Alice was home. ALL stood for Alice Lee Longworth.

44. JLL to ARL, 16 October 1943, JSP.

45. Melvin Dubofsky and Warren Van Tine, *John L. Lewis* (Chicago: University of Illinois Press, 1987), 285; JLL to ARL, 16 October 1943, JSP.

46. "Doubted whether Franklin," Belle Roosevelt Diaries, 29 March 1943; FDR's view of Winant, Belle Roosevelt Diaries, 20–21 March 1943, KBR.

47. Archibald Roosevelt to Ethel Roosevelt Derby, 26 June 1943, RFPH.

48. "Mrs. Roosevelt, Sr., Gains," *NYT*, 17 November 1935, 17.

49. Sylvia Jukes Morris, *Edith Kermit Roosevelt* (New York: Coward, McCann, & Geoghegan, 1980), chap. 38; "Services Are Held for Gen. Roosevelt," *NYT*, 25 July 1944, 9; Renehan, 233–240; *Medal of Honor Recipients, 1863–1978* (Washington, D.C.: U.S. Government Printing Office, 1979), 668; "Brig. Gen. Roosevelt Dies," *Chicago Tribune*, 14 July 1944, 1.

50. For Archie's service in WWII, see Renehan, 232–33.

Chapter 20: **"Full Sixty Years the World Has Been Her Trade"**

1. "The Reporters: Jonathan Aitken Interview with Alice Roosevelt Longworth," Yorkshire Television, [January 1969].

2. William Fulton, "Wives of Eisenhower's Aides Are Busy Buying New Plumage for Capital Whirl," *Chicago Tribune*, 8 December 1952, B2.

3. Darrah Wunder, "A Funny Thing Happened to Me on the Way to the White House," *Leeword* (September [?]), 4, MssVP2386, CHS.

4. "War is an inevitable thing," "Alice and Ruth Are Here!'" unidentified clipping, 22 June 1944, JSP. Alsop on Mrs. L from Alsop's unpublished memoir, author's possession.

5. ARL preservation tape, ICD 16031, 20 September 1967, JSP. Alice's evening with Hubble, her daughter, and her friends Mildred and Robert Bliss and Mary Beale took place around 1939. By that date, Hubble had published three books of lectures. Alice likely read *The Realm of the Nebulae* (London: Oxford University Press, 1936).

6. Rachel Carson to ARL, 15 June 1951, JSP.

7. Author's interview with Bill Walton, 27 May 1994.

8. ARL preservation tape, ICD 16031, 20 September 1967, JSP.

9. Larry McMurtry, *Walter Benjamin at the Dairy Queen* (New York: Simon & Schuster, 1999), 138.

10. Hope Ridings Miller, "Capital Whirl," *Washington Post*, 18 June 1942; "Paulina Longworth Makes Her Debut at Cincinnati Club," unidentified clipping, [1942]; "Paulina Longworth Makes Bow Tonight at Cincinnati," *Washington Evening Star*, [1942], all JSP. Angela Meeske, a contemporary of Paulina's, recalled that on the night of the debut, "Alice was mighty imposing, but very agreeable." Angela Meeske to author, n.d. 2004. On the engagement, see "Engagement of Interest," *Cincinnati Enquirer*, August 1944, Paulina Longworth Sturm Princeton File, CHS; Judith Cass, "Ex-Chicagoan to Wed Miss Longworth," *Chicago Tribune*, 7 August 1944, 13.

11. Kermit Roosevelt to John C. Greenway, 28 November 1924, Greenway AHS. "Alice Longworth Asks Mellon to Spare Building," *NYT*, 16 February 1936, 28. It was the Hunt and Riding School, at Twenty-second and P Streets in Washington, D.C. Author's interview with David Mitchell, 26 October 2001; and with Bazy Tankersley, 19 July 1996. Mrs. Tankersley thinks that Paulina's stutter may have been the result of her having been forced to use her right hand when she was innately left-handed, as mentioned earlier. Like her godfather, David Mitchell, Joanna Sturm believes that her mother was very fond of "Waldie" (Dorothy Waldron), and that the affection was returned. Author's interview with Joanna Sturm, 11 June 2006.

12. Margaret [Blake?], 10 August 1943, JSP. See also Herbert Bayard Swope to ARL, 18 August 1944, JSP; JSG to ARL, 10 August 1944, JSP.

13. Howard Teichmann, *Alice* (Englewood Cliffs, N.J.: Prentice Hall, 1979), 189. For more about "Dewey was a frightful bore—an incompetent little man," see ARL preservation tapes, ICD 16035, [summer 1968], JSP; Clayton Fritchie, "A Politician Must Watch His Wit," *NYT*, 3 July 1960, SM8.

14. Isabel Kinnear Griffin to ARL, 13 November 1968, JSP. For an example of Alice denying the quip, this one from her ninetieth year, see Norma Milligan, "She Says What She Thinks," *Modern Maturity*, June–July 1974, 10. Alice told Michael Teague that she thought she had overheard

it at a party. See Michael Teague, *Mrs. L* (Garden City, N.Y.: Doubleday, 1981), xiv.

15. Taft helped Alice find hotel rooms. See Robert A. Taft to Katharine Kennedy Brown, 18 May 1944, in Clarence E. Wunderlin Jr., ed. *The Papers of Robert A. Taft, Volume 2, 1939–1944*, (Kent, Ohio: Kent State University Press, 2001), 548; "Alice and Ruth Are Here!'" For Paulina as a page, see Thalia, "Chicago Host to Many Noted G.O.P. Women," *Chicago Tribune*, 2 July 1944, E1; Penciled draft, n.d. "There seems to be at least a serious…," JSP.

16. For Bricker, see Lewis L. Gould, *Grand Old Party* (New York: Random House, 2003), 296; Richard Norton Smith, *Thomas E. Dewey and His Times* (New York: Simon & Schuster, 1982), 278–279. Benzedrine is an amphetamine. "Outthink almost everyone," is from Richard Langham Riedel, *Halls of the Mighty* (New York: Robert B. Luce, 1969), 150. See Robert A. Taft to Henry F. Pringle, 4 March 1938, in *The Papers of Robert A. Taft, Volume 1*, (Kent, Ohio: Kent State University Press, 1997), 559. See also "Taft Takes Critic on Congress Tour," *NYT*, 16 June 1944, 21; Marcia Winn, "Front Views & Profiles," *Chicago Tribune*, 30 June 1944, 10.

17. "Politics Losing Hatred's Spice, Alice Laments," *Chicago Tribune*, 23 June 1944, 9; Author's interview with Robert Hellman, 25 April 2005.

18. "Miss Longworth Becomes Bride in East Today," *Chicago Tribune*, 26 August 1944, 13; Katherine McCormick Sturm to ARL, 28 August 1944, JSP.

19. Ruth's health failing, Albert Simms to ARL, 16 February 1945, JSP; Bazy McCormick Miller to ARL, 8 March 1945, JSP. See "Mrs. Simms, G.O.P. Leader, Dies in Sleep," *Chicago Tribune*, 1 January 1945, 1; "Ruth Hanna Simms, Republican

Figure," *NYT*, 1 January 1945, 19. Triny was Ruth's eldest daughter—Katharine Augusta McCormick. She married Courtlandt Barnes Jr. and became publisher of *Common Sense*. Ruth and Alice as monkeys, author's interview with Bazy Tankersley, 31 May 2006. See also Kristie Miller, *Ruth Hanna McCormick* (Albuquerque: University of New Mexico Press, 1992) 132. "Freud and religion and sex," 2 August 1917, ARL Diary, JSP.

20. ER to ARL, 18 April 1945, JSP; Joseph Alsop, *I've Seen the Best of It* (New York: W. W. Norton, 1992), 91.

21. Isabella Greenway King to John Selmes Greenway, 20 August 1945, Greenway AHS. For more on Alice's worries about Paulina and Alex, see JLL to ARL, 21 August 1945, JSP; JLL to ARL, 12 August 1945, JSP.

22. "For Relief to Austria," *NYT*, 1 November 1945, 25.

23. David Mitchell, Alex Sturm's college roommate, said the "marriage was in terrible trouble because of alcohol." Author's interview with David Mitchell, 26 October 2001. JLL to ARL, n.d., 1946, JSP.

24. "Mrs. Edith Roosevelt 85 Years Old Today," *NYT*, 6 August 1946, 35; EKR to ARL, 27 August 1946, JSP.

25. Archie Roosevelt to ARL, 6 August 1950, JSP; Edith Kermit Roosevelt Barmine to ARL, 25 September 1948, JSP. Clipping enclosed, Cholly Knickerbocker, "The Smart Set," 23 September 1948, *New York Journal-American*; Selwa Roosevelt, *Keeper of the Gate* (New York: Simon & Schuster, 1990), 159.

26. Philip B. Perlman to ARL, 24 August 1951, JSP; Felix Frankfurter to ARL, n.d.; 15 January 1955; 15 July 1955; 3 December 1955; all JSP; Frances Spatz and David Camelon, "Legendary Ladies: Rebellious 'Princess Alice,'" *American Weekly*, 12 November 1950, 25.

27. Robert Ingrim, "Alice Roosevelt Longworth," draft, 12 June 1946, for *Die Weltwoche*, 5, and 6, JSP.

28. C. D. Bachelor to ARL, n.d., JSP; for a reproduction of the cartoon, see Teague, 192; online transcript of Walter Trohan interview by Jerry N. Hess, 7 October 1979, 61, 62; Harry S Truman Presidential Library, Independence, Missouri, http://www.trumanlibrary.org/oralhist/trohan.htm#transcript. See also "Walter Trohan to Head Staff at Convention," *Chicago Tribune*, 6 August 1956, 4. Malcolm Muggeridge to ARL, 24 August 1947, JSP. Muggeridge's conversion to Christianity was a quarter century in his future.

29. See, for example, "These Charming People," *Washington Times-Herald*, 4 June 1944, for a photograph of Senator and Martha Taft, and Cissy and Alice, who are holding hands and smiling. See also Ralph Martin, *Cissy* (New York: Simon & Schuster, 1979), 293–294.

30. Author's interview with Bazy Tankersley, 19 July 1996. See also the following articles from the *Chicago Tribune*: "Ruth Elizabeth McCormick to Be Married," 24 June 1941, 15; "Miss Ruth Elizabeth McCormick Wed in Little Country Church," 30 August 1941, 11; "Ruth McCormick Miller and Husband Buy a Paper," 12 October 1946, 13; "Illinois Judge Grants Divorce to Mrs. Miller," 13 January 1951, 10; "Newsman Wed to Mrs. Miller in Washington," 1 June 1951, 4.

31. Edith Hamilton to ARL, 28 January 1947 and 8 February 1951, both JSP; JLL to ARL, 9 February 1947, JSP.

32. For this story, see James A. Michener, *The World Is My Home* (New York: Random House, 1992), 287–288. For a competing story, see Peter Khiss, "Hemingway Lost Pulitzer in 1941," *NYT*, 20 April 1966, 49, which states that Krock, in response to ARL's telephone call, "forcefully relayed the opinion" to the rest of the committee, which then resulted in Michener's winning the prize.

33. William Wright, *The Washington Game* (New York: E. P. Dutton, 1974), 21, 20; author interview with David Mitchell.

34. "Draw people out," Bazy Tankersley quoted in Kristie Miller e-mail to author, 22 May 2003; "It was fun," author interview with Janie McLaughlin, 26 May 1994.

35. Dean Acheson to Joseph Alsop, 26 May 1947, JSAP. On Acheson's resemblance to the tiger, see Page-A-Day Notes to author from Joanna Sturm and Kristie Miller, n.d. 2003, and "The Reporters: Jonathan Aitken Interview with Alice Roosevelt Longworth," Yorkshire Television, [January 1969].

36. Ingrim, 4.

37. Ruth Montgomery, "D.C. Wash," *Chicago Tribune*, 10 March 1951, 7. Alice and Martha Taft were photographed in 1947, for example, at the hearings on "Greek-Turkish loans," and the Senate Education and Labor Committee. See "Personalities," *NYT*, 6 April 1947, SM8 and 16 February 1947, SM24. William Moore, "Invite Yourself Out, A Senator Advises Pauley," *Chicago Tribune*, 21 February 1946, 11; Phillip Dodd, "Leahy Helped on Plane Deal, Kaiser Claims," *Chicago Tribune*, 30 July 1947, 1.

38. "White House Wins on Reorganization," *NYT*, 19 March 1938, 1; Willard Edwards, "Urges Horse Whipping of Wheeler Smearers," *Chicago Tribune*, 18 July 1946, 1.

39. Gould, 311.

40. Louis Starr, "Hits Government," *NYT*, 8 March 1947, 1 (for "extended his hand") and 3 (for the "wordplay").

41. JLL to ARL, 16 January 1952 and 31 December 1957; "tired man," JLL to ARL, 27 November 1945; John Chamberlain to ARL, 21 August 1949 and; JLL to ARL, 7 September 1949, all JSP.

42. ARL quoted in James Brough, *Princess Alice* (Boston: Little, Brown, 1975), 192. The original source is a *Boston Globe* interview, 17 August 1975, JSP; "Be subtle," JLL to ARL, 17 May 1948, JSP.

43. The information in this paragraph comes from "Our Backing Asked for U.S. of Europe," *NYT*, 18 April 1947, 12, and "New Group Backs Federated Europe," *NYT*, 24 April 1947, 3.

44. Harold L. Ickes to Joseph Alsop, 21 July 1948, JSAP.

45. "Film Stars, Writers, and Artists Promise to Work for Taft," *Chicago Tribune*, 27 April 1948, 8. "Women in their 20's Organized for Taft," *NYT*, 23 April 1948, 16; "Spur 'Twenties for Taft,'" *Chicago Tribune*, 24 April 1948, 2. Ruth's daughter Bazy Tankersley has no memory of Paulina being meaningfully involved with the campaign, or interested at all in politics. Author telephone interview with Bazy Tankersley, 1 June 2006. Didn't vote for Dewey ARL to Joseph Lash, 27 January 1972, JSP; "Soufflé" "New New Deal," *NYT*, 14 November 1948, E1. In 1945, when Truman ascended to the presidency, Alice Longworth may have said, "Henry Wallace talked about the common man, and lost the Presidency. Harry Truman was the common man, and got it." It would have been just as appropriate in 1948. Charles Poore, "Common Man-Hunt," *NYT*, 19 September 1948, BR5.

46. "My strength," EKR to ARL, 27 April 1944, JSP; "Dearest Alice," EKR to ARL, n.d. [1948], JSP.

47. ARL, scrap on The Ritz-Carlton's stationery, 12 February [1948], JSP.

48. Dorothy Pound to ARL, 4 April 1949, JSP; Joseph Alsop to Robert Lowell, 11 March 1949, and Robert Lowell to Joseph Alsop, n.d. [1949], JSAP. For Marcella Comes Winslow, see Teresa Moore, "A Washington Life," *Washington Post Magazine*, 9 July 1989, 27. For Alice's memories, see Jean Vanden Heuvel, "The Sharpest Wit in Washington," *Saturday Evening Post* 238, 24 (4 December 1965), 32.

49. This background information comes from Nathaniel Weyl, *Treason* (Washington, D.C.: Public Affairs Press, 1950) and Tim Redman, *Ezra Pound and Italian Fascism* (Cambridge: Cambridge University Press, 1991). Redman clearly exposes the racism and anti-Semitism of both Ezra and Dorothy Pound.

50. E. Fuller Torrey, *The Roots of Treason* (New York: McGraw Hill, 1984), 219, 239; author's interview with Joanna Sturm, 25 April 2005. Poetry anthology, see J. J. Wilhelm, *Ezra Pound* (University Park: The Pennsylvania State University Press, 1994), 280.

51. Catherine Seelye, ed., *Charles Olson and Ezra Pound* (New York: Viking, 1975), xv. For Olson's phrase, see page 18; for the list of judges instrumental in awarding Pound the Bollingen Prize, see Wilhelm, 277–278. For the controversies, see the rest of that chapter, especially page 280, which also explains that it was Cairns who first brought ARL to see Pound.

52. "Intellectually damaging," Anthony Lewis, "Poets Carry Day for Ezra Pound," *NYT*, 20 April 1958, E7. For Pound's release, see Wilhelm, 308–311; Torrey, 253–60; "Not a danger," Author interview with Robert Hellman, 25 April 2005.

53. For pass, Mary A. Cassidy to ARL, 14 November 1949, JSP; Eleanor Butler Roosevelt to "Lloyd," 17 December 1949, Lewis L. Gould Collection, Monmouth College Archives, Hewes Library, Monmouth College, Monmouth, Illinois; the book Eleanor was reading was probably written by Francis L. Wellman (New York: Macmillan, 1946); "Emily" [no last name] to ARL, 5 November 1950, JSP.

54. Drew Pearson, *Drew Pearson Diaries, 1949–1959* (New York: Holt, Rine-

hart, and Winston, 1974), 171. The entry for 19 June 1951, called Taft, "a great pal of McCarthy's."

55. "Visits Chicago," *Chicago Tribune*, 4 August 1950, 5.

56. "Turn our country away," "Wedemeyer Hails Taft as 'Realist,'" *NYT*, 6 May 1952, 23; "You know where TAFT stands," advertisement, *NYT*, 26 May 1952, 15; Eleanor Page, "Arlington Races Share Spotlight with Visitors," *Chicago Tribune*, 5 July 1952, A3; Eleanor Page, "Meet the Women Leaders at the Convention," *Chicago Tribune*, 7 July 1952, B7; Elizabeth Rannells, "Have You Heard?" *Chicago Tribune*, 20 July 1952, E3.

57. Eisenhower quote, Teague, 194; Richard M. Nixon, *RN*, (New York: Warner Books, 1978), 103–104; the quote is on page 104.

58. "Daughter of a President Helps Eisenhower Drive," *NYT*, 4 October 1952, 8; Dwight D. Eisenhower to ARL, 15 January 1953, JSP; Doug Wead, *All the Presidents' Children* (New York: Atria Books, 2003), 357. According to Wead, John Roosevelt also campaigned for Richard Nixon; ARL to Ethel Roosevelt Derby, 23 December 1952, ERDP.

59. ARL draft of a letter to Eisenhower, 2 February 1953, and Dwight D. Eisenhower to ARL, 14 February 1953, both JSP; Bess Furman, "White House Plans Old Social Whirl," *NYT*, 4 October 1953, 62; Dwight D. Eisenhower to ARL, 14 February 1953, JSP.

60. From Ethel's letter to Alice it appears that the two sisters most often stood opposed to Archie when dissention arose concerning their father. Ethel Roosevelt Derby to ARL, 1 August 1957, JSP. Ruby Douglas Evans, "Sagamore Hill, Old Home of 'T.R.,' Soon May Be a Presidential Shrine," *NYT*, 19 March 1951, 28; Edith Evans Asbury, "T.R.'s Descendants Stir Echo of Past," *NYT*, 15 June 1953, 1;

"The Texts of Eisenhower Speeches at Dartmouth and Oyster Bay," *NYT*, 15 June 1953, 10.

61. John Morton Blum, *A Life with History* (Lawrence: University Press of Kansas, 2004), 89–90.

62. "Hoover to Head Foundation Set Up as Taft Memorial," *Chicago Tribune*, 14 July 1954, 16; "Utah Snubs U.N. Day," *NYT*, 7 October 1954, 7.

63. "With Pat Nixon," Anthony Leviero, "Stennis Asserts McCarthy Poured 'Slime' on Senate," *NYT*, 13 November 1954, 1; "Detached malovolence," unidentified clipping, Hermann Hagedorn, Interviews Relating to Roosevelt Women, Harvard University; Author interview with Bill Walton. See also Teague, 197, for "perfect jay" and 199 for "truckman." The "friend" mentioned was Robert Hellman; author interview with Hellman, 25 April 2005.

64. Richard M. Nixon to ARL, 28 December 1954, JSP. See "The Tragedy of McCarthy," *Los Angeles Times*, 9 December 1954, which Richard Nixon included in his letter to Alice and called "just about the best analysis which has been written with regard to the unhappy ending of the McCarthy affair." For the McCarthy-Pearson fight, Nixon, 170; "political advantage ARL preservation tape, ICD 16021, 25 May 1967, JSP; for invitation assistance, Laura Gross to ARL, 7 February 1951, JSP; "took time off," "Nixon Is Briefed on Key Subjects," *NYT*, 2 October 1955, 49; ARL appointment calendar, 1959, JSP. And the summer months are virtually empty, as Alice would have been out of Washington then. The conversation is about Washington parties in general, but would apply to Longworth's dinners. The quote is from Donald R. Matthews, *U.S. Senators and Their World* (Chapel Hill: The University of North Carolina Press, 1960), 74–75.

65. Halo, Milligan, 11; Dwight D.

Eisenhower to ARL, 21 January 1957, JSP; "The Eisenhowers Star at 4 Dances," *NYT*, 22 January 1957, 18; "Paulina Sturm, Grandchild of T.R., Dies at 31," *Chicago Tribune*, 28 January 1957, 1.

66. See Paul Lewis, "William B. Ruger, 86, Founder of Gun Company," *NYT*, 10 July 2002, A18; Alan Farnham, "He Knew Quality," *Forbes* 170, 4 (2 September 2002), 206–207; "Mrs. Justin Sturm, Novelist's Widow," *NYT*, 8 May 1971, 32, states that Mrs. Sturm "backed her late son, Alexander, in founding a firearms company, the Sturm Ruger Company, in Southport"; Katherine Sturm to ARL, postmarked 28 September 1949, JSP; "Alexander Sturm Dies," *NYT*, 14 November 1951, 31.

67. Dorothy Day, "On Pilgrimage, *Catholic Worker*, 23, 7 (February 1957), 1, 7.

68. Charles G. Herbermann, et al., eds., *Catholic Encyclopedia* (New York: The Gilmary Society, 14:1912), 326. See also Stanislaus Woywod, *A Practical Commentary on the Code of Canon Law* (New York: Joseph F. Wagner, 1957), 545–546. Author's interview with Bill Walton. The information on Paulina Sturm comes from several interviews with Joanna Sturm, Robert Hellman, Bazy Tankersley, and Kristie Miller. See also "Mrs. Longworth [*sic*] Daughter Dies," *NYT*, 28 January 1957, 23; "Paulina Sturm, Grandchild of T.R., Dies at 31," *Chicago Tribune*, 28 January 1957, 1; and "Death Is Ruled Accidental," *NYT*, 7 March 1957, 44. The neighbors at 1222 Twenty-eighth Street, NW, were the late Gertrude Kirkland and Ann Caracristi. The former was an intelligence operative and the latter was deputy director of the National Security Administration and recipient of the Distinguished Civilian Service Award given by the department of defense.

69. ARL to Paulina Longworth Sturm, n.d., JSP; author's interview with Janie McLaughlin, 26 May 1994; Alice Longworth kept the mastectomy quiet. For get-well wishes, see Herbert Hoover to ARL, 20 September 1956; Dwight D. Eisenhower to ARL, 21 January 1957; JLL to ARL, n.d. ("Wed—26—56"), all JSP; "Second chance," author interview with Bazy Tankersley, 19 July 1996.

70. "Aerie," author's interview with Kristie Miller, 10 October 1990. The "free spirit" quote is from Teichmann, 199. ER to ARL, 5 July 1957, JSP; author's interview with Kristie Miller, 10 October 1990.

71. Ethel Roosevelt Derby to ARL, 1 August 1957, JSP.

Chapter 21: **"The Most Fascinating Conversationalist of Our Time"**

1. "Nixon's Favorite Dinner Partner," clipping, [12 February 1974], JSP. See also "Alice at 90 Rated as No. 1 Dinner Partner," *Alexandria* [Va.] *Daily Town Talk*, 13 February 1974, C2, JSP. For John F. Kennedy, see Ethel Kennedy to ARL, 20 January 1967, JSP; and Myra McPherson, "Trio of Individualists Revamp the GOP Image," clipping *Washington Post*, 27 October 1968, JSP. Katharine Graham, *Personal History* (New York: Knopf, 1997), 391.

2. ARL preservation tape, ICD 16021, 25 May 1967, JSP.

3. Joseph W. Alsop, *"I've Seen the Best of It"* (New York: W. W. Norton, 1992), 430; Patricia Nixon to ARL, 18 January 1962, JSP. For examples of the books, see Richard Nixon to ARL, 28 November 1960; Rose Mary Woods to ARL, 12 January 1960; Richard Nixon to ARL, 13 March 1962, all JSP; "more than generous," Richard Nixon to ARL, 24 September 1962, ARL; Henry Brandon, "A Talk with an 83-Year-Old Enfant Terrible," *NYT Magazine*, 6 August 1967, 72.

4. ARL preservation tape, ICD 16037, 26 September 1967, JSP.

5. Arthur Schlesinger Jr., *A Life in the Twentieth Century* (New York: Houghton Mifflin, 2000), 378. See also Arthur Schlesinger Jr. to Joseph Alsop, 9 December 1949, JSAP. See "Random Notes in Washington: Schlesinger Now Half of Faculty," *NYT*, 11 December 1961, 37; "Random Notes in Washington: Fall Term at Hickory Hill U.," *NYT*, 24 September 1962. Alice Longworth's quotes on Schlesinger come from the ARL preservation tape, ICD 16034, 19 August 1968; all other Hickory Hill quotes are from tape ICD 16037, 26 September 1967, JSP. David Halberstam, *The Best and the Brightest* (New York: Random House, 1972), 292.

6. Katharine Graham, *Katharine Graham's Washington* (New York: Random House, 2002), 131–32. Robert W. Merry, *Taking on the World* (New York: Viking), 397.

7. "Passport," Henry Brandon, "Visitors' Guide to the White House," *Sunday Times* (London), 16 July 1967, 13; "even presidents came, Selma Roosevelt, *Keeper of the Gate*, (New York: Simon & Schuster, 1990), 159; James Brough quoted in Howard Teichmann, *Alice* (Englewood Cliffs, N.J.: Prentice Hall, 1979), 197; for the "classified tidbits," Felix Frankfurter to ARL, 19 December 1960, JSP; Robert Bob Kintner to ARL, 20 July 1966, JSP; Kintner to Joseph Alsop, 7 February 1950, JSAP; Roosevelt, 159.

8. Roosevelt, 159; Ethel Roosevelt Derby to ARL, [1950], JSP; Ethel Kennedy to ARL, [1962], JSP; A. Robert Smith and Eric Sevareid, "Washington After Five," *Chicago Tribune*, 20 February 1966, S28.

9. Jean Vanden Heuvel, "The Sharpest Wit in Washington," *Saturday Evening Post* 238, 24 (4 December 1965), 30; her recipe was quoted widely: "Take a loaf of good unsliced bread.... Butter with sweet butter. Cut a thin slice with a sharp knife. Repeat." It can be found in the *Kennedy Center Performing Artists Cookbook* (Washington, D.C.: Museum Press, 1973), 169. For the loudly boiling teapot, see Michael Teague *Mrs. L* (Garden City, N.Y.: Doubleday, 1981), ix and x. Teague makes the point that Mrs. L and guests could ignore the boiling water, and one can hear it on the preservation tapes; for teas, author's interview with Janie McLaughlin, 26 May 1994.

10. "Face is mobile," Nicholas Von Hoffman, "Snap-Shots at the Hot Shoppe," *Washington Post*, 26 February 1967, 7. Henry Brandon called her beautiful in his August 1967 article "A Talk With an 83-Year-Old Enfant Terrible," 8; author's interview with Janie McLaughlin; "Hell on earth," ARL preservation tape, ICD 16037, 26 September 1969, JSP; Ethel Roosevelt Derby to ARL, 19 May 1962, JSP.

11. Andrew and Betsy Wyeth to ARL, n.d., JSP; Otto Von Habsburg to ARL, n.d., JSP; McGeorge Bundy to ARL, 21 August 1961, JSP.

12. Transcript of Mary Hagedorn interview with Mrs. Richard M. Bissell, 23 May 1955, Harvard University.

13. Bashful guests, James K. Galbraith, e-mail to author, 29 June 2006; author's interview with Kristie Miller, 15 February 2005; author's interviews with Bill Walton, 27 May 1994, and with Robert Hellman, 26 June 2006; Graham, *Katharine Graham's Washington*, 131.

14. Alice's views of Kennedy, Vanden Heuvel, 31, 32; "Cellist Pablo Casals Feted by Kennedys," *Chicago Tribune*, 14 November 1961, B7; "Casals Plays at White House," *NYT*, 14 November 1961, 1; "Washington Steps Out to Greet 'Mr. President,'" *Chicago Tribune*, 26 September 1962, D3; "Mr. President Seen in

Capital," *NYT*, 26 September 1962, 36; "Kennedy Unveils a Marble Mantle in White House," *NYT*, 3 July 1962, 10; "Building Honors Speakers," *NYT*, 23 May 1962, 28.

15. "Sobbing," Merry, 406–407; "boy stood-on-the-burning-deckish," Page-A-Day Notes to author from Joanna Sturm and Kristie Miller, n.d. 2003; Brandon, "A talk," 74.

16. Edward M. Kennedy telegram to ARL, 23 November 1963, ARL to Jacqueline Kennedy (draft), 12 December 1963; ARL to Robert Kennedy (draft), 3 March 1963; all JSP.

17. Ethel Roosevelt Derby to ARL, 12 July 1964, JSP.

18. Teresa Moore, "A Washington Life: Marcella Comes Winslow," *Washington Post Magazine*, 9 July 1989, 27.

19. ARL to Jacqueline Kennedy, 14 December 1968; Jacqueline Kennedy to ARL, 10 January [1969], both JSP.

20. "Royalty," Dorothy Marks, "A Long, Colorful Life," *Deseret News* [Salt Lake City, Utah], 10 February 1971, C1, JSP; "rogue elephant," Norma Milligan, "She Says What She Thinks," *Modern Maturity*, June–July 1974, 11; Lady Bird Johnson to ARL, 31 October 1964, JSP; Lady Bird Johnson, *A White House Diary* (New York: Holt, Rinehart, and Winston, 1970), 394–395; "Alice Longworth Will Cast a Vote for Johnson Today," *NYT*, 3 November 1964, 23; "Bull Moose," ARL Preservation tape, ICD 16021, 25 May 1967, JSP.

21. Johnson, 65, 263. Alice Longworth's story on ARL preservation tape, ICD 16034, 19 August 1968, JSP.

22. Johnson, 394–95.

23. ARL preservation tape, ICD 16024, 20 September 1967, JSP; unidentified clipping, 23 March 1966, JSP; Author interview with Robert Hellman, 25 April 2005. Alice Longworth gave mostly to environ-

mental causes, but her childhood sense of never having enough money never left her. Her Lee inheritance still trickled in as a monthly allowance, and she had investment income, which was based upon what Nick left her—including the odd railroad lease that came due—and from the proceeds of the sales of one hundred acres of land around Rookwood in 1950. The land had been sold to the Myers Y. Cooper Company and subsequently turned into suburbs, which grew apace in the postwar decades.

See Eleanor Adams, "Tea with Washington's Grande Dame," *Cincinnati Enquirer*, 2 January 1977; "Old Longworth Lot Now Being Cleared," *Cincinnati Post*, 1 May 1956; both ARLPF. For the railroad lease, see Landon L. Wallingford to ARL, 9 January 1969, JSP. Alice received $1,413.15 from a one-third share of railroad leases during 1968.

24. Lyndon B. Johnson to ARL, 6 January 1965, JSP. That letter and Jack Valenti to Lyndon B. Johnson, 5 January 1965; the press release of 6 January 1965, and ARL to Lyndon B. Johnson, 6 January 1965, all Folder FG 2/Q-T, Lyndon B. Johnson Library, Austin, Texas. See also McGeorge Bundy to ARL, 9 January 1965, JSP. LBJ's letter was really written by aide Eric Goldman. "Memorial to Theodore Roosevelt Dedicated October 27, 1967," *Theodore Roosevelt Association Newsletter* 2,1 (January 1968), 1; "Mrs. LBJ and Lynda Tour Teddy's Home," unidentified clipping n.d., JSP; for the biography, Johnson, 770.

25. "S-i-g-h-t," Betty Beale, "Prime 'Preservers' Feted," clipping, *Washington Evening Star*, 16 October 1969, F6; McPherson, "Trio of Individualists," both JSP.

26. ARL to Lyndon B. Johnson (draft), [July 14], JSP; Alice Longworth on Vietnam, ARL preservation tape, 16026, 28

September 1967, and ICD 16028, 10 October 1967, JSP. The latter contains the quote. In speaking, Mrs. Longworth drew out the two "longs."

27. Vanden Heuvel, 30.

28. Transcript of Jewell Fenzi interview with Joanna Sturm and Kristie Miller, 9 September 1989, 50 and 54 (hereafter called Fenzi interview).

29. Fenzi interview, 49. See page 54 of that interview for Kristie Miller's memory of Alice in the lotus position, trademark hat on head. See the diary of Mrs. George Dewey for evidence that TR knew yoga. Dewey Diary excerpts, 28 October 1907, JSP.

30. Fenzi interview, 50; Braden and "such fun," typescript of an interview, entitled "Return to the Far East," n.d., JSP; Moscow, Llewellyn E. Thompson to ARL, 10 July 1967, JSP.

31. Katharine Graham, *Personal History* (New York: Knopf, 1997), 391–95; quote on 394; for the headline, William F. Buckley, "The Politics of the Capote Ball," *Esquire*, December 1967, 159.

32. "Guilt Admitted in Longworth Theft," unidentified clipping; "Smelter Bares Longworth Loot," unidentified clipping; Jim Mann, "Mrs. Longworth in Court," *Washington Post*, 26 July 1972, JSP; *Auflick v. Longworth*, complaint for damages; *Auflick v. Longworth*, civil action no. 1650–72; all JSP.

33. "Beatles," *Boston Sunday Herald*, 6 June 1965, B49; Hermann Hagedorn, Interviews Relating to Roosevelt Women," Harvard University; "Edwardian," "The Grande Dames Who Grace America," unidentified clipping, JSP.

34. Mask, David Bowes, "In Search of Cincinnati," *Cincinnati Post*, 30 November 1973, 19; Portia Washington, ARL preservation tape, ICD 16034, 19 August 1968, JSP; Turner story, Nicholas Von Hoffman, "Snap-Shots at a Hot

Shoppe," *Washington Post*, 26 February 1967, 7–8.

35. "Conversations on the Phone," typescript, n.d., JSP; Bella S. Abzug to ARL, 24 March 1972, JSP; Milligan, 10; Grandaughter's insight, Susan Watters, "Here's a Capital Denizen Who Pooh-Poohs Politics," *Chicago Tribune*, 9 October 1977, D10; Alice's views, Sally Quinn, "Alice Roosevelt Longworth at 90," *Washington Post*, 12 February 1974, B3; Joseph P. Duggan, "A Tea Party, Just a Trifle Mad, with 'Princess Alice' Longworth," unidentified clipping, n.d., Papers of Huntingon Cairns, LC.

36. Milligan, 10. See Sally Quinn's interview at the time of ARL's ninetieth birthday when she responded, "I don't think that's nasty, why I think that's lovely, so nice. I'm so glad to hear she is," when told that Alice Barney was "claiming to be in love with Alice"; Quinn, B3; Teague, 81; GayPatriot.Net, a politically conservative blogspot, lists her as "one of our divas." See GayPatriot.Net: http://gay-patriot.net/2005/12/11/who-are-our-conservative-divas.

37. The friend at tea was James K. Galbraith, e-mail to author, 29 June 2006; "outgrew her hormones," June Bingham, "Before the Colors Fade," *American Heritage*, February 1969, 43, 73; "secret of youth," Teague, 199; tear gas, Milligan, 10; Twiggy, Marks, C1.

38. Quoted in Don Hewitt, *Minute by Minute* (New York: Random House, 1985), 74; Teichmann, 237.

39. "Dullest thing," ARL preservation tape, ICD 16034, 19 August 1968; draft of telegram to Richard Nixon, 4 November 1969, both JSP. Phoning friends, Teichmann, 211.

40. "'65 Horse Show Opens on Nov. 4," unidentified clipping, n.d.; McPherson, "Trio of Individualists"; "Alice Roosevelt Longworth at 85 Retains Impishness,"

and "'Lady Alice's' Wit Still Sharp at 85," unidentified clippings, n.d.; "Alice a Sensation on TV," *San Francisco Sunday Examiner & Chronicle*, 23 February 1969, 7, all JSP.

41. Richard Nixon to ARL, 12 February 1969; Grace Frances Borah to ARL, 13 February 1969, JSP; Lyndon B. Johnson telegram to ARL, 12 February 1969; Mamie and Ike Eisenhower telegram to ARL, 12 February 1969; For examples of her self-depreciating humor, See "'Lady Alice's' Wit Still Sharp at 85," unidentified clipping, n.d.; Peter Hurd to ARL, 1 June 1969; the Achesons to ARL, 15 February 1969, all JSP.

42. R. Buckminster Fuller to ARL, 21 March 1969, JSP; Norman Cousins to F. Buckminster Fuller, 17 March 1965, JSP.

43. Hyman G. Rickover to ARL, 11 December 1969; ARL preservation tape, ICD 19021, 25 May 1967, both JSP. The precise "royal visitor" is unclear. Quarks and quasars is from tape ICD 16031 [n.d.], JSP; "Lyndon Attends Frankfurter's Private Service," *Chicago Tribune*, 25 February 1965, B12.

44. Betty Beale, "She's Witty, Elegant—She's the Grooviest," June 14, 1970, unidentified clipping in Papers of Huntington Cairns.

45. Hellman's dissertation was entitled "*Die Freien:* The Young Hegelians of Berlin and the Religious Politics of 1840 Prussia" (Ph.D. diss., Columbia University, 1977); author's interviews with Robert Hellman, 25 April 2005 and 26 June 2006.

46. Ymelda Dixon, "A Former Envoy Returns," clipping, *Washington Evening Star*, 16 May 1969, JSP. The only photo accompanying this news story is of the former ambassador and Alice. Invitations for all of the other events are in the JSP. Billy Graham to ARL, 30 April 1973, JSP.

47. For "Washington's topless octoge-

narian," see Teichmann, who quotes a letter from Mrs. Longworth's physician (on page 229). Jane Howard, "Forward Day by Day," *NYT*, 8 December 1974, 324. Betty Ford to ARL, 4 October 1974, JSP; Henry Cabot Lodge Jr. to ARL, 13 November 1970, JSP.

48. Marks, C1.

49. Horace M. Albright, "Memories of Theodore Roosevelt," *Theodore Roosevelt Association Journal*, n.d., 5, JSP.

50. Ann Wood, "Just One of the Roosevelt Showoffs," *Sunday News*, 29 October 1972, 91, JSP; "Of Politics and Politicians," unidentified typescript, 4, JSP.

51. All invitations in JSP; Richard Nixon to ARL, 9 January 1973, JSP. "Mrs. Longworth could never resist anything political...." in Richard Nixon, *RN* (New York: Warner Books, 1978), 210.

52. Maxine Cheshire, "Very Interesting People," unidentified clipping, JSP. This happened in the mid-1960s, as several of the ARL preservation tapes make mention of it; "second footman," ARL preservation tape, ICD 16020, 7 February 1967, JSP; for stamp, Gary Clinton, e-mail to author, 17 February 2005; Vanden Heuvel, 32–33, 33.

53. "Capital's Grande Dame Laughs Off Those Watergate Blues," unidentified clipping, n.d., JSP; "Alice Longworth Marks*%$& Birthday," unidentified clipping, n.d., JSP.

54. Richard Nixon to ARL, 21 June 1973, JSP; "Asinine things," David Bowes, "In Search of Cincinnati," *Cincinnati Post*, 30 November 1973, 19; "an old friend," Milligan, 11; "state of shrug" and "dick-dick-dicking," Page-A-Day notes, JSP.

55. Milligan, 11, for "old crone," and cavier; Ethel Roosevelt Derby to ARL, 12 July 1964, JSP; guest list from "Alice Roosevelt Longworth, GOP Grande Dame, Is Dead," *Houston Chronicle*, 21

February 1980; Louise Le Claire, "Princess Alice Still Reigns," unidentified clipping, 8 September 1974, 24, both JSP.

56. The pillow still exists, but in a second incarnation. The first one may have read slightly differently, probably "If you can't think of something nice to say, sit right down here by me." That wording is from her reading off the pillow on 10 October 1967 on an ARL preservation tape, ICD 16029, JSP. The second version of the pillow has a Siamese cat's face in needlepoint at the bottom curl of the initial "I." Jean Vanden Heuvel first gave the pillow publicity in her 1965 *Saturday Evening Post* interview, "The Sharpest Wit in Washington." William Wright, *The Washington Game* (New York: E. P. Dutton, 1994), 60.

57. For one historian's suggestion that Nixon chose that quote to refer to happier days with his wife, see Fawn M. Brodie, *Richard Nixon* (New York: W. W. Norton, 1981), 143–44. Richard Nixon to ARL, 21 January 1974, JSP, and Dorothy McCardle, "A Daughterly Advantage," unidentified clipping, n.d., JSP.

58. Author's interview with Bill Walton, 27 May 1994.

59. Teague, viii; author interviews with Robert Hellman, 25 April 2005, Bazy Tankersley, 1 June 2006, and Alexandra Roosevelt Dworkin, 7 October 2001. "Darling Puss-Cat," also from Hellman, 2005.

60. Author's interview with Hellman, 26 June 2006.

61. Author's interviews with Hellman, 25 April 2005 and 26 June 2006. Hellman thinks that Mrs. Longworth "really remembered" the White House employee. I have tried unsuccessfully to track down his name. It is possible that he came back to the White House for that event, either to assist in the dinner and reception, or to reconnect with former White House employers, Alice Longworth among them. See also "State Dinner for Queen Elizabeth," *NYT,* 7 July 1976, 49.

Epilogue

1. Author's interview with Robert Hellman, 26 June 2006. He said she "was just being funny." "Alice Roosevelt Longworth Dies," *NYT,* 21 February 1980, 1.

2. Doug Wead, *All the Presidents' Children* (New York: Atria Books, 2003), 350. Esther Cleveland was born in the White House in 1893. Alice's sister, Edith, died in 1977, and her brother Archie died in 1979. Helen Taft Manning was very nearly Alice's age when she died (1 August 1891–21 February 1987).

3. "An extra piece of baggage" is how Alice Longworth characterized it to Bill Walton. Author's interview with Walton, 27 May 1994.

4. Lady Bird Johnson, *A White House Diary* (New York: Holt, Rinehart, and Winston, 1970), 486–487.

5. Books—along with oysters and maple sugar, according to Kristie Miller. "The Procession" (Glenn Kowalski); "Alice Roosevelt's House," on Haunted By Memories (Flaming Disk, 1987). See www.flamingdisk.com for the song. Anita Wilburn Darras, e-mail to author, 11 April 2006.

6. "Serious," In Search of Cincinnati," *Cincinnati Post,* 30 November 1973, 19; MacArthur, Teague, xv; childbirth, Teague, xiv–xv; purse, Jean Vanden Heuvel, "The Sharpest Wit in Washington, *Saturday Evening Post,* 4 December 1965, 30; poison ivy, Susan Sheehan, "Washington's Wittiest Woman," *McCall's,* January 1974, 64; LBJ, William Wright, *The Washington Game* (New York: E. P. Dutton, 1974), 231.

7. Ann Wood, "'Just One of the Roos-

evelt Showoffs," *Washington News*, 29 October 1972, 91, JSP; ARL's dresses were also cut loosely because of the double mastectomy, according to Kristie Miller and Bazy Tankersley.

8. Author interview with Joanna Sturm, 25 April 2005.

9. June Bingham, "Before the Colors Fade," *American Heritage*, February 1969, 43; TR to ARC, 10 April 1890, in ARC, *Letters from Theodore Roosevelt to Anna Roosevelt Cowles, 1870–1918* (New York: Charles Scribner's Sons, 1924), 108–9; author interview with Alexandra Roosevelt Dworkin, 7 October 2001.

10. Author interview with Bazy Tankersley, 19 July 1996.

11. Joseph M. Sheehan, "Fight to Protect Diamond Is Lost," *NYT*, 22 September 1955, 37.

12. Louise Hutchinson, "White House Weddings" Famous Brides Reminisce About Their Ceremonies," *Chicago Tribune*, 13 July 1966, B1.

Selected Bibliography

Manuscript Collections

American Antiquarian Society, Boston, Mass.
    Theodore Roosevelt Papers
Arizona Historical Society, Tucson, Ariz.
    Dinsmore Family Papers
    Greenway Papers
Chicago Historical Society, Chicago, Ill.
    Theodore Roosevelt Collection
Churchill Archives Center, Churchill College, Cambridge, England
    The Papers of Sir Cecil Spring-Rice
Cincinnati Historical Society Library, Manuscript Division, Cincinnati, Ohio
    Papers of Nicholas Longworth III (Mss801)
    Wulsin Family Papers (Mss844)
    Katherine Elizabeth Roelker Wulsin Correspondence (Mss589)
    Darrah Wunder Autobiographical Sketch (MssVF2386)
    Princeton Files:
        Judge Nicholas Longworth
        Nicholas Longworth
        Alice Roosevelt Longworth
        Paulina Longworth Sturm
        Susan Longworth
        Joseph S. Graydon
Cortauldt Institute, London, England
    Lord Lee of Fareham Papers
Herbert Hoover Presidential Library, West Branch, Iowa
    Commerce Papers
    President's Personal File
    Lou Henry Hoover Papers
    Lewis L. Strauss Papers
    Westbrook Pegler Papers
    Robert E. Wood Papers
Houghton Library, Harvard University, Cambridge, Mass.
    Theodore Roosevelt Collection

　　Anna Roosevelt Cowles Papers (bMS Am 1834.1)
　　Alice Roosevelt Longworth Family Papers (bMS Am 1541.9)
　　Archibald Bulloch Roosevelt Family Papers (bMS Am 1541.3)
　　Edith Kermit Carow Roosevelt Family Papers (*87M-101)
　　Ethel Roosevelt Derby Papers (87M-100)
　　Herman Hagedorn. Interviews Relating to Roosevelt Women (R200.H12i)
　　Roosevelt Family Miscellaneous Papers (bMS Am 1834.2)
　　Theodore Roosevelt Miscellaneous Papers (*93M-11)
　　Alexander Woollcott Papers
Idaho Oral History Center, Boise, Idaho
Idaho State Historical Society Library and Archives, Boise, Idaho
　　William E. Borah Papers (MS605, MS608)
Indiana Historical Society, Indianapolis, Ind.
　　Robert Hunter Papers
Library of Congress, Washington, D.C.
　　Joseph and Stewart Alsop Papers
　　Daniel C. Beard Papers
　　Mabel T. Boardman Papers
　　William E. Borah Papers
　　Huntington Cairns Papers
　　Joseph H. Choate Papers
　　William Dudley Foulke Papers
　　James R. Garfield Papers
　　Lillian Gish Papers
　　Harold Ickes Papers
　　Alice Roosevelt Longworth Papers
　　Alice Roosevelt Longworth Scrapbook
　　Nicholas Longworth Papers
　　Evalyn Walsh McLean Papers
　　Amos R. Pinchot Papers
　　Cornelia Bryce Pinchot Papers
　　Archibald Roosevelt Papers
　　Kermit and Belle Roosevelt Papers
　　Theodore Roosevelt Jr. Papers
　　Everett Sanders Papers
　　Eric Sevareid Papers
　　Ruth Hanna McCormick Simms Papers
　　Mark Sullivan Papers
　　Robert A. Taft Papers
Manuscripts Department, Lilly Library, Indiana University, Bloomington, Ind.
　　Samuel McClure Papers
Abraham Lincoln Presidential Library, Springfield, Ill.
　　Joseph Cannon Papers
　　H. H. Kohlsaat Papers
National Archives, London, England
　　Papers of the British Embassy (F.O 800/241-242/9/1)

Naval War College, Naval Historical Collection, Newport, R.I.
    Fred Leith (Ms. Coll. 89)
Newberry Library, Chicago, Ill.
    John T. McCutcheon Papers
    Carter H. Harrison Papers
    Alice French Papers
    Edith Franklin Wyatt Papers
    Papers of the Illinois Central Railroad Company
Privately held
    Joanna Sturm Papers
Franklin D. Roosevelt Library, Hyde Park, N.Y.
    Eleanor Roosevelt Papers
    Elliott Roosevelt Sr. Papers
    Roosevelt Family Papers Donated by the Children
Southern Historical Collection, Wilson Library, University of North Carolina at Chapel
    Hill, Chapel Hill, N.C.
    Peter Hagner Papers
University of Chicago, Special Collections Library, Chicago, Ill.
    Frank O. Lowden Papers
    Salmon O. Levinson Papers
University of Vermont, Special Collections, Burlington, Vt.
    Grace Goodhue Coolidge Collection
Washington State University Libraries, Manuscripts, Archives, and Special Collections,
    Pullman, Wash.
    Claudius Osborne Johnson Papers

Other Media

"The Reporters: Jonathan Aitken Interview with Alice Roosevelt Longworth," York-
    shire [U.K.] Television. [January 1969].

Microfilm Collections

Willard Dickerman Straight Papers, Division of Rare and Manuscript Collections, Cor-
    nell University Library, Ithaca, N.Y.
Presidential Papers of Theodore Roosevelt, Library of Congress, Washington, D.C.
William H. Taft Papers, Library of Congress, Washington, D.C.
Eleanor Roosevelt Papers, Franklin D. Roosevelt Presidential Library, Hyde Park,
    N.Y.

Oral Interviews

Allen, Robert S., transcript. Interviewed by Raymond Henle. 11 November 1966. Her-
    bert Hoover Presidential Library.
Alsop, Susan Mary. Interviewed by author. 24 May 1994.
Benn, Stephen. Telephone interview by author. 2 August 2004.

Borah, Mary McConnell, transcript. Interviewed by Rosita Artis. 18 October 1969. [OH#0013] Idaho Oral History Center, Boise, Idaho.

Borah, Mary McConnell, transcript. Interview by Maureen Bassett. 15 October 1971. Oral History Project, Latah County Museum Society, Moscow, Idaho.

Catt, Ann. Telephone interview by author. 30 May 2006.

Davison, F. Trubee, transcript and addenda to transcript. Interviewed by Raymond Henle. 14 September 1969. Herbert Hoover Presidential Library, West Branch, Iowa.

Dworkin, Alexandra Roosevelt. Telephone interview by author. 7 October 2001.

Emmerson, Dorothy, transcript. Interviewed by Hope Meyers. 28 September 1987. Association for Diplomatic Studies and Training, Arlington, Va.

Hagedorn, Mary, transcript. Interview with Mrs. Richard Aldrich, 30 March 1955. Interviews Relating to Roosevelt Women, R200.H12i. Houghton Library, Harvard University, Cambridge, Mass.

Hawley Jr., Jess, transcript. Interviewed by Barbara Pulling. 14 November 1989. [OH#1042] Idaho Oral History Center, Boise, Idaho.

Hellman, Robert. Interviewed by author on several occasions, 1993–2007.

Lane, Cora Rubin, transcript. Interviewed by Jackie Day-Ames. 25 May 1976. [OH#0905] Idaho Oral History Center, Boise, Idaho.

Longworth, Alice Roosevelt, Preservation Tape Collection. Various Dates. Library of Congress, Washington, D.C.

Macgruder, Lynn. Interviewed by author. 14 October 2001.

McLaughlin, Janie. Interviewed by author. 26 May 1994.

Meeske, Angela. Telephone interview by author. 19 April 2004.

Miller, Kristie. Interviewed by author on several occasions, 1992–2007.

Mitchell, David. Telephone interview by author. 26 October 2001.

Mitchell, Frances Binger. Telephone interview by author. 26 January 2007.

Reed, Mary. Telephone interview by author. 30 May 2006.

Roosevelt, Robin. Interviewed by author. 27 May 1994.

Roosevelt, Selwa. Interviewed by author. 13 October 2001.

Silvercruys, Robert, transcript. Interviewed by Raymond Henle. 7 November 1968. Herbert Hoover Presidential Library.

Sturm, Joanna. Interviewed by author on several occasions, 1993–2007.

Sturm, Joanna, and Kristie Miller [Twaddell] transcript. Interviewed by Jewell Fenzi. 9 September 1989. Association for Diplomatic Studies and Training, Arlington, Va.

Tankersley, Bazy. Interviewed by author. 19 July 1996. Telephone interviews by author. 31 May and 1 June 2006.

Teague, Michael. Interviewed by author. 3 August 1989.

Tomb, Jeanne. Telephone interview by author. 24 February 2007.

Totenberg, Roman. Telephone interview by author. 24 March 2005.

Walton, William. Interviewed by author. 27 May 1994.

Westerman, Whillock, transcript. Interviewed by Jeffrey G. Seward. 8 January 1974. [OH#0147] Idaho Oral History Center, Boise, Idaho.

Wolfe, Preston, transcript. Herbert Hoover Presidential Library.

Books and Articles

Abbott , Lawrence F., ed. *The Letters of Archie Butt, Personal Aide to President Roosevelt.* Garden City, N.Y.: Doubleday, Page, 1924.

———, ed. *Taft and Roosevelt: The Intimate Letters of Archie Butt, Military Aide.* 2 vols. Garden City, N.Y.: Doubleday, Doran, 1930.

Abels, Jules. *In the Time of Silent Cal.* New York: G. P. Putnam's Sons, 1969.

Acceptance of the Statue of William Edgar Borah Presented by the State of Idaho. Washington, D.C.: Government Printing Office, 1948.

Adams, Samuel Hopkins. *A. Woollcott, His Life and His World.* New York: Reynal & Hitchcock, 1945.

Aldrich, Nelson. *Old Money: The Mythology of America's Upper Class.* New York: Knopf, 1988.

Allgor, Catherine. *Parlor Politics.* Charlottesville: University Press of Virginia, 2000.

Alsop, Joseph. *I've Seen the Best of It: Memoirs.* New York: W. W. Norton, 1992.

Alsop, Stewart. *Stay of Execution: A Sort of Memoir.* Philadelphia: J. B. Lippincott, 1973.

Amory, Cleveland. *The Proper Bostonians.* New York: E. P. Dutton, 1947.

———. *Who Killed Society?* New York: Harper & Brothers, 1960.

Anderson, Isabel. *Presidents and Pies: Life in Washington, 1897–1919.* New York: Houghton Mifflin, 1920.

Anderson, Judith Icke. *William Howard Taft: An Intimate History.* New York: W. W. Norton, 1981.

Anthony, Carl Sferrazza. *First Ladies.* vol. 1. New York: William Morrow, 1990.

———. *Nellie Taft: The Unconventional First Lady of the Ragtime Era.* New York: William Morrow, 2005.

Ashby, Leroy. *The Spearless Leader: Senator Borah and the Progressive Movement in the 1920s.* Urbana: University of Illinois Press, 1972.

Auchincloss, Louis. *The Vanderbilt Era: Profiles of a Gilded Age.* New York: Charles Scribner's Sons, 1989.

Bacevich, A. J. *Diplomat in Khaki: Major General Frank Ross McCoy and American Foreign Policy, 1898–1949.* Lawrence: University Press of Kansas, 1989.

Bacon, Donald C. "Nicholas Longworth: The Genial Czar," in *Masters of the House: Congressional Leadership Over Two Centuries.* Roger H. Davidson, Susan Webb Hammond, and Raymond W. Smock, eds. Boulder, Colo.: Westview Press, 1998.

Bailey, Thomas A. *Theodore Roosevelt and the Japanese-American Crisis.* Stanford, Calif.: Stanford University Press, 1934.

Baker, John D. "The Character of the Congressional Revolution of 1910." *Journal of American History* 60, no. 3 (December 1973): 679–691.

Barrymore, Ethel. *Memories: An Autobiography.* New York: Harper & Brothers, 1955.

Beal, Merrill D. "'Instructing the People:' Recollections of William E. Borah." *Rendezvous: Idaho State University Journal of Arts and Letters* 18, nos. 1–2 (1983): 43–46.

Beale, Howard K. *Theodore Roosevelt and the Rise of America to World Power.* Baltimore: Johns Hopkins University Press, 1956.

Beran, Michael Knox. *The Last Patrician: Bobby Kennedy and the End of American Aristocracy.* New York: St. Martin's Press, 1998.

Berlin, Isaiah. *Flourishing: Letters, 1928–1946.* London: Chatto & Windus, 2004.

Bingham, June. "Before the Colors Fade: Alice Roosevelt Longworth." *American Heritage,* February 1969:42–43, 73–77.

Birmingham, Stephen. *The Grandes Dames.* New York: Simon & Schuster, 1982.

———. *The Right People: A Portrait of the American Social Establishment.* Boston: Little, Brown, 1968.

Blum, John Morton. *A Life with History.* Lawrence: University Press of Kansas, 2004.

———. *The Republican Roosevelt.* Cambridge, Mass.: Harvard University Press, 1954.

Boardman, Mabel T. "A Woman's Impressions of the Philippines." *Outlook* 82 (24 February 1906): 435–446.

Boehle, Rose Angela. *Maria Longworth: A Biography.* Dayton, Ohio: Landfall Press, 1990.

Boorstin, Daniel. *The Image: A Guide to Pseudo-Events in America.* New York: Atheneum, 1962.

Borah, Mary E. *Elephants and Donkeys: The Memoirs of Mary Borah.* Moscow: University Press of Idaho, 1976.

Borah, William E. *Bedrock: Views on Basic National Problems.* Washington, D.C.: National Home Library Foundation, 1936.

Braden, Joan. *Just Enough Rope: An Intimate Memoir.* New York: Villard Books, 1989.

Braden, Waldow W. "Some Illinois Influences on the Life of William E. Borah." *Journal of the Illinois Historical Society* 40, no. 2 (June 1947): 168–175.

———. "William E. Borah's Senate Speeches on the League of Nations, 1918–1920." *Speech Monographs* 10 (1943): 57–68.

Bradlee, Ben. *A Good Life: Newspapering and Other Adventures.* New York: Simon & Schuster, 1995.

Brands, H. W. *T.R.: The Last Romantic.* New York: Basic Books, 1997.

Braudy, Leo. *The Frenzy of Renown: Fame and Its History.* New York: Oxford University Press, 1986.

Brent, Charles H. "The Visit to the Philippines of Secretary Taft and His Party." *Outlook* 81 (14 October 1905): 369–372.

Brodie, Fawn M. *Richard Nixon: The Shaping of His Character.* New York: W. W. Norton, 1981.

Brooks, Gladys. *Boston and Return.* New York: Atheneum, 1962.

Brough, James. *Princess Alice.* Boston: Little, Brown, 1975.

Browder, Robert Paul, and Thomas G. Smith. *Independent: A Biography of Lewis W. Douglas.* New York: Knopf, 1986.

Bulkey, Barry. *Washington Old and New.* Washington, D.C.: W. F. Roberts, 1913.

Burchett, Richard Lee. "The Political World of Nicholas Longworth III: 1887–1903." PhD diss., University of Cincinnati, 1971.

Burke, Arthur M., ed. *Prominent Families of the United States of America.* New York: Heraldic Publishing, 1975.

Burke, Robert E, ed. *The Diary Letters of Hiram Johnson, 1917–1945.* Vols. 1–7. New York: Garland, 1983.

Burns, James MacGregor, and Susan Dunn. *The Three Roosevelts: Patrician Leaders Who Transformed America.* New York: Atlantic Monthly Press, 2001.

Burton, David. *Cecil Spring-Rice: A Diplomat's Life*. Rutherford, N.J.: Fairleigh Dickinson University Press, 1990.

Butler, Nicholas Murray. *Across the Busy Years: Recollections and Reflections*. New York: Charles Scribner's Sons, 1939.

Cairns, Huntington. *The Limits of Art: Poetry and Prose Chosen by Ancient and Modern Critics*. Washington, D.C.: Bollingen Foundation/Pantheon Books, 1948.

Caroli, Betty Boyd. *The Roosevelt Women*. New York: Basic Books, 1998.

Cassini, Marguerite. *Never a Dull Moment*. New York: Atheneum, 1956.

Champagne, Anthony. "John Nance Garner," in *Masters of the House: Congressional Leadership Over Two Centuries*. Roger H. Davidson, Susan Webb Hammond, and Raymond W. Smock, eds. Boulder, Colo.: Westview Press, 1998.

Chanler, Margaret. *Autumn in the Valley*. Boston: Little, Brown, 1936.

Cincinnati: A Guide to the Queen City and Its Neighbors. Cincinnati, Ohio: Wiesenhart Press, 1943.

Clapper, Olive Ewing. *Washington Tapestry*. New York: McGraw Hill, 1946.

Clinton, Gilbert. *The Mirrors of Washington*. New York: G. P. Putnam's Sons, 1921.

Coker, William S. "The Panama Canal Tolls Controversy: A Different Perspective." *Journal of American History* 55 (1968): 555–564.

Cole, Wayne S. *America First*. New York: Octagon Books, 1971.

———. "The America First Committee." *Journal of the Illinois State Historical Society* 44, no. 1 (Spring 1951): 305–322.

Coletta, Paolo E. *The Presidency of William Howard Taft*. Lawrence: University Press of Kansas, 1973.

Colman, Elizabeth Wheeler. *Mrs. Wheeler Goes to Washington*. Helena, Mont.: Falcon Press, 1989.

Collier, Peter. *The Roosevelts*. New York: Simon & Schuster, 1994.

Collin, Richard H. *Theodore Roosevelt, Culture, Diplomacy, and Expansion: A New View of American Imperialism*. Baton Rouge: Louisiana State University Press, 1985.

Commager, Henry Steele, ed. *Documents of American History*, 4th ed. New York: Appleton-Century-Crofts, 1948.

Contosta, David R., and Jessica R. Hawthorne. "Rise to World Power: Selected Letters of Whitelaw Reid, 1895–1912." *Transactions of the American Philosophical Society* 76, no. 2 (1986): 1–171.

Cook, Blanche Wiesen. *Eleanor Roosevelt*. 2 vols. New York: Viking, 1992, 1999.

Cooper, John Milton. *Breaking the Heart of the World*. Cambridge: Cambridge University Press, 2001.

———. *The Warrior and the Priest: Woodrow Wilson and Theodore Roosevelt*. Cambridge, Mass.: Harvard University Press, 1983.

———. "William E. Borah: Political Thespian." *Pacific Northwest Quarterly* 56, no. 4 (October 1965): 145–158.

Coudenhove-Kalergi, Richard N. *Crusade for Pan-Europe: Autobiography of a Man and a Movement*. New York: G. P. Putnam's Sons, 1943.

Cowles, Anna Roosevelt. *Letters from Theodore Roosevelt to Anna Roosevelt Cowles, 1870–1918*. New York: Charles Scribner's Sons, 1924.

Cox, James M. *Journey Through My Years*. New York: Simon & Schuster, 1946.

Cravens, Hamilton. *The Triumph of Evolution: The Heredity-Environment Controversy, 1900–1941*. Baltimore: Johns Hopkins University Press, 1988.

Croly, Herbert. *Willard Straight*. New York: Macmillan, 1925.

Cross, Wilbur, and Ann Novotny. *White House Weddings*. New York: David McKay, 1967.

Dalton, Kathleen. *Theodore Roosevelt: A Strenuous Life*. New York: Knopf, 2002.

———. "Theodore Roosevelt: Knickerbocker Aristocrat." *New York History* 67, no. 1 (January 1986): 39–65.

Danforth, D. N. "Contemporary Titans: Joseph Bolivar DeLee and John Whitridge Williams." *American Journal of Obstetrics and Gynecology* 120, no. 3 (1 November 1974): 577–588.

Daniels, Jonathan. *Washington Quadrille*. Garden City, N.Y.: Doubleday, 1968.

Davis, Kenneth S. *FDR: Into the Storm, 1937–1940*. New York: Random House, 1993.

Davis, M. Edward. "Joseph Bolivar DeLee, 1869–1942: As I Remember Him." *Lying-In: The Journal of Reproductive Medicine* 1, no. 1 (January–February 1968): 33–44.

Davis, Oscar King. *Released for Publication: Some Inside Political History of Theodore Roosevelt and His Times, 1898–1918*. Boston: Houghton Mifflin, 1925.

Deacon, Desley. *Elsie Clews Parsons: Inventing Modern Life*. Chicago: University of Chicago Press, 1997.

DeBenedetti, Charles. "Borah and the Kellogg-Briand Pact." *Pacific Northwest Quarterly* 63, no. 1 (January 1972): 22–29.

DeCamp, Graydon. *The Grand Old Lady of Vine Street: A History of* The Cincinnati Enquirer. Cincinnati: The Cincinnati Enquirer, 1991.

De Chambrun, Clara Longworth. *Cincinnati: Story of the Queen City*. New York: Charles Scribner's Sons, 1939.

———. *The Making of Nicholas Longworth*. New York: Ray Long & Richard R. Smith, 1933.

———. *Shadows Like Myself*. New York: Charles Scribner's Sons, 1936.

Ditzen, Eleanor Davies Tydings. *My Golden Spoon: Memoirs of a Capital Lady*. New York: Madison Books, 1997.

———. *The Hero: Charles A. Lindbergh and the American Dream*. Garden City, N.Y.: Doubleday, 1959.

Documents Diplomatiques Francais II. Paris: Imprimerie Nationale, 1931.

Doenecke, Justus D., ed. *In Danger Undaunted: The Anti-Interventionist Movement of 1940–1941 as Revealed in the Papers of the America First Committee*. Stanford, Calif.: Hoover Institution Press, 1990.

Donn, Linda. *The Roosevelt Cousins: Growing Up Together, 1882–1924*. New York: Knopf, 2001.

Douglas, William O. *The Court Years, 1939–1975: The Autobiography of William O. Douglas*. New York: Random House, 1980.

Dows, Alice. *Idle Hours*. Philadelphia: Dorrance Publishers, 1927.

———. *Illusions*. Philadelphia: Dorrance Publishers, 1931.

Dubofsky, Melvin, and Warren Van Tine. *John L. Lewis: A Biography*. Urbana: University of Illinois Press, 1987.

Duffey, Eliza Bisbee. *Ladies' and Gentlemen's Etiquette*. Philadelphia: Porter & Coates, 1887.

Duncan, Bingham. *Whitelaw Reid: Journalist, Politician, Diplomat*. Athens: University of Georgia Press, 1975.

Edge, Walter Evans. *A Jerseyman's Journal: Fifty Years of American Business and Politics*. Princeton, N.J.: Princeton University Press, 1948.

Egerton, George. "Diplomacy, Scandal and Military Intelligence: The Craufurd-Stuart Affair and Anglo-American Relations, 1918–1920. *Intelligence and National Security* 2, no. 4 (October 1987): 110–134.

Ellis, Anne. *The Life of an Ordinary Woman*. [1929] Boston: Houghton Mifflin, 1999.

Esthus, Raymond A. *Theodore Roosevelt and the International Rivalries*. Claremont, Calif.: Regina Books, 1970.

Fausold, Martin L. *James W. Wadsworth, Jr.: The Gentleman from New York*. Syracuse, N.Y.: Syracuse University Press, 1975.

Felsenthal, Carol. *Alice Roosevelt Longworth*. New York: G. P. Putnam's Sons, 1988.

Fenzi, Jewell. *Married to the Foreign Service: An Oral History of the American Diplomatic Spouse*. New York: Twain, 1994.

Ferrell, Robert H. *The Presidency of Calvin Coolidge*. Lawrence: University Press of Kansas, 1998.

————. *Woodrow Wilson and World War I: 1917–1921*. New York: Harper & Row, 1985.

Fishbein, Morris, with Sol Theron DeLee. *Joseph Bolivar DeLee: Crusading Obstetrician*. New York: E. P. Dutton, 1949.

Fleming, Karl, and Anne Taylor Fleming. *The First Time*. New York: Simon & Schuster, 1975.

Ford, Worthington, ed. *The Letters of Henry Adams*. New York: Houghton Mifflin, 1938.

Freidel, Frank. *Franklin D. Roosevelt: A Rendesvouʒ with Destiny*. Boston: Little, Brown, 1990.

Fruhauf, Aline. *Making Faces: Memoirs of a Caricaturist*. Washington, D. C.: Seven Locks Press, 1977.

Gable, John Allen. *The Bull Moose Years: Theodore Roosevelt and the Progressive Party*. Port Washington, N.Y.: Kennikat Press, 1978.

Gamson, Joshua. *Claims to Fame: Celebrity in Contemporary America*. Berkeley: University of California Press, 1994.

Gann, Dolly. *Dolly Gann's Book*. Garden City, N.Y.: Doubleday, 1933.

Gardner, Joseph L. *Departing Glory: Theodore Roosevelt as Ex-President*. New York: Charles Scribner's Sons, 1973.

Garraty, John A. *Henry Cabot Lodge: A Biography*. New York: Knopf, 1953.

Garrett, Wendell, ed. *Our Changing White House*. Boston: Northeastern University Press, 1995.

Gibson, J. Timberlake. "The Million Dollar Drop-Out." *Washingtonian*, April 1967: 40–43.

Godfrey, Donald G., and Val E. Limburg. "The Rogue Elephant of Radio Legislation: Senator William E. Borah." *Journalism Quarterly* 67, no. 1 (Spring 1990): 214–224.

Goll, Eugene W. "Frank R. Kent's Opposition to Franklin D. Roosevelt and the New Deal." *Maryland Historical Magaʒine* 62, no. 2 (1968): 158–171.

Goodwin, Doris Kearns. *No Ordinary Time*. New York: Simon & Schuster, 1994.

Gould, Lewis L. *Grand Old Party*. New York: Random House, 2003.

———. *The Most Exclusive Club*. New York: Basic Books, 2005.

———. *The Presidency of Theodore Roosevelt*. Lawrence: University Press of Kansas, 1991.

———. "The Price of Fame: Theodore Roosevelt and Celebrity, 1909–1919." *Lamar Journal of the Humanities* 10, 2 (Fall 1984): 7–18.

Graham, Katharine. *Katharine Graham's Washington*. New York: Random House, 2002.

———. *Personal History*. New York: Knopf, 1997.

Graves, Louis. *Willard Straight in the Orient*. New York: Asia Publishing, 1922.

Green, Constance McLaughlin. *Washington: Capital City, 1879–1950*. Princeton, N.J.: Princeton University Press, 1963.

Green, Harvey. *The Light of the Home*. New York: Pantheon, 1983.

Green, Horace, ed. *American Problems: A Selection of Speeches and Prophecies by William E. Borah*. New York: Duffield & Company, 1924.

Green, Marguerite. "The National Civic Federation and the American Labor Movement, 1900–1925." Ph.D. dissertation, Catholic University, 1956.

Greenbaum, Fred. *Robert Marion La Follette*. Boston: Twayne, 1975.

Greiner, Betsy. "The Day Alice Came to Town." *Timeline* 4, no. 1 (February–March 1987): 16–25.

Griscom, Lloyd. *Diplomatically Speaking*. Boston: Little, Brown, 1940.

Grover, David H. "Borah and the Haywood Trial." *Pacific Historical Review* 32, no. 1 (February 1963): 65–77.

———. *Debaters and Dynamiters: The Story of the Haywood Trial*. Corvallis: Oregon State University Press, 1964.

———. "Diamondfield Jack A Range War in Court." *Idaho Yesterdays* 7, no. 2 (1963): 8–14.

Hagedorn, Hermann. *Leonard Wood: A Biography*. 2 vols. New York: Harper & Brothers, 1931.

———. *The Roosevelt Family of Sagamore Hill*. New York: Macmillan, 1954.

Halberstam, David. *The Best and the Brightest*. New York: Random House, 1972.

Harbaugh, William H. *The Life and Times of Theodore Roosevelt*. New York: Oxford University Press, 1975.

Harlow, Alvin F. *The Serene Cincinnatians*. New York: E. P. Dutton, 1950.

Harriman, Daisy. *From Pinafores to Politics*. New York: Henry Holt, 1923.

Hathorn, Guy B. "The Political Career of C. Bascom Slemp." Ph.D. dissertation, Duke University, 1950.

Healy, Paul. *Cissy: The Biography of Eleanor M. "Cissy" Patterson*. New York: Doubleday, 1966.

Helm, Edith Benham. *The Captains and the Kings*. New York: G. P. Putnam's Sons, 1954.

Henderson, Amy. "Media and the Rise of Celebrity Culture." *OAH Magazine of History* 6, no. 4 (Spring 1992): 49–54

Herbermann, Charles G., et al., ed. *The Catholic Encyclopedia*. vol. 14. New York: The Gilmary Society, 1912.

Hewitt, Don. *Minute by Minute*. New York: Random House, 1985.

History of Medicine and Surgery and Physicians and Surgeons of Chicago. Chicago: Biographical Publishing Corporation, 1922.

Hoge, Alice Albright. *Cissy Patterson.* New York: Random House, 1966.

Holmes, Sarah C., ed. *The Correspondence of Ezra Pound and Senator William Borah.* Urbana: University of Illinois Press, 2001.

Homes for Ambassadors. New York: American Embassy Association, 1910.

Hoover, Irwin Hood. *Forty-two Years in the White House.* New York: Houghton Mifflin, 1934.

Horgan, Paul. *Tracings: A Book of Partial Portraits.* New York: Farrar, Straus and Giroux, 1993.

Hoyt, Edwin P. *Alexander Woollcott.* New York: Abelard-Schuman, 1968.

Hurd, Charles. *Washington Cavalcade.* New York: E. P. Dutton, 1948.

Ickes, Harold L. *The Autobiography of a Curmudgeon.* New York: Reynal & Hitchcock, 1943.

Jeffries, Ona Griffin. *In and Out of the White House.* New York: Wilfred Funk, 1960.

Johnpoll, Bernard K. *Pacifist's Progress: Norman Thomas and the Decline of American Socialism.* Chicago: Quadrangle Books, 1970.

Johnson, Claudius O. *Borah of Idaho.* Seattle: University of Washington Press, 1936.

Johnson, Evans C. *Oscar W. Underwood.* Baton Rouge: Louisiana State University Press, 1980.

Johnson, Lady Bird. *A White House Diary.* New York: Holt, Rinehart and Winston, 1970.

Johnson, Robert David. *The Peace Progressives and American Foreign Relations.* Cambridge, Mass.: Harvard University Press, 1995.

Jones, V. C. "Before the Colors Fade: Last of the Rough Riders." *American Heritage* 20, no. 5 (August 1969): 42–95.

Kasson, John F. *Rudeness and Civility: Manners in Nineteenth-Century Urban America.* New York: Hill and Wang, 1990.

Kelly, Frank K. *The Fight for the White House: The Story of 1912.* New York: Thomas Y. Crowell, 1961.

Keyes, Frances Parkinson. *Capital Kaleidoscope.* New York: Harper & Brothers, 1937.

Kerr, Joan Paterson. *A Bully Father: Theodore Roosevelt's Letters to His Children.* New York: Random House, 1995.

Klein, Nora C. *Practical Etiquette.* Chicago: A. Flanagan, 1888.

Kohlsaat, H. H. *From McKinley to Harding: Personal Recollections of Our Presidents.* New York: Charles Scribner's Sons, 1923.

Kroebel, Emma. *Wie ich an den Koreanischen Kaiserhof kam.* Berlin: Verlag von R. Jacobsthal, 1909.

Lahr, John. *Automatic Vaudeville.* New York: Knopf, 1984.

Lane, Jack C. *Armed Progressive: General Leonard Wood.* San Rafael, Calif.: Presidio Press, 1978.

Lash, Joseph. *Eleanor and Franklin.* New York: Signet, 1971.

Lee, Mary. *A History of Chestnut Hill Chapel.* Chestnut Hill, Mass.: The History Committee of the First Church in Chestnut Hill, 1937.

Leonard, Lewis Alexander, ed. *Greater Cincinnati and Its People: A History*. Vol. 6. Chicago: Lewis Historical Publishing Company, 1927.

Lensen, George A., ed. *The D'Anethan Dispatches from Japan, 1894–1910*. Tallahassee, Fla.: The Diplomatic Press, 1967.

Leuchtenburg, William E. *The Perils of Prosperity*. Chicago: University of Chicago Press, 1958.

Levin, Phyllis Lee. *Edith and Woodrow: The Wilson White House*. New York: Scribner, 2001.

Lindbergh, Charles. *Of Flight and Life*. New York: Charles Scribner's Sons, 1948.

Longstreet, Abbey Buchanan. *Social Etiquette of New York*. New York: D. Appleton, 1887.

Longworth, Alice Roosevelt. *Crowded Hours*. New York: Charles Scribner's Sons, 1933.

————, with Theodore Roosevelt Jr. *The Desk Drawer Anthology*. New York: Doubleday, Doran, 1938.

Looker, Earle. *The White House Gang*. New York: Fleming H. Revell, 1929.

McAllister, Ward. *Society As I Have Found It*. New York: Cassell, 1890.

McCarthy, Michael P. "The Short, Unhappy Life of the Illinois Progressive Party." *Chicago History* 4, no. 1 (Spring 1977): 2–12.

McCullough, David. *Mornings on Horseback*. New York: Simon & Schuster, 1982.

McHale, Francis. *President and Chief Justice: The Life and Public Services of William Howard Taft*. Philadelphia: Dorrance & Company, 1931.

McKee, Delber L. "The Chinese Boycott of 1905–1906 Reconsidered: The Role of Chinese Americans." *Pacific Historical Review* 55, no. 2 (May 1986): 165–191.

McKenna, Marian C. *Borah*. Ann Arbor: University of Michigan Press, 1961.

McLean, Evalyn Walsh. *Father Struck It Rich*. Boston: Little, Brown, 1936.

McMurtry, Larry. *Walter Benjamin at the Dairy Queen*. New York: Simon & Schuster, 1999.

MacNeil, Neil. *Forge of Democracy*. New York: David McKay, 1963.

Madaras, Lawrence H. "Theodore Roosevelt, Jr., Versus Al Smith: The New York Gubernatorial Election of 1924." *New York History* 47 (1966): 372–390.

Maddox, Robert James. "Keeping Cool with Coolidge." *Journal of American History* 53, no. 4 (March 1967): 772–780.

————. *William E. Borah and American Foreign Policy*. Baton Rouge: Louisiana State University Press, 1970.

————. "William E. Borah and the Crusade to Outlaw War." *Historian* 29, no. 2 (1967): 200–220.

Maney, Richard. *Fanfare: The Confessions of a Press Agent*. New York: Harper & Brothers, 1957.

Manners, William. *TR and Will: A Friendship That Split the Republican Party*. New York: Harcourt, Brace, 1969.

Margulies, Herbert F. *Reconciliation and Revival: James R. Mann and the House Republicans in the Wilson Era*. Westport, Conn.: Greenwood Press, 1996.

Marie, Queen of Roumania. *Ordeal: The Story of My Life*. New York: Charles Scribner's Sons, 1935.

Martin, Asa E. *After the White House*. State College, Penn.: Penns Valley Publishers, 1951.

Martin, Ralph G. *Cissy: The Extraordinary Life of Eleanor Medill Patterson*. New York: Simon & Schuster, 1979.

Matthews, Donald R. *U.S. Senators and Their World*. Chapel Hill: The University of North Carolina Press, 1960.

Means, Marianne. *The Woman in the White House*. New York: Random House, 1963.

Merry, Robert W. *Taking on the World: Joseph and Stewart Alsop—Guardians of the American Century*. New York: Viking, 1996.

Merz, Charles. "Borah's One-Man Party." *New Republic*, 10 June 1925: 66–70.

Michener, James A. *The World Is My Home: A Memoir*. New York: Random House, 1992.

Miller, Karen. *Populist Nationalism: Republican Insurgency and American Foreign Policy Making, 1918–1925*. Westport, Conn.: Greenwood Press, 1999.

Miller, Kristie. *Ruth Hanna McCormick: A Life in Politics*. Albuquerque, N.M.: University of New Mexico Press, 1992.

———. "Ruth Hanna McCormick and the Senatorial Election of 1930." *Illinois Historical Journal* 81 (Autumn 1988): 191–210.

Miller, Nathan. *The Roosevelt Chronicles*. Garden City, N.Y.: Doubleday, 1979.

———. *Theodore Roosevelt: A Life*. New York: William Morrow, 1992.

Miller, William "Fishbait," with Frances Spatz Leighton. *Fishbait: The Memoirs of the Congressional Doorkeeper*. Englewood Cliffs, N.J.: Prentice Hall, 1977.

Miller, Zane L. *Boss Cox's Cincinnati: Urban Politics in the Progressive Era*. Columbus, Ohio: Ohio State University Press, 2000.

Mills, C. Wright. *The Power Elite*. New York: Oxford University Press, 1956.

Mooney, Booth. *Mr. Speaker: Four Men Who Shaped the United States House of Representatives*. Chicago: Follett, 1964.

Morgan, Ted. *F.D.R.: A Biography*. New York: Simon & Schuster, 1985.

Morison, Elting E., and John Morton Blum, eds. *The Letters of Theodore Roosevelt*. 8 vols. Cambridge, Mass.: Harvard University Press, 1951–1954.

Morris, Edmund. *The Rise of Theodore Roosevelt*. New York: Coward, McCann & Geoghegan, 1979.

———. *Theodore Rex*. New York: Random House, 2001.

Morris, Sylvia Jukes. *Edith Kermit Roosevelt: Portrait of a First Lady*. New York: Coward, McCann & Geoghegan, 1980.

Mowry, George E. *Theodore Roosevelt and the Progressive Movement*. Madison: University of Wisconsin Press, 1946.

Murray, Robert K. *The Harding Era: Warren G. Harding and His Administration*. Minneapolis: University of Minnesota Press, 1969.

———. *The Politics of Normalcy*. New York: W. W. Norton, 1973.

Myers, Gustavus. *History of the Great American Fortunes*. New York: Modern Library, 1936.

Naylor, Natalie A., Douglas Brinkley, and John Allen Gable, eds. *Theodore Roosevelt: Many-Sided American*. Interlaken, N.Y.: Heart of the Lakes Publishing, 1992.

Nesbitt, Henrietta. *White House Diary*. New York: Doubleday, 1949.

Nicolson, Harold. *Diaries and Letters, 1930–1939*. New York: Atheneum, 1966.

Nixon, Richard M. *RN: The Memoirs of Richard Nixon* New York: Warner Books, 1978.

Ornig, Joseph R. *My Last Chance to Be a Boy*. Baton Rouge: Louisiana University Press, 1994.

Osgood, Robert E. *Ideals and Self-Interest in America's Foreign Policy*. Chicago: University of Chicago Press, 1953.

O'Toole, Patricia. *When Trumpets Call: Theodore Roosevelt After the White House*. New York: Simon & Schuster, 2005.

Page, William Tyler. "Mr. Speaker Longworth." *Scribner's Magazine*, March 1928:272–280.

Parsons, Elsie Clews. "Congressional Junket in Japan: The Taft Party of 1905 Meets the Mikado." *New-York Historical Society Quarterly* XLI no. 4 (October 1957).

Patterson, James T. *Mr. Republican: A Biography of Robert A. Taft*. Boston: Houghton Mifflin, 1972.

Pearlman, Michael. *To Make Democracy Safe for America: Patricians and Preparedness in the Progressive Era*. Urbana: University of Illinois Press, 1984.

Pearson, Drew. *Drew Pearson Diaries, 1949–1959*. New York: Holt, Rinehart and Winston, 1974.

———, and Robert S. Allen. *The Washington Merry-Go-Round*. New York: Blue Ribbon Books, 1931.

Peters Jr., Ronald M. *The American Speakership: The Office in Historical Perspective*. Baltimore: Johns Hopkins University Press, 1997.

Pinchot, Amos R. *History of the Progressive Party*. New York: New York University Press, 1958.

Pincus, Anne Terry. *Kennedy Center Performing Arts Cookbook*. Washington, D.C.: Museum Press, 1973.

Ponder, Stephen. "The President Makes News: William McKinley and the First Presidential Press Corps, 1897–1901." *Presidential Studies Quarterly* 29, no. 4 (Fall 1994): 823–836.

Powell, E. Alexander. *Yonder Lies Adventure!* New York: Macmillan, 1932.

Pringle, Henry F. *The Life and Times of William Howard Taft*. 2 vols. New York: Farrar & Reinhart, 1939.

———. "The Real Senator Borah: Twenty Years in Washington Has Not Weakened Him." *World's Work*, December 1928:133–144.

———. *Theodore Roosevelt*. New York: Harcourt, Brace, 1931.

Randolph, Mary. *Presidents and First Ladies*. New York: D. Appleton-Century, 1936.

Ratliff, Lucy Graydon. *The Graydons of Cincinnati, 1850–1984*. Cincinnati: n.p., 1984.

Redman, Tim. *Ezra Pound and Italian Fascism*. Cambridge: Cambridge University Press, 1991.

Rein, Irving J., Philip Kotler, and Martin R. Stoller. *High Visibility*. New York: Dodd, Mead, 1987.

Renehan Jr., Edward J. *The Lion's Pride: Theodore Roosevelt and His Family in Peace and War*. New York: Oxford University Press, 1998.

Reston, James. *Deadline: A Memoir*. New York: Random House, 1991.

Rhodes, Edward J. M. *China's Republican Revolution: The Case of Kwangtung, 1895–1913*. Cambridge, Mass.: Harvard University Press, 1975.

Riedel, Richard Langham. *Halls of the Mighty: My 47 Years in the Senate*. New York: Robert B. Luce, 1969.

Rixey, Lillian. *Bamie: Theodore Roosevelt's Remarkable Sister*. New York: David McKay, 1963.

Robinson, Corinne Roosevelt. *My Brother Theodore Roosevelt*. New York: Charles Scribner's Sons, 1921.

Rollins Jr., Alfred B. *Roosevelt and Howe*. New York: Knopf, 1962.

Roosevelt, [Anna] Eleanor. *The Autobiography of Eleanor Roosevelt*. New York: Harper & Row, 1978.

———. *This I Remember*. New York: Harper & Brothers, 1949.

———. *This Is My Story*. New York: Harper & Brothers, 1937.

Roosevelt, Archibald. *For Lust of Knowing: Memoirs of an Intelligence Officer*. Boston: Little, Brown, 1988.

Roosevelt, Eleanor Butler Alexander. *Day Before Yesterday: The Reminiscences of Mrs. Theodore Roosevelt, Jr.* Garden City, N.Y.: Doubleday, 1959.

Roosevelt, Elliott, ed. *F.D.R. His Personal Letters: The Early Years*. New York: Duell, Sloan, and Pearce, 1947.

———, and James Brough. *An Untold Story*. New York: G. P. Putnam's Sons, 1973.

Roosevelt, Felicia Warburg. *Doers & Dowagers*. Garden City, NY: Doubleday, 1975.

Roosevelt, Nicholas. *Theodore Roosevelt: The Man as I Knew Him*. New York: Dodd, Mead, 1967.

Roosevelt, James, with Bill Libby. *My Parents: A Differing View*. New York: Playboy Press, 1976.

Roosevelt, Robert B. *Is Democracy Dishonesty?* New York: Journeymen Printers' Co-operative Association, 1871.

———. *Progressive Petticoats*. New York: G. W. Carleton, 1874.

———. *The Washington City Ring*. Washington: F. & J. Rives & G. A. Bailey, 1873.

Roosevelt, Selwa. *Keeper of the Gate*. New York: Simon & Schuster, 1990.

Roosevelt, Theodore. *An Autobiography*. New York: Charles Scribner's Sons, 1929.

———. *In Memory of My Darling Wife Alice Hathaway Roosevelt and of My Beloved Mother Martha Bulloch Roosevelt Who Died in the Same House and on the Same Day on February 14, 1884*. New York: G. P. Putnam's Sons, 1884.

———. *Letters from Theodore Roosevelt to Anna Roosevelt Cowles, 1870–1918*. New York: Charles Scribner's Sons, 1924.

Rorabaugh, William J. *The Alcoholic Republic*. New York: Oxford University Press, 1979.

Rosenberg, Charles E. "Sexuality, Class and Role in 19th-Century America," *American Quarterly* 25, no. 2 (May 1973), 131–153.

Ross, Ishbel. *Grace Coolidge and Her Era*. New York: Dodd, Mead, 1962.

———. *The Tafts: An American Family*. New York: World Publishing, 1964.

Rothman, Ellen K. *Hands and Hearts: A History of Courtship in America*. New York: Basic Books, 1984.

Russell, Francis. *The Shadow of Blooming Grove: Warren G. Harding and His Times*. New York: McGraw Hill, 1968.

Sands, W. F. "Korea and the Korean Emperor." *Century Magazine* 69, no. 4 (February 1905): 577–584.

Sarasohn, David. *The Party of Reform: Democrats in the Progressive Era*. Jackson: University Press of Mississippi, 1989.

Sarles, Ruth. *A Story of America First*. Westport, Conn.: Praeger, 2003.

Saxbe, William B., with Peter D. Franklin. *I've Seen the Elephant: An Autobiography*. Kent, Ohio: Kent State University Press, 2000.

Scanlan, Nelle. *Boudoir Mirrors of Washington*. Philadelphia: John C. Winston, 1923.

Schacht, John N., ed. *Three Faces of Midwestern Isolationism: Gerald P. Nye, Robert E. Wood, John L. Lewis*. Iowa City: Center for the Study of the Recent History of the United States, 1981.

Scharff, Virginia. *Taking the Wheel: Women and the Coming of the Motor Age*. New York: Free Press, 1991.

Schickel, Richard. *His Picture in the Papers*. New York: Charterhouse, 1973.

————. *Intimate Strangers: The Culture of Celebrity*. Garden City, N.Y.: Doubleday, 1985.

Schlesinger Jr., Arthur M. *Learning How to Behave: A Historical Study of American Etiquette Books*. New York: Macmillan Company, 1946.

————. *A Life in the Twentieth Century*. New York: Houghton Mifflin, 2000.

————. *The Crisis of the Old Order*. Boston: Houghton Mifflin, 1957.

Schmidt, Richard T. F. "Stokowski in a May Festival Coup." *Cincinnati Historical Society Bulletin* 25, no. 2 (April 1967): 130–135.

Schriftgiesser, Karl. *This Was Normalcy: An Account of Party Politics During Twelve Republican Years: 1920–1932*. Boston: Little, Brown, 1948.

Schwartz, Abby S. "Nicholas Longworth: Art Patron of Cincinnati." In *The Taft Museum: A Cincinnati Legacy*, Dottie L. Lewis, ed. Cincinnati: Cincinnati Historical Society, 1988: 18–32.

Seagrave, Sterling. *Dragon Lady: The Life and Legend of the Last Empress of China*. New York: Knopf, 1992.

Seale, William. *The President's House: A History*. 2 vols. Washington, D.C.: White House Historical Association, 1986.

Seelye, Catherine, ed. *Charles Olson and Ezra Pound: An Encounter at St. Elizabeth's by Charles Olson*. New York: Viking, 1975.

Selden, Charles A. "The Father Complex of Alice Roosevelt Longworth and Ruth Hanna McCormick." *Ladies' Home Journal*, March 1927: 6–7, 72–74.

Sherman, Richard B. "Republicans and Negroes: The Lessons of Normalcy." *Phylon* 27, (First Quarter 1966): 69–71.

Sherwood, Mary Elizabeth W. *Manners and Social Usages*. New York: Harper, 1897.

Silverman, Elaine L. "Theodore Roosevelt and Women: The Inner Conflict of a President and its Impact on his Ideology." Ph.D. diss., UCLA, 1973.

Slayden, Ellen Maury. *Washington Wife*. New York: Harper & Row, 1962.

Slemp, C. Bascom, ed. *The Mind of the President as Revealed by Himself in His Own Words*. Garden City, N.Y.: Doubleday, 1926.

Smart, James Getty. "Whitelaw Reid: A Biographical Study." Ph.D. diss., University of Maryland, 1964.

Smith, Marie. *Entertaining in the White House*. Washington, D.C.: Acropolis Books, 1967.

Smith, Ira R. T. *"Dear Mr. President…": The Story of Fifty Years in the White House Mailroom*. New York: Julian Messner, 1949.

Smith, Richard Norton. *The Colonel: The Life and Legend of Robert R. McCormick, 1880–1955*. Evanston, Ill.: Northwestern University Press, 1997.

————. *Thomas E. Dewey and His Times*. New York: Simon & Schuster, 1982.

Stenehjem, Michele Flynn. *An American First: John T. Flynn and the America First Committee*. New Rochelle, N.Y.: Arlington House, 1940.

Stevenson, Robert Louis. *Prince Otto: A Romance*. New York: Charles Scribner's Sons, 1925.

Stevens, Harry R. "The First Cincinnati Music Festival." *The Historical and Philosophical Society of Ohio History Bulletin* 20, no. 3 (July 1962): 186–196.

Stimson, Henry L., and McGeorge Bundy. *On Active Service in Peace and War*. New York: Harper & Brothers, 1947–1948.

Stokes, Thomas L. *Chip Off My Shoulder*. Princeton, N.J.: Princeton University Press, 1940.

Stone, Ralph. "Two Illinois Senators Among the Irreconcilables." *Mississippi Valley Historical Review* 50, no. 3 (December 1963): 443–465.

Sullivan, Mark. *The Education of an American*. New York: Doubleday, Doran, 1938.

————. *Our Times: The Twenties*. Vol. 6. New York: Charles Scribner's Sons, 1935.

Taft, Helen H. *Recollections of Full Years*. New York: Dodd, Mead, 1914.

Teague, Michael. *Mrs. L: Conversations with Alice Roosevelt Longworth*. Garden City, N.Y.: Doubleday, 1981.

————. "Theodore Roosevelt and Alice Hathaway Lee: A New Perspective." *Harvard Library Bulletin* 32, no. 3 (Summer 1985): 225–238.

Teichmann, Howard. *Alice: The Life and Times of Alice Roosevelt Longworth*. Englewood Cliffs, N.J.: Prentice Hall, 1979.

Torrey, E. Fuller. *The Roots of Treason: Ezra Pound and the Secrets of St. Elizabeth's*. New York: McGraw Hill, 1984.

Ts'ai, Henry. *China and the Overseas Chinese in the United States, 1868–1911*. Fayetteville: University of Arkansas Press, 1983.

Ts'ai, Shih-shan. "Reaction to Exclusion: The Boycott of 1905 and Chinese National Awakening." *Historian* 39, no. 1 (November 1976): 95–110.

Tuchman, Barbara W. *Practicing History*. New York: Knopf, 1981.

Van Rensselaer, Mrs. John King. *The Social Ladder*. New York: Henry Holt, 1924.

Vare, Daniele. *The Last Empress*. Garden City, N.Y.: Doubleday, Doran, 1938.

Varg, Paul A. *Open Door Diplomat: The Life of W. W. Rockhill*. Urbana: University of Illinois Press, 1952.

Vidal, Gore. *Palimpsest*. New York: Penguin Books, 1995.

Vinson, John. *William E. Borah and the Outlawry of War*. Athens: University of Georgia Press, 1957.

von Dakke, John F. "Grape Growing and Wine Making in Cincinnati, 1800–1870." *CHS Bulletin* 25, 3 (July 1967): 197–212.

Wagenknecht, Edward. *The Seven Worlds of Theodore Roosevelt*. New York: Longmans, Green, 1958.

Waldrop, Frank C. *McCormick of Chicago*. Englewood Cliffs, N.J.: Prentice Hall, 1966.

Walker, Stanley. *Mrs. Astor's Horse*. New York: Frederick A. Stokes, 1935.

Walters, Ronald G., ed. *Primers for Prudery*. Baltimore: Johns Hopkins University Press, 2000.

Ward, Geoffrey. *Before the Trumpet: Young Franklin Roosevelt, 1882–1905*. New York: Harper & Row, 1985.

————. *A First-Class Temperament*. New York: Harper & Row, 1989.

Warner, Hoyt Landon. *Progressivism in Ohio, 1897–1917*. Columbus: Ohio State University Press, 1964.

Warner, Marina. *The Dragon Empress: The Life and Times of Tz'u-Hsi*. London: Weidenfeld & Nicolson, 1972.

Wead, Doug. *All the Presidents' Children: Triumph and Tragedy in the Lives of America's First Families*. New York: Atria Books, 2003.

Weyl, Nathaniel. *Treason*. Washington, D.C.: Public Affairs Press, 1950.

Whipple, Wayne, and Alice Roosevelt Longworth. *The Story of the White House and Its Home Life*. Boston: Dwinell-Wright, 1937.

White, Ralph. "The Europeanism of Coudenhove-Kalergi." In *The European Unity in Context: The Interwar Period*. Peter M. R. Stirk, ed. London: Pinter Publishers, 1989.

White, William Allen. *The Autobiography of William Allen White*. New York: Macmillan, 1946.

————. *A Puritan in Babylon: The Story of Calvin Coolidge*. New York: Macmillan, 1958.

Wilensky, Norman M. *Conservatives in the Progressive Era: The Taft Republicans of 1912*. Gainesville: University of Florida Press, 1965.

Wilhelm, J. J. *Ezra Pound: The Tragic Years, 1925–1972*. University Park: The Pennsylvania State University Press, 1994.

Willets, Gilson. *Inside History of the White House*. New York: The Christian Herald, 1908.

Wister, Owen. *Roosevelt: The Story of a Friendship*. New York: Macmillan, 1930.

Woodward, Stanley. "Protocol: What It Is and What It Does." *Department of State Bulletin*, 3 October 1949: 501–503.

Woollcott, Alexander, Beatrice Bakrow Kaufman, and Joseph Hennessey, eds. *The Letters of Alexander Woollcott*. New York: Viking, 1944.

Worthington, C. Ford, ed. *The Letters of Henry Adams*. New York: Houghton Mifflin, 1938.

Woywod, Stanislaus. *A Practical Commentary on the Code of Canon Law*. New York: Joseph F. Wagner, 1957.

Wright, William. *The Washington Game*. New York: E. P. Dutton, 1974.

Wunderlin Jr., Clarence E., ed. *The Papers of Robert A. Taft*. 2 vols. Kent, Ohio: Kent State University Press, 1997 and 2001.

Young, Nancy Beck. *Lou Henry Hoover: Activist First Lady*. Lawrence: University Press of Kansas, 2004.

Zieger, Robert H. *John L. Lewis: Labor Leader*. Boston: Twayne, 1988.

Index